BIG IDEAS

Big Ideas

A Guide to the History of Everything

Cameron Gibelyou
University of Michigan

Douglas Northrop
University of Michigan

New York   Oxford
OXFORD UNIVERSITY PRESS

Oxford University Press is a department of the University of Oxford.
It furthers the University's objective of excellence in research, scholarship,
and education by publishing worldwide. Oxford is a registered trade mark of
Oxford University Press in the UK and certain other countries.

Published in the United States of America by Oxford University Press
198 Madison Avenue, New York, NY 10016, United States of America.

For titles covered by Section 112 of the US Higher Education
Opportunity Act, please visit www.oup.com/us/he for the latest
information about pricing and alternate formats.

Library of Congress Cataloging-in-Publication Data

Names: Gibelyou, Cameron, author. | Northrop, Douglas Taylor, author.
Title: Big ideas : a guide to the history of everything / Cameron Gibelyou,
    University of Michigan, Douglas Northrop, University of Michigan.
Other titles: Guide to the history of everything
Description: First edition. | New York : Oxford University Press, 2020. |
    Includes bibliographical references and index. | Summary: "A higher
    education history textbook that covers the history of the universe,
    Earth, life, and humanity as a single unified whole, integrating
    knowledge from across the natural sciences, social sciences, and
    humanities"—Provided by publisher.
Identifiers: LCCN 2020005788 (print) | LCCN 2020005789 (ebook) | ISBN
    9780190201210 (paperback) | ISBN 9780190201227 (epub) | ISBN
    9780197500118
Subjects: LCSH: Civilization—Philosophy. | Cosmology. | Human evolution. |
    World history.
Classification: LCC CB19 .G475 2020 (print) | LCC CB19 (ebook) | DDC
    901—dc23
LC record available at https://lccn.loc.gov/2020005788
LC ebook record available at https://lccn.loc.gov/2020005789

Printing number: 9 8 7 6 5 4 3 2 1
Printed by LSC Communications, Inc., United States of America

CONTENTS

DETAILED CONTENTS

ACKNOWLEDGMENTS

We received generous help from a wide variety of people in putting this book together.

First, we thank those who read a draft of the entire book and gave us encouragement and thoughtful feedback. Foremost among this group is Nicole Gibelyou, who read a draft of every section in the book and, in some cases, multiple drafts. Her feedback, ideas, vision, and suggestions contributed to this project immeasurably. We are likewise deeply grateful to Dave Burzillo, who also read and responded to the entire manuscript and whose wide-ranging knowledge of nearly every topic was a great help—as was his enthusiasm for the project. Thanks to David Christian, whose input on the initial manuscript was thoroughly appreciated and made several sections of the book stronger. We particularly appreciate his graciousness and generosity in supporting this project even as our book engages and sometimes challenges parts of his own work. We also thank the other reviewers for Oxford University Press, for pointing out many ways in which we could improve the final product. We carefully considered all of their advice, and we adopted much of it. The book has benefited greatly from their input.

Experts from a wide variety of backgrounds gave us input on specific portions of the book, ranging from individual paragraphs to multiple chapters. One of our central goals was to provide an introduction to subjects that experts in the corresponding fields would regard as clear, accurate, and precise. We sought out many such experts to verify that what we had written squared with their knowledge, and we greatly appreciate the many generous and enthusiastic responses we received. In this vein, we thank the following people: in the natural sciences, John Bratton, Scott Collins, Mark Ditzler, Chris Fink, Jamie Gleason, Dragan Huterer, Alex Lechler, Leo Michelotti, and Carolina Simao Roe-Raymond; in the humanities and social sciences, Jay Crisostomo, Christian de Pee, Ray De Vries, Daniel Hirschman, David Manley, Aaron Michka, C.S.C., Sarah Mills, Janet Richards, Perrin Selcer, John Speth, and Tom Trautmann. Whether this input consisted of an encouraging message that we already had things basically right, or whether it pointed to issues needing revisions (major or minor), we are grateful for this help.

We are also deeply grateful to the team at Oxford University Press for their unstinting, expert work on the book. We are especially indebted to Charles Cavaliere, who has been the absolute model of an editor, encouraging our progress and thoughtful in overseeing the book's emergence, and to Anna Russell and Danica Donovan, whose enthusiasm and attention to detail were much appreciated. Thanks also to the OUP production editor Brad Rau, and copy editor Wesley Morrison, both of whom helped enormously with matters of style, expression, consistency, and coherence. Thanks to Irina Maisuradze, whose patient artistic work contributed greatly to both the aesthetic appeal and the accuracy of many graphics.

We take full responsibility for any remaining mistakes, omissions, or unclarities on any of these levels.

On a personal level, we each want to thank the multitude of others who encouraged and enabled us in this project. In particular:

Cameron Gibelyou: My contributions to this book drew in some way on almost everything I have ever learned, and I am grateful to all the great many people who have taught, mentored, and inspired me in the pursuit of truth and understanding over the years. I cannot list more than a tiny fraction of them here, but I am deeply thankful for each and every one and for all they have shared with me. Thanks especially to Doug Northrop, for his immense help and support over the past decade, for his outstanding mentorship and friendship, and for bringing me into the field of Big History and helping me turn my love of learning, teaching, and sharing ideas into a career. It has been great working on this book with you. Thanks to Dragan Huterer, Phil Deloria, Angela Dillard, Tim McKay, and Bob Bain, for your thoughtful mentorship and friendship over the years. Thanks to my Big History co-instructors Doug Northrop, Sarah Hamilton, Perrin Selcer, and Phil Deloria, who have been great to teach with and from whom I have learned a great deal. And thanks to all my students, whose thoughtful conversations about history and the future and, in a few cases, direct feedback on drafts of this book helped to inspire material in it; thanks especially to Rachel Beglin and Audrey Schwartz. Thanks to my wife Nicole Gibelyou, who has been a wonderful companion in working on this book, as in all other things. I can't wait to work with you on the joint projects we have been putting on hold in our efforts to finish this one. Thanks to our son Joshua Gibelyou, who was eager to join our family team from the start and, among many other things, listened with rather extraordinary patience to me as I worked out my thoughts about the subject matter of this book when he was less than one year old. I hope you enjoy this book, especially about 15 years from now. Thanks also to my wider family, especially my parents, grandmother, and sister, for encouraging and enabling my love of learning from a young age, and also for making sure that I did not spend all my time in the abstract world of ideas. I owe you for that one! I dedicate my contributions to this book to my teachers, friends, and mentors from my sophomore year of high school, the formative time of my life when I first grew fascinated by the questions discussed in this book.

Douglas Northrop: Many thanks to Cameron Gibelyou, for traveling this journey with me—dating all the way back to 2009, when he first sat in on the perhaps-crazy venture of "Zoom," my attempt at framing a new approach to Big History. It has been a privilege to work with, and learn from, him in the years since. I admire his voracious intellect and boundless good cheer; a better collaborator could hardly have been designed. My gratitude also to the University of Michigan, and especially its Department of History and College of Literature, Science, and the Arts, for encouraging this unusual kind of intellectual / pedagogical work and offering me a home as I pursued it. Bob Bain, Anne Berg, Kathleen Canning, Geoff Eley, Will Glover, Gabrielle Hecht, Sue Juster, Michael Kennedy, Val Kivelson, Olga Maiorova, Farina Mir, Ellen Muehlberger, Perrin Selcer, Minnie Sinha, Ron Suny, Jeff Veidlinger, Penny Von Eschen, and Jason Young played particularly important roles as colleagues and friends—along with many others, including all the guest lecturers and students who participated in "Zoom," whose contributions are manifold and whose names would overspill this page. Beyond that, I truly would not have made it through the adventures (and misadventures) of the years in which this book was written without my children, Jeremy and Sawyer, and the support of an extraordinary personal "team," including a group of U-P friends and professional helpers whom I scarcely deserve but treasure beyond words. They know who they are. Above all, my work on this book is undergirded by, and enmeshed with, new chapters in my own life—foremost the support and love of Sarah Koenig, who in her sustaining presence has taught me not only that the universe is indeed full of surprises, but that when approached with hope and faith, they can sometimes be the most unexpected, and wonderful, gifts of all.

Ann Arbor, Michigan
April 2020

REVIEWERS

Bob Bain, University of Michigan, Ann Arbor
David Christian, Macquarie University
Timothy Doran, California State University, Los Angeles
Todd Duncan, Portland Community College
Lowell Gustafson, Villanova University
Deborah Johnston, Keystone Academy
Jonathan Markley, California State University, Fullerton
Barry H. Rodrigue, University of Southern Maine
Kären Wigen, Stanford University

PREFACE

The American anthropologist Clifford Geertz once wrote that certain big ideas "burst upon the intellectual landscape with a tremendous force. They resolve so many fundamental problems at once that they seem also to promise that they will resolve all fundamental problems, clarify all obscure issues."[1] As Geertz further points out, however, one ultimately realizes that a given idea, no matter how powerful, "does not explain everything, not even everything human, but it still explains something; and our attention shifts to isolating just what that something is, to disentangling ourselves from a lot of pseudoscience to which, in the first flush of its celebrity, it has also given rise."[2]

This book, titled *Big Ideas*, contemplates a wide range of big, powerful ideas—from the Big Bang, plate tectonics, and evolution to culture, contingency, and sustainability—and subjects them all to the kind of analysis that Geertz describes: considering exactly how powerful these ideas are, how they connect with one another, and where their limitations lie. But this is not a generic exploration of ideas. Rather, it is a profile of ideas relevant to what we refer to as "universal history": the history of the universe, Earth, life, and humanity—hence the subtitle, *A Guide to the History of Everything*. As we turn from one big idea to another, we offer, and also critique, a powerful core narrative that threads throughout the book: a concise "history of everything" that combines disciplines like cosmology and astrophysics, the Earth and life sciences, anthropology and history. In other words, we tell a universal-historical story and analyze the ingredients of that story as we go.

This book was both fun and immensely challenging to write. We, the co-authors, are scholars and teachers by training, one whose academic training is in astrophysics (Cameron Gibelyou) and one whose expertise is in history (Douglas Northrop). We both have strong interests in a variety of fields outside our own, each of us reading widely and having done formal academic work in both the sciences and the humanities. Gibelyou has taught at the college level in physics, astronomy, history,

1. Geertz, *The Interpretation of Cultures*, p. 3 (citing Susanne Langer, *Philosophy in a New Key*).
2. Ibid., p. 4.

English, and psychology, and has created courses on "Predicting the Future" and "Popular Science." Northrop teaches world / global history as well as Eurasian and imperial history and created the college course ("Zoom: A History of Everything") that introduced Gibelyou to the fascinating integrative field of Big History, which systematically generates and contemplates universal-historical narratives. Between the two of us, we are well-versed in various religious and philosophical intellectual traditions from around the world. But even with two authors having complementary expertise and fairly wide-ranging knowledge, it is more than a little daunting to put together a book on the history of everything. Still, we found the exercise to be a very worthwhile adventure over the course of about six years.

We offer this book, not unambitiously, as an attempt to create a novel framework for thinking about the history and future of everything. We grapple throughout with issues at the intersection of the natural sciences, history, literature, philosophy, religion, and the humanities in general. We attempt to make a reasoned analysis of worldviews that underlie historical writing across many fields. We bring a wide range of voices to bear on fascinating questions of where everything—from the universe as a whole to any particular thing within it—came from, how it got to be the way it is today, and where things might be headed in the future. Our aim has been to treat scientific explanation and humanistic interpretation as partners, inviting those with primarily scientific interests into a humanistic discussion about science and history, and those with core interests in the humanities into a discussion of how humanities-based ways of thinking might connect with and apply to the natural sciences. As much as possible, we directly quote authors from across disciplines and across centuries, placing our own commentary on each "big idea" within a broader set of intellectual traditions. (For this reason, there is no separate Suggested Readings section: the text itself, along with footnotes, captions, and the Appendix, will point the way toward sources to help interested readers explore any given issue more deeply.)

We also offer the nature of our collaboration itself as a possible model—and a promising approach to integrating disciplines. Many of the insights necessary for an all-encompassing work of history are insights that experts working in disciplines isolated from one another cannot ever "get to" by virtue of their isolation from one another. We would argue that the antidote to this intellectual isolation is precisely the kind of collaboration we have engaged in while writing this book. Our historian-scientist collaboration is an example of what one might call "deep multidisciplinarity": the full integration of thinking across fields. Our writing process supported this full integration of our thoughts: Northrop, the historian, had a vision for a book based on a series of connected essays about big ideas across the history of the universe, Earth, life, and humanity, that arose from the university course he had designed and taught; Gibelyou, who was trained as an astrophysicist and had experienced (and later co-taught) that course, agreed to co-author and fleshed out what the big ideas would be. We agreed that rather than writing within our own specialized fields (Gibelyou writing science sections, Northrop writing history sections), it would be better to fully co-write a book that both of us could agree to "own" every word of. This was both challenging and exciting, and it proved thoroughly worthwhile. We spent the next few years working to develop the ideas presented here, with Gibelyou formulating ideas, developing them in conversation with Northrop, and composing a first draft; Northrop then leading multiple rounds of editing; and then a final process of collaborative discussion and debate going back and forth to choose the words that would ultimately appear here. Along the way, we took the input of experts from a great diversity of academic backgrounds, worldviews, and career paths. Our process was consistent for the entire book. In the end, we both stand by every word as the outcome of an intense, mutually illuminating, multiyear collaboration.

We have come to think that this is how interdisciplinary collaboration should work: not only by independent thinkers developing their own lines of thought, but also by fully thinking together and converging on a way of thinking about things to which both can fully agree. To find the place of each discipline, the boundaries of each discipline, the proper relations of one with another in the pursuit of overarching insight and truth, each disciplinary perspective must be open to completion and correction by other disciplines and by philosophical reflection and a careful comparison and integration of worldviews. The people involved must be similarly open as well. Putting the history of everything together in one place is inevitably an act of synthesis, re-collecting the past, and it can be an opportunity for people with knowledge of different pieces of the puzzle, as well as different understandings of what is fundamental and how the world works, to come together as well.

We recognize that in writing about the worldviews underlying universal histories, we are developing and expressing a worldview of our own. We make no claim to be omniscient narrators! We hope that the perspective we have developed will push everyone—whether reading this book in a classroom context or out of general interest—to think more deeply about their own worldviews, as it has done for us, and about universal history and the big ideas that contribute to it.

ABOUT THE AUTHORS

Cameron Gibelyou is a faculty member at the University of Michigan, where he develops and teaches original, innovative multidisciplinary courses, including "Popular Science," "Predicting the Future," and "Tours of the Past." He has taught courses on Big History—the history of the universe, Earth, life, and humanity—at both the high-school and college levels and serves as science advisor and teacher consultant for the Big History Project. His PhD is in physics, with a specialization in astrophysics and cosmology.

Douglas Northrop is Professor of History and Middle East Studies at the University of Michigan, where he teaches world / global and Big History, Central Asian studies, and the history of empire, environment, and culture. His other books include *An Imperial World: Empires and Colonies Since 1750, A Companion to World History*, and the prize-winning *Veiled Empire: Gender and Power in Stalinist Central Asia*. He is now working on a study of natural disasters along the Eurasian frontier.

BIG IDEAS

1

INTRODUCTION

Overview

This is a book on universal history: the history of the universe, Earth, life, and humanity. Books like this tend to begin in a certain way. You, the reader, may even have expected this before you opened it—a book with "history of everything" in the title might begin with a soul-stirring meditation on the vastness of the universe in both space and time, and the smallness and fragility of the planet we call home.[1] Or perhaps with an ancient creation story from a long-vanished civilization whose flaws show how much better we understand the world, thanks to science, than people did hundreds or thousands of years ago.[2] Or with a reflection on the inadequacy of short time scales for understanding the large patterns of human history as a whole, and the need to put humanity in cosmic context.[3]

But that is not how this book begins. It begins, well, the way it just began, because we do not intend only to retell the history of everything, but also to contemplate the way these universal stories are told.

A Brief History of Histories of Everything

Recent years have seen an explosion of "histories of everything." From professional scientists and historians to travel writers and authors of science fiction, fantasy, and popular science, an impressively wide range

---

1. Like Carl Sagan's *Cosmos*, Robert Hazen's *The Story of Earth*, or Cynthia Stokes Brown's *Big History: From the Big Bang to the Present*.

2. Like Steven Weinberg's *The First Three Minutes*, David Christian's *Maps of Time*, Eric Chaisson's *Epic of Evolution*, or Stephen Hawking's *A Brief History of Time*.

3. Like Fred Spier's *Big History and the Future of Humanity*, David Christian's *This Fleeting World*, or Walter Alvarez's *A Most Improbable Journey: A Big History of Our Planet and Ourselves*.

of writers have sensed the excitement of living at a time when human knowledge seems to touch everything from the deepest reaches of space to the depths of the oceans, from the ages before dinosaurs walked the Earth to the whole history of humankind. Authors have synthesized the best scientific and historical scholarship, trying to understand how we got where we are now, why the world looks the way it does, and what we might be able to say about where that world is headed. The history of the universe, Earth, life, and humanity may not be complete, but a basic outline feels visible, with a great many important details that seem firmly in place.

In addition to sharing a set of core facts, such grand stories cannot help but touch some common levels of meaning—including, perhaps especially, what it means to be human, to be alive in the cosmos. Whether modern or premodern, human hearts seem to stir in the presence of these questions. Hence, it is not surprising that "histories of everything" are not purely a modern creation but have their own deeper history. Creation myths are one major predecessor, with ancient roots: these were and are the ways many cultures have expressed an understanding of the origins of the universe and everything in it, including humankind. While many such creation stories may sound fanciful or just plain false to modern ears, they are grounded in the specific knowledge of the world that the people who composed them possessed, and they often express deep truths in story form.

In the last two or three centuries, a range of scientifically based origin stories have taken the findings of different natural-science disciplines and united them with human history to tell one apparently seamless story. Such science-based universal histories go back at least as far as the mid-19th century, with *Vestiges of the Natural History of Creation* (1844).[4] Though its scientific merit was questionable even at the time and its content is long outdated, *Vestiges* influenced the subsequent pattern of these narratives that drew on science in an attempt to capture the history of everything. In the 20th century, H. G. Wells wrote *The Outline of History* (1919–1920) and *A Short History of the World* (1922), works whose ambitions to bring together the history of the Earth, life, and humanity echoed *Vestiges* and also Charles Darwin's work in *On the Origin of Species* (1859) and *The Descent of Man* (1871). By the mid-20th century, Maria Montessori's educational initiatives emphasized cosmic history, and continue to do so to this day. Popular-science writers, Carl Sagan foremost among them, have been putting human history in planetary and cosmic context for decades. And these are far from the only examples of 19th- and 20th-century grand scientific-historical narratives.

"Big History," the name for a more recently emerging field of multidisciplinary scholarship that addresses cosmic and human history as a single unified whole, is one of the most prominent recent examples of these efforts to integrate evidence-based

---

4. See James Secord's *Victorian Sensation* for an account of this unique book's publication and reception. Originally published anonymously, *Vestiges* was later revealed to have been written by Robert Chambers.

scientific and historical knowledge into a single "history of everything." It responds to the institutional and intellectual conditions of the 21st century, in which knowledge of the past is unavoidably scattered throughout the landscape of academic disciplines: not only historians but astronomers, geologists, physicists, chemists, biologists, paleontologists, archaeologists, anthropologists, and others have much to say about the past on different time scales. Big History seeks to bring the insights of all these different fields together. While Big History does not by any means represent the first foray into universal history, it has achieved a new level of prominence. Courses in Big History at the secondary level and in higher education are on the rise throughout the world, and some of the most successful Big History authors have found a mass readership.

Information and Interpretation

So why write another book of universal history? Does the world need more books on the history of the universe, Earth, life, and humanity? We ourselves might say "no" if we intended simply to retell the same story that so many other authors have already captured. But while this book does include a concise account of universal history, sharing such a universal narrative is not our primary goal. Instead, we seek fundamentally to step back and evaluate the approach to universal history that these and many other modern accounts of science and history have taken, examining the basic ideas and core assumptions that underlie grand stories about the past. We intend not only to tell such a story, but to contemplate how it is told, to analyze it, and to critique aspects of it.

Why do this when much of modern-day knowledge about the past seems essentially certain and beyond critique? Our generation and its scientific culture have certainly gained new insights into the workings and history of the world, and we appreciate that Big History and similar approaches can provide a forum for thinkers to consider fundamental issues of origins, and of change and continuity over time. There can indeed be impressive coherence as we cross boundaries of time, space, and discipline to understand the world's past.

However, universal histories—just like every other kind of history, and indeed every kind of story—always operate at two levels, the *informational* and the *interpretive*. At the informational level, one finds a basic set of facts and evidence regarding what happened in the past: the conditions of the universe in its infancy, for example, or which dinosaur species existed when, or how agriculture began to take root in different areas of human settlement. The informational level is subject to a certain amount of debate, but many important questions at this level have been settled within the various domains of science and history. The interpretive level, meanwhile, has more to do with the big-picture, "What does it all mean?" kinds of questions—including questions about what our cosmic and planetary history means for our present and future, for who we are as humans and where we are going. Our goal in this book is to narrate the "history of everything" at the informational level, drawing on fields of study across the sciences and humanities, but simultaneously to contemplate the meaning of that history at the interpretive level.

The two levels are always inescapably intertwined. Even in the selection of which facts and evidence to take into account when constructing a historical narrative, information and interpretation come together: an author makes *interpretive* choices even about the apparently basic matter of which *information* to include in the first place. Such choices are partly driven by the kind of story the author wishes to tell and the lessons the story is designed to communicate.

Themes

The relationship between worldviews and universal histories, and between the informational level and the interpretive level, is one theme that appears regularly throughout this book. A given universal history never just communicates a set of observational facts about the past; it reflects an entire worldview and set of philosophical ideas about how the natural world and human existence "work." The same set of facts about the past might be given very different meanings and interpretations depending on the intellectual framework, culture, and philosophical dispositions of the authors. In particular, the intellectuals who have produced many recent universal histories usually interpret scientific and historical knowledge within a particular modern, secular, Western worldview. So one might ask how the events of the past—from the beginning of the universe over 13 billion years ago to the history of life to the arrangement of human societies over time—could take on different meanings when set against the backdrop of different understandings of the world. The *story* of the history of everything can be framed or interpreted in many different ways, and invested with distinct kinds of meaning and very different "takeaways."

To be clear, it is not a "bad thing" that universal histories involve interpretation: it is part of what makes them interesting to engage with, and it is unavoidable. Ideally, the interpretive level is the realm of insightful and carefully justified analysis rather than "subjectivity" or mere opinion. But we hope to make it clear just how many interpretive choices go into the writing of any grand story about the past, including our own, and how strongly an author's worldview may color the choices made. Accordingly, in every chapter, we raise questions and discuss issues of interpretation, including but not limited to:

- Does the size of the universe mean that humans are cosmically insignificant (chapter 2)?
- How should we interpret the fact that Earth is not at the center of the universe, or that humanity's existence occupies such a short span in the grand scheme of deep time (chapter 3)?

- Does evolution by natural selection show us that the natural world is merci-lessly competitive, harmoniously cooperative, or something else (chapter 4)?
- What does it mean to be human, and how does taking an evolutionary and biological view of human origins affect our view of human beings (chapter 5)?
- How important in the overall course of history are the relative contribu-tions of individual people, humans acting collectively, and impersonal forces (chapter 6)?
- How do modern ways of conceptualizing reality color our perceptions of the bigger history of everything (chapter 7)?
- Should we expect the future to bring overall progress to the state of human beings, or is that an unhelpful way to frame the question (chapter 8)?

These are all deeper issues of interpretation that do not fall straight out of the scientific and historical evidence. They bear on issues of framing, the meaning with which stories are invested, and the complex relationship between evidence and story. We hope that attending explicitly to the interpretive level, and compar-ing alternative interpretations, will help to open or re-open questions about "what it all means" and invite a broad range of voices into that conversation. And since interpretive questions like those listed here necessarily move beyond the realm of empirical (observational) evidence, we explore how different interpretive conclu-sions might be justified, and what might make a given answer stand out as more compelling than others.

A second theme, closely related to the first, involves the implications of univer-sal histories for views of humanity. By their very nature, universal histories attempt to connect natural history (the history of the universe, Earth, and life) with human history. To the extent that such stories make the passage between the non-human and the human as seamless as possible, the narrative that emerges will naturally em-phasize those aspects of humanity that are most legible within the terms of the natural sciences—how humans eat, how population numbers change, what biologi-cal universals extend across cultures, and so forth—but, when seen from a social-scientific or humanistic view, risk taking a reductive, strictly "positivist" view of humanity. We will consider the relationship between universal histories and these understandings of humanity throughout the book, especially in the second half.

A third and final theme is that of scale and discipline. Universal histories stitch together scales in time and space, from fractions of a second to billions of years, from the tiniest subatomic particles to galaxies and the whole universe. They also knit together widely disparate academic disciplines, from cosmology to archaeol-ogy to history. In what ways do these scales and disciplines genuinely "speak" to one another, and in what ways does the act of uniting them actually force them into a misleadingly singular box? Can a universal history incorporate the sciences and the humanities on equal footing, making room both for appropriate kinds of reductionism and for human agency and purpose? We will attend to these kinds of questions when discussing many of the individual "big ideas" that make up this book. A general insight that emerges from this analysis is that different sources of evidence and methods of investigation lend themselves to understanding each scale. There is no automatic or necessary relationship between the size of a thing and its importance: the fact that galaxies are big does not make them all-important, and the fact that elementary particles are small does not make them fundamental to the exclusion of the larger entities that they compose. A full understanding of most phenomena requires considering the interactions and feedback loops that exist between different scales; for instance, in the biological realm, a full understanding of life must incorporate an understanding of everything from the level of molecules and cells to the level of ecosystems and the entire biosphere.

Organization and Layout

The purpose of this book is to explore how universal histories are told, and to provide readers with the tools for thinking about them constructively and critically. We seek to probe the worldviews behind modern universal histories while sketching the scientific and historical evidence that they claim as their basis: to tell the story, in other words, but also to analyze the story. To that end, our exploration will be both specific and concise: we discuss 42 "big ideas" that serve as major ingredients in universal narratives. These big ideas come out of the sciences and humanities, and they shape how universal histories are told. They include key concepts such as the Big Bang, plate tectonics, evolution, the biosphere, technology, culture, contingency, and sustainability. We not only address what these ideas mean and why they are important in the context of the fields of study that generated them, but also evaluate their strengths and limitations for understanding universal history—that is, how well they work as ingredients in grand stories of the past, beyond the disciplinary domains that originated them.

The chronological sequence of these ideas provides an order to the book: ideas come first that especially help make sense of the history of the universe, followed by those that illuminate the history of the Earth, then life, then humanity. Such a sequence in time is also a sequence in academic discipline; we discuss underlying ideas that originate in cosmology, geology and the Earth sciences, biology and paleontology, anthropology, and disciplinary history. The basic structure of the book is captured in the chapter titles, each of which is a big idea in itself, addressing the universe, Earth, life, humanity, history, modernity, and the future.

Our goal in organizing the book this way is to carefully analyze the intellectual power of these ideas for understanding the world, as well as the often-unacknowledged difficulties that universal histories face in taking these ideas out of their specialized contexts and putting them to work in such a grand project of synthesis. It also allows us to make explicit the philosophical assumptions that underlie modern universal histories, and to treat these assumptions on their own terms.

Hence, the final big idea in each chapter is more explicitly philosophical, including topics such as the role of mathematics, the nature of time, the character of science, and questions of agency and determinism.

Each of the 42 big ideas has its own "section," with its relevant "subheadings." This way of dividing up the text helps to facilitate our basic approach: presenting ideas, then analyzing their strengths and limitations. Along the way, we analyze not just works that explicitly combine natural history with human history, but that discuss any aspect of the history of the universe, Earth, life, and humanity. The core narrative of universal history that we are analyzing—the informational story of what happened in the history of the universe, Earth, life, and humanity—is present throughout.

Points and Purposes

In short, this book is designed to reveal where various lines of thought in modern scholarship have converged on a single understanding about what happened in the past, while also identifying and analyzing the basic worldview behind these narratives. We hope to show that modern universal histories are shaped not only by the best scientific and historical evidence, but also by a specific vision of humanity's nature and place in the world and a Western secular value system, which are *not* necessarily outcomes of this same evidence. There is, in other words, a basic worldview behind these stories that is sometimes seen as also arising *from* the evidence, and as being necessary for anyone who takes scientific and historical scholarship seriously, but actually is analytically separable from it. That worldview includes a wide variety of philosophical presuppositions about the nature of the universe itself, about human beings, and about the human mind, free will, religion, causation, time, and even what "counts" as an explanation. We will attempt to get far enough outside these underlying assumptions that they themselves become subject to questioning.

We offer this book in the hope of sparking reflection and discussion. We want it to serve as a starting point rather than the final word. In a few hundred pages, we cannot be all-encompassing, but we hope to create space to talk about fundamental assumptions and first principles among students, teachers, enthusiasts, and readers of universal histories.

Creation

What happened in the earliest moments of the universe's existence? Why is there something rather than nothing?

It may not be obvious at first glance, but these two questions are profoundly different. The first is a question about *beginnings*, about *history*, and empirical evidence—physical vestiges of the past—yields many clues about how to answer it.

The second question, however, is of a very different type. It is a question about the ultimate *origins* of all that exists, and about what the universe *depends on* for its existence. Different answers to this question correspond to different views about the fundamental nature and origin of *being*, of existence itself. It is difficult to imagine how one could, even in principle, answer the question of why there is something rather than nothing using empirical evidence as the decisive factor: the evidence itself is part of the "something."

The scientist and author Carl Sagan put the difficulty this way: "If you wish to make an apple pie from scratch, you must first invent the universe."[5] In other words, there is no such thing as doing anything really "from scratch," at least in human experience. Baking, or any other form of work, is always directed at transforming matter that already exists rather than making something truly new. The "nothing" in the question "Why is there something rather than nothing?" is not just a vacuum governed by the laws of physics; it is the absence of anything at all—including the vacuum, and including the laws of physics. The question of the universe's earliest moments, meanwhile, deals with how the matter in the universe transformed from earlier states into later states. To explain the development of things is not necessarily to explain the source of things.

Science-based universal histories almost by definition base themselves in empirical evidence, the kind of knowledge that can be observed in the world of matter and light that human senses can receive (perhaps with help from instruments like telescopes and microscopes that augment our natural abilities) and that human brains can process. Empirical evidence is the raw material that physics, chemistry, biology, history, and many other disciplines build on as their foundation. And empirical evidence has contributed much to a scientific understanding of the early history of the universe. (We discuss details of the science in chapter 2.) But it can only get us so far when responding to the question of why there is something rather than nothing.

That question is worth taking seriously at the outset when embarking on a study of the history of everything. In some ways, it is the grandest of questions, and it demands some real thought. And thought really ought to get us somewhere in contemplating these issues. It is here that ideas about Creation—that is, grand ideas about the ultimate origin and fundamental nature of the universe, from the entire history of human thought, especially those ideas outside the realm of what we normally call "science"—may be the best and most appropriate place we can turn. The next subheading illustrates a range of such ideas about creation, without delving into the full philosophical justifications for each perspective or rigorously comparing their relative merits.

---

5. Carl Sagan, *Cosmos*, p. 179.

A Quick Tour of Ideas About Creation

A reasonable first question to ask about the universe is whether it even *had a beginning* in the first place. Speaking very generally, the Hindu and Buddhist religious and philosophical traditions deriving from India say "no," while the philosophical traditions of the largest Abrahamic religions—Judaism, Christianity, and Islam—say "yes."

The Buddha, in the moment of his enlightenment, is said to have understood everything there is to understand. While he admonished his disciples not to concern themselves with metaphysical questions about the nature and origins of the universe, various Buddhist sects and traditions nevertheless have developed a widely shared vision of the universe, all said to go back to that singular moment of enlightenment. That vision of the universe is one in which beings live, die, and are born again in a new form; in which change and flux are the only constants; and which has no beginning in time but has always existed: a cyclic, beginningless universe.

The religious philosophies associated with Hinduism, meanwhile, tend to share this idea of an eternal cosmos, with a handful of variations on the theme. The Samkhya school of thought within Hinduism treats both Prakriti and Purusha—roughly translated as "matter" and as "spirit" or "consciousness," respectively—as primordial realities, neither reducible to the other, that have always existed. It affirms the existence of the gods of the Hindu pantheon like Vishnu, Shiva, Indra, and others, but no God who reigns supreme over all others. The Yoga school (a philosophical system, not just a set of techniques or practices) thinks similarly but adds the existence of a God (Ishvara) who resembles the God of Abrahamic monotheism in being spirit rather than matter, all-knowing, wise, and compassionate, but who is not the Creator of the universe—matter and spirit being viewed as uncreated. The Vaisheshika school likewise treats matter as uncreated, having always existed, but holds that there is a supreme God who acts as a potter or weaver or carpenter; though not the creator of matter itself, God shapes otherwise-shapeless matter into the forms it takes. Advaita Vedanta, another school of thought, holds that all being is essentially One in a mysterious way that transcends human reason. The appearance of a multiplicity of diverse entities in the world, then, is not the ultimate reality; absolute oneness and unity is, and always has been.

These orthodox philosophical systems within Hinduism all rely, in different ways, on the most ancient Hindu scriptures, the Vedas[6]—including the most

---

6. Including the parts of Vedic literature known as the Upanishads.

ancient of these, the Rig Veda, which implicitly draws the same distinction we have drawn between beginnings and origins:

> But, after all, who knows, and who can say
> whence it all came, and how creation happened?
> The gods themselves are later than creation,
> so who knows truly whence it has arisen?
> Whence all creation had its origin,
> he, whether he fashioned it or whether he did not,
> he, who surveys it all from highest heaven,
> he knows – or maybe even he does not know.[7]

By contrast, Abrahamic monotheism has tended to be much more explicit about both the beginning and the origin of the universe: the first sentence in the Bible is "In the beginning, God created the heavens and the Earth."[8] For the most part, Judaism, Christianity, and Islam share a common view of the universe as having a past beginning and a future end, and God as the sole Creator, without beginning or end.

Still, even within this mainstream Abrahamic view of God and the cosmos, philosophical arguments about the nature of creation are in some ways comparable to the considerations raised by Indian philosophers, and by others around the world. In particular, the Middle Ages saw an interreligious tradition of philosophical inquiry arise that could cross the boundaries of Judaism, Christianity, and Islam, as well as geographical boundaries of Christendom and the Islamic world, which included figures such as Ibn Sina (a.k.a. Avicenna, c. 980–1037), Al-Ghazali (c. 1058–1111), and Ibn Rushd (a.k.a. Averroes, 1126–1198) in Islam; Moses Maimonides (c. 1135–1204) in Judaism; and Thomas Aquinas (1225–1274) in Christianity. The later thinkers drew on the thoughts of the earlier ones, engaging, quoting, agreeing, and disagreeing as they would with any fellow philosopher, even across religious lines. They all drew on the ancient Greek philosopher Aristotle's philosophical categories and language, and wrestled with many of the same questions, arriving at different but related answers.

For example, Aristotle (384–322 BCE) had claimed to prove that the world had always existed, based in part on the principle that things arise and change only from preexisting prior states: there could be no ultimate beginning because any supposed

---

7. Translation by A. L. Basham; for this and others, see http://www.creationmyths.org/rigveda-10-129-indian-creation/rigveda-10-129-indian-creation-10-table-versions.htm .

8. Variously translated from the somewhat more ambiguous Hebrew original, but the translation given here has been, and is, both mainstream and profoundly influential in the history of Western philosophy.

beginning would have to be preceded by something before it. This was a position that Ibn Sina and Ibn Rushd supported, while Al-Ghazali, Maimonides, and Aquinas all challenged it, each in different ways and with different justifications. Various Islamic philosophers, including Al-Ghazali, developed the counterargument that far from being provably eternal, the universe *must* have had a beginning and, therefore, an ultimate cause. In shortened form, the argument is that there cannot be an actual infinity of past days (or years, or any unit of time); hence, there must have been a first moment in time. And since something that begins to exist must have a cause, there must be a cause of the universe. This argument is based in reason, not specifically in divine revelation and faith, although philosophers in monotheistic traditions would almost unanimously identify the cause of the universe as the Creator God of religious revelation.

Similarly, Aquinas argued that the universe must depend on a self-sufficient Creator for its very being. Unlike everything within the physical universe, God must require no cause, be eternally unchanging, exist outside the limits of space and time, have no preceding state or condition, and be the cause of the existence of all things: the one and only Uncaused Cause.[9] While Aquinas held it as true that the universe had a beginning in time, he also argued that *even if* the universe had always existed and had no beginning in time, it would still be sensible to say that it is created. In other words, the universe could—speaking on the basis of reason alone, without making reference to revelation or faith—be both *created* and *eternal*: the universe simply does not contain the explanation of its own existence, and thus requires an explanation outside itself, not just in its first moment but from moment to moment, regardless of whether the universe has existed forever or had a single beginning point in time.

Behind this view of origins is the understanding that *creatio non est mutatio*: creation is not a change. In other words, creation is not a one-time event that happened at the beginning of the universe's existence, the initial moment when the universe first came into being, but is instead the originating and *sustaining in existence* of all that is—without which the universe would utterly cease to exist. A "watchmaker deity" that sets the universe in motion and then abandons it, as a watchmaker might build and wind up a watch and then leave it behind, is "later than creation" (as in the Rig Veda quotation presented earlier) and a totally different kind of being than God as described by Aquinas, who is the ultimate cause of the entire natural order, including all the "natural causes" within it, the cause of the very existence of natural causes in the first place. God, as described by Aquinas, provides the ultimate underpinning of all that is: Being itself and the source of being, the root of the world and the reality who is the Creator of all other realities.

---

9. Note that basically every position outlined in this section holds that *something* must be eternal, either the world, or God, or both.

Creation Myths and Universal Histories

Ideas about creation often find expression not only in philosophical treatises but in stories, in creation myths. Historically, creation myths have given people both *explanations* at the informational level and *ideas and attitudes toward the world* at the interpretive level. And, speaking very broadly, science-based universal histories have often seen themselves as a modern version of creation myths, as modern knowledge put into story form. David Christian, a founding figure in the field, has referred to Big History as a "modern creation myth" or "modern origin story," where the word "myth" means "grand story that provides a framework for thinking about origins." Christian sees Big History as the project of taking what modern scientists and historians have observed about the world and weaving it into a single, coherent story that can show us who we are as human beings, where we have been, and where we are going, both as a species and as a planet.

There are two main considerations to keep in mind when thinking of a universal history as the counterpart of myth. First, insofar as they are *stories*, evidence-based narratives always include interpretive framing, and they must—because they are stories—make choices as to what to include and what to exclude. These choices cannot themselves be made through empirical evidence alone; they always answer to other criteria. And so the path from hard evidence to coherent story is never straight, nor is it necessarily uncontroversial. It is easy enough to appreciate that this is the case when dealing with a politically charged controversy in which the same historical facts are set into radically different narratives. But it is also true when we create an apparently universal narrative out of the natural sciences and scholarship in history and the humanities.

Evidence-based narratives therefore deserve to be analyzed *as narratives*, lest the interpretive framing become invisible. The question of ultimate origins is one example. As discussed earlier, empirical evidence alone is inconclusive about ultimate origins, and not necessarily the best way of approaching the question, yet different answers to the question of origins place the world within radically different frameworks. The same transformation of matter in the history of the universe, Earth, and life, and the same basic outline of human history, may take on vastly different meanings within these different frameworks.

Second, many narratives may hold deep insights at the interpretive level, a core value that should not be lightly discarded. This is true both of ancient creation myths and the modern myths of the sort found in science fiction and fantasy— J. R. R. Tolkien's goal of creating a mythic narrative through his writing on Middle-earth is one example. Such stories may not try to be historically accurate, or to provide an evidence-based picture of what happened, but still offer commentary and insight about the nature of the universe and what it means to be human in it. Poetic or symbolic descriptions of real or fictional events, primordial or present-day, stand alongside evidence-based narratives. Treating a modern evidence-based story of the past as if it is in precisely the same genre as ancient creation myths risks doing justice to neither.

Take the biblical account of Genesis as a paradigmatic example. Jewish and Christian commentaries have long mined this account for fundamental insights about humanity and the world, often recognizing the genre in which the beginning of Genesis is written not as a blow-by-blow history, but as a poetic and symbolic narrative that communicates deep truths in story form. As just one example, the humanist philosopher Leon Kass calls the reading of Genesis "the beginning of wisdom," and writes:

> The stories cast powerful light, for example, on the problematic character of human reason, speech, freedom, sexual desire, the love of the beautiful, shame, guilt, anger, and man's response to mortality. The stories cast equally powerful light on the naturally vexed relations between man and woman, brother and brother, father and son, neighbor and neighbor, stranger and stranger, man and God.[10]

Joseph Campbell writes of myth in general as

> showing you what the shape of the universe is, but showing it in such a way that the mystery again comes through. Today we tend to think that scientists have all the answers. But the great ones tell us, "No, we haven't got all the answers. We're telling you how it works – but what is it?" You strike a match, what's fire? You can tell me about oxidation, but that doesn't tell me a thing.[11]

A fundamental function of a good myth, Campbell argues, is to help the reader in "realizing what a wonder the universe is, and what a wonder you are, and experiencing awe before this mystery."[12] Literature and story do that in a creative and symbolic way, and proper recognition of genre is key to interpretation.

In the end, this is essentially an argument in favor of meeting each story, ancient or modern, on its own terms—as a story—and engaging with each story not only at the informational level but at the interpretive level as well. All grand stories, whether based in modern scientific knowledge or not, deserve a careful, charitable, and critical reading. A modern evidence-based narrative may be more accurate

10. Leon Kass, *The Beginning of Wisdom*, p. 10.

11. Joseph Campbell, *The Power of Myth*, p. 39.

12. Ibid., p. 38.

informationally, but others may yet be more authentic, true to life, and resonant with reality in ways that go beyond the simply informational. And one can live in multiple stories at once.

Discipline

If we define history broadly, as the study of change and continuity over time, then "historians" are not the only experts who study "history": cosmologists, geologists, paleontologists, and representatives of several other academic disciplines are also involved in historical pursuits. Universal histories are a powerful tool for integrating many such disciplines, bringing together these different sources of knowledge.

This kind of integration is not the norm within the academic world. Especially throughout the 20th century, expert specialization more often has increased, to the point where experts in one discipline now rarely speak to experts in other disciplines. Opportunities to integrate knowledge systematically are rare.

Remarkably, despite this isolation of disciplines, scholars working more or less independently in domains from cosmology to history have managed to assemble evidence for a basic story of the past that is impressively coherent at the informational level: the universe began 13.8 billion years ago in the Big Bang, according to cosmologists; stars formed perhaps a hundred million years later, producing new elements when they later exploded as supernovae; the Sun and Earth formed over 4.5 billion years ago, as matter came together in our area of the Milky Way under the influence of gravity, according to astronomers and planetary scientists; life on Earth began over 3 billion years ago and has evolved to take on countless forms, according to geologists and biologists; human ancestors appeared within the last 6 to 7 million years, and the human body, human societies, human technology, and human ideas about the world have changed over recent ("historical") time in various ways that have been extensively studied by anthropologists and historians.

Even the simple fact that the dates in this outline work out sensibly is an indication that there is some basic agreement about, and reliability to, this story. By contrast, through much of the 19th century, geologists' best estimates for the age of the Earth were much smaller (on the order of millions rather than billions of years) and did not seem to provide sufficient time for evolution to produce the present diversity of life (see Plate 1). Those disciplinary stories, in other words, did not fit together. And through part of the 20th century, cosmologists' best estimates for the age of the universe were smaller than geologists' best estimates for the age of the Earth—a rather striking inconsistency! So it is not trivial, and in fact is quite impressive, that further work and evidence within each field have led to a remarkably self-consistent, cross-disciplinary timeline, especially when disciplines are so compartmentalized that experts do not necessarily, or intentionally, connect their ideas with those in other disciplines.

The Challenges of Integrating Different Disciplines

That said, moving from one discipline to another does not just mean switching from one set of ideas (or time scale) to another. Each discipline is not merely a content area, but also a set of methods and sources of evidence, and it often unfolds within a distinctive set of philosophical assumptions about how the world works. And while there may be consistency between the content of different disciplines at the informational level, there may yet be significant differences of worldview from one discipline to another, especially about what is truly fundamental. For instance, if you ask a physicist, chemist, biologist, and psychologist to describe what a human being fundamentally *is*, you will likely get four different answers: everything from a collection of particles subject to deterministic laws[13] to a set of neurons with supplementary tissue. These examples are admittedly extreme, and any individual member of a discipline may have a more nuanced view of the relationship among all the possible viewpoints. However, it is always tempting for practitioners of a given discipline to assume that whatever *they* study is absolutely fundamental: for physics, subatomic particles or the laws of nature; for psychology, the brain; for history, social interactions and culture. Every individual discipline is already presented implicitly within a framework of a larger view of the world and a sense of how to think about it.

Each discipline is also itself both human and historical, which means that each discipline has a distinct culture and institutional framework of its own, built up over decades or centuries. Cosmology, Earth science, biology, history, and other disciplines are not just bodies of knowledge, but also communities of people. And as with any group of people, a dominant culture may emerge and evolve over time, influencing (although never controlling absolutely) how experts in the discipline think and speak about their subject matter.[14] It should not be surprising, then, that such cultural and social factors come into play during the production of knowledge, not as an obstacle to perfect "objectivity" but as an integral part of the process: knowledge is produced by people.[15] So despite many points of coherence at the informational level, integrating disciplines at the interpretive level can be much more challenging, and also requires a balanced evaluation of the many disparate cultures and worldviews represented in different disciplines.

To illustrate these general observations, we turn to a specific example: the issue that different disciplines do not necessarily have the same standards for what kinds of explanations are considered *admissible*. In other words, what is considered a good

---

13. "A physicist is the atoms' way of thinking about atoms" (anonymous; quoted in Bill Bryson, *A Short History of Nearly Everything*, p. 113).

14. Introductory textbooks, and the writings of outspoken members of a given discipline, are good places to look if one is interested in probing the culture of that discipline.

15. Even the word "discipline" itself contains hints of this, as it comes from the same root as "disciple"—the idea being that one learns a discipline by becoming a disciple (graduate student, in today's world) of those who have mastered (become experts in) the field.

explanation is different depending on which discipline one is working in. The example here, of simplicity vs. complexity, demonstrates the tensions that can emerge.

Example: What Counts as an Explanation? Simplicity vs. Complexity

Physicists love simple, elegant explanations. While every physicist would affirm the necessity both of rigorously self-consistent mathematics and of experimental evidence, the physics community has also developed a culture of favoring mathematical theories that are aesthetically appealing. Perhaps surprisingly, this has a track record of success. The Nobel laureate Frank Wilczek writes, "Plato valued beauty over accuracy. . . . And when trying to guess what will come next, I often follow Plato's strategy, proposing objects of mathematical beauty as models for Nature."[16] Or as the physicist and mathematician Hermann Weyl put it in the mid-20th century, when looking back on his own distinguished career, "My work always tried to unite the Truth with the Beautiful, but when I had to choose one or the other, I usually chose the Beautiful."[17]

Wilczek and Weyl do not say these things as flighty or unrigorous members of the discipline: their theories have found a great deal of success. Beauty and aesthetics are never the only criteria for the selection of models in physics, but physicists retain a sense that explanations in this discipline should usually be simple and elegant.[18] The Big Bang is an "exception that proves the rule." During the mid-20th century, while the evidence was still up in the air regarding the accuracy of the Big Bang model, the theory was often dismissed on the grounds that the idea of a beginning of time seemed inelegant and arbitrary to physicists. And even now that the Big Bang has become widely accepted based on evidence, the prominent theoretical physicist Steven Weinberg writes that the Big Bang "is not the most satisfying theory imaginable of the origin of the universe," and that physicists "would prefer a greater sense of logical inevitability in the theory,"[19] though they almost universally accept it based on the strength of the evidence.

Historians, by contrast, tend to balk at any explanation that feels too elegant, "beautiful," or "logically inevitable" as being incapable of having accurately captured all the relevant evidence:

> Scholars are and must be cautious: a good story is not necessarily the one that incorporates all of the data at hand. Some "good stories" are simply wrong.[20]

---

16. Frank Wilczek, *A Beautiful Question*, pp. 4–5.

17. Quotation from William O. Straub, http://www.weylmann.com/ .

18. It is this sense that leads them to search for a "theory of everything."

19. Steven Weinberg, *The First Three Minutes*, p. 8.

20. Patricia A. McAnany and Norman Yoffee, *Questioning Collapse*, p. 7.

History as well as life itself is complicated—neither life nor history is an enterprise for those who seek simplicity and consistency.[21]

In most circumstances, there would be nothing problematic about physicists and historians having different approaches. The approaches that physics and history have developed are both well-suited to their subject matter. The potential problem comes when, in a universal history, the approach of one discipline is used on another discipline's subject matter without adequate attention to the implications of doing so. That is, should a "history of everything" answer primarily to simplicity, elegance, and general principles, or to complexity, distinction, and particularity? In practice, one can narrate different parts differently. But that requires specific attention to disciplinary cultures and worldviews, and to the reasons why they exist: combining disciplines not by abolishing all boundaries, but by understanding the boundaries in as much detail and with as much precision as possible. A jigsaw puzzle, after all, is not put together by simplifying the boundaries of each piece, but by understanding the shape of each piece well enough to see where the pieces do or do not fit together—and not the shape only, but also the color and design of the piece. Thus, by analogy, the content, methods, and cultural approach of a given discipline are all important for proper interpretation and integration, especially if we are to avoid arbitrarily privileging the values, culture, and worldview of one discipline over others. To see how disciplines connect with one another, one must ideally understand the languages and cultures of the disciplines just as much as their content, and be able to interpret what experts in a given field write in light of the culture of that field.

Integrating the Humanities and Sciences: The Interpretive Level

We invoked physics and history in the previous section not only because they are the fields in which we (the authors) were trained, but because they exemplify perhaps the most fundamental fault line between disciplines: that between disciplines within the sciences and those within the humanities. Broadly speaking, the humanities study human culture past and present, including what the historian William Cronon calls the "cultural values of people as storytelling creatures struggling to find the meaning of their place in the world,"[22] while the sciences engage in observation and experimentation on the natural world.

As the physicist and philosopher Martin Eger has proposed, attempts to construct a universal history or "epic of evolution" represent attempts to interpret the

---

21. Jared Diamond, *Collapse*, p. 349.

22. William Cronon, "Kennecott Journey," in *Under an Open Sky: Rethinking America's Western Past*, p. 32.

meaning of the findings of the natural sciences for everyone, scientists and non-scientists alike. Authors of works of popular science that contribute to this genre see themselves as filling in key pieces of a single, meaningful big picture. In other words, a universal history is fundamentally a blend between the sciences and the humanities, not just in the sense that both the natural sciences and disciplinary history lend content knowledge, but also in the sense that a universal history often attempts to *reflect* and *transmit* the "cultural values" of certain scientific disciplines while *influencing* the cultural values of a broader audience. It is a humanities-oriented project, drawing on scientific content.[23]

It is precisely this "humanistic" focus on discerning the *meaning* of science (and history) that may be one of the most promising, intellectually generative, and also provocative features of Big History. Universal histories share scholarly knowledge, acknowledging the reliability of evidence-based knowledge drawn from a variety of fields while grappling with the larger worldviews and stories in which individual scientific and historical ideas become embedded. Since Big History organizes the composition of universal histories into a coherent field, those who work in this field have a great opportunity not only to transmit existing interpretations of science and history, but also to challenge them productively. In other words, Big History, as a field, could contribute to distinguishing the informational level from the interpretive level at the foundations of several disciplines. Were this to happen, the field would provide a forum for efforts at integration rather than a prepackaged way of going about that integration, a place where cross-disciplinary syntheses could be attempted and connections made, a much-needed space to discuss big ideas in public, with rigor. As Eger has argued in the context of popular-science writing—before Big History became an organized field of its own—this contestation and debate are precisely what make a field sustainable and "[save] it from being merely an intellectual fad, a passing ideology, the hobbyhorse of philosophically untutored scientists."[24]

In practice, however, doing this requires a clear set of standards: How can we identify some universal histories as being better than others, not only at the informational level but also at the interpretive level? In a universal history, or any other intellectual endeavor that attempts to integrate many disciplines, how does one justify an argument in a way that will resonate across disciplines? For example, to return to the simplicity-vs.-complexity example: Is a universal history better if it is distilled down to a simple, elegant explanation of what one needs to know, or is it better if it is more open, nuanced, and complicated? Without an identifiable set of first principles and standards to assess quality, the field of Big History could expect a simple proliferation of universal histories, not necessarily an increase in quality.

---

23. See, especially, Martin Eger, "Hermeneutics and the New Epic of Science," pp. 261–279 in *Science, Understanding, and Justice: The Philosophical Essays of Martin Eger*, ed. Abner Shimony.

24. Ibid., p. 274.

One way to begin answering these questions is to consider how existing disciplines handle these same questions, and to see whether Big History might proceed in the same way. To be rigorous, convincing, and nuanced, any field must have transparent *methods* that produce *evidence* subject to *interpretation*. And the final interpretation must be subject to a range of possible critiques, so that anyone engaging with the field can start at the ground level and query the nature of the methods and evidence upon which the interpretation is based. Otherwise, the interpretive level becomes mere opinion. The field must also acknowledge situations where multiple interpretations are possible. In the case of Big History, people of many different disciplinary backgrounds, including both those trained in the humanities and those who are better versed in the sciences, must be able to participate in such a process.

Treating Big History as the disciplinary ground for contesting the humanistic interpretation of science has a tremendous payoff. Returning to the example of disciplinary "models" of a human being, each one of these models of reality is based in a set of ideas that adds new insight to the nature of a human being: they become fundamentally misleading only when seen in isolation from—that is, to the exclusion of—the others. What if, instead of competing with each other, we saw each of these models as contributing something distinct, a different dimension to our understanding of humanity? What if Big History could hold all these models of the person together, without taking any one of them to be the final reality?

There are vastly different disciplinary cultures—and yet there is only one world, or universe. Disciplines intersect, overlap, and shade into one another all the time, whether practitioners recognize it or not. Organizing an effort to integrate historical disciplines better may be what Big History as a field can do best, and it is a project to which we hope to contribute substantially throughout this book.

Scale

Imagine that the Earth were shrunk down to the size of the smallest objects currently visible to the human eye, about a tenth of a millimeter—that is, the size of a large amoeba, or the width of a human hair. The Sun would then be the size of a small grape and would sit a meter away from the Earth in the Solar System, while the nearest star other than the Sun would be about as far away as San Diego is from Los Angeles. The outer reaches of the Milky Way Galaxy in this scaled-down universe would be 25 times as far away as the Moon is from Earth in reality. Or, alternatively, if you were shrunk to the size of a bacterium, an ordinary-sized human host you might live within would "look" roughly as big as Japan does now. On the other hand, if an atom were the size of a tennis ball, then the bacterium *Escherichia coli* would be nearly a kilometer across, and an adult human being's height would reach five times beyond the orbit of the Moon.

Looking at time scales rather than spatial scales, if the 13.8 billion years of the universe's history were laid out on a 100-yard American football field, then the extinction of the dinosaurs 66 million years ago would occur about a half-yard from the end zone corresponding to the present. All of the history of *Homo sapiens*, roughly 300,000 years, would occupy the final two-thousandths of a yard, approximately two millimeters. Or, on the other side of the spectrum, if you could experience a typical time scale of a neuron firing in your brain (approximately 1 millisecond) as noticeable in the way the duration of short-term memory (on the order of 10 seconds) is now, then the length of an average human life would "feel" like a million years.

Space and Time Tell a Story

The scale analogies described here are a familiar staple of universal histories, going back at least to the time of *Vestiges of the Natural History of Creation*. To study universal histories is to encounter a range of scales well beyond human experience and to consider how they relate to, and connect with, one another; analogies can be immensely helpful for grappling with the sheer unfamiliarity of exceptionally large or exceptionally small scales.

An alternative approach, for the more numerically inclined, would be to simply report the sizes of things.[25] But analogies or no, the scale of things can never *really*

Side Note: Powers of Ten

This section, especially in the footnotes, will occasionally make use of mathematical expressions like 10^{12} or 10^{-12}. The positive exponent (the "12" in 10^{12}) expresses a large number, 1 with 12 zeros after it: 1 trillion, or 1,000,000,000,000. The negative exponent (the "–12" in 10^{-12}) expresses a small number, one-trillionth, or 0.000000000001. In general, "powers of ten" are a convenient way to express numbers that are inconvenient to write out: 10^n represents a 1 with n zeros after it, and 10^{-n} represents a 1 with n zeros before it, one zero before a decimal point and the rest after it.

---

25. The numerical comparisons are precise but, even for professional scientists, usually do not give as much of an intuitive feel for the relative scale of things—even as the numbers are the basis for constructing the analogies that provide such an intuitive feel. Converted so that all the units are meters (m), the diameter of the Earth is around 10^7 m, the diameter of the Sun around 10^9 m, the distance from the Earth to the Sun around 10^{11} m, the distance from Earth to the nearest star around 4×10^{16} m, the diameter of the Milky Way around 10^{21} m, the diameter of the observable universe around 8×10^{26} m, the width of a human hair around 10^{-4} m, the width of the bacterium *E. coli* around 10^{-6} m, an atomic diameter around 10^{-10} m, and the height of a human roughly 2 m.

be "just reported." There is always a larger point being made: behind all Science, there is Story. Even a dry numerical report of the sizes of things would communicate something—if only by the author's choice of which sizes to report and which comparisons to make.

For example, a cosmologist might report on the large scales, as in the first paragraph of this section, perhaps wishing to emphasize how small we are as human beings, and stressing the apparent cosmic insignificance of human life:

> The size and age of the Cosmos are beyond ordinary human understanding. Lost somewhere between immensity and eternity is our tiny planetary home. In a cosmic perspective, most human concerns seem insignificant, even petty.[26]

Meanwhile, a biochemist might wish to emphasize how intricately made (or gigantic!) we are, stressing the elegance of all the mechanisms that underlie and enable human life:

> There are billions [of times] more atoms in a teaspoon of water than there are stars in the Milky Way.[27]

Both perspectives would be consistent with what we know at the informational level. Human beings occupy the middle of the range of known scales in the universe, both of space and time. (See "Side Note: We Are Intermediate-Scaled.") Thinking of scales *logarithmically*, where we ask how many *times* larger or smaller, longer or shorter, one scale is than another,[28] quickly reveals that a wide range of interpretations of humanity's place within the "grand scheme" of scales in the universe would be consistent with the raw data. At the interpretive level, it seems that multiple interpretations, multiple perspectives, must be held together here—or perhaps size just does not say as much about the significance of a thing as we sometimes think it does.

It is not easy (and perhaps not desirable) to avoid privileging a certain set of scales as "fundamental" or "more important" and then interpreting other scales accordingly. Especially with regard to time, the way a history organizes and interprets scale is a fundamental aspect of the story it tells; the organization of time within the story reveals something of what the author's purpose was in writing.

---

26. Carl Sagan, *Cosmos*, p. 1.

27. Michelle Francl, "The Best Chemistry Books," https://fivebooks.com/best-books/chemistry-michelle-francl .

28. A very common approach in the sciences.

Side Note: We Are Intermediate-Scaled

The largest known structures in the universe (the superclusters and filaments of the "cosmic web"; see chapter 2) occupy spatial scales a trillion trillion times larger[29] than the human body, while the smallest known structures are the quark composites known as protons and neutrons, which are roughly a thousand trillion times smaller. The scale of a large city is precisely in the middle of the largest and smallest scales of structures in the universe. Seen in this light, humans are neither huge nor tiny.

A similar statement could be made with respect to time: the longest time scale in our universe is the age of the universe,[30] about two hundred million times longer than a human lifespan, while the shortest time scale known to physics is the so-called Planck time, 10^{53} (a hundred thousand trillion trillion trillion trillion) times shorter than a human life span. Seen in this perspective, human lives are actually on the long end of time scales in the universe, though still in the middle. To take another example: one second, a good unit of time in which to measure human conscious awareness, is *shorter* than the longest time observation known to science (the age of the universe) by almost exactly the same factor as it is *longer* than the shortest direct time observations currently known to science (studied in "femtochemistry" and "attophysics"—around a hundred million billion times).[31] Again, we find ourselves in the middle. And it is not just time and space where we find ourselves of intermediate scale: If the mass of a proton were scaled up to one kilogram, a human being would be as massive as a typical star.[32]

For instance, consider David Christian's magisterial work of Big History, *Maps of Time*. As shown in Table 1.1, the chapters are divided up in such a way that the first several cover time spans of millions to billions of years, while the last several cover hundreds to thousands of years.

To organize time in this fashion is itself a device for picking out a narrative thread: one could imagine telling a very different kind of story "just" by changing the way the page numbers were allotted. This particular organization is also

---

29. All measured in one dimension; cube the numbers to get three dimensions.

30. Many known *processes*, however, take longer than this, such as the life cycle of red-dwarf stars or the radioactive decay of certain isotopes (see chapters 2 and 3). They just have not been completed yet!

31. Numbers: 4×10^{24} m, 10^{-15} m, 1.4×10^{10} y $= 4 \times 10^{17}$ s, 10^{-17} s.

32. The astronomer Martin Rees suggested this comparison; see, e.g., TED, "Sir Martin Rees: Earth in Its Final Century?," https://www.youtube.com/watch?v=3qF26MbYgOA .

Table 1.1 Organization of Chapters in *Maps of Time*

Chapter of *Maps of Time*	Number of Years Covered Within Chapter	Approximate Percentage of the Universe's 13.8 Billion Years Covered by End of Chapter	Percentage of the Book's Total Page Count Covered by End of Chapter[1]
1 (ends on p. 38)[2]	300,000	0.000000007%	8%
2 (p. 56)	~9,000,000,000	65%	11%
3 (p. 75)	~800,000,000	71%	15%
4 (p. 105)	~300,000,000	73%	21%
5 (p. 136)	~3,500,000,000	Over 90%	28%
6 (p. 169)	7,000,000	99.95%	34%
7 (p. 203)	200,000	99.999%	41%
8 (p. 244)	11,500	99.99992%	50%
9 (p. 282)	5,000	99.99996%	57%
10 (p. 332)	5,000	99.99996%	68%
11 (p. 363)	1,000	99.999993%	74%
12 (p. 405)	700	99.999995%	82%
13 (p. 439)	250	99.999998%	89%
14 (p. 464)	100	99.9999993%	95%
15 (p. 491)	Futures: $10^{10^{76}}$	N/A	100%

1. Based on a page count of 491 (omitting preface, appendices, and other back matter).
2. Slightly misleading, as this includes the book's introduction (pp. 1–14) in the fractions, but that only accentuates how weighted the proportions are toward more recent material.

convenient for giving roughly equal time to different scientific fields; in a sense, time is partitioned up according to discipline.[33]

Value, Significance, and Scale: Small Matters Too

The strategy used in Christian's *Maps of Time* is one way of narrating a universal history, but one can imagine alternative histories with a much different kind of framing. While we do not attempt to write such a history here, an interesting example might

33. Cosmologists certainly speak about billion-year time scales far more often than historians do. But no discipline operates on one time scale exclusively; all work on multiple time scales, within certain ranges. Cosmologists analyze billions of years of cosmic history in part by studying supernovae that last for a matter of days; Earth scientists recognize the importance both of the changing composition of the ocean over hundreds of millions of years and the rare meteorite impact that remakes the surface of the Earth in a matter of hours. All disciplines know macroscales and microscales.

be to explore what a universal history would look like that emphasized very short time scales—the time scales that may be less than fully visible in grand, sweeping narratives. Yet the small scales matter too: without quark-quark interactions on time scales of 10^{-24} seconds, or chemical reactions on time scales of 10^{-15} seconds, or molecular-level processes within living cells that occur on time scales of 10^{-6} seconds, or neural processes on time scales of 10^{-3} seconds, there would be no longer-scale story of the history of the universe, Earth, life, and humanity.[34] The short and the long are equally necessary; the trends we see are, at least in part, a relic of what we choose to pick out.

There are an infinite number of ways to tell the story, and stories emphasizing the small might well cast human life in a different light than the usual cosmic narratives do. Humans may look radically insignificant on the scale of the universe, with our tiny bodies in a huge universe and our short life spans measured against the duration of stars or planets. But if we spend more time thinking about subatomic particles or molecules or cells, it becomes easier to see human beings as wondrous, complex living organisms. Human history also is shaped by both long and short trends: institutions that endure for many human life spans shape the nature of lived experience, but so do the choices made by particular people in particular moments. Looking at one side without the other can produce a one-sided picture of the whole.

One could go too far in this direction. Reductionism, which is explored further in chapter 3, is the assumption that smaller means more basic and more fundamental, and that all explanations must ultimately *reduce* down to these levels. When we assume that genes or molecules or subatomic particles are where the "real" causes or explanations lie, we have given a reductionist explanation.

But just as we asked what it would take to avoid privileging one discipline at the expense of others, we might—and do, periodically, throughout this book—ask what it would take to avoid privileging one scale in space or time at the expense of the others. The astrophysicist Subrahmanyan Chandrasekhar once wrote, "The greatest sculptures can be viewed—indeed, should be viewed—from all distances since new aspects of beauty will be revealed in every scale."[35] The world is largely unfamiliar at both the largest and smallest scales in the universe. Yet the scales underpin each other, and their interweavings allow their different stories to unfold. As small scales provide underpinnings for larger-scale stories, larger scales provide new contexts and influences for those small scales. By exploring a variety of scales, we not only see a great deal more of the connections between scales, but also have greater opportunity to reflect on the choices inherent in crafting any singular "universal" history.

---

34. Respectively, these numbers are based on Gerard 't Hooft, *Time in Powers of Ten*, p. 116; 't Hooft, p. 134; Maya Shamir, Yinon Bar-On, Rob Phillips, and Ron Milo, "SnapShot: Timescales in Cell Biology," https://www.cell.com/cell/pdf/S0092-8674(16)30208-2.pdf; and 't Hooft, pp. 171–172.

35. Subrahmanyan Chandrasekhar, *Truth and Beauty: Aesthetics and Motivations in Science*, p. 72.

2 UNIVERSE

This chapter's five sections explore several topics at the intersection of science, storytelling, and philosophy. The first section ("Universe") is a kind of "grand overview" of ideas about the universe as a whole. The second ("Big Bang") presents and analyzes the scientific big idea that has come to frame the overall history of the universe. The third and fourth describe key principles ("Gravity" and "Entropy") for understanding how the history of the universe has unfolded. The fifth and final section ("Mathematics") is more specifically philosophical, focusing on the question of why mathematics has such seemingly gratuitous explanatory power in the physical sciences.

Universe

The entities visible in the sky—the Sun, the Moon, the stars—have always been part of our reality as humans, and they have figured prominently in our stories. This is no less true in the modern world. The expert observers of the sky we call "astronomers" and "cosmologists" have done much to show that the universe is not only a part of our reality, but a part of our history: the atoms in our bodies were generated in the early universe and in stars, the planet we stand on formed from a swirling gas cloud like some of the distant nebulae we see through telescopes, and the Sun that "governs the day" is a star just like the ones we see at night and formed some 4.6 billion years ago.

Scientific cosmology, the observation-driven study of the physical universe on its largest scales in space and time, shows us much that is invisible to the unaided eye. In this chapter, we will meet several nonvisible entities, including dark matter, dark energy, and the cosmic microwave background. Cosmology also expands our understanding of the size of the universe, which turns out to be unimaginably vast.[1] It shows that the heavens and the Earth are made of the same stuff, the same kind of matter: protons and neutrons and electrons are building blocks for the matter in stars and planets just as surely as they are for every bit of matter on Earth.

Still, modern universal histories, especially those communicated through popular science and Big History, do not just stitch together a number of facts or insights that cosmologists have discovered about the physical universe; they attach meanings and interpretive stories to it. In other words, they go beyond the realm of the purely informational and venture into the territory of philosophy and storytelling. Science may tell us about ourselves as humans, but it does so especially in the hands of those who become scientific storytellers. And rightly or wrongly, those storytellers impart their own philosophical leanings to their scientific stories.

The Size of the Universe

The size of the universe is perhaps one of the most mind-stretching discoveries of modern cosmology. Our own Milky Way Galaxy is only one of perhaps 2 trillion galaxies or more in the observable universe.[2] Each of these galaxies is a huge system of stars, interstellar dust and gas, and unseen "dark matter," all held together by their mutual gravitational pull. The distance from one end to the other of a large galaxy like our own is about 60 trillion times larger than the diameter of the Earth, yet even large galaxies have diameters hundreds of thousands of times smaller than the total distance it is possible to see into the universe.[3]

---

1. Literally, "unimaginably." In important ways, the human brain cannot process or understand it. Cosmologists thus expend much effort in trying to develop metaphors or thought experiments to help.

2. See Christopher J. Conselice, Aaron Wilkinson, Kenneth Duncan, and Alice Mortlock, "The Evolution of Galaxy Number Density at $z < 8$ and its Implications": https://iopscience. iop.org/article/10.3847/0004-637X/830/2/83 , for the research that brought the estimated total number of galaxies up from about two hundred billion to perhaps two trillion. Exactly three galaxies outside the Milky Way are visible to the naked eye: the Andromeda Galaxy, the Large Magellanic Cloud, and the Small Magellanic Cloud (the latter two are usually considered dwarf galaxies).

3. In addition to being mind-stretching, the scale of the universe is also unexpected. As recently as 1920, prominent scientists were debating whether the Milky Way Galaxy was the entire universe. (Leading astronomers Harlow Shapley and Heber Curtis met at the Smithsonian for a "Great Debate" about this question in 1920, and each could support their opposing positions based on the scientific evidence available at the time.) Professional astronomers were consistently underestimating the true size of the observable universe by a factor of 100,000. But even early 20th-century estimates of the universe's size dwarf previous estimates. For instance, medieval Arab astronomers, whose estimates were state-of-the-art for the time, estimated the radius of the universe as 90 million miles—which we now know to be quite close to the distance between the Earth and the Sun.

And what cosmologists have observed to date may not be all there is. In fact, it may not be even close. The universe may go on infinitely in all directions, and there may still be galaxies no matter how far out one goes. If this were the case, we would only be able to observe those galaxies close enough that their light has had enough time to reach us. Light does not travel instantaneously: it moves at about 186,000 miles (or about 300,000 kilometers) per second, roughly one foot per nanosecond, so it can only travel a certain distance, even in the billions of years the universe has existed. Since nothing travels faster than light, we simply have no way of observing any part of the universe from which light has not had enough time to travel to us. Those unknown and unobservable parts of the universe are said to be beyond our "cosmic horizon," the limit of what is observable; and the parts of the universe from which light *has* had enough time to travel are referred to as the "observable universe." The cosmic horizon is just like a normal earthly horizon in that it is a distance we cannot see beyond; to do so is beyond the current limits of scientific cosmology, and perhaps beyond what science can achieve even in principle. The observable universe is huge, but it may be only a speck within the entire universe.

This is the present state of cosmological knowledge regarding the universe's size. In the context of universal histories and the intellectual world that informs them, however, the vastness of the universe is never merely reported, but always *interpreted*. And very different interpretations of the vastness of the universe are consistent with what scientists have found. A common reflection is that the cold cosmic loneliness of the Earth mirrors the cosmic insignificance of human beings:

> Who are we? We find that we live on an insignificant planet of a humdrum star lost between two spiral arms in the outskirts of a galaxy which is a member of a sparse cluster of galaxies, tucked away in some forgotten corner of a universe in which there are far more galaxies than people.[4]

Meanwhile, others who take part in the broader interpretive conversation that informs universal histories view the grandness of the universe as clear evidence of the work of an even greater and more wonderful Creator, whose magnificence is manifested in the beauty and incomprehensible vastness of the universe and who both loves the universe and takes care of human beings:

> And so God is still around. All of our knowledge, all of our developments, cannot diminish his being one iota. These new advances have banished God neither from the microcosmic compass of the atom nor from the vast, unfathomable ranges of interstellar space. The more we learn about this universe, the more mysterious and awesome it becomes. God is still here.[5]

---

4. Carl Sagan, *Cosmos*, p. 159.

5. Martin Luther King, Jr., *The Measure of a Man*, p. 54.

Or, alternatively, that matter is itself sacred in some way, so the amount of it and the physical place of the Earth in the cosmos are secondary or irrelevant:

> God, ultimate reality, permeates all material manifestations, and hence . . . there is no fundamental antagonism between matter and spirit, world and God.[6]

The sheer number of thoughtful people who have addressed this issue, with different people finding different interpretations compelling or even self-evident, is a good reminder that even well-established physical facts about the universe, like its size and structure, can be taken to mean strikingly different things.

The Centrality of the Earth

A second illustration of the distinction between scientific observations and the stories that are told about them deals with the question of whether the Earth is at the center of the universe. Modern cosmology holds that there is no center and no edge to the universe, while writers in ancient and medieval Europe, along with the Islamic world and many other places, almost universally placed the Earth at the center of the universe. Countless works of popular science and Big History have couched the geocentric (Earth-centered) view of the universe as also being egocentric (self-centered), an example of people in the past making the Earth seem important so as to satisfy the human ego or gratify some basic human need:

> Earth was presumed to be the stable hub of the Universe. After all, the Sun, Moon, and stars all appear to revolve around our planet. It was natural to conclude, not knowing otherwise, that home and selves were special. This centrality led to a feeling of security or at least contentment—a belief that the origin, maintenance, and fate of the Universe were governed by something more than natural, something supernatural.[7]

The Scientific Revolution that took Earth out of the center is then taken as a "dethronement" of humanity:

> We must be appallingly silly to imagine we can find any importance for ourselves at all. Yet we are trying to do just that, despite our apparent mediocrity, which became evident when Renaissance scholar Nicolaus Copernicus decentralized Earth from the solar system around 500 years ago.[8]

---

6. Sangeetha Menon, "Hinduism & Science," in *The Oxford Handbook of Religion and Science*, p. 11.

7. Eric Chaisson, *Epic of Evolution*, p. ix.

8. Caleb Scharf, "Is Earth's Life Unique in the Universe?," http://www.scientificamerican.com/article/is-earth-s-life-unique-in-the-universe/ .

But this is an incorrect understanding of what Earth's centrality meant to many people who held this theory, and a misrepresentation of the possible range of interpretations of Earth's non-centrality.

The perception of Earth's centrality was mostly a matter of commonsense observation, not self-importance. It certainly *looks* like everything in the sky is circling around the Earth, and it seemed absurd to suggest that the Earth is moving—as it must be if it is orbiting the Sun, rather than being motionless at the center of the universe. In ancient and medieval Europe, heliocentric (Sun-centered) views were routinely rejected on the basis of *evidence*: if the Earth is not fixed in place, then when one throws something up in the air it should not fall straight down; the number and distribution of stars on one side of the sky is basically the same as the other side, so it makes sense that we are at the center; and so forth. Even Nicole Oresme (c. 1320–1382), a 14th-century philosopher who did not find such arguments against the Earth's motion conclusive, wrote that "everyone maintains, and I think myself, that the heavens do move and not the Earth"[9]—on the basis of this being the commonsense interpretation of everyday phenomena.

Moreover, European thinking, particularly in the Middle Ages, viewed the center of the universe as the place where impure, "weighty" material collected, as in Aristotle's understanding of physics; the Earth was the domain of corruption and change, while the heavens were perfect and unchanging:[10]

> Another modern misconception about the medieval Christian worldview is that people thought the central position of the earth meant that it was somehow exalted. In fact, to the medieval mind, the reverse was the case. The universe was a hierarchy and the further from the earth you travelled, the closer to Heaven you came. At the center, underneath our feet, the Christian tradition placed Hell. Then, surpassed in wickedness only by the infernal pit, was our earth of change and decay.[11]

Dante's *Inferno*, which was representative of thinking at the time (the early 1300s), placed Earth at the center of the universe, Hell at the center of Earth, and the devil at the center of Hell. The center was not necessarily a good place to be.

Correspondingly, while modern science has taken the Earth out of the center of the universe, it is not clear that this is a "demotion" of the Earth. If the change of cosmic address demotes anything, it demotes the heavens. Saying that something is "celestial" is still a compliment in everyday language, but we now understand that the objects in the sky are neither perfect nor unchanging, and we lack the absolute

---

9. Nicole Oresme, *Le Livre du ciel et du monde*, Book II, chapter 25, fol. 144b, eds. Albert D. Menut and Alexander J. Denomy, trans. Albert D. Menut, p. 537.

10. See, e.g., David Lindberg, *The Beginnings of Western Science*, pp. 53, 55.

11. James Hannam, *The Genesis of Science*, p. 31.

sense of "up" and "down" that the medieval vision of the cosmos offered. As for the Earth, there is a certain continuity over hundreds or thousands of years in associating the Earth or the ground with humility (a word related to the Latin *humus*, meaning earth or soil)—think of someone who is "down-to-earth," or the statement that "the meek shall inherit the earth."

In any case, scientific narratives of the past century have tended to imply that Earth's non-centrality must be a sign of its insignificance, but attaching any grand meaning to the Earth's physical location in the universe is a relatively recent phenomenon. The idea that the center was a place of importance, and that moving away from the center is a demotion, would have been foreign to Copernicus and many thinkers hundreds of years before as well as after him.

The Moral Meaning of the Universe

Writings about modern science also often claim that science has discovered that the universe is amoral: the universe does not care about us or how we act; morality is not written into the cosmos; it is not embedded in the way the world works; it is a purely human and social construct. The novelist Carlos Ruiz Zafón puts the idea succinctly:

> Man is a moral animal abandoned in an amoral universe and condemned to a finite existence with no other purpose than to perpetuate the natural cycle of the species.[12]

The wording may vary, but the general trend is clear. Modern thinkers often diverge from a common pattern in the premodern world as well as in many societies and belief systems today—namely, seeing the universe as having a moral grain that a person or a society can be in or out of tune with, according to their choices and actions, and seeing human society as having the ability to conform or not conform to the order of an inherently moral cosmos.

The ancient Chinese provide a case study of a way to envision or perceive a moral order embedded in the universe itself. Not only did they build capital cities on a cosmic grid oriented on the cardinal directions and name parts of the palace after the Milky Way and stars, but ancient Chinese thinkers perceived connections between the cosmos and human behavior. Confucians taught that correct performance of ritual and proper demeanor toward others would bring human society into conformity with the inherently moral cosmos, setting humans in their proper place in the universe. The emperor, the "Son of Heaven," bore the ultimate responsibility for the alignment of human society with the cosmos. He sacrificed to Heaven

---

12. Carlos Ruiz Zafón, *The Angel's Game*, p. 202.

and Earth as a son to his parents, and he performed agricultural rites to ensure the progress of the seasons. The correct observance of this responsibility would bring bountiful harvests, popular support, and heavenly approval; neglect would cause disasters, uprisings, and the loss of Heaven's mandate. Daoists believed that government and ritual were artificial human inventions that violated the natural order, and therefore had their own proposals for living in harmony with the cosmos, in small, self-sustaining communities.[13]

The Roman orator Cicero provides a capsule summary of a related idea, from a very different time and place:

> True law is right reason in agreement with nature; it is of universal application, unchanging and everlasting; it summons to duty by its commands, and averts from wrongdoing by its prohibitions. . . . It is a sin to try to alter this law, nor is it allowable to attempt to repeal any part of it, and it is impossible to abolish it entirely. We cannot be freed from its obligations by senate or people. . . .[14]

A similar link was forged, albeit more indirectly, by Immanuel Kant:

> Two things fill the mind with ever new and increasing admiration and awe . . . the starry heavens above me and the moral law within me.[15]

While thinkers in Big History and similar circles have "argued that we need to start exploring the links between different domains of knowledge, from cosmology to ethics,"[16] it is worth pointing out that this connection has already been forged elsewhere, and many times over. In fact, secular Western thinkers are the exception to the rule in *not* perceiving the cosmos as inherently moral in nature. From Dao (Chinese) to Dharma (Indian and widespread in Buddhist contexts) to Ma'at (Egyptian) to natural law (Western and elsewhere), an immense variety of people

---

13. We are grateful to Christian de Pee for material in this paragraph. See also Benjamin I. Schwartz, *The World of Thought in Ancient China*, and Angus C. Graham, *Disputers of the Tao: Philosophical Argument in Ancient China*.

14. Cicero, *De re publica* III, XXII, 33, trans. Clinton Walker Keyes, *Cicero in Twenty-Eight Volumes, XVI, De Re Publica, De Legibus*, p. 211. Cicero's "nature" here is more properly "human nature" than "the universe," and the Western "natural law" tradition is generally focused not on aligning oneself with the general rhythm of the universe so much as with the moral duties inherent in *human* nature. Still, there is broad consonance between this view and that of a moral cosmos: moral duties can be identified, at least in part, through reason and observation, and the "way the world works" includes moral demands.

15. Immanuel Kant, *Critique of Practical Reason*, trans. Lewis White Beck.

16. David Christian, *Maps of Time*, p. 4.

have shared some sense of an inherently moral cosmos, even if they differ significantly in their understanding of what precisely that entails.[17]

Does the absence of a moral meaning to the universe in modern science indicate that no such meaning exists? The question of moral meaning cannot be decided from within modern science. The physical sciences as such are not designed to answer questions of meaning, purpose, and morality. The theoretical physicist Steven Weinberg has commented that "the more the universe seems comprehensible, the more it also seems pointless,"[18] but to the extent that scientists who study the physical universe find this to ring true, it is because the natural sciences, as disciplines, are not equipped to engage issues of meaning and values in the way that they engage physical facts.[19] Mechanisms are legible to science, but the mechanism is not the meaning—just because one can identify a mechanism for how something works does not mean it has no meaning. If one considers science as the only reliable way of knowing about the world, then questions of meaning and morality will be excluded, because they are not part of science. But even this position is itself a philosophy rather than a consequence of scientific observations.

Defining the Universe

If you ask what the universe itself *is*, the answer you will likely get in a scientific or Big History context is that the universe is all the matter, energy, space, and time in existence. Sagan, again, from the very beginning of his masterwork *Cosmos*: "The Cosmos is all that is or ever was or ever will be."[20] As expansive as that might sound, defining "universe" in this way has serious implications for what a universal history considers real, because the universe is the playing field for all of universal history. Limiting the definition of the universe to matter and energy and time and space entails a philosophical assumption that we might call *physicalist* or *materialist*: that the material world is all that is real.

Materialism has worked well as a methodological assumption within the sciences; it is part of the "rules of the game" that the scientist must assume natural

---

17. Even Carl Sagan spoke of the "moral depth" of the world, sometimes as if it had an independent existence.

18. Steven Weinberg, *The First Three Minutes*, p. 154.

19. The Islamic philosopher Seyyed Hossein Nasr (b. 1933) argues that "there is no logical link in the modern world between science and ethics . . . What is needed is knowledge of the cosmos that is congruous and shares the same universe of meaning with ethical norms," to remake modern science by baking ethics into the "very theoretical structures and philosophical foundations of science." (Seyyed Hossein Nasr, "Islam and Science," in *The Oxford Handbook of Religion and Science*, eds. Philip Clayton and Zachary Simpson, p. 83.)

20. Carl Sagan, *Cosmos*, p. 1.

causes for every observation wherever possible. But in a universal history, a physicalist definition of the entire playing field has implications for all the questions one asks down the road, and it sets the terms of the discussion from the outset. The terms of every worldview other than the secular materialist is automatically excluded, and a certain philosophy of mind—which we explore in chapter 5—is essentially guaranteed. This may not seem to be a problem to anyone who is already convinced of physicalism, but viable alternative views exist: many people in the modern world accept scientific explanations of physical and natural phenomena while also arguing that there are more things in Heaven and on Earth than are dreamt of in a strictly physicalist philosophy—to slightly paraphrase Shakespeare's famous words in *Hamlet*. Along similar lines, the historian Marshall Hodgson once referred to the common dismissal of non-physical entities and causes among Western thinkers as a "narrowing in the range of reality that Occidentals [people of the West] were prepared to invest greatly in exploring."[21] Especially as we move forward to considering the human experience, which is rich in experiences that do not easily reduce to purely physical explanations, defining the universe in physicalist terms risks being "positivistic" or "scientistic"—that is, assuming that all valid knowledge comes through scientific study, to the exclusion of other methods and viewpoints. And it is not just a question of whether there are non-physical realities, but of how we interpret the material world itself. A physicalist starting point identifies material things as what "matters," while historians and other scholars of the humanities take it for granted that human history and culture are not entirely material.[22]

The lesson of all these examples is that any grand overall vision of the universe is always shaped and colored by a value system, and that these value systems must be considered and evaluated on their own terms rather than excluded or rendered invisible simply because they do not function according to scientific terms. While modern science has proven extremely successful at discovering new facts and insights about the nature of the physical universe, the broader *meaning* of the universe is not reducible to these factors. A reductive scientific view of the universe may drop important realities from consideration and, at the very least, can close one off to understanding how others see the world or closely examining the underlying philosophical assumptions of many modern scientists.

---

21. Marshall G. S. Hodgson, "The Great Western Transmutation," in *Rethinking World History: Essays on Europe, Islam and World History*, p. 62.

22. Physicalists usually accept that the "non-material" aspects of human experience, like thoughts and ideas and cultural norms, are in an important sense *real*, but physicalism posits that these things are all fundamentally *physical*, a position that, in practice, arguably still biases one's thinking toward a certain kind of positivism.

Big Bang

Apparent breakthroughs that seem to fundamentally change a field may garner press coverage, but arguably the biggest story in cosmology over the past few decades has not been a single breakthrough, but rather the convergence of many lines of evidence on a single set of ideas, collectively known as the Big Bang, scientific cosmology's central model for the beginning and history of the universe. The essence of the Big Bang model is that our universe began at a certain time in the past (13.8 billion years ago, according to the best current estimates, although this number is subject to ongoing revision), was very hot and dense in its early years, and has been expanding and cooling ever since. As the universe has expanded, matter in the universe has, under the influence of gravity, collected into the large-scale structures—galaxies and clusters of galaxies—that we see today.

The Big Bang stands not only as a theoretical story but as an evidence-based model that continues to be refined by observations, almost universally accepted among cosmologists and an indispensable part of science-informed universal histories. Ever since it became clear in the late 1920s that the universe is expanding, theorists have gradually built a story of the universe by analyzing the conditions that would have prevailed throughout the universe at each stage in its history. Essentially, they have taken present-day conditions—including temperature, density, and rate of expansion—and "rewound the tape" of the universe's history, extrapolating backward to determine the likely conditions in the past. Meanwhile, observers have found ways to test those extrapolations.

The Story

The basic story of the universe's history, generated by extrapolating backward from the present-day expansion and components of the universe (with appropriate proportions of matter, light, etc.), includes the following basic sequence.

In the first second of its existence, the universe went through several distinct phases. Temperatures in these earliest moments were so high that many forms of matter as we know them in the present-day universe could not exist stably; even subatomic particles like protons and neutrons were constantly disrupted and unstable in the earliest fraction of a second. The fundamental forces, which govern how matter and energy interact, separated—one at a time—from one another. This means that gravity, electromagnetism, the weak nuclear force, and the strong nuclear force (discussed later, in the "Gravity" section of this chapter) all became distinct from one another, as they are to this day. As the temperature of the universe rapidly fell, new forms of matter became stable, so that protons, neutrons, and electrons were distinct entities by the end of that first second.

For the next few minutes after that, the entire universe was still so hot and dense that it acted as a kind of nuclear reactor, combining protons and neutrons to produce nuclei of the three lightest elements: hydrogen, helium, and lithium.

However, the vast majority of elements could not be formed at this time, because the temperature and density of the universe swiftly fell too low to sustain the nuclear reactions as the universe continued expanding. Only later, when stars formed, would heavier elements be made.

For hundreds of thousands of years after this point, the universe remained so hot that atoms did not exist: some atomic nuclei (the tiny central part of the atom containing protons and neutrons) had been formed as just described, but the high temperatures that prevailed everywhere in the universe prevented electrons from joining up with nuclei to form stable atoms. However, by about 370,000 years after the Big Bang, the temperature had fallen far enough for nuclei and electrons to combine into stable atoms. Before this, the unbound electrons would have scattered light, just as a dense fog does. So although light was present in the universe—a great deal of light having been generated in the first fraction of a second—it could not travel freely, and the universe was opaque. But once electrons became bound to nuclei, the universe became transparent, meaning that light could travel freely through it. The light from this early stage of the universe's history is still present today; it is called the cosmic microwave background.

Up until this point, the matter in the universe had been distributed in an almost perfectly uniform way: no part of the universe had more than a tiny fraction[23] more or less matter than any other part of the universe. But as the universe expanded even more, this nearly featureless distribution of matter began changing: certain regions attracted more matter, and others emptied out. Over hundreds of millions of years, this process ultimately led to the formation of stars and galaxies.

As a theory and a model, the Big Bang makes the "predictions" about the universe's history described earlier based on mathematics and laws of physics. But the real power of the Big Bang model is in the observations that support it, leading cosmologists to the conclusion that this theory closely describes what actually happened billions of years ago.

The Evidence

The three most powerful pieces of evidence for the Big Bang are the expansion of the universe, the cosmic microwave background, and the relative amounts of hydrogen, helium, and lithium in the universe.

The first pillar of evidence, the expansion of the universe, is supported by the observation that light from almost every galaxy in the universe is *redshifted*. When light is redshifted, the wavelength of the light becomes longer. The reason this is called a "redshift" is that for visible light, increasing wavelength corresponds to a shift toward the red end of the spectrum. Redshift can be measured using telescope optics that are specially designed for *spectroscopy*, the measurement of the

---

23. Based on observations, the number turns out to be about 1/100,000.

spectrum[24] of incoming light received by the telescope—like what a prism does in splitting white light into a rainbow. Certain features of a spectrum are known to occur at specific wavelengths in a non-shifted spectrum, so if these features occur at longer wavelengths, cosmologists know there is a redshift. (See Plates 2 and 3.)

To explain the redshift of light from distant galaxies, cosmologists invoke the expansion of the universe: as space expands, light waves traveling through space are stretched out, meaning that their wavelengths become longer.[25] The farther away a galaxy is, the more redshifted its light is—a trend that is now called the Hubble-Lemaître Law. This is exactly what one would expect if the redshifts were due to the expansion of the universe, since the farther away one point is from another in an expanding space, the faster the points recede from one another, much like dots drawn on the surface of an inflating balloon.[26]

A second pillar of evidence for the Big Bang is the cosmic microwave background (CMB), sometimes called the cosmic microwave background radiation. Unlike every other wavelength of light, microwaves can be detected coming almost identically from every direction in the sky. It is called "cosmic" because it pervades the cosmos, providing a "background" over the entire sky, and "microwave" refers to the fact that it is radiation (light) in the microwave part of the electromagnetic spectrum. (See Plate 2.) The CMB was first discovered by accident in the 1960s,[27] but cosmologists now observe it in great detail using specially designed instruments such as the Planck, Wilkinson Microwave Anisotropy Probe, and Cosmic Background Explorer satellites.

---

24. A "spectrum" is the intensity of light as a function of frequency (or wavelength): the amount of light emitted at different frequencies.

25. The expansion of the universe is not an explosion outward *into* space; it is the stretching of all space itself. There need not be any "frontier" dividing the part of the universe that has matter in it from an infinitude of totally empty space beyond. The universe is still able to expand even if it has no center and no edge: the distances between objects can still increase regardless of whether there is something to expand into.

26. This "cosmological redshift" is related to, but not quite the same as, the Doppler effect, which is the blueshifting or redshifting of light due to the motion of an object toward or away from an observer. Cosmological redshift is due to the *expansion of space itself*, while the Doppler effect is due to the motion of objects *within space*. This means that the distance between two objects gets "stretched out" as space expands, so that some objects in the observable universe are more than 46 billion light-years from Earth even though the universe itself is less than 14 billion years old. Even as the universe expands, however, galaxies, stars, and planets do not expand, because they are held together by gravity.

27. Though its existence had been predicted nearly 20 years earlier. Steven Weinberg argues that the lack of any serious experimental effort to detect the CMB is a testament to how difficult physicists found it in the mid-20th century to take theories of the early universe seriously, as well as being due to a breakdown in communication between experimenters and theorists. (Steven Weinberg, *The First Three Minutes*, pp. 122–132.)

The CMB's existence is consistent with the view that the entire universe was much hotter and denser in its early stages. As early as the 1940s, physicists had predicted that microwave background radiation should pervade the universe if the Big Bang was correct, since the early universe would have been filled with light (as described earlier). So the discovery of the CMB was taken as powerful evidence in favor of the Big Bang.

In addition to its existence being predicted, the CMB shows all the signs of truly being light "left over" from an early, hot, dense phase of the universe's existence, both in its spectrum and in its anisotropies (the differences from one direction in the sky to another), which are observed in great detail and match theoretical predictions precisely. In particular, the temperature of the CMB is almost exactly the same from one point in the sky to another, varying only by about a hundred-thousandth of a degree. This kind of variation, which corresponds to tiny variations in the density of matter, is perfectly consistent with an early-universe origin for the CMB: the early universe had to have been nearly uniform (with the same mix of particles, the same density, the same temperature, etc.) or the present-day universe would be far "lumpier" than it is, but it also had to have some variation in order for structures such as stars and galaxies to eventually form. A universe without any variation from point to point would simply have stayed uniform forever, since gravity would hold all matter in perfect balance. (See Plate 4.)

The third pillar of evidence for the Big Bang is the amount of hydrogen, helium, and lithium in the universe. The Big Bang model makes strict predictions, based on well-established knowledge in thermodynamics and nuclear physics, about how much of each element should have been formed in the first few minutes of the universe's existence, when the entire universe was so hot and dense that nuclear fusion could create them. Observations of the actual amounts of hydrogen, helium, and lithium in the universe closely match these predictions, which would be an extraordinary coincidence if the Big Bang model were not accurate.

Beyond these three pillars is other evidence for the Big Bang. One such piece of evidence is that the nature of objects cosmologists see in the universe changes the farther away they look. This is significant, because looking out into space entails looking back in time. Since light takes time to travel from one point to another, observers on Earth see objects in space as they were a certain amount of time in the past, because it took light that amount of time to travel from there to here. The more distant the source, the further back in time: We see the Moon as it was more than a second ago, the Sun as it was somewhat over eight minutes ago, nearby stars as they were tens to hundreds of years ago, and distant galaxies as they were millions to billions of years ago. And when cosmologists use telescopes to look at the most distant galaxies, they see not full-fledged galaxies but "proto-galactic clouds," which seems to indicate that the objects in the universe have changed substantially over cosmic time, as the Big Bang holds.

Another point in favor of the Big Bang is that the estimated ages of objects that astronomers and cosmologists find in the universe are always, at most, 12 to 13 billion years. This suggests that the universe has a finite age, which the Big Bang predicts. It is also reassuring that the best detailed models of the Big Bang indicate that the universe itself is over 13 billion years old, comfortably older than any particular object in the observable universe.

A final piece of evidence for the Big Bang comes from telescopic surveys of galaxies. These surveys confirm that the large-scale distribution of galaxies in the universe matches, with considerable precision, the distribution that one would expect if those galaxies formed under the influence of gravity pulling matter from less dense regions of the universe into more dense regions of the universe over hundreds of millions of years.

In short, the Big Bang model makes specific predictions about a variety of observations, and by and large, the observations agree with the predictions. If the Big Bang model is substantially on the right track, this is exactly what we would expect. With so much evidence in accord with the Big Bang, its presence in science-based cosmic histories is a given, but that does not mean every aspect of the model is equally well-tested, or equally likely to stand up to continued scientific scrutiny over the next 10 or 20 or 100 years.

Side Note: The Lithium Problem

Some cosmologists argue that the abundances of light elements in the universe present the single most powerful piece of evidence in favor of the Big Bang model, because the theoretical predictions range over ten powers of ten—the predicted amount of hydrogen is 10 billion times the predicted amount of lithium—and are so closely matched by observational results. Yet there is a stubbornly persistent problem: the amount of lithium observed in the universe is off by a factor of three from the theoretical predictions of the Big Bang model. That is, the observed amount of lithium is about three times less than predicted.

It is a fascinating problem, in part because it is a relatively small issue—it can hardly be said to disprove the Big Bang, given that the observational results have no reason to be within a factor of a *billion* of the theoretical predictions if the Big Bang model is inaccurate. But even a small issue is a genuine problem, and while possible explanations have been given, the difference has never been convincingly explained. The lithium problem has not yet gone away, and provides food for thought in what is otherwise a stunning confirmation of a set of ideas about what happened in the early universe.

Levels of Confidence

Graphics like the ones in Figures 2.1 and 2.2 suggest that the history of the universe is equally well-known in each of its earliest stages. But in reality, substantially different types of evidence, with different levels of reliability, lie behind the claims made about these different stages.

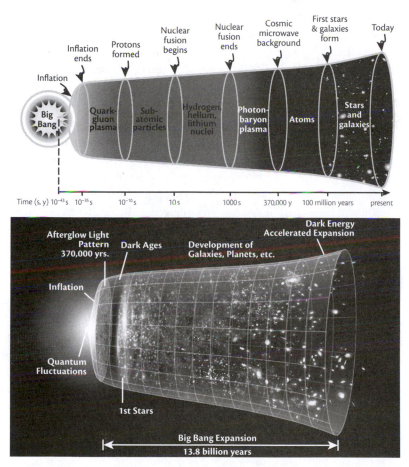

FIGURES 2.1 and 2.2 Two Ways of Representing the History of the Universe Note the difference in emphasis: The image in Figure 2.2 devotes almost all its space to the most observable parts of the universe's history, while the image in Figure 2.1 devotes more than half its space to the earliest, less directly observable parts of that history. To see this difference, compare where the cosmic microwave background ("Afterglow Light Pattern 370,000 yrs.") appears in each figure, or where the first stars appear.

Source (2.1): Based on https://phys.libretexts.org/Bookshelves/University_Physics/Book%3A_University_Physics_(OpenStax)/Map%3A_University_Physics_III_-_Optics_and_Modern_Physics_(OpenStax)/11%3A_Particle_Physics_and_Cosmology/11.7%3A_Evolution_of_the_Early_Universe

Source (2.2): NASA/WMAP Science Team

The most direct evidence has to do with the evolution of galaxies, clusters of galaxies, and the overall large-scale structure of the universe during the last several billion years of cosmic history. This part of the Big Bang story is directly observable—more directly, in a way, than any other aspect of history, because as described earlier, looking out into space means looking back in time. So while we only get to see what a given galaxy looked like at a single moment in its history, observing many galaxies reveals trends over time in what galaxies looked like and shows how the large-scale structure of the universe took shape over time.

The CMB is also powerful and direct evidence for the conditions of the early universe, in this case going back to 370,000 years after the Big Bang. As with the light from distant galaxies, the light from the CMB comes to us largely unaltered from the conditions in which it was emitted ages ago, still bearing the imprint of the early universe. While theoretical physics is necessary as a framework for interpreting what the CMB tells us and for comparing theoretical predictions with observational results, the CMB is still a direct observation of the past.

Before the 370,000-year mark, however, we can no longer rely on direct observation. Since the universe was opaque before that time, no light can reach us that is older (more distant) than the CMB. Still, there is evidence of the conditions in the universe at earlier times, in the form of the elements hydrogen, helium, and lithium. The amount of these elements, which can be detected using current instruments, is essentially a relic, an artifact, from the first few minutes of the universe's existence. It is not a direct observation of the light from that era, but the match between predicted and observed amounts of these elements gives us a window on the conditions in the universe at that time.

Before the era in which these nuclei were formed—called the era of Big Bang nucleosynthesis—the evidence becomes more and more indirect and remote as the conditions in the universe become more and more extreme (hotter, denser, higher energy). There are no observations of light or relics from these earlier times. However, the conditions in the universe at earlier times, back to less than 10^{-14} seconds,[28] have been re-created on Earth in particle accelerators, and the laws of physics that govern such conditions are known and tested. So the theoretical predictions as to what the universe was like at that time seem to be on solid footing— there is just no way, at present, for astrophysicists to make direct observations of this era to verify that these actually *were* the conditions of the universe at that time.

Earlier than this, the conditions that would have prevailed in the universe are so extreme, so high-energy, that they have never been re-created even in a laboratory, and so before 10^{-14} seconds, there is a complete absence of relevant observations. Before roughly 10^{-36} seconds, the laws of physics themselves are unknown.

---

28. See, e.g., SpaceMath@NASA, "Space Math," https://spacemath.gsfc.nasa.gov/universe/6Page91.pdf.

Before roughly 10^{-43} seconds, the laws of physics are not only unknown, but are thought to break down entirely. Time itself may cease to be well-defined in this earliest "fraction of a second."

So, in general, the further back in time we go, the less confident we can be about the story, and the more we are speculating or extrapolating from well-founded observations. There is, however, one exception: most cosmologists argue that a stage of "inflation" took place some 10^{-35} seconds after the Big Bang, in which space expanded incredibly rapidly, explaining (among other things) how far-flung parts of the universe that ought never to have been in contact with one another are at the same temperature now.[29] It may be possible to observe relics from inflation— particularly the so-called B-modes in the CMB polarization—similar to how it is possible to observe the relics of Big Bang nucleosynthesis.[30]

It may seem like a somewhat trivial issue that the story of the universe's history is not really as seamless as it might appear at first glance. After all, does it really matter if we get the initial second of the universe's history partially wrong, if most of the billions of years of cosmic history after that are directly visible to us? Well, first of all, a lot happened during that second. But also, as we argued in the previous section, the way a universal history deals with the history of the universe sets the tone for how it deals with the rest of history. So it is worth making explicit just how different the types of evidence underpinning various aspects of the universe's history are—not only to judge different aspects of that history with nuance, recognizing that future research could substantially change the picture of what happened in those first moments, but to prepare to make similar judgments in other aspects of history. For instance, much of the history of life is well-documented using the artifacts we know as fossils, but the initial origin of life itself over 3 billion years ago is investigated primarily through informed speculation and the re-creation (in laboratories) of conditions analogous to those in specific environments on the early Earth. There is a difference between these parts of the story in terms of the confidence with which we can access them. Keeping these different kinds of evidence in focus will remain a goal throughout this book.

---

29. Inflation is consistent with current evidence from observations of the CMB and the large-scale structure of the universe. Detailed observations provide some reason to think that inflation happened; the theory passes observational tests that could have ruled it out. But it is not on the same kind of evidential footing as much of the rest of the Big Bang model.

30. Only one group of scientists (the BICEP2 collaboration) has ever claimed to observe these B-modes, and they were later shown to be mistaken. Other aspects of the universe's large-scale structure, however, give what many cosmologists would consider strong circumstantial evidence of inflation. As an aside, it is also conceivable that the cosmic neutrino background, a sea of particles that—like the CMB—carries the imprint of conditions in the early universe, might be directly detected someday. The cosmic neutrino background is predicted to be a relic from roughly one second after the Big Bang.

Gravity

Physicists identify four fundamental forces that allow matter to interact with other matter: gravity, electromagnetism, and the strong and weak nuclear forces. Gravity is the force of attraction between any two objects with mass, and it is a force with unlimited range: two objects with mass will attract one another gravitationally no matter how much distance is between them (though the force does grow weaker the farther apart two objects are).[31] At the same time, gravity is a feeble force. Ordinarily, huge masses must be involved in order for its effects to be noticeable, as with the Earth and the Sun. Gravity is easily overpowered by any competing forces, as demonstrated by the fact that a small magnet can hold another magnet up against the gravitational pull of the entire Earth.[32]

If gravity is a weak force, though, it is an exceptionally powerful idea. It is fundamental to how material objects move and influence each other. And applied to the history of the universe, gravity provides a central unifying principle, for it plays a huge role in the formation of everything from planets and stars to galaxies and the overall pattern of matter in the universe.

Gravity in the History of the Universe: Galaxies, Stars, Elements, Planets

Gravity shapes the overall structure and clustering of matter in the cosmos through what cosmologists call "structure formation." As already mentioned, every part of the universe was nearly identical to every other part in the early days; the CMB, which carries the fingerprint of what the universe was like 370,000 years after the Big Bang, is 99.999 percent uniform. However, the universe was never 100 percent uniform, which means that gravity could act in such a way as to make those tiny non-uniformities grow. Regions with slightly more matter would produce a slightly greater gravitational force of attraction, drawing in the surrounding matter. Denser areas would thus become denser, and areas with less matter would grow even less dense with time.

In the early universe, hundreds of thousands to millions of years after the Big Bang, gravity thus produced clumps of matter separated by emptier regions. Small clumps then came together to produce larger clumps, which themselves came together, and so on, in a process known as "bottom-up" or "hierarchical" structure formation, that ultimately resulted in the formation of galaxies. Galaxies themselves then gathered together to form clusters. At the very largest scales, matter in

---

31. Though gravitational influences are not transmitted instantly, but instead travel across distances at the speed of light.

32. Most of the forces we experience in everyday life, such as the force of one object pushing against another, are fundamentally electromagnetic, resulting from the repulsion of like charges at the atomic level.

the present-day universe is distributed in a manner reminiscent of the inside of a sponge, with large clusters and long filaments of galaxies surrounding mostly empty voids: the so-called "cosmic web." Computer simulations of matter clumping under the influence of gravity can be compared with actual telescopic observations of the cosmic web, and the close match between the two suggests that the sponge-like pattern can be regarded as the result of gravity operating on matter throughout the universe over cosmic time scales. (See Plate 5.)

In addition to these largest of all structures, gravity also helps us describe how stars have formed throughout the history of the universe. A star is essentially a ball of gas held together by gravity. From the first stars forming perhaps on the order of 100 million years after the Big Bang to the stars that continue to form in to-day's universe, the basic process of star formation is the same. Clouds of gas (almost entirely hydrogen and helium) collapse under their own gravity to form spinning disks, and matter slowly falls toward the center of the disk until that center becomes hot enough for nuclear fusion to combine hydrogen nuclei into helium.[33] Once fusion begins, internal pressure in the star[34] holds it up against further collapse, stabilizing the star for most of its life cycle.

For the first 90 percent of its life cycle, every star fuses hydrogen into helium at its core. Relatively massive stars, however, are also able to produce heavier elements in that last 10 percent of their life cycles, either by fusion, which produces elements up to and including iron, or by another nuclear process called neutron capture, which produces a huge variety of elements heavier than iron. Supernovae, the stellar explosions that occur at the end of the lifetime of the most massive stars, are an especially important part of this story: they not only generate many new elements,[35] but eject those elements far into interstellar space, where they can eventually become incorporated into new stars. The elements produced in stars—every element heavier than lithium has its origins in stars—provide the building blocks of all the matter we find within and on planets. As Carl Sagan put it, "We are made of starstuff."[36] (See Plate 6.)

Planetary systems seem to form by the same basic process as stars. Gravity collects matter in interstellar space into spinning disks of gas, incorporating elements generated by past generations of stars. The center of the disk becomes a star, while the outer parts of the disk may collapse to form one or more planets through a

---

33. Extreme conditions are necessary for nuclei to fuse together. Ordinarily, they would repel one another strongly rather than joining together, since all nuclei carry positive charges.

34. Generated by the radiation produced by fusion.

35. Recent evidence suggests that merging neutron stars are also an important source of new elements.

36. Carl Sagan, *Cosmos*, p. 190.

gradual process known as accretion.[37] The planets of our own Solar System contain many hints of how they formed: the planets all revolve in the same direction, including the Moon's revolution around Earth; most of the planets and the Sun rotate about their axes in the same direction; and the planets and the Sun all sit in the same plane. These observations are all consistent with the Solar System having its beginnings in a swirling disk of gas pulled together by gravity. And telescopes can observe such swirling disks at various stages of forming planets around other stars and protostars. While the exact arrangement of planets differs from one stellar system to another, the process of planet formation seems to be a routine outcome of how gravity operates on matter.[38]

So the evidence is strong that gravity plays a direct role in the formation of planets, stars, galaxies, and the cosmic web, and stars enable the formation of the wide variety of chemical elements. This is why gravity has an honored place in universal histories; it gives much information about the origins of order on many scales. However, for all gravity's explanatory power, the story is still changing around the exact nature of gravity, and the role it has played in the history of the universe. And those changes call into question key aspects of the contents of the universe as well.

Ideas About Gravity

Theories of gravity—that is, ideas and explanations of how gravity works—have a long history. Before Isaac Newton's mathematical theory of gravity in the late 1600s, people knew that apples fall to the ground, and they knew that the Moon orbits the Earth. But no one had argued convincingly that the two phenomena were related. Gravity provided a unified explanation of celestial and earthly phenomena; it is a prime example of physics showing that the same matter and the same physical laws operate in the heavens and on the Earth.

Albert Einstein added nuance to the scientific community's understanding with his theory of gravity, the general theory of relativity, which models gravity as being a result of the curvature of spacetime: the presence of mass causes space itself to curve, and the curvature of space affects the motion of other matter. Since general relativity makes even more accurate predictions of how celestial objects move than Newton's theory of gravity, Einstein's theory is considered the better model of how gravity works. Observations of gravitational phenomena, both experiments done in Earth-based laboratories and observations of the Solar System, Milky Way Galaxy, and universe, confirm—sometimes in exquisite detail—the predictions of general relativity.

---

37. The word is used to indicate the gradual collecting of matter in a concentrated place, so one can say that both stars and planets form through accretion.

38. The accretion of planets probably begins with electrostatic forces rather than gravity, and gravity takes over once the building blocks have grown large enough.

Still, theoretical physicists are not fully satisfied with the state of gravitational theory. One issue is that general relativity stands in some tension with quantum mechanics, the theoretical framework underlying the other three fundamental forces. This produces an awkward situation in which all of physics rests on two theoretical frameworks that are difficult to reconcile with one another. A major frontier of theoretical physics is finding a compelling theory of quantum gravity— that is, an understanding of fundamental physics that explains gravity in the same terms as the other three forces.[39] Better yet, for theoretical physicists, would be a "theory of everything" that not only explains all the forces in the same terms, but fully unifies the four forces as expressions of a single phenomenon, in the way that electricity and magnetism are both expressions of electromagnetism. String theory, which treats the smallest units underlying all matter as tiny strings rather than particles, is currently the most popular attempt among physicists at a theory of everything, but the level of acceptance of string theory as a legitimate form of science is mixed within the physics community, especially due to concerns about whether string theory is empirically testable.

Observational Challenges: Dark Matter and Dark Energy

In addition to these theoretical challenges for understanding the nature of gravity, there are observational challenges in understanding how gravity has operated over the history of the universe. In fact, there is a rather big caveat to the statements above regarding the consistency between cosmological observations and general relativity, as well as the earlier statement that computer simulations of the universe's history produce a distribution of matter in the universe similar to what is observed: These statements are only true if one posits the existence of a great deal of unseen "dark matter." Gravity acting on the *visible* matter in the universe fails to explain the motions of matter at almost every scale the size of a galaxy or larger. Objects in the outer reaches of spiral galaxies rotate around their centers much faster than they ought to according to general relativity (and Newtonian gravity). The motions of galaxies within galaxy clusters are also much faster than general relativity predicts. And computer simulations show that the amount of visible matter in the universe does not produce enough gravity to have pulled the large-scale structure of the universe together into the cosmic web in the first place.

---

39. Particle physicists unattached to the geometric (curvature-of-spacetime) interpretation of general relativity point out that only one particle-physics theory of gravity (involving particles called "gravitons") is consistent with very basic observations of gravitational phenomena, and that it is mathematically exactly equivalent to general relativity. This may suggest less dissonance between fundamental theories than that suggested in the main text. (Rachel Rosen, "A Massive Gravity Status Report," talk at COSMO16 conference, http://cosmo16.physics.lsa.umich.edu/talks.html .)

Why, then, do cosmologists not abandon the general-relativistic understanding of gravity on these large scales? A few do, but most argue that dark matter provides a single, simple, and elegant solution to all of these problems. Dark matter is a form of matter that does not interact with light—so it is dark not in the sense of being black, but of being invisible or transparent to all wavelengths of light. It is an elegant explanation of the problems outlined earlier, because the *same total amount* of dark matter explains each of the discrepancies: the same total amount of dark matter in the universe is the right amount to explain the rotation of spiral galaxies, the motion of galaxies in clusters, and the large-scale structure of the universe. This would be a sizable coincidence if dark matter were not really there. Observations of ordinary visible matter, in galaxies, clusters, and the cosmic web, are all consistent with dark matter being about five times more abundant in the universe than ordinary matter. Moreover, the presence of dark matter can be more directly probed through a phenomenon called gravitational lensing, in which concentrations of mass bend the path of light. Such bending of light can reveal where mass is present, and observed patterns of gravitational lensing provide strong evidence for huge clumps of unseen matter within clusters of galaxies. So dark matter is well-established in cosmology as an explanation for what might otherwise have been interpreted as gravitational anomalies. Many searches are underway to detect dark-matter particles and determine whether their identity matches that of one or more particles predicted to exist by theorists. There are tantalizing, but inconclusive, hints that already-existing observational results may actually be definitive evidence for dark matter.

Even more mysterious than dark matter is "dark energy," a term cosmologists use for whatever is causing the acceleration of the universe's expansion. This acceleration was discovered in the 1990s, resulting in a Nobel Prize[40] in 2011. Dark energy functions as a sort of antigravity, which repels rather than attracts, but no compelling model exists for what it is or why it behaves the way it does. All that is clear is that the universe's expansion is accelerating, rather than slowing down as would be expected if the attractive force of gravity went unopposed at the universe's largest scales. Dark energy can be fitted into general relativity fairly easily by introducing a "cosmological constant" into Einstein's equations, representing an energy associated with empty space. In fact, Einstein himself inserted it into his equations, but he took it out because of its ad-hoc quality, calling the insertion of the cosmological constant his biggest blunder. Cosmologists now routinely put this "blunder" back into the equations, however, in response to observations. What remains unclear is whether this kind of modification to general relativity actually captures the true nature of dark energy.

In any case, many different lines of evidence in cosmology and astrophysics suggest that ordinary matter is only some 5 percent of the total matter and energy

---

40. To the physicists Saul Perlmutter, Brian Schmidt, and Adam Riess.

in the universe. Some 25 percent is dark matter, and 70 percent is dark energy. Cosmologists often speak as though it is an embarrassing situation for science to only "know about" 5 percent of the universe, or for us to be made of that 5 percent:

> We are in the embarrassing position of not knowing what most of the universe is made of.[41]

> Adding insult to injury, cosmologists have found that we're not even made of the majority substance.[42]

If pressed, however, most will admit that the percentage of total matter and energy is not really what determines *importance*—an interpretive assessment if there ever was one! In particular, ordinary matter seems to interact with other matter and light in a wider variety of ways than do dark matter and dark energy, allowing it to form more complex structures, from planets to plants. Ordinary matter, one might say, is more "interesting."[43] Still, without dark matter and, perhaps, dark energy, ordinary matter would never have clumped together to the extent that it has, so dark matter and dark energy help enable ordinary matter to do what it does, creating the conditions for our existence.

Side Note: Unseen Matter and Gravity

Observations of anomalies in the rotation patterns of galaxies, the motions of galaxies in clusters, and so forth are usually interpreted by cosmologists to indicate that unseen (dark) matter is present in the universe, rather than that the laws of gravity are incorrect. This is a problem that has come up repeatedly in the history of astronomy: When gravitational theory fails to match up with celestial observations, should we assume that there is unseen matter we do not know about? Is there an error in our observations or inferences? Or is it that the laws of gravity as we know them are wrong?

In fact, all of these explanations have been invoked successfully before. Anomalies in how Uranus was observed to orbit the Sun led to the discovery of extra matter in the form of the planet Neptune. Later anomalies in how Neptune was orbiting the Sun turned out to be due to incorrect data on Neptune's mass. Anomalies in how Mercury was observed to orbit the Sun turned out to be a byproduct of Newtonian physics, and were resolved by general relativity—a change in our understanding of the laws of physics.

---

41. David Christian, *Maps of Time*, p. 41.

42. Max Tegmark, *Our Mathematical Universe*, p. 393.

43. For a discussion of the possibility that dark matter actually *is* as "interesting" as ordinary matter, see Lisa Randall, "Does Dark Matter Harbor Life?," http://nautil.us/issue/48/chaos/does-dark-matter-harbor-life .

Gravity as a Metaphor

Gravity goes a long way toward providing a single "driving force" behind the formation of everything from planets to stars to galaxies to the cosmic web. But there is
still much active research, both theoretical and observational, to understand gravity
and the role it plays in the history of the universe.

This is especially important to remember when we consider that gravity is not
only a powerful explanation for features of our universe but also a powerful metaphor, and one that is deployed frequently in entirely different settings, whenever
things attract or coalesce. In *Maps of Time*, David Christian talks about "social gravity" drawing communities of humans together into villages and cities.[44] Physicists
in the 20th century created "demographic gravitation" equations that turned this
sort of metaphor into a set of mathematical statements and attempted to apply it to
contemporary society.[45]

Such metaphors and analogies, whether mathematical or not, are clever in principle, but they run a real risk of giving the illusion of a unified explanation where
one does not even exist within physics. Though powerful within physics, the idea
of gravity cannot reliably be applied to human society at any level more detailed
than "some things attract each other." When scientific metaphors are used as a way
of characterizing social changes, it is important to be particularly clear about the
limitations of those metaphors, to avoid misunderstandings of social change and of
scientific explanation alike.

Entropy

Entropy is a favorite topic of popular-science writers, often presented as one of the
truly all-encompassing ideas in the natural sciences. The second law of thermodynamics, which states that entropy tends to increase in any spontaneous natural process, is frequently said to imply that the universe is growing more disordered over
time and, eventually, will reach a state of "heat death" in which nothing new will
ever happen for the rest of time. However, understanding the role that entropy plays
in the history and future of the universe requires a great deal of care and nuance,
because there is some distance between the scientific concept of entropy and the
grand metaphor of deterioration and decay to which entropy is often reduced.

---

44. David Christian, *Maps of Time*, p. 245; see also p. 188.

45. See John Q. Stewart, "Demographic Gravitation: Evidence and Applications," https://
www.jstor.org/stable/2785468 . Meanwhile, in astrophysics, the clumping and clustering of
matter into dense regions at the expense of less dense regions is often referred to as "the rich
getting richer and the poor getting poorer," another physics-society gravity analogy that could
easily be taken too far.

What Is Entropy?

Entropy is not easy to describe or understand intuitively. It was first defined in the 1800s with respect to thermodynamic processes and the efficiency of heat engines, as a measure of how much energy is unavailable to do *work*. (Work is done when energy is transferred to the surroundings so as to produce an effect like rotating a shaft, compressing a spring, or moving an object.) In any process involving the transfer of heat, some energy will be dissipated: energy becomes spread out, dispersed, and therefore unavailable to do work. A classic example of this pattern is that a hot object and a cold object, when put together, eventually come to the same temperature. In this case, the energy differential, which could have been harnessed to do work just as water falling from a greater height to a lesser height can be harnessed, has been eliminated. But even if the energy differential were harnessed to do work, some energy would likewise be dispersed and thus "lost." Entropy gives a way to quantify how much energy is spread out in this way.

Later in the 1800s, a microscopic definition and analysis of entropy showed why energy tends to disperse and entropy tends to increase in a spontaneous process: In the absence of other constraints, the dispersal of energy is simply more probable than its concentration. The reason is that at the microscopic level, there are far more ways for energy to be dispersed than for it to be concentrated.

A classic analogy here is that a drop of ink added to water tends to spread out rather than becoming more concentrated. If we assume that the ink diffuses randomly, so that each molecule can diffuse in any direction, it is actually possible that the ink drop would become more concentrated rather than spreading out. Molecules could move in precisely such a way that all of them go closer to where the ink hit the water. But this is highly improbable, since there are many directions each molecule could go that would result in spreading but very few directions that would result in further concentration. And this is true for each and every one of the unimaginably large number of molecules in the ink drop (on the order of 10^{20} for even a tiny drop), so the combined effect is that spreading out is far, far more probable.

Similarly, the oxygen molecules in a room could all, by chance, move in the same direction at once and concentrate themselves in one corner, making the air in the rest of the room unbreathable. But this never happens, because there are far more ways for the unconfined, randomly moving oxygen molecules to distribute themselves uniformly throughout the room. The probability of molecules clustering in a corner is so low that it would almost certainly never happen even if you waited for trillions of years.

The *second law of thermodynamics* applies similar reasoning to processes involving the transfer of heat and energy. For instance, why does a hot oven cool down when turned off, rather than heating up further? Why does salt go into solution (up to a point) rather than separating from water? Why do oil and water avoid mixing?

In all cases, a careful analysis of the microscopic situation shows that while it is theoretically possible for the opposite to happen, it is simply far more probable that these processes occur in the way they do, because there are far more ways for this to happen. In other words, there are more microscopic states ("microstates") associated with the macroscopic state ("macrostate") that does occur. Equilibrium—the condition in which there are no temperature differentials, no net flows of matter or energy, and no macroscopic changes—is reached in each case because it is a maximum-probability state. The maximum-probability state is the state with the highest *entropy*.

Entropy, Order, and Complexity

Entropy is often explained as being a measure of how disordered a system is. In a sense, the hot oven with cooler surroundings is a highly ordered system, with energy concentrated in a specific place and not in others, while the cooled-down oven has that energy dissipated and, therefore, less order. Similarly, the drop of ink is concentrated and ordered before it spreads out haphazardly in all directions. A common analogy for these situations is that of a neat and tidy room, as opposed to a highly disordered room with papers and objects strewn everywhere. There are far more possible configurations of the room in which there is disorder and far fewer in which there is order, meaning that the tendency for the room is to go from order to disorder over time. (Entropy is a common excuse among physicists who find it difficult to keep their offices clean!)

The "disorder metaphor" sometimes helps to clarify the microscopic meaning of entropy and the reason why thermodynamic processes tend to increase entropy. But one might begin to wonder how ordered structures in the universe, such as stars and life and human societies, are possible at all: Does their presence violate a fundamental law of nature? Part of the resolution of this apparent paradox is that the analogy between entropy and disorder is imprecise and potentially misleading, a holdover from a description of energy by the physicist Ludwig Boltzmann in the late 1800s. "Disorder" at the microscopic level may or may not correspond to a macroscopic appearance of disorder—as is the case when water and oil *maximize* entropy by *not* mixing, which gives the appearance of macroscopic order.

In fact, for each form of complexity or highly ordered structure in the universe, there is a corresponding explanation, which depends on the nuances of each case, for why no violation of the second law of thermodynamics occurs. For instance, a star forms by collapsing from an amorphous cloud of gas, which seems like it would *decrease* entropy—the cloud of gas was unstructured, random, and "disordered," and the star appears much more organized. But while the contraction of the cloud really does contribute a reduction in entropy because the gas becomes less dispersed (the opposite of the ink drop) and its atoms have fewer available microstates, the process of star formation increases entropy overall because of the release of radiation, which carries heat from a hotter region to a colder region and also increases the total number of particles, thus increasing the dispersal of energy more than enough to compensate for the contraction of the gas cloud.[46]

Life is another case in point. How can the intricate order and complexity of even a single cell form, or evolution of new ordered structures occur, when the second law of thermodynamics would suggest that the dispersal of energy and dissolution of order should be the rule? Actually, there is no conflict here. Entropy only has to increase in a "closed" system in which energy is neither coming in nor going out, and in this case, the Earth is not the whole system. Instead, a full analysis would include the Sun and the Earth, with the total entropy increasing thanks to nuclear fusion in the Sun even when the entropy of specific living systems on Earth may decrease. That said, the tendency of energy to disperse is part of why the maintenance of life's order requires a constant input of energy, and why living things must channel and manage these energy flows. Equilibrium, the state in which nothing new happens and entropy is maximized, generally means death for living organisms.[47] Yet at the same time, the cellular and biochemical processes of life often take advantage of processes that increase entropy in precisely such a way as to *create* order and *enable* life, as when a cell "imports" useful materials from its surroundings in ways that increase entropy or when oxygen diffuses from the lungs to the bloodstream.[48]

So it can be misleading to think of entropy strictly as a disordering and disorganizing influence. The chemist Peter Atkins's contention that the second law of thermodynamics means "things get worse"[49] all the time in the universe can seriously mislead as a guiding principle. The amount of useful energy always decreases in any spontaneous process. But that does not imply that every process makes the universe more disordered in the usual sense of the term; stars and life, for example, can maintain their order not just *in spite of* entropy increase but actually *because of* entropy increase, properly harnessed. As Christian discusses,[50] complex objects both channel and disperse energy, and greater complexity creates new opportunities for microscopic "disorder" (the dispersal of energy) as well as (sometimes) new forms of order. Structures that seem more ordered to us often deal with greater

---

46. David Wallace, "Gravity, Entropy, and Cosmology: In Search of Clarity," https://academic.oup.com/bjps/article-abstract/61/3/513/1395297 ; Steven Frautschi, "Entropy in an Expanding Universe," https://science.sciencemag.org/content/217/4560/593 .

47. A fact alluded to in everything from Erwin Schrödinger's essay "What Is Life?" to Primo Levi's memoir *The Periodic Table*.

48. See John Tooby, "Falling into Place: Entropy and the Desperate Ingenuity of Life," in John Brockman (ed.), *This Explains Everything*, p. 190.

49. Peter Atkins, "Why Things Happen," in John Brockman (ed.), *This Explains Everything*, p. 192.

50. David Christian, *Maps of Time*, p. 505 ff.

energy inputs and outputs (for their size), in part because they are also effective dispersers of energy and, therefore, need more energy to start out with.[51]

So there really is no paradox in the fact that ordered structures exist in a universe where entropy tends to increase. Part of the issue here is that complexity is an ill-defined concept physically but is very intuitive, while entropy is not intuitive but is well-defined physically. And the other part of the issue is that it is misleading to think of the second law of thermodynamics as a drive toward disorder, or as driving anything at all. It is rather a statement of probability, based on the availability of microscopic states corresponding to macroscopic states. The second law does not make order impossible, and as a metaphor for the deterioration of things, it has its limits.

Entropy in an Expanding Universe, Past and Future

Applied to the history of the entire universe, gravity and entropy may seem like they work in opposition to one another. Planets, stars, galaxies, and the cosmic web are all ordered patterns within the universe sculpted by gravity, but increasing entropy means increasing dispersal of energy and, therefore, loss of energy available for work. Taken to its logical conclusion, the second law of thermodynamics is often said to guarantee an eventual "heat death" in which the universe itself "dies"—in the sense that a final equilibrium is reached and nothing new can ever happen again. Equilibrium has every appearance of being the *end*, for living things and for the universe alike.

The idea of "heat death" goes back to 19th-century physics, but modern cosmology presents a somewhat more complicated picture than this, in large part because the expansion of the universe and the influence of gravity both make it quite difficult to analyze the history and future of the universe in terms of entropy. The early universe, with its random mix of particles and light, seems at first glance like it should have been in a *high*-entropy state and already in equilibrium, which begs the question of how anything new could happen at all without violating the second law. But there are two reasons why this is not a paradox. First, a system dominated by gravity does not have an equilibrium state, because gravity causes matter to clump together but not disperse; that is, there is no opposing process to balance out the clumping.[52] And second, the early universe was not in thermal equilibrium, because it was expanding. Energy can still disperse and entropy increase in an expanding universe, but as space itself expands, the *maximum* entropy possible increases even faster: there is more space for energy to disperse into, and so entropy does

---

51. See Eric Chaisson, *Epic of Evolution*, pp. 132–145.

52. David Wallace, "Gravity, Entropy, and Cosmology: In Search of Clarity," https://academic.oup.com/bjps/article-abstract/61/3/513/1395297 .

not readily reach a maximum. Thus, the expanding universe actually moves away from equilibrium. In this sense, the expansion of the universe makes possible the temperature and pressure differentials that ultimately allow for the formation of all ordered structure.[53]

As for the future, a "heat death" involving a final, universe-wide equilibrium in which all activity ceases no longer seems inevitable. It still may very well be the case that everything in the universe will "die" in the sense of degrading to a uniform bath of separated particles in which nothing new ever forms again—and depending on the behavior of dark energy, it is even possible that the fabric of spacetime itself might be ripped apart at some distant time billions of years or more in the future. But these results are not an automatic consequence of the second law of thermodynamics, since the expansion of the universe tends to pull the maximum-entropy state further and further out of reach even as entropy increases within the universe.

Like gravity, entropy provides a powerful metaphor that is easy to apply excessively or even recklessly, especially in matters of order and complexity. It can be, and has been, used to imply that everything from the universe to human society "runs downhill" and decays. While entropy does help to inform questions of complexity, order, and even the fate of the universe, the temptation is to turn entropy from a genuinely important physical principle into a much grander, metaphysical principle from which we can draw sweeping conclusions about the nature of change. Entropy is a powerful idea, but like all the ideas that we highlight, it must be deployed carefully and held in balance with other big ideas. Just like gravity lends itself as a metaphor for attraction, entropy lends itself as a metaphor for deterioration, but in both cases, excessive or imprecise use of the metaphor is a common problem.

Mathematics

A fascinating aspect of the physical world is the mathematical regularity with which a wide range of phenomena behave: everything from falling bodies, to magnets, to subatomic particles, to the large-scale structure of the universe seems to display patterns and regularities of behavior that can be described with mathematics. Many physicists, philosophers, and other thinkers have asked the question of why these regularities should exist in the first place, and why mathematics should be helpful in describing them. Without the existence of precise, predictive, verifiable, mathematical regularities, it is hard to envision modern science—and, hence, science-based universal histories—existing at all. We now turn to a deeper analysis of these so-called "laws of nature" as the topic of our first philosophical exploration.

---

53. See David Christian, *Maps of Time*, p. 508.

Laws of Physics

What is a "law of nature"? Outside the scientific community, the term is often used to indicate a scientific concept that is practically certain, as in "you cannot break the law of gravity." Within the scientific community, however, and especially in physics, the word "law" has a more specific meaning: it usually indicates a mathematical relationship between measurable quantities.[54] So one might speak of Newton's "theory" of gravity to indicate his whole theoretical framework for explaining gravity, but Newton's "law" of universal gravitation is the specific mathematical statement that the gravitational force between two bodies is proportional to the product of the bodies' masses divided by the square of the distance between them. The physical laws of nature seem to stay the same over the history of the universe, and in fact, cosmological observations can sometimes place limits on how much a given law might have changed over cosmic time, based on how alterations in these laws[55] would have affected observable properties of matter in the universe.[56] By all appearances, the laws are stable through time, and likewise do not vary from one part of the universe to another.

Many questions could be asked about these laws: Do they have to take the form they do? Could other universes exist with different laws? Why do laws "exist" in the first place? Why does mathematics work so well for describing regularities in nature, and what implications does this have?

The association between mathematics and the study of the natural world goes back a long way. In ancient Greece, Pythagoras (c. 570–c. 495 BCE) and his followers identified numerical relationships underlying musical harmonies and were among the first to argue that the Earth is a sphere, though probably based on aesthetic considerations more than on observation.[57] Plato (c. 429–c. 347 BCE) envisioned the physical world being made of atoms that took the form of "perfect" geometric solids. In medieval Europe, Copernicus (1473–1543)—and essentially everyone before him—assumed that celestial orbits followed circles because circles were considered to be perfect, while Kepler (1571–1630) thought that the distances between planets were based on a different kind of geometrical perfection, that of Platonic solids.[58]

---

54. The use of the term "law" may or may not be a strong indicator of how well-verified the relationship is.

55. And the constants that appear in them.

56. See, e.g., Venkat Srinivasan, "Are the Constants of Physics Constant?," http:// blogs.scientificamerican.com/guest-blog/are-the-constants-of-physics-constant/ .

57. See Mario Livio, *Is God a Mathematician?*, p. 19.

58. See Frank Wilczek, *A Beautiful Question*, or Mario Livio, *Is God a Mathematician?*

Many of these ideas sound bizarre to modern ears, but perhaps they should not. For in fact, physicists like the Nobel laureate Frank Wilczek report the strong sense that mathematics is fundamental to how the physical world works:

> The most daring hopes of Pythagoras and Plato to find conceptual purity, order, and harmony at the heart of creation have been far exceeded by reality.[59]

Of what he referred to as the "unreasonable effectiveness of mathematics in the natural sciences," the physicist Eugene Wigner wrote:

> The mathematical formulation of the physicist's often crude experience leads in an uncanny number of cases to an amazingly accurate description of a large class of phenomena. This shows that the mathematical language has more to commend it than being the only language which we can speak; it shows that it is, in a very real sense, the correct language.[60]

A classic example is Maxwell's equations of electromagnetism. All of classical electromagnetic theory, a huge body of knowledge about the phenomena of electricity and magnetism, can be condensed and summarized in four compact equations, which James Clerk Maxwell helped to identify in the 1860s. The compactness of expression embodied in these equations strikes many physicists as well-nigh miraculous in its own right, but there is even more to the story: by combining and manipulating these equations mathematically, Maxwell was able to predict the existence of *electromagnetic waves*, and was even able to identify the speed with which those waves must travel, which turned out to be numerically the same as the measured speed of light. This suggested for the first time that light was in fact an electromagnetic wave, a notion that was verified experimentally some two and a half decades later by Heinrich Hertz.

It is difficult to overstate how extraordinary this is. By performing pencil-and-paper manipulation of mathematical equations, Maxwell correctly predicted the existence of a previously unknown phenomenon (electromagnetic waves) and identified the underlying nature of a known phenomenon (light), predicting that in addition to visible light, there should be a whole spectrum of frequencies and wavelengths of electromagnetic waves that are invisible to the human eye. These were subsequently discovered and are now known as radio waves, infrared radiation, X-rays, gamma rays, and so forth (see Plate 2). It is as if the mathematics were

---

59. Frank Wilczek, *A Beautiful Question*, p. 322.

60. Eugene Wigner, "The Unreasonable Effectiveness of Mathematics in the Natural Sciences," https://www.dartmouth.edu/~matc/MathDrama/reading/Wigner.html .

so thoroughly baked into the physical phenomena of electricity and magnetism that all one had to do was skillfully manipulate equations in order to more deeply probe the nature of the physical world. Experiments were needed only as confirmation of what math had been used to "discover."

Limitations of Laws

Mathematical laws of nature provide broad-ranging descriptions and predictions of natural phenomena. But at the same time, no known physical law holds true at every scale, or applies to everything without any limitations.[61] Even Maxwell's equations fail to hold in certain situations, particularly when the smallest possible amounts of light (photons, or "particles" of light) are involved. It is interesting that any given mathematical law may have incredible predictive power, yet that predictive power is never unlimited. As Wigner put it, the laws of nature are "of almost fantastic accuracy but of strictly limited scope."[62]

This observation has implications for considering how much of the physical world can actually be described by physics, and for whether a "theory of everything," as described in the "Gravity" section of this chapter, is even possible:

> Every empirical law has the disquieting quality that one does not know its limitations. . . . Alternatively, it is possible that there always will be some laws of nature which have nothing in common with each other. . . . It is even possible that some of the laws of nature will be in conflict with each other in their implications, but each convincing enough in its own domain so that we may not be willing to abandon any of them. . . . We may lose interest in the "ultimate truth," that is, in a picture which is a consistent fusion into a single unit of the little pictures, formed on the various aspects of nature.[63]

In other words, perhaps the laws of physics, expansive and all-encompassing as they feel to physicists, are simply much more limited in scope than they seem. It is a particularly interesting question whether mathematical laws of physics can be extended to adequately describe the full behavior of complex systems, such as living organisms. There is no doubt that this is difficult in practice, but what about in principle? We will return to this question in the philosophical discussion of chapter 3, on reductionism.

---

61. See, e.g., Lawrence M. Krauss, "The Trouble with Theories of Everything," http://nautil.us/ issue/29/scaling/the-trouble-with-theories-of-everything .

62. Wigner, "The Unreasonable Effectiveness of Mathematics."

63. Ibid.

Another question one might pose about the limits of mathematical laws is some-times referred to as the "problem of underdetermination"—that is, even if a math-ematical model of a certain phenomenon turns out to be fantastically accurate, the universe could actually be working according to a totally different, unknown set of "rules" that simply mimic the results of mathematical laws in the situations we are able to observe. A famous example of this argument came from Pope Urban VIII, a longtime friend of Galileo under whose auspices Galileo would later be prosecuted and sentenced to house arrest. Urban tried to reduce Galileo's confidence that the Earth orbits the Sun rather than the other way around by pointing out that even if a heliocentric model gave better predictions of the motions of planets across the sky, the reality of how the Solar System worked might be much different than that suggested by the model.[64]

Galileo and many others have viewed this argument as a cheap way out of giving one's assent to a physical theory, and it certainly can be used as such. But it is also a genuine problem, without a wholly satisfactory solution. Many science writers would here invoke the principle of parsimony, "Occam's Razor," that simpler expla-nations are to be preferred over more complex ones. But simplicity does not always lead to accuracy, and a universe with dark matter and dark energy (among many other things) is complex in ways that cosmologists failed to anticipate. Moreover, several episodes in the history of physics confirm that when one fundamental law replaces another, the accuracy of the predictions may increase only slightly, while the fundamental image of physical reality suggested by the law changes radically.[65] This seems to suggest that the interpretation of what a given physical law *means* for what is "really going on" should be viewed as subject to considerable revision, even if the law produces highly accurate results.

Laws and Discipline

These considerations are all worth taking into account when considering to what extent mathematical explanations and law-like behavior should appear in dis-ciplines outside of physics and the natural sciences. The apparent universality,

---

64. See James Hannam, *The Genesis of Science*, pp. 325–326.

65. For example, the laws of general relativity only make very slightly more accurate predic-tions than Newton's law of gravity about how bodies move under the influence of gravity. But Einstein's theory greatly shifts the picture of what gravity *is*—from a force that acts instantly at a distance in Newton's conception, to a manifestation of the curvature of spacetime whose influence propagates at the speed of light. A similar shift occurred in many branches of physics with the advent of quantum theory in the early 20th century: the mathematical predictions of the laws involved became only a little more accurate in many cases (though in other cases, the difference was much bigger), but the underlying physical reality implied by the theory changed radically—suggesting that the world of the very small behaves in bizarre and almost paradoxi-cal ways, alien to the neatly mechanistic Newtonian system.

predictability, and reliability of mathematical laws has appealed to a variety of people as a potential way of explaining everything from the behavior of star clusters to the behavior of crowds of people. The field of "cliodynamics,"[66] for instance, attempts to explain large patterns of human history as instantiations of universally applicable mathematical laws. Or in a more mainstream manifestation of the mathematical impulse, financial markets are often a target for mathematical modeling. In both cases, the idea is that if one understands the mathematical laws underlying the behavior of a complex system, it becomes possible to predict the future and reap the corresponding benefits. Meanwhile, others resist the sense of inevitability that attends mathematical laws—especially mainstream historians, who are more sensitive to the "exceptions to the rule" and the influence of human agency, and tend to gravitate toward multicausal explanations rather than anything that can be neatly summed up in a set of equations.

In all of this, bear in mind that it is not even clear whether mathematical laws explain everything within the domain of *physics*, let alone whether there are full-blown mathematical laws to describe or explain anything outside of physics. Even within the natural sciences, it is harder to apply mathematics profitably outside of physics: the mathematical biologist I. M. Gelfand is quoted as having said, "There is only one thing which is more unreasonable than the unreasonable effectiveness of mathematics in physics, and this is the unreasonable ineffectiveness of mathematics in biology."[67] Perhaps the "rules" of other natural sciences, as well as the patterns discerned by the social sciences and the humanities, are not fully reducible to the underlying physics. Or it may be that certain phenomena are simply not describable in mathematical terms. The physicist Richard A. Muller writes, "Physics is arguably that tiny subset of reality that is susceptible to mathematics. No wonder physics yields to math; if an aspect of existence doesn't so yield, we give it a different name: history, political science, ethics, philosophy, poetry."[68]

In any case, overapplication of mathematical laws can easily turn into "physics envy," the sense that physics serves as a model for all other disciplines because of its success at describing its subject matter mathematically. This is another reason why understanding the limitations of the laws is important when integrating fields in a universal history. Stories drawn from the history of life and of humanity are typically stories of apparent *contingency* and *particularity*, but a cosmic framing situates these stories within a context of seemingly *deterministic* and *universal* laws. Yet it is a relatively open question to what extent those laws themselves, successful as they have been over a wide range of scales and phenomena, provide the deterministic and universal context they seem to.

---

66. See, e.g., Peter Turchin's work.

67. Quoted in Mario Livio, *Is God a Mathematician?*, p. 245.

68. Richard A. Muller, *Now: The Physics of Time*, p. 255.

Why the Unreasonable Effectiveness?

Leaving aside these limitations of scope and interpretation of mathematical theories, it is still a source of wonder and fascination for physicists that mathematics works so well in describing many phenomena of the natural world. Is there a reason why mathematics is so useful in physics? One might contemplate three broad classes of explanations:

1. Matter has mathematical *properties* that can be abstracted and studied independent of the matter itself. That is, the nature of matter includes certain mathematical propensities. This explanation was advocated by Aristotle in the fourth century BCE, as well as by the many medieval philosophers who drew on Aristotle's work—all long before the most impressive modern connections between mathematics and natural science emerged.[69]
2. Mathematical realities *control* matter. In some sense, mathematical laws have an existence independent of matter and control matter. They do not just *describe* natural phenomena, but *cause* them. A related, if somewhat extreme, suggestion is that reality is itself mathematical. The physicist Max Tegmark has recently advocated this position.[70]
3. The appearance of mathematical structure in nature has nothing to do with nature itself and everything to do with our perception of it. In extreme form, this explanation could take the form of an "idealist" theory holding that matter does not exist independent of mind, and that the mathematical laws we seem to be discovering in nature are actually, in some fashion, a projection of our own minds. The astronomer and physicist James Jeans was a prominent advocate of this position in the early 20th century.

Although one of these three types of explanation will probably stand out to any given reader as being the most intuitive and compelling option, it is possible to mount a reasonably sophisticated defense of any of them. For now, we simply make the point that how one speaks about the laws of nature matters. For example, physicists often speak of systems "obeying" laws or being "governed" by laws, instead of speaking of laws as being ways of describing or categorizing regularities that exist within nature and our study of it. This is just a way of speaking; there is nothing in modern physics that requires physicists to speak in this way. But the way of speaking suggests a certain philosophical attitude, namely explanation 2, at the expense of others.

---

69. For an interesting analysis, see James Franklin, "The Mathematical World," https://aeon.co/essays/aristotle-was-right-about-mathematics-after-all .

70. See, e.g., Max Tegmark, *Our Mathematical Universe: My Quest for the Ultimate Nature of Reality*.

Physical Laws and the Nature of Explanations in Physics

The question of why mathematics is so useful in physics also makes a difference in the context of universal histories. If we assume explanation 1 from the previous list, that matter has mathematical properties, then a universal history might aspire to contemplate not only the origins of matter, but also the origins of its mathematical propensities. Assuming explanation 2, a universal history might aspire to explain where these laws came from as well. Both of these projects would seem to draw on some combination of physics and philosophy. Assuming explanation 3, meanwhile, might imply the need for a completely different kind of universal history, one in which mind would have to be treated as more fundamental than matter.

Considering any of these three possibilities raises deep questions about what it means to *explain* an observed phenomenon. If the laws of physics seem to explain how various phenomena in the natural world work, can the origin of the laws of physics themselves be explained? For example, one can explain how matter behaves according to the laws of gravity, but at a more fundamental level, why do two masses "know" of each other's existence and behave in any predictable way at all?

Physicists typically consider a phenomenon "explained" when it can be shown to be a particular instance of a general principle (as laws of gravity explain how the Moon orbits the Earth and how apples fall from trees), or when the principles themselves can be shown to derive from more general or fundamental, accurate or predictively powerful principles (as Newton's law of gravity is "explained" as a special application of general relativity in situations where objects are not moving close to the speed of light and spacetime is not strongly curved). So physics might, by its nature, be able to *characterize* how the natural world behaves through the laws of nature, showing which laws are fundamental and which can be derived from others. But it cannot explain why the laws *exist* in the first place, except perhaps by reference to something else that would itself be outside the domain of physics. Physics is not designed to give an account of being or existence itself. And in the same way that physics cannot address why there is something rather than nothing, it cannot address why the "something" that does exist takes the basic form it does, as opposed to some other form. Why is there such a thing as charge, or mass, or space, or energy, or light, or mathematical laws? Perhaps some items on this list can be explained in terms of others, but there will always be *some* list of basic, elementary constituents of the universe. Physicists have to take something as given, or there would be nothing to "do physics" with.

More generally, any discipline's explanations must reach a "ground zero." Each discipline must have some kind of reasonably well-defined endpoint, where experts in the discipline consider a phenomenon under study to be explained as fully as the discipline can explain it. Biologists, for instance, may consider the workings of a cell to be explained when these workings can be described in terms of known chemical reactions and physical processes—as when the workings of a cell membrane are explained in terms of the chemical properties of the lipid bilayer that comprises it. Many psychologists consider their explanatory work finished when they can show that a behavioral phenomenon corresponds directly to some function of the brain—as when certain impairments in the use of language are fully "explained" when areas of the brain like Broca's area or Wernicke's area are shown to be damaged. The exact placement of the "ground zero" of explanation may shift over time for a given discipline, but each discipline must be able to identify an end to the "why" questions. It is precisely this ultimate grounding that allows the rest of the work in the discipline to be intelligible.

Where does this ultimate grounding come from for physics, a discipline often appealed to as the ultimate grounding for other scientific disciplines? One could argue that the question of why anything, and why certain fundamental types of things, exist in the first place is most directly addressed by philosophy, specifically metaphysics:

> It is an observable character of all metaphysical doctrines that, widely divergent as they may be, they agree on the necessity of finding out the first cause of all that is. Call it Matter with Democritus, the Good with Plato, the self-thinking Thought with Aristotle, the One with Plotinus, Being with all Christian philosophers, Moral Law with Kant, the Will with Schopenhauer, or let it be the absolute Idea of Hegel, the Creative Duration of Bergson, and whatever else you may cite, in all cases the metaphysician is a man who looks behind and beyond experience for an ultimate ground of all real and possible experience.[71]

Étienne Gilson (1884–1978), the philosopher who penned this passage, later identifies that "ultimate ground" with "the cause of all causes, or first cause, whose discovery has been for centuries the ambition of the metaphysicians."[72] It is not physics but philosophy, and perhaps theology, that considers and tries to illuminate the *origins* or *purpose* of being itself.

Fine-Tuning

The apparent "fine-tuning" of the laws of nature provides another angle to consider in determining how one might explain why there are mathematical laws at all. Of gravity, Bill Bryson writes:

> What is extraordinary from our point of view is how well it turned out for us. If the universe had formed just a tiny bit differently—if gravity were fractionally stronger or weaker, if the expansion had proceeded just a little more slowly or swiftly—then there might never have been stable elements to make you and me and the ground we stand on. Had gravity been a trifle stronger, the universe itself might have collapsed like a badly erected tent, without precisely the right values to give it the right dimensions and density

---

71. Étienne Gilson, *The Unity of Philosophical Experience*, p. 247.

72. Ibid, p. 248.

and component parts. Had it been weaker, however, nothing would have coalesced. The universe would have remained forever a dull, scattered void.[73]

And the gravitational example is not the only one: it appears that whatever the limits of the laws of nature may be, these laws—and in particular, the constants in the equations that express those laws—have to be almost exactly as they are in order for any structure at all, let alone complex entities like life, to exist in the universe. As Stephen Hawking writes, "The laws of science, as we know them at present, contain many fundamental numbers, like the size of the electric charge of the electron and the ratio of the masses of the proton and the electron. . . . The remarkable fact is that the values of these numbers seem to have been very finely adjusted to make possible the development of life."[74] It was observations like these that led the physicist Freeman Dyson to remark, "As we look out into the Universe and identify the many accidents of physics and astronomy that have worked together to our benefit, it almost seems as if the Universe must in some sense have known that we were coming."[75]

On the other hand, not every physicist is convinced there is really something to be explained here. First, it is not clear that the fundamental constants have to be as fine-tuned as suggested above in order for life to appear in the universe. Arguing that even relatively large changes in some constants could be compensated for by other physical effects, the astrophysicist Fred Adams writes that "the parameters of our universe could have varied by large factors and still allowed for working stars and potentially habitable planets. . . . Universes have many pathways for the development of complexity and biology, and some could be even more favorable for life than our own."[76] This is especially relevant if it turns out that there can be living things wildly different than "life as we know it" on Earth—perhaps a form of life not based on carbon, or not dependent on water, or made of dark matter rather than ordinary matter. In that case, completely different physical laws might be able to support life that takes a completely different physical form.[77] To draw a related image from the science-fiction writer Douglas Adams, a puddle might think that the hole in which it finds itself is fine-tuned for it to fit so perfectly into the hole,

73. Bill Bryson, *A Short History of Nearly Everything*, p. 15.

74. Stephen Hawking, *A Brief History of Time* (2017 edition), p. 129.

75. Different versions of this quote appear in different places. This one is the version in John D. Barrow and Frank J. Tipler, *The Anthropic Cosmological Principle*, p. 318. A somewhat different version is quoted in Bill Bryson, *A Short History of Nearly Everything*, p. 237.

76. Fred Adams, "The Not-So-Fine Tuning of the Universe," http://nautil.us/issue/44/luck/the-not_so_fine-tuning-of-the-universe .

77. Moreover, physicists are not yet certain how many distinct and independent fundamental constants there are. Perhaps some of the constants are linked with other constants, and determine their values, in ways that physicists have not yet realized. In other words, there may be fewer "independent parameters" than the arguments from fine-tuning usually imply.

but the water in the puddle is adapted to the hole, not the other way around.[78] Perhaps life is adapted to the universe, not the universe to life.[79]

Still, even granting these counterarguments, it is remarkable that life in the universe exists despite the fact that a great many possible combinations of laws and constants would have precluded the existence even of stars or planets or any kind of ordered structure at all. It begs the questions: Did the laws in fact have to take the form they did, and the constants the values they did?[80] If so, why? If not, why the apparent coincidence that the laws do permit life to arise? For now, at least, physicists' best answer to the first question is *no*. It appears that there is no logical reason why these laws and constants *had* to take the form they did. To the latter question, physicists who advocate the idea of a multiverse argue that there are huge numbers of universes, all with different laws, and we exist in one that seems fine-tuned for our existence simply because it is the one in which we *could* exist.

The existence of multiple (quite possibly unobservable) universes is not as outlandish an idea as it may at first seem. Various proposed theories of fundamental physics actually *predict* that multiple universes would be formed as a byproduct of natural processes. If those theories turn out to be robust at predicting features of our own universe, that could lend at least circumstantial "evidence" in favor of a multiverse.

Debates about fine-tuning and the multiverse, however, seem to miss the more basic question: Whether fine-tuned or not, why is there a law of gravity at all? If there are multiple universes, why do *any* of those universes exist? The existence of many universes would seem to require even more explaining than the existence of only one. The puddle analogy gives a plausible image for understanding why there is a strong fit between the characteristics of the universe and the life that inhabits it, but whether there is one hole (universe) and one puddle (life) or many holes and many puddles, why any of it? And why is there any kind of intelligible order, especially as expressed in the structures of matter and the forms of mathematical laws, in any universe at all?

Such considerations lead some to infer divine creation. Physicists comfortably write books with titles like *Is God a Mathematician?* and *The Mind of God* while

---

78. See Douglas Adams, *The Salmon of Doubt*, p. 131.

79. There is also the objection that if the universe were not suitable for life, we would not be here to discuss the matter. The philosopher Thomas Nagel replies to this concern: "One doesn't show that something doesn't require explanation by pointing out that it is a condition of one's existence. If I ask for an explanation of the fact that the air pressure in the transcontinental jet is close to that at sea level, it is no answer to point out that if it weren't, I'd be dead." (Thomas Nagel, *Mind & Cosmos: Why the Materialist Neo-Darwinian Conception of Nature Is Almost Certainly False*, p. 95, footnote.)

80. Einstein once commented: "What I'm really interested in is whether God could have made the world in a different way; that is, whether the necessity of logical simplicity leaves any freedom at all." (Albert Einstein to Ernst Straus, as quoted in *Einstein: A Centenary Volume*, ed. A. P. French, p. 128.)

routinely quoting Einstein's line that "God does not play dice with the universe."[81] There is certainly precedent among physicists (including the inventor of the Big Bang model, the Catholic priest and astrophysicist Georges Lemaître) for appealing to an all-powerful creative intellect to understand the ultimate origins of order in the cosmos. Whether this creative intellect should be identified with the God of any particular religious revelation is a further step that some (like Lemaître) take and some (like Einstein) do not.[82]

And yet within physics, there is also a common view that explanations invoking divine causation not only are empty, but give up on the very idea of scientific explanation itself. Many physicists see little room for supernatural agency as an appropriate explanation of anything, since virtually any phenomenon could be "explained" by saying "God did it" without really contributing a deeper understanding of the phenomenon itself. Concern is heightened by the prevalence of "God-of-the-gaps"-style explanations among advocates of "intelligent design," where the divine explicitly becomes a category to explain what science does not presently understand.[83] Another objection to divine creation is that it simply begs the question by raising another—namely, who or what created God?

Yet the idea of *causality*—that effects have causes—is precisely what may address both these concerns. The universe exists, and at least to a great extent, it is intelligible and ordered. These things seem like *effects*—the sorts of things that require a causal explanation. And if the chain of causal reasoning is to hit bedrock somewhere, if the physical world and its laws are to have an ultimate grounding, then the cause of the universe's existence and intelligibility must not require a cause itself: an uncaused cause. As we saw Aquinas argue in chapter 1, an uncaused cause must lie beyond the natural world, for all things within time and space are finite and limited and seem to require a cause to explain their existence. An uncaused cause beyond nature, unlimited by space and time, does not undermine scientific explanation, but is instead a philosophically reasonable conclusion—one that provides ultimate grounding and rationale for the project of further explanation at the level of physics, and justification for why mathematical laws would exist in the first place.

---

81. As Bryson points out, this is what physicists always say Einstein said; the actual quote is "It seems hard to sneak a look at God's cards. But that He plays dice and uses 'telepathic' methods . . . is something that I cannot believe for a single moment." (Bill Bryson, *A Short History of Nearly Everything*, p. 146.) Einstein made similar observations in other settings, so the general idea was clearly on his mind. (Ralph Keyes, *The Quote Verifier*, p. 51.)

82. In the early European scientific tradition, part of the reason why mathematical laws were sought in the first place is precisely that natural philosophers and scientists commonly believed that the universe had a creator who behaved consistently and not arbitrarily, making a search for regularities justifiable.

83. "God-of-the-gaps" explanations have been criticized not just on scientific grounds, but on religious grounds: in this picture, as scientific knowledge advances, those gaps that God is the God of, close up. Within a God-of-the-gaps framing, as we know more and more, we seem to need God less and less.

3 EARTH

Paralleling chapter 2, we begin our exploration of Earth's place in universal history with a section ("Earth") analyzing ideas about the Earth itself: the scientific frameworks that view the Earth as a set of systems, a planet, and a living organism. The second section explores a major unifying scientific theory ("Plate Tectonics") that helps to frame and explain the history of Earth, and the third and fourth sections present two big principles that advance one's understanding of that history ("Deep Time" and "Ordering by Separating"). The final section explores a major philosophical issue ("Reductionism") that becomes increasingly relevant as complex entities like the Earth and living things come into view in our analysis of universal history.

Earth

The Earth has existed for more than four and a half billion years. In the context of universal history, this enormously long history of the Earth itself takes on a life of its own. As with the universe, scientists studying the Earth have crafted distinctive ways of thinking about the planet we call home—first of all, by thinking of it as a planet. Thinking of the Earth as a unit, with a history that has left traces in rocks and elsewhere on and below the Earth's surface, gives us an indication both of the deep processes that have shaped the ground we walk on and also what lies much farther beneath our feet, inside the Earth.

Forming the Earth

The Earth's initial formation connects us back to the cosmic narratives of chapter 2. Astronomers using the most powerful telescopes in the world can directly observe young stars still in the process of formation; these stars usually have a rotating disk of matter around them that is coalescing to form planets—a byproduct of gravity pulling matter together into a star. Our own Solar System shows many hints, discussed in chapter 2, of having formed in this manner. We cannot directly see the Earth in this process of formation (although if someone were observing us right now, from a position over 4.5 billion light-years away, they might be able to), but the Earth and other planets of the Solar System are thought to have formed by *accretion*, a process we will say more about later in this chapter. In essence, though, accretion means that our planet—like many others—was built over time from smaller rocky building blocks. Computer simulations of such processes in a swirling disk of matter around a young star suggest that building a planet takes only a short time (in cosmic terms), measured on the order of millions of years.

Very little direct evidence survives from this time in the "prehistory" of Earth, but a consistent picture emerges from observations of other star systems, from computer simulations, and from meteorites—especially certain small rocky bodies called carbonaceous chondrites—that fall to Earth and provide the closest thing to a "fossil," a physical artifact, from the period of the Solar System's initial formation. (Carbonaceous chondrites often include small mineral grains trapped within the body of the meteorite that date to almost 4.6 billion years ago, and these are probably among the first solids that formed in the Solar System. More generally, the asteroid belt—the source of nearly all meteorites—is an important source of evidence for conditions in the early Solar System; the rocky bodies that make up the asteroid belt were never able to combine into a stable planet and have largely retained the characteristics they had at their formation.) As with some early stages of the universe's history, scientists use extrapolations, comparisons, and pieces of indirect physical evidence to paint a plausible and reasonably detailed portrait of the Earth's very early past. (See Plate 7.)

Earth as a Planet

The Earth's status as a *planet* is familiar enough. It formed alongside a set of several other planets; as a "rocky"[1] planet, its composition is much like that of Mercury, Venus, and Mars. Most of the chemical elements it contains were formed in aging stars and supernovae. Many of its characteristics (e.g., mountains) and processes (e.g., volcanism and earthquakes) are common to some other planets and moons in, and presumably also outside of, the Solar System.

All of this sounds straightforward. Still, it is worth taking the time to unpack the implications of classifying the Earth in this way. Earth itself went from being considered a non-planet to being classified as a planet in the transition from Ptolemaic (geocentric) astronomy to Copernican (heliocentric) astronomy. The word "planet" means "wanderer." Since Ptolemaic astronomy considered Earth to

---

1. As opposed to "gas giant."

be stationary at the center of the Solar System, it did no wandering or moving at all and so was not considered a planet, whereas the Copernican system classified Earth with the other bodies, like Mercury and Mars and Jupiter, that orbit the Sun—a change both in the meaning of "planet" and in Earth's status.

Much more recently, astronomers clarified the definition of "planet" once again, to include objects that are large enough to have been rounded by their own gravity and to have cleared debris from the area of their orbit. Because it had not cleared its orbit of debris, Pluto, a body in the Kuiper Belt of the outer Solar System, was reclassified as a dwarf planet after spending over seven decades classified as a planet. In the public discussion that ensued, it became clear that the general public has a great deal of investment in which objects are referred to as planets.

In a sense, the very act of calling the Earth a planet means taking an outsider's view, observing Earth from the cosmos rather than taking an Earth-centered view of the cosmos. Earth then becomes the third rock from the Sun, not the starting point and center of all observation. Any history of the Earth that likewise places it in cosmic context has the interesting feature of zooming in on the Earth from outside, with the cosmos being the story's starting point. We have already discussed the fact that the deeper meaning of Earth's non-centrality is debatable and often misrepresented. But imaginations are certainly influenced by what we can see, and now we do, in fact, have the opportunity to see Earth from outside: there are photographs of the Earth from space. (See Plate 8.) And something interesting happens when we do that; many people feel emotional resonances when seeing the Earth as a whole, in cosmic context. As Robert Hazen begins his book *The Story of Earth*:

> One of the most arresting images of the twentieth century is a photo of Earthrise, taken in 1968 by a human traveler in orbit around the Moon. We have long known how precious and special our world is: Earth is the only known planet with oceans of water, with an atmosphere rich in oxygen, with life. Nevertheless, many of us were unprepared for the breathtakingly stark contrast between the utterly hostile lunar landscape, the lifeless black void of space, and our enticing marbled white-on-blue home. From that distant vantage point, Earth appears alone, small, and vulnerable but also more beautiful by far than any other object in the heavens.[2]

Some would take this even further. Carl Sagan, commenting on an image of Earth from the Voyager 1 spacecraft when it was looking back at Earth from the outer edges of the Solar System (see Plate 9), wrote:

> From this distant vantage point, the Earth might not seem of any particular interest. But for us, it's different. Look again at that dot. That's here. That's

---

2. Robert Hazen, *The Story of Earth*, p. 1.

home. That's us. On it everyone you love, everyone you know, everyone you ever heard of, every human being who ever was, lived out their lives . . . on a mote of dust suspended in a sunbeam. . . . Our posturings, our imagined self-importance, the delusion that we have some privileged position in the universe, are challenged by this point of pale light. Our planet is a lonely speck in the great enveloping cosmic dark. . . . There is perhaps no better demonstration of the folly of human conceits than this distant image of our tiny world. To me, it underscores our responsibility to deal more kindly with one another, and to preserve and cherish the pale blue dot, the only home we've ever known.[3]

In a strikingly similar passage written some seven centuries earlier and from a completely different worldview, Dante turns back to look at the Earth as he is ascending through Heaven in *The Divine Comedy*, and intones the following:

> My eyes went back through the seven spheres below,
> and I saw this globe, so small, so lost in space,
> I had to smile at such a sorry show.
> Who thinks it the least pebble in the skies
> I most approve. Only the mind that turns
> to other things may truly be called wise.[4]

In addition to serving as a powerful reminder that Dante, and medieval Europe in general, did not see the Earth's centrality in the universe as a point in the Earth's favor, the similarities in these passages suggest the impact of an imaginative or actual view of the Earth as a whole, against a cosmic background, that crosses a variety of worldviews.

Earth as a Set of Systems

In addition to being a planet, the Earth is also a *set of systems*. Earth scientists conceive of the Earth as a set of concentric, near-spherical shells,[5] each of which is an identifiable system that interacts with the other systems. For example, the *atmosphere* is the mixture of gases that circle the planet above its surface; the *biosphere* is the sum total of all life on the planet, which forms a thin layer at the surface as well as just above and just below the surface; the *lithosphere* is the combination of crust and upper

---

3. Carl Sagan, *Pale Blue Dot: A Vision of the Human Future in Space*, pp. 6–7.

4. Dante, *Paradiso*, Canto 22 (trans. John Ciardi).

5. Technically, they are not quite concentric, and there is substantial interpenetration between systems. For example, the biosphere penetrates several other "spheres."

mantle that is rigid and split into tectonic plates; and the *asthenosphere* is the weak and ductile solid portion of the mantle below the lithosphere that flows slowly over geologic time. In addition to these, we could identify many other "sphere" systems: the *hydrosphere*, which includes all of Earth's liquid water; the *cryosphere*, which includes frozen water; and so forth. These systems are, by definition, global in nature—not just in the sense of "worldwide," but in the sense that they are (hollow) globes, approximately spherical and three-dimensional, each with different thicknesses.[6]

This way of "dividing up" the Earth is different from dividing it up into the more familiar three layers of core, mantle, and crust, which are defined by composition and density. What makes up the crust, for example, is different than what makes up the mantle. Meanwhile, the crust and the upper mantle are grouped together into the lithosphere, even though their makeup is not the same, because the lithosphere and other "spheres" are defined as units that play a certain *role* and *behave* as a unit in some fundamental way. (See Plate 10.)

Looking through the lens of these "spheres" powerfully illuminates the sense that everything on Earth is intricately connected to everything else, that *the Earth is an interconnected whole*.[7] Earth systems co-evolved through the long history of the Earth and continue to mutually influence each other. In particular, the biosphere is integrally connected with everything else; as we discuss later in this chapter and in chapter 4, the Earth and life have developed and changed together, with the history of life and the geological makeup of the planet influencing one another in a variety of ways.[8]

An often-underappreciated example of this pattern is the Earth's magnetic field. Generated by motions of molten iron in the outer core of the Earth, its effects span the range of the other "spheres." The existence of the magnetic field has enabled the continued existence of the atmosphere, because the magnetic field shields atmospheric gases from bombardment by particles streaming from the Sun (and other more distant cosmic sources), which otherwise could sweep these gases away over time. Likewise, the biosphere is protected from harmful radiation in part by the magnetic field and in part by the atmosphere that the magnetic field helps to preserve. In many such ways, the systems of Earth are deeply interconnected.

Earth as Alive

Earth may be described as small, fragile, and lonely when placed against the historical or physical backdrop of the cosmos, but once we look at it closely, we also see that it is alive, energetic, with a "life" of its own. These are metaphorical ways of

---

6. We have drawn on Robert Hazen's "seven core truths" about the Earth in *The Story of Earth*.

7. Hazen's fifth "core truth."

8. Hazen's seventh "core truth."

speaking, which "enliven" the Earth and transform a scientific account into a story that non-specialists can grasp and enjoy. But such metaphors also feed back into the scientific questions that Earth scientists think to ask.

The metaphor is frequent in Earth science that the Earth is itself a living thing. Some have even gone so far, based at least in part on James Lovelock and Lynn Margulis's Gaia hypothesis, as to claim that the Earth—with its complex, interlocking systems and its mechanisms for self-regulation and stability—should be considered one giant living thing. While most do not take it that far, this is nonetheless a powerful metaphor and storytelling device, and one that encourages the search for interconnections and feedback among Earth's systems.

In a way, the cosmic view of Earth as a planet and the Earth scientist's view of Earth as a set of interconnected systems work together. The cosmic view makes it easy to see Earth as a single system, to conceive the "global" as a category, to see the unity of Earth as a planet. This in turn makes it easy to conceive of Earth as deeply interconnected, or intraconnected—that is, everything connected to everything else at a planetary scale. They are different, but complementary, ways of making sense of the Earth: one being the astronomer's view, starting from outside and moving toward Earth while seeing the Earth itself as a product of the cosmos, and one being the Earth scientist's view, starting from the Earth itself and treating it as a set of systems of its own.

The metaphor of Earth as a living thing also has implications for how we think about life, a subject to which we turn in chapter 4. While many things in this world are unquestionably alive by any definition, there are others—viruses being the quintessential example—where the precise definition of "life" really matters. Can the Earth genuinely be considered a living organism? Can viruses? The answers to these questions have implications for how we conceptually divide up the world, both in our science and in our storytelling. This is true not least because the "life metaphor" infiltrates all science: we hear of stars being born and dying, going through life cycles, and having different generations. We hear of the universe itself being born and dying. There are choices being made in describing things this way, choices that are aesthetic and interpretive rather than based purely on scientific evidence. And if we are interested not only in the raw evidence but in the story that we weave out of science, the power of the life metaphor cannot be ignored.

Plate Tectonics

Plate tectonics, an idea barely a half-century old, now stands as the great unifying theory for Earth science. It plays a role in geology similar to that of the Big Bang in cosmology, to atomic theory in chemistry, to evolution in biology, and to quantum field theory and general relativity in physics. Each of these scientific disciplines has developed a central theory or theories, a set of explanations that synthesizes a wide range of observations into a core set of ideas that produces a coherent and well-tested understanding of some aspect of how the world works. Plate tectonics unites observations ranging from the distribution of volcanoes and earthquakes over the Earth's surface to the magnetic striping around the mountain ranges in the middle of the oceans. It unifies our explanation of many geological processes, and it explains the question of "tectonics"—that is, how geological features are constructed (the Greek *tekton* means "builder").

Universal histories almost invariably discuss plate tectonics, because like the Big Bang and evolution, it is a theory that not only provides a core explanation of some aspect of the world, but also key ingredients of a story. Each of these three theories is not just mechanistic, explaining how something works, but is also temporal, giving an account of change over time. Plate tectonics provides a central touchstone for some major processes that have helped to shape Earth for at least a billion years.

The Idea and the Evidence

The basic idea of plate tectonics is that the Earth's lithosphere (the upper mantle plus the crust) is broken into large plates. New lithosphere forms by welling up from the Earth's interior at the mid-oceanic ridges—the mountain ranges that are submerged in the middle of every ocean on Earth. New lithosphere slowly spreads outward to form ocean basins, while old oceanic lithosphere plunges downward along plate boundaries and is recycled back into the lower mantle in a process called subduction. This conveyer-belt-like motion, involving both the generation of new lithosphere at the mid-oceanic ridges and the destruction of that lithosphere at plate boundaries, is known as seafloor spreading.[9] (See Plate 11.)

The modern theory of plate tectonics builds on the much older idea of continental drift. Continental drift is the idea that the continents are not fixed in place, that they can move. But without a mechanism for how huge slabs of rock could move around the surface of the Earth, the idea remained largely speculative from its origins in the 1500s (when world maps were first circulated after the joining of the Old World and New World) until the 1960s.

Alfred Wegener, a meteorologist with deep interest in geology, amassed a considerable amount of evidence for continental drift in the early 1900s, including the jigsaw-puzzle fit between coastlines, especially South America and Africa, that cartographers had noticed since the 1500s. Beyond this, Wegener and others pointed out that the jigsaw-puzzle fit between continents should be even better if

---

9. Remove all the water in the world's oceans and you would find that, to first approximation, there are basically two elevations for the surface of the Earth: that of the oceans and that of the continents. Oceanic crust, which occupies the lower elevation, is denser and thinner than the lighter but thicker continental crust. For this reason, continental lithosphere is not easily subducted.

one looked at continental shelves rather than coastlines. (Continental shelves are extensions of the continents that are submerged in shallow water off the coasts of continents, before the steeper downward slope that drops off into the deep ocean. During times in Earth's history when the sea level was lower, the edge of the continental shelf would be the coastline rather than present-day coastlines.) Wegener showed continuities in geological structures, such as mountain ranges, and in the ages and types of rocks on opposite sides of the Atlantic. He pointed out that certain types of fossil organisms had only been discovered in locations that were now separated by an ocean, but that this could be easily explained if the landmasses had been joined in the past. And he pointed to evidence that there were once glaciers in Africa, such as "scratch marks" / striations on various rocks that are telltale signs of past glaciers dragging debris over the rocks, and other mismatches between present-day geography and ancient climate.[10]

What Wegener was missing, which caused many fellow scientists to be dismissive of continental drift, was a plausible mechanism for how continents could possibly drift apart from each other over geologic time.[11] Evidence for a mechanism awaited development of the technology to map the ocean floor in detail, around the globe.

From the mid-1800s to the 1950s, improving technologies for surveying the ocean floor gradually revealed that it is not flat and featureless, but that a continuous mountain range runs along the middle of the ocean floor around the world.[12] Moreover, the oceanic crust is, on average, much younger than the continental crust, with almost none of it older than about 180 million years (continental interiors are typically much older, from 500 million to almost 4 billion years old). And the oceanic crust is younger near the mid-oceanic ridges and older toward the continental margins, in a symmetric form suggesting that new crust emerges at the mid-oceanic ridges and spreads outward. (See Plate 12.) Even beyond that, a strongly magnetic mineral (called, appropriately enough, magnetite) in the rock around the mid-oceanic ridges shows a striping effect. Magnetite grains act as small bar magnets, with a north pole and a south pole. The magnetic striping effect means that if one

---

10. Some ancient glacial features can also be explained by "Snowball Earth" episodes in which the entire Earth may have been frozen over. Other systematic geography-climate mismatches, however, can only be explained through detailed reconstructions of how continents have drifted over time, explaining what climate zones the various landmasses were in at different times in the past.

11. Naomi Oreskes additionally argues that the nature of the evidence assembled by Wegener was quite different, and less compelling, than the highly quantitative and geophysical evidence on which the full-fledged theory of plate tectonics would ultimately be based. See Naomi Oreskes, "The Rejection of Continental Drift," *Historical Studies in the Physical and Biological Sciences* 18, no. 2 (1988): 311–348.

12. For a fuller and very readable account, see W. Jacquelyne Kious and Robert I. Tilling, "Developing the Theory," http://pubs.usgs.gov/gip/dynamic/developing.html .

were to start at the mid-oceanic mountain range and move outward toward a continent, the magnetic polarity produced by the alignment of the magnetite grains in the crust would effectively "flip" every so often. Near the mid-oceanic ridge, the north poles of the grains would all point south. A bit farther out, the north poles would all point north. Farther out than that, they would all point south again—and so on.

What do all these various pieces of evidence add up to? As geologists deduced in the late 1950s and early 1960s, everything fits comfortably with the seafloor-spreading hypothesis: new seafloor is constantly produced at the mid-oceanic ridges and moves away from the ridge, explaining why the youngest seafloor is near the mid-oceanic ridge; the Earth's magnetic field leaves an imprint in the molten rocks when they first come to the surface and cool; the fact that Earth's magnetic field switches polarity every several hundred thousand years (on average) explains the alternating polarity; and the destruction of old oceanic lithosphere as it subducts back into the lower mantle explains why almost no seafloor on Earth today is older than 180 million years.

Plate tectonics supplies the mechanism that Wegener's ideas about continental drift lacked, and it rests on a wide range of precise geophysical measurements that complement and extend Wegener's observations, putting continental drift on firm scientific footing. Continents move because they are taken along for the ride with the motions of the lithospheric plates. These plates move thanks to both the "ridge push" along the mid-oceanic ridges where new lithosphere is generated, and the "slab pull" from heavy oceanic lithosphere diving back into the mantle and pulling along the lithosphere connected with it, all driven by convective motion in the Earth's mantle (see the next subheading, "Plate Tectonics and the Earth's Interior").[13] The process of seafloor spreading connects what happens on the ocean floor with the surface motions of entire continents, and with motion in the mantle below.[14]

GPS satellites can now measure the motion of the continents, and the pace—some 3 cm/year, a thousand times slower than Wegener's initial estimates—matches up with the rates extrapolated from geological measurements. This provides a final piece of evidence that continental drift really does happen.

Plate Tectonics and the Earth's Interior

Ultimately, the whole process of plate motion is driven by the internal heat of the Earth. How does this happen? The Earth's internal heat produces large-scale motions (convection) in the mantle, including in the weak, syrupy solid of the

---

13. The fastest-moving plates are being subducted along a large fraction of their boundaries, indicating slab pull's importance, but ridge push is invoked to explain why continents break apart after they come together, as in the case of Pangaea (see the subheading "Plate Tectonics and the Earth's Interior"). (John Grotzinger et al., *Understanding Earth* (5th edition), pp. 37, 40.)

14. Thanks to Alex Lechler for several helpful conversations about this topic (and many others).

asthenosphere, which in turn produce motion of the lithospheric plates that ride atop the asthenosphere. Earth formed by accretion, the colliding of many small rocky bodies, and heat is produced in such a formation process, which—along with decay of radioactive elements in its interior—still powers Earth's internal "engine." Just as hot air rises and cold air falls, so too the motions of rocks in the interior of the Earth bring heat from the interior up to Earth's surface. This is what ultimately drives motions in the mantle and supplies energy to melt rock, move continents, and lift up mountains.

While the asthenosphere is immediately below the lithosphere and thus "carries" the lithospheric plates, the entire mantle contributes to plate tectonics. One indication of this can be seen from studying the fate of subducted seafloor. Almost no seafloor on Earth is older than 180 million years, which means that essentially all the seafloor from the time of Pangaea, the "supercontinent" in which all the continental landmasses were combined some 250 million years ago, has long since subducted. An amount of lithosphere equivalent to the entire ocean floor has been recycled back into the mantle, and geologists can actually "see" this cold subducting material—that is, infer where it is now—by examining how seismic waves are transmitted through the Earth. The cold subducting material can extend all the way down to the boundary between the core and the mantle, indicating the participation of even the lowest parts of the mantle in the processes that drive plate tectonics.[15]

Though Earth scientists are confident of their inferences, knowledge of the Earth's interior is generally based on indirect evidence, such as that from seismic waves. Drilling has never gotten us even halfway through the crust, and certainly not to the mantle.

Side Note: Does Plate Tectonics Itself Have a History?

It is unclear when the movement of rigid plates of lithosphere began. Very early in Earth's history, when the planet was newly formed and still very hot, the lithosphere would have been too hot for rigid plates to form and move around coherently. The planet has been cooling continuously since then, however, and at some point, the crust cooled down enough for plate tectonics to operate as it does today. Current evidence points to this having happened at least 1 billion years ago, as there are rock features that suggest collisions between continents and relative motion of continents going that far back. Further back into the past, the evidence becomes less clear and conclusive.[16]

---

15. Grotzinger et al., *Understanding Earth*, p. 41.

16. For a helpful but technical discussion, see Julie Baldwin and Staci Loewy, "When Did Plate Tectonics Begin?": http://serc.carleton.edu/NAGTWorkshops/earlyearth/questions/tectonics.html .

Shifting the Conceptual Ground

Part of what makes plate tectonics such a compelling theory, and the unifying theory for the Earth sciences, is that it unites different aspects of the Earth itself. It explains how mountains are built up through the collision of continents, as well as the jigsaw-puzzle fit of continents noted by Wegener. It explains the planet's pattern of earthquakes and volcanic activity, which occur most frequently along plate boundaries. (See Plate 13.) It connects seismic observations of what happens under the surface of the Earth throughout its three-dimensional volume with the features we see on the surface. It accounts for several of the couplings that we see between Earth systems, and it helps to describe the interconnectedness of the different parts of the Earth—for example, helping to unite the climate system with the lithosphere, since mountains and other features influence climate.[17] The theory is a story of convergence not only of continents but of disciplines: Alfred Wegener was himself a meteorologist, and many subfields of Earth science informed the discovery and ongoing application of the theory. Petroleum geologists, for instance, have located oil-bearing rock formations on one continent by matching them up with their predrift continuations on another.[18]

Plate tectonics also takes us back in time. It gives the Earth dynamism and a mechanism for change over time that includes even seemingly eternal structures like mountains, which are built up and eroded away over tens and hundreds of millions of years. It links the initial formation of the Earth with ongoing geological processes.

Moreover, it provides a key to understanding the co-evolution of Earth and the biosphere: continental drift sets a stage for the history of life. As continents drift around, landmasses go through different latitudes; areas that were at the poles may end up at the equator, and vice versa. And there are different proportions of different habitats—mountains, shallow-water areas in the oceans, and so forth—as a function of how the continents are arranged at a given time. Even though the motions of plates produce earthquakes and volcanoes, which can be destructive, in the long view these motions may be generative, and they certainly influence the patterns of, and the possibilities for, evolutionary change.

And yet, despite its fundamental importance to the story that science-based universal histories tell, plate tectonics is a surprisingly new idea. As recently as the 19th century, earthquakes were narrated and understood in ways totally foreign to anyone whose understanding of Earth is shaped by plate tectonics. The study of earthquakes was a part of meteorology through the 19th century. The weather

---

17. Mountains are built up through plate-tectonic processes, and the more mountains there are on Earth at a given time in geological history, the more of Earth's water gets "locked up" in ice at high elevations, other factors being equal.

18. Grotzinger et al., *Understanding Earth*, p. 37.

bureau would report them—as a form of weather—precisely because there was no scientifically comprehensible mechanism for understanding why they happen. And not only earthquakes, but the whole edifice of geological theory we have unfolded in this section would have been conceived differently. Even in, say, 1955, a "history of everything" would not have mentioned plate tectonics.

So one might ask: If plate tectonics can come along and produce a seismic shift in our understanding of the Earth's workings and history, what other ideas might produce similar shifts in the future? It is, of course, impossible to say. But scientific inquiry has a way of turning up surprises that change significant aspects of the story a universal history might tell,[19] as with dark energy, which leads us to extrapolate a totally different future for the universe than was predicted just five years before its discovery. How else might new developments—even developments at the informational level, as all of these are—change the picture, the context we use to frame scientific evidence in a history of everything, the importance we attach to different aspects of the story? We expect such changes to happen, and so too expect elements of this apparently well-known and firmed-up story to be, in fact, provisional and open to future change.

To Ponder: Plate Tectonics as a Metaphor

Gravity, natural selection, and life are taken up outside their respective disciplines as broader metaphors. Could plate tectonics work as a broader metaphor outside the Earth sciences?

Deep Time

Often portrayed as a fragile home for humanity and life, the Earth is anything but fragile in at least one regard: it has existed for a third of the age of the universe. While small in terms of spatial size, the Earth—perhaps alone of all places in the universe—has provided a place for life to thrive for billions of years and has survived traumas (another metaphor!) of many sorts along the way.

---

19. The evidence used to validate plate tectonics came in good measure from technologies and techniques that were developed for entirely different purposes than geological investigation. For example, wartime submarine detection provided the impetus to develop sonar and magnetometers that could probe the ocean floor. Even coastline mapping in the 1500s, although it would prove to be a geologically useful set of observations, was not done primarily for scientific purposes. Part of the reason *why* scientific inquiry turns up surprises is that new technologies sometimes reveal patterns in the natural world that no one had thought of or noticed before, and there is no reason to expect that trend to cease in the future.

The ancientness of the Earth is often called "deep time." It is "deep" both in the sense of deep in the past and also deep under the ground. Geologists came to the conclusion that the Earth must be very old long before astronomers were able to determine the age of the universe (see Plate 1). Before the Big Bang was proposed, models of the universe generally were mechanistic (explaining how it works, independent of time[20]) rather than temporal (explaining how it changes over time). So even though the universe is indeed older than the Earth—how could it not be?—deep time is an idea that "belongs" to the Earth sciences, where it was first discovered and "unearthed."

A Brief History of Earth

The geologic time scale organizes the Earth's deep past into intervals known as (from longest to shortest) eons, eras, periods, epochs, and ages. A brief look at the conditions on Earth during each of the four eons gives us a basic sense of how the Earth has changed over time. (See Figure 3.1 and Plates 14 and 15.)

During the Hadean eon (4.5–4.0 billion years ago), geologists believe that the Earth started out rapidly rotating,[21] hot, barren, and waterless; was routinely bombarded with meteorites and intense cosmic radiation; and exhibited widespread volcanism. The Hadean, named after Hades because of its initially "hellish" conditions, was not a time when life is likely to have existed, though a stable planet with conditions suitable for life slowly took shape during this half-billion-year eon. Earth scientists surmise that as the planet cooled and the loose rocks in the early Solar System were gradually swept into the Earth or out of its orbit, volcanism and meteorite bombardment decreased. The Moon formed, likely as the product of a collision between the Earth and a Mars-sized object, at some point during this eon. (See "Side Note: How Did the Moon Form?") The Earth had no atmosphere, no oceans, and no magnetic field initially, but each of these began to take shape during the Hadean. The atmosphere is thought to have come originally from gases expelled by volcanoes. The oceans are thought to have come from water vapor expelled by

---

20. As the Ptolemaic and steady-state models alike did.

21. The idea that the Earth rotated more rapidly in the past is based on extrapolating present-day conditions backward: the Earth's rotation is slowing down incrementally even now, so that the length of a day becomes very slightly longer all the time. Therefore, it stands to reason that the rotation was more rapid, and the days shorter, in the past. Fossilized corals from more than 400 million years ago (much more recent than the Hadean) preserve indications that there were over 400 days in a year at that point in Earth's history, consistent with Earth's rotation rate being faster and the day being shorter than it is now; see, e.g., Kate Golembiewski, "How Ancient Coral Revealed the Changing Length of a Year," https://www.theatlantic.com/science/archive/2016/02/fossilized-coral-calendar-changes-leap-day/471180/ . For a related discussion, see G.E. Williams, "Precambrian Length of Day and the Validity of Tidal Rhythmite Paleotidal Values," https://agupubs.onlinelibrary.wiley.com/doi/pdf/10.1029/97GL00234 .

EON	ERA	PERIOD	Beginning (millions of years ago)	Geologic Highlights
PHANEROZOIC	CENOZOIC	Quaternary	3	Human history (Holocene—10,000 years) Ice Age (Pleistocene)
		Neogene	23	
		Paleogene	66	PETM (55 million years ago) Mammals diversify Giant birds
	MESOZOIC	Cretaceous	145	*Dinosaur extinction* Atlantic Ocean opens First flowering plants
		Jurassic	201	*Mass extinction* Age of the reptiles begins
		Triassic	252	
	PALEOZOIC	Permian	299	*Greatest mass extinction in Earth history* Pangaea formed
		Carboniferous	359	Widespread coal swamps *Mass extinction*
		Devonian	419	First amphibians
		Silurian	444	Widespread coral reefs *Mass extinction*
		Ordovician	485	First land plants First fish
		Cambrian	541	Modern animal phyla appear
PRECAMBRIAN	PROTEROZOIC	NEO-PROTEROZOIC	565	Ediacaran organisms
			700	Snowball Earth
		MESO-PROTEROZOIC		"Boring Billion": time of unusual climatic and geochemical stability
			1600	Baraboo mountains form (Wisconsin)
		PALEO-PROTEROZOIC	2100	Banded iron formations are precipitated as O_2 accumulates in atmosphere
			2500	
	ARCHEAN	NEOARCHEAN	2800	Modern-style plate tectonics (subduction)
			3200	Oldest rocks in Wisconsin
		MESOARCHEAN		
		PALEO-ARCHEAN	3800	Oldest rocks in U.S. (Minnesota) Earliest evidence of life (Greenland)
		EOARCHEAN	4000	Oldest rocks on Earth
	HADEAN		4500	No rocks from this period on Earth; known from meteorites, Moon rocks, and a few Australian zircon crystals

Note: Intervals are not shown in proportion to duration.

FIGURE 3.1 Simplified Geologic Time Scale One (simplified, and approximated) representation of the geologic time scale.

Source: Based on Marcia Bjornerud, *Timefulness: How Thinking Like a Geologist Can Help Save the World* (Princeton: Princeton Univ. Press, 2018), pp. 184–185.

those same volcanoes, or possibly deposited by comets, or a combination thereof, that saturated the atmosphere and, ultimately, came to the surface as rain. The magnetic field, without which atmospheric gases would eventually have been swept away by the stream of particles from the Sun known as the solar wind, probably came into being once nickel and iron had sunk into the Earth's core in a process known as differentiation (explained more fully in the next section, "Ordering by Separating").

During the Archean eon (4.0–2.5 billion years ago), the Earth's oceans, magnetic field, and climate system were established, and stable continental masses had accumulated. Plate tectonics may have already been operating by this point, but this is unclear. The atmosphere, formed initially during the Hadean, was probably composed largely of carbon dioxide, methane, water vapor, and nitrogen. The Archean saw the emergence of the first life on Earth: single-celled organisms that we will "meet" again in chapter 4.

By the Proterozoic eon (2.5 billion to 541 million years ago), the plate-tectonic and climate systems were most likely operating as they do today. Oxygen in the atmosphere increased, for reasons that will be more fully explored under "Biosphere" in chapter 4. The first traces of multicellular life are found in the Proterozoic. There is also significant evidence for one or more "Snowball Earth" episodes, in which the entire planet may have become so cold as to freeze over.

The Phanerozoic eon (541 million years ago to present) is the eon of "visible life," when nearly all fossils are found, since few hard-bodied macroscopic organisms existed previously. It began with the "Cambrian explosion," when most of the major phyla of animals came into existence, and it continues to the present day. It is worth pointing out that although most of what follows in this book occurred in the Phanerozoic, this eon represents only about one-ninth of the Earth's history. Just as visible matter is only some 5 percent of the universe, the Earth's past is much deeper than what meets the eye.

How Do We Know?

What kind of evidence do geologists use to craft this story of the Earth's history?

The understanding of the Hadean eon involves some speculation, but this speculation is based on a well-considered central idea: that the present is the key to the past. Comparatively few rocks have been found dating to the first half-billion years of Earth's existence, so geologists often use more indirect methods to infer what the conditions were and how they changed. For instance, the idea that water vapor in the atmosphere rained down to create our oceans, and that it originally came from within the Earth and was outgassed volcanically, is arrived at by taking rates of current volcanic water vapor outgassing, asking how much water vapor would be released over a 500-million-year period, and determining at what concentration the atmosphere would become supersaturated. Geologists combine that with thermal models of the Earth's interior and surface to calculate when the Earth might have been cool enough to sustain liquid water. As with the universe, the earliest parts of this story require more modeling and extrapolation than the later parts do, though the accepted picture has been worked out as precisely as limited evidence permits.[22]

The Earth's conditions during the other three eons are much less speculative, because we have more direct evidence. Stable rocks existed on Earth, and those rocks can be dated. There are only a few such rocks from the Hadean; almost all dated rocks from the Earth are dated to the Archean or later.

The crudest way of dating rocks is to observe their relative positions: rocks that are deeper under the Earth's surface are usually older. But this is only a relative measurement, and it says nothing of the absolute age of the rocks, the actual number of years ago that they formed. For that, geologists turn to radiometric dating.

Radiometric dating takes advantage of the radioactive decay of certain atomic nuclei. Recall from chapter 2 that an atomic nucleus is the tiny central part of the atom containing protons and neutrons, around which electrons "orbit."[23] Two nuclei are considered *isotopes* of the same element if they have the same number of protons but different numbers of neutrons.[24] An isotope is identified by the number of protons plus neutrons it has. So, for instance, all isotopes of lead have 82 protons, but lead-206 has 124 neutrons (82 + 124 = 206) while lead-207 has 125 neutrons (82 + 125 = 207).

Certain isotopes decay radioactively; for instance, uranium-238 and uranium-235 are isotopes that exist only for a certain period of time, on average, before they spontaneously change into other forms. Uranium-238 decays to lead-206 (passing through many other nuclei on the way), while uranium-235 ultimately decays to lead-207. The precise moment at which any given nucleus will decay is unpredictable, but in a large sample, it is quite predictable how long it will take for half the nuclei to decay: this is called the "half-life." By measuring how much of the original "parent" isotope remains in a rock and comparing this quantity to how much "daughter" isotope (the stable end product of radioactive decay) has accumulated, geologists can determine how many half-lives have passed since the rock formed. The half-life of an isotope useful for radiometric dating must be long enough for a measurable amount of the isotope to be left in whatever rock is being dated. Uranium-238 has a half-life of about 4.5 billion years; uranium-235 has a half-life of about 700 million years. Both are good isotopes to use for radiometric dating, since uranium-containing rocks from most or all of Earth's history still have

---

22. Thanks to Alex Lechler and Nathan Niemi for helpful discussions of several points here.

23. In quotes because it is not an especially precise way to describe the electron cloud known to quantum mechanics.

24. For example, helium-3 and helium-4 are both forms of helium because they both have two protons. Helium-3 has one neutron (for a total of 3 [two protons + one neutron]), however, while helium-4 has two neutrons (for a total of 4 [two protons + two neutrons]).

appreciable quantities of both. There are several other helpful isotope "systems" as well, though, including potassium-40 (decays to argon-40; half-life, 1.3 billion years), rubidium-87 (decays to strontium-87; half-life, 49 billion years), and carbon-14 (decays to nitrogen-14; half-life, 5,730 years—hence useful for dating the much more recent past).[25]

It is convenient for Earth scientists that such "clocks in rocks" exist. But applying radiometric-dating techniques comes with many complications. Cross-calibration is helpful and necessary; by studying samples from different portions of the same rock, or different minerals within the same sample, or different isotopes within the same rock, geologists can check the results they find.[26] The field of geochronology has advanced dramatically in recent years. State-of-the-art measurements can now date rocks that are 250 million years old to within about 100,000 or 200,000 years, precise to within 0.1 percent.[27]

Radiometric dating enables an understanding of how continental landmasses came to be: the interior regions of present-day continents often date as being much older than the outer regions, suggesting that they were built up over time. The dating of rocks can also provide information about the conditions of the ocean and atmosphere in the past, because rocks indirectly record this information. For instance, certain minerals like pyrite and uraninite, which are unstable at Earth's surface when there is appreciable oxygen in the atmosphere, are more abundant in rocks having ages more than about 2.4 billion years. From this and other evidence found in sedimentary rocks, geologists infer that the atmosphere contained little to no oxygen before this time. In fact, geologists can use rock evidence to characterize how oxygen built up in the atmosphere as a function of time. Rocks also respond to the climate in ways that will be partially described in the next section, giving Earth scientists the opportunity to understand the planet's climate as a function of time. Understanding the past of the atmosphere and hydrosphere are, in turn, crucial to understanding the history of life.

While the ages of rocks can often be determined very accurately and precisely,[28] this does not end all debates about what precisely happened at a given time or in a given place. With regard to the earliest forms of life, Archean sediments show the first tantalizing evidence for life on Earth, in the form of telltale biochemical signatures in rocks and fossilized imprints of unicellular organisms. But given that

---

25. Grotzinger et al., *Understanding Earth*, p. 182.

26. Also helpful for consistency and precision is the fact that certain minerals exclude the daughter (end-product) nucleus when they first form (by cooling from a melted state), thus fixing the initial conditions in a way that allows calibration of other systems.

27. See Mark D. Schmitz and Klaudia F. Kuiper, "High-Precision Geochronology," https://pubs.geoscienceworld.org/msa/elements/article-abstract/9/1/25/137938 .

28. *Accuracy* has to do with how correct the number is; *precision* has to do with how consistently the same result is produced.

Side Note: How Did the Moon Form?

The origin of the Moon is another subject of debate. The abundances of isotopes of oxygen on the Moon, as well as certain other aspects of its isotopic and chemical composition, closely match those on Earth, providing strong evidence that the Earth and Moon probably came from the same progenitor material and formed in the same part of the Solar System. However, mathematical and computer models, along with direct analysis of Moon rocks sampled during the Apollo missions, demonstrate the near-impossibility of the Moon spontaneously breaking off from the early Earth, and suggest that the Moon formed relatively late in the planetary-growth stage of the early Solar System. These findings have led to the suggestion, first proposed in the 1970s, that the Moon formed as a byproduct of a high-energy collision between the proto-Earth and a smaller, Mars-sized object. Computer modeling and isotope geochemistry support the likelihood of this "giant impact hypothesis," but many questions remain: Could the Earth and Moon have both emerged from a single post-impact cloud of vaporized rock material?[29] Or did a glancing blow vaporize rocky material from both the proto-Earth and the impacting body into a ring that eventually coalesced into the Moon? Earth scientists judge the collision scenario to be by far the most likely, but research on many important details is ongoing.

---

non-living processes can sometimes generate structures that look like such fossilized imprints of life, the exact timing of life's origin is difficult to date, even if individual rock samples with candidate fossils can be dated accurately.

Telling the Story of Deep Time

This is the Earth's story. But humans are the ones writing the story, and humans often pick out the details of Earth's history that show how it ultimately became habitable for us. This helps to explain why, for example, we traced how oxygen got into the atmosphere rather than, say, argon: oxygen is the gas that we think of as being most vital for us. We track the Moon primarily because it is an object of curiosity for people, being a large object in the sky and having a prominent place in nearly every human being's awareness of the world—though it may also have helped stabilize Earth's early climate swings, paving the way for habitability. And we track what is happening on the crust of the Earth, only rarely turning our attention to the layers beneath, not only because more obvious changes happen on the surface and

---

29. See, e.g., Simon J. Lock et al., "The Origin of the Moon Within a Terrestrial Synestia," https://agupubs.onlinelibrary.wiley.com/doi/full/10.1002/2017JE005333 .

we have readier access to the evidence of what happened there compared to beneath it, but also because the surface is where we and most other familiar life forms exist.

One does have to pick out certain details at the expense of others: 4.5 billion years is, after all, a very long time to narrate. But the choices made in forming a narrative of Earth's history say a lot about how that narrative views the place of humanity. One could narrate the history of the Earth as if humans are the point of that history, by picking out all the details that "led" to us. G. S. Kutter, in perhaps the first attempt (in 1987) to put together a college textbook narrating a comprehensive scientific history of the universe, Earth, and life, expressed a fear that the order in which he was presenting topics "might mislead the reader into thinking that there is purpose to evolution, whose ultimate aim is the making of mankind," and he commented instead that "nothing could be further from the truth, at least as far as is known from science."[30] Many authors have included similar statements. But if the structure of a narrative presents a linear sequence of events that culminate in the existence of humans, that structure itself can, at least potentially, create the impression that everything "leads to us."

On the other hand, one could narrate the Earth's history as if humans are not the point of that history, emphasizing that the whole 200,000 or 300,000 years of our species' history are a tiny blip on the map of the Earth's whole story. The structure of the narrative, in this case, might stress those events that did not directly lead to making the Earth human-habitable in the recent past—which could include the vast majority of events in the 4.5 billion years of the planet's history. Or it might attempt to dwell on a given topic in strict proportion to how long it lasted, relegating 0.007 percent (300,000/4.5 billion) of the narrative to human beings. Or it could focus explicitly on how everything led to something other than humans: bacteria,[31] or ants,[32] or grass,[33] or the non-living structures and formations of the Earth itself.[34]

As we discussed in chapter 1 under "Scale," there is a sense in which both perspectives—that the history of Earth is a preparation for the coming of humankind, and that it is not—make valid points. By many measures, humans are a very small part of the Earth's story. But it is also the case that a lot had to happen for our existence to be possible, not only on the surface but throughout the Earth, including the mantle and the core as well. There are deep reasons why our species could not,

---

30. G. S. Kutter, *The Universe and Life*, pp. xii–xiii.

31. As in Lynn Margulis and Dorion Sagan, *Microcosmos: Four Billion Years of Evolution From Our Microbial Ancestors*.

32. As in several works of E. O. Wilson.

33. As in Jonathan Markley, "A Child Said, 'What Is the Grass?': Reflections on the Big History of the *Poaceae*," http://worldhistoryconnected.press.illinois.edu/6.3/markley.html .

34. Or it could attempt to avoid giving the impression that the history of the Earth led to anything at all—perhaps the most difficult option, given the human affinity for narrative arc.

in fact, have existed for a large fraction of Earth's history: too many other things had to happen first, like the origin of oxygen in the atmosphere, the evolution of multicellular organisms, and the evolution of the brain. And the story of how events in Earth's history led up to us is a fascinating story in its own right, one that deserves to be told.

Deep time is sometimes treated as a discovery that diminishes the centrality or importance of humanity, as Copernicus decentralizing the Earth within the Solar System is said to do. But as with Copernicus, the opposite interpretation of the meaning of deep time is also justifiable and legitimate: human life might appear even more remarkable when we recognize how long it took for the Earth to become habitable by creatures such as ourselves, and for life to take on the variety of forms it currently does. That it took such a long time to "prepare the way" for the appearance of human beings on the Earth (i.e., for the Earth to become human-habitable) is part of what makes human beings interesting and special and important. And the impact our species has had on this planet, both positive and negative, is impressive in part because it has happened in a comparatively short time.

It is not "unscientific" to elevate humanity to a position of importance even in the context of deep time, despite the interest that Kutter and others show in avoiding such elevation. Evaluating the *meaning* of deep time lies at the interpretive level rather than the informational level. And in any case, demonstrating how the history of Earth led to our species' existence is not mutually exclusive with the insight that it also took a long time to prepare the way for many other living and non-living aspects of the present-day world.

Another easily overlooked aspect of the storytelling of deep time is how we divide up and label the Earth's history—into eons, eras, and so on. The exact way we subdivide and label may seem unimportant: a given set of events happened in history no matter when we decide the Triassic, the Pleistocene, or the Middle Ages began or ended, just as the Solar System body called Pluto goes on orbiting the Sun regardless of whether or not we call it a planet. However, at the same time, the way we narrate a story matters at the interpretive level, and subdividing time into defined intervals (called "periodization" by historians) is an important ordering, or interpretive, device. In choosing how to periodize, one is implicitly making arguments about which changes matter most.

For instance, much of Earth's history is periodized not by strictly geological markers, but according to the history of life.[35] During the Phanerozoic, subdivisions of the geologic time scale are marked by distinctive sets of fossils; the time scale places the boundaries of the intervals at times when these sets of fossils changed abruptly.

---

35. This is largely for historical reasons. William Smith recognized that it was not the order of types of rocks that determined their age, but the order of fossils within the rocks themselves, and that these could be used to date and correlate strata across geographical areas. (Peter Ward and Joe Kirschvink, *A New History of Life*, p. 10.)

One might ask how a periodization based entirely on non-living aspects of Earth's history would look. Perhaps the operation of plate tectonics would come to the foreground[36]—though even in the case of plate tectonics, there seems to be a close relationship between the history of the Earth and the history of life, to the point where subduction may stabilize life by helping to cycle water, carbon dioxide, and other substances important to living things between the surface and the deep interior of the Earth.[37] The co-evolution of Earth and life, such that living and non-living systems constantly feed back on one another, provides strong reason why life may be a good basis for periodizing Earth's history: it is not just that living things are interesting to us. Nonetheless, a different choice could be made, and different periodizations would provide distinct framings and alternative ways of thinking about Earth's history.

These two issues—the role of human beings in the Earth's history, and the question of periodization—come together in a surprising way in debates over the Anthropocene.[38] The Anthropocene is an unofficial name that has been proposed recently for the geological epoch we are currently in; the "anthropo" (human) part reflects the fact that, by many measures, humans are the most influential species on the planet. The argument is that if geologists thousands or millions of years from now might find traces of our current activity in the Earth's strata, the naming of the present epoch could, and should, reflect this reality.

Periodization provokes debate in human history partly because the "human story" has different waystations for different groups—for example, the word "medieval" applies much more readily to Europe than it does to China. Periodization is thus about geography and culture as well as time. Interestingly, the idea of the Anthropocene brings such debate into the dating of geological time divisions too. It is a global periodization, with little room for recognition that conditions vary from place to place around the globe. It seems to imply that the present-day diversity of human beings, modes of social organization, and relationships with the natural environment is negligible—for geological purposes, at least. It presupposes a certain dichotomy between humans and nature, suggesting that at some point, the relationship or balance of power between the two shifted and now humanity is in charge of, or at least influencing, Earth's future. It suggests that "letting nature take its course" is no longer a possibility—though whatever dominant position humans may have is one that we possess only through interacting with other organisms, including the plants and animals we eat and the microbes inside our bodies. Many implications are packed into this single, apparently neutral, scientific term.

---

36. With, e.g., time periods based on the configuration of continents, or on the timing of prominent episodes of mountain-building.

37. See, e.g., Steve Nadis, "Why Aliens and Volcanoes Go Together," http://nautil.us/issue/12/feedback/why-aliens-and-volcanoes-go-together .

38. Thanks to Perrin Selcer for identifying this connection.

To Ponder: The Anthropocene

In what contexts might the term "Anthropocene" seem most appropriate? In what contexts might it seem least appropriate?

While the Anthropocene may be a more "loaded" term than more ancient subdivisions of geological time (see "Sustainability" in chapter 8 for more detail), these considerations bring us back to the overall question of whether, in narrating the story of deep time, it is the Earth's history or humanity's history we are narrating. The very word "Anthropocene" implies certain arguments about the place of humans in nature, or the relationship between humans and nature. But the framing and narrating of Earth's history in general does something similar, producing a planetary narrative in space and time, often with life as the focus. Just as the Anthropocene obscures the local in favor of the global, so too any narrative of deep time produces a certain storyline of global change that captures a very different flavor than what living an actual lifetime at any point in time, and at any particular place on Earth, would reveal.

Ordering by Separating

The Earth is a dynamic place. Much remains stable from one day to the next: the input of solar energy, the cycling of water and various other substances, many aspects of the climate system.[39] But at the same time, there is also long, slow change, the processes that unfold over geologically long periods of time and eventually add up: the oxygenation of the atmosphere, the motion of the continents. And there are also dramatic events—the meteorite impacts, the supervolcanic events—that reconfigure the Earth and alter the long-term co-evolution of Earth systems and life.

In any history, the dramatic (apparently contingent) one-time events are often more exciting to place in the foreground than the slow (apparently inevitable) change. The choice of which events to consider as "foreground" and which to consider as "background" is another issue that affects the framing of the story and influences its interpretation. In this section, we focus on the long, slow "background" changes in Earth's history, and we briefly describe several of the processes that order

---

39. Even the stasis, however, is usually a steady-state equilibrium of competing processes rather than a truly static arrangement; cycles of opposing processes persist over time. Many arguments for a young Earth that persist in some circles are extrapolations of one half of a competing process without the other.

matter within, on, and above the planet, often by separating one type of matter from another.

This question of how to separate background from foreground in telling the Earth's history goes back to one of the fundamental tensions in the history of geology: that between uniformitarianism (seeing continuous processes as the primary driver of change on Earth) and its opposite, which we might call contingency, or singularity, or in the extreme case, catastrophism (seeing the Earth's history as driven by major events—cataclysms—that remake the workings of the planet). A history of any sort can become fixated on singularity, on exceptions to the rule, but the rules themselves give structure and a place for the exceptions to unfold. And one can explain much of how the Earth operates, and how it got to be the way it is, through these long, slow, geological processes. Modern geology takes Earth science beyond the field's initial impulses toward catastrophism and uniformitarianism and into a more nuanced understanding that Earth's history shows both long periods of relative stasis and catastrophic or otherwise unique and irreversible events.[40]

Accretion and Differentiation

Accretion is our first example of a long, slow process important to Earth's story. In general, the word "accretion" means building something up over time by collecting matter to it: something small becomes bigger as it gathers matter to itself. The Sun, for example, formed by accretion from a cloud of gas and dust. Planets also form by accretion: the disk around the Sun, or any young star, is called an accretion disk, because planets accrete within the disk (see Plate 7). The Earth formed by accretion, from the small rocky building blocks (themselves formed through accretion) called "planetesimals." The continents formed on Earth's surface by an accretionary process in which rock was gradually added to them over time.

Accretion is a process that can easily be thought of as one in which uniqueness and contingency play no part. It does not seem to matter exactly which rocks end up in a planet, or which atoms end up in the Sun, because the average composition is going to be the same, give or take any particular rock (or atom). And yet this seemingly universal and deterministic process forms the basic structure within which unique and contingent events become possible in Earth's history.

Not long after the Earth had formed, another process, called differentiation, is thought to have occurred within the Earth: another long and slow process, in which heavier elements sank toward the core of the spherical Earth and lighter elements rose toward the outer portion of the sphere, which became the Earth's crust. This could happen because the molten early Earth was a fluid, and as in water or any other fluid, denser material sinks while less dense material rises. Differentiation

---

40. Hazen's sixth "core truth."

provides an explanation of why there are chemical differences in the composition of the Earth depending on how far down into the planet one "looks." The same process of differentiation occurs today in molten rock: components with different compositions separate out, if they have sufficient time to do so before the molten rock cools.

Differentiation and accretion are quite distinct processes, but both may play a role in explaining the presence of water on Earth. Two competing explanations for how the hydrosphere came to exist are, first, that water came from comets and, second, that water came from inside the Earth and was initially released in vapor form by volcanoes. In one case, the explanation relies on further accretion (water collects on Earth's surface from outside), and in the other case, the explanation relies on further differentiation (as water escapes from the Earth's interior). Both explanations are currently plausible based on geological evidence.

Sedimentation and Isotope Fractionation

Another process that is key to geology is sedimentation. Sedimentation occurs when loose particles, such as sand or silt, are carried by the processes of weathering and erosion into beds where they form layers—a certain kind of ordering by separating.[41] Sediments turn into sedimentary rocks over time, so these rocks provide records of the conditions when and where the sediments were deposited. From this, geologists can reconstruct the history of some rock formations, learning much about past conditions.

Another example of an Earth process that is key to our understanding of what has happened on this planet in the past is "isotope fractionation." The basic idea is that isotopes of the same element will separate from one another under certain conditions. Geologists can use knowledge of those conditions to describe how various Earth systems have operated in the past.

For example, when water turns from liquid to gas by evaporation, H_2O molecules with the lightest stable isotope of oxygen (oxygen-16) are slightly more likely to evaporate than are those with heavier isotopes (especially oxygen-18). This means that water molecules that include oxygen-16 are slightly more able to move across Earth's surface; that is, they are slightly more likely to be "liberated" by evaporation into the gas phase at lower latitudes and then move through the atmosphere as part of water vapor. This makes them more likely to find their way to higher latitudes, where their mobility ends when they leave the atmosphere as precipitation and ultimately become "locked up" in glaciers, unable to return to the states or locations they were previously in. So during times of colder climate (more

---

41. "Weathering" indicates the processes that break up rocks into fragments. "Erosion" indicates the processes that loosen and transport soil and rock particles, which are often deposited in layers. "Lithification" is the process by which sediments are converted into solid rock. (Grotzinger et al., *Understanding Earth*, p. 65.)

glaciers) in Earth's history, ocean water had slightly less oxygen-16, and glaciers had slightly more oxygen-16, than during times of warmer climate (fewer glaciers). This basic observation is regularly used to probe global temperatures at different times in the past by analyzing the relative abundance of oxygen isotopes in ice cores.

Similarly, carbon goes through isotope fractionation during biological processes. Depending on how a plant takes in carbon dioxide during photosynthesis, it may separate out carbon isotopes to a greater or lesser extent. Changes in the relative abundance of carbon isotopes in the rock record can therefore indicate changes over time in what plants lived in a given area. A similar analysis can be performed on fossilized animals: a technique called stable-isotope analysis uses the fractionation of isotopes of various elements by animals to track everything from aspects of their life cycle to where they lived to what they ate to their place in the food chain (called "trophic level"). Information about all of these things can be drawn out by tracking the amount of different isotopes that ended up where.[42]

Ordering by Separating, Past and Present

Examining in detail various "background" geological processes, as we have done in this section, reveals a good deal about the long, slow, cumulative changes in the Earth's history. As demonstrated especially with isotope fractionation, it also sheds light on how geologists can make credible claims about events that happened thousands, or millions, or even billions of years ago.

These background processes continue today. Sedimentation and isotope fractionation still occur constantly, and even planetary accretion still happens: it is estimated that a million tons of meteorites hit the Earth every year, mostly burning up high in the atmosphere. Of course, this accretion happens at a much slower rate than it did in the early Solar System, or life never would have been able to arise. Many processes that have shaped the Earth for a long time are so slow that they allow the perception that Earth is static. But it is not: there is, everywhere, a set of background processes going on that allows for the stability and order we see and the many changes that the Earth has seen in its long history.

Reductionism

It appears that all matter in the universe is made of particles: atoms, or subatomic particles that are even smaller than atoms. And yet a universal history that told

---

42. Isotope fractionation is also the principle by which a mass spectrometer, a key laboratory instrument in geology, works. Mass spectrometers separate isotopes by mass: a spectrum is a range, and just like a prism separates light into a range of colors, a mass spectrometer physically separates different isotopes, which have different masses, using a magnet. This is used to do the isotope analysis in radiometric dating and the various analyses discussed in this section.

a story only of subatomic particles might be rather boring—at least, to everyone other than elementary-particle physicists. Rather, it is the *composites* those subatomic particles form that are of greater interest: stars and galaxies, planets and asteroids, living organisms, and human beings.

That said, it is not just a need for more interesting storytelling that leads people to speak of composites rather than focusing only on subatomic particles or other constituent parts. Many people have the sense that the entities that populate the world, past and present, are *real*, that they can be treated on their own terms and "deserve" a history of their own.

The set of philosophical ideas known as "reductionism" provides a challenge to this way of telling the story. Reductionism takes many forms, but at its core is the idea that a composite entity—that is, something made of multiple parts or elements—should be treated as nothing more, and nothing less, than the sum of its parts, that the whole can be understood entirely by analysis of the parts.

What is "really happening" in a complex system? Can a composite entity influence its own components, or are the components all that matter? Is a stable whole, like a red-dwarf star or a yeast cell, really a "whole" at all, an entity in itself, or just a temporarily stable arrangement of parts? These are all questions that have to do with reductionism. Spending some time pondering the issue of reductionism gives us an opportunity to reflect on all the major themes of this book: the relationships between scales and between disciplines, the views of humanity implicit in universal histories, and the interplay of the informational and interpretive levels.

What Is Reductionism?

The word "reductionism" is used in many different ways in different contexts, so we give a short overview of what precisely we mean by that term here.

What is being "reduced" in reductionism? "Higher-level" composite entities are being reduced to their "lower-level" parts, as when we treat a forest as a collection of trees, a tree as a collection of cells, or a cell as a collection of atoms.

In what might be called "strong reductionism" or "ontological reductionism," the claim is that the whole *is* nothing but the sum of the parts. (Ontology is the philosophical study of being, what *is*, hence the emphasis.) Closely related is "causal reductionism," which claims that only the lowest levels—the most basic parts, the fundamental building blocks—can actually *cause* anything to happen. If we were to engage in strict reductionism of these varieties, we would maintain that it is correct to describe everything that exists in terms of particles and the physical laws that govern them, and that it is ultimately incorrect or illusory to speak of higher levels of organization, like stars or cats or people, having the ability to cause anything: their constituent particles are all that we would think of as having that ability. As the Greek philosopher Democritus put it more than two millennia ago, "By convention sweet and by convention bitter, by convention hot, by convention cold, by convention color; but in reality atoms and void."[43] Or as the co-discoverer of the double-helical structure of DNA, Francis Crick, wrote:

> "You," your joys and your sorrows, your memories and your ambitions, your sense of personal identity and free will, are in fact no more than the behavior of a vast assembly of nerve cells and their associated molecules. As Lewis Carroll's Alice might have phrased it: "You're nothing but a pack of neurons."[44]

These are representative statements of the strong-reductionist viewpoint, in which the forest *is nothing but* a collection of trees, the tree *is nothing but* a collection of cells, and the cell *is nothing but* a collection of atoms—and, hence, the forest itself is nothing but a collection of atoms (or the subatomic particles that compose atoms).

A very different flavor of reductionism is what might be called "methodological reductionism," which is not a set of ideas about the way reality itself works, but rather a scientific strategy that attempts to *explain* the properties and behaviors of systems in terms of smaller components. A classic example of reductionism in the physical sciences is the behavior of gases: the temperature of a gas can be explained as a manifestation of the average kinetic energy of the atoms or molecules in the gas, while the pressure of a gas can be explained in terms of how many atoms or molecules "bump up" against the sides of the container. The gas, which is a composite of atoms or molecules, is a higher-level entity with higher-level properties of pressure and temperature, properties that turn out to correspond to the actions of the constituent parts in a well-defined and consistent way. In that sense, the actions of the parts explain the higher-level properties. Moreover, the existence of mathematical relationships between pressure, temperature, volume, and amount of gas (expressed in the "ideal gas law" and similar equations) can then be explained in terms of the motions of molecules or atoms. As the Earth scientists Charles Langmuir and Wally Broecker remark in *How to Build a Habitable Planet: The Story of Earth from the Big Bang to Humankind*, "Understanding how laws that operate at small scales manifest on much larger scales is one of the great triumphs of the scientific method."[45]

Natural scientists have had a remarkable degree of success "explaining" phenomena in this way, by demonstrating connections between the behavior of

---

43. Quoted in *Stanford Encyclopedia of Philosophy*, "Democritus," https://plato.stanford.edu/entries/democritus/ .

44. Francis Crick, *The Astonishing Hypothesis: The Scientific Search for the Soul*, p. 3.

45. Charles Langmuir and Wally Broecker, *How to Build a Habitable Planet: The Story of Earth from the Big Bang to Humankind*, pp. 5–6.

higher-level systems or composite entities on the one hand and their constituent parts on the other. This success has led to a widespread sense among scientists that methodological reductionism is a valuable approach to understanding *why* various systems behave the way they do, and it also stands at the root of less widespread, but still moderately prominent, arguments that ontological and causal reductionism ought to be adopted as well.[46]

Scale and (Anti-)Reductionism in Universal Histories

In all forms of reductionism, weak or strong, there is the sense that smaller means more basic, more fundamental, and in a way, more important. Physicists do not say that pressure and temperature explain molecular motion, for example, but that molecular motion explains pressure and temperature. On the other hand, universal histories must almost by definition work at a range of scales simultaneously and illuminate the relationships between scales. In some ways, these histories demonstrate, and illustrate, the limitations of reductionism.

In *Maps of Time*, David Christian (drawing on the work of the physicist Eric Chaisson) puts forward a scheme of increasing levels of complexity that come into existence in the history of the universe: stars, elements, planets, life, human beings, and human societies. Each, he argues, is not just a composite, but a composite that obeys a set of "rules" and follows a set of patterns *distinct* from the rules and patterns of its constituent parts. Christian effectively implies that across-the-board reductionism to the lowest levels would be not only uninteresting but also inappropriate for understanding the actual patterns that emerge in universal history, that each whole is more than the sum of its parts:[47]

> The lighting up of the first stars was a momentous turning point in the history of the universe, for it marked the appearance of a new level of complexity, of new entities operating according to new rules. What had been billions and billions of atoms, drawn together by the force of gravity, suddenly became a new organized structure. . . .[48]

---

46. There is, however, a lingering question of whether "too much" reductionism is unhelpful. It seems that genetics, for instance, is best illuminated by studying chemistry and the molecular level, but reduction to the level of quantum physics would cease to be illuminating in the same way.

47. Christian also argues that the higher-level patterns are important, because "we are pattern-detecting organisms" (*Maps of Time*, p. 26), thus locating the importance of the patterns not in themselves but in our storytelling (see also *Maps of Time*, p. 505). Still, he argues that these patterns are also "really there," and that "their existence is one of the great puzzles of the universe." (*Maps of Time*, p. 506.)

48. David Christian, *Maps of Time*, pp. 44–45.

But at the biological level of complexity, new rules appear as well. Living organisms operate according to distinctive and more open-ended rules of change, which are superimposed on the simpler and more deterministic rules of physics and chemistry.[49]

As chemicals combine to form living organisms, emergent properties appear that we cannot explain simply by studying the chemicals from which organisms are constructed. So, to understand living things, we need a new paradigm, one that takes us beyond the rules of nuclear physics, chemistry, or geology and into the realm of biology.[50]

Similarly, in their more science-focused universal history, Langmuir and Broecker comment:

A cell is much more than a collection of reactions among chemicals. It has functions that cannot be inferred or understood from the atomic scale. It has a history, is descended from ancestors going back in time to the origin of life, and relates to its surroundings in ways that must be observed to be understood. It has a relationship both to the underlying molecular scale and the next larger scale (e.g., the organism) of which it is a part.[51]

Systems thinking asserts that the whole is greater than the sum of the parts, and that there are "emergent properties" that arise from the whole that could never be understood or predicted from a reductionist approach.[52]

Contextual Emergence

In seeking to tell a history of how these "wholes," these higher levels, came to be, *Maps of Time, How to Build a Habitable Planet,* and other works in the universal-history genre become *histories of emergence*: they give an account of how different scales relate to one another in such a way that lower-level parts give rise to higher-level wholes. These parts not only give rise to the higher levels, but also set certain constraints on what is possible for them. For example, people cannot pass through walls at will because of the nature of the atoms that make up human bodies (and walls). At the same time, higher-level wholes set the context in which lower-level parts function, arranging and directing their action, as when one instructs "many

---

49. Ibid., p. 81.

50. Ibid., p. 82.

51. Charles Langmuir and Wally Broecker, *How to Build a Habitable Planet: The Story of Earth from the Big Bang to Humankind,* p. 13.

52. Ibid., p. 13.

millions of electrons and protons what to do" by deciding to move one's arm.[53] There is a feedback between scales.

The argument here is not only that emergent properties are found at the higher levels, but that those higher levels exert a *causal influence* on the lower levels, undermining the basis of causal reductionism. It seems difficult to explain how the universe, Earth, life, and humanity got to be the way they are without invoking such "top-down" causal influences.

There are several reasons for this, both in practice and in principle. One practical obstacle to reducing all explanations to the laws of physics is that natural systems are often extremely complicated in their details, open to many influences rather than being simple and closed systems; for these reasons, they are impossible to perfectly model at any given moment. Chaos is a second issue: many systems are so sensitive to their initial conditions (the state in which the system starts) that even very small changes in the initial state result in gigantic changes in the final state. This principle has been called the "butterfly effect," which refers to the idea that the flapping of a butterfly's wings in one part of the globe can lead to a tornado in another part of the globe—or, more precisely, that the tiniest differences in the initial state of the system (butterfly vs. no butterfly) can, in combination with all the other causes at play, lead to radically different outcomes (tornado vs. no tornado).[54] As Langmuir and Broecker summarize, "In practice, even a straightforward phenomenon such as water flowing out of a garden hose cannot be predicted quantitatively from first principles. There is a gap between our practical experience of nature and the pure laws governing phenomena."[55]

The limitation of scope is not just in practice, however. It is also in principle. As the cosmologist and mathematician George Ellis has argued, many systems and aspects of the world make little sense if we think of them as determined entirely by their constituent parts. Objects like airplanes and computers, for example, exist not because they are natural outcomes of the laws of physics and the initial conditions of the universe but because *ideas* about how to *manufacture* them have causal efficacy. No physics-based explanation could, even in principle, make sense of why the electrons and protons in a pawn move around a chessboard in different ways than the electrons and protons in a rook. And brains "mindlessly" following the laws of

---

53. The example and quote are from George Ellis, "Physics, Complexity, and the Science-Religion Debate," pp. 752–753 in *The Oxford Handbook of Religion and Science*, eds. Philip Clayton and Zachary Simpson.

54. That is, the butterfly does not directly cause the tornado. It is just one tiny part of an initial global state, and many other causes are at play. But even this small a difference in the initial conditions can make a big difference in what eventually happens—that is the point of the butterfly effect.

55. Our discussion follows Charles Langmuir and Wally Broecker, *How to Build a Habitable Planet: The Story of Earth from the Big Bang to Humankind*, pp. 6–12; the quote is from p. 12.

physics cannot explain the selection of some sentences as writeable and others as not writeable; the composition of sentences is not in strict conformity with what the particles or neurons in one's brain *must* do, but instead relate to higher-level *meanings* that in turn affect how those particles and neurons behave. It is not just a matter of not having discovered sufficiently powerful laws of physics. It is a matter of what physics could ever do, in principle.[56]

Universal histories that treat these higher-level patterns and entities as real, then, have reasonable philosophical ground for doing so. This does not mean that every composite is identified correctly. Seeing the Earth as a living being, as in extrapolations of the Gaia hypothesis mentioned earlier, is contestable as a correctly identified composite. But we have to identify *some* composites. Otherwise:

> The implication is that the particles that existed at the time of decoupling of the cosmic background radiation in the early universe just happened to be placed so precisely as to make it inevitable that 14 billion years later, human beings would exist and Crick and Watson would discover DNA, Townes would conceive of the laser, and Witten would develop M-theory.[57]

It seems that one almost must make room for emergence and top-down causation in order to make any sense of universal history.

Discipline, Reductionism, and the Overall Shape of Knowledge

Another way to approach the issue of reductionism is to speak not of scales or causality or emergence, but of discipline. Reductionist positions are often stated (sometimes comically, as in Figure 3.2) in terms of relationships among disciplines,

---

To Ponder: Wholes and Parts

This section has discussed some shortcomings of the idea that the whole is generally determined entirely by the parts that make it up. Could it be the case that instead of the whole being determined by the parts, the parts are determined by the whole? Could atoms come together in a certain way not because they are driven by their own inner logic, but because they are driven by the inner logic of the forms that they are combining to create? (This idea echoes a principle behind the Aristotelian ideas of form and formal cause; see "Purpose" in chapter 7.)

---

56. All these examples are from George Ellis, "Physics, Complexity, and the Science-Religion Debate," in *The Oxford Handbook of Religion and Science*, pp. 752–753.

57. Ibid., p. 757.

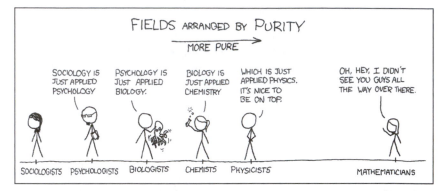

FIGURE 3.2 **Relationships Among Fields** A (humorously presented) popular view of the relationships among academic disciplines, which is often challenged—implicitly or explicitly—by universal histories.
Source: xkcd.com

with the study of culture and society reducing to psychology and biology, which in turn reduce to chemistry, which in turn reduces to physics:

> Reductionism is the view that the central concepts that characterize macro-level phenomena in fields such as psychology, religion, art, and morality can be translated into micro-level concepts such as those that figure in genetics; and these in turn can be translated into the concepts of physics.[58]

Reductionism of this sort certainly has some basis: chemistry and biology are based on physical principles; the behavior of people is at least partially illuminated by studying the brain biologically; the study of culture can be enriched by understanding something about individual psychology. But experts in humanities-oriented disciplines tend to oppose strong reductionism, in part because the knowledge their disciplines produce is rendered somehow less "real" if it is assumed that knowing about the particles (or the cells, or the neurons, or the brains, etc.) means knowing everything there is to know.

In an integrative field like Big History, which brings together the sciences and the humanities, it is fair to ask what the relationship between disciplines is, or should be. Should certain disciplines, like physics or cosmology, be regarded as more "fundamental" than others? What grounds the knowledge produced in Big History, or determines which discipline's approach is at the "right level" of reductionism? Is there a "best" scale at which to tell a universal story, or particular

58. Dale Jamieson, "Book Review: Consilience," http://issues.org/15–1/jamies/# (quoted in William Katerberg, "Myth, Meaning, and Scientific Method in Big History," https://ibha.wildapricot.org/resources/Documents/Origins/Origins_V_12.pdf, p. 5) .

portions of the story? Where possible, should one prefer smaller scales and constituent parts rather than larger scales and composites?

As the historian William Katerberg has argued, Big History as a field favors "pluralist modes of explanation rather than a reductionist consilience."[59] That is, instead of assigning physics or any other discipline the "fundamental" role, Big History creates space for a meeting ground of disciplines, ostensibly as equal partners.

As explored under "Discipline" in chapter 1, this strategy opens up opportunities to contribute to the philosophical foundations of the various disciplines on which universal histories draw, challenging extreme reductionist visions by giving the "higher-level" and "lower-level" disciplines attention alongside one another. It also has the potential to open up discussion of the relationship between disciplines at the interpretive level. Rather than a pyramid or hierarchy of disciplines that reduce to physics, another model might look more like a hub and spokes, with all the disciplines that contribute to universal histories arranged around the outside and the philosophical analysis at the interpretive level in the center.

In the end, Christian, Langmuir and Broecker, and many other authors of universal histories have sided with the view that the right level of analysis depends on the question you are asking. Knowing the position of every atom in a painting does not help one understand the painting.[60] Different levels of explanation tend to be more profitable for different things, though all go together and are present at once.

---

59. Katerberg, "Myth, Meaning, and Scientific Method in Big History," p. 6.

60. Cf. Huston Smith, *The World's Religions*, p. 24.

4 LIFE

The first four sections of this chapter explore life on Earth and its history: in "Life," we consider how biologists view living things at scales from the molecular to the planetary; in "Evolution," we introduce evolution as the central unifying scientific idea for understanding how the history of life has unfolded; in "Biosphere," we discuss how one might give an account of the history of all life on Earth; and in "Biochemistry," we consider the origin of life and return to the question of what it means to say that something is alive. In the final section ("Science"), we contemplate the philosophy of science as we look back at the cosmological, geological, and biological scientific disciplines encountered so far in this book.

Life

Consider what comes to mind when you think about "life," "the living world," "living things," or "nature." Just as we observed with respect to the history of the universe and Earth, the very words we use to describe and categorize the subject matter of universal histories carry a wide range of meanings and connotations, which in turn affect our interpretation of the events, the causal relationships, and the mechanisms that scientific research reveals. In the case of life's history, the stories we hear are bound up with ideas about what life even *is* in the first place, what it means to say that life has changed through evolution, and our ideas about the scales of life—from the stunningly intricate molecular and biochemical world that underpins it, through the range of different entities that we think of as being individually "alive," to the sum of all life on the planet, which is known as the biosphere.

Life and Levels of Biological Organization

Imagine an invisibly small entity, long and thin, that "walks" upright on two tiny "legs" and carries a load as it moves along a slender tube that stretches into the distance as far as you can perceive. The picture you imagine is similar to what a molecule known as a kinesin actually does. A kinesin is a motor protein, a type of molecule that uses energy to create motion within a living cell. It carries loads along microtubules, long and thin structures that, among other functions, provide a kind of support structure or scaffolding within cells. The kinesin's simple stepping motion plays a crucial role in the process of cell division that stands at the root of reproduction throughout the living world.[1] It is just one small element of the hidden intricacy within living beings that emerges when you zoom in on the tiny molecular world that enables life, and without which life as we know it could not exist.[2]

What, exactly, separates the living world from the (also intricate, in different ways) non-living world? What is "life"? We will return to this question at a more philosophical level toward the end of the chapter, but for now, we begin with a more descriptive approach—as biologists typically do, having long struggled to agree on an appropriate definition. A common approach among biologists to describing life is to speak both of *characteristics of living things* and of *levels of organization within the living world*.[3]

A list of characteristics of living things would customarily include self-regulation (maintaining steady internal conditions; homeostasis), energy processing (metabolism), growth and development, reproduction, evolutionary adaptation, interaction with living and non-living surroundings, and a perhaps hard-to-nail-down but crucial sense of *order*. As with nearly any attempt to define a complex notion using a list, there is ambiguity in practice; one can find examples of things that are obviously non-living but still have several characteristics on the list. Clouds, for example, are ordered structures, interact with surroundings, "reproduce" in a certain sense, and may grow and develop over time. And there are other entities that sit somewhere in between, having all or nearly all the characteristics, but that by most estimations are not considered truly living: viruses are a classic example, since they resemble living organisms in their molecular composition, their ability to reproduce and evolve, and their close relationships with living things but lack metabolism of their own and cannot reproduce outside of

---

1. Kinesins are found specifically in eukaryotes; see later in this section for distinctions between eukaryotes and prokaryotes.

2. For much more of this, see the video titled "Inner Life of the Cell" at https://www.youtube.com/watch?v=FzcTgrxMzZk .

3. See, e.g., Neil A. Campbell et al., *Biology* (8th edition), chapter 1, by which this particular description is inspired.

a host. Despite these complications and shortcomings, however, such a list is a good starting point for understanding the characteristics we associate with the *concept* of "living things."

A complementary approach to defining and characterizing life is to give an account of how living systems[4] appear at many different scales and many different levels of organization, ranging from atoms and molecules to cells to organisms to ecosystems to the entire biosphere. Life is characterized by an interplay of structures and processes at different scales, and in an echo of the wider patterns of universal history, different sources of evidence and methods of analysis lend themselves to understanding each level.

At the *molecular* level, we find an enormous range of tiny parts in any living system. The kinesin motor protein that "walks" is just one example of a tremendous array of molecules that play indispensable roles in living cells. Yet while there is great variety in the large molecules that the structures of life are built from and that the processes of life use, these molecules fall into only four basic classes: carbohydrates, lipids, proteins, and nucleic acids. *Carbohydrates*, examples of which include glucose, starch, and cellulose, serve as fuel for living organisms or provide structural support. *Lipids*, examples of which include fats and oils, play a variety of roles and are the type of molecule that cell membranes are composed of—the chemical properties of a certain type of lipid (phospholipids) make them perfectly suited to form membranes that can enclose and protect the sensitive biochemistry of the cell's inner workings. *Proteins* carry out many of the cell's activities, doing everything from transporting substances within or between cells, to providing structural support for the cell, to aiding in cell movement or cell-to-cell signaling. (Kinesin is an example of a protein.) *Nucleic acids*, especially *deoxyribonucleic acid* (DNA), store a cell's "blueprints" for building the proteins that do so much else in the cell.[5] Mechanisms within the cell "translate" a sequence in DNA[6] into a corresponding sequence of amino acids, the relatively small molecules that serve as the building blocks of proteins, using *ribonucleic acid* (RNA) as an intermediary. Once an amino-acid chain is formed, it "folds" to form a full, three-dimensional structure—a complete protein.

Today, DNA is often seen as a symbol of life because of its role in providing the "instructions" for how to build the proteins that compose the cell and perform its work. DNA not only contains these instructions used in the growth and development of an *individual* organism, but it provides the primary molecular basis for

---

4. Loosely, a "system" is a combination of components that function together. See "Systems" in chapter 7.

5. See Campbell et al., *Biology*, chapters 1 and 5.

6. That is, a sequence in base pairs.

passing characteristics on from one generation to the next. Nucleic acids are unique among molecules[7] in that they provide the directions for their own replication and, hence, enable traits and even the entire design of an organism to be passed on through time, creating the conditions for life to have continuity through time and thus *history*. Yet neither DNA, nor proteins like kinesins, nor any of the other molecular "ingredients" in life are themselves alive: they lack several of the "qualifications" just discussed. At the molecular scale, then, life may appear as an extraordinarily complicated and exquisitely interwoven aggregation of molecular structures and chemical reactions, but these components are not themselves alive.

The *cellular* level is the smallest scale that biologists typically consider to be truly alive: "In life's structural hierarchy, the cell has a special place as the lowest level of organization that can perform all activities required for life. Moreover, the activities of organisms are all based on the activities of cells."[8] All known living organisms are composed of cells,[9] and organisms may be either single-celled or multicellular. There are two basic types of cells, *prokaryotic* and *eukaryotic*, comprising and underpinning all forms of life on Earth. Eukaryotic cells are usually much larger and have both a *nucleus* containing the cell's genetic material (DNA) and *organelles*, structures inside the cell that are enclosed by membranes and carry out various functions (e.g., energy production in *mitochondria* or storage and transportation of molecules in *vacuoles*). But although the simpler prokaryotic cells, which seem to have existed on Earth for at least a billion years before eukaryotic cells appeared, lack a nucleus and organelles, they still have extraordinarily complex inner workings. Nearly all multicellular organisms, including all plants and animals, are composed of eukaryotic cells; unicellular organisms, on the other hand, may be either prokaryotic (e.g., bacteria or archaea) or eukaryotic (e.g., amoebas or diatoms). (See Plate 16.)

The level of the *organism* is the level at which non-biologists are accustomed to thinking about life. In the case of single-celled life, the cell is itself an organism, an independent entity that reproduces and responds to its environment as a coherent whole. Multicellular organisms contain more than one cell, which allows the possibility of multiple types of cell, each of which has the same genetic information (unique to the organism) but specializes in a distinct function, that work together within that same organism. Human heart muscle cells, for example, perform different functions than human nerve cells, despite containing the same genetic information. As at the molecular and cellular levels, *structure* and *function* are related at the

---

7. Campbell et al., *Biology*, p. 86.

8. Ibid., p. 7.

9. Unless one considers viruses to be alive, but their non-cellular structure is itself one argument against classing them in the same category as living things.

level of the organism: the way a given part of an organism is structured correlates with the function that part serves for the organism as a whole.[10]

At larger scales than the organism, biologists analyze populations and communities of organisms. A *population* consists of a group of individuals of the same species inhabiting a given area, while a *community* consists of all the organisms—usually of many different species—that inhabit such an area. An even larger unit of biological organization is the *ecosystem*, which is a collection of many different kinds of organisms in an area plus the non-living physical factors with which those organisms interact, including the flow of energy through the system and the cycling of substances and chemical elements (like water or nitrogen) that takes place within it. Ecologists attempt to study ecosystems holistically; although the reductionist tendencies in many domains of science would usually treat the molecular and cellular levels as fundamental and the ecosystem level as mere superstructure, ecology focuses on the "higher" levels in their own right as well – not just on the parts of which they are composed. There are many reasons to do this, including that the interactions between living organisms and their environments inform how the "lower," smaller-scale levels operate. To take one striking example, an organism's DNA is determined in large part by its ancestors' evolutionary history of adapting to a changing environment—a coupling of the organismal level, the molecular level, and the ecosystem level, past and present.[11] As we have seen before, neither small-scale nor large-scale phenomena are all-important: they interact with and influence one another.

At the highest level of organizational scale in the living world, at least unless (until?) life is discovered on other planets, is the *biosphere*: the sum total of all life on Earth, the combination of all ecosystems. It is a "sphere" because it literally forms a (nearly) spherical shell. Thinking of the Earth as a whole, life rests in a thin shell on the Earth, just below the surface (including the oceans and at least the upper portions of the solid crust), and just above the surface (the atmosphere).[12] The biosphere, like every other level, can be thought of as a *system*, with certain inputs and specific processes that control outputs. It is strongly coupled to other Earth systems, like the atmosphere and the hydrosphere of chapter 3. For example,

---

10. Campbell et al., *Biology*, p. 7.

11. See the next section, "Evolution," for more detail.

12. Life can actually be found at rather extraordinary altitudes. Scientists have been aware of "tropospheric biota" for decades, but only in the last few years have they recognized the diversity of this portion of the biosphere, which probably includes "thousands of *species* of bacteria, fungi, and untold viral taxa." (Peter Ward and Joe Kirschvink, *A New History of Life: The Radical New Discoveries About the Origins and Evolution of Life on Earth*, p. 30.) Life below the Earth's surface is even more remarkable and diverse: as much as 70 percent of Earth's bacteria and archaea may exist below the surface. (Deep Carbon Observatory, "Life in Deep Earth Totals 15 to 23 Billion Tonnes of Carbon—Hundreds of Times More than Humans," https://deepcarbon.net/life-deep-earth-totals-15-23-billion-tonnes-carbon)

biogeochemical cycles—pathways through which a chemical element or type of molecule moves between the living and non-living components of an ecosystem— are a prime example of mutual interaction between life ("bio"), the Earth ("geo"), and the elements and molecules ("chemical") that make up the matter both of living creatures and of inanimate objects.

Very few biologists, however, would claim that an ecosystem or the entire biosphere should itself be considered *alive* or a *living thing*; rather, these are collections of living things, plus the non-living substances with which those living things interact. The Gaia hypothesis, mentioned in chapter 3, pushes back against this reasoning to some extent, emphasizing the unity of the biosphere as a system. Be that as it may, at all these levels, from molecules to biosphere, the living world is marked by self-regulation. Through various feedback mechanisms, living systems characteristically succeed in maintaining stable conditions in everything from the concentration of solutions at the molecular and cellular level, to internal temperature at the organismal level, to nutrient availability at the ecosystem level, to (arguably) the Earth's climate at the level of the biosphere.[13] And there is interplay and feedback *between* the levels, not just *within* a given level: The smaller scales can only be understood fully through their relationship with the larger scales, and vice versa.[14]

Life: Discipline and Reductionism

Understanding life and the nature of living systems clearly presents challenges of navigating and connecting scales. Biologists must balance the often-successful reductionist approach of understanding a system in terms of its parts with the holistic objective of understanding the relationships between levels of organization in biological systems. This is complicated by the fact that different levels of organization are often "claimed" by different disciplines or subdisciplines within the biological sciences. While *molecular and cellular biologists* (who study the smallest scales of life) may examine the same living organisms as *ecologists and evolutionary biologists* (who study the largest scales of life), their perspectives do not necessarily speak to one another in practice, and at an institutional level, biology departments often split apart along these fault lines.

Universal histories, in turn, face a similar question of how best to treat the relationships between biological scales in narrating a history of life. The *study* of life may be fragmented, but life itself functions as an integrated whole. Should any one

---

13. See, e.g., Jamie Davies, "A Closed Loop," https://aeon.co/essays/the-feedback-loop-is-a-better-symbol-of-life-than-the-helix . For the biosphere, James Lovelock and Lynn Margulis's Gaia hypothesis is one example of an argument that feedback loops at the level of the entire biosphere operate to preserve a stable environment for life.

14. This is the domain of "systems biology." Cf. Charles Langmuir and Wally Broecker, *How to Build a Habitable Planet: The Story of Earth from the Big Bang to Humankind*, p. 14.

Side Note: Scales of Life

Living things are tiny in the grand scope of the universe, but gigantic compared with the basic building blocks. As discussed in chapter 1, they occupy the middle of the scales in the universe. As the astrophysicist Gregory P. Laughlin writes:

> The size of things in our universe runs all the way from the tiny 10^{-19} meter scale that characterizes quark interactions, to the cosmic horizon 10^{26} meters away. In these 45 possible orders of magnitude, life, as far as we know it, is confined to a relatively tiny bracket of just over nine orders of magnitude, roughly in the middle of the universal range: Bacteria and viruses can measure less than a micron, or 10^{-6} meters, and the height of the largest trees reaches roughly 100 meters. The honey fungus that lives under the Blue Mountains in Oregon, and is arguably a single living organism, is about 4 kilometers across. When it comes to known sentient life, the range in scale is even smaller, at about three orders of magnitude.[15]

Laughlin argues that physical and chemical constraints make it likely that life *must* occupy this range of scales, that nothing like the functions of life could be carried out by entities much larger or smaller, anywhere in the universe. For example, the weaker the surface gravity of a planet (or a moon), the larger the planet's organisms could be, but that planet would also need to have strong enough gravity to "hold on" to an atmosphere, as Earth does. This places a lower limit on how strong the gravity could be on a life-supporting planet, and a corresponding upper limit on how large the organisms could grow.

---

level of organization be treated as fundamental, as each level may appear to practitioners of the subdiscipline that focuses most on it? A history of life at the molecular level would look quite different than a history of organisms or ecosystems, even though the physical "stuff" being described is the same in all cases. (See "Side Note: The Same Entity Can Be Treated at Multiple Levels.")

This may be another point where universal histories, and especially the scale-switching they engage in, may be a valuable aid to established disciplines like biology. By making judicious choices of how to narrate the relationships between scales, such histories may give scientists new opportunities to consider how their own specialized research and disciplinary perspective fit into a larger whole. In this chapter, we focus on tracing the history of life at the largest and the smallest scales—in the "Biosphere" and "Biochemistry" sections, respectively—and then ask how different

---

15. Gregory Laughlin, "Can a Living Creature Be as Big as a Galaxy?," http://nautil.us/issue/34/adaptation/can-a-living-creature-be-as-big-as-a-galaxy .

Side Note: The Same Entity Can Be Treated at Multiple Levels

An individual molecule could never be a cell, and an individual ecosystem could never be the entire biosphere. But a cell can be an organism, and an organism can be an ecosystem. All single-celled organisms are examples of the former. Each and every human being provides an example of the latter: each human plays host to a huge array of microorganisms known collectively as the microbiome, a word that draws on "biome," a classic term in ecology that means a large community of plants and animals occupying a distinct region, such as a desert or grassland or tropical rainforest. From a microbial perspective, a single human being is, in effect, an entire region, and a variety of invisible organisms inhabit that region. The total number of cells in a given human being's microbiome appears to be at least as great as the total number of human cells in that human's body, and may even exceed that number.[16] *Microbial ecologists*[17] operate at this scale and often use classical ecological approaches to understand the interactions of organisms within the microbiome, which may differ widely from one another genetically.[18]

It is worth remembering that while studying a human being as an *organism* is different than studying a human being as an *ecosystem*, which in turn is different than studying human beings at the *cellular level*, the physical matter of which the person is made up is the same in all cases. Similarly, whatever happened in the history of life, happened, and left the observational traces that it did—but there are many ways to tell a story about it, even while remaining scrupulously true to the evidence.

---

disciplinary perspectives might bear on the question of what life is and how we should think of it. Before getting there, though, we turn to the subject of biological evolution, which is necessary preparation for talking about the history of life.

Evolution

Evolution is a fundamental organizing principle of biology; as a founding figure in modern biology, Theodosius Dobzhansky, commented: "Nothing in biology makes

---

16. Old estimates of the number of cells in the microbiome suggested that they outnumbered human cells by as much as 10 to 1, but according to more recent studies, the difference in number is probably not that great. In any case, the exact composition of a given person's microbiome is unique to that person, and disturbances to the microbiome can produce illness and disease while a healthy microbiome can help to ensure the person's health.

17. "Microbial ecology" literally means, in its Greek roots, the "study [*logos*] of the house [*eco*] of small [*micro*] living things [*bios*]."

18. The Human Microbiome Project is an interesting reference here. See https://www.hmpdacc .org/ .

sense except in the light of evolution."[19] Evolution gives life a dynamic history in which things change rather than staying static—similar to what the Big Bang does for the universe. It is the unifying theory, a broad framework for explaining a wide variety of phenomena, for the history of life and for the biological sciences.

The story of how the modern theory of evolution came together, through the work of naturalists and biologists of the 19th and 20th centuries, shows the interplay of theory and observation in producing new scientific understanding. Meanwhile, current debates over the proper place of evolution in a broader understanding of the world provide a prime illustration of the interplay between the informational and interpretive levels.

The History of Evolution: Darwin's Time and Before

The name associated most strongly with biological evolution is Charles Darwin (1809–1882). But Darwin did not come up with the idea of "transmutation of species"—that species have the ability to change into other species over long spans of time. Evolution in this sense was, one might say, "in the air" in England, France, and elsewhere before Darwin was even born. Paleontologists and geologists of the late 1700s and early 1800s had established that species in the past had become extinct, and that the fossil record revealed a succession of organisms of different forms. The idea that species change over time was a matter of public discourse in England by the time *Vestiges of the Natural History of Creation* came out in 1844, and scientists and non-scientists alike discussed the topic a great deal.[20]

It was harder, however, to come by convincing and comprehensive explanations of how and why such change might have happened. Like continental drift, which could never have become central to Earth science without a mechanism to explain how huge landmasses could move around the face of the planet, evolutionary theory required a plausible mechanism for how and why species might change over time. Darwin provided this plausible mechanism in his ideas about natural selection, which laid many of the foundations for modern evolutionary theory. But he never once used the word "evolution" in the first five editions of *On the Origin of Species* (the first of which was published in 1859).[21] Instead, he spoke of "descent with modification."

_____

19. Quoted in Campbell et al., *Biology*, p. 12.

20. See James Secord's *Victorian Sensation* for a detailed account of the book and surrounding public discourse. Written by Robert Chambers, *Vestiges* was published anonymously; Chambers was only revealed as the author years after his death in 1871.

21. The word "evolution" had been used to refer to the transmutation of species for decades by the time Darwin published, and it was certainly clear that his book was an attempt to explain exactly that.

So much has been written in the past two centuries about this "descent with modification" that it is difficult to describe the core of the idea without adding embellishments or explanatory devices that were suggested later, whether by Darwin himself or by his many commentators. But the idea of descent with modification boils down to this: Organisms reproduce, and the characteristics of one generation tend to differ from the characteristics of the previous generation. Over long periods of time, the accumulation of changes from one generation to the next, and the accumulation of different changes in different populations, leads to gradual branching off of species from one another, with new and diverse forms of life ultimately arising.

Drawing on some more modern terminology may help to clarify. When the changes in question are changes in the frequency of a trait *within* a species, this is now called "microevolution." Meanwhile, "macroevolution" is the broad pattern of change in species themselves, and in the overall diversity of life, over long spans of time. The link between microevolution and macroevolution is the process known as "speciation": as changes accumulate over time, populations of organisms descended from one and the same species may no longer be able to breed with one another, producing multiple species where there was only one before. Differences that produce this kind of separation[22] lead to speciation. Differences of many kinds accumulate over time and become more pronounced, leading eventually to the formation of new groups of organisms that differ greatly from one another and from their ancestors.[23]

Although the terminology of the previous paragraph was not in use at the time, this is the idea of descent with modification that Darwin used, drawing on ideas that many thinkers before him had employed. What these early evolutionary thinkers lacked, however, was a clear mechanism for how and why this might happen. Jean-Baptiste Lamarck, whose major works on evolution appeared some 50 years before Darwin's, was one of the few who had actually proposed such a mechanism. He argued that organisms change in response to their environment and are also subject to a natural tendency toward increasing complexity, an attempt

---

22. The separation could be a separation in physical location, behavioral compatibility, or biochemical compatibility. Collectively, these forms of separation are known as "reproductive barriers."

23. This account of speciation relies on the "biological species concept," in which two types of organisms are considered to be members of different species if they cannot typically mate and produce offspring that are themselves fertile. This is only one working definition of "species," however, and it is difficult (in principle) to apply to microorganisms or to anything that reproduces asexually. Also, it is difficult (in practice) to apply to fossils, since reproductive incompatibility is very difficult to discern from body shape alone and often has nothing to do with morphology, but rather with biochemistry or behavior that becomes invisible in the fossil record.

at explaining both why organisms would change over time and why they appeared to become more complex.[24]

Natural Selection

Darwin, therefore, did not generate the idea of evolution, but he did put it on firmer ground as an explanation for biodiversity and biological change over time. With his idea of natural selection[25] and the evidence he amassed for it, Darwin provided a more compelling proposal for how and why evolution could happen than did Lamarck or any previous theorist.[26]

The basic idea of natural selection is that in each generation of a given population, some individuals are more likely to survive and reproduce—perhaps because they are more adept at avoiding predators, perhaps because they have immunity to a common infection, perhaps because they display a set of behaviors that make them likely to leave more offspring or that make their offspring more likely to survive. To the extent that these characteristics can be inherited (meaning that the characteristics pass systematically from one generation to another), the more viable offspring an organism will leave, and the more those inherited characteristics will be represented in later generations. So there is a tendency for those organisms best suited to their environment to thrive and for others to die off, thus "selecting" certain traits and leading to changes in the frequencies of different traits in a population. And as the environment keeps changing, so too species keep changing. Each species is part of the "environment" for other species in the area, so the changes respond to, and influence, one another. (Note that it is *populations* of organisms, not individual organisms, that evolve.)

Natural selection is not the only mechanism of evolution—*genetic drift* and *gene flow*, e.g., are also important mechanisms. However, we do not go into detail

---

24. Despite his contributions, Lamarck is remembered now mostly for his (later discredited, but recently at least partially revived) idea that characteristics *acquired* later in life can be passed along to the next generation—an idea that was not unique to him but in fact was held in common by most scientific thinkers of the time. The classic example of Lamarck's thinking is that a giraffe could develop such a long neck by progressively stretching it out in order to reach leaves that provide its food source; he suggested that the stretched-out neck could then be inherited and stretched still further by later generations.

25. Alfred Russell Wallace independently originated the idea of natural selection before Darwin published the idea, but many years after Darwin first thought of and began developing it. Wallace approached Darwin with the idea before Wallace tried to publish it himself, and came to acknowledge that Darwin's thinking came first, driving Darwin to compose *Origin* as promptly as possible.

26. Darwin also proposed the idea of common descent, that all organisms now alive are descended from one early form. Lamarck and many others had worked with a combination of spontaneous generation and transmutation of species in which certain small living things could be spontaneously generated on an ongoing basis and then evolve into a variety of other forms.

about them here, because only natural selection consistently leads to "adaptive" evolution that improves the match between organisms and their environment.

Modern Evolutionary Synthesis

The language in the previous discussion is intentionally minimalist, emphasizing variation, heredity, and selection but avoiding any mention of modern genetics, molecular biology, and cell biology. Why? Because Darwin originally formulated his theory of "descent with modification" in the absence of almost everything biologists now know about these fields.[27] Yet findings since Darwin's time not only have failed to disconfirm evolution, they have vaulted it into the central place in biology and filled many of the gaps in Darwin's own understanding. Biologists have built Darwin's initial insights about natural selection into a more self-consistent and all-encompassing idea of how descent with modification happens, drawing on 20th-century genetics and molecular biology to craft the *modern evolutionary synthesis*.

A small amount of historical background here goes a long way toward clarifying why the modern evolutionary synthesis stands as one of the most successful scientific ideas of the past century. Before roughly 1900, it was not yet clear to biologists how genetics, evolution, and cell biology fit together. In particular, it was not yet clear how, exactly, genetic inheritance worked, how precisely traits were passed down from one generation to another. Darwin's own proposed mechanism of genetic inheritance[28] implied that inheritance would generally result in offspring whose traits were a blend of their parents' traits, which seems logical enough at first glance. However, "blending inheritance" stood in tension with Darwin's ideas about natural selection (as well as with a host of observations of how heredity actually works), because it would tend to *reduce* variation rather than preserving it for natural selection to act on. For example, descendants of a mother with blue eyes and a father with brown eyes would have eyes of intermediate blue-brown color, and continued blending of traits in that generation and future generations would lead to a population in which everyone had a similar intermediate eye color. If variation is reduced or eliminated over time, natural selection would not have the "opportunity" to select certain traits at the expense of others; differences in traits would instead be eliminated by the blending.

Gregor Mendel, a Catholic monk who laid the foundations for modern genetics by experimenting on pea plants in a monastery, actually solved this problem

---

27. Darwin even made key mistakes, including accepting flawed ideas about the inheritance of acquired characteristics that are now associated with Lamarck's name but were widely accepted by naturalists of the time (see, e.g., chapter 5 of *Origin*).

28. Called "pangenesis"; see Darwin's book *The Variation of Animals and Plants Under Domestication*, and also Kate Holterhoff, "The History and Reception of Charles Darwin's Hypothesis of Pangenesis," https://link.springer.com/article/10.1007%2Fs10739-014-9377-0 .

during Darwin's lifetime, although it appears that Darwin remained unaware.[29] Mendel's work showed that offspring receive a combination of genetic contributions from their parents that result in the expression of one trait or another, not (usually) a blend. Rather than reducing variation, the actual biological mechanism preserves the variation that natural selection could work on as its "raw material."

The connection between Darwinian evolution and Mendelian genetics did not become widely recognized until later, in the 1920s. Biologists in the late 1800s and early 1900s tended to communicate poorly across specializations, and evolution remained in the background of biology. But when evolution and Mendelian genetics did come together, the result was powerful. Mendelian genetics at an *organismal* level came into its own by the late 1800s, but only in the 1900s did *molecular* genetics emerge in earnest. DNA was identified as a distinct molecule by Friedrich Miescher in 1869, and was recognized as the molecule associated with heredity through experiments done in 1928 (by Frederick Griffith), 1943 (by Oswald Avery, Colin MacLeod, and Maclyn McCarty), and 1952 (by Alfred Hershey and Martha Chase). In 1953, James Watson and Francis Crick proposed that DNA had a double-helix shape, based on an X-ray diffraction image taken by Rosalind Franklin and Raymond Gosling in 1952. Only with this information about shape did it become clear *how* DNA could carry genetic information.

The discovery of the double helix and subsequent work in molecular genetics have demonstrated the molecular mechanisms that allow DNA to copy itself with great fidelity, but also with room for a mistake here and there—in other words, a mutation, which helps to provide the raw genetic variation on which natural selection works.[30] More recently, the biological subfield of evolutionary development ("evo-devo") has shown that small changes in key genes that control the rate and timing of an organism's embryonic development can sometimes result in large changes to the body plan of an organism, thus generating significant evolutionary change in a relatively short period of time. "Horizontal gene transfer," in which genetic material moves directly between organisms rather than only passing "vertically" from parent to offspring, is also increasingly recognized as an important factor in evolutionary change, especially among microbes. And new windows are opening onto the importance of "epigenetics" in evolution: molecules that help to determine which DNA sequences are active and which are inactive in a given cell can sometimes be passed

---

29. On the other hand, Mendel was aware of Darwin, and seems to have thought favorably of his work. The life and work of these two men who never met each other, one a devout Catholic monk and the other an agnostic naturalist, and whose work would later be seen as twin pillars of modern science, certainly provide food for thought in modern debates about the relationship between religion and science.

30. Mutations can produce new alleles entirely, while sexual reproduction reshuffles them. (An "allele" is a variant of a gene; for example, we might speak of a brown allele and a blue allele for the gene of eye color.)

from generation to generation and, therefore, are able to influence evolution. In all these phenomena, the study of molecular genetics contributes greatly to a more precise and detailed understanding of how evolution works.

The modern evolutionary synthesis relies both on evidence from the past (fossils, which can situate descent and evolution in time and can be used to create a history) and the present (genetics experiments, observations of present biodiversity, and so on). It brings together all the scales of biology. Evolutionary theory turns out to explain, and to be explained by, mechanisms at the cellular and molecular level, and also to drive change at the level of ecosystems and the entire biosphere. It likewise brings together the subdisciplines of the biological sciences, both with one another and with other natural sciences. Modern evolutionary biology descends more fully from this synthesis than strictly from Darwin, crucial as his contributions were.

Extended Side Note: Evidence for Evolution

Like the Big Bang and plate tectonics, the modern evolutionary synthesis is a unifying theory supported both by direct evidence and by indirect observations that are consistent with its tenets. The most direct evidence that evolution happens is that descent with modification can be observed in "real time" in laboratory and field settings with organisms having short enough life spans to observe changes in populations across generations. These are observations of microevolution and speciation. Macroevolution generally occurs over much longer time spans and must be inferred from indirect—but still powerful—evidence, such as:

- *The fossil record.* Fossils of ancient organisms give "hard evidence" both that past life was different from present life, and that a relationship exists between them. Fossils provide some of the raw material with which to construct evolutionary sequences of organisms, and they can sometimes give an indication of the ways organisms interacted with their environments. Fossils are of three types:
  - *Body fossils,* the best-known type of fossil, preserve some part of the body of an organism. Since soft tissues preserve very rarely, body fossils are usually found only for creatures with shells, skeletons, or other hard body parts.
  - *Trace fossils* are artifacts not of the body of an organism, but of something an organism left behind: burrows, footprints, tracks, feces (coprolites), nests, and so forth. They can give helpful clues regarding the *behavior* of an organism in a way that body fossils usually do not.
  - *Chemical fossils* are chemical compounds found in rocks that provide a "signature" of life—for example, certain molecules or ratios of isotopes do not occur naturally in rocks, so far as scientists know, except as an artifact of living systems.

Each type of fossil is especially useful for obtaining particular kinds of information: anatomy and function from body fossils, habits and behavior from trace fossils, metabolism from chemical fossils. The fossil record is strongly consistent with the basic idea of "descent with modification." Using the modern methods of radiometric dating and stratigraphy described in chapter 3, paleontologists can sequence fossil remains in time and demonstrate patterns of descent and relatedness of form.

- *Homology and vestigial structures.* The word "homology" refers to shared traits among different organisms, while the term "vestigial structures" refers to structures that no longer serve a function in the organism but seem to have done so in an ancestor. An example of homology is that mammalian forelimbs not only have the same bones, but also the same joints, nerves, and blood vessels—which is striking given that these forelimbs take the form of an arm in humans, a front paw in cats, a wing in bats, and a flipper in whales. The similarities exist, in the light of evolutionary theory, because all these appendages were inherited from a common ancestor.[31] The wings of flightless birds like ostriches and emus, which make little functional sense but can be explained as relics or holdovers from ancestral birds that did fly, are examples of a vestigial structure.
- *Biogeography.* Organisms within a given region tend to be similar to one another and not necessarily to organisms elsewhere, even ones that play analogous ecological roles. For example, the flora and fauna of Australia and New Zealand are largely unique to these large and fairly isolated islands, with animals that are similar to one another in ways that they are not similar to animals anywhere else in the world. Descent from common ancestors makes sense of this pattern.

These are not the only pieces of evidence that are strongly consistent with evolution. For example, microbiology and cell biology have shown that many of the same chemical processes and pathways, and almost exactly the same genetic code (the "rules" for translating DNA sequences into proteins), operate in all living organisms. There is no evident reason why this should be the case unless all living organisms are actually related to one another and derive fundamental aspects of their biochemistry from the same universal common ancestor. Also, the DNA molecule replicates in exactly the way it would have to in order to be consistent with evolution: replication of DNA is highly precise and accurate, but with rare mutations. Studies of life at the molecular level have turned out to be profoundly consistent with evolution in ways that corroborate that evolution is a real process.

---

31. Campbell et al., *Biology*, p. 16.

Evolution as Information, Evolution as Interpretation

Evolution has proved to be a very powerful idea. As a scientific framework, it makes sense of an enormous range of observations on an equally wide range of scales. The modern evolutionary synthesis stands at the center of biological science in the way that plate tectonics stands at the center of Earth science and the Big Bang at the center of cosmological science. Its footing in evidence and observation of the living world is deep and solid. (See "Extended Side Note: Evidence for Evolution.") There are many debates and active research at the informational level about the details of evolutionary relationships past and present, the relative importance of the various mechanisms of evolution, and other topics. But the overall picture of "descent with modification" and natural selection as a primary driver of evolution is well-established.

That said, when we say the evidence for evolution is overwhelming, we need to be careful: Which "evolution" are we talking about? The word in general simply means "change over time." And within biology, the word can be used to mean everything from observed changes in organisms over time, to common descent of all organisms from a universal common ancestor, to natural selection and the other mechanisms responsible for these changes. More broadly, it can mean the modern evolutionary synthesis, complete with genetic and molecular underpinnings; it is this level that the side note on evidence for evolution addresses.

In public discourse beyond the biological sciences, including universal histories, however, "evolution" can mean something even bigger than that. If evolution were nothing but a set of well-established, technical-scientific ideas about the unequal reproductive success of individuals within a species and consequent changes to populations of organisms over time, it would never receive the public attention that it does. Other great unifying theories within the sciences (plate tectonics, atomic theory, quantum field theory in physics, the Big Bang) receive a certain amount of attention in the public eye and coverage in school curricula, but no scientific idea raises attention—and sometimes ire—like evolution. In discussing evolution, we quickly find ourselves discussing philosophical as well as biological matters, and it is crucial for universal histories to be clear on what questions about evolution are fully answerable through scientific evidence, what questions science can inform but not answer, and what questions lie outside the realm of science. In other words, we have to distinguish, as best we can, the informational level from the interpretive level.

Evolution, Progress, and the Value of Animals

The relationship between *evolution* and the idea of *progress* provides an example of the constant interplay of information and interpretation. Biologists often resist the idea that evolution represents progress—that it necessarily results in organisms that are in any sense "better" or "higher" than the ones that came before. Natural selection may favor certain traits, but which traits are favored always depends on the environmental context, which changes over time and from place to place. "What constitutes a 'good match' between an organism and its environment can be a moving target,"[32] and there is, according to the known mechanisms of evolution, no inherent drive toward greater "complexity" or "perfection" or anything of the sort (as Lamarck and others had suggested).[33] There is only adaptation and response to a shifting set of environmental constraints.

And yet the idea that "evolution" means "progress" continues to show up in subtle ways.[34] For example, being land-dwellers ourselves, humans often associate movement from sea to land with progress, so we think of organisms evolving to come out of the water and onto land as a "step forward." But organisms can go back the other way, evolving so as to move from land to sea. Whales, for instance, are descended from animals that walked the land, which in turn descended from sea creatures. If one's ideas about progress are deeply embedded, it may sound somehow improper that evolution would produce movement from land to sea as well as from sea to land. It might prompt the question, "Aren't species on land more evolved than species in the sea?"

Equating evolution with progress in this way, however, simply does not work in practice. One reason is that all species alive on today's Earth have just as long an evolutionary history as human beings or lions or oak trees do, all having descended from the last universal common ancestor over the same period of time. Just as the tips of the branches of a tree may all be a similar distance from the trunk, all species in the present-day "tree of life" have been evolving for the same amount of time. In fact, the relevant measure of "how much evolution" a given species has undergone is not how many years have passed but how many *generations*, since evolutionary changes take place from one generation to another. And in that regard, microbes, with their short generation times—not to mention their ability to directly exchange genetic material[35]—may actually be regarded as "more evolved" than plants and animals.[36] We may assign higher value to plants and animals for other reasons, but doing so is not an automatic outgrowth of knowledge about evolution.

Yet even Darwin speaks the language of progress throughout *On the Origin of Species*, making repeated references to species being "improved" or "perfected." Take, for example, these selections from the final two paragraphs of *Origin*:[37]

---

32. Campbell et al., *Biology*, p. 481. A good example is the peppered moth, which observers in England found became darker in body color in polluted environments during the Industrial Revolution, presumably because predators could more easily identify and consume lighter-colored moths against tree trunks made dark by pollution. When pollution was cleared up, lighter-colored moths were again favored, better able to blend in against tree trunks, and so became more common again.

33. In fact, the simplest types of organisms (single-celled prokaryotes) have proved incredibly durable, continuously inhabiting the Earth for longer than any other type.

34. As the philosopher Michael Ruse has chronicled extensively in his book *From Monad to Man*.

35. The phenomenon called "horizontal gene transfer," discussed earlier.

36. Unicellular organisms are often as genetically different from one another as plants and animals are from one another.

37. Also see chapter 4 of *Origin*, which is particularly full of these kinds of references.

And as natural selection works solely by and for the good of each being, all corporeal and mental endowments will tend to progress towards perfection. . . . Thus, from the war of nature, from famine and death, the most *exalted* object of which we are capable of conceiving, namely, the production of the *higher* animals, directly follows.[38]

Speaking of "exalted" results and "higher" animals draws more heavily on the medieval conception of the Great Chain of Being and related ideas about the "hierarchy" of existence than it does on Darwin's own ideas about evolution by natural selection. It is true that evolution sometimes results in the production of new *capacities*—like photosynthesis, or the complex biochemistry of eukaryotic cells, or the ability to live on dry land, or sociality, or various forms of intelligence.[39] But even if we regard certain capacities as "higher" than others, we are making a judgment that cannot be justified strictly in evolutionary terms, even if it may be justified on philosophical grounds not directly tied to the process of evolution.[40]

This does not necessarily mean that "all animals are equal"[41]—or all plants, or all microbes. The issue is *not* that it is impossible to assess the relative "value" of

---

38. Charles Darwin, *On the Origin of Species*, in *From So Simple a Beginning: The Four Great Books of Charles Darwin*, ed. Edward O. Wilson, p. 760; italics added.

39. We are here drawing on Robert Bellah, *Religion in Human Evolution: From the Paleolithic to the Axial Age*, pp. 60–65, who in turn draws on Marc W. Kirschner and John C. Gerhart, *The Plausibility of Life: Resolving Darwin's Dilemma*. Note also a certain directionality in terms of the production of biodiversity: as Terrence Deacon writes in *The Symbolic Species*, evolution is like entropy: a diversification, a spreading out (p. 29). Or E. O. Wilson: "The overall average across the history of life has moved from the simple and few to the more complex and numerous. During the past billion years, animals as a whole evolved upward in body size, feeding and defensive techniques, brain and behavioral complexity, social organization, and precision of environmental control—in each case farther from the nonliving state than their simpler antecedents did." "Progress, then, is a property of the evolution of life as a whole by almost any conceivable intuitive standard, including the acquisition of goals and intentions in the behavior of animals." (Quoted in Michael Ruse, *On Purpose*, p. 103.)

40. The ease with which discussions of evolution slip into the language of progress is just one manifestation of the complexities in assessing the (moral / aesthetic) *value* of non-human living organisms. As Hal Herzog explores in his book *Some We Love, Some We Hate, Some We Eat: Why It's So Hard to Think Straight About Animals*, it seems to be nearly impossible to think in a strictly, rationally consistent way about the moral status of animals: How many people have truly self-consistent ideas about whether *and which* animals should be eaten, used in medical research, kept as pets, kept in zoos, killed for use in consumer products, protected *from other animals*, and so forth? A similar conundrum comes when trying to assess the value of microbes, which we often characterize as "good" or "bad" according to their effects on human health when in fact the role any given bacterium plays with respect to health depends greatly on context: "The same microbes can be beneficial in the gut but dangerous in the blood . . . Just as a garden flower can be considered a weed if it shows up in the wrong place, our microbes might be invaluable in one organ but dangerous in another, or essential inside our cells but lethal outside them" (Ed Yong, "Microbes have no morals," https://aeon.co/essays/there-is-no-such-thing-as-a-good-or-a-bad-microbe). Metaphors that put the natural world in familiar "human" terms can be valuable aids to understanding, but they can also mislead just as easily as they can help.

41. To quote the sardonic, allegorical view of George Orwell's *Animal Farm*.

organisms in contemplating how we ought to treat them: presumably, very few people would try to argue that mosquitoes or mushrooms deserve to be treated with the same dignity as a human being. The evolutionary process simply seems to be of little help in making judgments of this sort, because what counts as "progress," or what makes one organism "higher" than another, is a matter that must be addressed at the interpretive level through philosophical consideration, not strictly at the informational level through empirical evidence.

Evolution, Progress, and the Value of Human Beings

The importance of being clear on the relationship between "evolved-ness" and "value" becomes even greater when considering the evolution of human beings. To see why, one again needs to look no further than Darwin himself. His book *The Descent of Man*, published 12 years after *On the Origin of Species*, applies natural selection to understand the origin of the human body and various human behaviors, including moral behavior. In the book's first three chapters, he argues that the human body clearly bears the imprint of animal origins, and that the human mind reveals differences only in degree and not in kind as compared to animals. He frames human life naturalistically in an attempt to show how human morality flows not from any genuinely external or binding moral law, but from the biological history of humanity, and he traces the origins of morality to persistent social instincts drawn from a primate past.

This is a mixture of science and philosophical framing, of the informational level and the interpretive level. Explaining the history and diversity of life, or the historical origins of the form of the human body, has turned out to be well within the capabilities of biological science. Biology also has something to say regarding the origins of some human social tendencies, behavioral patterns, and even emotions. But whether this fully explains the nature of the human mind, or answers the question of how one *ought* to act (especially as opposed to how people *do* act), is another matter.

One might say that in *The Descent of Man*, evolution by natural selection transitioned from being a scientific explanation for the diversity of life (as it was in *On the Origin of Species*) to also being proposed as a philosophical framing for human life—a project that fundamentally reaches beyond science and should be recognized as philosophical and interpretive rather than stemming directly from scientific research. Yet subsequent works based in evolutionary biology likewise have often blended the interpretive level with the informational level, extrapolating from an evidence-based, scientific understanding of life to express a much larger worldview that bases itself in biology but philosophizes well beyond it. Philosophical interpretation of the science thus begins to seem like a part of the science, or a necessary outcome of the science, when in fact other well-considered interpretations are possible and, indeed, can be equally faithful to the science.

When thinking about the evolution of human beings, instances of stepping too quickly from the informational level to the interpretive level have often resulted in various kinds of eugenic thinking that Darwin and many evolutionary theorists after him have advocated, or at least been on friendly terms with. Eugenics, a system in which people deemed "unfit" are encouraged or forced not to have children while those deemed more "fit" are encouraged to breed, was seen by much of the scientific and cultural elite—at least of the modern West through the mid-20th century—as an important and necessary means to achieve social progress and a good "gene pool." Darwin himself discussed related ideas at some length, especially in *The Descent of Man* (although the term itself, "eugenics," was not coined until after he died). For instance, he wrote in *Descent*:

> The term, general good, may be defined as the means by which the greatest possible number of individuals can be reared in full vigour and health, with all their faculties perfect, under the conditions to which they are exposed. As the social instincts both of man and the lower animals have no doubt been developed by the same steps, it would be advisable, if found practicable, to use the same definition in both cases, and to take as the test of morality, the general good or welfare of the community, rather than the general happiness; but this definition would perhaps require some limitation on account of political ethics.[42]

In the context of his work, Darwin's suggestion of a possible "limitation on account of political ethics" may refer to his seemingly conflicted sense that a morality based in compassion and protection for the weak was a good and noble thing, even if also "highly injurious to the race of man."[43] As he wrote:

> Hence we must bear without complaining the undoubtedly bad effects of the weak surviving and propagating their kind; but there appears to be at least one check in steady action, namely the weaker and inferior members of society not marrying so freely as the sound; and this check might be indefinitely increased, though this is more to be hoped for than expected, by the weak in body or mind refraining from marriage.[44]

On the other hand, he sometimes came closer to directly advocating what we would now see as eugenics:

---

42. Charles Darwin, *The Descent of Man*, in *From So Simple a Beginning*, p. 833. The term "eugenics" was coined by Darwin's half-cousin, Francis Galton, soon after Darwin's death.

43. Ibid., p. 873.

44. Ibid.

Both sexes ought to refrain from marriage if in any marked degree inferior in body or mind; but such hopes are Utopian and will never be even partially realised until the laws of inheritance are thoroughly known. All do good service who aid towards this end. . . . All ought to refrain from marriage who cannot avoid abject poverty for their children; for poverty is not only a great evil, but tends to its own increase by leading to recklessness in marriage. On the other hand, as Mr. Galton has remarked, if the prudent avoid marriage, whilst the reckless marry, the inferior members will tend to supplant the better members of society. . . . The most able should not be prevented by laws or customs from succeeding best and rearing the largest number of offspring.[45]

In any case, Darwin's suggestions of fundamental criteria of morality seem to provide another example of thoughts at the interpretive level being discussed alongside basic scientific information, thus giving the philosophical judgments an air of authority (and perhaps greater authority than they deserve) precisely because they are mingled with scientific observations. When Darwin's readers have too easily attached *value* to the process of evolution or the passage of time, rather than more deeply considering what the real criteria of value ought to be, it has not exactly ended well. Notably, in the 20th century, it was not new or better scientific research that discredited eugenic programs, but the association of eugenics with Nazi ideology, which itself was based in important ways on eugenics programs and ideas then at play in the United States.[46]

Darwin did not write *The Descent of Man* (or *On the Origin of Species*) in a vacuum; he was responding to scientific, cultural, religious, and moral concerns of his time, both as a scientist and as a human being.[47] The question of how to regulate reproduction and produce a "well-bred" population had been discussed at length in Victorian England, and Darwin was only adding to that discussion. Some 70 years before *The Descent of Man*, for instance, Thomas Malthus[48] had proposed that human populations would always tend to grow faster than the resource base supporting them, leading to various checks on population and helping to determine who would live and who would die. Some 30 years before the publication of *Descent*, Charles Dickens had the miserly character Ebenezer Scrooge (of *A Christmas Carol*) make a sneering comment about the "surplus population"

---

45. Ibid., p. 1247.

46. The laws of 1933 in Germany were based in part on the California sterilization statutes of 1929, plus the scientific conversation among eugenicists crossed borders and included both German racial scientists and Americans.

47. In this, Darwin was like all scientists, although *Descent* makes Darwin's philosophical commentary more explicit than many works of science.

48. Malthus's ideas will be explored further in chapter 6 ("Population").

among the poor, implying that the world would be better off if such people were dead. *The Descent of Man* should be viewed not in isolation but against the backdrop of this ongoing discussion.

Survival, Struggle, and the Nature of Nature

Even the famous phrase "survival of the fittest" is to some extent an interpretation, and it shows how evolutionary theory has been bound up, from the beginning, with ideas about how "Nature" should be viewed: Is Nature ultimately beneficent, calm and harmonious, or instead brutal and violent, competitive, "red in tooth and claw"[49]? In short, what is Nature "like"?

Darwin and his contemporary, the polymath intellectual Herbert Spencer, both personified Nature as violent and competitive. Spencer originally coined the phrase "survival of the fittest," not Darwin; but Darwin framed the evolutionary process as a struggle for existence and used Spencer's phrase in some of his own later work.[50] (The full title of *Origin* was, in fact, *On the Origin of Species by Means of Natural Selection, or the Preservation of Favoured Races in the Struggle for Life*.) Darwin sought to re-train our vision of Nature, so that any apparent state of balance, harmony, and equilibrium appears not as the outcome of an *absence* of struggle or competition, but rather as the outcome of extreme but equally matched *pressures*, which lead to extinction and death for many organisms when they acquire the slightest disadvantage in the struggle. Darwin argued that without a clear-sighted vision of the "universal struggle for life,"[51] "the whole economy of nature, with every fact on distribution, rarity, abundance, extinction, and variation, will be dimly seen or quite misunderstood."[52]

Living after this Darwinian re-drawing, many people today have inherited such views of Nature, largely without realizing it, and find these views embedded in the dominant ways of speaking about evolution, life, and the history of life. For example, on the first page of their sweeping *A New History of Life*, the geobiologists Peter Ward and Joe Kirschvink call natural selection "the most pitiless of all phenomena"[53]—an interpretation that would not cause many readers to blink, but

---

49. From Alfred Lord Tennyson, *In Memoriam A. H. H.*, published in 1849 (10 years before *Origin*). In the poem, Tennyson laments the death of his friend Arthur Henry Hallam at the age of 23, and he struggles with faith, reason, and doubt in a characteristically Victorian way, strangely echoing Darwin's later writing in *The Descent of Man* even though Tennyson came to opposite religious conclusions and wrote in poetry instead of prose.

50. See, e.g., Charles Darwin, *The Descent of Man*, in *From So Simple a Beginning*, p. 870.

51. Charles Darwin, *On the Origin of Species*, in *From So Simple a Beginning*, p. 489.

52. Ibid.

53. Ward and Kirschvink, *A New History of Life*, p. 1.

that draws upon an entire history of developing reflections on the nature of Nature in general and of natural selection in particular.

Such violent metaphors for evolution and for Nature can be misleading, however, or at least one-sided. Darwin himself frequently spoke in the opposite way, presenting Nature and natural selection as benevolent, or even caring: "Man selects only for his own good; Nature only for that of the being which she tends."[54] He admired Nature's "workmanship"[55] and praised natural selection as superior to artificial selection: "as immeasurably superior to man's feeble efforts, as the works of Nature are to those of Art."[56] He spoke of "the wonder" of common descent[57] and the "grandeur in this view of life."[58] He saw natural selection as working "solely by and for the good of each being."[59] Even with regard to the struggle for existence, he wrote: "When we reflect on this struggle, we may console ourselves with the full belief, that the war of nature is not incessant, that no fear is felt, that death is generally prompt, and that the vigorous, the healthy, and the happy survive and multiply."[60]

These less competitive views of Nature and of natural selection did not end with Darwin. In fact, at the leading edges of today's biological science, a short answer to the question "What is evolution?" may not emphasize competition for scarce resources but instead variation, heredity, and differential reproductive success. Differential reproductive success can and does occur because of success or failure in a competition for scarce resources, but this is not the only reason why some members of a species might have more offspring than others do. Darwinian evolution is not only about the death of a "surplus population," but about which individuals have the most offspring; as Darwin stated in writing about the struggle for existence and sexual selection, "success in leaving progeny" was "more important" than "the life of the individual."[61] More recent thinkers have confirmed this perspective and carried it forward: "The neo-Darwinians of the beginning of this century put forward a much richer concept and showed, on the basis of quantitative theories, that the decisive factor in natural selection is not the struggle for life, but—within a given species—the differential rate of reproduction."[62] Moreover, "specialists all

54. Charles Darwin, *On the Origin of Species*, in *From So Simple a Beginning*, p. 503.

55. Ibid.

56. Ibid., p. 489.

57. Ibid., p. 532.

58. Ibid., p. 760.

59. Ibid.

60. Ibid., p. 500.

61. Ibid., p. 490.

62. Jacques Monod, *Chance and Necessity*, p. 115.

agree in thinking that direct strife, Spencer's 'struggle for life,' has played only a minor role in the evolution of species."[63]

In any case, painting evolution as fundamentally *about* competition for scarce resources, or suggesting that evolution implies a particularly violent or competitive view of Nature, is an interpretation—and not a consistently fitting one. It does not always capture the basic science accurately, and some scientists have even argued that cooperation drives evolution more than competition does.[64] Species quite frequently cannot survive without one another, and Darwin recognized in *Origin* that organisms create ecological niches for one another (albeit without conscious intent to do so). As the mathematical biologist Martin Nowak has put it, "Life is therefore not just a struggle for survival—it is also, one might say, a snuggle for survival."[65]

Regardless of the details of such debates, metaphors of "friendliness" or "violence" in nature clearly matter a great deal for how we interpret what evolutionary biology *means* for our understanding of the world. This is true not least because evolution, in a generalized sense, has been taken up as a way to understand not only life, but the universe and Earth as well. The power of the life metaphor, explored in chapter 3, that paints stars or universes or planets as "living" and "dying," comes through clearly yet again. Evolution and life are themselves such powerful metaphors that other disciplines deploy them as well, even if not always conscious of the interpretive consequences of doing so.

Evolution: Interpret with Care

The power of evolution and natural selection as "big ideas" is considerable. Within the biological sciences, evolution provides a unifying framework for understanding a wide array of phenomena. Outside of biology, the idea of evolution remains powerful, but one must use it as an interpretive lens only with great care. Careless or malicious interpretive applications of the Darwinian framework have led to everything from misleading understandings of the natural world to the destruction of human lives in the name of "survival of the fittest" and the "general good" of society, through such approaches as eugenics. Information from the biological sciences can certainly play a role in discussing the significance of evolution for how we think about humanity and the natural world, but it is just as crucial to preserve a robust role for philosophical, moral, and humanistic reasoning in contemplating these topics as well.

---

63. Ibid., p. 151.

64. Such as, for example, Lynn Margulis: see, e.g., Lynn Margulis and Dorion Sagan, *Microcosmos*, pp. 28-29. For another example, see Anna Lowenhaupt Tsing, *The Mushroom at the End of the World*, pp. 137–144.

65. Martin A. Nowak, "Why We Help," https://www.scientificamerican.com/article/why-we-help/ .

Biosphere

The biosphere is the Earth system that includes all life on Earth. Like the lithosphere, asthenosphere, atmosphere, hydrosphere, and the other "spheres" of chapter 3, the biosphere has a history of enormous changes and an ongoing, ever-changing relationship with the rest of the planet. The evolutionary framework for understanding the history of all life reveals that all living organisms in the biosphere are related to one another, however distantly. And all organisms, past and present, share certain features. At the same time, the life present on Earth at any given point in Earth's history is very different from the life present at any other point. The evolution of entirely new life forms, new capacities, and new habitats is common, as is the extinction of species.

The Beginnings of the Biosphere: 3+ Billion Years Ago

The biosphere began over 3 billion years ago, with the first appearance of life on Earth. How life originated presents a genuine puzzle. The details are usually thought to be bound up with physics and chemistry, so we will cover this in the next section, "Biochemistry." But regardless of what happened to bring it about, there are almost certainly traces of ancient, single-celled life in rocks from more than 3 billion years ago.

These cells were prokaryotes—that is, cells without an organized nucleus or organelles (see the "Life" section at the start of this chapter). Prokaryotes were the only form of life on Earth for roughly half the history of the biosphere, and they profoundly shaped the biosphere and the Earth itself. Without them and their contributions to the atmosphere and oceans, past and present, today's biosphere full of both multicellular and unicellular organisms would not be possible.

Genetic commonalities between modern organisms indicate that the last universal common ancestor (LUCA) of all present-day living organisms may have lived some 3.6 billion years ago. LUCA is not necessarily the first organism, but rather the most recent organism that is related to all living things alive today. Any and all ancestors of LUCA would also be shared ancestors of all living things today.

A World of Microbes: 3 to 1.5 Billion Years Ago

While there are hints that life existed as long as 3.8 billion years ago, or even earlier, in the form of cell-like structures and chemical traces found in rocks that date from this time, it is difficult to establish beyond doubt that these are actual cellular structures or products of cellular metabolism, rather than non-living structures and chemicals in rocks.[66]

---

66. Or contamination from scientific instruments used to isolate and examine them. For a discussion, see Ward and Kirschvink, *A New History of Life*, p. 76.

Clearer evidence for the presence of living cells exists 3 billion years ago and after. Many of the remains from this time take the form of stromatolites. Stromatolites are structures left by colonies of single-celled organisms,[67] prokaryotic cells that trap and bind sediments and deposit them in layered structures which readily fossilize. (See Figure 4.1.)

A major innovation in the history of the biosphere probably took place during this period, between 2 and 3 billion years ago, in the form of organisms called cyanobacteria, a kind of bacteria that engage in oxygenic photosynthesis, a biochemical process of "fixing" carbon (taking carbon atoms from the non-living world, such as carbon dioxide in the air, into living structures) and harvesting energy from the Sun. This process uses carbon dioxide and water as ingredients to produce glucose (a sugar molecule that carries energy that organisms can use) and, as a byproduct, oxygen. This was surely not the only novel piece of cellular biochemistry developed

FIGURE 4.1 Modern-Day Stromatolites in Shark Bay, Australia These structures are deposited, layer by layer, by colonies of microbes. They are rare today, but were more common billions of years ago. Fossilized stromatolites provide some of the earliest evidence for the presence of microbial life on Earth over 3 billion years ago.
Source: Robert Goldstein

---

67. The fact that they are colonies is helpful for paleontological purposes, because the aggregation of single-celled organisms can produce macroscopic remains.

during this time, but it was one of the most significant developments in the entire history of life—not least because oxygen subsequently built up around Earth's surface, was absorbed in the ocean and in land surfaces, and then could accumulate in the atmosphere, which previously held at most trace amounts of oxygen. After about 2.4 billion years ago, rocks that are unstable in the presence of oxygen become much less abundant in the rock record, as mentioned in chapter 3, indicating that there was significant oxygen in the atmosphere around that time;[68] rocks that are still present today thus serve to indicate when oxygen began to accumulate in the atmosphere.

People often think of oxygen as being necessary for life, because human beings and much of the rest of today's biosphere rely on it. But the biosphere had thrived in the absence of oxygen for hundreds of millions of years. In fact, introducing it to the oceans and atmosphere in large quantities may have produced an "oxygen holocaust"—a mass extinction of the microbes that existed at the time. Oxygen is a highly reactive element; it is possible that much of the then-existing biosphere found oxygen toxic, though the rareness of microbial fossils makes it difficult or impossible to assess this idea directly. Also, the presence of oxygen in the oceans would lead to the removal of other key elements, such as the iron dissolved in ocean water, which combines with oxygen to produce solid iron oxide that comes out of solution and falls to the ocean floor.[69] With much less iron available in a form useful to living cells, many of the organisms alive at the time may have died. Changes in one part of the biosphere can, through a variety of mechanisms, affect the circumstances of the whole.

That said, the fact that *any* life could survive the introduction of significant oxygen into the atmosphere indicates that many life forms may have been exposed to trace amounts of oxygen long before it began accumulating in large quantities. Without some exposure, it is difficult to explain why biochemical systems would have evolved that could protect at least some cells against the potentially harmful effects of oxygen.[70] The biochemist Nick Lane even suggests that LUCA may have used trace amounts of oxygen to respire, and he points out that "there is no solid evidence that oxygen ever caused a mass extinction."[71]

---

68. Analysis of sulfur isotopes has also converged on roughly 2.4 billion years ago as the time when ozone (O_3) was first present in the atmosphere. One major question still lingers about the timing of the oxygenation of the atmosphere, which is why manganese oxide, usually taken as a strong indicator of the *presence* of oxygen, is also present in sediments alongside the pyrite and uraninite that usually indicate the *absence* of oxygen. For further discussion, see Ward and Kirschvink, *A New History of Life*, p. 77 ff.

69. Iron oxides precipitated in this way are thought to contribute to iron-oxide layers of sedimentary rock commonly found in "banded iron formations."

70. See Ward and Kirschvink, *A New History of Life*, p. 71 ff.

71. Nick Lane, *Oxygen: The Molecule That Made the World*, p. 21.

In any case, atmospheric oxygen was a prerequisite for the later development of the kinds of complex life we know now. Oxygen's chemical properties make it possible for cells to harness a great deal more energy, so the presence of plentiful oxygen in the atmosphere meant that more free energy was available.[72] The first eukaryotic cells, far larger and with much greater internal structure than prokaryotes, appeared after the shift to an oxygenated atmosphere, some 2 billion years ago.[73] The first eukaryotes were still unicellular organisms, but they were much larger than prokaryotes; eukaryotic cells are some 10 to 100 times larger in diameter than prokaryotic cells and, hence, may enclose a volume more than 1,000 times greater. As already discussed, eukaryotic cells include various organelles, membrane-bound compartments within the cell that carry out various cellular functions.

The size and complexity of eukaryotic cells may sound like a point in eukaryotes' favor, but there is a problem with such large size: the ratio of surface area to volume is much *smaller* for a large cell than for a small cell, which means that nutrients cannot so readily be taken in and diffuse to where they need to be in the cell. In a sense, the size of eukaryotic cells *requires* specialized compartments like organelles to solve this logistical problem that prokaryotic cells simply do not face. In any case, eukaryotic cells never made prokaryotes obsolete. The two types of cells have coexisted on Earth for some 2 billion years, and the activities of prokaryotes (including those incorporated in our own human microbiomes, and the billions of prokaryotes contained in every gram of soil[74]) continue to be necessary for the survival of eukaryotes. Today's biosphere is shaped heavily by the "collaboration" between these two very distinct, but interdependent, types of cells.

How did eukaryotes come to be in the first place? As Nick Lane has pointed out, all eukaryotic cells have an astonishing number of similarities, despite the fact that they are adapted to massively different environments. This suggests that cells more complex than prokaryotes originated exactly once in life's history; otherwise, why should all cells be either prokaryotic or eukaryotic, with such a wide gulf of size and complexity between them? It may be that it is at least as difficult for cells more complex than prokaryotes to form from prokaryotic ancestors as it is for prokaryotes to form from non-living materials, so that this happened only once in 3 to 4 billion years of evolution.

---

72. To get a sense of the difference oxygen makes: anaerobic respiration of glucose produces 2 ATP molecules (the energy currency of the cell) per glucose molecule, while aerobic respiration (with oxygen) produces 36 ATP molecules per glucose molecule. (Charles Langmuir and Wally Broecker, *How to Build a Habitable Planet*, p. 469.)

73. Today, nearly all eukaryotes—including almost all known animals and plants—incorporate oxygen in the metabolic processes that produce energy for their cells.

74. "If I could do it all over again, and relive my vision in the twenty-first century, I would be a microbial ecologist. Ten billion bacteria live in a gram of ordinary soil, a mere pinch held between thumb and forefinger. They represent thousands of species, almost none of which are known to science." (Edward O. Wilson, *Naturalist*, p. 364.) Our thanks to David Burzillo for this reference.

As for the question of how specific organelles came into being, this is largely a matter of speculation and ongoing biological research,[75] but mitochondria and chloroplasts are major exceptions. All eukaryotes include mitochondria, organelles that are commonly called "the powerhouse of the cell" because they carry out the biochemical reactions that supply the cell with energy. According to the biologist Lynn Margulis's endosymbiotic theory, mitochondria are derived from ancient prokaryotic cells that were engulfed by other prokaryotic cells and then retained through the generations. This explains why mitochondria have their own DNA, which turns out to be closely related to the DNA of certain prokaryotes alive today. Meanwhile, chloroplasts are organelles in modern plants[76] that give plants the ability to perform photosynthesis; they likewise have their own DNA, which suggests they are closely related to cyanobacteria, the dominant photosynthesizing microbes for hundreds of millions of years.

A World of Microbes . . . Plus Other Stuff: 1.5 Billion Years Ago to the Present

While the first multicellular eukaryotes may have appeared some 1.2 to 1.5 billion years ago, fossil evidence suggests that multicellular life really "came into its own" much later, some 600 million years ago, with the appearance of a diverse range of macroscopic life known as the Ediacaran biota. Nearly all the large organisms of that time, however, would look unusual and unfamiliar to us today. More "modern" macroscopic life, patterned on similar "templates" as today's large organisms, did not appear until closer to 500 million years ago, during the Cambrian period.

As discussed in chapter 3, the history of Earth is divided into four "eons," each lasting half a billion years to 2 billion years: the Hadean, the Archean, the Proterozoic, and the Phanerozoic. The Phanerozoic, the eon of "visible life,"[77] began 541 million years ago with the Cambrian period. The Cambrian featured an "explosion" of different forms of macroscopic animal life, especially those with hard shells, bones, and other structures that more easily fossilize (hence, "visible life"—visible to paleontologists, and to the naked eye). A wide variety of basic body plans came into existence, with patterns and symmetries that are still familiar today—for example, bilateral symmetry, where the left and right sides of an organism are mirror images of each other, as in human beings; or radial symmetry, where an organism looks the same as it is rotated through an angle, as in starfish. There are indications of considerable mobility in the animals of the Cambrian oceans, such as limbs, fins, and tails. Predation and defense against predation, including

---

75. See Nick Lane's *The Vital Question* for an interesting take on this topic.

76. And in some protists (eukaryotic organisms that are not plants, animals, or fungi).

77. The meaning of the Greek roots of the word.

body features like body armor and behaviors like burrowing, also became common at this time.

What triggered the Cambrian explosion remains a matter of debate, and the most prominent ideas are difficult to test. Some evolutionary or environmental threshold may have been reached that allowed a slew of changes to occur in a comparatively short period of time (several million years): perhaps oxygen levels rose to a critical threshold, making more energy available for the development of larger and more active bodies; perhaps changes in the chemistry of the ocean made the chemical ingredients of shells and bone more readily available to organisms; perhaps nervous systems became sufficiently developed to enable predator-prey relationships in which predators could hunt well enough to eat while prey could hide well enough to survive, thus in turn enabling rapid predator-prey co-evolution and the opening of new ecological niches for animals to fill. Or maybe the genome of the last common ancestor of the modern animal phyla changed in such a way as to allow the evolutionary exploration of many body plans.[78] Or changes in climate, especially the transition from a "Snowball Earth" to a much warmer Earth, might have led to rapid evolution. Perhaps several factors converged at the same geological "moment" to enable unprecedented evolutionary change among macroscopic organisms. Evidence is lacking that would show the precise roles of these and other possibilities.

The rest of the Phanerozoic would see much diversification of the animal body plans and patterns that were established in the Cambrian. Species diversity among plants and animals rose as new relationships between species became possible and new ecological niches opened up, particularly with the colonization of the land by plants, animals, and fungi starting in the Ordovician period, some 450 million years ago. Life on land was challenging and required a vast array of new adaptations for organisms suited to a buoyant, liquid world. But aquatic habitats were already full of living things, many of them competing for limited resources. The land, however, offered new habitats with less competition and, for some organisms, refuge from predators. New selection pressures on land favored adaptations that helped organisms survive there, including those that helped organisms move about and maintain their structure on land—such as sturdy skeletons, stiff vascular tissue in plants (e.g., wood), and the amniotic egg with its watertight membrane.

The broadest trends in the Phanerozoic biosphere, including the rise and fall of dominant animal groups,[79] also reflect the effects of continental drift, mass extinctions, and adaptive radiations. Continental drift alters habitats: for example, most marine species inhabit shallow waters, and the formation of supercontinents

---

78. See, e.g., Scott Freeman, *Biological Science* (4th edition), pp. 487–488. Thanks also to Catherine Badgley for pointing out several of these possibilities.

79. Such as fish and insects in the Paleozoic, reptiles in the Mesozoic, and mammals in the Cenozoic.

like Pangaea would destroy a considerable amount of that habitat. Continental drift also produces climate change and can lead to speciation due to geographical separation. Mass extinctions are geologically short periods of time in which a great number of species die out; paleontologists have traditionally counted five of them in the Phanerozoic. Extinction at a smaller scale is a routine part of evolution and the history of life on Earth, with perhaps one species going extinct every few years on average. Mass extinctions, however, typically feature sustained extinction rates at least thousands of times greater—as in the aftermath of the asteroid impact that many geologists believe wiped out the non-avian dinosaurs and a great many other species 66 million years ago.[80] Not just species but ecosystems too are affected by mass extinctions; complex interactions determine which species go extinct and which survive. But mass extinctions pave the way for adaptive radiations, evolutionary processes in which many new groups of organisms appear, adapted to ecological roles ("niches") vacated by species that became extinct.[81] Ecosystems thus "recover" from a mass extinction, over the course of millions of years, although the new ecosystems often look quite different from those that came before.[82]

Fossils supply much of the "hard evidence" for the conditions of the biosphere during the Phanerozoic. While most fossils are not as well-preserved as the sort that find their way into museum displays, the fossil record yields a great deal of information about what changes happened and when. And the story constructed from the fossil record can be supported or challenged by phylogenetics, another line of evidence and reasoning based on *comparisons* of currently living organisms, both at a genetic / molecular level and at a structural / morphological level. Finally, evolutionary theory provides the understanding of intrinsic biological mechanisms that underlie evolutionary change. These theoretical frameworks and sources of evidence provide an integrated way of approaching the changes and continuities of life's history.

How Historians Can Help Scientists

There is an interesting point of contact between the sciences and humanities in considering how to construct a narrative of life's history out of the basic biological evidence. On any scale, one's thinking about the past may fall into a pattern of

---

80. While there is no controversy about an extinction event having happened about 66 million years ago, a determined subset of the geological community maintains that the evidence is weak for asteroid impact being the primary cause. Volcanic activity associated with the Deccan Traps in present-day India may have had sufficiently catastrophic atmospheric consequences to produce a mass-extinction event. (See Bianca Bosker, "The Nastiest Feud in Science," www.theatlantic.com/magazine/archive/2018/09/dinosaur-extinction-debate/565769/.)

81. Mammals, for instance, diversified to fill many niches opened up by the extinction of the non-avian dinosaurs.

82. Campbell et al., *Biology*, pp. 519–525.

straightforward linear narrative: "this happened and then that happened," or "this caused this, which caused that." But the real world is almost always more complicated. In the history of the natural world, as in the history of humanity, many causes and conditions are at work simultaneously;[83] there are interconnections between causes, as well as feedbacks between scales; and the context of an event (at multiple scales) may matter a great deal for the proper interpretation of the event. Historians trained in multicausal, contextual thinking about the past[84] can make important contributions to how science-based histories of the universe, Earth, and life are told, and can do this precisely because they have pondered deeply the nature of storytelling and the construction of narratives.

As an example of contextual thinking, Peter Ward and Joe Kirschvink,[85] in their *A New History of Life*, argue for a focus not just on species or the biosphere as a whole in narrating the history of life, but specifically on ecosystems—on trying to understand fossils and the history of life in the context of ecosystems, including the completely new kinds of ecosystems that appeared when the land or the air was colonized, or when atmospheric oxygen created an entirely new niche for organisms to occupy in how their metabolism operated.[86] At an even larger scale, the geological contexts of different points in time during Earth's history can differ enormously, with the entire Earth being frozen over at certain points and much warmer conditions prevailing at others.

Historians are also well versed in the challenges of how to balance continuity and change. In addition to landmark turning points like the oxygenation of the atmosphere or the evolution of eukaryotes, there were also long periods of comparative stasis in the history of life, which are harder to narrate than the hinge points.[87]

---

83. So, e.g., we attempted to emphasize in our own (very condensed) history of life that prokaryotes and unicellular organisms were never *replaced* by eukaryotes and multicellular organisms, but instead exist in a dynamic relationship with them and, in many ways, continue to enable their existence. Another way of saying this: prokaryotes did not "evolve into" eukaryotes; rather, prokaryotes evolved into prokaryotes and eukaryotes.

84. See chapter 6.

85. Two scientists who have clearly thought a good deal about what it takes to "do history" with science.

86. Ward and Kirschvink, *A New History of Life*, pp. 5–6. The mechanism for evolutionary change may exist at the level of species, but there is interplay between the scales of life, and ecosystems could play a much more central role than they did in our story.

87. "But of bliss and glad life there is little to be said, before it ends; as works fair and wonderful, while still they endure for eyes to see, are their own record, and only when they are in peril or broken for ever do they pass into song." (J. R. R. Tolkien, *The Silmarillion*, p. 95.) On a more strictly biological note, the paleontologists Stephen Jay Gould and Niles Eldredge's idea of "punctuated equilibrium" is an elaboration of the modern evolutionary synthesis that places particular emphasis on the importance of these periods of relative stasis in evolutionary history.

Side Note: Stromatolites and Hunter-Gatherers

A common trend in multiple fields that contribute to universal histories is to use modern-day examples as "analogues," or windows into past realities that bear some similarity to a modern parallel. For instance, paleontologists have often used modern-day stromatolites in places like Australia's Shark Bay (see Figure 4.1)—which features many stromatolites that are not fossils, but rather structures currently inhabited by living microbes, and still being built up—as examples for gaining a better understanding of stromatolites in the Archean.[88] On the one hand, this is an important way of building one's intuition and ability to reason about the past. On the other hand, there are limits to the approach, especially since many other (modern!) organisms inhabit Shark Bay, meaning that the entire ecological, atmospheric, and biospheric context of modern stromatolites is quite different than the Archean context of now-fossilized stromatolites. We will see the power and limitations of using modern analogues as "evidence" about the past again when we consider the difficulties of using modern hunter-gatherers as analogues of past hunter-gatherers in chapter 6: while certain elements of a foraging lifeway may bear resemblances across time, the broader context of foragers as a small minority in the world of today is much different than that of Paleolithic foragers who inhabited a world where fully agricultural societies had never existed.

Finally, the way narratives are constructed can sometimes be driven as much by the perceived implications and lessons of the narrative as they are by the available evidence—another idea that is deeply familiar to historians. For example, the story of changes in the atmosphere leading to a mass die-off at the time of the oxygenation of the atmosphere makes a good morality tale for us today, in an age that is deeply concerned about the implications of greenhouse-gas emissions for the future of humanity, but the very ease with which this analogy can be drawn should perhaps make us wary. That the atmosphere went from (nearly) oxygen-free to oxygenated is no longer seriously questioned, but the idea that atmospheric oxygen produced a mass extinction is not as firmly established, for the reasons discussed earlier. Such careful distinctions need to be made, and remembered; both the story and the lessons will change in content and in confidence over time as the available evidence itself evolves.

The Place of Humans in Life's History

In our telling of the history of the biosphere, we have tried to sketch landmarks, changes, and transitions with significance for the biosphere *as a whole*, rather

---

88. For further discussion, see Ward and Kirschvink, *A New History of Life*, p. 69.

than focusing on, or only narrating, the path leading to human beings. One could imagine many other ways of telling the story, each different depending on the underlying purpose. If instead we cared mostly about the story of what led to us as human beings, a more detailed narrative would have turned in the direction of the fraction of the biosphere that inhabits the land. Such a history would focus on vertebrates, animals with brains, mammals, and so forth. Or if we wished to emphasize the world of very small living things, a more detailed narrative might trace the emergence of new microbial groups in the oceans and below the Earth's surface, perhaps de-emphasizing the whole world of macroscopic life. Which is the better approach? None has an absolute claim on being "better"; it would depend on one's purpose in writing. (See Figure 4.2.)

Tree of Life

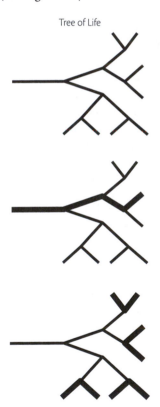

FIGURE 4.2 **Focusing on Different Parts of the Evolutionary Tree** Different approaches to narrating life's history correspond to focusing on different parts of a commonly used metaphor: the evolutionary "tree of life." A variety of trade-offs and issues arise when using any such singular metaphor to describe the entire history of life, but at the same time, the "tree" image does offer helpful insights. (Top) Attempting to narrate the history of the biosphere as a whole corresponds to looking at the tree as a whole. (Middle) Attempting to narrate the specific "lineage" that led to human beings corresponds to tracing the origin of a single branch. (Bottom) Discussing the present-day condition of the biosphere would correspond to focusing on all the tips of the tree's branches.
Source: Authors.

That said, it is not that one must strictly choose between focusing on matters of significance to humans and focusing on the biosphere as a whole. Even if one's purpose in narrating life's history is ultimately to understand humanity, we are profoundly interdependent with the rest of the biosphere, and always have been. As discussed in chapter 3, a great deal had to happen in the past in order to make life "like us" possible, and only by interacting constantly with the rest of the biosphere—from our own microbiomes that help sustain us internally to the ecological processes that give us food, drinkable water, and an atmosphere we can breathe—can we survive now. Past or present, everything has interacted with everything else to make everything what it is now, so it is helpful to understand as much of the biosphere and its history as possible, even if only to understand the context of human life.

Biochemistry

As humans, we often think of ourselves as modern organisms, and from a certain perspective, we are. The biological ancestors of modern humans and the biological ancestors of modern chimpanzees diverged from a common ancestor only some 6 to 7 million years ago, according to the best current estimates. Even our most distant primate ancestors are relative latecomers to the scene of life on Earth, which started billions of years ago.

But while that is true on a species level, it is also true that some parts of us are very old indeed. Many biochemical pathways—sequences of chemical reactions that human cells use to generate energy, to make proteins, and to replicate DNA—originated billions of years ago. And the universal genetic code seems to be common to all life. Every cell ever known to science "translates" nucleotide sequences (the "language" of DNA) to amino-acid sequences (the "language" of proteins) in almost exactly the same way. Vestiges of the first ancient prokaryotes are still present in our own cells and the cells of every other living organism.[89]

Life is one huge family. (See Plates 17 and 18.) Everything is related to everything else, as far as we know, however distantly. Although the family resemblance between a dog and an amoeba may not be instantly obvious, there are points of striking unity amidst the diversity of life, especially at the molecular and cellular levels, deriving in part from the common ancestry of all life.[90] Every living organism is a mosaic of ancestral and derived features, a mix of the ancient and the novel, at

---

89. As Darwin wrote in a more macroscopic context, "Man still bears in his bodily frame the indelible stamp of his lowly origin" (Charles Darwin, *The Descent of Man*, in *From So Simple a Beginning*, p. 1248). One might argue that this is not necessarily a "lowly" origin at all, however, but a rather profound one.

90. It also derives from environmental / ecological similarities (convergent evolution), as discussed under "Contingency" in chapter 6.

each scale.[91] And just as the idea of the biosphere provides a way of thinking about the history of life on its largest scales in both space and time, biochemistry provides a way of thinking about the history of life on its smallest scales.[92]

The Beginnings of Life: How, Where, Why?

All living cells are extraordinarily complex. Even the simplest bacterium contains several thousand kinds of molecules, linked through an intricate set of chemical reactions vital to the life of the cell.[93] Given this remarkable complexity, by what path, process, or mechanisms did life come into being in the first place?

The short answer is that no one knows. At present, there is no complete, evidentially supported, systematic explanation for how life began—or anything close to it. Scientists have not found it easy to even approach the question of how such complex entities *could* come to be, given their diverse components interacting in highly specific ways to produce an array of functions, let alone to show that there was a particular pathway through which they *did* come about. But there have been suggestive experiments, observations, and theoretical frameworks for getting a handle on this question, resulting in a sort of scientifically informed speculation about the how, where, and why of the origins of life.

How?

Scientists who work on the problem of the origin of life identify four basic pieces that needed to be in place for life to begin. One might call them "steps," though their proper order is itself part of the debate. Be that as it may, there first must be small organic (that is, carbon-containing) molecules available, such as amino acids, the building blocks of proteins. Second, these small molecules must combine into the far more complex and large molecules, such as proteins and nucleic acids, that form the building blocks of cellular structures. Third, some kind of compartmentalization must put these building blocks into contact with one another and localize them. Fourth, certain large molecules, or (proto-)cellular compartments, must have the ability to self-replicate—and more specifically, to self-replicate with modifications or "errors" that are themselves replicable, so as to give rise to Darwinian evolution.[94]

The first piece seems to be by far the easiest. A famous experiment in 1952, named for the scientists who devised it (Stanley Miller and Harold Urey), provided the first proof of principle that basic building blocks of life, and in particular the

---

91. We are grateful to Diarmaid O'Foighil for this insight.

92. Thanks to Mark Ditzler for substantial help framing the current state of research described in this section.

93. Ward and Kirschvink, *A New History of Life*, p. 42.

94. Ibid., pp. 47–48.

How old is the Earth? The Universe?

Varying scientific estimates of the age of the Earth and Universe over time

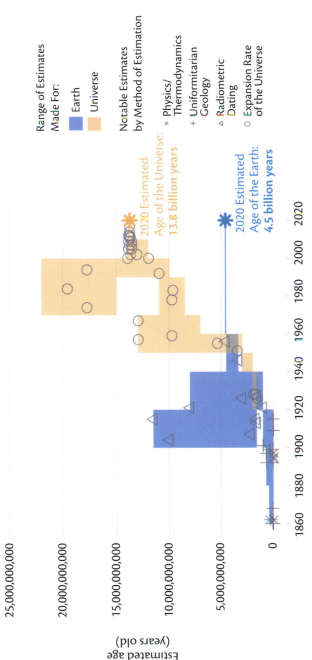

PLATE 1 **Estimates of the Age of the Earth and the Age of the Universe, 1860–2020** This graph shows how scientific estimates of the ages of the Earth and the universe have changed over time. The blue and orange bars represent a given time period's prevailing expert opinion as to what the age of the Earth (blue) and the universe (orange) likely would turn out to be, with some particularly notable individual age estimates plotted as points whose shapes depend on the method used to obtain the estimates. For a more detailed description of the content of the graph and the storyline communicated by it, see Appendix, pp. 419–420.

Source: Graphic-Design by Carolina Simao Roe-Raymond

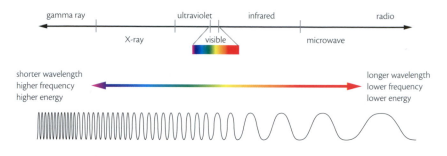

PLATE 2 The Electromagnetic Spectrum Radio waves, microwaves, infrared radiation, visible light, ultraviolet radiation, X-rays, and gamma rays are all electromagnetic waves, distinguished from one another by their different wavelengths. A scientific understanding of electromagnetic radiation has been key to probing the universe, as astronomers have made significant new discoveries each time they have surveyed the heavens at a new range of wavelengths. Electromagnetic waves were "discovered" through the mathematical manipulation of equations in theoretical physics before they were detected experimentally, as described under "Mathematics" in chapter 2.
Source: NASA

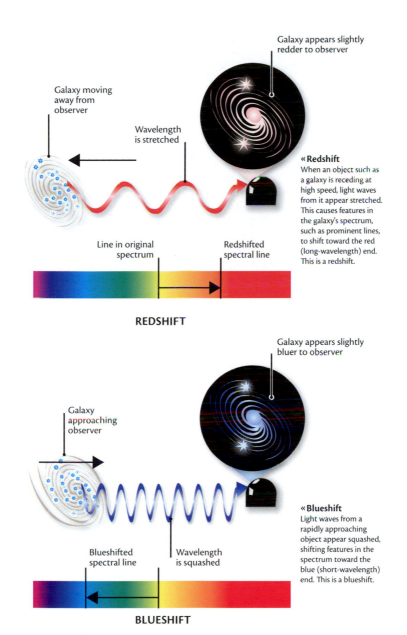

Galaxy appears slightly redder to observer

Galaxy moving away from observer

Wavelength is stretched

«Redshift
When an object such as a galaxy is receding at high speed, light waves from it appear stretched. This causes features in the galaxy's spectrum, such as prominent lines, to shift toward the red (long-wavelength) end. This is a redshift.

Line in original spectrum

Redshifted spectral line

REDSHIFT

Galaxy appears slightly bluer to observer

Galaxy approaching observer

«Blueshift
Light waves from a rapidly approaching object appear squashed, shifting features in the spectrum toward the blue (short-wavelength) end. This is a blueshift.

Blueshifted spectral line

Wavelength is squashed

BLUESHIFT

PLATE 3 **Redshift and the Expansion of the Universe** A key piece of evidence that the universe is expanding is the *redshift* of light from distant galaxies. When light is red-shifted, the wavelength of the light becomes longer. The reason this is called a "redshift" is that for visible light, increasing wavelength corresponds to a shift toward the red end of the spectrum. Certain features of a spectrum (like a spectral line, as pictured, or like a peak in intensity) occur at specific wavelengths in a non-shifted spectrum, so if these features occur at longer wavelengths, cosmologists infer that the stretching of space has produced a redshift. See the discussion under "Big Bang" in chapter 2.

Source: Based on Helen Fewster, ed., *Big History: Examines Our Past, Explains Our Present, Imagines Our Future* (New York: DK Publishing, 2016), p. 29.

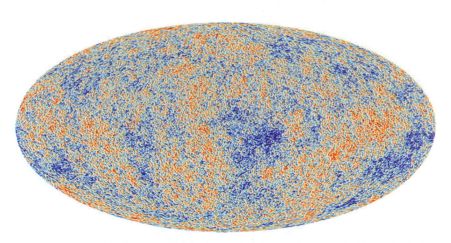

PLATE 4 Cosmic Microwave Background Another major piece of evidence for the Big Bang comes from observations of the cosmic microwave background (CMB). This image, a product and central symbol of modern cosmology, represents actual data from observations of this "oldest light in the universe." See the discussion under "Big Bang" in chapter 2.

Source: ESA and the Planck Collaboration

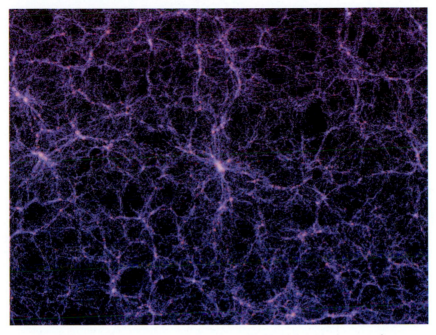

PLATE 5 The Cosmic Web A computer simulation of the distribution of matter in the universe on its largest scales; roughly speaking, each dot in this image represents an entire galaxy. At the very largest scales, matter in the present-day universe is distributed in a manner reminiscent of the inside of a sponge, with large clusters and long filaments of galaxies surrounding mostly empty voids: the so-called "cosmic web." Computer simulations of matter clumping under the influence of gravity can be compared with actual telescopic observations of the cosmic web, and the close match between the two suggests that the sponge-like pattern can be regarded as the result of gravity pulling matter together throughout the universe over cosmic time scales, as described under "Gravity" in chapter 2. *Source:* Dr. Volker Springel/Max-Planck-Institute for Astrophysics

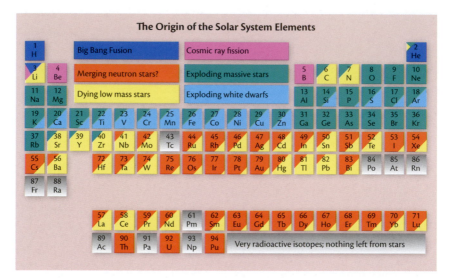

PLATE 6 Where Do Elements Come From? Most of the elements in the Solar System, and in the universe in general, are "manufactured" in stars. There are several known mechanisms through which this happens, including the stellar explosions called supernovae. Most elements are produced through more than one mechanism, as shown in the diagram above—a representation of the results of ongoing research. See the discussion under "Gravity" in chapter 2.

Source: Jennifer Johnson

PLATE 7 Planets in Formation (Artist's Interpretation) Astronomers using the most powerful telescopes in the world can directly observe young stars still in the process of formation, which usually have a rotating disk of matter around them in the process of co-alescing to form planets—a byproduct of gravity pulling matter together into a star. This image is an artist's interpretation of that process. As discussed under "Gravity" in chapter 2 and "Earth" in chapter 3, our own Solar System shows many hints of having formed in this manner, with Earth being built over time from smaller, rocky building blocks.
Source: NASA

PLATE 8 Earthrise Taken by William Anders, an Apollo 8 astronaut, from lunar orbit on December 24, 1968, this famous photo has inspired many people to reflect on the Earth as a whole. See the discussion under "Earth" in chapter 3.

Source: NASA/Bill Anders

PLATE 9 Pale Blue Dot An image of Earth from the Voyager 1 spacecraft, when it was looking back toward our planet from the outer edges of the Solar System. Our home planet is a small, "pale blue dot" when viewed from so far away. The idea of seeing Earth from a great distance has inspired many, from the medieval Italian poet Dante to the 20th-century astronomer Carl Sagan, to reflect on the place of human life in the grand scheme of things. While Earth's relative physical smallness and non-central position in the universe are sometimes taken as indications of its ultimate insignificance, chapter 2 ("Universe") and chapter 3 ("Earth") question the idea that Earth's size and position should be interpreted in this way.
Source: NASA/JPL-Caltech

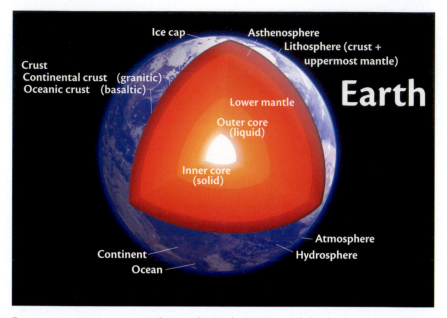

Ice cap
Asthenosphere
Lithosphere (crust +
uppermost mantle)
Crust
Continental crust   (granitic)
Oceanic crust   (basaltic)
Lower mantle
Outer core
(liquid)
Earth
Inner core
(solid)
Atmosphere
Continent
Hydrosphere
Ocean

PLATE 10 Diagramming the Earth Earth scientists subdivide the Earth's interior into core, mantle, and crust, which are defined by composition and density: what makes up the crust, for example, is different than what makes up the mantle. The crust and the upper (rigid) mantle are grouped together into the lithosphere, which is broken up into tectonic plates that ride atop the asthenosphere, the weak and ductile solid portion of the mantle below the lithosphere that flows slowly over geologic time. See the discussions under "Earth" and "Plate Tectonics" in chapter 3.

Source: Based on Kelvinsong/Wikipedia

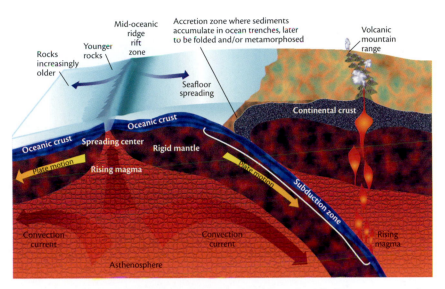

Labels in figure:

Rocks increasingly older

Younger rocks

Mid-oceanic ridge rift zone

Accretion zone where sediments accumulate in ocean trenches, later to be folded and/or metamorphosed

Volcanic mountain range

Seafloor spreading

Continental crust

Oceanic crust

Oceanic crust

Spreading center

Rigid mantle

Plate motion

Rising magma

Plate motion

Subduction zone

Convection current

Convection current

Rising magma

Asthenosphere

PLATE 11 Diagramming Plate Tectonics The basic idea of plate tectonics is that the Earth's lithosphere (the upper, rigid part of the mantle plus the crust) is broken into large pieces ("plates"). New lithosphere forms by welling up from the Earth's interior at the mid-oceanic ridges, the mountain ranges that are submerged in the middle of every ocean on Earth. New lithosphere slowly spreads outward to form ocean basins, while old oceanic lithosphere plunges downward along plate boundaries and is recycled back into the lower mantle in a process called subduction. This conveyer-belt-like motion, involving both the generation of new lithosphere at the mid-oceanic ridges and the destruction of that lithosphere at plate boundaries, is known as seafloor spreading. See the discussion under "Plate Tectonics" in chapter 3.

Source: Based on https://www.geosci.usyd.edu.au/users/prey/ACSGT/EReports/eR.2003/GroupD/Report1/web%20pages/assignment_1.html

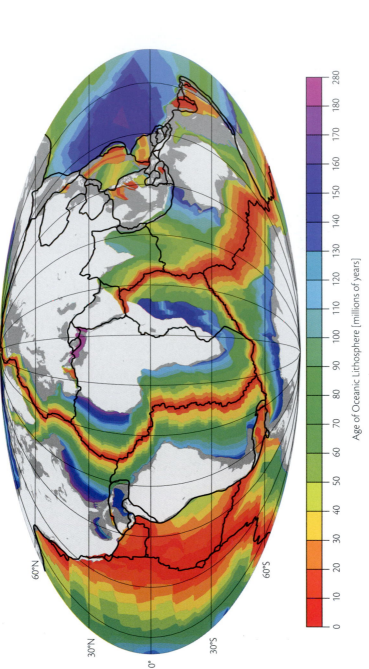

Age of Oceanic Lithosphere [millions of years]

| 0 | 10 | 20 | 30 | 40 | 50 | 60 | 70 | 80 | 90 | 100 | 110 | 120 | 130 | 140 | 150 | 160 | 170 | 180 | 280 |

PLATE 12 Age of the Earth's Seafloor While the Earth is over 4.5 billion years old, the ocean floor is almost everywhere less than 180 million years old, and it is youngest near the underwater mountains of the mid-oceanic ridges. New seafloor is constantly produced at the mid-oceanic ridges and moves away from the ridges, explaining why the youngest seafloor is found close to the ridges and the oldest is found close to plate boundaries, where it subducts. See the discussion under "Plate Tectonics" in chapter 3.

Source: Based on https://en.wikipedia.org/wiki/Seafloor_spreading#/media/File:Age_of_oceanic_lithosphere.jpg

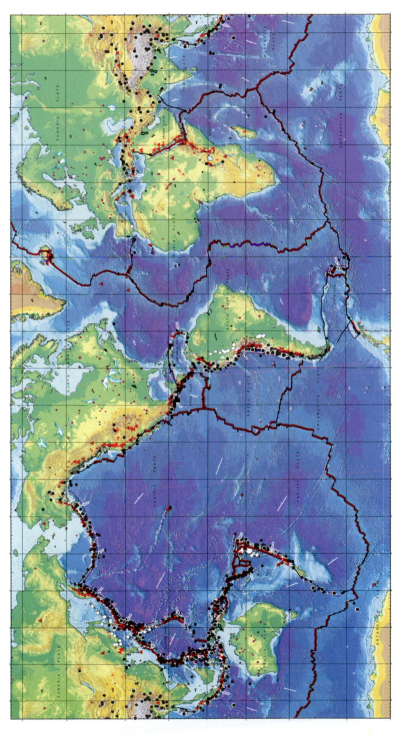

PLATE 13 Earthquakes, Volcanoes, and Plate Tectonics Part of what makes plate tectonics such a compelling and important theory for the Earth sciences is that it unifies different aspects of the Earth itself. It explains how mountains are built up through the collision of continents, as well as the jigsaw-puzzle fit of the continents. It also explains the planet's pattern of earthquakes and volcanic activity, which occur most frequently along plate boundaries, as shown here and discussed under "Plate Tectonics" in chapter 3.

Source: USGS

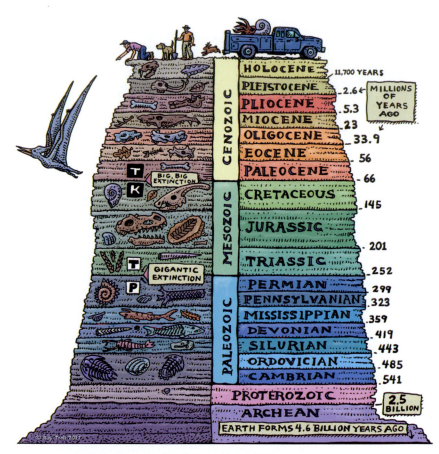

PLATE 14 Partial Geologic Time Scale, Illustrated The ancientness of the Earth is often called "deep time": it is deep both in the sense of deep in the past and also deep under the ground. The geologic time scale organizes the Earth's deep past into intervals known as (from longest to shortest) eons, eras, periods, epochs, and ages. Most of this image is devoted to the Phanerozoic eon (lasting from 541 million years ago to the present), when nearly all macroscopic fossils originated. The Phanerozoic is subdivided into the Paleozoic, Mesozoic, and Cenozoic eras. The subdivisions on the far right of this image include two different kinds of time scale: periods (Cambrian through Cretaceous) and epochs (Paleocene through Holocene). See the discussion under "Deep Time" in chapter 3.

Source: Ray Troll

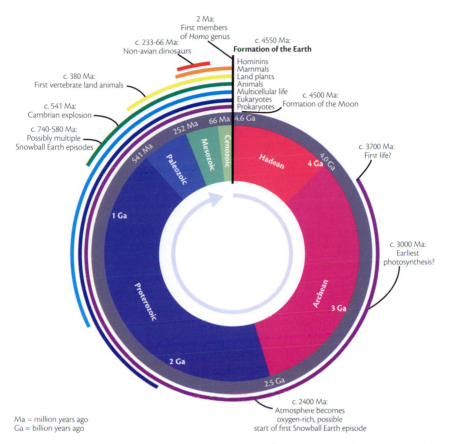

2 Ma:
First members
of *Homo* genus

c. 233–66 Ma:
Non-avian dinosaurs

c. 4550 Ma:
Formation of the Earth

Hominins
Mammals
Land plants
Animals
Multicellular life
Eukaryotes
Prokaryotes

c. 380 Ma:
First vertebrate land animals

c. 541 Ma:
Cambrian explosion

c. 740–580 Ma:
Possibly multiple
Snowball Earth episodes

c. 4500 Ma:
Formation of the Moon

c. 3700 Ma:
First life?

c. 3000 Ma:
Earliest
photosynthesis?

252 Ma   66 Ma   4.6 Ga

541 Ma   Hadean   4.0 Ga

Paleozoic   4 Ga

Mesozoic   Cenozoic

1 Ga

Proterozoic   Archean

3 Ga

2 Ga

2.5 Ga

c. 2400 Ma:
Atmosphere becomes
oxygen-rich, possible
start of first Snowball Earth episode

Ma = million years ago
Ga = billion years ago

PLATE 15 A Geological "Clock" In another way of representing geologic time, Earth's formation occurs at 12 o'clock, and time progresses clockwise until reaching the present. In the innermost circle, the Hadean, Archean, and Proterozoic eons are labeled, along with the Paleozoic, Mesozoic, and Cenozoic eras of the Phanerozoic eon. The outer rings label various important events in the history of the Earth, most of which are discussed further under "Deep Time" in chapter 3 and "Biosphere" in chapter 4.

Source: Based on https://en.wikipedia.org/wiki/Geological_history_of_Earth#/media/
File:Geologic_Clock_with_events_and_periods.svg

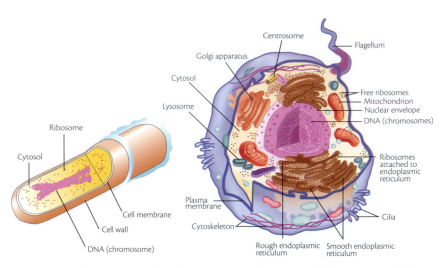

Centrosome

Flagellum

Golgi apparatus

Cytosol

Lysosome

Free ribosomes
Mitochondrion
Nuclear envelope
DNA (chromosomes)

Ribosome

Cytosol

Ribosomes
attached to
endoplasmic
reticulum

Plasma
membrane

Cilia

Cell membrane

Cytoskeleton

Cell wall

DNA (chromosome)

Rough endoplasmic   Smooth endoplasmic
reticulum   reticulum

PLATE 16 Comparison of Prokaryotic and Eukaryotic Cells (Not to Scale) There are two basic types of cells, prokaryotic and eukaryotic, comprising and underpinning all forms of life on Earth. Eukaryotic cells are usually much larger and have both a *nucleus* containing the cell's genetic material (DNA) and *organelles*, structures inside the cell that are enclosed by membranes and carry out various functions. Although the simpler prokaryotic cells, which seem to have existed on Earth for at least a billion years before eukaryotic cells appeared, lack a nucleus and organelles, they still have extraordinarily complex inner workings. See the discussion under "Life" in chapter 4.

Source: Based on http://web2.mendelu.cz/af_291_projekty2/vseo/files/191/13405.jpg

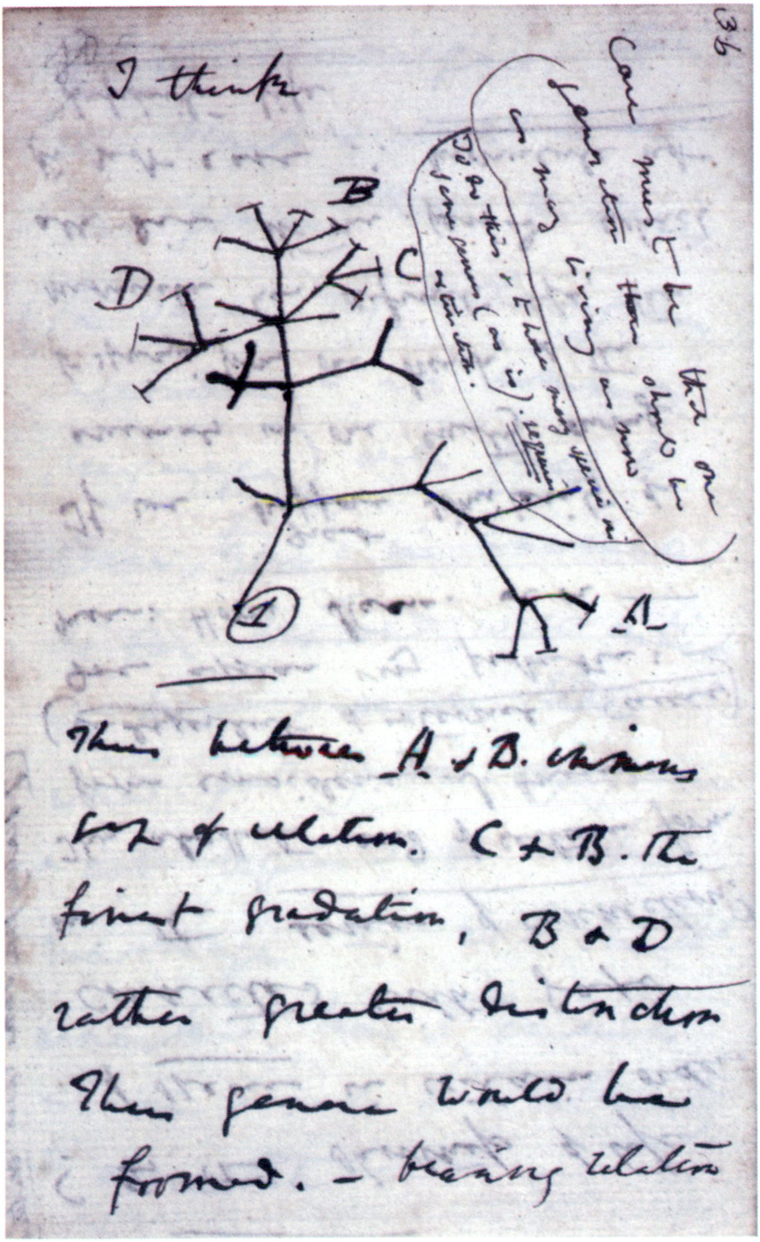

PLATES 17 and 18 Darwin's "Tree of Life," and "Tree of Life" with Updates From Charles Darwin's notebook sketch to a modern representation of the relationships among organisms, evolutionary biology indicates that life is one huge "family": all life is related, as far as we know, however distantly. The history of life can look very different, though, depending on how one chooses to tell the story. See the discussion under "Biosphere" in chapter 4.

Source (Plate 17): https://en.wikipedia.org/wiki/Tree_of_life_(biology)#/media/File:Darwin_Tree_1837.png.

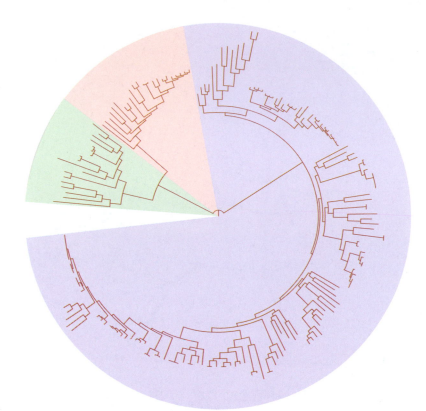

PLATE 18 Darwin's "Tree of Life" with updates.

Source (Plate 18): Based on image generated at https://itol.embl.de/itol.cgi.

PLATE 19 The "Lost City" The "Lost City," a small portion of which is shown here, is a deep-sea alkaline hydrothermal vent field, the sort of place that could have been a site where life originated over 3 billion years ago. As discussed under "Biochemistry" in chapter 4, the questions of how, where, and why life might have originated are closely interrelated and the subject of ongoing research and speculation. How far science can proceed in developing a compelling explanation of life's origin is an open question.
Source: NSF, NOAA, University of Washington. Image courtesy: National Science Foundation

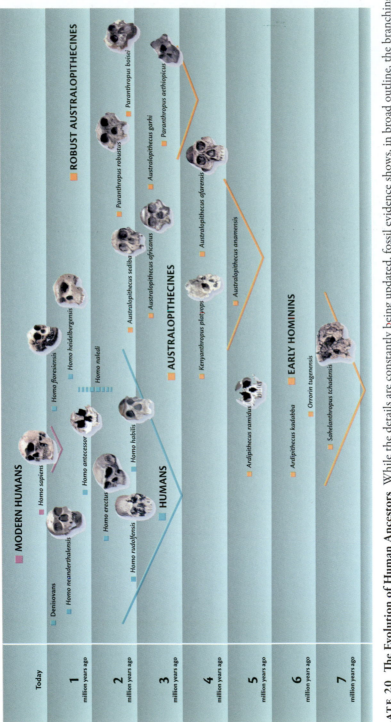

PLATE 20 The Evolution of Human Ancestors While the details are constantly being updated, fossil evidence shows, in broad outline, the branching pattern that gave rise to various human "ancestors" and "relatives." While evidence-based scientific research tells us much about the human past and evolution of the human body, the deeper questions of what it means to be human still loom as large as ever. See the discussion under "Humanity" in chapter 5.

Source: Natural History Museum

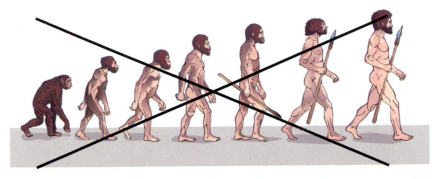

PLATE 21 **The "March of Progress": A Wrong Way to Think About Evolution** While
the "March of Progress" image is a staple of popular culture, imitated or parodied in a
great many settings, nearly everything about it is misleading or incorrect. In particular,
evolution is a story of branching and diversifying, not of linear progression. Perhaps even
more importantly, the idea that evolution means progress can become treacherous when
applied to human beings and human societies. See the discussions under "Humanity" and
"Culture" in chapter 5 as well as under "Evolution" in chapter 4.

Source: Usagi-P/Shutterstock

Human Migration

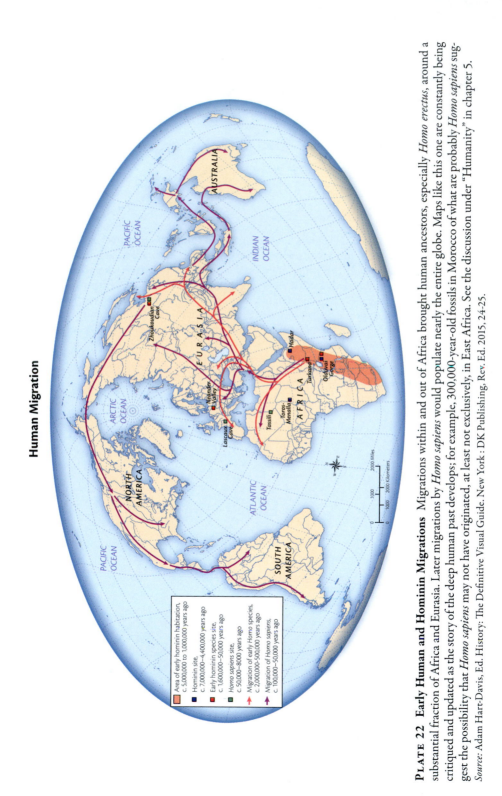

PLATE 22 **Early Human and Hominin Migrations** Migrations within and out of Africa brought human ancestors, especially *Homo erectus*, around a substantial fraction of Africa and Eurasia. Later migrations by *Homo sapiens* would populate nearly the entire globe. Maps like this one are constantly being critiqued and updated as the story of the deep human past develops; for example, 300,000-year-old fossils in Morocco of what are probably *Homo sapiens* suggest the possibility that *Homo sapiens* may not have originated, at least not exclusively, in East Africa. See the discussion under "Humanity" in chapter 5.
Source: Adam Hart-Davis, Ed. History: The Definitive Visual Guide. New York: DK Publishing, Rev. Ed. 2015, 24-25.

PLATE 23 Cave Art from Spain, Altamira The Cave of Altamira in Spain, in which this cave painting is found, includes art from over 30,000 years ago.

Source: Thomas Quine/Wikipedia

PLATE 24 Rock Art from South Africa Rock art in South Africa, like the panel depicted here, may be only a few thousand years old or less, but the nature of the symbolism that such art contains has provided scholars with insights that have been helpful in interpreting much older cave paintings elsewhere in the world.

Source: Iziko Museums of South Africa, Social History Collections and SARADA. Photo: Neil Rusch.

PLATE 25 Cave Art from France, Chauvet Cave Cave and rock art from the "Stone Age," tens of thousands of years ago, is not at all "primitive": Pablo Picasso is said to have commented that painters from this time left him little to accomplish (see Ian Tattersall, *Masters of the Planet*, p. xiv). These paintings are one of the many indicators of what anthropologists call "behavioral modernity": when members of the *Homo sapiens* species began to behave in ways that seem familiar to us now, and indicate cognitive traits and symbolic activity that are universal to all human groups alive today. Scholars debate when this shift happened, and whether the shift occurred gradually or suddenly. See the discussion under "Humanity" in chapter 5.

Source: Bradshaw Foundation

Present-day language families

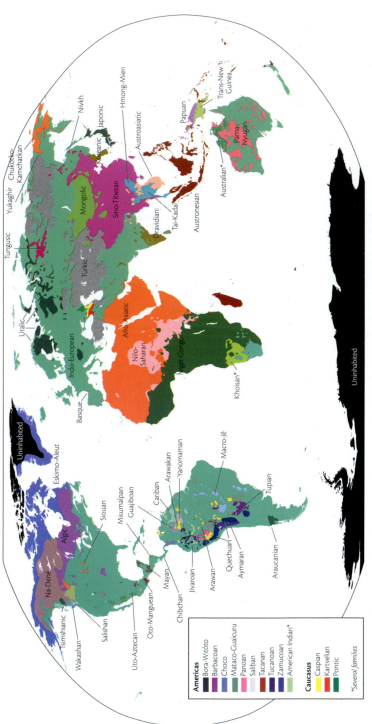

PLATE 26 Present-Day Language Families Languages change constantly. Although dictionaries and grammar lessons may make it seem as though there is such a thing as a "proper" way of speaking that is frozen in time, any given language changes so rapidly that it is functionally no longer the same language 1,000 years later. This constant change means it is almost impossible to trace the histories of languages back more than a few thousand years. It is also the basis of the conclusion that languages themselves are related to one another. A "language family" is a set of languages that all "descend" from one common ancestral language. This map represents the distribution of language families in the world today. See the discussion under "Language" in chapter 5.

Source: Alumnum/Wikipedia

cm

PLATE 27 Clovis Points The Paleolithic (Stone Age) was not a static, unchanging time during which all humans lived in caves and spent every day searching for food and trying to escape predators. Instead, it was a diverse and dynamic time, one of tremendous innovation and cultural diversity. The great continental migrations carried humans into totally new and highly varied environments, from dense equatorial jungles to the barren tundras of far northern latitudes and everything in between. These migrations were supported by—and produced—a variety of technological and artistic cultures. One example of a Paleolithic culture known to modern archaeology is the Clovis culture that featured distinctive fluted stone projectile points, widespread across much of the Americas about 13,000 years ago. See the discussion under "Context" in chapter 6.

Source: Billwhittaker at English Wikipedia

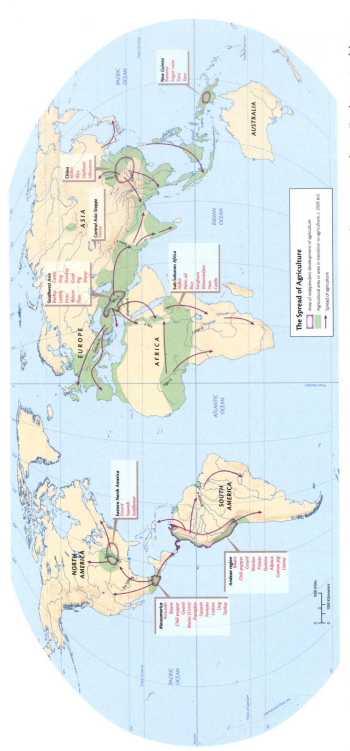

PLATE 28 **The Origins and Spread of Agriculture** Agriculture first appeared some 11,000 years ago, but most people on Earth remained hunter-gatherers for thousands of years after that. Agriculture emerged independently in several places around the world, and it spread from those places of origin, slowly—and not without reversals—only becoming the dominant way of acquiring food around the world perhaps 3,000 years ago. See the discussions under "Technology" in chapter 5 and "Context" in chapter 6.

Source: Adam Hart-Davis, Ed. *History: The Definitive Visual Guide.* (New York: DK Publishing, Rev. Ed. 2015), 36–37.

PLATE 29 Geographical Terms Used in World History, Part 1 Many of these terms are referenced at different points throughout the text of this book, especially in chapter 5 and after.

Source: Map from OUP database, labels added by artist

PLATE 30 Geographical Terms Used in World History, Part 2 Many of these terms are referenced at different points throughout the text of this book, especially in chapter 5 and after. Note the effect on one's perception of the relative importance and relationships of places when using different map-projection techniques to draw the Earth's surface on a flat page.

Source: Map from OUP database, labels added by artist

PLATE 31 **The Origins of Writing** Writing originated, as far as scholars are aware, a little over 5,000 years ago, in Sumer (southern Mesopotamia). Shown here, on a tablet describing a beer allocation, is an early form of cuneiform, the first-ever script used to write Sumerian. Cuneiform endured, with some modifications, for over 3,000 years, and it was used to write in many different languages. Historians commonly associate the origin of writing with the beginning of "history," as opposed to "prehistory," because written sources have traditionally been seen as indispensable to—or even the defining feature of—historical scholarship. But the divide between history and prehistory is arbitrary, and scholars can use many other sources to investigate the deep human past. See the discussions under "History" and "Context" in chapter 6.

Source: © The Trustees of the British Museum

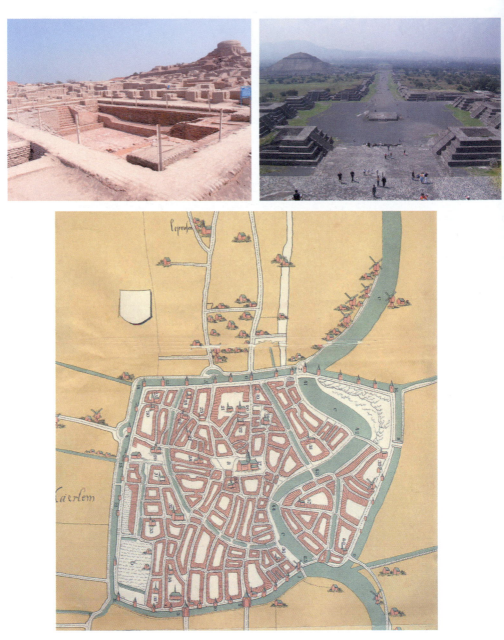

PLATE 32 Cities in the Pre-modern World (**a**) Mohenjo-daro was one of the first major cities on Earth, part of the Indus Valley civilization and settled by perhaps a few tens of thousands of residents at its peak. (**b**) Teotihuacan was a major city in the Valley of Mexico, with a peak population perhaps three times that which Mohenjo-daro had contained at its own peak some 2,000 years earlier. (**c**) Haarlem is a Dutch city that has been continuously inhabited since the European Middle Ages; this map shows it around 1550. These three cities exemplify both diversity and similarity in the urban settings of the pre-modern world. See the discussion under "Context" in chapter 6 and "Modernity" in chapter 7.

Sources: (a) Saqib Qayyum/Wikipedia

(b) & (c) Wikipedia

building blocks of proteins (amino acids), can be synthesized under conditions similar to those that existed on the early Earth. Miller and Urey passed an electric current through a mixture of gases that they thought simulated atmospheric conditions on the early Earth, and they found that amino acids formed spontaneously. In the years since this experiment, the mixture of gases they used has been shown to be inappropriate as a representation of what Earth's atmosphere was like at the time. But their proof of principle nevertheless remains, as amino acids turn out to be *more* easily synthesized than was expected in the 1950s: they appear to be present even in places like interstellar gas clouds, comets, meteorites, and interplanetary dust particles. The most basic building blocks of life seem to be relatively easy to synthesize under a wide range of conditions, even those that at first glance seem inhospitable, and regardless of the composition of the early Earth's atmosphere, organic molecules would have found their way to Earth's surface in large quantities through meteorites and dust particles striking the planet.

The other three "steps," however, have turned out to be much more resistant to conclusive scientific understanding. Explaining how these basic building blocks could combine into highly complex molecules like DNA is difficult, as is explaining the initial formation of cells and their mechanisms for self-replication.

Living things cannot live without input of energy, and an immense network of chemical reactions harvests energy for the cell. This network of reactions is what the word "metabolism" refers to at a cellular level. In other words, living things require both the *replication* of *information* stored in DNA and the *chemistry* and *energy* associated with metabolism, which requires a diverse array of proteins in today's organisms. So what came first, metabolism or reproduction? As James Trefil, Harold Morowitz, and Eric Smith point out:

> The essential problem is that in modern living systems, chemical reactions in cells are mediated by protein catalysts called enzymes. The information encoded in the nucleic acids DNA and RNA is required to make the proteins; yet the proteins are required to make the nucleic acids. Furthermore, both proteins and nucleic acids are large molecules consisting of strings of small component molecules whose synthesis is supervised by proteins and nucleic acids. We have two chickens, two eggs, and no answer to the old problem of which came first.[95]

For over 30 years, much attention has focused on the possibility that in the earliest precursors of life, the nucleic acid RNA substituted for both DNA and proteins, and played the roles of both. This "RNA world" is an appealing possibility,

---

95. James Trefil, Harold J. Morowitz, and Eric Smith, "The Origin of Life: A Case Is Made for the Descent of Electrons," https://www.jstor.org/stable/27859328?seq=1 .

because RNA is capable of both storing information like DNA does and catalyzing reactions[96] like proteins do. And even though they also include DNA and proteins, cells across the living world still use RNA (in interactions with DNA and proteins) for both purposes. RNA, in fact, plays the role of mediator between DNA and proteins: the process of translation, which produces proteins based on DNA-sequence templates, heavily involves RNA. Even cellular RNA that cell biologists previously thought was "junk RNA"—the term coined for bits of RNA that seemed to play no role in genetics and translation—turns out to be used by the cell for various purposes previously thought to be reserved only for proteins, including catalysis and gene regulation. If RNA did, in fact, play both genetic and catalytic roles in the earliest forms of life, this would help to explain why it plays such diverse roles in all cells now and why it functions as an intermediary between DNA and proteins.

So the RNA-world scenario has some compelling features, but the principal difficulties of this scenario are that RNA is (1) a very complex molecule that is essentially impossible to form without a detailed network of chemical reactions already in place to build it up from simpler precursor molecules and (2) not especially stable. As Ward and Kirschvink summarize: "In fact, it appears that there are many steps required in making RNA, and each step would require different conditions, or a different chemical environment."[97] So while it seems likely that early life did rely heavily on RNA, the RNA-world scenario does not necessarily clarify how that RNA formed in the first place; we have not really answered the question of how life formed, only, perhaps, pushed it back one step.

An alternative scenario proposes that the first precursors of life were not RNA or any nucleic acid, but rather a small handful of chemical reactions involving small organic molecules, which are still preserved as the core reactions common to all cellular metabolism on Earth. This "metabolism-first" scenario has the advantage of explaining why all cells rely on the same core set of reactions, and it also provides a foundation for explaining the formation of large nucleic-acid molecules: nucleic acids could plausibly emerge as a product of a progressively expanding network of early metabolic reactions. Although the metabolism-first approach is promising in certain regards, it remains unclear by what pathways such reaction networks might have emerged, or precisely why, and how, exactly, they came to support the basic processes of intergenerational inheritance and Darwinian evolution.

Where?

Another important question, which may shed light on the *how*, relates to *where* life might have originated. Darwin's proposed answer, which he put in a letter to the

---

96. That is, speeding reactions up so that they actually happen, rather than being so slow that they effectively do not happen at all.

97. Ward and Kirschvink, *A New History of Life*, p. 55.

botanist Joseph Hooker, was "some warm little pond"[98] with the right mixture of chemicals present and energy from the Sun or lightning providing the "spark" to make them combine. Darwin knew full well that this was speculation, without any empirical evidence, and neither he nor any other scientist of his time understood anything like the full biochemical and molecular complexity of living cells. Even so, the idea of life emerging spontaneously from a "primordial soup" on the surface of the Earth has greatly influenced the imaginations of generations of biologists, as well as the broader public.

With what they know now about the early Earth,[99] cellular biochemistry, and the wide gulf in molecular complexity that separates even the simplest living organisms from non-life, scientists today recognize what a tremendous challenge it is to form a convincing, detailed account of how a chemical-rich pond warmed by the Sun could produce the first living things. Considerable effort goes into simulating, in laboratory settings, the conditions of such a site, and examining details of how its chemistry might have played out. The formation of life would require a site where the "raw materials" of life (especially small organic molecules) could accumulate, with energy to "feed" the chemical reactions, along with a certain amount of compartmentalization—if not an actual protocell, then at least the pores of a rock or mineral surface that could protect the stability of the reaction networks and concentrate the raw materials and the reaction products in one place. Many recent ideas about the origins of life have focused on various mineral surfaces that could provide templates or compartments for the formation of life.[100]

In addition to shallow ponds, deep-sea alkaline hydrothermal vents (see Plate 19) have emerged more recently as plausible sites for the formation of life, because they possess all the attributes outlined in the previous paragraph. These vents, which are fissures in the ocean floor that release a constant stream of superheated water (sometimes over 400 degrees Celsius, but it does not boil because of the extreme pressure), are rich in chemicals and geothermal energy, and the rocks around them tend to have a porous structure and contain minerals that help to facilitate a variety of chemical reactions. Moreover, they sustain full ecosystems

---

98. Charles Darwin, letter to Joseph Hooker, February 1, 1871, http://www.darwinproject. ac.uk/DCP-LETT-7471 .

99. E.g., for at least part of the Hadean eon, there was relatively little solid land area, the ocean was hot and (to today's organisms) toxic, a great deal of volcanic activity occurred, and the Earth was periodically bombarded by asteroids and comets. In addition, the ocean may have been routinely vaporized, in whole or in part, and then restored by millennia-long rainfalls thousands of years later. For life to come into being at Earth's surface, the most extreme environments of the Hadean would likely need to have passed away. Life may conceivably have come into existence earlier in a place insulated from the asteroid and comet bombardment, like the deep ocean or within the crust.

100. For a discussion, see Ward and Kirschvink, *A New History of Life*, p. 53.

today in the otherwise cold and dark depths along the ocean floor, including mi-crobes that thrive in an extremely hot and sulfur-rich environment and that may be similar to the first prokaryotes.

While deep-sea vents are now considered a leading possibility for the site of life's origin, the RNA-world scenario likely is incompatible with it, because the RNA molecule is stable only at much lower temperatures than those found near these vents. Still, the existence of deep-sea vents[101] is a reminder that the origin of life not only may have tolerated, but actually may have required, what seem like extreme conditions to us.

Whether or not deep-sea vents are, in fact, the site of life's origins, the discovery of these vents has expanded the scientific imagination for the possible *where* of life's origins. Another direction where we might expand our speculation is out into the rest of the Solar System: the *panspermia* hypothesis proposes that life on Earth did not originate here, but instead began on another planet or body—the leading candidate being Mars—and was delivered to Earth via comet or asteroid. Unfortunately, this does not really help to explain *how* life formed; it only expands the possibilities for *where*. Interestingly, "warm little ponds" and deep-sea vents may be possible sites for the formation of life even on other bodies in the Solar System. It appears there may have been both ponds and vents on Mars when that planet had liquid water in its deep past, and planetary scientists expect that vents should be relatively common when liquid water is in sustained contact with underlying rock, as in subsurface oceans like those on Jupiter's moon Europa and Saturn's moon Enceladus.[102]

Why?

Was the origin of life inevitable, or was it an improbable fluke? The answer depends not only on what you consider the most likely *how* and *where*, but also on how you approach the question of *why* life formed. Did the formation of life depend on processes that unfold naturally under the right conditions, or did it depend on a single, unexpected but pivotal event that occurred by random chance or divine intervention?

That the origin of life is often spoken of in terms of probabilities is, in part, a relic of early speculation about the primordial-soup hypothesis. Aleksandr Oparin and J. B. S. Haldane, who conjectured in the 1920s that chemical processes on the early Earth might have filled the oceans with organic molecules, suggested that in this "prebiotic soup" (Haldane's term), molecules would have plenty of opportunity to come together *by chance* to produce a self-replicating system. Once self-replicating systems existed, some of them would presumably be more stable in their

---

101. Only discovered in 1976–1977, a few years after a human being first walked on the Moon!

102. See, e.g., Rachel Brazil, "Hydrothermal Vents and the Origins of Life," https://www.chemistryworld.com/features/hydrothermal-vents-and-the-origins-of-life/3007088.article .

environment, better able to "survive and reproduce," at which point the known mechanisms of evolution by natural selection could "take over" in explaining the continued development of life.[103]

With updated knowledge of cellular biology, biochemistry, and molecular biology today, it is possible to evaluate this scenario in greater detail. Oparin and Haldane constructed their hypothesis long before scientists were aware of the intricacies of self-replicating molecules like RNA and DNA, but it now seems relatively clear that RNA and DNA are much too complex to form by chance—even given an entire ocean, perhaps an entire universe of oceans, full of organic molecules.

What may be necessary is to frame the question of life's origin in terms of step-by-step, incremental processes rather than in terms of a single leap. While it might seem that a wide gulf now exists between life and non-life, perhaps there are many intermediate states between living and non-living, making the gulf incrementally bridgeable. If so, then perhaps the *why* is fully explicable in terms of the ordinary laws of physics and chemistry, operating under the right conditions. As Trefil, Morowitz, and Smith point out, when trying to understand the origin of highways in the United States, we do not ask whether it was roads or cars that came about first, or suspect that the whole transportation infrastructure came about at one time, but instead consider how trails, paths, and roads "co-evolved" with modes of transport.[104]

But in that case, what are the "right conditions"? Even if it is possible for life to self-assemble spontaneously through natural processes, questions of probability and chance still reappear. Did the conditions that would allow for this self-assembly require an extraordinary combination of circumstances, so that we might expect even microbial life to be rare or unique in the universe? Or do natural processes operating in conditions that prevail on or below the surface of many Earth-like planets and moons throughout the universe lead to the self-assembly of the earliest cells, so that we can expect at least comparatively simple and microscopic forms of life to be common to practically every rocky body in the universe with liquid water? (These are questions that fall squarely in the domain of astrobiology, an interdisciplinary field that addresses the possibilities for life in the universe and what life might look like more broadly if Earth life is but one case out of many.)

The right answer to these questions, and even the right way to approach the questions in the first place, remain unclear. Part of the reason is that the molecular and biochemical complexity of cells makes their origin an extraordinarily difficult research question in theoretical and applied chemistry. But it is also difficult because of the

---

103. The modern evolutionary synthesis, which Haldane did a great deal of work to develop, helps to explain why evolution gets invoked to explain not just the history of life but also the origins of life itself. Mechanisms of "molecular selection" or "chemical selection" (David Christian's term) are extrapolations, but they can be powerful ones.

104. Trefil, Morowitz, and Smith, "The Origin of Life," pp. 208–209.

character of the available evidence. Paleontologists who work with, for example, dinosaur fossils have the advantage of working with direct physical evidence, a remnant of past conditions that carries an imprint of those past conditions. It would be extremely helpful to scientists who work on the origin of life to have similarly direct evidence of the molecular precursors of life. Rocks often do preserve specific indications of the chemical environment in which they formed, and the molecular precursors of life may have left signatures of their presence in Earth's rock record. But at least for the time being, scientists have not been able to identify any such signatures definitively and unambiguously. Rocks older than about 3.4 billion years sometimes contain organic material that might be a product of life, of life's precursors, or of processes unrelated to life; there is as yet no way to conclusively distinguish among these possibilities.[105]

Where does this leave us in our overall assessment of life's origins? It seems that scientific speculation about life's origins does solidify over time into something more informed and, perhaps, accurate, thus producing better-informed and more sharply reasoned plausibility arguments. But we are generally still dealing with plausibility arguments rather than with evidence, and problems and questions still surround every proposed scenario.

Ongoing research into the origin of life attempts to understand the "rules" of organic chemistry in a wide variety of geophysical environments, to experimentally model the geochemistry of these environments, and to illuminate how the network of basic metabolic reactions common to all life may have been built up over time through a series of intermediate steps.[106] Perhaps a future experiment, informed by these considerations, will actually succeed in placing non-living components in a test tube and producing either a living cell or a simpler, but self-sustaining, precursor. But it is worth pointing out just how speculative such a scenario is, at least for now. And even if a cell were to self-assemble in a test tube one day, we still would not have demonstrated conclusively that this is how life *did* form on Earth, only that it *could* have formed by such a pathway. We would have a convincing model and a (very) plausible scenario, but quite possibly still no direct evidence in analogy to a fossil. We would have a general process, not an airtight knowledge of the particular circumstances that prevailed when life first came into being on Earth.

Why does this lack of direct evidence matter? In chapter 2, we argued that different aspects of the universe's early history stand on very different evidential footing

---

105. See, e.g., E. A. Bell, P. Boehnke, T. M. Harrison, and W. L. Mao, "Potentially Biogenic Carbon Preserved in a 4.1-Billion-Year-Old Zircon," *Proceedings of the National Academy of Sciences* 112, no. 47 (2015): 14518–14521; or C.P. Marshall, G. D. Love, C. E. Snape, A. C. Hill, A. C. Allwood, M. R. Walter, et al., "Structural Characterization of Kerogen in 3.4 Ga Archaean Cherts from the Pilbara Craton, Western Australia," *Precambrian Research* 155, no. 1–2 (2007):1–23. We are grateful to Mark Ditzler for these references.

106. See Trefil, Morowitz, and Smith, "The Origin of Life," p. 213.

and, as such, should be treated with different levels of confidence. The origin of life seems similar in this regard: we have the tools of inference and extrapolation, but as yet no uncontroversial, direct observation or direct relics from the past.

Moreover, in the previous discussion, we postulated that although a great many details remain unclear, natural causes can be invoked to explain how life formed from non-living components. This remains a common assumption[107] within the biological community—that life can form spontaneously through natural processes that are known to present, or that will be known to future, science. But even this basic premise has not been rigorously demonstrated to be true, either by empirical observation or by theoretical deduction. The absence of a compelling naturalistic explanation is often taken by advocates of "intelligent design" as a sign of divine intervention, and even the atheist philosopher Thomas Nagel argues that the improbability of life forming by chance indicates that the fundamental assumptions of naturalism are likely wrong.[108]

On the other hand, if scientists do find a convincing naturalistic explanation, would that disprove divine involvement? A common argument among secular thinkers is that explaining the origin of life naturalistically would render God unnecessary, superfluous: If natural causes explain even something as complicated and fundamental as the origin of life, what room is left for God to be actively working in the world?

Religious thinkers, meanwhile, ask: Where did those natural causes come from in the first place? And why are the "laws" and causes within the natural world "set up" in such a way that the spectacular complexity of life could emerge as a seamless outcome of basic causes? A purely naturalistic explanation for life's origin leaves such questions unexplained. In the 13th century, Thomas Aquinas argued that a seamlessly integrated natural order, which does not require constant miraculous divine intervention in order to bring forth life, is a greater testament to God's "governance" of the world than an incomplete natural order that requires arbitrary interventions. That is, Aquinas argued that the power of natural causes is a reflection of the power of God—that God is like a shipwright who, instead of building a ship directly, grants to the timbers the (rather more impressive) ability to build themselves into a ship.[109] Siding with Aquinas, the Orthodox Christian writer David Bentley Hart argues that a natural order requiring arbitrary divine intervention to bring forth life "might well suggest some *deficiency* in the fabric of creation. It might suggest that the universe was the work of a very powerful, but also somewhat

---

107. Or perhaps a postulate, or an informed speculation, or an extrapolation.

108. See Thomas Nagel, *Mind and Cosmos: Why the Materialist Neo-Darwinian Conception of Nature Is Almost Certainly False.*

109. "It is as if the shipbuilder were able to give to timbers that by which they would move themselves to take the form of a ship." (Thomas Aquinas, *Commentary on Aristotle's Physics (Sententia super Physicam),* II.xiv.268.)

limited, designer. It certainly would not show that the universe is the creature of an omnipotent wisdom, or an immediate manifestation of the God who is the being of all things."[110]

Unexpected though it may be, both many atheistic thinkers and many religious thinkers rooted in classical monotheistic philosophy expect that the life / non-life gap can likely be bridged incrementally, using the basic laws of physics and chemistry. If scientific work ultimately shows that natural causes are sufficient to explain the origin of life, both "sides" of this debate may see their interpretive expectations as having been confirmed.

Life's History—A Biochemical Story?

Typically, in scientific universal histories, the beginning of life is a biochemical story, but most of the rest is told as a story of organisms. This is a subtle shift of focus in both scale and discipline, albeit an understandable one—given that the beginnings of life require basic chemical patterns to emerge, and organisms build upon that. However, one might ask: What if, instead of changing the focus from biochemistry to organisms, we continued to narrate the history of life from the standpoint of atoms and molecules? We do not attempt this approach in detail here, but merely outline what it might look like.

The story would lean heavily on the field of molecular evolution, the biological subfield that studies changes over time in the molecular constituents of life, including DNA, RNA, and proteins. Molecular evolution helps to illuminate how new alleles and entire new genes have come into being, how amino-acid sequences in proteins have changed over time to produce proteins with new structures and functions, and how other changes at the molecular level have correlated with evolutionary changes in life's history. For instance, the previous section outlined how life's major metabolic pathways might have formed in the first place, but these pathways did not stop developing after life formed. An entire history of metabolism could be told.

A history of metabolic pathways might emphasize living things' attempts to harness available elements. The proportions of different elements represented in a cell are quite similar to the proportions of those same elements in the ocean, suggesting that life formed out of the elements that were available at the time of its formation. But living things have higher concentrations of carbon, nitrogen (prominent especially in amino acids), phosphorus, and iron, among a few other elements. Iron is a particularly good example of the challenges that living things face in acquiring specific elements from their environments: humans and many other present-day organisms need far more iron to survive than is available, proportionately, in today's

---

110. David Bentley Hart, *The Experience of God: Being, Consciousness, Bliss*, p. 39; italics added.

oceans. It thus seems likely that the common ancestor of all present-day life lived in, and was adapted to, an ocean with far more iron in it than today's ocean; once most of the iron precipitated out in the form of iron oxide, organisms still required iron but had to find new ways of acquiring it. Just as organisms fill ecological niches, there are chemical niches to which organisms adapt, and the story of adaptation plays out at a molecular level just as much as it does at a more macro-level.

What Is Life?

The word "biochemistry" should itself be enough to make one pause and return to the question of what life *is*. It implies that one approach to studying life ("bio") is to study chemistry, bringing the domain of atoms and molecules and chemical reactions together with the domain of living things. The word itself encapsulates a crucial, but now easily overlooked, intellectual innovation. The idea that the same chemicals and principles apply to both the living and the non-living world came as a profound surprise in the 1820s, when the chemist Friedrich Wöhler synthesized urea, a compound previously thought to be produced only by living things, from non-biological precursors. Wöhler's synthesis of urea stands as the first demonstration that life and non-life are made of the same "stuff," just as physicists and astronomers have shown that the heavens and the Earth are made of the same stuff.

Physicists, always eager to conquer new domains, have tried to take this insight even further, by considering the workings of living organisms in terms of basic physics, as the 20th-century physicist Erwin Schrödinger did in his 1944 book, appropriately titled *What Is Life?*[111] And in a statement that brings us back to our discussions of reductionism and scale, another physicist, Eric Chaisson, writes: "When examined closely, living systems do not differ basically from the non-living."[112]

The key word here, however, is "closely." It is true that the components of living systems—especially at the atomic and subatomic scales—do not differ from the components of non-living systems: the same elements compose both, often in similar proportions.[113] But at larger scales, living and non-living systems differ a great deal, which also means that the context and function of molecular-level activity differ greatly. The letters in this book do not differ from those used in the Dr. Seuss classic *The Cat in the Hat*, for example, yet that does not mean that the books have similar content or meanings.

---

111. Biologists themselves do not typically devote much attention to the question of what life is, apart from the occasional public article (often about viruses or extraterrestrial life) and the first several pages of an introductory textbook. The question comes up at intersections of fields, like biophysics, astrobiology, and geobiology—in other words, the intersections with biology of fields we have met in previous chapters.

112. Eric Chaisson, *Epic of Evolution*, p. 284.

113. With a few exceptions, carbon being the most prominent example of an element more common in living than in non-living systems.

Life as we know it clearly *requires* a set of highly organized chemical reactions, but only if we focus exclusively on the molecular scale could we be tempted to state that life is *nothing but* a set of organized chemical reactions. No, there is more to life than that—important and illuminating as the domains studied by molecular biology, biochemistry, and cellular biology are. Even the molecule DNA records the history of *organisms*, in that the DNA received by a new organism has been affected by billions of years of natural selection operating on organisms in their environments. An understanding of life always requires an understanding of the interplay and feedback among scales in space and time, as well as among levels of biological organization.

So definitions of life that rely exclusively on the molecular and biochemical levels begin to appear reductive.[114] It seems that the level of the organism—what it is, what it does, what it can become—is an especially important aspect to empha-size, and in some ways, the organism explains the underlying biochemistry more than the biochemistry explains the organism. Organisms behave with a certain unity or autonomy.[115] We, as humans, are an example: we have a unified experience and way of responding to the world, despite the fact that the physiological and biochemical processes within our bodies occur at different rates.[116] Although the biochemical mechanisms of life are important, a given protein usually exists for only about two days; "it is the constant reproduction and renewal of the life form that defines life itself."[117] Immanuel Kant pointed out that machines can be disas-sembled and put back together again, but organisms, when disassembled, die.[118] And if organisms were then put back together again in exactly the same configura-tion, it seems that they would not be "the same." Moreover, the molecular and bio-chemical components of a living being assemble in the precise way they do because of a larger context, which is the organism. Understanding life in a purely reductive and mechanistic mode risks missing the whole nature of living things.[119]

---

114. One popular approach, inspired by Carl Sagan and proposed by a NASA committee in 1994, defines "life" as "a self-sustaining chemical system capable of Darwinian evolution" (see, e.g., https://astrobiology.nasa.gov/research/life-detection/about/). Note how the level of the organism is implicitly included in the definition via the reference to Darwinian evolution, which operates at a higher level than the molecular and biochemical while still having conse-quences for the operations of living things at these levels.

115. Ward and Kirschvink, *A New History of Life*, p. 34. The ancient and medieval idea of a "sensitive soul" was designed to account for this very aspect of life, its unity and "vital prin-ciple"; see "Mind" in chapter 5.

116. See "Time" in chapter 8.

117. Ward and Kirschvink, *A New History of Life*, p. 34.

118. Bellah, *Religion in Human Evolution*, p. 114.

119. Likewise, it is much different to say that the Earth acts *like* a living organism than to say that the Earth itself *is alive*.

The kinesin protein stepping along a microtubule that we met at the beginning of this chapter may not look much different than the molecular activity of a given non-living system when looked at in isolation. But the *context* of that protein's stepping motion makes all the difference.

Science

What does it mean to say that an idea, perspective, or approach to knowledge is "scientific"? Alternatively, what does it mean to say that an idea is "not scientific" or is "unscientific"?

We have argued in this book that not all knowledge is scientific knowledge. The project of interpreting the deeper meaning of scientific conclusions reaches well beyond the domain of science itself, and other disciplines complement, critique, and contextualize scientific work in the scope of human knowledge. The fact that the interpretation of science, as well as the subject matters of other disciplines, are not themselves scientific does not make them invalid or lacking in rigor: it only means that they are not science, and that is as it should be.

This approach stands in contrast to a perspective often called "scientism" (a word with negative connotations) or "positivism" (a word with different connotations in different communities). Positivists argue that all reliable knowledge stems from empirical observation. A little more loosely, scientism (or positivism) can be defined as the view that the observation, experimentation, and reasoning associated with science provide the only reliable path to truth. Almost no one would label their own views as "scientistic," the adjective form of the word "scientism," because the word itself has negative connotations. But scientism still informs a great deal of popular writing about science, and it affects how universal histories treat the relative merits of scientific, historical, religious, and philosophical ideas.

Scientism may take subtle forms. When one sees the claim that it is impossible to know something because it lies outside of science, we are usually dealing with some form of scientism. (A common example: "It's impossible to know why there is something rather than nothing.") Another example is that the "social sciences" of psychology, sociology, political science, and economics are often defended by practitioners as being "real sciences too," a claim that implicitly appeals to the idea that it is better to be a science than a non-science. Even the term "social sciences" invokes the sense that "real" knowledge ought to "look like" the natural sciences. Scientism also manifests in how the humanities are sometimes seen as less valuable, or less capable of generating genuine knowledge, than the sciences. (Jared Diamond, who is critical of how historians write about history: "At best, history is classified among the social sciences, of which it rates as the least scientific."[120])

And yet scientific disciplines do not operate in a vacuum; they exist within philosophical, historical, and social contexts. The very question of what science is, and

---

120. Jared Diamond, *Guns, Germs, and Steel*, p. 420.

what makes scientific knowledge reliable or trustworthy, is to a large extent a philo-sophical question. Like philosophy, both history and sociology can also shed light on what science is and what scientists do. There are, for example, historical reasons why science so often appears to be generating "objective," impersonal knowledge when in fact it is always *people* who produce scientific knowledge—as we will discuss later.

In short, science is not the sum total or the only criterion of all knowledge, but rather fits into a broader whole: a historical, social, philosophical, and interpretive framework. Science does not become less powerful or less illuminating when placed in this context and when its limits are recognized—quite the opposite, in fact. It is worth spending some time examining the implications of this point, reflecting back on chapters 2 through 4 as we transition from primarily discussing the sciences in our exploration of universal histories to primarily addressing the humanities.

Science Is Philosophical

Philosophy incorporates many subfields, including metaphysics and ontology, epistemology, and ethics: the study of what reality is, what knowledge is, and how we ought to act, respectively. Applied to science, philosophy poses questions about the relationship between scientific knowledge and reality, the nature of the "scientific method," and the values and ethical standards that ought to guide and govern science—none of which are themselves scientific questions, strictly speaking, though they inform the practice of science at every level.

The philosopher Ronald Giere points out that a great deal of scientific knowledge consists of models that *represent* the reality of the physical universe in the same way that a map represents the reality of a particular place. Just as the map is a representation rather than the thing itself that is being represented, so too scientific concepts like "electrons," and even great unifying theories like plate tectonics or evolution by natural selection, are representations. And just as some maps are better than others, some models are better than others, in that they more closely correspond to what they represent.

How does one determine whether one model is better or worse than another? For example, how would we determine whether a model of the universe that in-cluded dark matter was better than one that did not? Each model generates predic-tions, which can be compared to observations of the real world. If the predictions of the model match the observations of the world (in this case, telescopic observa-tions of distant galaxies), so much the better for the model. As Giere "maps" it:

$$
\begin{array}{ccc}
\text{Real World} & \leftrightarrow & \text{Model} \\
\downarrow & & \downarrow \\
\text{Observations} & \leftrightarrow & \text{Predictions}^{[121]}
\end{array}
$$

---

121. Ronald N. Giere, *Understanding Scientific Reasoning*, p. 32.

We have seen this kind of reasoning at work many times in this book. Galileo argued for the heliocentric model of the Solar System on the basis of its predictions being somewhat more in accord with actual observations than were the predictions of the geocentric model. Einstein's theory of gravity, general relativity, replaced Newton's gravitational theory on the basis of a better match between observations and theoretical predictions. In chapter 2 ("Gravity"), we saw that cosmological research often involves creating computer-simulation models of the universe and comparing the predictions of those models with observations, as in our dark-matter example. Similarly, a multitude of observations in geology and biology *make sense* in light of the ideas of plate tectonics and evolution by natural selection, which adds to the credibility of these theories; that is, they are considered very good scientific models precisely because they explain so many observations in a unified way. While even these models will surely be adjusted and (ideally) improved in the future, fitting a wider range of observations even better than they do now, any model that hoped to outright *replace* one of them would have to explain all the same observations they do, and others as well.

Are models "true," or are they just "useful" in the same way that a map may be useful? Some critics have been especially harsh in attributing to modern science very little ability to illuminate truth and reality. The modern Islamic philosopher Seyyed Hossein Nasr writes that science's "prestige emanates not from the illumination that it provides of the nature of reality, but from the fact that it leads to the acquiring of wealth and power over nature, as claimed by one of its founders, Francis Bacon."[122] Indeed, the Nobel laureate Frank Wilczek points out that physicists consider the "fertility"[123] of a scientific idea to be the test of its value, with "truth" being "highly desirable, but . . . not the only, or even the most important, criterion"[124] in judging a theory. And the astrophysicist Mario Livio writes similarly of a model's "predictive power."[125] As long as we think in terms of models, what we are getting at is not truth but representations of what is true, representations which are judged according to their usefulness in predicting the observations and experimental results we get.[126]

---

122. Seyyed Hossein Nasr, "Islam and Science," in *The Oxford Handbook of Religion and Science*, eds. Philip Clayton and Zachary Simpson, p. 75.

123. Frank Wilczek, *A Beautiful Question: Finding Nature's Deep Design*, p. 318.

124. Ibid.

125. Mario Livio, *Is God a Mathematician?*, p. 223.

126. It is interesting to think about the interpretation of quantum mechanics in this light. Light (or matter) is often said to be both wave and particle, but neither the wave "model" nor the particle "model" works in all situations—suggesting that light (or matter) at the smallest scales is something else entirely, something that behaves like a wave in some situations and like a particle in others.

Along related lines, the philosopher Karl Popper proposed that what marks an idea as truly "scientific" is that it is *falsifiable*—that is, capable of being shown, through observation and experiment, to be false. The work of scientists, then, is to propose ideas about how the natural world works, and then intentionally try to demonstrate their falsehood. The best that a scientific theory can hope for is not being "proven true," but rather being tested in many ways and not shown to be false.

In a somewhat similar spirit, the historian and philosopher of science Thomas Kuhn saw scientific paradigms as being *incommensurable* with one another. What does that mean? Kuhn argued that scientists in a given disciplinary community (like physics, or chemistry, or evolutionary biology) normally work under a "paradigm"—a framework of ideas about how the world works and what methods one ought to use in order to gain new scientific knowledge.[127] The modern evolutionary synthesis might be called a paradigm insofar as it not only provides knowledge about nature, but also helps to set a certain research agenda for furthering our knowledge of the biological world, helping to define what constitutes a legitimate research question to pursue. Under conditions of "normal science," essentially no one in the scientific mainstream questions the dominant paradigm, but if and when "anomalies" accumulate to the point where it seems the paradigm itself is flawed, then a paradigm shift may occur, in which a scientific disciplinary community completely alters the framework of what they think they know and how they do research. Kuhn's argument about the incommensurability (the lack of full comparability) of paradigms implies that a new paradigm is not necessarily "better" or "worse" than a previous paradigm; there is not necessarily progress in understanding, only change. Therefore, under a strict interpretation of Kuhn's ideas, one might be forced to say that the Big Bang, plate tectonics, the modern evolutionary synthesis, and even atomic theory or general relativity are no better than the scientific ideas that came before and that they replaced—in other words, they are just different.[128]

These trends in 20th-century philosophy (with deeper roots in the past) are only the tip of the iceberg among modern and postmodern critics of science who have sought to undermine the idea that scientific ideas are "true." And yet it seems that these critics not only go too far, but perhaps much too far: a careful and nuanced view of science does show that real scientific knowledge, at least in the sense of models that represent quite well a reality of how something works or what actually happened in the past, is possible. One theoretical framework can improve upon another in the sense of being empirically validated over a wider range of circumstances, better explaining existing data, or bringing conceptual clarity where before

---

127. This is not quite how he used the word originally, but it is how many have picked it up in practice.

128. For Kuhn's presentation of his basic system of thought, see Thomas Kuhn, *The Structure of Scientific Revolutions*.

there was confusion. And empirical observations can themselves become sharper, wider-ranging, and more detailed over time. Scientific models can also incorporate uncertainty, probability, relative confidence, and states of belief. Some ideas enjoy a very high degree of certainty. Others are merely speculative. And many are somewhere in between, which is usually where the active research happens. Science is not a binary "know / not know," but rather an approach to testing competing hypotheses, a way of arriving at reliable claims that exist on a spectrum of confidence.

Herein lies the balance we are trying to strike throughout this book: not denying the legitimacy of scientific (or historical) knowledge closely grounded in the research methods of physics, astronomy, Earth science, biology, or chemistry, but also performing a careful analysis of the relationship between scientific knowledge and grand claims about the nature and meaning of the universe, Earth, life, and humanity.

Side Note: How the Philosophy of Statistics Influences Cosmology

Philosophy is important not only to the interpretation of science, but also to the practice of science, sometimes in important ways. To give a concrete example, the question "What is probability?" may seem too abstract for even physicists to find it valuable, yet it turns out to be a very practical question in cosmology.

Cosmologists routinely generate computer-simulated "model universes," each of which has a given rate of expansion, amount of dark matter, amount of dark energy, and other fundamental parameters (quantities that define the model). Running these simulations, in turn, yields predictions about other aspects of the universe, such as how galaxies should be distributed in space, which can then be compared to observations in order to test the models.

The "initial conditions" given to a model—that is, what the universe looks like at the beginning of the simulation, corresponding to the beginning of the universe—cannot be fully and uniquely specified, however, because the randomizing effects of quantum mechanics are thought to have come into play in the earliest moments of the universe's history. Due to this randomness, a given set of parameters does not uniquely specify a single outcome, but rather corresponds to a range of possible "universes."

Dealing with the randomness inherent in the models is where the philosophy of probability comes into play. If you are a "frequentist" in your interpretation of probability, you take a given model, generate simulated data corresponding to that model a large number of times to get the range of possible universes corresponding to the model's parameters, and then compare the observations to the simulated data to see how often that observation occurs within the simulated data. You repeat this procedure for each model, and see which models produce simulated data similar to the actual observations. In contrast, if you are a "Bayesian" in your interpretation of probability, you begin with a probability distribution for which models you suspect are most likely, and through mathematical manipulation allow the data from the actual observations to modify that distribution—in some ways, the reverse of the frequentist approach.

For example, say you flip a coin 100 times and get 60 heads and 40 tails. Does this mean the coin is weighted, or is it a fair coin that just happened to come up heads more often by chance? Both the frequentist and the Bayesian will try to determine whether the "50/50 model" of the coin is an acceptable fit to the data. The frequentist will take the 50/50 model, simulate 100 coin flips many times over assuming this model, and see how rare it is for 60 heads to occur. The frequentist then rules out the "null hypothesis" that the coin is fair if this outcome is sufficiently rare. Meanwhile, the Bayesian might start with the assumption that all models (50/50, 51/49, 52/48, etc.) are equally likely, and through some clever mathematical manipulation use the data from the actual 100 flips to determine an updated likelihood for the different models. The Bayesian can then assess whether the 50/50 model is so unlikely that it can be effectively ruled out.

As the cosmology community has shifted to almost universally adopting a Bayesian approach—a change not in ideas about the physical universe, but rather about the meaning of probability—an entire research agenda has shifted too, including the questions that cosmologists ask about the universe, how they attempt to build and rule out models of the universe, and even what telescopes they attempt to build and what kinds of evidence they seek.

Ethical thinking about science provides another example of the need for a careful understanding of the relationship between scientific knowledge and its contexts. It is not difficult to find examples of people claiming that certain ethical stances—for example, those for or against embryonic stem cell research, or cloning, or certain kinds of artificial-intelligence research—are "scientific" or "unscientific," "for science" or "against science." But ethical questions about what research should be conducted and what should not, or how the results of scientific research should be used, are not scientific questions at all: they are questions of values. As the philosopher Charles Taylor has pointed out, values to guide science come from outside the "immanent frame" within which science views things.[129] Everyone agrees that a certain set of ethical principles and values ought to guide scientific research—without some set of guidelines, terrible abuses can and have occurred[130]—but they disagree about what those principles ought to be. Science does not provide direction

---

129. See Charles Taylor, *A Secular Age*, and Craig Calhoun, "This Philosopher Has Reimagined Identity and Morality for a Secular Age," https://www.huffingtonpost.com/entry/charles-taylor-philosopher_us_57fd00dde4b068ecb5e1c971 .

130. As in the Tuskegee study of the mid-1900s, when the United States Public Health Service not only left syphilis in African-American men untreated despite the fact that a treatment was available, but did not even inform the participants that they had the disease; or in Nazi Germany, where Josef Mengele and other doctors performed torturous and lethal forms of human experimentation.

or purpose even to itself. Science provides no reason to cure diseases or save lives; ethical and moral principles do that. Science cannot determine whether physical health and longer life expectancies are the highest goods, or even worthwhile goods, to pursue; philosophical reasoning must engage in that task.[131]

Science Is Social

Science is often said to be a way of gaining knowledge about the world that relies on reasoning, logic, and above all, empirical evidence, experimentation, and observation, and in which one need not appeal to authority: "take nobody's word for it," the motto of England's Royal Society commands.[132] Scientific knowledge appears to be impersonal. There are human beings called scientists who do the work to produce that seemingly impersonal knowledge, but (so the story goes) they are disinterested observers, skeptically designing experiments and other observations of the world that will put their ideas to the test and, perhaps, challenge much of what they thought they knew. And a rightly conducted observation can be replicated by any other observer, regardless of the observer's identity. So even if research yields an inaccurate conclusion, the scientific method is self-correcting. Nature may hide her secrets, but the impartial inquiry of the scientific method will eventually illuminate them.

There is some truth to all this. Some results that were landmark discoveries decades or centuries ago are now routinely replicated every day in college-level lab courses.[133] The ideas of the Big Bang, plate tectonics, and evolution are so central to cosmology, Earth science, and biology in part because they unify so many apparently unrelated observations; evidence from many different areas converges to verify the central tenets of these theories. And many scientists do make earnest efforts to disprove their own favored ideas, leaving those ideas much stronger and well-verified when they pass the test. And yet it would seem that science must also feature an elaborate system of establishing whom to trust, whose word is trustworthy, because no one, scientist or otherwise, can repeat even a significant fraction of the observations and experiments that have gone into building the edifice of modern scientific knowledge.

Consider this: The ideas of modern science are not exactly obvious to the casual observer. Scientists ask us to believe that the universe began over a hundred million human life spans ago in conditions where literally nothing that presently exists could be found in the same form that it is now. Add to this that gravitational fields affect the flow of time, that the continents beneath our feet move around, that

---

131. John Sexton, "A Reductionist History of Humankind," http://www.thenewatlantis.com/publications/a-reductionist-history-of-humankind .

132. See https://royalsociety.org/about-us/history/ .

133. Like Robert Millikan and Harvey Fletcher's oil-drop experiment to determine the charge of an electron, or Henry Cavendish's experiment to "weigh the Earth" (find its mass, or its density).

everything is composed of particles too small to be seen, that every living organism is related to every other living organism, and various other ideas that might strike someone who did not know better as not just wrong but laughable. In each case, specialists have assembled a vast array of evidence to support the claims involved. But most people would never even stop to consider this evidence if science and scientists had not achieved a cultural status in which they are seen as worthy of some amount of trust. As the physicist Anthony Rizzi writes:

> Consider what you actually know about the earth's motion. Do you feel as if the earth's surface is moving at 1,000 miles an hour due to its rotation? Do you feel like the earth is moving 67,000 miles an hour around the sun? Indeed, we still use language that indicates how strongly we do not sense any motion of the earth. Any of us might say: "It's getting dark, because *the sun is going down*." Even among those with an advanced scientific education, many have not considered on what grounds they believe and say these things. Hence, for most, the motion of the earth is more than a matter of faith; it is a matter of *unconscious* faith. That is, it is one thing to trust an expert's word, but it is another level of faith completely to not even be conscious of the fact that one is taking another's word.[134]

And the historian Steven Shapin argues that although people often think science has eliminated the need to rely on authority, in favor of direct experience, in practice we rely on authority all the time:

> What we know of comets, icebergs, and neutrinos irreducibly contains what we know of those people who speak for and about these things, just as what we know about the virtues of people is informed by their speech about things that exist in the world.[135]

It is not random whom one trusts. In practice, scientists themselves rely on trust in order to determine whose articles and books to take most seriously. They know their colleagues' reputations for doing good or poor work, and reputations are based at least in part on whose research is most rigorous, replicable, and insightful. But practitioners of science do not perform all observations themselves.[136] Even when knowledge has come to seem institutionalized, de-personalized, and remote, it always ultimately has a foundation in the immediate and personal—that is, basic interpersonal trust.

---

134. Anthony Rizzi, *The Science Before Science: A Guide to Thinking in the 21st Century*, p. 1.

135. Steven Shapin, *A Social History of Truth*, p. xxvi.

136. Shapin points out how this practice of relying on trust and authority while advancing a rhetoric of direct observation and direct experience took shape, with a focus on early modern England, in *A Social History of Truth*.

To Ponder: Crackpots

This section has explored how certain people and institutions come to be regarded as trustworthy because of their association with science. Meanwhile, other ideas that "sound scientific," at least at first, come to be regarded as "crackpot," illegitimate, and not even worth considering. The "crackpots" (or, especially in medical science, "quacks") who espouse these ideas are written off, often in dismissive tones. Consider this situation philosophically, historically, and socially, from as many angles as possible: What conditions, within scientific communities and among the broader public, produce the phenomenon of "crackpots"?

Science is irreducibly social. It is an interpersonal endeavor, practiced in certain institutional settings, communicated through journals, engaged with a broader public, making use of specific ways of speaking, and funded not through an abstract process of reasoning but by the will of the public or specific benefactors. Even the most solitary researchers work in and answer to communities, to whom certain ideas and research questions will resonate more strongly than others. And so the social contexts of scientific work, including the cultural narratives built up around science and drawn on in universal histories, help to determine which questions scientists view as even worth asking in the first place.

Science Has Limits

Science can be a reliable way of probing how the natural world works, as well as the history of the universe, Earth, and life—especially when phenomena can be measured, quantified, and investigated through empirical evidence. Scientific evidence often converges on a single set of evidentially justified conclusions—as it has with the Big Bang, plate tectonics, and evolution, to take three examples we have explored in this book. In these cases, the analysis and integration of scientific evidence produce strong, solid, coherent understandings of the phenomena in question. But the assumption that scientific knowledge is the only kind of knowledge tends to produce unnecessarily narrow visions of reality. Universal histories, drawing on many scientific disciplines as well as history and the humanities, are in a uniquely good position to recognize the *boundaries* and *limits* of science, and to illuminate the relationship that the natural sciences have with other disciplines.

In addition to the "practical" limits that all scientists acknowledge they face (constraints imposed by finite funding and time, inaccessibility of desired evidence, technical difficulty of the research itself, and so forth), there are also limitations of science "in principle." It could not be otherwise. As a cultural practice subject to historical and sociological analysis, and a way of knowing that fits within a broader philosophical framework rather than serving as the criterion of all knowledge, science has limits.

It explores pockets of the total "space" of possible knowledge, and it is especially successful at answering specific questions about mechanisms by which aspects of the natural world work. But science cannot be all-encompassing: empirical evidence unfolds only within the space of the questions one thinks to explore in the first place. Even positivism itself is a philosophical position—it is difficult to envision performing an experiment to verify that science is the only reliable way of knowing the world.[137]

Scientists have often found it useful to treat science as if it is both isolated from other disciplines and also an inherently superior way of knowing.[138] Speaking of the limits of science may seem like an attempt to undermine science itself, but it is not. The good news about science having limits is that it gives us a bigger world to explore. The careful integration of science into universal histories might help us return to a vision of science and related disciplines more closely corresponding to the medieval discipline of natural philosophy—that is, the part of the "love of wisdom" (what "philosophy" means, in its Greek roots) that deals with nature. As William Katerberg writes:

> Retrieving and rethinking older concepts such as "natural philosophy" and "natural history," which are broader in conception than notions of "science" from the nineteenth century, might help us to understand better both the diverse practices and metaphysical assumptions associated with science in the present and the science-like practices in the past.[139]

As the Nobel laureate physicist Polykarp Kusch has said, "Science cannot do a very large number of things, and to assume that science may find a technical solution to all problems is the road to disaster."[140] It must instead remain "one finger of the hand of humanity,"[141] as the Dalai Lama put it, and indeed, one finger on the hand of universal histories, which themselves put science to work in service of a larger *interpretive* context and goal.

---

137. Positivism is sometimes justified on the basis of a minimalistic philosophy, that "entities are not to be multiplied without necessity," a statement of what has come to be known as Occam's Razor (see chapter 2). But if minimalism or parsimony is to be preferred, why should that be? It is still at least partially a philosophical question. (And, appropriately, Occam refers to William of Ockham, a philosopher.)

138. And one that has roots at a definite moment in the past, usually identified as the "Scientific Revolution," an idea that has been much critiqued by historians but is used strategically by scientists to indicate an abrupt transition from flighty and unreliable ways of knowing to the rigor of science. (The word "scientist" was first used in the year 1833, but this does not mean that there were no people who engaged in recognizably scientific activity, or no real knowledge, before then—or before Galileo and Newton in the 1600s and 1700s, for that matter.)

139. William Katerberg, "Myth, Meaning, and Scientific Method in Big History," https://ibha.wildapricot.org/resources/Documents/Origins/Origins_V_12.pdf, p. 7 .

140. Quoted in Stanley L. Jaki, "The Limits of a Limitless Science," in *The Limits of a Limitless Science: And Other Essays*, p. 21.

141. Dalai Lama, *The Universe in a Single Atom: The Convergence of Science and Spirituality*, p. 11.

5

HUMANITY

While evidence-based scientific research tells us much about the human past, the deeper questions of what it means to be human loom as large as ever. In the five sections of this chapter, we explore various dimensions of these questions. In "Humanity," we consider scientific investigations of human ancestry and contemplate what they assume or imply about what it means to be human. In "Culture," we discuss culture as a unifying framework for anthropologists and what it means to think of humans as cultural animals. In "Technology," we examine human tool use and some of the stories that are told about its early history. In "Language," we ponder the origins of this uniquely human mode of communication. And in "Mind," we contemplate the philosophy of mind and how careful thinking about the relationship between mind and brain could inform universal-historical writing.

Humanity

In most forms of Buddhism, the traditional belief is that human life is an almost unimaginably precious opportunity. Traditional Buddhist cosmology holds that there are six realms where a being can be reborn: from highest to lowest, these are the realm of the gods, who are not immortal even though they live very long lives; the realm of the demigods, who like the gods possess supernormal powers; the realm of humans; the realm of animals; the realm of the hungry ghosts (*pretas*), who live long but miserable lives; and the realm of the hell-beings, who suffer excruciatingly. Although life spans in all except the human and animal realms are very long, death and rebirth come for every being, over and over, in a potentially endless cycle.

Endless, and also pointless: Buddhist traditions view this cycle of rebirth not as cause for joy but as a disaster for beings who remain trapped within it, suffering constantly—even when one is reborn as a god—and destined to spend most of their existence suffering horribly in various hells. Human life is so precious, in this view, because it represents the only good opportunity to escape the cycle of rebirth, through enlightenment: the lower realms contain such awful pain that no one could focus on pursuing enlightenment, while the higher realms contain too many pleasurable distractions. So being born as a human, especially a human who has access to the teachings of the Buddha and who can live a morally upright life, is the best rebirth possible. The Tibetan Buddhist teacher Patrul Rinpoche makes the point especially vividly:

> Imagine the whole cosmos of a billion universes as a vast ocean. Floating upon it is a yoke, a piece of wood with a hole in it. . . . This yoke . . . never stays in the same place even for an instant. Deep down in the depths of the ocean lives a blind turtle who rises up to the surface only once every hundred years. That the yoke and the turtle might meet is extremely unlikely. . . . Nevertheless, by sheer chance the turtle might still just slip its neck into the yoke. But it is even more difficult than that, the sutras say, to obtain a human existence with the freedoms and advantages.[1]

This vision of humanity places value on certain capabilities of human beings and assesses the value of human life according to a set of standards and priorities that make sense within a particular worldview.

The modern scientific enterprise may appear to operate quite differently. Biological anthropology, archaeology, and the universal histories that draw on them seem to build up a vision of human nature by studying human origins, examining the vestiges that humans and human ancestors left behind, rather than imposing a vision of human nature on the evidence from the outset. But science imposes a definition of humanity too: as we have put it before, behind all Science, there is Story. One cannot look for the origins of something without first identifying what that "something" is—in this case, what it means to be human. Scientific investigations of humanity's past will naturally focus on those aspects of humanity that are empirically observable in the evidential record of the past, like bipedalism or tool use, but these observable qualities—which constitute only one limited dimension of humanity—can become a de facto philosophical definition of what it means to be human. And so, just as in Buddhism, ideas and assumptions about human nature get mixed into science-based narratives of human development and human origins.

---

1. Patrul Rinpoche, *Words of My Perfect Teacher*, pp. 33–34. The original version of this analogy can be found in the Mahayana Mahaparinirvana Sutra.

This is a fundamental aspect of the study of human origins, and being explicit about it can help to produce a more responsible universal history, one that opens up deep questions about humanity.

Human Ancestry

How did human beings come to be the way they are today? This is a fundamental question that science-based universal histories address, drawing on the disciplines of archaeology and anthropology. Anthropology studies the full range of human diversity and analyzes people, culture, and institutions. It includes physical or biological anthropology, archaeology, linguistic anthropology, and cultural anthropology.[2] Within biological anthropology, paleoanthropologists study human evolution through the fossil record, and primatologists study living and fossilized non-human primates. Evidence used to address the question of human origins comes from the fossil record (the physical remains of past organisms), the archaeological record (the remains of artifacts they left behind), DNA evidence, and the study of other primates. What follows is a capsule summary of the typical story of human origins that universal histories tell, based on the work of several generations of anthropologists.[3]

Bipedalism (walking upright on two legs) was perhaps the first distinctly human trait to emerge among ancient primates. Six to seven million years ago, the lineage of chimpanzees and bonobos, humanity's closest living relatives genetically, diverged from the lineage that would lead to humans, and the line that would ultimately produce human beings included bipeds.[4]

Subtle skeletal changes associated with bipedalism are visible in the fossil record—in order to walk habitually on two legs rather than four, slight but distinct changes are necessary in the knees, pelvis, foot, lower back, and even skull. These skeletal changes provide evidence for *when* bipedalism evolved, but not necessarily *why*. Biological anthropologists have suggested many reasons why bipedalism may have evolved; many of these have to do either with the relatively high efficiency of this form of locomotion[5] or with the advantages conferred by freeing up the hands

2. See Kenneth J. Guest, *Cultural Anthropology: A Toolkit for a Global Age*, chapter 1.

3. Going back to Darwin, who laid the foundations for applying an evolutionary framework to human ancestry in *The Descent of Man*.

4. Note that this does not mean that humans evolved from chimpanzees; instead, chimps and humans evolved from a common ancestor that was different from both. The common ancestor of chimps, bonobos, and humans may have been bipedal—it is unclear whether the chimp and bonobo lines or the human line is the one that diverged from the ancestral condition.

5. Many quadrupeds are faster than humans, but humans can better endure moving over long distances.

to carry tools or food. Which of these reasons were actually operative at the time is difficult to assess, however, and is more a matter of making plausibility arguments than of relying on direct evidence.

In the fossil record of roughly 3 to 7 million years ago, only bipedalism and very subtle dental differences distinguish the first hominins (primates that are more closely related to modern humans than to any other organism alive today) from the evolutionary line that would lead to chimps. Brain size had not increased when bipedalism emerged, nor would it for another few million years after the emergence of habitual bipedalism. The cranial capacity of human ancestors 6 to 7 million years ago was roughly 300 to 400 cubic centimeters, giving them space inside their skulls for brains roughly one-quarter the size of present-day human brains. According to fossil evidence, cranial capacity in human ancestors began to increase substantially only some 2.5 million years ago.

Fossils of the earliest bipeds are rare but include bones from a few different specimens: *Sahelanthropus*, *Orrorin*, and *Ardipithecus*, hominins that lived 4 to 7 million years ago and that seem to have left only the most fragmentary remains, albeit enough to discern their bipedality. There are many more fossils of later bipeds, however, including those belonging to the australopithecines, a group of hominins that existed in Africa some 5.6 to 1.2 million years ago. This group, which includes the famous fossil skeleton known as Lucy, was bipedal and would eventually use simple stone tools, but still remained rather ape-like in appearance and brain size. One species of australopithecines (though which one is still debated) is ancestral to the genus *Homo*, our own genus, which emerged 2 to 3 million years ago and was initially distinguished primarily by an increase in brain size to some 600 cubic centimeters. Species within the genus *Homo* include *Homo habilis* (the first *Homo* species), *Homo erectus* (*ergaster*), *Homo heidelbergensis* (probably the last common ancestor of Neanderthals and modern humans), and *Homo sapiens* (us). (See Plates 20 and 21.)

The archaeological record begins some 3 million years ago, when the first simple stone tools appeared, which were used by australopithecines and members of the genus *Homo*. (The history of tool-making among human ancestors will be spelled out in more detail in the "Technology" section of this chapter.)

As far as we know, the story of human ancestors took place entirely in Africa up until some 1.8 million years ago, when the first known major migration out of Africa occurred. *Homo erectus / ergaster*, which may even have been able to control fire (though there is no indisputable evidence for this) left Africa and quickly spread over the temperate regions of Eurasia, getting as far as Indonesia. This meant that *Homo* lineages existed, and continued to evolve, in Africa, Europe, and Asia from this time forward; fossils of *Homo erectus* appear in Africa, Asia, and Europe.

This migration, and subsequent migrations,[6] happened against the backdrop of the geological epoch known as the Pleistocene, which started nearly 2.6 million

---

6. Including, perhaps, an "out-of-Africa" migration of *Homo heidelbergensis*.

years ago and featured repeated glaciations over periods of tens of thousands of years. Migrations may have been, at least in part, responses to shifts in climate. (See Plate 22.)

The first known appearance of our species, *Homo sapiens*, also occurred in Africa, perhaps some 300,000 years ago, and over time *Homo sapiens* migrated and expanded within Africa. Starting perhaps around 100,000 years ago, some groups of anatomically modern humans then began expanding out of Africa, into Europe and Asia and, eventually, the Americas. This means that at least two "out-of-Africa" migrations occurred, one by *Homo ergaster* nearly 2 million years ago and one by *Homo sapiens* within the last 100,000 or so years. Each of these migrations was itself spread out over hundreds to thousands of years, involved many groups, and did not happen all at once. This means that as they expanded into new environments, *Homo sapiens* would have encountered a variety of hominins, and there appears to have been a considerable amount of interbreeding between *Homo sapiens* and these "archaic humans,"[7] including the species (or subspecies) known as Neanderthals and Denisovans. Exactly how much gene flow had been occurring all along in these populations, the extent of the interbreeding between modern and archaic humans, and the extent to which *Homo sapiens* displaced other *Homo* species by violence or competition for key resources are all subjects of ongoing debate—as are many of the dates we have given here, which change rapidly with new evidence.[8] Evidence from genetic analysis[9] combines with the fossil record and the archaeological record to produce a constantly shifting and updated picture.[10]

At some point, members of the *Homo sapiens* species[11] began to behave in ways that seem familiar to us now and that indicate cognitive traits and symbolic activity that are universal to all human groups alive today, including figurative or icono-graphic art, personal adornment, invention and standardization of much more creatively designed and sophisticated tools than were already in use, and burial of the dead (especially with grave goods). This apparent cognitive-behavioral shift is called "behavioral modernity." Scholars debate when this shift happened—the

---

7. A choice of language that rather naturally disposes us to see these species as "incomplete" or "underdeveloped" versions of ourselves, though there may be much better ways of thinking about them.

8. Even the initial peopling of the Americas, long thought to have occurred 14,000 to 16,000 years ago, may be pushed back by many thousands of years, and there may have been multiple peoplings of the Americas.

9. Both mitochondrial and nuclear DNA.

10. Linguistic analysis of the relationships of languages spoken by different human groups today is also a helpful source of evidence for the movements and interactions of human popu-lations during the more recent past.

11. And also, possibly in a more limited way, Neanderthals.

estimates seem likely to end up over 100,000 years ago[12]—and whether the shift occurred gradually or suddenly. There is also the question, difficult or perhaps even impossible to determine based on fossil and archaeological evidence, of how long human cognitive capacity for symbolic thought and communication existed before they left archaeological traces—art and personal adornment in forms that preserve long enough for us to see them today. If a Paleolithic Mona Lisa were painted in sand or on wood, after all, we would never know. (See Plates 23 to 25.)

Throughout essentially all of the past 6 million years, many human ancestral species co-existed at once. New species emerged as small groups became isolated and diverged, but considerable interbreeding also may have occurred among ancestral species,[13] making human ancestry neither a linear progression nor even a branching tree, but rather a tangled and densely intertwined branching more reminiscent of a muddy delta.[14]

The Search for Human Origins and the Anthropologist's Proxies for Humanity

At the informational level, it is not the role of a universal history to dispute any of the basic details in this story, any more than to dispute the details of how the Milky Way formed, or of when mammals first evolved. These are the subjects of primary research in their respective scientific fields. That said, it is worth pointing out that even the basic outline of human ancestry is still very much in flux: stable as it may appear when narrated seamlessly, the timeline and overall story have changed tremendously with new evidential developments—and will likely continue to do so.

For example, the discovery in Ethiopia of the roughly 3.2-million-year-old Lucy and accompanying fossils in 1974, and a set of trace-fossil footprints discovered in 1976 in Laetoli, Tanzania, showed conclusively that bipedalism predated an increase in brain size, whereas earlier anthropologists and biologists, ever since

---

12. Recent discoveries of human remains and artifacts at caves in Israel and South Africa, including those at Qafzeh, Skhul, and Blombos, have pushed back the estimates of when modern behaviors began by tens of thousands of years from the original estimates of 50,000 years ago. (See, e.g., Genevieve von Petzinger, "The Modern Mind May Be 100,000 Years Old," http://nautil.us/issue/40/learning/the-modern-mind-may-be-100000-years-old .) Note also that earlier dates for behavioral modernity have these changes taking place in Africa, and many discoveries of indicators of behavioral modernity have been made in Africa.

13. Interbreeding among different species may seem like a contradiction in terms, but recall from the previous chapter that the "biological species concept," in which two types of organisms are considered to be members of different species if they cannot typically mate and produce offspring that are themselves fertile, is only one way of defining a species and, in any case, is difficult to apply to fossils, since reproductive incompatibility is very difficult to discern from body shape alone and can be contradicted by genetic evidence.

14. John Hawks, "Human Evolution Is More a Muddy Delta than a Branching Tree," https://aeon.co/ideas/human-evolution-is-more-a-muddy-delta-than-a-branching-tree .

Darwin's time, had proposed that bipedalism and brain-size increase happened at the same time.[15] Bipedal human ancestors older than 4 million years were discovered only in the period from 1992 to 2002, and now far more lineages among human ancestors are known than was the case even 15 years ago. New ways of analyzing DNA in the 21st century[16] have also convinced anthropologists that *Homo sapiens* did interbreed with Neanderthals, after that possibility had long seemed ruled out, and with Denisovans, whose very existence was unknown until 2010. The early history of human ancestors is thus hard to resolve, and we can be confident that the story will continue changing substantially as the evidential record continues to grow.

At the interpretive level, however, we can pose a different sort of question, one that exerts a particular fascination for human beings who write and read universal histories—namely, where does *humanity* first appear in this story? At the beginning of a chapter on human origins in *Maps of Time*, David Christian writes: "To know ourselves, we must know the history of *Homo sapiens*."[17] But one could argue that it should be the other way around: to understand the history of *Homo sapiens*, we must know ourselves. If we are trying to identify human origins through fossil and archaeological evidence, we must first identify what makes a human being a human being—that is, we must *operationalize* "humanity," give "humanity" a working definition.[18] (To *operationalize* means to take a concept and make it measurable.)

There is a certain alignment between the type of evidence we seek and the conclusions we can draw about human origins. If our evidence is physical and biological, then the conclusions we draw based on that evidence will relate to the physical and biological aspects of human beings. This is the dimension of humanity most

---

To Ponder: What Does It Mean to Be Human?

Make a list of possible answers to this question. Which of these could be said to be "scientifically observable" in the present? How about in the past, through fossils, artifacts, and genomes?

---

15. Lucy is, by the standards of biological anthropology, a fantastically complete fossil skeleton, but it is also worth noting this means it is only something like 40 percent complete.

16. Especially nuclear DNA, the DNA in the nuclei of cells, and not just mitochondrial DNA.

17. David Christian, *Maps of Time*, p. 139.

18. As the anthropologist Philippe Descola writes in a different context, "we should emphatically remind ourselves that only knowledge of the structure of any phenomenon can make it possible to inquire relevantly into its origins." (Descola, *Beyond Nature and Culture*, p. xviii.)

readily accessible to science. For example, when discussing what makes humans unique and considering the question of human origins, Christian speaks of qualities like bipedalism, hunting, large brains, language, general "ecological creativity,"[19] and the ability to learn collectively, as well as sociability, dexterous hands, meat eating, and a "long period of childhood learning."[20] He points out that there is only a tiny difference (less than 2 percent) between the chimp genome and the human genome.[21] In a similar vein, Stephen Hawking has commented, "We are just a slightly advanced breed of apes on a little planet, which circles around a most average star."[22] Rabbi Jonathan Sacks, summarizing the statements of various popular-science writers, writes that "the scientisation of the human person"[23] is "deeply embedded in popular science. We have become 'the naked ape,' 'a gene's way of making another gene,' an organism among organisms, without freedom or virtue, neither sacred nor unique."[24] Indeed, it is not hard to find even more minimalistic assessments of human nature than these, spoken in the name of "science."[25]

If we wish to avoid the scientism that would reduce human persons to "nothing but" physical and biological objects of scientific study, however, we must acknowledge another dimension of human nature, the origins of which are not so easily inferred from fossils, artifacts, or DNA studies—and the expressions of which are best found in poetry, philosophy, religion, and the humanities, as well as introspection and even (or perhaps especially) everyday life. As the neuroscientist Adam Zeman, drawing on the philosopher Roger Scruton, has written, "We are 'persons,' free, accountable, self-conscious, rational. . . . As persons, we require a different 'order of

---

19. Christian, *Maps of Time*, p. 145.

20. Ibid., p. 153; see chapter 6 of *Maps of Time* for a full discussion.

21. That said, as Steven Pinker points out, a 1 percent difference in DNA strands could produce a 100 percent different set of proteins if the differences were in the right places, so comparing DNA strands alone can be misleading, even at a purely biological level. (Pinker, *The Language Instinct: How the Mind Creates Language*, p. 361.) Or as Skye Cleary puts it, citing Kevin Laland, "that small percentage translates into thousands of structural changes at the genetic level, which in turn can be combined to yield millions of ways in which humans are distinct from chimpanzees. Just because the difference is small in percentage, it doesn't mean it is not both very obvious and highly consequential." (Skye C. Cleary, "Human Nature Matters," https://aeon.co/essays/theres-no-philosophy-of-life-without-a-theory-of-human-nature ; see Kevin Laland, *Darwin's Unfinished Symphony*, p. 16 ff.)

22. Hawking's original words were published in German, in an interview with *Der Spiegel* (October 17, 1988, http://www.spiegel.de/spiegel/print/d-13542088.html). Translation by Anne Berg.

23. Jonathan Sacks, *The Great Partnership: Science, Religion, and the Search for Meaning*, p. 125.

24. Ibid., p. 115.

25. E.g., the cosmologist Sean Carroll: "We humans are blobs of organized mud." (Sean Carroll, *The Big Picture: On the Origins of Life, Meaning, and the Universe Itself*, p. 3.)

explanation' to that offered by biology."[26] The poet Robert Browning wrote, "Love, hope, fear, faith—these make humanity; / These are its sign and note and character."[27] And as John Martin, an academic cardiologist and poet, has put it: "I take apart their insides, discover the insides of their insides, until I know the atoms of the molecules that make the cells stick. But where is man desiring beauty?"[28] Even Hawking adds to the "advanced breed of monkeys" statement, indulging a bit of the scientist's pride in science: "But we can understand the universe, and that makes us something very special."[29]

These deep, fundamental, "poetic" aspects of humanity are not straightforward to detect in the deep past, to put it mildly. No matter how important we consider self-consciousness, or moral responsibility, or the use of reason, or the capacity for self-sacrificial love of another person, these leave little direct physical evidence. Scholars searching for human origins end up looking for the things they can see: things like bipedalism, tool use, control of fire, body structure, brain size, and indirect indicators of cognition and language and cooperation. The evolutionary origins of the human body, and artifacts created by creatures with those bodies, are what the fossil and archaeological records display, and bipedalism, brain size, and other traits can be inferred from them. When thinking about human origins through an archaeological lens, it can be tempting to think that these ultimately define what it means to be human—because the evidence pushes us to see it this way.[30]

Yet both dimensions, the animal nature of humans and the qualities that are less scientifically definable and observable, are equally real—as has often been acknowledged by thinkers the world over. A Jewish sage of the late 1700s and early 1800s, Rabbi Simcha Bunim of Peshischa, reportedly said that a person should have two pockets, "so that he can reach into the one or the other, according to his needs."[31] One pocket should contain the words "For my sake was the world created," and the other should include the saying "I am earth [dirt] and ashes."[32] Another proverb

26. Quoted in Adam Zeman, "Anything Dennett Can Do, Scruton Does Meta," https://standpointmag.co.uk/issues/march-2017/critique-march-2017-adam-zeman-daniel-dennett-roger-scruton/ .

27. Robert Browning, "Paracelsus," Part III.

28. Also quoted in Adam Zeman, "Anything Dennett Can Do."

29. Again, Hawking's original words were published in German, in the interview with *Der Spiegel* (http://www.spiegel.de/spiegel/print/d-13542088.html).

30. Other "human sciences" like psychology have their own process of redefining and "scientizing" humanity.

31. Quoted in Martin Buber, *Tales of the Hasidim: The Later Masters*, pp. 249–250.

32. Ibid., p. 250. Cf. Psalm 8: "When I look at thy heavens, the work of thy fingers, the moon and the stars which thou hast established; what is man that thou art mindful of him, and the son of man that thou dost care for him? Yet thou hast made him little less than God, and dost crown him with glory and honor." (Psalm 8:3–5, RSVCE.)

implies something similar: "Be humble, for you are made of earth; be noble, for you are made of stars."[33]

It matters that we avoid reductionism about the human person and, in particular, that we avoid exclusive focus on the aspects of human beings that are most accessible to science. The Holocaust survivor and psychotherapist Viktor Frankl issued this stern warning:

> The gas chambers of Auschwitz were the ultimate consequence of the theory that man is nothing but the product of heredity and environment; or as the Nazi liked to say, of "Blood and Soil." I am absolutely convinced that the gas chambers of Auschwitz, Treblinka, and Maidanek were ultimately prepared not in some Ministry or other in Berlin, but rather at the desks and in the lecture halls of nihilistic scientists and philosophers.[34]

Even if one is not willing to go as far as Frankl, we are *both* animals *and* unique within the animal kingdom. The scientific investigation of human origins through biological anthropology and archaeology reveals considerable insight about how certain dimensions of humanity came to be, as well as the origins of a number of specific human characteristics. But the full depth and dignity of what it means to be human involves more than just a list of characteristics, and thus remains inaccessible to these disciplines. As Scruton writes:

> What a thing is and how it came to be are two different questions, and the answer to the second may not be an answer to the first. It may be as impossible to understand the human person by exploring the evolution of the human animal as it is to discover the significance of a Beethoven symphony by tracing the process of its composition.[35]

We should not expect to find a full-fledged answer to the question of the origins of humanity in any historical investigation based purely on scientific evidence.

---

33. Sometimes said to be a Serbian proverb, though that provenance is very uncertain. For an informal discussion, see https://www.reddit.com/r/GetMotivated/comments/280lhf/be_humble_for_you_are_made_of_earth_be_noble_for/ .

34. Viktor Frankl, *The Doctor and the Soul*, p. xxi. A somewhat more moderate version of a similar point comes from the sociologist Christian Smith: "Few representations of the human in social science theories make it at all clear why such objects should be bearers of rights, equality, or self-determination." (Smith, *What Is a Person?*, p. 3.)

35. Roger Scruton, *On Human Nature*, p. 19.

Culture

The Big Bang, plate tectonics, and evolution provide unifying theoretical frameworks for the history of the universe, Earth, and life within the disciplines of cosmology, Earth science, and biology. David Christian has proposed "collective learning" as a unifying framework for understanding the history of human beings. A related, but perhaps more all-encompassing, unifying framework for human history might be found in the idea of *culture*, a powerful theoretical framework in the discipline of anthropology.[36]

Culture is a concept that can be applied to nearly any community of human beings, of any size: one could speak of the culture of an empire, a city, a tribe, a club, a family, or even a couple. For anthropologists, the word refers to a group's shared ways of interpreting and making sense of the world. One prominent 19th-century anthropologist, Edward Burnett Tylor, defined culture as "that complex whole which includes knowledge, belief, art, morals, law, custom, and any other capabilities and habits acquired by man as a member of society."[37] Clifford Geertz, an influential 20th-century cultural anthropologist, viewed culture as "a system of inherited conceptions expressed in symbolic forms by means of which men communicate, perpetuate, and develop their knowledge about and attitudes toward life."[38] In any case, culture has to do with interactions that build through time, across generations, and produce patterns that shape and structure the ways in which groups of people live. "Material culture" is the subset of culture that involves physical manifestations, including all material artifacts—whether forms of art, tools, or anything else—produced by a group.

To an anthropologist, then, culture is not simply a matter of having different ideas about what tastes good, or when you eat, or how you show politeness to others, or what constitutes great artwork. An anthropologist's vision of culture includes all these things but is more all-encompassing, incorporating behaviors, thought patterns, and the crafting and use of material objects. Culture lies at the root of how human lives are lived and how human ideas about the world are formed in concrete times and places.

Biology and Culture

The forms and varieties of culture can be rich expressions of our humanity. But why do humans have culture at all? How did it get started in the first place?

---

36. The Greek roots of "anthropology" mean "study of man."

37. Edward Burnett Tylor, *Primitive Culture: Researches into the Development of Mythology, Philosophy, Religion, Art, and Custom, Volume 1*, p. 1.

38. Clifford Geertz, *The Interpretation of Cultures*, p. 95. Geertz and Tylor intended their words to apply to all humans, but expressed these points using the gendered language of their day—as, presumably, we today use expressions that will seem dated or limited to future audiences.

Universal histories, almost by definition, frame the history of humanity against a backdrop of the history of the universe, Earth, and life; this framing might lead one to approach culture through an evolutionary lens. What would follow from that choice? Should culture be considered purely a biological adaptation, with different cultures developing different practices because they are responding to different environmental selection pressures? Is everything from religious practices to hygiene explainable in terms of what helps the human organism survive and reproduce? Do cultures "evolve" primarily in response to biological constraints?[39] Or to the contrary, is culture a separate realm from the biological world, a realm that does not answer to Darwinian logic? One could also phrase these same questions in terms of disciplines: Are disciplines such as anthropology and history, which emphasize the role of human ideas and interactions and, therefore, rely on culture as a theoretical framework, largely reducible to biology (as some scientists might say), or are they more independent of the sciences (as historians and anthropologists usually like to think)?[40]

As Robert Bellah points out in his sweeping history of human religious phenomena, the past is always with us; our bodies bear traces of the entire history of the universe, Earth, and life.[41] So biology certainly provides a set of basic prerequisites to culture. Without the evolution of the human brain or the vocal tract's capacity to produce sounds for language, for instance, there could be no human culture as we know it. Or to take another example, the biological need to consume food lies behind a dizzying array of practices and attitudes around what a person is encouraged or discouraged to eat in a given culture.

That much seems uncontroversial. But does biology determine more about culture than this? A common assumption is that once human culture came into existence—whenever that was—culture essentially "took over" from biology, reducing or ending the Darwinian biological evolution of human beings, because human cultural, social, and technological activity allowed humans to master their environments. As James Burke has commented, "The moment man first picked up a stone or a branch to use as a tool, he altered irrevocably the balance between him and his environment."[42] Similar but more nuanced is the anthropologist Franz Boas's view that cultures develop in the ways they do because of their unique histories, so differences between cultures are due more to their different historical trajectories than to biological factors. Boas likewise held that similarities between

---

39. Arguing that behavioral traits can be adaptive, just like physical traits, goes back to Charles Darwin and to the zoologist Konrad Lorenz.

40. See Philippe Descola, *The Ecology of Others*, p. 12.

41. See, e.g., Robert Bellah, *Religion in Human Evolution: From the Paleolithic to the Axial Age*, p. x. See also "Biochemistry" in chapter 4.

42. James Burke, *Connections*, introduction (page unnumbered).

cultures are not primarily due to general laws like evolution, but rather to "cultural diffusion," where groups borrow from one another.[43]

On the opposite end of the spectrum, some scholars have argued that cultural changes are *nothing but* adaptive responses to the environment, in a classic Darwinian mode, transmitted through the generations because they are useful for survival and reproduction. From this point of view, cultural phenomena like art, religion, and even science can be reduced to adaptive responses to environmental pressures. The anthropologist Marvin Harris takes this rather aggressively reductive approach, which would appear promising if we wanted to ground the origins of human cultures in a framework of evolutionary biology. But as Philippe Descola points out, such universal explanations of cultural particulars fail to explain the particularity: why should different groups have such different taboos against eating certain foods, for instance, if all the food taboos are simply adaptive?[44] It seems that human culture is too diverse and malleable, and in ways that are not merely responding to the physical environment, for the idea of adaptation to the environment to give us a full understanding of where culture comes from in the first place.

Many thinkers fall somewhere in the middle between emphasizing biology at the expense of culture or culture at the expense of biology. For example, Julian Steward, actually a predecessor of and inspiration for Harris, divided a given society's culture into a "core"—aspects of the culture that have to do with biological realities like food production and use of natural resources—and "secondary traits" like "aesthetics, moral values, mythology, [and] certain religious beliefs or ritual attitudes."[45] The core biological realm would then be responsive to Darwinian selection pressures from biology, but the secondary traits would not. Therefore, these secondary traits might display considerably more diversity across cultures, unbound as they are from universal biological requirements and not subject to "ecological determinism."

Not only anthropologists but biologists too have attempted to address these questions about the relationship between biology and culture. E. O. Wilson, a founding figure in the field of sociobiology (the study of social behavior across the living world, within an evolutionary framework), argues that culture cannot be viewed as a phenomenon independent of biology, but that it is also important to avoid a crude biological-genetic determinism.[46] He proposes that biology and

---

43. Guest, *Cultural Anthropology*, p. 47.

44. See Descola, *The Ecology of Others*, p. 2 ff.

45. Ibid., p. 14.

46. See E. O. Wilson, *Consilience*, pp. 181, 204–205. Wilson also contends that a study of social systems must be grounded in an understanding of the biology and behavior of the individuals who compose them. He proposes a unified framework for understanding social phenomena across the animal world, in which sociologists study recent "particular complex societies" (Ibid., p. 207), anthropologists study many kinds of human societies, primatologists study social arrangements in primates in general, and sociobiologists study social arrangements and "social behavior in all kinds of organisms" (Ibid., p. 208).

culture are linked via epigenetic rules—that is, behavioral "rules of thumb"[47] or "soft instincts"[48] that "direct the individual toward those relatively quick and accurate responses most likely to ensure survival and reproduction" but "leave open the potential generation of an immense array of cultural variations and combinations."[49] Bellah echoes this approach, speaking of "cultural developments from biological beginnings."[50]

These various approaches inform how one might think about when and how human culture came into being, how biological evolution affects culture, and also how culture affects biological evolution. Although rarely in perfect agreement about the details, a wide variety of thinkers seem to converge on a *co-evolutionary* framework, in which culture is neither fully independent of nor fully reducible to biology, but in which the two constantly interact: Once humans (or human ancestors, or even other primates) developed the capacity for practices like tool-making or the use of language, these cultural realities became part of the "environment" that exerted Darwinian selection pressures on them. In other words, *culture influences biological evolution* even while environmental pressures also influence at least certain aspects of culture, with the implication that, as the anthropologist Marshall Sahlins writes, "humans evolved biologically under *cultural* selection."[51]

As one potential example of this pattern, the primatologist Richard Wrangham argues that the (cultural) practice of cooking food, which was made possible by the practice of harnessing fire, in turn made more energy-rich food available to human ancestors, enabling the shortening of the digestive system, various changes in the shape of the head, and ultimately, evolution of the modern human body and brain.[52] Just as the *biological* ability to tolerate lactose is an evolutionary innovation that evolved as an adaptation to the *cultural* practice of dairy farming in certain parts of the world over the last 10,000 years, so too it is at least plausible that biological features like brain size may result, in part, from cultural practices like cooking. It also works the other way: biological selection must apply at the cultural level. One example is attitudes toward fertility and bearing children; a culture that discourages having children will not, in general, last especially long.

As with so many things, there is an interplay and a feedback loop: biology and culture affect one another. It is tempting to assign the "more important" or "more fundamental" role to one or the other, perhaps depending on one's disciplinary

---

47. Ibid., p. 210.

48. Not Wilson's words, though he writes that "the hard instincts of animals are translatable into epigenetic rules of human behavior." (Ibid., p. 212.)

49. Ibid., p. 210.

50. Bellah, *Religion in Human Evolution*, p. xii.

51. Marshall Sahlins, *The Western Illusion of Human Nature*, p. 104; italics added.

52. See Richard Wrangham, *Catching Fire: How Cooking Made Us Human*.

sympathies or training, but it is impossible to fully tease biology and culture apart once both are in play. The language one chooses can obscure this, however, especially if it suggests thinking in a hierarchical way of biological "foundations" and cultural "superstructure." As we discussed in chapter 3 ("Reductionism"), it is tempting to see all of these disciplines as existing in a certain hierarchy, where cultural anthropology reduces to biology, which reduces to chemistry, which reduces to physics.[53] But none of these "levels" stands alone, nor is one more fundamental or "real." They all play a powerful role and mutually interact and influence one another, suggesting that their approaches stand *alongside* one another more than the "levels" metaphor would suggest.

Biology and Culture as Interpretive Framing

One might go even further than co-evolutionary thinkers and deny the reality of any sharp dividing line between "biology" (or "nature") and "culture." A strong distinction between nature and culture is far from universal across societies: dividing the world up in this way has been a specifically Western phenomenon, and

---

Side Note: Cultural Evolution

Early evolutionary frameworks for understanding culture, like that of Edward Burnett Tylor (1832–1917), James George Frazer (1854–1941), and Lewis Henry Morgan (1818–1881), thought of the history of "cultural evolution" as a progress narrative, a line leading upward from the lowly states of "savages" to those of "barbarians" and, finally, to the "civilized." Later anthropologists rejected this set of ideas as being far "too Eurocentric, too hierarchical, and lacking adequate data to support its grand claims."[54] But one can still hear echoes of such ideas when, for instance, present-day Native Americans or Australian Aborigines are invoked as something like "fossils" of a bygone human past. It is worth bearing in mind that modern industrial-capitalist societies cannot be said to be "more evolved" than "primitive" foraging or agricultural societies; all present societies, industrial or agricultural or forager, have had the same amount of time to change and have undergone many changes. More generally, to equate some measure of complexity with a relatively greater level of "evolved-ness," progress, and value holds serious implications for how one views other people and other groups. The concept of evolution applied at a human, societal level can become treacherous.

---

53. Tempting partly in order for specialists, especially those who work in fields considered more "fundamental," to keep control of the broader intellectual agenda within reach of the tools their field controls.

54. Guest, *Cultural Anthropology*, p. 46.

a relatively recent one at that, as Descola has pointed out in *Beyond Nature and Culture*. Although a division between nature and culture may seem self-evident to many people influenced by present-day Western cultural forms, many other societies see what we would call culture among animals and even plants, and even in the West, medieval observers treated nature as a "unifying arrangement of things" rather than "a domain of objects that were subject to autonomous laws that formed a background [for human activity]."[55] Perhaps questions about the origins of human patterns and habits could, or even should, be situated in a different interpretive scheme than one that draws such a hard line between nature / biology and culture.

Looking at the behavior of animals, especially highly social and/or intelligent animals like whales, dolphins, elephants, wolves, and many birds, suggests that "nature" and "culture" may not be so separable. Adult killer whales teach their young how to hunt food. Canaries and finches "learn at least some aspects of their song from others"[56] of their species, and whale pods engage in pod-specific songs, taught by parents to their offspring. Chimps teach their young to create rudimentary tools. Many different animals engage in play, and a variety of species engage in forms of social learning that can be transmitted through generations or that vary among groups. Even plants are constantly responding to their environment and communicating with one another via chemical signals; although they do not have brains, and one only rarely hears it argued that they truly *experience* anything, even they have at least some of the basic trappings of culture, if one is attuned to the chemical mode in which they connect.[57] In a book that applies the word "culture" to whales and dolphins, Hal Whitehead and Luke Rendell write that "to biologists like us, culture is a flow of information moving from animal to animal";[58] what unites all animal cultures is "being a shared collection of socially transmitted knowledge and behavior"[59] that travels between individuals and across generations independent of genes and can influence the dynamics of evolution itself.

In this more general sense, without words like "belief," "art," "morals," and "law," as in Tylor's human-specific definition, culture can be a meaningful and powerful idea to take up outside its original anthropological context, opening up new modes by which to understand at least some animals. Culture is something that can be

---

55. Ibid., p. xv.

56. Hal Whitehead and Luke Rendell, *The Cultural Lives of Whales and Dolphins*, p. 3.

57. In his book *The Strange Order of Things*, the neuroscientist Antonio Damasio goes one step further in writing that "simple bacteria have governed their lives for billions of years according to an automatic schema that foreshadows several behaviors and ideas that humans have used in the construction of cultures" (p. 221). At the same time, Damasio reminds us, "*foreshadowing* minds and feelings is not the same as *generating* minds and feelings" (Ibid., p. 27; italics added).

58. Whitehead and Rendell, *The Cultural Lives of Whales and Dolphins*, p. 3.

59. Ibid., p. 205.

adaptive: having the capacity for culture can improve an organism's ability to survive and reproduce in its environment,[60] especially when that environment encourages cooperation among members of a species.[61] Whitehead and Rendell even raise the possibility of gene-culture co-evolution in whales and dolphins. Culture, defined in this more general way, may be a fairly common evolutionary development.

The extension of the idea of "culture" to other present-day species may also be a way of throwing light on how we might think about human ancestors one or two million years ago, who used stone tools (a form of material culture) and may have had relatively complex social structures. One might take the approach that culture is, indeed, older than *Homo sapiens*, and that it is also widely present in today's world across the animal kingdom. As Whitehead and Rendell write, to say "that culture has been intertwined with human evolution for 2.5 million years . . . one has to accept a reasonably broad concept of culture."[62]

This does not, however, mean that there is nothing distinctive about human culture. Even if culture in general is not a uniquely human phenomenon, *human* culture, in all its variety and diverse expressions, is. The anthropologist Jonathan Marks writes: "Labeling ape behavior as 'culture' simply means you have to find another word for what humans do."[63] Whitehead and Rendell point out that many features of human culture may be unique to humans, including language, cumulative technology, shared meanings, moral codes, and symbolic objects.[64] Other scholars have identified the unique role of family ties in the building of human societies: "Humans are the only primates that maintain lifelong relationships with dispersing offspring."[65] Sustained kinship networks, enabled and "facilitated by a unique ability to maintain relationships in the absence of spatial proximity,"[66] allow us to build relationships and networks across communities and across great distances. And Christian emphasizes collective learning and the benefits of symbolic language, which greatly increase the benefits of cooperation, allowing knowledge to be both collective (within groups) and cumulative (cultural transmission through

---

60. See Daniel Lord Smail, *On Deep History and the Brain*, p. 94, or Whitehead and Rendell, *The Cultural Lives of Whales and Dolphins*, p. 246.

61. Whitehead and Rendell, *The Cultural Lives of Whales and Dolphins*, p. 223.

62. Ibid., p. 206.

63. Quoted in Ibid., p. 203.

64. Ibid., pp. 203–205. Also note: "If culture must include systems of meaning like languages, then cetaceans (and other non-humans) cannot have culture on current evidence, and it is not clear how we would ever obtain such evidence in the future." (Ibid., p. 204.)

65. Lars Rodseth et al., "The Human Community as a Primate Society," *Current Anthropology* 32, no. 3 (1991): 221.

66. Ibid., p. 241.

generations).[67] Moreover, as the biologists Peter Medawar and Jean Medawar have written, "Only human beings guide their behavior by a knowledge of what happened before they were born and a preconception of what may happen after they are dead: thus only human beings find their way by a light that illumines more than the patch of ground they stand on."[68]

Perhaps that is going too far. Perhaps people have a tendency to underestimate what whales or dolphins know, or what our primate ancestors knew. But there does seem to be at least a difference in degree, and perhaps even in kind, where culture is concerned, between the human and non-human worlds. As we alluded when discussing the idea of behavioral modernity, there is much debate about how to connect non-human (pre-human? proto-human?) culture to the kind of artistic and symbolic culture that one sees clearly in the past 100,000-plus years. But whatever may be happening elsewhere in the animal kingdom or may have happened deep in the history of human ancestors, the history of *Homo sapiens* certainly involves cultural transmission and collective learning. And this collective learning helps to make human history particularly well-suited for the kind of *historical* analysis that we will see in chapter 6. Yet across the animal kingdom and the living world in general, talk of culture and history may also be applicable: perhaps there are more histories than our own to tell.

Technology

The word "technology" comes from the Greek *techne*, which means "art," "skill," or "craft." Today, the word conjures images of small electronic devices and complex machines, but technology—the skillful use of tools, or the crafting of means to do things that could not otherwise be done—is not only much, much older, but arguably older than humanity itself. Yet our "modern" forms of technology, and especially modern ideas about technology, shape how stories of the development and use of technologies in the deep past are usually told. Whether we are talking about stone tools or airplanes, hunting implements or computers, the harnessing of fire or the harnessing of nuclear energy, stories about technology often take the form of *progress narratives* of increasing sophistication and growing human mastery over nature.

One can, indeed, pick out certain forms of progress in the history of the kinds of tools that humans and human ancestors have used. But here, we identify three

---

67. See Christian, *Maps of Time*, especially pp. 147–148.

68. Quoted in the epigraph of Karl Popper and John Eccles, *The Self and Its Brain*, p. v. See also Daniel Lord Smail, who agrees that collective learning is "what separates human culture from the culture of other animals" (Smail, *On Deep History and the Brain*, p. 101), or E. H. Carr: "The essence of man as a rational being is that he develops his potential capacities by accumulating the experience of past generations" (Carr, *What Is History?*, p. 150).

narratives from the history of technology that illustrate the need for nuance in telling such stories: the development of stone tools 3 million years ago, the hunting of large animals 70,000 to 10,000 years ago, and the development of agriculture about 11,000 years ago.

Stone Tools

The date of the first stone tools used by human ancestors has been pushed back deeper and deeper into the past as new evidence has been uncovered; the best estimates currently stand at over 3 million years ago. The first known stone tools were simple, followed over time by composite and more stylized tools used for a wide variety of purposes. Even the very earliest stone tools, though, were non-trivially difficult to make. A number of archaeologists have engaged in "experimental archaeology" through "flint knapping"—that is, striking stones against one another to create replicas of early stone tools and then using those tools to do things like butcher animals, scrape hides, or chop wood in an effort to see what the tools might have been used for.[69] In addition to finding ancient tools themselves, archaeologists have also discerned the effects of tools in the fossil and archaeological records; for instance, some animal bones bear visible signs of human modification, like cut marks or certain characteristic fractures that appear to result from blows delivered by a tool.

From the start, the stone tools that human ancestors made displayed certain patterns in their makeup. Archaeologists call the earliest widespread stone-tool "industry" (a word that, when used in an archaeological context, means a stable pattern in the collection of tools made and used by people of a given time and region) the Oldowan, and the Oldowan "toolkit" included a variety of stones modified to create chopping and cutting edges, formed by striking stone surfaces against one another.[70] The next most ancient stone-tool "industry" was the Acheulean. Acheulean stone tools are associated especially with *Homo erectus* and include specialized hand axes. These tools were more varied than Oldowan tools and could presumably be used to accomplish a greater diversity of tasks.

Similar choices of style and design across wide geographical areas and through long spans of time, as archaeologists see in the Oldowan and especially the Acheulean stone tools, appear to indicate standardization, an impressive level of planning, and even mental templates for what to do with the stones. However, this kind of conclusion may be reading too much into the shapes of the stones: up to a

---

69. See, e.g., Nicholas Toth, "The First Technology," *Scientific American* 256, no. 4 (1987):112–121.

70. These tools probably served many different tasks. Butchering an animal, for example, requires many different processes, and different tools would be useful for different parts.

certain point, the shapes we find could simply be the shapes these stones naturally took when flakes were struck away.[71] (See Figure 5.1.)

Given the character of the evidence available, it is easy to tell the history of tools as a story of progress—in terms of function, size, or fineness of detail. It may even be difficult to imagine telling this history in any other way, especially given that there really was an increase in the sophistication, power, and versatility of some of

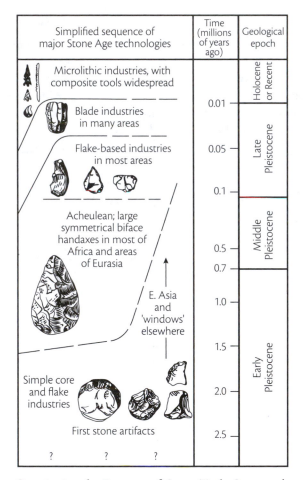

FIGURE 5.1 Questioning the Progress of Stone Tools Stone tools took different forms over time, as this (simplified) graphic shows. To what extent this should be interpreted as a sign of technological progress, however, is an open question.

Source: Based on Steven Jones, Robert Martin, and David Pilbeam, eds., *Cambridge Encyclopedia of Human Evolution* (Cambridge: Cambridge University Press, 1992), p. 357.

71. Or for that matter, could be the shapes of the blocks of raw material (the "cores") from which flakes were removed.

the tools developed in the past 2 to 3 million years. New technology often builds on old technology, so tracing a narrative thread of progressively increasing sophistication, from the first stone tools to the present day, is certainly possible. As the archaeologist Nicholas Toth writes:

> Yet every modern technology—including those for exploring other parts of the solar system, splitting the atom, engineering genetic material and performing organ transplants—is linked in an unbroken line of culture with the inception of flaked-stone tools between two and three million years ago.[72]

There are other pieces of this puzzle, however, that we must also bear in mind, calling some of this steady-progression narrative into question. First, it seems that the Oldowan and the Acheulean industries were sometimes used together; the Acheulean never completely supplanted the Oldowan, even over the course of a million years of use—which means they do not really form a "sequence" as a typical progress narrative might assume. Second, there was a great deal of stasis in these tool-making industries, each of which did not change appreciably over hundreds of thousands of years. Such protracted stasis is not just interrupted progress; it may indicate a lack of inherent directionality. Third, it is very difficult for us now to discern what, exactly, these tools, or even naturally available objects (like river-smoothed stones) that did not require modification to become useful as a tool, were used for. Scholars' informed guesses about such questions may simply be wrong. And fourth, a whole range of tools that may have been used at different points in the past may be invisible to us now, either not yet discovered or not preserved in the archaeological record at all. Wood, for example, does not typically preserve. Bamboo can make a sharp cutting edge, but does not last for long periods of time. The parallel story of wooden tools,[73] therefore, and of tools made from other organic substances that rarely preserve, could perhaps call into question the apparent progress narrative of stone tools, but for the most part, we do not have access to that story.

There are also significant implications to thinking of the line from stone tools to modern technology as an "unbroken" one. A subtle implication is that humans have been progressively mastering the environment for millions of years. For example, consider the James Burke quotation mentioned earlier: "The moment man first picked up a stone or a branch to use as a tool, he altered irrevocably the balance

---

72. Toth, "The First Technology," p. 121.

73. Archaeologists do have some access to the history of wood*working*: Working different materials leaves different microscopic "polishes" on the edges of some stone tools, giving an indication of whether a given stone tool might have been used to shape wood or softer vegetation, or to butcher an animal. (Toth, "The First Technology," p. 120.)

between him and his environment."[74] A certain view of humanity, and of humanity's relationship with technology, is implicit—that tool use is a (or even *the*) defining feature of what it means to be human, that to be human is to stand above nature, and that tool use enables this. Modern technological society, from this point of view, begins to look like the inevitable, or at least favored, outcome of a process of "ascent," so that the modern West, with all its technological "achievement," appears as the highest form of humanity.

Caution is required here, though, if for no other reason than that people today who do not use the most "advanced" technology are neither "archaic" nor somehow less human than those who carry powerful computing devices everywhere they go. In fact, they have various advantages that those who are more dependent on technology have often lost, as when the introduction of writing (a much more basic kind of technology) leads to a considerable reduction in people's memory for the spoken word.

As much as our identity as humans may seem bound up in our relationship with technology, human nature does not primarily consist in technological capacity. And while humans are unique in the extent to which we develop and rely on an incredible variety of tools, the use of tools is widespread across the animal kingdom—as noted in the previous section. Not only other primates, but also other mammals, birds, octopuses, insects, and other animals are users of tools.[75] The story of early stone tools is certainly interesting, and there is no question that there really are long-term trends in the sophistication of tools. Still, for many reasons, a history of tool use must be careful about its tone and cautious about its implications.

Hunting and Extinction of the Megafauna

A second example of a technological story whose complexity can be obscured by simple progress narratives is that of the hunting and extinction of Pleistocene megafauna (large animals) in human-inhabited continents over the last several tens of thousands of years. The Pleistocene is the geological epoch that extends from about 2.6 million years to about 12,000 years ago, and it was characterized by cycles in which glaciers advanced to cover a substantial fraction of the globe, retreated, and advanced again, repeating every 100,000 years or so.[76] During this epoch, a

---

74. Burke, *Connections*, introduction (page unnumbered).

75. See Edward O. Wilson, *Sociobiology: The New Synthesis, Twenty-Fifth Anniversary Edition*, pp. 172–175, for a classic list and discussion, or Amanda Seed and Richard Byrne, "Animal Tool-Use," DOI 10.1016/j.cub.2010.09.042, for a more recent one. We are grateful to Dave Burzillo for these references.

76. Depending on a given author's usage of the term "ice age," the Pleistocene is either referred to as "the ice age" due to the cycle of glaciation and warming or as a time when "ice ages" came and went as global temperatures fluctuated from glacier-inducing lows to the highs of the warmer (interstadial) periods.

huge variety of megafauna, including mammoths and mastodons, saber-toothed tigers, giant sloths, cave bears, and a variety of other creatures, roamed all continents except Antarctica. Over a roughly 60,000-year-long period, though, starting some 70,000 years ago and ending approximately 10,000 years ago, and beginning mostly in Australia and then spreading around the globe, these animals died off. The timing of these extinctions largely coincides with the arrival of humans on the continents where the extinctions were occurring, so we know that humans were around when the animals went extinct. In many cases, humans moved into a given region immediately before the extinction occurred.

Many writers have therefore suggested that humans were not merely present at the time of the extinctions, but in fact caused them through overhunting. Correlation does not imply causation, however, so the case is not conclusive. There could be a third factor that drove both human migration and megafaunal extinctions to occur at the same time. The most likely candidate for such a third factor would be climate change, a reasonable possibility since the global climate was unstable during the Pleistocene, cycling between periods when glaciers covered much of the globe and much warmer times. That said, such cycles had been going on for over 2 million years, so something would have had to be different about the most recent glacial cycle to explain why the megafauna died out this time, and not during the two dozen or so previous cycles.[77] A plausible candidate for this "something" is growing human populations migrating to new continents and new habitats, and the hunting capabilities they brought with them. (While human ancestors may have used weapons like wooden spears to hunt for hundreds of thousands of years, the hunting capabilities that behaviorally modern *Homo sapiens* developed in the last 100,000 years were, or at least seem to be, much more formidable than before. Bone tools, blade technology, and new composite tools like spear-throwers may have given humans increasing capacity for killing animals.)

How might one assess the likelihood of any given scenario for why the megafauna died out? There is, in some cases, direct evidence of human hunting, especially for mastodons and mammoths. There are also cave paintings that suggest the hunting of a few now-extinct megafauna. Such evidence makes it clear that there was, indeed, human hunting of at least some megafauna.

A more detailed way of testing what led to the extinctions is to use modern laboratory methods to essentially perform an autopsy on animal remains that are sufficiently well-preserved—even tens of thousands of years after the animal's death. It is possible, for example, to reconstruct parts of the life history of a mastodon based on chemical[78] analysis of its tusks: how fast the animal grew and matured, when it was

---

77. See, e.g., Paul L. Koch and Anthony D. Barnosky, "Late Quaternary Extinctions: State of the Debate," https://www.annualreviews.org/doi/10.1146/annurev.ecolsys.34.011802.132415 .

78. Technically, isotopic.

weaned, at what age it died. Climate change leading to lack of availability of food should show itself in slower growth, later maturation, and lower fecundity. Deaths brought about by human hunting, meanwhile, would not display these effects, or would display their opposites.[79] At present, the balance of evidence seems to indicate that climate change did not impact mastodons negatively. Evidence from Siberian mammoths shows a decrease in weaning age, as opposed to the increase that would be expected if climate change had produced nutritional deficiencies.[80] This is the kind of analysis scientists can perform: examining how certain species went extinct in particular locations, and testing different hypotheses for the cause of extinction. A preponderance of evidence may then point in one direction or another.

The extinction story of the Pleistocene megafauna is not always narrated with this kind of nuance, however. The two leading hypotheses for why the megafauna went extinct are that humans, aided by their technologies, hunted them to extinction or that changes in climate drove them to extinction. Either way, the story and its moral practically write themselves, given modern concerns and present-day narratives. In one case, we have a cautionary tale about the destructive effects of human technologies—a different kind of progress narrative, in which increasingly powerful technologies increase humans' ability to destroy existing things as well as to create new things. In the other, we have a narrative of the potential adverse effects of climate change, itself a product of human impacts in the present, although not in the Pleistocene.

Yet the reality must almost certainly be more complex than either of these scenarios would, at first glance, suggest. Humans certainly did not kill all the megafauna directly—even the most extreme overhunting scenario does not involve the direct killing of every animal. Hunting a species to extinction does not mean killing every individual, but rather hunting until populations are too small to remain viable, leading to population collapse. In addition, humans may not have directly hunted predators like the saber-toothed tiger, but they could have reduced the populations of their prey, a development that in turn would have starved the predators.[81] Alternatively, predator populations may have been directly hunted and

---

79. Michael Cherney, "Records of Growth and Weaning in Fossil Proboscidean Tusks as Tests of Pleistocene Extinction Mechanisms," http://hdl.handle.net/2027.42/120909 ; D. C. Fisher, "Paleobiology and Extinction of Proboscideans in the Great Lakes Region of North America," pp. 55–75 in *American Megafaunal Extinctions at the End of the Pleistocene. Vertebrate Paleobiology and Paleoanthropology*, ed. G. Haynes.

80. D. C. Fisher, "Paleobiology of Pleistocene Proboscideans," *Annual Review of Earth and Planetary Sciences* 46, May (2018):229–260.

81. Grover S. Krantz, "Megafaunal Extinctions: Man's Modification of the Environment May Have Caused the Demise of Some Large Pleistocene Mammals," https://www.jstor.org/stable/27828993 .

collapsed, leading to the enlargement of prey herbivore populations, which could in turn have meant overexploitation of the land and subsequent collapse of the herbivores. Moreover, humans may not have always been the only "invasive species" to migrate into a new area at a given time, meaning that there may have been other sources of ecological disruption. And human activities other than hunting may also have disrupted habitats of the megafauna; in particular, human use of fire to clear forests in Australia could have led to a loss of food for the herbivore megafauna there. And to complicate matters still further, climate change may have produced ecological changes that made populations more vulnerable to what humans could do by hunting.

Any of these ecological "storylines" is a viable possibility. To add even further to the complexity, the story need not be the same on every continent, or for different ecosystems. Such an enriched, multicausal explanation, with the possibility of several narratives at work, is harder to pin down fully, difficult to summarize concisely, and may be less satisfying to some than a single-cause explanation with a powerful moral. But it is exactly this kind of nuance that is so crucial for thinking through not only past relationships with technology, but present ones too.

In addition, even if humans do bear the primary responsibility for the extinction of the Pleistocene megafauna, one can envision telling the story with different moral tones. In one version, humans appear as destructive creatures that disrupt ecosystems and destroy life. In another, humans are protagonists looking out for their own safety and well-being and destroying terrifying, deadly beasts that have no regard for their lives, like a prehistoric version of "Godzilla." Both possible "morals" are consistent with the same basic story.

That humans have the capacity for destructive uses of their technologies is not in doubt. But if what we seek is a deep understanding of the dynamics of the megafaunal extinction, we need rigorous, well-contextualized, nuanced explanations, and we should be aware that even while a certain amount of evidence is available to us, there remain significant limitations to what that evidence can tell us.

Agriculture

A third example of the complicated relationship between technology and progress is the development of agriculture, the cultivation and domestication of plants and animals for human food and other uses. The technology and practice of agriculture arose as a means of acquiring food only quite recently in the history of humans and their ancestors. While experiments with plant cultivation may have been happening for a very long time, agriculture as a primary means of human subsistence is less than 1/100 as old as stone tools, and more recent than nearly all of the megafaunal extinctions. The first unmistakable signs of systematic cultivation of crops for food by settled farmers are from the Middle East,[82] roughly 11,000 years ago.

Even after this point in time, foraging remained the dominant method of food acquisition across most of the world for several thousand years. But those groups that became agricultural experienced fairly sweeping changes in their technologies and ways of life. For example, most foragers carry everything they own, but farmers, settled as they are in a particular place, do not. Farmers use a different set of tools, including heavier and more stationary ones: everything from sickles to stone axes, hoes, and grindstones. Later agriculturalists developed pottery for storage and cooking, kilns for baking, means of irrigation, and plows—a much different toolkit than would be necessary, helpful, or feasible among foragers.[83]

Why did agriculture arise so late in the history of technology? There are several logical possibilities, including that agriculture was simply a great invention that no one thought of earlier, that it was driven by particular environmental conditions unique to that time, that population sizes or densities had to reach a critical threshold before farming became beneficial, or that agriculture depended on previous technological, cognitive, and/or cultural changes that required a long period of time to lay the groundwork for (so that humans did not have the means to implement agriculture until relatively recently). The general idea that agriculture was a single great invention dominated scholarship for much of the 20th century. But the dominant idea now is that a combination of factors was at work: a warming climate made agriculture possible, just when population pressure in human communities that had recently finished spreading over the entire globe made some innovation in food supply necessary in order to feed all mouths.

In this model, no one sat down one day and thought that life would be much better if their community could live in large settlements, with permanent housing, and cultivate crops, and then made that happen. Instead, it was a much longer, slower, and perhaps less thought-out process. Food production by agriculture was probably something that various human communities "backed into" and then became trapped by, or "tried on for size" as a seasonal adaptation, with some switching back to foraging either temporarily or permanently.[84] Agriculture initially appeared only in a few places around the globe, not necessarily the most ecologically suitable ones; and it did not always spread immediately or irresistibly. It produced

---

82. Sometimes called the "Near East," an older term, which arose within European scholarly circles—using Europe's geographic position to determine what was "Near" and "Far." (The "Far East" was what we would now call East Asia.) Also sometimes called "Southwest Asia."

83. See, e.g., J. R. McNeill and William McNeill, *The Human Web: A Bird's-Eye View of World History*, p. 37.

84. David Graeber and David Wengrow, "How to Change the Course of Human History (At Least, the Part that's Already Happened)," https://theanarchistlibrary.org/library/david-graeber-david-wengrow-how-to-change-the-course-of-human-history?v=1532544909 .

the conditions for continued, and perhaps sometimes increased, conflict, whether between farmers or between foragers and farmers: some plots of land are more valuable than others for the cultivation of crops, so it matters who owns what land. And it did not necessarily produce improvements in nutrition or health or longevity, which seem to have decreased in the initial aftermath of the introduction of farming.[85] Even in the modern world, foragers (hunter-gatherers) are often content to remain foragers rather than adopt agricultural practices, at least when their area of foraging is abundant; they may have more reliable food, greater leisure time, shorter work days, and less vulnerability to disease, famine, and undesirable social control[86] than many in farming societies.[87] While this modern example cannot be applied directly to the past, it is at least plausible that the same reasoning would have applied in many times and places: "As the economist Ester Boserup and others have observed, there is no reason why a forager in most environments would shift to agriculture unless forced to by population pressure or some form of coercion."[88]

In any case, the time scales involved for a transition to farming were too long for agriculture to have been a single discovery or invention by an individual or group. In the words of Jared Diamond, "Even in the cases of the most rapid independent development of food production from a hunting-gathering lifestyle, it took thousands of years to shift from complete dependence on wild foods to a diet with very few wild foods."[89] And even among groups that eventually adopted agriculture fully, a combination of collecting and cultivating must have prevailed for a long time, perhaps with cultivated gardens appearing initially as a reserve food source.[90] Revolutions are rarely as revolutionary as they seem.

Whatever the initial impetus for the spread of agriculture, its presence had far-reaching consequences. Because of the need to give specific plots of land sustained attention, reliance on agriculture tends to give rise to sedentism, living in one place permanently or semi-permanently. This in turn can give rise to denser collections of people, settling in villages and cities. The reverse is also true: sedentism can give rise to agriculture, though it does not always do so. The Natufian settlements of

---

85. See, e.g., Jared Diamond, "The Worst Mistake in the History of the Human Race," http://discovermagazine.com/1987/may/02-the-worst-mistake-in-the-history-of-the-human-race .

86. See James C. Scott, *The Art of Not Being Governed*.

87. A couple examples of scholars who have made the case for the superiority of foraging and inferiority of agriculture are Marshall Sahlins, "Notes on the Original Affluent Society," pp. 85–89 in *Man the Hunter*, eds. Richard B. Lee and Irven DeVore with the assistance of Jill Nash-Mitchell; and Jared Diamond, "The Worst Mistake in the History of the Human Race." For a powerful counterpoint and nuanced discussion, see "Hunter-Gatherers: Noble or Savage?," https://www.economist.com/christmas-specials/2007/12/19/noble-or-savage .

88. Scott, *The Art of Not Being Governed*, p. 20.

89. Jared Diamond, *Guns, Germs, and Steel: The Fates of Human Societies*, p. 107.

90. Ibid., pp. 107–108.

"affluent foragers" in the preagricultural Near East show that sedentism did sometimes arise in areas of abundance even without agriculture, and the hunter-gatherer
monumental architecture of sites like Göbekli Tepe in modern-day Turkey indicate
that people might also gather in one place for cultural, religious, or political reasons
even though they are doing no farming.[91] In any case, sedentism and agriculture
can, at least potentially, exist in a feedback loop: Once one is committed to getting
one's food from a small area of land, there is a permanency of settlement, which
leads to denser collections of people in one place, which in turn can lead to continued farming and set the stage for the development of still larger settlements.

The story of agriculture started out as a classic progress narrative in the 1920s,
when V. Gordon Childe presented it as the "Neolithic Revolution," leading to villages, cities, and ultimately "civilization," with each of these viewed as rungs of a
ladder leading to ever-better social arrangements. Modern scholarship, meanwhile,
has tended to present agriculture as either negative or neutral: a necessary invention in order for certain communities to survive, but one that had radically unforeseen consequences thousands of years later. Even this story can take on a flavor of
technological determinism, however, as if there is an inevitable or law-like "progression" from foraging lifeways to settled agricultural life in dense settlements. As with
the story of prehistoric tool use, there certainly is an identifiable, long-term trend
over the course of thousands of years—but care must be taken to recognize the
great many exceptions that exist to any "rule."

Progress Narratives and the Interpretation of Prehistoric Technologies

Many aspects of the stories that we hear in universal histories about the history of
human technologies are not in dispute: human ancestors created and used tools,
the megafauna are gone, and agriculture came into use as a means of providing food
at a certain point in the past, before which it did not exist. The history of human
technology includes various long-term trends, and in each case, there are reasons
for those trends: technologies build on one another over time, expanding and diversifying and changing the "toolkits" of different societies in different ways.

Progress narratives, however, risk not only oversimplifying the story, but also
obscuring deeper questions about technology. They can play into the sense that
technology advances, that it "marches forward," independent of human choices,
social and political structures, and cultural context. This is a deterministic view of
technological progress, separated from its cultural and social roots. In addition,
technological progress narratives may subtly place modern standards of comfort,
convenience, and efficiency in a consumer-capitalist society as the standard by

---

91. See, e.g., Charles C. Mann, "The Birth of Religion," https://www.nationalgeographic.com/
magazine/2011/06/gobeki-tepe/ .

which to measure both technology and humanity itself. Progress, almost by definition, must be measured with respect to some goal,[92] and the temptation is to think of "us," in the here and now, as that goal. Of course, modern technology is not exactly an unqualified good: how technology is deployed matters a great deal, as shown by the examples of dynamite (which Alfred Nobel created as a safer alternative to explosives used in construction and mining, but which can also be used as a weapon to destroy property and human lives), the guillotine (which is now a symbol of brutal execution and the Reign of Terror, but was originally advocated as a more humane and even egalitarian form of capital punishment[93]), or nuclear power (for both bombs and power plants). The introduction of a new technology always brings consequences, many of which are not foreseen or intended. And more technology is not always better.

What is the alternative to technological progress narratives about the past, present, and future? Like natural selection, technology has to do with adaptation to an ever-changing environment, and new technologies themselves become part of this environment—that is, the technology itself becomes part of the environment that people then seek even more technology to respond to. In other words, the use of technology produces the need for more technology.[94] Necessity may be the mother of invention, but invention is also the mother of necessity. And while progress in both constructive and destructive capabilities is one thread that one may pull out of the history of technology, it is worth remembering that as we observed with biological evolution, everything is just as "evolved" as everything else in terms of the opportunity it has had to adapt to its environment: different environments have simply called out the need for different adaptations. As in so many other situations, modeling technological change as a set of interconnected feedback loops captures the nuances of historical change better than modeling that history as a single line.

Language

In *The Language Instinct*, Stephen Pinker writes, "Simply by making noises with our mouths, we can reliably cause precise new combinations of ideas to arise in each other's minds. The ability comes so naturally that we are apt to forget what

---

92. Marshall Hodgson: "[Progress] implies movement toward a goal, or at least in a good direction." (Hodgson, *The Venture of Islam: Conscience and History in a World Civilization, Volume Three: The Gunpowder Empires and Modern Times*, p. 178.)

93. Joseph-Ignace Guillotin, an advocate for use of the guillotine who ended up with his name on it (although he did not invent it), actually opposed the death penalty but saw the guillotine as more humane than other methods of execution.

94. "Man spends his time devising techniques of which he afterwards remains a more or less willing prisoner" (Marc Bloch, *The Historian's Craft*, p. 39). Arguably, this is true not only of technology, but of social arrangements and behavior patterns too.

a miracle it is."[95] Language is both an apparent miracle and the object of scholarly study in a variety of fields; just as humanity does not "belong" to anthropology alone, language does not belong to linguistics alone but to the study of literature, psychology, sociology, anthropology, philosophy, and a host of related disciplines. An inherently multidisciplinary subject, language and its origins provide a central topic for universal histories.

Language also ties in with questions about what it means to be human, about the human brain, and about the human mind. While humans can in some sense think without using language (as an example, think about playing the piano), a great deal of human thought is tied to language and makes use of language, and language shapes the forms that ideas can take. In addition to shaping the interior life of a person, language also shapes communication between people; it is the means by which something as intangible as an idea can be shared and made effective in the external world. Without language, it is hard to believe that many of our technologies would be possible, and human culture would surely be much different, if even possible at all.

Language and mind, the subjects of the final two sections of this chapter, are thus closely interrelated—with one another and with culture, technology, and humanity. Considering their origins raises extremely difficult questions both methodologically and scientifically, and it also leads us to ask questions about the interior lives and communicative abilities of the rest of the animal kingdom. In the context of a history of everything, what place does language have? How can we probe it— in the human past, the non-human past, and the non-human present—and what does it mean for how we think about humanity?

Some Basic Properties of Language

The word "language" comes from the Latin *lingua*, meaning "tongue"—an implicit reference to the key role the human tongue plays in articulating the sounds of spoken language. There are well over 100 distinct sounds ("phonemes") that the human vocal tract can produce, with a subset of this full range of possible sounds being used by any given language. (For example, linguists say that English uses about 40 of these, with other languages using anywhere from 11 to more than 100.) While a large number of people in today's world routinely encounter *written* language, it is *spoken* language that is primary: non-literate (non-reading, non-writing) individuals or societies past and present still have spoken languages, but no one uses writing without having a spoken (or signed) language. When we discuss "language" in this section, therefore, we are referring to spoken and signed languages rather than to written language.

---

95. Pinker, *The Language Instinct*, p. 1.

Languages are *symbolic*. With a few exceptions, words (whether spoken or gestured) function as "signs" that do not sound (or look) like what they represent. The word "tree" in no way *resembles* a tree, for example, but instead is an arbitrary sound made meaningful because of its use as part of a language.

All languages have what linguists refer to as syntax and semantics. Syntax refers to the *rules* for combining words into sentences, including in what order words can be placed (e.g., subject-verb-object). Semantics refers to the *meaning* of words. The rules of syntax have a logic of their own, largely independent of semantics; a sentence may make grammatical sense but have no decipherable meaning ("colorless green ideas sleep furiously"—Noam Chomsky's classic example). Syntax helps to enable the great flexibility of language by ensuring that all who speak a given language are "playing by the same rules."

Language also has the property of generativity or productivity, meaning that words can be combined and recombined to create totally original sentences. Most sentences in this book, for instance, have literally never been written, spoken, or even thought before, not in the exact form in which they appear here. This is true even when a sentence expresses an idea that others have expressed, and it is also true that language allows the expression of entirely new ideas. Language enables, or at least greatly expands, humans' ability to communicate about things that are remote in time and space (displacement), and likewise greatly expands humans' powers of cooperation and imagination—and deception.

Linguists use the term "natural languages" to refer to languages that are used in everyday life, as opposed to, say, only in religious texts or rituals or technical languages like those in computer programming. There are some 5,000 to 7,000 natural languages in use today, with the precise number depending on what counts as a separate language, which is a matter of debate. They are, moreover, not entirely separate in practice, given that more than half of the world's population speaks more than one language. One possible criterion for distinguishing languages from one another is whether they are *mutually intelligible*, meaning that speakers of the languages can readily understand one another without exerting extra effort.

There is no single language "part of the brain" or "language gene." But there are parts of the brain, and at least one gene, that appear to bear some special connection with language. In particular, language is usually lateralized, meaning that one hemisphere (left half or right half) of the brain is dominant in the processing and production of language.[96] Language also seems to be compartmentalized

---

96. Which hemisphere is dominant correlates to some extent with another kind of lateralization—namely, handedness. One neurological study found that speech was processed in the right side of the brain for only 4 percent of strongly right-handed people, increasing to 27 percent for strongly left-handed people. (Knecht et al. [2000], cited by George F. Michel et al., "How the Development of Handedness Could Contribute to the Development of Language," *Developmental Psychobiology* 55:6 (2013):608–620.)

(or modularized) in the brain in surprisingly specific ways. For example, syntax and semantics are processed in largely separate regions of the brain. We know this because injuries to different parts of the brain can cause people to lose their ability to process syntax but not semantics (Broca's aphasia, in which the person understands and produces language only with great difficulty and cannot speak grammatically) or to lose semantics but not syntax (Wernicke's aphasia, in which the person speaks fluidly but nonsensically). As for genetics, there has so far been only one gene, called *FOXP2*, clearly linked to language production; mutations in this gene can produce severe congenital language impairment.

Despite the Latin roots of "language" referring to the tongue, one does not need a tongue or even a vocal tract at all to produce language; the world has over 100 sign languages based on movement of the hands rather than sounds. Sign languages are not exalted forms of body language, but instead fully developed natural languages just like spoken languages: they have the same basic structure as spoken languages, they have the same productivity, the same brain areas are activated in processing them, and babies go through the same developmental stages when learning them—including "babbling" with their hands.[97]

Children are better at learning languages than adults, even though adults are better at learning many other things. When exposed to a spoken or signed language in the normal course of development, a child swiftly becomes fluent. It seems that there is a sensitive period for learning a language: if a child is not exposed to any language at all before roughly age 9 to 12, the child may later develop some ability to use language if exposed to it but will likely never be fluent in any language.[98] There is also a sensitive period for learning languages beyond a first language: learning a language is seemingly effortless for very young children, but it becomes more difficult after about age 7. Languages learned after this age are rarely learned as well as those learned before this age, and they are usually spoken with an accent.

Languages change constantly over time. Dictionaries may make it seem as though there is a "proper" way of speaking that is frozen in time, but any given language changes so rapidly that it functionally is no longer the same language 1,000 years later. Modern-day English speakers, for example, find Chaucer, who wrote in the 1300s, largely incomprehensible.[99]

---

97. As an additional note, American Sign Language is not translated English; the two languages have totally different syntax.

98. See, e.g., Pinker, *The Language Instinct*, p. 298. Pinker gives the example of a woman who was deaf but neurologically unimpaired and who did not acquire any language at all until age 31, but was still able to learn some 2,000 words and hold a job. (Ibid., pp. 297–298.)

99. Chaucer wrote in Middle English. Old English, the language in which (for instance) *Beowulf* was composed, is totally incomprehensible to English speakers and more similar to modern German than to modern English.

This tendency to change is the basis of the fact that languages themselves are related to one another. For instance, the "Romance" languages include Spanish, French, Italian, and Portuguese, all of which have roots in a common ancestor, Latin ("Romance" in this context means "from Rome"). The Germanic languages include German, Norse, Dutch, Swedish, and English (which also has strong Romance influences due to the conquest of England by the Normans, who spoke Norman French, in the year 1066). The Romance languages and the Germanic languages, in turn, are also related, but more distantly; they all fall within the larger Indo-European language family.[100] A language family is a set of languages that all "descend" from one common ancestral language.[101] (See Plate 26.)

Origins of Language: When, How, Why?

The presence of language in humans of the past is not an easy thing to track. The question of when, how, and why language originated has been called the hardest problem in science, and it has no straightforward or easy answers. One must rely on highly indirect approaches rather than anything resembling direct physical evidence.

When?

Language and writing are strongly associated in most present-day societies, so much so that "the origins of language" and "the origins of writing" almost seem like they should be the same thing. But they are not even close! Writing emerged for the first time, as far as we know, less than 5,500 years ago. There is a wide range of estimates for how old language is, but ballpark figures put it at 10 to 100 times older than writing. The capacity for language lies very deep in our past and may be part of what makes us human, but writing is more of an aberration, developed in the relatively recent past.[102] Perhaps this is reflected in the fact that learning to read

---

100. If no known language is related to a given language, then that language is in a language family of its own and is referred to as an "isolate." Sumerian, the oldest language ever to be written down and thus known in relative completeness, appears to be an isolate.

101. Drawing a parallel that might be especially noticeable in this context, Charles Darwin wrote: "The formation of different languages and of distinct species, and the proofs that both have been developed through a gradual process, are curiously parallel." (Quoted in Pinker, *The Language Instinct*, p. 242.) Just as in biological evolution, differences among languages result from variation, heredity, and isolation. (Ibid., p. 243.)

102. That said, graphic communication—the use of visual symbols or markings that communicate some meaning, that allow messages to be transmitted and preserved beyond a single moment in time—may be much older than full-fledged writing systems. More on this under "Connection" in chapter 7. See also Genevieve von Petzinger, "Why Are These 32 Symbols Found in Ancient Caves All over Europe?," https://www.ted.com/talks/genevieve_von_petzinger_why_are_these_32_symbols_found_in_ancient_caves_all_over_europe?language=en ; and Genevieve von Petzinger, *The First Signs*.

and write is laborious for children, while learning to speak and comprehend speech is not.[103] It is also reflected in the fact that almost every person who is illiterate still speaks or signs. So how would one investigate the origins not of writing, but of language itself?

One approach to probing the origins of language might involve trying to directly reconstruct a common ancestor of all present-day languages, and then tracking how languages evolved as humans migrated over the Earth—perhaps even reconstructing an original language of humankind. Some very old languages can, indeed, be partially reconstructed. Just as the relationships of modern organisms can tell us something about the history of life, the relationships of modern languages can tell us something about the history of language, because languages change over time in fairly regular and predictable ways.[104] For example, the languages of Europe and northern India turn out to be related (hence, the "Indo-European language family"). This was a surprise when it was first recognized,[105] but there is a historical explanation: the migrations of an original group of people who spoke "Proto-Indo-European," a language that can be partially reconstructed even though it was never written down. Unfortunately, this method can only carry us a certain distance back in time. It may be the case that all languages on Earth derive from a single, original language.[106] However, languages change so swiftly that it is almost impossible to trace the histories of languages back more than a few thousand years. Our ability to reliably reconstruct past languages largely dies out some 6,000 years ago, not long before the first writing systems came into being, and such reconstruction may be entirely impossible before 10,000 years ago.[107]

A slightly more helpful way of trying to track the origins of language is through the archaeological record. As David Christian points out, language enables collective learning and the accumulation of knowledge over many generations, which

---

103. Pinker, *The Language Instinct*, p. 186.

104. The analysis is similar to phylogeny in biology, and the analogy between language and evolution (again) goes back to Darwin.

105. The relationship between certain words in Indian and Iranian languages and in European languages had been noticed off and on in the 1500s and 1600s, but in the early 1800s, a close connection between the languages spoken in Persia and northern India and various languages in Europe and Russia was systemically recognized. The Dravidian languages of southern India are not related to Indo-European languages—so most of the languages of northern India are much more closely related to most of the languages of Europe than they are to the languages of southern India.

106. Noam Chomsky has pointed out that a visitor from Mars would think that all human beings speak the same language, with minor regional variations. See Big Think, "Noam Chomsky on Language's Great Mysteries," https://bigthink.com/videos/noam-chomsky-on-languages-great-mysteries .

107. See Cynthia Stokes Brown's *Big History: From the Big Bang to the Present*, p. 63.

allows us to create things that would not be possible without language.[108] But it is very difficult to identify unequivocally that some technological or artistic artifact would have been impossible to create without language, and before the relatively recent invention of writing, language left few unmistakable and uncontroversial traces of its presence.[109] That said, the relative stasis of tools and art made by hominins before *Homo sapiens*, compared to the aesthetic and utilitarian productivity of *Homo sapiens* over a comparatively short time, points in a certain direction. The paleoanthropologist Ian Tattersall summarizes:

> Only beginning around 100–80 thousand years ago do we begin to find (also in Africa) intimations that early *Homo sapiens* began to show symbolic behaviors. These indications include evidence of bodily ornamentation, highly complex multi-stage technologies, overtly symbolic objects (such as geometrical engravings) and, most importantly, evidence of a new and questing spirit of innovation. Previously, change had been only sporadic and rare.[110]

This relates to what we stated earlier about "behavioral modernity" in modern humans. Anatomically modern humans have been around for perhaps 300,000 years. Anthropologists long thought that the "creative explosion" of modern human behavior, tool use, and art occurred some 50,000 years ago in Europe, but as Tattersall and also Genevieve von Petzinger point out, a variety of sites in the Near East and Africa are pushing that number back to at least 80,000 to 100,000 years, with evidence like heat-modified ochre, burials with grave goods, and strong hints of the use of shells for personal adornment—all suggestive, if circumstantial, indications of symbolic thought.[111] The paleoanthropologists Sally McBrearty and Alison Brooks have even argued that some of the archaeologically visible indicators of behavioral modernity start appearing around the same time as anatomical modernity, in Africa, some 250,000 years ago or more.[112] The picture is still far from

---

108. See, e.g., Christian, *Maps of Time*, p. 182.

109. There are geometric carvings on stone in Blombos Cave in South Africa from 90,000 years ago. This at least seems to indicate the kind of symbolic thinking that language draws upon, but even it is not an outright proof that language existed at that time.

110. Ian Tattersall, "Who and What Are We? And When Did We Get Here?," https://web .archive.org/web/20180908134524/https://www.bigquestionsonline.com/2017/04/13/ who-what-are-when-did-get-here/ .

111. Genevieve von Petzinger, "The Modern Mind May Be 100,000 Years Old."

112. Sally McBrearty and Alison S. Brooks, "The Revolution that Wasn't: A New Interpretation of the Origin of Modern Human Behavior," https://www.sciencedirect.com/science/article/ pii/S0047248400904354?via%3Dihub .

complete, though, and any conclusions based on this kind of evidence remain speculative. It is at least plausible, however, that the origins of language may be located in time near the origins of our biological species, bringing anatomical modernity and behavioral modernity together with the origin of language.

Another way of attempting to track the origins of language is to examine the changes in the vocal tract and brain from the fossil record, and then attempt to match these sources of evidence with genetic evidence. Such reasoning can be used, at most, to argue that our hominin ancestors may have had certain capabilities associated with language, like the production of a range of sounds or some of the neurological underpinnings of language—they cannot show definitively that any particular hominin actually used language. That said, many primates have sufficient control of their hands to create signs in sign language, and the voice box was probably capable of making a sufficient range of sounds for language some 2 million years ago (though vocalization is difficult to infer from skeletal remains).[113] Broca's area is large and prominent in *Homo habilis* skulls bearing faint imprints of the wrinkle patterns of the brain, and it is larger in the left hemisphere, indicating some of the lateralization (dominance of one hemisphere with regard to a given task) that we see in the present. But this area may not have been associated with language at that point in time.[114] Meanwhile, analysis of the origin of the *FOXP2* gene suggest that it may have taken its present form some 150,000 years ago (as a very rough estimate),[115] pointing again toward the same vicinity of time as the appearance of anatomically modern humans in Africa (or somewhat thereafter).

The overall picture seems to be that various neurological and anatomical features necessary for language took shape over a protracted period of time stretching back millions of years, probably helping to enable the forms of communication used by hominins at those earlier times. But these features may not have been put to use in the service of the production of syntactical human language until much more recently.

How?

Is it possible to envision *how* language might have come into being? Basically every animal—and a great many other organisms too—could be said to communicate in some fashion: visually, vocally, chemically, or through other modes.[116] Some

---

113. Thanks to Laura MacLatchy for pointing this out (personal correspondence).

114. Pinker, *The Language Instinct*, p. 363. Stone tools indicate right-handedness quite early on, over 1 million years ago.

115. Guest, *Cultural Anthropology*, p. 117.

116. For example, songbirds use specific songs to convey different messages. Chimpanzees use vocalizations and visual displays. Honeybees have their "waggle dance." Vervet monkeys use different alarm calls for different predators; all vervets appear to use the same sounds to communicate the same meanings.

animals, primates in particular, communicate in quite sophisticated ways through a wide array of vocalizations and can even pick up elements of signed human languages. But no animal matches the vocabulary of even a 4-year-old human child, or appears capable of anything like the productivity of human language.[117] The structure and flexibility associated with human syntax comes to animals only in limited ways and with considerable effort, if at all, not naturally and spontaneously as it does to human children. Even the most sophisticated animal communication systems seem to have an essentially finite range of meanings, whereas human languages draw on a finite array of sounds and a finite set of words and rules yet put them together to produce an essentially infinite range of meanings.[118] E. O. Wilson writes that animal communication is "repetitious to the point of inanity."[119] Despite the fact that various animals share the capacity for certain components of human language, one finds a wide gap between language and animal communication systems, and hence something to be explained.

The question is further complicated by the fact that there are several good reasons for evolution *not* to favor the development of language. It may seem self-evident that language, along with general intelligence and a big brain, are evolutionarily adaptive traits, but this is not entirely true. Consider that spoken language requires the vocal tract to be configured in a way that increases the chances of choking on food, and that a large brain requires a great deal of energy to keep it running—and also puts women in appreciably greater danger during childbirth due to the large head size of human infants. There are plenty of organisms, including primates, that get by quite well, evolutionarily, without language and a human-sized brain. So how did we come to possess them?

A number of thinkers respond to this question by positing a co-evolutionary framework of the sort introduced earlier in this chapter. In a widely cited book, *The Symbolic Species: The Co-evolution of Language and the Brain*, Terrence Deacon has argued that the brain size of human ancestors increased and linguistic capabilities improved over the course of hominin evolution because brain size and language became locked into a mutually reinforcing feedback loop. He suggests that more sophisticated language capabilities proved beneficial precisely because everyone

---

117. Elephants remain an intriguing possible exception. As much as three-quarters of their sounds are below the frequency range audible to human ears, and their full communicative capacity is only beginning to be studied. See Caitrin Keiper, "Do Elephants Have Souls?," https://www.thenewatlantis.com/publications/do-elephants-have-souls .

118. An "infinite use of finite means," as Noam Chomsky has put it, enabling an "unprecedented mode of communication." (Cited in Terrence W. Deacon, *The Symbolic Species: The Co-evolution of Language and the Brain*, p. 13.)

119. Cited in Pinker, *The Language Instinct*, p. 349. The E. O. Wilson article cited is "Animal Communication," https://www.jstor.org/stable/24927427 , though this quote does not seem to actually appear in Wilson's article.

else in the species (or in a given community) was using (a simple form of) language. At the same time, exploiting the advantages of language, developing it from simple beginnings, and responding to new demands generated by the social use of language may have resulted in increases in size and deep reorganization of the brain. The start of the process may have come when the capacity for symbolic thought came into being, producing the conditions for a true—albeit "simple"—natural language.

Although we today find complex languages in all human beings and non-linguistic communication systems throughout the animal kingdom, these ancestral simple languages are now nowhere to be found.[120] Deacon writes:

> From this perspective language must be viewed as its own prime mover. It is the author of a co-evolved complex of adaptations arrayed around a single core semiotic innovation that was initially extremely difficult to acquire. Subsequent brain evolution was a response to this selection pressure and progressively made this symbolic threshold ever easier to cross. This has in turn opened the door for the evolution of ever greater language complexity.[121]

Deacon's interpretation is related to the "social-brain hypothesis," which posits that improved ability to navigate increasingly complex social situations, including through language-based communication, was the selective pressure that drove the evolution of bigger brains, greater levels of cooperation and sociality, as well as language. In Steven Pinker's words, "*When individuals matter*—when you're a 'who'—you need a social brain capable of reasoning, planning, rewarding, punishing, seducing, protecting, bonding, understanding, sympathizing."[122] The "adaptive environment" that pushes brain development onward, then, "consists primarily of other humans."[123]

Attractive as these ideas appear, they need to be at least partially qualified. It is not just "a bigger brain" overall, or a general symbolic capacity, or the raw size and shape of the brain that make language possible; it is instead dependent on the existence of very precise wiring of the brain's internal microconnections.[124] As already noted for Broca's aphasia and Wernicke's aphasia, brain damage to specific regions

---

120. Terrence W. Deacon, *The Symbolic Species*, pp. 12, 41.

121. Ibid., p. 44.

122. Pinker, *The Language Instinct*, p. 346.

123. Smail, *On Deep History and the Brain*, p. 146.

124. Pinker, *The Language Instinct*, p. 375.

has the effect of impairing specific language functions, such as syntax or semantics, without impairing other language functions or necessarily affecting general cognitive capacity. Also, both newborn humans and adult macaque monkeys, for example, are unable to process syntax, because they literally lack a neural pathway for it: developing this capacity requires a rewiring of the brain that happens developmentally for human infants but does not happen for any non-human animal, including the macaque.[125]

It is also worth emphasizing that any explanation, whether evolutionary or otherwise, must account for the unique role that human childhood plays in the acquisition of a language. Explanations that emphasize how language might help a person survive or reproduce in adulthood must be complemented by a mechanism for picking it up during childhood in the first place.[126] Children are better at learning languages than adults, so acquiring language cannot be a simple function of a particularly strong ability to learn. And children acquire the accent of peers, not parents, so they are not simply imitating their caregivers. Children also make certain mistakes in language use that no one could have taught them, as when trying to form the past tense of an irregular English verb by adding "-ed" or "-d" to it—giving, for example, "bited" rather than "bit." They master the basic rules of syntax even when not directly taught, and they display the productivity of language from an early age. They pick up an incredible variety of words and syntactical rules without much obvious reinforcement and without many repeated trials.[127] Taken as a whole, these facts suggest that human children are clearly primed to pick up language.

Some hints for the role children play in the formation of a new language come from examples where children spontaneously develop a syntax for a language when none already existed, as when a child learns a "pidgin" (a simplified mode of communication that has no native speakers, but that draws words and a few basic grammatical rules from at least two languages spoken fluently by adults in a mixed-language community) as their first language and spontaneously converts it into a

---

125. Robert C. Berwick, "Why Only Us: The Origin of Human Language," https://www.catholicscientists.org/events/20170421-origins ; see also Robert C. Berwick and Noam Chomsky, *Why Only Us: Language and Evolution*.

126. Cf. Kenneth Kaye, *The Mental and Social Life of Babies: How Parents Create Persons*, p. 186: "Although it clearly involves cognitive processes within the child, the progressive development of symbols is a social process whose evolution in our species must have involved the behavior of parents and other adults, as well as the behavior of their imitators. No symbolic system could have survived from one generation to the next if it could not have been easily acquired by young children under their normal conditions of social life."

127. This is the argument from the "poverty of the stimulus" (Noam Chomsky's phrase) that the ability to acquire language must be innate.

"creole," with a full syntactical structure similar to any natural language.[128] While none of these observations of present-day human children can be used to conclude anything definite about the ancient past, they point strongly toward the importance of socialization in communities that include young children for any explanation of how language came into being and could be sustained across generations.

Side Note: Language and Thinking

Language is not simply a tool for communication that leaves our basic cognition unaffected; the way we think is itself also structured, conditioned, and constrained in important ways by our capacity for language.[129] But does *which* language we speak also condition our thoughts? The Sapir-Whorf hypothesis argues that this is true.

There are many shades of this hypothesis, and a discussion of the nuances quickly gets into very technical matters of 20th-century philosophy. Keeping it simple, the "strong" version of the Sapir-Whorf hypothesis holds to linguistic determinism, the view that a given language *determines* thought—in other words, that all thinking is dependent on the particular language in which it is done. A "weak" version of this hypothesis argues for linguistic relativity, the view that a particular language *shapes* or *influences* thought without determining it.

It is surely true that our imaginative worlds are colored by particular languages. For example, languages that have the feature of "evidentiality" and include "evidentials" force their speakers to attend to *how* they know what they articulate, and with how much confidence. Speaking such a language must certainly affect which features of reality one keys into and communicates. But there also seem to be significant limits to how far particular languages structure our thoughts. After all, people sometimes find thoughts difficult to articulate, or remember the "gist" but not the words, or have a sense of understanding something without being able to articulate it, or coin new words, or learn new words, or fail to remember which language they read or heard something in—none of which should be possible if all thought is language-based.[130]

---

128. A dramatic example comes from Nicaragua, where deaf children—who had previously been isolated and not exposed to any language at all—were brought together for the first time ever in the late 1970s / early 1980s and spontaneously created a (signed) language of their own, Nicaraguan Sign Language. (Educators tried to teach them an existing sign language, but this effort failed.) This was a pidgin initially, but it became a creole when young deaf children were subsequently brought in and spontaneously added syntactic rules, making it into a full-blown natural language. As another example, deaf children of hearing parents learn sign language from non-native speakers, creolizing it. "Creolization by a single living child" has been documented, picking up near-perfect American Sign Language (ASL) from highly imperfect parental ASL. (Pinker, *The Language Instinct*, p. 27.)

129. See, e.g., Terrence W. Deacon, *The Symbolic Species*, p. 22.

130. See Pinker, *The Language Instinct*, pp. 46–47.

Why?

If the discussion so far has pointed in the direction of possible processes or mechanisms for *how* language capacity could evolve, a further issue remains: *Why* do human beings have language? This question could be posed in a way that would take us outside the realm of scientific inquiry, but we will frame it more narrowly, following the scholars Robert C. Berwick and Noam Chomsky by asking: Why only us? Why, that is, are communication systems found across the animal kingdom, and yet language and all the capabilities that come with it are found in only *Homo sapiens* (and perhaps only ever appeared in *Homo sapiens*)?

Berwick and Chomsky have pointed out that the basic trait of language distinguishing it from other communication systems is that one can "glue" smaller pieces, like words, into larger pieces, like prepositional phrases. The ability to vocalize a range of sounds seems to have long been available to many animals. But even the widest range of sounds, useful though they might be, are not language if they cannot be *combined* according to definite rules to produce a huge, perhaps infinite variety of meanings and the ability to think and talk about things that are distant in time and space. It seems that only *Homo sapiens* has the specific ability to glue together units of meaning, and then to glue those larger units together into still larger units, and so forth. Hence, only humans possess a communication system with the flexibility and scope of language.[131]

There is a rather strong analogy between attempts to explain the origin of language and attempts to explain the origin of life. The logic and mechanisms of language change, on the one hand, and of species change, on the other, are well-understood within linguistic and biological domains, respectively. But the core questions of how life and language came into being in the first place leave us grasping at possibilities more than finding definitive answers. As with the origin of life, we are again in the realm of making plausibility arguments, engaging in informed speculation, and sketching areas of active research rather than being able to retell uncontroversial conclusions based on solid evidence.

Mind

It is not easy to sit and tune in to all that you hear during a given moment. But close your eyes and try—there are soft sounds you probably were not aware of at all, and there may be louder sounds that you had been "tuning out."

What is happening to allow you to hear these sounds? The sound waves your ears detect are vibrations in air molecules. These vibrations ripple through the air and come into contact with the eardrum, a tiny membrane inside the ear, after having

---

131. See Robert C. Berwick and Noam Chomsky, *Why Only Us*, and Robert C. Berwick, "Why Only Us."

been funneled and amplified there by the shape of the ear. The eardrum vibrates like the surface of a drum,[132] at the same frequency as the incoming sound wave. These vibrations are then funneled through the tiny bones of the middle ear (the hammer, anvil, and stirrup) to the cochlea of the inner ear. The cochlea is a spiral, snail-shaped organ that, through the basilar membrane and organ of Corti, "transduces" the signal to a neural signal, transforming the physical vibration into an electrical signal. This electrical signal, in turn, is passed along from neuron to neuron, and it ultimately goes to the auditory cortex in the temporal lobe of the brain. All this happens in an instant, a small fraction of a second after the sound reaches your ears.

This may sound like a perfectly good, straightforward, scientific explanation of how and why we hear. But did any of this information actually clarify why your *conscious experience* of sound in this exercise was the way that it was, or why you had a conscious experience of sound at all? One could multiply this question to any other sense as well, and apply it also to the question of why we have a conscious experience of anything, whether thoughts, feelings, or sensations. What is the relationship between first-person conscious experience and the physical, "objective" world of vibrations, electricity, and brains? Is understanding the *origins of mind* the same as, or necessarily connected with, understanding the *evolution of the brain*?

Mind, Consciousness, Physicalism

The brain is a physical thing. You could hold one in your hand, or measure its physical properties—its length and width and height, for example, or the electrical activity within it while it sits inside someone's head. The mind, meanwhile, seems non-physical. Your conscious experience does not seem like something that is part of the external, physical world. It is thus reasonable to pose the question: How did it come to be that in a physical world, the world that usually frames universal history, we as physical beings have a non-physical experience of the mind?

Perhaps unsurprisingly, philosophers all over the world have been pondering the relationship between mind and body, between conscious experience and the physical world, for many centuries. By giving us a deeper understanding of how the brain works, modern neuroscience has added a new dimension to the questions that philosophers can pose, but without fully answering those underlying questions.

One philosophical approach to the relationship between mind and brain is what philosophers of mind call physicalism. (We encountered this word before, in a more general context, in chapter 2.) According to this view, there is nothing fundamentally separate from the brain that ought to be called the "mind"; everything that seems like a mental or conscious experience is just a physical event in the physical world, subject to the same laws of physics (and chemistry, and biology) as

---

132. The eardrum is also known as the tympanic membrane: think "tympani."

everything else. Physicalists maintain that we can, in principle, describe any conscious experience in terms of neurons and electric potentials and neurotransmitters, and that this level of explanation puts us more in touch with reality, with what is really going on, than using our normal "mentalistic" language of thoughts and feelings and sensations. According to this view, the physical facts are all the facts there are.

Physicalism is, arguably, a radical philosophical position. It runs counter to the intuition, cultural beliefs, and linguistic tendencies of nearly every human society. And yet it is popular among present-day Western philosophers, and it is a common working assumption of many specialists in the natural sciences and social sciences. Advocates of physicalism would point to various pieces of evidence for it, including the fact that brain injuries can substantially change one's personality and perception of the world—that is, changes in the physical world can, at least apparently, permanently or semi-permanently alter a person's conscious experience—and the fact that conscious experiences sometimes seem to follow physical experiences, rather than the other way around. In a famous experiment by Benjamin Libet, brain waves appeared to "jump" distinctly before the conscious experience to which they corresponded (see "Causation" in chapter 6).[133]

Far from everyone in philosophy and the sciences is convinced by physicalism, however, and as mentioned in chapter 2, people who work in the humanities tend to contend that "immaterial" things, like mental states and ideas, have paramount importance for understanding why people act the way they do and, indeed, why human history has unfolded the way it has. This does not stand in outright contradiction to a physicalist philosophy of mind, since most physicalists think that mental states are real, even if not ultimately distinct from physical events. But arguably, the very fact of first-person "subjective" experience is itself an argument against a strict physicalist interpretation: because conscious experience seems not only so profoundly different than physical events, but also to behave according to such a different set of rules, one would be hard-pressed to even define what, precisely, it would *mean* to say that the mental is "really" physical. As the philosopher Thomas Nagel has written, "Physicalism is a position we cannot understand because we do not at present have any conception of how it might be true."[134]

---

133. Benjamin Libet, Curtis A. Gleason, Elwood W. Wright, and Dennis K. Pearl, "Time of Conscious Intention to Act in Relation to Onset of Cerebral Activity (Readiness-Potential): The Unconscious Initiation of a Freely Voluntary Act," https://academic.oup.com/brain/article-abstract/106/3/623/271932 . See also Benjamin Libet, "Unconscious Cerebral Initiative and the Role of Conscious Will in Voluntary Action," https://www.cambridge.org/core/journals/behavioral-and-brain-sciences/article/unconscious-cerebral-initiative-and-the-role-of-conscious-will-in-voluntary-action/D215D2A77F1140CD0D8DA6AB93DA5499 .

134. Thomas Nagel, "What Is It Like to Be a Bat?," *The Philosophical Review* 83, no. 4 (1974):446.

Examples of non-physicalist ideas about the relationship between mind and brain include property dualism and substance dualism. Property dualism posits that although the physical world is all that is real, it has two distinct sets of properties: physical properties and mental properties. According to this way of thinking, the mental world arises from, or is produced by, the brain and nervous system. Thus, consciousness is a property of, for example, any organism with a sufficiently complex nervous system, but the mental world is still *distinct* from the physical world—hence, the word "dualism," since in this case the mental and the physical are considered as two distinct kinds of properties of matter. Some property dualists would argue that the physical world can affect the mental world, but that the mental world does not, in any way, affect the physical world: this perspective holds that the mind is an epiphenomenon of the brain, a byproduct of the brain's activities.[135] Other property dualists treat the mind as an emergent property[136] of the brain, and see mental processes as also genuinely capable of affecting physical processes: thoughts can cause neurons to fire (and, correspondingly, lead to other actions in the world), just as neurons firing can produce thoughts.[137]

Substance dualism, meanwhile, treats mental phenomena as connected with a fundamentally non-material reality—such as a non-material *soul* that is a completely distinct kind of entity ("substance") from anything existing in the physical world, including the brain, and that is the basis of a person's essence and conscious experience. There must be significant interaction between the brain and any non-physical soul that gives rise to consciousness, since conscious experience is ordinarily affected strongly by the state of the brain. But substance dualists argue that conscious experience cannot be *reduced to* the state of the brain. Unlike property dualists, substance dualists further argue that conscious experience also does not *arise from* the state of the brain. Instead, brain states and non-physical souls are distinct things that interact with one another, so that mental processes, like thoughts, can produce effects in the physical world and physical processes, like those of the nervous system, can produce effects in conscious experience.

Positing a whole order of reality beyond the material world may seem excessive to some, but this does have its explanatory advantages. Substance dualism, and even property dualism, arguably have an easier time than strict physicalism in explaining why each person has an individual perspective, the ability to "own" one's mental experiences, and to experience them as one's "own" experience. Likewise, if consciousness

---

135. On the other hand, recall the old saying that "correlation does not imply causation." Even if brain events are correlated with conscious thoughts, this does not mean that brain events cause all thoughts in such a way that thoughts have no causal efficacy of their own.

136. See "Reductionism" in chapter 3.

137. For an interesting account of a brief discussion between the Dalai Lama and some neuroscientists at an American medical school about this issue, see Dalai Lama, *The Universe in a Single Atom: The Convergence of Science and Spirituality*, pp. 127–128.

is not reducible to the physical, it would seem to be easier to account for the fact that conscious thoughts and intentions appear to have causal power in their own right: ideas and desires and purposes seem to have the ability to cause things to happen. Mind-body dualism (whether property dualism or substance dualism) could also help to explain why consciousness has a unified experience of the world even though the biochemical processes that may appear to underlie it happen at different rates. And it could be argued that mind-body dualism is the simpler explanation of basic observations: there seem to be (at least) two orders of reality, the mental and physical, and dualism argues that, indeed, there are. Physicalism is simpler in the sense that it posits that only the physical is real, and that the mental is actually physical, yet dualism takes at face value just how profoundly different the mental "world" is than the physical world. Minds can perform actions that it seems physical objects cannot: like *be aware*, consciously *know* things, *feel* pleasure or pain, or *experience* sounds and sights and tastes. It is reasonable enough to posit that distinct substances, or at least distinct properties, underlie such distinct-seeming orders of reality.

That said, *all* of these options—physicalism, property dualism, and substance dualism—are relatively recent Western philosophical categories.[138] Religious and philosophical traditions around the world sometimes split up questions about mind, body, and soul along very different lines. For example, the Samkhya school of thought within Hindu philosophy posits two fundamental realities, Purusha and Prakriti (spirit and matter),[139] but places mind and its activities (reflecting, reasoning, feeling, etc.) under the category of *matter*. Only when illuminated by Purusha, pure consciousness, does *mind* become *conscious*. Or to take a different example from Western philosophy before René Descartes (1596–1650) introduced modern substance dualism, Aristotle and Thomas Aquinas offered the idea that soul and body are not two substances but one unified substance: that spirit and matter are distinct, yet so intertwined that it is "as pointless to ask whether soul and body are one as it is to ask whether the seal and the wax are one."[140] These approaches offer thought-provoking, alternative viewpoints from which to consider the relationship between mind and body.

In any case, if a strict reductive physicalism were demonstrably complete and correct, universal histories would, in principle, have no need for a separate account of the origins and effects of mind and could focus only on the evolution of the brain. However, as we have already seen in the co-evolutionary accounts of

---

138. It is not that the basic ideas underlying these philosophical categories are completely novel; variations on them have been articulated or implied in many times and places. But the particular set of alternatives presented here, especially as framed in connection with science and the workings of the brain, has been characteristic of Western philosophy in recent decades.

139. See "Creation" in chapter 1.

140. Stanford Encyclopedia of Philosophy, "Saint Thomas Aquinas," https://plato.stanford.edu/entries/aquinas/ , drawing on Aristotle's *De anima II.1.*

the origins of culture, language, and the physical structure of the brain itself, many historical accounts of the evolution of the brain implicitly agree, or even assume, that the most *non-physical-seeming* aspects of human experience—like ideas, communicated through language and culture—have the ability to cause changes in the *physical* world, including in the physical structure of the brain.

The problems posed by strict physicalism are only compounded when we consider non-human animals and ask the question of whether there are "other minds." Peter Godfrey-Smith points out that we humans have a sense of *engagement* with many animals (as anyone who has ever interacted with a pet cat or dog knows) that points to some kind of conscious experience in them. He argues that there may be a distinction between sentience (the ability to feel or perceive) and consciousness, where sentience is a byproduct of the "evolution of sensing and acting"[141]—a kind of property dualism applied widely throughout the animal kingdom and reminiscent of the distinction made in the ancient world by Aristotle, and in medieval Europe by the Scholastic philosophers, between the "rational soul" of humans and the "sensitive souls" of many animals. If, indeed, the brain (or other nervous systems) gives rise to sentience or to consciousness, as property dualists maintain, it fits well with the observation that we share many brain features with other mammals, and fewer brain features with those animals that seem to have minds that are less familiar or engage-able (to us): a lizard, say, or an octopus.[142]

Even in this case, however, there is a question that universal histories, as well as philosophers, have difficulty addressing and thus often avoid: How and why does the mental arise from the physical? The philosopher David Chalmers writes, "It is widely agreed that experience arises from a physical basis, but we have no good explanation of why and how it so arises. Why should physical processing give rise to a rich inner life at all? It seems objectively unreasonable that it should, and yet it does."[143] Similarly, Robert Bellah argues, "Despite some extravagant claims made by a

---

141. Peter Godfrey-Smith, *Other Minds: The Octopus, the Sea, and the Deep Origins of Consciousness*, p. 79.

142. In speculating about any non-human organism's experience of the world, there is a real danger of imposing human categories and reading human experiences into something that must be profoundly different. Strictly speaking, we do not know the experiences of other animals, at all, even if we can make many guesses. As Brandon Keim writes, paraphrasing the neuroscientist Joseph LeDoux, "Animals might have subjective experiences . . . but people shouldn't hasten to understand them in terms of our own." (Keim, "Animal Minds: The New Anthropomorphism," http://www.chronicle.com/article/Animal-Minds/237915 .) Or as the philosopher Thomas Nagel writes, "I want to know what it is like for a *bat* to be a bat. Yet if I try to imagine this, I am restricted to the resources of my own mind, and those resources are inadequate to the task. I cannot perform it either by imagining additions to my present experience, or by imagining segments gradually subtracted from it, or by imagining some combination of additions, subtractions, and modifications." (Nagel, "What Is It Like to Be a Bat?," p. 446.)

143. David Chalmers, "Facing Up to the Problem of Consciousness," *Journal of Consciousness Studies* 2, no. 3 (1995):201.

few adventurous souls, we actually don't have a clue as to how consciousness emerges from the underlying physics; we don't even know the appropriate questions to ask."[144]

Whether human minds are the only truly conscious minds, or whether there are other minds, there seems to be fertile ground for productive interaction between history and philosophy as well as psychology—literally, the "study of the soul," from the Greek *psyche*—even if psychology too has often focused strongly and intentionally on the physical and the measurable. Universal histories could benefit from sophisticated engagement with the philosophy of mind, just as they could benefit from engagement with other philosophical domains explored in other parts of this book. The full role of mind in universal history, and its interactions with matter, are issues that could be much more deeply explored.

Perhaps philosophy could benefit as well from interactions with universal history. The philosophy of mind presents some difficult questions no matter what one's basic stance is. But as we have sketched here, perhaps asking these questions against a universal-historical backdrop provides a new angle from which to respond, since universal histories consider the broad sweep of living organisms in general, the history of life, and the place of human beings within it all.

Extended Side Note: Other Minds

Having explored the domains of culture, technology, language, and especially mind enables us to speak again to the question of human distinctiveness. What seems to be emerging is a vision in which animals—that is, non-human animals—are far smarter, more capable, more complexly social, and more mentally present than many strands of 20th-century science acknowledged. Our primate ancestors are certainly part of this story. But it does not seem a major leap to say that humans really do have a unique way of engaging with and understanding the world. We have explored this in different ways throughout this chapter, comparing human culture to the various forms of information exchange and social learning in animals, human technology to the forms of tool use in the animal kingdom, human language to animal communication, and human consciousness to animal sentience. As Terrence Deacon writes, "Biologically, we are just another ape. Mentally, we are a new phylum of organisms."[145] We have a rich internal world, a form of self-knowledge that is surely much different than what any non-linguistic animals have.

Yet there are pitfalls to speaking in this way. At the same time as we have unique forms of culture, technology, communication, and sentience, it also seems clear that forms of these phenomena exist widely throughout the animal

---

144. Bellah, *Religion in Human Evolution*, p. 758.

145. Terrence W. Deacon, *The Symbolic Species: The Co-evolution of Language and the Brain*, p. 23.

world, and perhaps even more broadly throughout the living world (i.e., including plants and microscopic forms of life). It has grown popular of late to undermine humanity's supposed superiority by showing that other animals are actually more similar to us than we realize. Defenders of human distinctiveness then emphasize equally real differences between humans and other animals. But arguments for or against human distinctiveness that are based on *capacities* or *abilities* to think, feel, or do certain things have the potential to deny value and worth not only to various animals, but also to many human beings, especially "the young, the old, the ill, and the disabled,"[146] some of whom may lack or have lost a given capacity. Instead of abilities or capacities defining our humanity (or our worth), perhaps it would be better to say that our humanity is what enables our spectrum of capacities. Language does not make us human; being human makes us capable of language. Consciousness does not make us human; being human makes us capable of consciousness— and likewise for culture and technology. A person raised in the wild, without language, would still be *human*, after all, but a parrot that learned an especially large number of words would not. Rather than emphasizing capacities to think, feel, or do certain things, therefore, perhaps it is better to treat humanity as an irreducible category, and to focus on what we as humans *are*, in our wholeness.

Universal histories should not need to justify including human history in their cosmic pictures on the basis of human *distinctiveness* from the rest of the animal world. The story of human history is worth telling in its own right, as, indeed, are other animal histories. Each exists as its own heading, with cosmic and terrestrial contexts as a backdrop and all life being interconnected from the beginning. If there are more similarities between human beings and other animals than were previously recognized, why would that mean we need to demote the human person's status, rather than promote (to some extent, in certain ways) that of the other animals? Caitrin Keiper writes:

> Animal science that describes their real abilities, where they can receive credit for intelligent or compassionate actions driven by more than mere instinct, would by extension elevate man's stature too – not flatten it with animals', but raise them both above the low bar of pure determinism.[147]

---

146. Caitrin Keiper, "Do Elephants Have Souls?" The main thrust of our argument in this paragraph owes much to Keiper's piece.

147. Ibid. In the same article, Keiper also writes: "It is interesting to consider how the everyday proximity to different kinds of creatures may have affected the development of these beliefs. That is, elephants, higher-order primates, and the like are not native to the West, and thus our basic common sense of what 'animals' can think or do calibrates at the level of, say, horses and dogs— not to malign the intelligence of horses and dogs, which we tend to underappreciate anyway. But in Asia and Africa, where there's been much more natural interaction between people and very smart animals—and not as novelties but as members of other communities—most cultures seem to take a more expansive view of animal potential." It is also worth pointing out that cruelty and indifference to animals often go along with cruelty and indifference to humans, and that empathy for suffering in animals often goes along with empathy for suffering in humans.

Integrating the Human Sciences: Human Beings and Being Human

A broad synthesis of the "human sciences"—including anthropology, psychology, evolutionary biology, sociobiology, linguistics, and neuroscience—might relate all the main topics we have explored in this chapter's sections to one another. Technology, for instance, is not just a scientific reality, but also a deeply human and cultural one. Language shapes our conscious experience and may have influenced the evolution of the brain even as changes in the brain may have enabled language. The mind is culturally situated and shaped by language and technology. Language enables much of human culture and activity.[148] And culture, language, and mind are all expressions of our humanity. Universal histories are important places where such integration of human sciences can, and does, occur.

At the same time, it is important not to reduce human beings to less than they are in the name of science. The human sciences all have their particular approaches and their forms of reductionism. A certain methodological reductionism (see "Reductionism" in chapter 3) may well be necessary in order to make research questions manageable within each of these domains. But if our ultimate goal is to see the whole human being more clearly, rather than closing off important dimensions of humanity from our understanding, then these disciplines ultimately must be placed within an interpretive framework that is broader and larger than all of them.

This means, among other things, the need to resist the "scientization" of the human person even as we learn various things about the biology and evolution of humanity, technology, culture, language, and the mind from science—with scientific knowledge ideally complementing rather than replacing the various forms of humanistic historical and cultural knowledge. Václav Havel, the famous Czech playwright, dissident, and politician, put it this way:

> The more thoroughly all our organs and their functions, their internal structure and the biochemical reactions that take place within them, are described, the more we seem to fail to grasp the spirit, purpose and meaning of the system that they create together and that we experience as our unique

---

148. Though the loss of language does not remove our humanity, or necessarily our mental presence: the French-Canadian monk known as Brother John experienced severe but temporary episodes of aphasia in which he lost all ability to express or comprehend language, but he remained conscious, aware, and capable in other regards. Peter Godfrey-Smith writes, "John would later describe these episodes as very difficult and confusing, but he did manage, and he was mentally *present* during them." (Peter Godfrey-Smith, *Other Minds: The Octopus, the Sea, and the Deep Origins of Consciousness*, p. 143.)

self. . . . Experts can explain anything in the objective world to us, yet we understand our own lives less and less.[149]

In a similar vein, the essayist Caitrin Keiper writes, while discussing the promise and peril of speaking anthropomorphically about elephants:

> In modern Western science, the whole concept of life is so mechanical that, if you look closely, not even people are supposed to be anthropomorphized. Emotional, holistic terms such as *love, sorrow,* and *concern* have no place in an impoverished language of chemical transactions at the micro level and selection pressures at the macro. Not that chemical transactions and selection pressures are not essential influences, because of course they are—but from our current knowledge of them, they are acutely inadequate to describing the subtleties of lived experience.[150]

If universal histories claim to tell us something about ourselves as human beings, where we came from and where we are going, we must be able to recognize our full selves in them, rather than being asked "to pretend that we are not what we know ourselves to be—thinking and feeling subjects, moral agents with free will, and social beings whose culture builds upon the facts of the physical world but is not limited to them."[151] An account of life and the world must include that which is recognizable as human, in this philosophical and humanistic sense, as fully as it sketches our place in the cosmos.

---

149. Václav Havel, "The New Measure of Man," https://www.nytimes.com/1994/07/08/opinion/the-new-measure-of-man.html . These same words, with slightly different punctuation, appear as the text of Havel's July 4, 1994, speech upon acceptance of the US National Constitution Center's Liberty Medal; see https://constitutioncenter.org/liberty-medal/recipients/vaclav-havel .

150. Caitrin Keiper, "Do Elephants Have Souls?"

151. John Sexton, "A Reductionist History of Humankind," http://www.thenewatlantis.com/publications/a-reductionist-history-of-humankind .

6

HISTORY

We turn now to the story of humans in history, the way that term is usually understood. In the first section, "History," we consider the place of human history in the wider contexts of universal history, and conversely also reflect on how universal histories fit in (or alongside) the broader landscape of existing historical scholarship. This brings up matters of scale, of contingency and context, of agency and determinism: all classic issues in *historiography*, the study of how history is written. In "Contingency," we discuss the idea of contingency as a unifying framework for understanding history. In "Context," we map three broad "eras" for all of human history and explore the power of large-scale histories to clarify the sometimes radically distinct contexts in which humans of different times have lived their lives. In "Population," we elaborate on the advantages and disadvantages of considering world population numbers as a fundamental driver of historical change, and in "Causation," we explore how larger philosophical questions about causation, human agency, and determinism apply to the writing of history.

History

"Well-behaved women seldom make history."

This famous saying, coming out of the mid-1970s, communicates the view that women had to break out of boundaries set for them in historically male-dominated societies in order to "make history." Perhaps surprisingly, especially for those used to hearing the phrase in "rebellious" contexts and seeing it emblazoned on bumper stickers, T-shirts, and coffee mugs, the line first appeared in a scholarly historical journal, in an article about Puritan funeral services penned by a graduate student at the University of New Hampshire. That author, Laurel Thatcher Ulrich—who later went on to win the Pulitzer Prize for history and to become a professor at Harvard—was not originally encouraging women to "misbehave." Rather, she offered this catchy dictum as a commentary on how history should be written, urging historians to more fully value the lives and contributions of "common" people, who are rarely written about in history textbooks:

> Cotton Mather called them "the hidden ones." They never preached or sat in a deacon's bench. Nor did they vote or attend Harvard. Neither, because they were virtuous women, did they question God or the magistrates. They prayed secretly, read the Bible through at least once a year, and went to hear the minister preach even when it snowed. Hoping for an eternal crown, they never asked to be remembered on earth. And they haven't been. Well-behaved women seldom make history; against Antinomians and witches, these pious matrons have had little chance at all. Most historians, considering the domestic by definition irrelevant, have simply assumed the pervasiveness of similar attitudes in the seventeenth century.[1]

On the scales of a universal history, individual lives—whether of a king or of an 18th-century midwife—have a tendency to disappear, too tiny to see in the grand landscape of historical time. We might hear instead of vast aggregates: agricultural societies and hunter-gatherers, villages and cities, empires and kingdoms, the Industrial Revolution and colonialism, the technology of warfare in the 20th century and of the internet in the 21st. It is easy to begin thinking that the individual—any individual—does not really change history, no matter how well- or ill-behaved she or he may be, but instead fades into the background against so many larger impersonal forces.

Yet it is actually easy to see that individual people, even the most ordinary and unnoticed of people, do matter—and not just because they have the dignity and worth of *being* a human being, but also because they change the course of history. Starting with the simplest possible way to make this point, consider the biological fact that everyone has two parents. This means that everyone has four grandparents, eight great-grandparents, and so forth. Going back n generations, each person has 2^n ancestors. But this would suggest that 40 generations ago, which takes us back no more than perhaps 1,200 years, each person has approximately 1 trillion ancestors. However, no more than a few hundred million people were alive on Earth at that time. How can this be?

The reason is that the ancestors are not all distinct from one another.[2] In fact, if one goes back far enough in history—and computer simulations show that it does

---

1. Laurel Thatcher Ulrich, "Vertuous Women Found: New England Ministerial Literature, 1668–1735," *American Quarterly* 28, no. 1 (1976):20.

2. Bill Bryson presents a similar argument, explained in a slightly different way for a somewhat different purpose. (Bryson, *A Short History of Nearly Everything*, pp. 397–398.)

not require going back all that far (just several thousand years)[3]—everyone who was alive at that time either has everyone currently alive as a descendant or has no presently living descendants at all. Contemplate that for a moment: if any one of those universal common ancestors had died before having children, or if his or her own parents had had one fewer child, then none of us would be here today. The planet would still be populated, presumably, but with a completely different set of people. And this is true not just of a single common ancestor, but of a whole host of them.

We can push the question one step further. Let's say that we remove one of those universal common ancestors, so that the humans populating Earth are now a different set of people. How did history unfold over those several thousand years with a different set of individuals on the planet? What would be the same as in the history of humanity that actually happened? What would be different? Would the Roman Empire, for instance, have been? Perhaps so, with a single ancestral change—but with enough changes, maybe not. Aggregating individual shifts, after all, could lead to larger and larger changes that propagate through the generations, and at some point, presumably even very large-scale entities would also take different shapes. If not Rome, would a similar but distinct empire have emerged? At around the same time? With similar characteristics, and if so, which ones? Would a series of giant land-based empires still have emerged from roughly 4,000 years ago to the present?

The answers to these questions are debatable, to say the least, and are at some level unknowable. Perhaps changing one person—or two, or ten, or a thousand, or even a million—would not materially alter such large-scale outcomes. But the thought experiment strikes at the root of fundamental questions at the foundations of any history, including universal histories. How much do large historical trends depend on the choices (or existences) of individuals? How much do they depend on collective human trends and institutions like culture or politics or religion? And how much do they depend on "impersonal" forces and frameworks of biology, geography, and environment that seem less likely to respond to individual agency? In a historical narrative, how much should we emphasize, how much weight should we give to, "basic" and universal biological matters of food production, water acquisition, disease and epidemiology, or demography, and how much should we emphasize the apparently irreducible choices of individuals, made in a particular moment and with every indication that a different choice, with different consequences, was also genuinely possible?

Universal Histories in the Context of History-Writing

While universal histories operate on more expansive time scales than most, many of the same problems and questions that they face confront other writers of history.

---

3. See, e.g., Douglas L. T. Rohde, Steve Olson, and Joseph T. Chang, "Modelling the Recent Common Ancestry of All Living Humans," https://www.nature.com/articles/nature02842 .

The subtitle of the present book notwithstanding, universal histories are not really histories of *everything*. They are frameworks for thinking about trends and patterns in history on a large scale, which leave out a great many details and observations just as surely as any other history does. As the historian S. A. M. Adshead has pointed out with regard to world history:

> World history can be as broad as an ideal of knowing everything about everything, a total history. It can be as narrow as the diplomatic relations between states, an international political history. It can take a middle course and study patterns, whether Hegelian, Marxist, Toynbean or Teilhardian, supposedly common to all histories: not the whole of history, but the whole in history.[4]

Regardless of which path a given history takes, some things must come into focus and others must go out of focus. In a certain sense, Christian's *Maps of Time* says it all in the title: a universal history is a map of time. And just as maps must highlight certain patterns and places while leaving much else "unsaid," so too must a universal history privilege certain forms of analysis, certain themes and methods, certain actors and places, while closing others off—or never even mentioning them at all. We have argued that this is true of the history of the universe, Earth, and life, and it is true likewise of human history.

The way present-day historians write, including universal histories, has itself taken shape over time. Certain ancient writers, such as Herodotus and Thucydides in ancient Greece or Sima Qian in ancient China, are regarded as "ancestors" of modern professional history-writing: they engaged in interpretive storytelling about the past that was closely grounded in evidence, and they sought to understand patterns of cause and effect in human actions.[5] History as a professional discipline, one that produced a particular kind of writing by a specific group of people identified as "historians," began much more recently, in a story conventionally told by reference to figures such as Leopold von Ranke (1795–1886), who sought to professionalize the writing of history in the 1800s, a time when many other academic disciplines were also professionalizing and taking the shape we know and recognize today. Von Ranke is particularly famous for the dictum that historians should report history "as it actually happened"—in other words, the historian must have a fundamental professional allegiance to integrity, accuracy, and fidelity to the *evidence* that is selected and used in studying, analyzing, corroborating, and understanding the past. The historian, according to this understanding, must draw conclusions that

---

4. S. A. M. Adshead, *Central Asia in World History*, p. 3.

5. See, e.g., Thomas R. Martin, *Herodotus and Sima Qian: The First Great Historians of Greece and China: A Brief History with Documents*.

are well-grounded and based on a disciplined interpretation of evidence, privileging such conclusions over any speculations that are not based on such evidence.

Mainstream professional history-writing, at least since von Ranke, has focused on history as written at the level of nation-states—with a general trend toward narrowing the focus to still smaller scales in time and space, but even then usually grounded in the context of a given nation. "History as a profession emerged hand in hand with the nation-state,"[6] and historical subfields thus often correspond to the scale of nation-states: someone who wishes to train as a historian might enter the field of American history, or Russian history, or Brazilian history, for instance. There are exceptions, such as those historians who zoom down to tiny scales, writing "microhistories" that relate individual life stories (although even these are often nested in, and can be read through the lens of, their subjects' local, regional, and national connections). Meanwhile, a comparatively small group of historians[7] have expanded their focus to larger scales, writing *transnational* history, *global* history, *world* history, *environmental* history, *deep* history, and *Big* History. Transnational history maintains nation-states as a framing idea but engages the histories of multiple nations, especially through crossings of national boundaries. In principle, some kinds of global history engage the history of the entire world, or patterns that stretch across it. World history, as a slightly different approach, attempts to treat nation-states not as a framing device but as one among many historically contingent phenomena,[8] focusing instead on other forms of connection between people and on comparison of different cultures and civilizations. Environmental history focuses on engaging biology, geology, and geography to understand the environmental context and effects of human communities. Deep history presents a planet-scaled human history, one that seeks the roots of human behavioral patterns and cultural expressions in a very long past stretching back to the Paleolithic. And Big History, as readers of the present book already know, situates the history of the entire human species in cosmic, geological, and biological context.[9]

Examples of these large-scale approaches can be found in scholarly writings published in the early twentieth century, and sometimes earlier. But by most

---

6. Sven Beckert, *Empire of Cotton: A Global History*, p. xxi.

7. The movement toward larger scales in history-writing, at least in the form of global or world history, is still at least slightly intellectually "fringe" in some scholarly circles. In the United States, it is mainstream and very common at the primary- and secondary-school (K-12) level, but has only recently started to achieve representation in many university history departments (and become a growth area in academic hiring). Big History, by contrast, is far less common. In fact it is almost absent at the postsecondary level as a specialty that defines hiring priorities or graduate admissions (the places where resources most matter).

8. That is, the nation-state is a historically situated form of political organization that often defines the contours along which histories are written, but world history tries to view history from outside the nation-state lens.

9. These brief profiles of each field are inspired by Matt Villeneuve and Phil Deloria.

measures, they have only really started to flourish in the last generation or so. Even now, mainstream historians mostly write histories at time scales measured by years or decades, and at geographical scales of the nation-state or smaller, covering at most the past 500 years. More ancient histories are only a small part of most history departments. World history, and especially Big History, are even further from the norm, and have long been comparatively absent in most university or college settings. So unlike past chapters, which dealt with fields of study that have considerable disciplinary consensus (astronomy, geology, paleontology, and so on), this chapter and chapter 7 address highly contested territory. Many historians—and perhaps even most—would not consider "the entire world" or "modern humanity as a whole" to be legitimate subjects for investigation, because they are seen as impossible to study with the necessary disciplinary grounding in original sources. Meanwhile, we aim to point out the interdependence of small and large scales, considering large scales as context for small scales and small scales as generators of large-scale patterns.

Evidence, Deep Time, and World History

To investigate and know anything about the past requires the discovery and interpretation of vestiges, or traces,[10] that the past leaves behind. For cosmologists, this takes the form of light from galaxies or the early universe, emitted millions or billions of years ago. For geologists, the interpretation of rocks is key, and paleontologists and archaeologists rely on bones or artifacts buried in the Earth. Customarily, the vestiges of the past that historians use have been written texts, which sometimes have been supplemented by other materials, such as visual or artistic products, or material culture of many kinds. To explore the ancient past, historians may consult archaeological evidence and, more recently, evidence drawn from the Earth

---

To Ponder: A History of You

Stop reading. Find a piece of blank paper, and then locate a (probably electronic) stopwatch or clock that shows both minutes and seconds. Ready? Come back to this page when you are set. Now—take *four minutes* (no more, no less) to write a history of yourself. That's right: a history of YOU. Don't think too much about it; the clock is already running. Just write! (Do this before continuing to read. There will be a follow-up Side Note a few pages later.)

---

10. See, e.g., Daniel Lord Smail, *On Deep History and the Brain*, p. 48.

sciences of environmental conditions (climate, local availability of water, etc.). The central emphasis on written texts has been strong enough, however, that the subject we today call "history" has traditionally been defined as beginning—that is, being *possible*—precisely when the first written texts appear.

The fact that disciplinary history has focused on such texts produces certain kinds of knowledge with characteristic patterns. For example, historians have traditionally focused on state-based agricultural and urban societies that used writing to preserve records, rather than on nomadic or foraging societies that avoided writing. This emphasis on a particular kind of source helped to reinforce a consistent, systematic bias toward viewing the landed societies that produced these sources as more knowable, relatable, or "advanced" than others. Also, we only have a small fraction of the writing that was originally produced by people in far-distant times—only those sources that survived. This means that historians have better access to anything that someone in the past thought was worth preserving and then later saved and categorized in an archive or library, or that simply was written on easily preserved materials. Textual evidence can produce a rich variety of information and make it possible to ask many new kinds of questions, but even leaving aside matters of potential bias or skewing within the sources (e.g., who was writing the text, for what purpose, and what they might have not known or intentionally left out), these materials give us access only to certain times, places, types of societies, and roles.

Perhaps even more notably for purposes of a universal history, this focus on writing has, for the most part, restricted historians to the study of the past 5,000 years or so, since that was, as far as we know, when writing was first invented. As practitioners of the emerging field of deep history have described, using texts as the primary form of evidence within the discipline of history is what created the familiar distinction between "history" and "prehistory"—an arbitrary divide based on writing as the line of demarcation. In other words, prehistory is *by definition* the time before writing. So dividing time in this way tends to suggest that the "historical" past is different, and perhaps more knowable and relatable, than the more nebulous and static-seeming "prehistoric" past.[11]

Yet for all its advantages in the modern world, writing is far from the only vestige of the past that gives us access to the stories of earlier humans; see chapter 5 for some of the many other sources of archaeological, linguistic, genetic, and geological evidence that converge on a picture of what human lives were like tens of thousands of years ago, long before any written records survived. Viewed against the backdrop of the entire human past—stretching over tens of thousands of years or

---

11. See, e.g., Andrew Shryock and Daniel Lord Smail, "Preface," in *Deep History: The Architecture of Past and Present*, p. x.

more—writing seems an activity that is not even common, let alone universal. The deep historian Daniel Lord Smail writes that "we should imagine a cone of increasing evidence, swollen but not fundamentally transformed in the past five thousand years by the addition of writing."[12]

Even where they exist, written records provide an *additional*, but not necessarily a *superior*, source of evidence. Accepting written sources at face value is not generally well-advised. As the historian E. H. Carr writes, "No document can tell us more than what the author of the document thought—what he thought had happened, what he thought ought to happen or would happen, or perhaps only what he wanted others to think he thought, or even only what he himself thought he thought. None of this means anything until the historian has got to work on it and deciphered it."[13] And on the flip side, orally transmitted histories have their own (albeit equally qualifiable) historical reliability. Remarkable examples include the Native Americans of the Pacific Northwest possibly having retained accurate oral traditions of the massive flooding that occurred when the Lake Missoula ice dam failed repeatedly, up to about 15,000 years ago. And Australian Aboriginal oral traditions appear to record geological events that can now be confirmed through other forms of evidence as having occurred over 10,000 years ago,[14] with some claims reaching even further back.

In summary, the act of writing something down does not make it magically accurate or more advanced. The additional kinds of hard evidence used by scholars working in fields like deep history and Big History go beyond the traditional historian's reliance on written texts: universal histories rely both on written texts and on non-written sources of evidence to fill in a more complete picture of human history, reaching more than the usual limit of 5,000 years back in time and including pieces of the larger puzzle that might otherwise be thrust to the margins.

---

12. Smail, *On Deep History and the Brain*, p. 66.

13. E. H. Carr, *What Is History?*, p. 16. As Marc Bloch writes, "the evidence of witnesses in spite of themselves" (Bloch, *The Historian's Craft*, p. 61) is often more telling than the face value of a document. Writing during World War II, Bloch poses the question: Would we not rather have a few confidential military reports than all the newspapers of 1938 and 1939? (Bloch, p. 62.) Conscious motives are not always reliable as guides to why people do what they do, even well-intentioned memory is fallible, and there are often multiple reasons behind any given individual's actions (see Carr, p. 57; Bloch, pp. 99, 195). The problem is not exactly that we are relying on the testimony of human beings, however; practically all knowledge is drawn from the testimony of others, as we saw under "Science" in chapter 4 (cf. Bloch, p. 50).

14. See, e.g., John Upton, "Ancient Sea Rise Tale Told Accurately for 10,000 Years," https://www.scientificamerican.com/article/ancient-sea-rise-tale-told-accurately-for-10-000-years/ . Also see David Montgomery, *The Rocks Don't Lie: A Geologist Investigates Noah's Flood*, pp. 176, 211–213.

To Ponder: Southeast Asian Inscriptions

Virtually the only writings that survive from early Southeast Asian history (more than several centuries ago) are inscriptions carved in hard surfaces, such as stone and metal, e.g. on temple walls and stelae (monuments). Due to the tropical conditions, nearly all other writing that had been committed to any kind of more perishable material has disintegrated. How do you think this kind of selective preservation of writing affects the stories historians can reconstruct about this period? Can you think of other potential ways to gain evidence about this time and place that would help to round out, and put in context, the writing that does survive?

Information and Interpretation in World History

This book has already focused on histories at the scales of the universe, Earth, and life, including the forms of evidence that lie behind such histories, the claims made by experts in the corresponding disciplines, and the big-picture interpretive stories that are woven out of them. One might think that a global history of humanity, so much shorter in time and with so many different forms of evidence behind it, would be more straightforward to assemble than these larger-scaled histories of the inanimate and living worlds, and that assembling a single, definitive account of the human past would be possible—even if not exactly easy. Yet it is often at this smaller scale, the human scale, that universal histories seem to be at their most ambitious. With respect to evidence, the character of historical claims that experts make, and the broader interpretation of what it all means, there is such richness in the sweep of human experience: How can we possibly integrate all of it into a single picture?

One potential response is that we can't, and that we shouldn't even try. Someone raising this objection might argue that while human beings inhabit one planet, there is such a bewildering variety of cultural worlds, and so much crucial detail that must drop out of any large-scale account, that composing a history of the world is a fundamentally flawed project. No one could possibly read all of the primary sources, of all humans around the world, in every language. So while certain kinds of basic information might be possible to assemble and put in one place, the interpretive consequences of presenting any single narrative as "the" history of everything would always make such a project misleading.

This is an important objection. A universal history aspires to speak broadly—so broadly, in fact, that any other historical narrative could, in principle, "fit within" it. But if we think of one narrative as being *the* overriding one, or of one framework as being *the* overarching one, we run the risk of selection bias and reductionism: viewing politics, or economics, or environment, or culture, or human agency, or cooperation, or conflict, or some such force or feature of the world as being uniquely fundamental, all-encompassing, or all-structuring in a way that it probably is not. Instead, all these features and more are mixed together—but even a world history that incorporates and integrates and blends all of these elements will have its shortcomings, its contestable points, its tendencies to emphasize certain things at the expense of others. Any particular universal history is only "a," not "the," history of everything. In any case, the writing of history is driven by what kinds of questions historians ask, and as long as the character of those questions continues to change through time, there can be no single, definitive account of history that is valid for all time.

Yet there *are* certain large-scale patterns we can focus on in writing world history that provide context or background for more specific, smaller-scale histories. A history of the United States would not tell a history of Michigan, then of Ohio, then of Indiana, and then of Illinois, as if they were all separate stories.[15] Similarly, a world history that focuses on regions of the world while ignoring their interconnections risks arbitrary separation of connected stories. Moreover, if we learn that, for example, Japan began as a collection of hunter-gatherer societies, some of which developed agriculture and denser settlements with time, leading to the later establishment of cities and states, and then we turn to Spain and find the same general pattern, and then we turn to Mesoamerica and find the same pattern, should we not make sense out of this by perceiving generally describable processes of settlement, food production, and social interactions? There will, of course, be exceptions to this, as there are to nearly any rule, but there is a larger story and set of dynamics that each region participates in. Learning about world history may not capture all the detail one would need in order to understand Japan, or Spain, or Mesoamerica in detail, but that is not its point. And the light that world history does shed on wider, often shared human experiences can set key contexts for smaller-scale histories.

More than that, the ultimate goal of world histories is rarely a mere *description* of change and continuity[16] over time, but rather an *explanation* or analysis of the dynamics of why and how changes over time took place, rooted in an understanding of human beings as a species and in the particularities of each culture, in each time, and in each specific place. This makes the writing of world history, like the history of the universe, Earth, and life, as well as smaller-scale human histories, a fundamentally *interpretive* task, even as it also rests on a foundation of evidence. The interpretation of historical significance is not a free-for-all in history any more

---

15. Thanks to Bob Bain for this analogy.

16. Historians often discuss their discipline as one that addresses both change and continuity, but as mentioned under "Biosphere" in chapter 4, the balance is a difficult one to strike: a good story seems to require the narration of change; continuities have a tendency to fade into the background, and so change often becomes the focus of historical writing. See the "Causation" section later in this chapter for more on the relationship between causation, continuity, and change.

than it is in science; it is not open to an infinite range of views. Historical stories must conform to the best available evidence. But as Carr writes:

> Every journalist knows today that the most effective way to influence opinion is by the selection and arrangement of the appropriate facts. It used to be said that facts speak for themselves. This is, of course, untrue. The facts speak only when the historian calls on them: it is he [or she] who decides to which facts to give the floor, and in what order or context.[17]

What historians do is the disciplined *interpretation* of evidence to convert it into a story. As Carr points out repeatedly in *What Is History?* (the title of his book), the historian is also part of history and writes with a set of sensibilities molded by a context of time and place. Hence, before you study the "facts" of history, it is worth studying not only the historian, but also the historian's historical and social environment.[18]

Side Note: Following Up on "A History of You"

Look back at your "History of Me" essay from the *To Ponder* feature. What is the earliest point in time, and the most distant geographical location, to which you referred? It is fairly likely that you did not mention anything more than a century or two ago, even though you could have (in accord with the approach of universal histories) begun anywhere—even with the Big Bang. If you did not, though, this may be, at least in part, because you fell into a certain *genre* of writing: a personal narrative.

To see the effects of having an implied genre, imagine you were going to tell your story in different settings—like a job interview, or a psychology class, or an interreligious-dialogue group, or a kindergarten classroom. In each case, you would highlight different things. You still have the same set of life experiences: we might say that the "informational level" of your life remains the same in all cases. But there are different ways to frame your story, interpret it, and invest it with a certain meaning, even if you are never lying or misrepresenting yourself. We have seen how the same set of raw materials in the history of the universe, Earth, and life can be invested with different meanings, and how choices of interpretation and framing and analysis can make different sense out of the same underlying events. This same theme, fundamental to how historical narratives work, repeats at the scale of human history.

---

17. Carr, *What Is History?*, p. 9.

18. Ibid., pp. 26, 54.

Large Scales and the Individual

What about the individuals discussed at the beginning of this chapter? Behind abstract social entities like cultures or empires or economies are particular *people* who lived their lives in conditions shaped by these larger structures.[19] Individuals are certainly shaped by the groups and the structures in which they participate. But groups are combinations of individuals; individuals are not combinations of groups. And as the first section of this chapter argued, not only groups and structures, but also individual persons—the "smallest" scale in world history—may have a real, almost incalculable influence on everything that comes after them. In the rest of this chapter, we will keep returning to the question of how we can think about history at all scales, uniting the smallest scales of individual persons with the largest forces and structures of history,[20] according each scale an integrity and importance of its own, and recognizing their profound interdependence.

Contingency

It has often been said (in an aphorism dating to the early 18th century) that nothing in life is inevitable except death and taxes—but even taxes are a relatively recent historical phenomenon in the grand scope of human history. We might say that taxes are not really *inevitable* at all, but arose as a *contingent* outcome of certain kinds of political structures.

The idea of contingency means that historical events are not fully predictable but, instead, are situationally produced—that is, they are conditional on previous events that may shape the range of possible outcomes but that do not predetermine any one result. To say that one event is contingent upon a prior event means that it depends on the prior event as a prerequisite to make it possible; one might say, for instance, that the rise of Baghdad as a center of Islamic scholarship was contingent upon the life of Muhammad and the rise of Islam in the first place: the earlier events did not directly *cause* the later events, but the later events could not have happened without the earlier. To state that an event was *contingent* in general, without further qualification, means that the event would not have been possible without a certain sequence of previous events or actions being taken by particular actors, that it did not have to happen the way it did. Contingency is not another word for randomness, chance,[21] or accident, but it does emphasize a lack of inevitability in the way

---

19. Echoing Bloch in *The Historian's Craft* (p. 151; cf. pp. 25–27).

20. Not unlike the way in which the Big Bang unites the smallest scales with the largest in the story of how structure in the universe first formed.

21. In a sense, chance is a human mode of explanation rather than something intelligible within nature. Things have causes.

that events unfold. Most historians view with visceral suspicion any and all historical narratives that appear overly neat, making the outcomes that *did* occur appear as though they *had* to occur.

Professional historians often consider contingency to be a central idea of their discipline and a crucial part of their toolkit in explaining historical change. What makes something "history," as opposed to (for example) an application of a scientific law, is that it is, in many ways, *not* predictable or known in advance. Instead, its outcome depends on the precise path that got it there, and on the specific contexts that surrounded it. Regular, predictable patterns such as those described by scientific laws may create conditions and provide constraints on what is possible in the first place. But historical contingency matters too, since the details of what happens (or may happen) in any moment also depend on what has gone on before that moment. Contingency emphasizes that today's events affect what is possible tomorrow, and in ways that are sometimes dizzyingly complex.[22]

Contingency's power as a way of explaining the past is not limited to disciplinary history. For example, the geologist Walter Alvarez uses a version of contingency as a framing device for all of Big History in his book *A Most Improbable Journey: A Big History of Our Planet and Ourselves*. While Alvarez's understanding of contingency is not the same as historians', the paleontologist Stephen Jay Gould also borrowed the concept, using it in a way that comes much closer to a typical historian's view, when he applied contingency to the history of life:

> I am not speaking of randomness . . . but of the central principle of all history—*contingency*. A historical explanation does not rest on direct deductions from laws of nature, but on an unpredictable sequence of antecedent states, where any major change in any step of the sequence would have altered the final result. This final result is therefore dependent, or contingent, upon everything that came before—the unerasable and determining signature of history.[23]

Contingency thus provides a central idea in several dimensions of a universal history, and a unifying idea that shapes the character of historical explanation at all scales—reaching well beyond the disciplinary terrain of merely human history.[24]

---

22. Or, to put it another way, today's contingencies help to set tomorrow's contexts. Time-travel narratives play with this: If you change something earlier in the story, what else must be carried along with that change?

23. Stephen Jay Gould, *Wonderful Life: The Burgess Shale and the Nature of History*, p. 283.

24. There is one more relevant sense of the word. In the domain of philosophy known as modal logic, "contingent" means *possible but not necessary*: one way of framing this is to say that a statement is contingently true if it is true in some, but not all, possible worlds. By analogy, historical contingency emphasizes that many outcomes are possible, though only some are realized.

Contingency in History

A few examples of contingency's role in historical explanation will illustrate these general principles.

Individual military battles provide conspicuous instances of contingent moments in world history, where different outcomes seem genuinely possible. In the Battle of Salamis, for instance, the (heavily outnumbered) Greeks repulsed the invading Persians, preserving political sovereignty for the Greek city-states at a time roughly 10 years before Socrates was born. Had they lost, things would have turned out in a different way, with potential ripple effects reaching into our world today. Or in 1241, when news that the Great Khan, Ogodei, had died reached the fearsome Mongol troops who had crossed the Danube and almost reached Vienna, their commanders withdrew quickly to travel home and participate in the deliberations to choose a successor—after which they never returned to eastern Europe. A generation later, in the Battle of Ain Jalut (1260), the Muslim Mamluks likewise stopped the military advance of the Mongols toward Egypt and North Africa. Had any of these encounters turned out differently, one might easily imagine today's world looking quite different.

Another example of contingency in history comes from what the historians J. R. McNeill and William McNeill refer to as "perhaps the greatest might-have-been of modern history,"[25] the Ming Dynasty's decision post-1440 to dedicate Chinese resources to internal needs, such as securing the northern frontier of the empire, rather than expanding Chinese imperial reach by sea—an option that could well have succeeded, given that at the time China's naval resources massively outclassed those of every other state, China was the world's biggest center of population and wealth, and the Chinese admiral Zheng He had already made convoy expeditions around the Indian Ocean, carrying about 20 times as many sailors as Columbus would bring on his largest expedition to the Americas a few decades later. The contingent decision by the Ming to abandon these far-flung voyages meant that China, the wealthiest and most powerful society of the 1400s, would not be the primary society to establish trade outposts (or colonies) throughout Afro-Eurasia, or to be the maker of new settlements and connections with the New World.

The presence of even highly contingent moments in history does not mean that absolutely *anything* is possible, however. There are surely conditional near-inevitabilities too, where a certain outcome is likely or even bound to follow once some other event has taken place. Historians and others argue about these cases. For example, Jared Diamond, who is not a disciplinary historian (he straddles several fields but holds an academic position in geography), contends in

---

25. J. R. McNeill and William McNeill, *The Human Web: A Bird's-Eye View of World History*, p. 126.

his Pulitzer Prize-winning book *Guns, Germs, and Steel* that many conquests, including those of New World societies like the Aztecs and the Inca by the Spanish, were inevitable—not because of any intrinsic biological, cognitive, or social superiority of one people to another, but because of the different environments in which they historically lived and to which they had adapted. In the case of joining Old World and New World, Europeans came from a part of the Earth where everything from crops and agricultural practices to metallurgy to disease epidemics (and, hence, disease resistance) could spread quite readily across a wide area, while the peoples of North and South America did not live in so strongly interconnected a society. This was all for the simple reason, Diamond argues, that Eurasian populations mostly lived at approximately the same latitude, situated on an east-west axis and sharing fairly similar climate and geographical conditions, while the American continents run mostly north-south and thus have greater climatic and geographical variation, hampering to some extent the mobility of crops, people, diseases, and technologies. J. R. and William McNeill, reasoning along similar lines, point out that the dense metropolitan webs and intense military competition within the Old World made Old World civilizations, especially China, the wealthiest, most powerful, and most formidable (epidemiologically as well as militarily) of the world.[26] Either way, geography may have militated in a particular direction, and perhaps even have made certain outcomes more or less inevitable. Still, there is much room for debate by considering questions of culture: What if, for example, the otherwise formidable peoples of the Old World had consistently come to the New World with more benign intentions than the desire for conquest and pillage? Things could well have turned out quite differently for all involved.[27]

The list of geographical factors that have influenced historical outcomes could be multiplied indefinitely: the great steppe grasslands of Central Asia that supported nomadic pastoralists such as the Mongols, who have a history of their own in addition to repeatedly playing the role of military invaders; the waterways and plains that made China comparatively easy to unify politically, while a lack of comparable features in Europe encouraged political fragmentation (and thus, perhaps, intense military competition and innovation); the regularity of the Nile's floods that made Egypt well-suited for an early adoption of agriculture and that set up conditions wherein Egyptians were rarely dominated by outsiders for the first 3,000 years of that kingdom's existence. To take a much more recent example, the historian Kenneth Pomeranz has argued that the presence of coal deposits in Britain close to the centers of population, compared with similar resources

---

26. Ibid., p. 162.

27. At the same time, this is debatable. Given the military history of Europe and Eurasia, how likely was a colonialism with benign intentions?

in China that were far from population centers, was a key reason why the Industrial Revolution started in Britain.[28]

A universal-historical approach, however, also makes clear that geography is itself contingent: geological processes had to shape the landscape to be what it is today. The accretion of continental landmasses billions of years ago, along with plate-tectonic processes operating over (at least) hundreds of millions of years, produced the arrangement and shape of continents that we have now. The evolution of the vast forests of the Carboniferous period more than 300 million years ago led to the presence of coal deposits, and plate-tectonic and other geological processes since then led to the present distribution of these coal deposits around the world. And so forth. A primary distinguishing feature of universal histories, especially of Big History, is that they allow contingency to be brought to bear not only on human history, but also on the terrestrial and cosmic context in which human history unfolds. Depending on the scale under consideration, these "background," seemingly predetermined elements of geography and natural resources become contingent as well, albeit on far different time scales.

These ideas may help us respond to the question posed near the beginning of this chapter, about whether the Roman Empire would have still emerged if one person whose descendants include everyone alive today had never been born. Perhaps certain processes, such as the drawing together of people into denser settlements and the ultimate formation of land-based empires, are "robust outcomes" of geographical and environmental conditions that—while themselves contingent upon long-term geological processes—were likely, or even very likely, to happen eventually given the conditions in which the past 200,000 or 300,000 years of human history unfolded, even if the precise nature of the Roman Empire (e.g., its culture, its practices, and its name) may be more contingent.

Agriculture itself provides an interesting thought experiment in this regard. Scholars now think that agriculture "began" independently in about seven locations across the globe—in the sense that people began farming without, as far as we can tell, being in any kind of communication with other people elsewhere who were already farming. From these seven locations, and perhaps others not yet discovered, agriculture spread. It did not spread everywhere, as even today there are hunter-gatherer societies that choose not to join the ranks of agricultural societies. But overall, it did spread, and by about 2,000 or 3,000 years ago, a significant majority of humans had oriented their lifestyles to acquire food primarily through farming. At a global scale, even hunter-gatherer and nomadic-pastoralist societies were strongly affected by this development.

---

28. Kenneth Pomeranz, *The Great Divergence: China, Europe, and the Making of the Modern World Economy*.

The facts that people began acquiring food through agriculture in multiple locations during a period that covered just a few thousand years, starting around 11,000 years ago in the Fertile Crescent (located in the Middle East), and that this happened after *Homo sapiens* had lived as hunter-gatherers for perhaps some 300,000 years, seem to suggest environmental (or other) constraints strongly pushed people in multiple parts of the world toward the same process. This was the first time after *Homo sapiens* had migrated around the entire globe when a warm interglacial period occurred, creating more favorable conditions in which agriculture *could* enable the feeding of more mouths. So there may be certain geographical and biological trends (not laws) that could help to explain the overall picture of why agriculture began when it did. These trends created the conditions in which it could flower, and perhaps also incentives to pursue it. But the details of *which* groups ended up with *which* agricultural practices, of which groups instead resisted agriculture, and so forth seem likely to be more contingent matters, depending upon individual and collective decisions and upon local conditions of abundance or scarcity.[29]

Contingency in the History of Life

In evolutionary biology, the interplay of open possibilities and constraints plays out in debates about whether life would look basically the same today if evolution started over again "at the beginning." That is, if the evolutionary history of life could be reset to 3 billion years ago or more and then allowed to proceed forward again, would today's world still include a mixture of prokaryotic and eukaryotic cells, groups of organisms resembling today's animals and plants, and intelligent organisms like human beings?

The process of evolution includes a great deal of apparent openness to multiple possible outcomes: the mutations that provide raw material for natural selection (see "Evolution" in chapter 4) arise due to irregular and unusual "mistakes" in the replication of DNA or from other forms of "damage" (i.e., change) to the DNA molecule. And a small number of such changes can result in large changes at the level of the organism as a whole, especially if a collection of mutations occurs to genes that regulate the body plan and life cycle / development of an organism. A single branching point—like the origin of eukaryotic cells, which may have been a highly contingent, one-time event—could have consequences for literally billions of years. Evolution in this sense is always structured by the past, making it a fully historical and inescapably contingent process.

The paleontologist Stephen Jay Gould has written extensively about contingency in the history of life, primarily in his book *Wonderful Life*, which argues that

---

29. One often says something is the way that it is "for historical reasons" when it does not make sense in the present, but in a sense, everything is the way that it is for historical reasons.

the existence of essentially all macroscopic life now on Earth—including human beings—hinged on the (at the time, apparently low-probability) survival of a few life forms from the Cambrian period. Several aspects of Gould's argument, including the idea that animal body plans were especially diverse in the Cambrian period compared to more recent times, have been called into serious question.[30] Still, his articulation of contingency's role in the history of life retains considerable power and validity. Gould acknowledges that some aspects of life's history are predictable, since "invariant laws of nature impact the general forms and functions of organisms; they set the channels [that is, the range of possibilities] in which organic design must evolve."[31] But Gould also argues that the "channels are so broad relative to the details that fascinate us."[32] In other words, the laws of physics and chemistry may affect the range of possibilities and broad outline of life's evolutionary history, but the details are historically contingent. Gould summarizes this conclusion as "*laws in the background* and *contingency in the details*."[33]

There seem to be at least a few key moments of extreme contingency in life's history. The asteroid impact 66 million years ago that may have led to a mass extinction, including the extinction of the non-avian dinosaurs, is an example.[34] If, indeed, the mass extinction's primary cause was the asteroid impact, then a slight change in that asteroid's trajectory could have meant that reptiles would not have vacated the ecological niches that mammals overtook during the millions of years that followed. Paul Braterman suggests that even the timing and location of the impact mattered: if the asteroid had come 10 minutes earlier or later, landing 150 miles to the east or west due to the Earth's rotation during those 10 minutes, the destructive effects of the impact might have been much more local, not global. The presence of the mineral gypsum in the impact zone of the asteroid may have allowed the impact to create a sulfuric-acid haze around the entire globe that sharply reduced sunlight long enough to cause global mass death.[35]

---

30. See, e.g., Simon Conway Morris, *The Crucible of Creation*.

31. Gould, *Wonderful Life*, p. 289.

32. Ibid., p. 289.

33. Ibid., p. 290.

34. As noted in chapter 4, many geologists ascribe a causal role to such an impact, but a minority have marshaled substantial countervailing arguments. The topic remains under dispute.

35. Paul Braterman, "How to Kill a Dinosaur in 10 Minutes," http://www.3quarksdaily.com/3quarksdaily/2017/08/ten-minutes-difference-that-doomed-the-dinosaurs.html . Richard Lenski's *E. coli* Long-Term Evolution Experiment, which has tracked genetic changes in 12 initially identical populations of the bacterium *E. coli* over more than 70,000 generations, provides an experimental approach to exploring the relationship of contingency and convergence in the course of evolution. For a review of related research, see Zachary D. Blount, Richard E. Lenski, and Jonathan B. Losos, "Contingency and Determinism in Evolution: Replaying Life's Tape," https://science.sciencemag.org/content/362/6415/eaam5979 .

On the other hand, the range of possibilities during the course of the history of life is limited. There is a phenomenon known as convergent evolution, more or less paralleling what we have sketched as constraints on the pathways taken in human history. Convergent evolution means that in response to similar environmental conditions and the (as far as we know) unchanging laws of physics and chemistry, very different organisms, following distinct evolutionary pathways, may nevertheless end up with strikingly similar adaptations. A classic example is wings used for powered flight, which evolved independently in birds, bats, and insects.[36] Complex eyes are another striking example: the eyes of an octopus or squid evolved along different lines from those of human beings, but their designs wound up being remarkably similar.[37] A less-well-known example is the group of sea creatures known as ctenophores, which look and move rather like jellyfish but have neurons, muscles, and other tissues that are built from totally different molecular building blocks than in the rest of the animal kingdom.[38] The fact that there are multiple molecular pathways to a similar set of tissues, and similar sets of functions achieved through divergent mechanisms, suggests that deep convergence can occur even at a molecular level.

Certain outcomes at the largest scales of life's history may also be quite robust. Charles Langmuir and Wally Broecker argue that both the total mass of all life on the planet and the amount of energy flowing through ecosystems have almost certainly increased over time through a consistent process: "If a network of organisms creates an environment more capable of sustaining life and processing energy—i.e., more habitable—this network will have an evolutionary advantage. . . . One of the natural consequences of a planet with life may be a progressive increase in planetary habitability, provided the external conditions for life can persist."[39] There are also certain aspects of the history of life that, even if their origins were not inevitable, are strongly *conserved*, or maintained, through time. The biologists Marc Kirschner and John Gerhart describe certain "conserved core processes," including the cell itself, various biochemical processes within the cell, and the eukaryotic cell, among others.[40] These conserved

---

36. And pterosaurs—though in different cases, the mechanisms are substantially different. See, e.g., Jonathan Losos, "Why Hasn't Evolution Made Another Platypus?," http://nautil.us/issue/52/the-hive/why-hasnt-evolution-made-another-platypus .

37. Both types of complex eye probably evolved from a simple cluster of light-sensitive cells present in a common ancestor. See, e.g., Neil A. Campbell et al., *Biology* (8th Edition), p. 529.

38. Douglas Fox, "Aliens in Our Midst," https://aeon.co/essays/what-the-ctenophore-says-about-the-evolution-of-intelligence .

39. Charles H. Langmuir and Wally Broecker, *How to Build a Habitable Planet*, p. 535.

40. Marc W. Kirschner and John C. Gerhart, *The Plausibility of Life: Resolving Darwin's Dilemma*, p. 39 (and throughout the book).

elements are not unlike analogous conserved institutions in human history, such as kinship networks or agricultural villages, which have a deep stability through time despite ongoing variation in their details.

The relative importance of possibility and constraint has been debated, most notably between Gould and fellow paleontologist Simon Conway Morris, whose scientific work formed a basis for Gould's writing about contingency but who disagreed with Gould's interpretation.[41] Still, the general idea that the history of life is an interplay between possibility and constraint is not controversial: whatever the exact proportions, both play significant roles.

Chance, Laws, and Contingency in Historical Explanation

Whether in human history or in the history of life and the Earth, historical change seems to result from this interplay of possibility and constraint. Especially in the context of evolutionary biology, and sometimes (but more rarely) in the realm of human history, experts sometimes draw a further conclusion—namely, that contingent processes result in outcomes characterized by "chance," or "randomness," or "accident." One need not look far in biological writing to find references to the Darwinian character of life's history framed in these terms. The evolutionary biologist Richard Dawkins writes:

> Natural selection, the blind, unconscious, automatic process which Darwin discovered . . . has no mind . . . It does not plan for the future. It has no vision, no foresight, no sight at all. If it can be said to play the role of watchmaker in nature, it is the *blind* watchmaker.[42]

This emphasis on the "blindness" or chance[43] nature of natural selection is not universal among biologists, but it is common. Historians, by contrast, are usually careful to avoid such language, but that does not stop other prominent intellectuals from writing about the character of historical change in these terms. For example, the Nobel-laureate psychologist Daniel Kahneman writes:

> The often-used image of the "march of history" implies order and direction. Marches, unlike strolls or walks, are not random. We think that we should

---

41. See, especially, Simon Conway Morris, *The Crucible of Creation*.

42. Richard Dawkins, *The Blind Watchmaker: Why the Evidence of Evolution Reveals a Universe Without Design*, p. 5.

43. Or "random walk."

be able to explain the past by focusing on either large social movements and cultural and technological developments or the intentions and abilities of a few great men. The idea that large historical events are determined by luck is profoundly shocking, although it is demonstrably true.[44]

Whether we are talking about human history or the history of life, however, good historical explanation does not rely on notions of randomness, any more than it carries out a search for ironclad laws. There are several reasons for this.

First, in common speech, "random" is often used to mean "uncaused," "meaningless," or "inexplicable" (admittedly not a very precise usage). It would seem that calling something random is not an explanation of historical change, but rather the absence of an explanation. Scientific and historical explanations rely on order and causation, while invoking randomness often signals the absence of a deeper understanding.

Second, what appears random from one perspective may not appear random at all from a different viewpoint, or at a different scale. Mutations may look unpredictable and random from the biologist's viewpoint, but a physicist's analysis might subject the same event—a change in an organism's genome—to an analysis in terms of cause and effect at a smaller scale.[45] As the author Tony Hillerman writes, "From where we stand the rain seems random. If we could stand somewhere else, we would see the order in it."[46] Moreover, true randomness is very difficult to obtain. In generating random numbers, for instance, computers often use a "pseudorandom number generator" that produces numbers with the same statistical variation as genuinely random numbers, but a reproducible deterministic process lies behind the generation of these numbers. In fact, in any apparently random process, some order may underlie the randomness. Even physicists, confronted with the apparently inherent randomness of quantum-mechanical processes, sometimes posit "hidden variables" that explain observed effects without invoking randomness. In short, it is difficult to demonstrate with certainty that true randomness is at

---

44. Daniel Kahneman, *Thinking, Fast and Slow*, p. 218. Kahneman goes on to point out that Adolf Hitler, Joseph Stalin, and Mao Zedong, each with their powerful influence on 20th-century history, had a 50/50 chance of being female rather than male, if we go back a moment before the relevant human egg was fertilized. Kahneman claims that this fact shows it is unimaginable how much the course of world history would have changed with an ever-so-slight tweak to a biological reality.

45. A different kind of randomness seems to be inherent in quantum-mechanical processes such as those that apply to this scale.

46. Tony Hillerman, *Coyote Waits*, p. 214.

work, and what seems random to us may indicate the lack of a deeper understanding of the subject.[47]

Finally, even apparent randomness is possible only within a highly ordered framework. Only because dice are designed in such a way as to be "fair" can we be confident that rolling them produces a random result. And only because there is a well-ordered car-manufacturing industry and highway system can we speak of an apparently random assortment of cars going down a highway.[48] Evolution is comprehensible to us because it shows strong patterns, as human history does too—and any role for apparent chance exists only because there is an order to the broader framework. There is a reason why even apparently random variations can lead to convergent evolution: universal physical and chemical constraints provide an ordered backdrop to the history of life. Ernst Mayr, a founding figure in the modern evolutionary synthesis,[49] wrote: "When it is said that mutation or variation is random, the statement simply means that there is no correlation between the production of new genotypes and the adaptational needs of an organism in the given environment."[50]

Overall, then, randomness as commonly understood is not the same thing as contingency, and contingent processes do not necessarily produce random outcomes. Contingency instead lies in a middle ground between randomness and inevitability. Historical processes, whether in biology or in human history, are neither the unfolding of events that *had* to happen the way they did, nor are they arbitrary or totally chaotic. Invoking contingency does not necessarily invoke pure chance and accident; rather, it denies that universal, deterministic scientific laws are sufficient to fully explain the details of historical change—even as those laws may be present as constraints that carve out the channels of what is possible in the first place. Historians do not generally focus on these laws, nor (usually) even find

47. There is a field of applied mathematics that studies "stochastic processes," which are processes with one or more randomly distributed variables. And there are statistical tests that one can apply to, for instance, a sequence of random numbers to determine whether it is genuinely random or has a previously undetected order. But it is hard to imagine how one could perform a test for true randomness of evolutionary or human-historical outcomes, given the uniqueness of any historical sequence of events and the inability to replay the process except in certain highly constrained experimental settings.

48. The sequence of cars on a highway exhibits a kind of randomness, but each trip is planned and fits into a life in an intelligible way even though the drivers' lives are not closely correlated with one another. (The example in text, and in the text of this footnote, is inspired by Stephen M. Barr, "The Design of Evolution," https://www.firstthings.com/article/2005/10/the-design-of-evolution .)

49. See "Evolution" in chapter 4.

50. Ernst Mayr, *Toward a New Philosophy of Biology: Observations of an Evolutionist*, p. 99.

Side Note: Counterfactuals

Contingency is a way of understanding how something came to be the way it is, by following a chain of causation back in time. To avoid the causal chain becoming an exercise in mere description of *what* happened, rather than an analysis and interpretive understanding of *how* and *why* it happened, one must recognize the lack of inevitability at each step and, perhaps, consider what could have been—and why it wasn't. This can bring us into the realm of "counterfactuals": scenarios that seem like they could have happened but did not. Why they did not is a question that can provide interesting material for thought experiments. What if the Axis powers had won World War II, for example? What if Siddhartha Gautama, later known as the Buddha, had died in infancy? What if the speakers of the Proto-Indo-European language had all been wiped out before their language could spread and morph, over the centuries, into a family of languages spoken by billions of people today? How would history be different?

Counterfactuals are, by their nature, speculative; they are not evidentially based or documented like "real" history. For this reason, historians usually regard excessive use of counterfactuals as a sign of poor historical thinking. E. H. Carr writes that only those on the losing side of history engage in counterfactuals, because they like to think that things could have turned out differently.[51] And yet counterfactuals can be illuminating in helping to evaluate the specific weights that may attach to different parts of a historical explanation. For this reason, even eminent historians occasionally indulge in such discussions.

them interesting. Instead, they focus on the *un*predictabilities—that is, on explaining which precise outcomes occurred within these broad channels. These outcomes in turn are governed by the kinds of particular, situationally determined, complex contingencies for which historians are trained to look.

Context

Trained historians balk at student essays or popular books that begin with phrases such as "Since the dawn of time . . . ," or "People have always . . . ," or "For all of history . . ." Such grand generalizations ignore the particular historical and social *context* that gives each time and place its own flavor and character, which historical analysis seeks to capture as fully as possible and understand in its nuances and specificities.

---

51. "In a group or a nation which is riding in the trough, not on the crest, of historical events, theories that stress the role of chance or accident in history will be found to prevail. The view that examination results are all a lottery will always be popular among those who have been placed in the third class." (Carr, *What Is History?*, p. 132.)

This is another way of saying that good histories must put events or people into proper, grounded historical context. Human life may have common threads that stretch across all times and places, but these universals, precisely because they are everywhere and all the time, will explain very little of the contingent outcomes of particular situations involving specific people. The behavior and thinking of people in different cultures, whether past or present, can be very difficult to understand without an understanding of context. The world and world-view of every individual child, woman, and man is profoundly and distinctively shaped by the context in which they live, and every aspect of life is affected—right down to the state of one's body in life and in death, as the historian Robin Fleming writes:

> Indeed, the impact of things like poor environment, diet, migration, even disease, are often dictated by social, political, and cultural practices. As we have seen, the remains of bodies carry memories of physical outrages and cultural practices, diseases endured, meals eaten, and childhood homes lost.[52]

Historical context matters, crucially, if you are trying to understand any individual life, including your own.

At the level of historical evidence, context is likewise important for the processes of identifying, selecting, reading, and understanding sources. Any textual evidence has already been run through a cultural filter in the mind of the writer, and one must understand that filter, as well as one's own filter(s), to understand what the texts meant to those who wrote them and what those texts can tell us now. Otherwise, we risk making assumptions about how similar other times, places, and cultures were to our own, assumptions that are often not valid, and in turn writing histories that reflect our own historical context more than the one about which we are writing.

Historians therefore do their best to *situate* historical actors, events, and narratives within appropriate contexts. World history provides a certain contextual framework for understanding the circumstances in which people lived out their lives, and why they faced the choices they had to make. It provides a "panorama"[53] view of the world's history, rather than a close-up of specific circumstances, that can broadly illuminate how distinct from one another various circumstances have been in different times and places.

---

52. Robin Fleming, "Writing Biography at the Edge of History," https://academic.oup.com/ahr/article/114/3/606/11693/Writing-Biography-at-the-Edge-of-HistoryRobin .

53. Use of the word in this context inspired by Ross E. Dunn and Laura J. Mitchell's book *Panorama: A World History.*

A Brief History of the World in Three Parts

Historians working at the level of a nation-state or other relatively well-contained region, and within time scales comparable to human lifetimes, can provide deep and rich context for individual lives and events. Those working in world history, meanwhile, paint with a broader brush, providing historical context at a larger scale and/or over longer periods of time.

To get a rough sense of historical context for lives and events throughout the global deep past, it is useful to have in mind a global "periodization." As discussed in chapter 3 in the context of Earth science, periodization is a major conceptual and interpretive tool for dividing history into a manageable number of distinct "slices" of time. Historical periods, such as the "Middle Ages" or the "early modern," are not usually labels that were used by the people who lived through them. Rather, they are *representations of time* devised by historians and filled with specific stories and meanings. Think of the connotations that come to mind when you hear "medieval times" or "the Middle Ages" or, even more powerfully, "the Dark Ages." As the historian Marc Bloch writes, "the name, as always, carries the idea along with it."[54]

Periods are also often tied to particular regions of the world. Europe may have had a Middle Ages, but it is less clear that one should try to map that term onto, say, China or India. As E. H. Carr puts it:

> The division of history into periods is not a fact, but a necessary hypothesis or tool of thought, valid in so far as it is illuminating, and dependent for its validity on interpretation. Historians who differ on the question of when the Middle Ages ended differ in their interpretation of certain events. The question is not a question of fact; but it is also not meaningless.[55]

Choosing a particular way of periodizing implies something about which times and places should "go together." Referring to both Venice in the year 1100 and Paris in the year 1250 as "medieval" implies a basic similarity that would not be shared by, say, Venice in 1100 and Paris in 1900—or, for that matter, by Venice in 1100 and Venice in 1900, or by Venice in 1100 and Angkor in 1100. A different periodization might group times and places together differently.[56]

---

54. Bloch, *The Historian's Craft*, p. 182.

55. Carr, *What Is History?*, p. 76.

56. Periodizations have their own history. The 14th-century scholar Petrarch, for example, labeled the centuries preceding his own era as the "Dark Ages"; later writers (who lived during the period we would call "early modern") talked about the "Middle Ages," which they thought of as a placeholder between the more noteworthy ancient and modern times.

While there are many possible ways to periodize the history of *Homo sapiens*, spanning the entire globe, we can start by following David Christian's three-part[57] division of deep human time. This periodization includes the era of foragers (300,000 to 10,000 years before the present), the agrarian era (10,000 to 250 years before present), and the industrial[58] era (250 years ago to present).[59] These eras follow broad trends in dominant modes of food production and economic activity, as well as in overall human population numbers and energy use. And while they are limited, imperfect representations and thus will miss important details, as any periodization scheme will—for instance, agrarian and foraging societies are not purely a thing of the past but continue to exist right up to the present—these periods do provide a "large-scale story to frame [one's] thinking," an overall "picture of global change and connections," "readily available and useful 'big pictures'" that can be "employed to narrate change over time and to locate, within the big story, historical details visible only at smaller scales."[60]

Foraging Era: "Many Worlds"

The period that Christian labels the "era of foragers," from the beginning of our species to 10,000 years ago, was a time when all human groups engaged in food collection rather than food production as their primary means of subsistence: all were hunter-gatherers. Population numbers, although impossible to estimate precisely, were low, likely no more than a few million worldwide at any given time, considering the geographical extent of land that humans occupied and the population densities that foraging can support.[61] Historical change, however, happened. This was, for instance, the era that saw large-scale migrations that brought anatomically and (probably) behaviorally recognizable *Homo sapiens* out of Africa and around the globe starting approximately 100,000 years ago, after having already spread out considerably within Africa.

---

57. As the deep historians Andrew Shryock, Thomas R. Trautmann, and Clive Gamble point out, it is strikingly common to divide history into three ages. European thinkers from the 1400s onward have divided historical time into the ancient world (classical antiquity), the Middle Ages, and the modern. Archaeologists commonly divide the history of certain parts of the world into Stone Age, Bronze Age, and Iron Age, based on the material basis for technologies at each time. Individual civilizations likewise may have three-part subdivisions: Ancient Egypt has the Old Kingdom, the Middle Kingdom, and the New Kingdom. Even the periods themselves may be subdivided by threes: the Middle Ages subdivided into the Early, High, and Late Middle Ages; the Stone Age into the Paleolithic, Mesolithic, and Neolithic (Old, Middle, and New Stone Ages). See Andrew Shryock, Thomas R. Trautmann, and Clive Gamble, "Imagining the Human in Deep Time," in *Deep History: The Architecture of Past and Present*, pp. 44–45.

58. Christian uses "modern" here.

59. See David Christian's books *Maps of Time* and *This Fleeting World*.

60. Bob Bain and Lauren McArthur Harris, preface to Christian's *This Fleeting World*, pp. x, xii, x, and x, respectively.

61. See, e.g., Christian, *Maps of Time*, p. 209.

It also included many other interactions, including episodes of both interbreeding and violence, between hominins of different species or populations, such as *Homo sapiens*, Neanderthals, and Denisovans. The peopling of the globe, moreover, was in one sense completed during this period, by the time humans had inhabited North and South America, from coast to coast, some 14,000 years ago.[62]

The era of foragers took place within the Paleolithic, also known as the Old Stone Age (to invoke another, parallel periodization). It was a time before there were cities, agrarian states and empires, or other institutions recognizable from today's world, *anywhere in the world*. If one looks to history to discern the connections between today's world and the past, therefore, the era of foragers can feel thoroughly disconnected and foreign. And yet it seems likely, at least based on the kinds of artifacts people produced that have survived until today, that humans of this time[63] were not so different from people today in many important ways, including their basic range of behaviors. What connects us with people of the Paleolithic? The emerging subfield of deep history, along with world history, has attempted to trace connections with our deep past using a number of themes, including the human body itself, energy use and activity within ecosystems, language, food, kinship, migration, the exchange of goods, disease, dance, and the brain. All of these human realities have changed over time, but historical narratives can use them to connect people of today with people of the deep past—and in a way that they cannot readily connect today's world with the deep past by writing about more modern phenomena such as cities, states, and empires.[64]

Although the era of foragers is by far the longest of Christian's three eras, population densities during this period were small enough that probably only some 10 percent of all the humans who have ever walked the Earth lived in this time.[65] Still, it would be a misrepresentation of the Paleolithic to assume (drawing on popular stereotypes) that it was a static, unchanging time, in which all humans lived in caves and spent all day searching for food and trying to escape predators.[66] Instead, we should imagine a diverse and dynamic time: a time of tremendous innovation and cultural diversity around everything from styles of tools and art, to practices for raising children and caring for the elderly, to negotiating relationships with other

---

62. The exact timing is heavily disputed. See, e.g., information about the Chilean archaeological site called Monte Verde.

63. Or, at least, part of this time. See chapter 5 for more detailed discussions.

64. Even the composition of historical narratives links us in some ways to people of the Paleolithic: as Smail points out, there were almost certainly Paleolithic oral histories, the forerunners of modern historical writing (Smail, *On Deep History and the Brain*, p. 59).

65. See Christian, *Maps of Time*, p. 208, drawing on M. Livi-Bacci, *A Concise History of World Population*.

66. To be fair, predators really are a greater threat in most hunter-gatherer societies than in most agricultural or industrial societies.

individuals and groups, to religious rituals and customs, to preferred foods.[67] The great continental migrations carried humans into totally new environments, from dense equatorial jungles to barren tundras of far northern latitudes to everything in between. And these migrations were supported by a variety of technological and artistic cultures. One example is the Aurignacian tradition of carved bone and flint tools and cave art (including the now-famous Chauvet cave in southern France) that appeared some 30,000 to 40,000 years ago in present-day Europe. Another is the Clovis culture that featured distinctive, fluted stone projectile points (see Plate 27), widespread across much of the Americas about 13,000 years ago and a probable forerunner of many other early cultures there. Many more examples of Paleolithic cultures could be added, and surely only a small fraction of the total have so far been unearthed and characterized by modern archaeology.

Traditions of tool-making are, presumably, only the tip of the iceberg: a material manifestation of entire cultural systems that had rich sets of traditions, social activities, and lifeways, which likely changed a great deal over time and mixed with or even replaced one another as people migrated and intermingled. If modern foraging societies are any indication, people of this early era certainly would not have spent all day looking for food. It is not even the case that all Paleolithic foraging societies were mobile and tiny: some late Paleolithic villages in areas of abundant resources appear to have had as many as a thousand people living in them; various goods like arrowheads and amber appear to have been traded over long distances;[68] and the complexity of religious sites such as Göbekli Tepe in modern Turkey suggests levels of social organization and coordination among at least some foraging societies that were previously thought to be impossible.[69] Social structures may have been extremely variable, both between societies and even seasonally within a given society:

> Within the same population, one could live sometimes in what looks, from a distance, like a band, sometimes a tribe, and sometimes a society with many of the features we now identify with states. . . . It seems inherently likely, and the evidence confirms, that those same pioneering humans who colonised much of the planet also experimented with an enormous variety of social arrangements.[70]

---

67. List partially inspired by Jared Diamond, *The World Until Yesterday: What Can We Learn from Traditional Societies?*

68. Smail, *On Deep History and the Brain*, p. 5.

69. See, e.g., Oliver Dietrich, Jens Notroff, and Klaus Schmidt, "Feasting, Social Complexity, and the Emergence of the Early Neolithic of Upper Mesopotamia: A View from Göbekli Tepe," pp. 91–132 in *Feast, Famine, or Fighting? Studies in Human Ecology and Adaptation*, eds. R. Chacon and R. Mendoza; and Ofer Bar-Yosef, "From Sedentary Foragers to Village Hierarchies: The Emergence of Social Institutions," pp. 1–38 in *The Origin of Human Social Institutions*, ed. Walter G. Runciman.

70. David Graeber and David Wengrow, "How to Change the Course of Human History (At Least, the Part that's Already Happened)," https://theanarchistlibrary.org/library/david-graeber-david-wengrow-how-to-change-the-course-of-human-history .

Lives lived in the era of foragers are not easy for us to understand or imagine, and we lack the benefit of written evidence. But there is still a historical context in which to place these people, and other forms of evidence are available about certain aspects of life at the time. Judging by the tremendous cultural diversity of modern foraging societies, this was very likely a time of many linguistic and cultural distinctions—of "many worlds," in Christian's framing.[71] It was certainly a period of *history*, of historical change, not an unchanging era frozen in time, or a piece of natural history at a time when humans were completely at the mercy of nature. Contingent, path-dependent change, affected by human choices, was just as operative then as now.[72]

Side Note: Evolutionary Psychology

If human history and contingent change over time began not with the advent of agriculture or of writing, but instead during the era of foragers, this implies a strong critique of the approach to human behavior suggested by the field of evolutionary psychology. By arguing that many human behavioral patterns took shape in a single context (hunter-gatherer societies vulnerable to predators), evolutionary psychology often ignores the reality of historical and cultural change during the Paleolithic. As the paleoanthropologist Ian Tattersall comments:

> There is a school of thought that we humans sometimes act so bizarrely because the evolution of our brains has not been able to keep pace with the rapid transformation of society that has occurred since humans began to adopt settled lifestyles at the end of the last glacial episode. Our minds, according to this view, are still responding, sometimes inappropriately, to the exigencies of a bygone "environment of evolutionary adaptedness." This view has a wonderful reductionist appeal; but in reality our brains are the ultimate general-purpose organs, not adapted "for" anything at all.[73]

Or as Daniel Lord Smail summarizes: "The human mind did not just adapt at some fixed moment in the past. It is, instead, continuously adapting."[74]

---

71. Christian, *Maps of Time*, p. 137. "Many worlds," "few worlds," and "one world" are quotations from section titles in Christian's *Maps of Time*. See *Maps of Time* pp. 137, 205, and 333; also see Table 8.1 on p. 210 in *Maps of Time*.

72. One point to contemplate is that Native American groups of the late 1400s and early 1500s were as far removed in time from the Clovis culture as Columbus and his crew were from the hunter-gatherers of western Europe 13,000 years ago.

73. Ian Tattersall, *Masters of the Planet: The Search for Our Human Origins*, p. 228.

74. Smail, *On Deep History and the Brain*, pp. 146–147. See also Philippe Descola, *The Ecology of Others*, pp. 2–3; David Bentley Hart, *The Experience of God: Being, Consciousness, Bliss*, p. 73; or Marshall Sahlins, *The Western Illusion of Human Nature*, p. 104 ff.

Agrarian Era: "Few Worlds"

If we frame the agrarian era of human history as beginning with the first known development of agriculture—in the Near East some 11,000 years ago—we have to allow for a long transition period. As discussed earlier, many groups actively or passively resisted the spread of agriculture long after this point. But agriculture can support much denser populations than foraging, so agricultural societies could grow to include far more people than any foraging society. Moreover, once adopted, agriculture can be difficult to turn away from, as a successful agricultural society may quickly have more people than can be supported by foraging. Over time, therefore, as more groups settled into the lifeways of agricultural communities and villages, agriculture slowly overtook foraging as the dominant mode of subsistence for most people on Earth, and the world population rose into the tens and then hundreds of millions of human beings. It is difficult to estimate precisely, but by perhaps 3,000 years ago, more than half of the people on Earth may have lived in agrarian societies, most as farmers who worked the land.[75] And even for those groups that remained foragers or that resumed foraging after experimenting with agriculture, the growing presence of these settled agricultural societies was consequential; interaction between settled agricultural societies and mobile foraging societies structured life for both groups for thousands of years.

During the first half of the agrarian era, agriculture was not, in fact, the dominant way of acquiring food. But it was on the rise, and it emerged in various places around the world. (See Plate 28.) The Neolithic (New Stone Age) is the name often given to this period, after the adoption of agriculture but before the advanced metal-working of the Bronze Age began in certain places about 5,000 years ago. People in various Neolithic settlements began making pottery, and a few villages grew large enough that we now call them "towns." A particularly large and famous Neolithic settlement, Çatalhöyük, flourished around 9,000 years ago in what is now Turkey; it contains wall paintings and figurines, as well as some of the first extant human-produced metallic artifacts.[76] The site was finally abandoned after being inhabited for an impressively long period of nearly 2,000 years.

Mesopotamia, an area located between the Tigris and Euphrates rivers mostly in modern-day Iraq and Syria, had the longest known tradition of agriculture. (See Plates 29 and 30 for maps labeled with many of the geographical terms commonly used in world history.) Many different cultures emerged in the 6,000 or so years between the first agricultural villages there and the Bronze Age civilization of Sumer

---

75. On this "Neolithic demographic transition," see, e.g., Livi-Bacci, *A Concise History of World Population*, [6th edition], pp. 36–42.

76. See, e.g., Thomas Birch, Thilo Rehren, and Ernst Pernicka, "The Metallic Finds from Çatalhöyük: A Review and Preliminary New Work," http://discovery.ucl.ac.uk/1474072/1/Birch%20et%20al%202013%20Catal%20Hoyuk%20copper%20a%20review%20and%20new%20work%20plus%20Appendices.pdf .

in southern Mesopotamia, including the Ubaid culture that existed some 8,500 to 5,800 years ago, which created a system of symbols upon which the world's first known writing system later drew. The grain-based agriculture of Mesopotamia and the broader Fertile Crescent allowed the storage and concentration of food surplus, making it easier for societies that relied on crops like wheat and barley—and likewise rice in East Asia or, later, maize and beans and squash in parts of the Americas—to support specialists like artisans, royalty and government officials, and religious figures like priests, who did not grow their own food.[77] The "secondary products revolution"—the exploitation of "secondary products" from animals like milk, wool, and traction power / plowing—seems to have begun in Mesopotamia about 5,000 to 6,000 years ago and spread across Eurasia, enabling agriculture to penetrate new areas and allowing even denser settlements.

The emergence of Mesopotamian cities, starting especially about 6,000 years ago, depended crucially on rural populations producing enough food (whether voluntarily or, probably more often, by force or threat) to support both themselves and the non-farmers of the city.[78] By 5,000 years ago, the city of Uruk, at its time almost certainly the largest in the world, had a population of 50,000 people, with well-fortified walls. Cities such as this brought new forms of social organization at all levels, as did the first states.[79] Writing then originated, as far as we know, some 5,200 years ago, also in this same area of Mesopotamia. (See Plate 31.) The first empire also came from the same area, nearly a millennium later, when Sargon of Akkad overran the city-states of Mesopotamia about 4,300 years ago, spreading his rule as far as the Mediterranean and creating a fundamentally new kind of political structure.[80]

There are thus many "firsts" associated with Mesopotamia, and one of these—the emergence of writing and city-states in Sumer a little over 5,000 years ago—is the point where traditional world history usually "kicks in." World history thereafter is

---

77. Cities are ecosystems too, and require much greater land area than what is needed to build the city itself. They do not exist in isolation from their natural / rural surroundings. Moreover, social differences of many sorts, including hierarchies of power and status, existed before these agricultural patterns appeared.

78. A "city" can be distinguished from other residential forms, such as villages and towns, in exactly this way: not so much by raw size as by functional profile, specifically an inability to feed itself. Cities need to import food either from nearby areas, like hinterlands where farmers live, or via merchant trade.

79. A "state" is a sovereign political unit, meaning that it controls a certain territory and can intervene in the lives of people living there. It can act in most cases independently of other states and carry out actions relative to them, such as making treaties or waging war. States thus need to be larger than a certain size: a nomadic kin group might be independent of state authority, for instance, but would not qualify as a state of its own.

80. An "empire" is a form of state in which power and authority are projected over long distances, over people who are perceived as meaningfully different, e.g., in language, culture, religion, or ethnicity. Empires often carry out exploitative practices on behalf of the imperial center.

often told as the story of a series of states and empires: the city-states of Mesopotamia; the empires of China and India; the empires of Persia and the Middle East; the Greek city-states and the Roman Empire, the Byzantine Empire, and the Ottoman Empire; and then the nation-states of the more recent past.[81] In the Americas, the great cities of Teotihuacan, Tenochtitlan, Tula, Chichen Itza, Cusco, and Machu Picchu receive attention, as do the civilizations of the Olmecs, Toltecs, and Aztecs of Mesoamerica; the Maya of the Yucatan Peninsula; the Inca of the Andes in South America; and perhaps the dispersed Mississippian culture[82] of North America. In Africa, one reads of Egypt, Nubia, and the kingdoms of Mali, Songhai, Ghana, and Zimbabwe. Readers of world history usually learn less about Australia, however, as it remained inhabited by foragers (not agrarian farmers) until the time of European colonization, and even less about the islanders of Pacific Oceania.

In our periodization, however, it is better to think of most of the last 5,000 years (up until a few hundred years ago) as simply the second half of the agrarian era. The dynamic historical change that characterized the Paleolithic applies in this era too, everywhere around the globe: the agricultural and foraging societies of the world were not static even in places where they did not ("yet") feature cities or become incorporated into imperial states.

As for those places that did, these early states—whether city-states or imperial states—commonly included features such as a division of labor and hierarchy, bureaucracy and writing, armies and taxation, frequent warfare, tribute-taking, and large monumental buildings.[83] These new social and political forms, "cities" and "states," made possible new occupations and lifestyles, not to mention new forms of wealth and power—at least for some fraction of the people, some of the time. The keeping of written records also changes what we can say about these places and people; new forms of evidence make the stories of some individuals and groups fairly accessible to us even now. But the vast majority of people during the final 2,000 years of the agrarian era were farmers living in agricultural villages or hamlets and rural settings, and they left few, if any, written records.[84] Life in an agricultural village that had been incorporated into a state was a very different context than an agricultural

---

81. The "nation-state" is a specifically modern phenomenon: a politically sovereign unit that defines itself as expressing the interests of one particular group, the "nation"—unlike an empire, which asserts control of people that do not share this single identity, and unlike other forms of state organization, such as monarchies in which power is usually not legitimated on the basis of a popular or collective identity.

82. Mound-builders who had several relatively dense population centers, including Cahokia in present-day Illinois.

83. Christian, *Maps of Time*, pp. 271–281.

84. For a discussion of the difference between "nucleated" vs. more dispersed patterns of settlement, see, e.g., Terry Hunt and Carl Lipo, *The Statues that Walked: Unraveling the Mystery of Easter Island*, pp. 121–123.

village independent of state power, since farmers were subjected to rents and taxes and military conscription. On the other hand, at least in theory, they also received a certain level of protection against raids and other forms of violence against persons and property.[85] However, although states and empires controlled increasing land areas over time, even 300 years ago they controlled no more than one-third of the land area that is now incorporated within modern states.[86] World-historical accounts that focus on early states and empires therefore tend to skew our vision in favor of the centers of political power. Considering the lives of common people is a way to return our focus to smaller scales, which were only partially influenced or disrupted by the politically powerful.[87]

The increasing adoption of agriculture and the slow, fitful clustering of people into larger settlements were processes that happened all over the world; this meant that even the great states and empires had world-historical contexts of their own, and were increasingly not isolated from one another. Egypt provides an example of a civilization whose history reflects this world-historical context. Because of the fertility of the Nile valley, Egypt was one of the earliest dense clusters of people, and its geographical features helped make it relatively immune to invasion by outsiders for 3,000 years. Yet after Alexander the Great finally conquered it, Egypt was continuously under foreign rule for more than two millennia. That the early adopters of agrarian civilization could be so overrun reflected the waxing of wealth and military might in other centers of power throughout the Old World, a process that had its parallels in the New World with the growth and contraction of major civilizations such as the Chavín or the Maya—and later, following the arrival of Iberian colonizers, the Inca and the Aztec.

Industrial Era: "One World"

The industrial era is by far the shortest of the three periods, but in some ways the most difficult to write about in a condensed way. Compared with the foraging and agrarian eras, it has a superabundance of textual and other sources of evidence for historians to study, and there has been less time for the consequences of recent events to play out compared with events of thousands of years ago. Prominent

---

85. McNeill and McNeill, *The Human Web*, p. 50.

86. Christian, *Maps of Time*, p. 305.

87. Discussing Jesus's words in the Gospel of Matthew, "Blessed are the meek, for they shall inherit the land," Pope Benedict XVI comments, "Of course, there is a sense in which the interplay between 'meekness' and the promise of the land can also be seen as a perfectly ordinary piece of historical wisdom: Conquerors come and go, but the ones who remain are the simple, the humble, who cultivate the land and continue sowing and harvesting in the midst of sorrows and joys. The humble, the simple, outlast the violent, even from a purely historical point of view." (Pope Benedict XVI, *Jesus of Nazareth: From the Baptism in the Jordan to the Transfiguration*, p. 83.)

features of the industrial era include the human population growing from several hundred million to several billion in just two centuries; a transition from a world with severe limits on energy use, speed of transport, and speed of communication to a world with access to huge supplies of energy, rapid global transportation by land and by air, and near-instant communication; deepening global interconnections; widespread industrialization and accompanying changes in the rhythms of daily life for most of the world's people; and (by some measures) greater inequalities between the world's wealthiest and poorest than ever before. The changes associated with the modern world are so unique and sweeping that it is not unreasonable to describe the past 200 to 300 years—despite being barely a blip in the longer time-lines discussed throughout this book—as an entirely new era of world history, certainly for humanity and, perhaps, even for the planet as a whole.

The global interconnections of the modern world have roots going back all the way into the migrations during the era of foragers, which established human populations in every corner of the world. But the "world zones" of Afro-Eurasia, the Americas, Australia / Papua New Guinea, and the Pacific Islands remained largely separate from one another until the 1500s.[88] While Vikings reached Newfoundland around the year 1000, and contact between Pacific islanders and South Americans almost certainly occurred decades or even centuries before 1492,[89] these did not lead to sustained connections between separated parts of the world. No new long-term trade networks or new global economies appeared.

The decades and centuries following 1492, however, were different. Historians often label the 1500s to the 1700s as the "early modern" period, a label that originated from histories of Europe but that is applied more broadly today. This period still fits rather well as part of the agrarian era, for all the reasons already discussed, yet it was a time when many of the political, economic, and social forms of the modern world began taking shape. The Afro-Eurasian and American world zones became tightly linked, both economically and ecologically. Animals, plants, and microbes traveled from the Americas to Eurasia, and from Eurasia to the Americas, in what has become known as the "Columbian Exchange."[90] A new intensification of agriculture occurred in both world zones, as crops such as tomatoes and potatoes (from the New World) and sugar, coffee, and cotton (from the Old World) found new and sometimes more suitable homes, and as new crops made it possible to

---

88. Following Christian's division of the world into zones in *Maps of Time*; see, e.g., p. 212 and the image on p. 213 in *Maps of Time*.

89. The sweet potato spread from Central and South America to the Pacific Islands; the chicken was introduced to South America by the Polynesians. See, e.g., Hunt and Lipo, *The Statues that Walked*, p. 4.

90. A term coined by the historian Alfred W. Crosby in his 1972 book *The Columbian Exchange: Biological and Cultural Consequences of 1492*.

farm lands that had not been suitable for farming at all.[91] Economically, European imperialist projects and the Atlantic slave trade also lay at the foundation of the first fully global economy. Slave labor in the Americas, using people forcibly taken from parts of sub-Saharan Africa and made into commodities for purchase, produced "cash crops" such as sugar, coffee, and cotton, products that found ready markets in the first mass consumer culture of Eurasia (not just Europe; China still received the lion's share of the benefits of economic activity worldwide well into the 1700s[92]). Many modern economic institutions, including insurance, accounting, and banking firms, grew larger and more sophisticated through the necessities of financing—and spreading the risk—of the voyages of slave ships.[93]

An even more sweeping global change to human life came with the changes wrought by the Industrial Revolution and the transition to what the historical demographer E. A. Wrigley calls an "energy-rich economy"[94] and what J. R. and William McNeill refer to as a "high-energy society."[95] Using coal—and, later, oil and natural gas—for a range of purposes liberated a tremendous supply of energy that had been buried underground for (in many cases) over 300 million years, and made it less necessary for those with access to these "fossil fuel" resources to rely on biomass (e.g., burning wood) for energy. This, in turn, made mass poverty "unnecessary,"[96] although poverty in actuality continued and, in some cases, grew. Even so, "the transition to a high-energy society amounted to a great liberation from drudgery and toil"[97] for many people. In the agrarian era, controlling energy had largely meant controlling *people*, hence the importance of labor regimes like slavery, serfdom, or indentured servitude. But controlling energy in the modern world also means controlling fossil fuels.

The pattern of global trade, mass consumption, industrialization, and expanding access to energy resources had profound consequences for large-scale economic trends, and also for individual lives around the world. It produced a move away from agricultural villages and toward cities that continues today, and a world where more than half the human population now lives in urban settings, with several hundred cities holding populations of more than a million people each. (Consider that only 1,000 years ago, there were probably, at most, five cities that had ever

---

91. McNeill and McNeill, *The Human Web*, pp. 207–208.

92. For example, "mid-eighteenth-century Chinese almost certainly consumed more sugar than Europeans." (Pomeranz, *The Great Divergence*, p. 18.)

93. As Sven Beckert writes, the foundations of global capitalism in the early modern involve "the realities of slavery, expropriation, and colonialism." (Beckert, *Empire of Cotton*, p. xviii.)

94. E.A. Wrigley, *Energy and the English Industrial Revolution*, p. 26.

95. McNeill and McNeill, *The Human Web*, p. 214.

96. Ibid., p. 232.

97. Ibid., p. 285.

reached this size: Alexandria in Egypt, Rome, Chang'an and Kaifeng in China, and Baghdad.[98] See Plates 32 through 34.)

The general pattern of the Industrial Revolution, at least when it started, was that poor, geographically concentrated workers were heavily exploited, then gradually, and very unevenly, conditions improved for a variety of contingent and contextual reasons. Considerable violence often was associated with workers protesting their plight and striking. But the parts of the world that industrialized first—in the sense that they built the first factories—also tended to benefit at the expense of parts of the world that industrialized later:

> By the second half of the nineteenth century, workers organized collectively, both in unions and political parties, and slowly, over multiple decades, improved their wages and working conditions. This, in turn, increased production costs, creating openings for lower-cost producers in other parts of the world. By the turn of the twentieth century, the model of industrial capitalism had traveled to other countries and was embraced by their modernizing elites. As a result, the cotton industry left Europe and New England and returned to it[s] origins in the global South.[99]

Global economic, transportation, and communication ties only became stronger with time. In the 19th century, steamships tightened connections across the sea, with railroads doing likewise over land. (See Figure 6.1.) And the telegraph created near-instantaneous connections between faraway places. By the early 1900s,

> a growing proportion of people depended on fossil fuels, on food raised on distant continents, in short, on the maintenance of global linkages. Long-distance trade increasingly involved items basic to human survival, such as food and fuel. In the nineteenth century, the worldwide web attained such efficiency that great gains followed from erecting an economy based on massive daily flows of energy and materials over great distances, a feat that required huge technical skill, investment, and constant maintenance.[100]

While the 19th and early 20th centuries saw many nations attempt to avoid reliance on global markets and supply their own economic needs through imperial expansion and acquisition of raw materials, the trend toward heavier reliance on

---

98. Estimates of city populations vary considerably. Classic estimates can be found in Tertius Chandler's *Four Thousand Years of Urban Growth: A Historical Census* and George Modelski's *World Cities: −3,000 to 2,000.* Ian Morris also provides estimates, including Kaifeng on this list.

99. Beckert, *Empire of Cotton*, p. xvii.

100. McNeill and McNeill, *The Human Web*, p. 213.

FIGURE 6.1 Mobility and the Industrial Revolution The industrial era has seen the creation of technologies, like railroads, that can move people and goods faster and on larger scales than ever before, helping to strengthen global economic, transportation, and communication ties.
Source: "B&A Steam Engine"/Unknown Author/Wikipedia.

global trade worldwide has been fairly widespread during the last few centuries. Networked electronic technologies of the late 20th and early 21st century only accelerated this tendency. But well before the internet, the transition to the modern world had already "locked us into a high-energy society, in which we must continue to mobilize, transport, and use vast quantities of basic items."[101] Once the modern industrial era had gotten underway, there was no going back, at least not without a hugely difficult transition and high social costs.

Political changes also accompanied this new, modern context. European colonial powers exerted political sovereignty over a large portion of the globe, peaking around the turn of the 20th century and declining after World War II. The 19th century had featured a large number of revolutions, especially between 1815 and 1870; in the Western Hemisphere, some of these revolutions led to broadened forms of political participation, first for men of property and then, in fits and starts, for other groups.[102] The nation-state, a relatively recent form of political organization that gained traction especially in the 19th century, became the worldwide norm in the 20th century. As the historian Adam McKeown writes:

As late as the turn of the twentieth century the world political map still contained a multiplicity of sovereign units: nation states, city states,

---

101. Ibid., p. 214.

102. Ibid., p. 229. In the Eastern Hemisphere, some such movements partly succeeded, as, for example, in Japan. But elsewhere, such as in China, massive upheavals like the Taiping Rebellion did not culminate, at least not as quickly, in political revolution.

princedoms, federations, empires old and new, protectorates, colonies, do-
minions, extraterritorial enclaves, customs receiverships, clans and other
kin-based units, with a broad spectrum of subordination and autonomy
among them all. By the early 1960s a mosaic of nation states with similar institutions and similar claims to autonomy covered most of the world. It was
a spectacular diffusion and homogenization of political forms. The national
units and boundaries that we now take for granted as the foundation of a
fragmented, unglobalized world were themselves a relatively recent product
of the globalization of political forms. Yet these forms are often seen as precisely the opposite of globalization.[103]

The ideological and political / economic costs of continued European imperialism—including rebellions by colonial populations—rose sufficiently high as to
provoke the widespread collapse of most empires by the mid-20th century.

Much more could be said about the industrial era, and chapter 7 addresses
"Modernity." But for now, it is worth taking a step back to notice just how much
of what we often take for granted about the world we live in was contingent upon
these global developments in the past 200 to 500 years. These developments have
made possible both incredible individual and collective wealth[104] as well as deep
inequality between rich and poor.

And yet the periodization given here—into the three eras of foraging, agrarian, and industrial—is far from the only possible approach, and it can even be
misleading if taken too far. For instance, many modern groups are still agrarian or even foragers, although their lives too are affected by the global context
of modern industrial society. Even regarding the basics of energy acquisition,
about half of the world's population today relies on biomass "as a major, often the
only, source of domestic energy for cooking and heating."[105] And fossil fuels also
enable things like chainsaws and logging trucks, which make it easier to exploit
biomass. Moreover, despite our global connectivity, an individual may struggle
just as much as ever, or even more, to feel connected with other people. Any
global, overarching periodization must leave room for other ways of categorizing
time and experience.

---

103. Adam McKeown, "Periodizing Globalization," *History Workshop Journal* 63 (Spring 2007):223–224.

104. Ramez Naam writes that even the extraordinarily wealthy of the ancient world could travel from place to place only slowly and laboriously, had no access to antibiotics or painkillers, could communicate over long distances only very slowly, and had no access to modern conveniences of temperature control, variability of diet, and the like. (Naam, *The Infinite Resource*, p. 32.)

105. H. W. de Koning, K. R. Smith, and J. M. Last, "Biomass Fuel Combustion and Health," https://www.ncbi.nlm.nih.gov/pmc/articles/PMC2536350/ .

The Multiple Contexts of Universal Histories

Walter Alvarez defines Big History as "the approach to history that places human history within the context of cosmic history, from the beginning of the universe up until life on Earth today."[106] Universal histories set individual lives and particular events into multiple contexts at multiple scales: the context of cosmic history, yes, but also of Earth history, the history of life, and the history of humanity. Ideally, this enables new angles from which to understand how things came to be the way they are, to see many contexts at once, and to appreciate their interplay in shaping a path-dependent, contingent story. This is the idea behind the so-called "Little Big Histories" that Esther Quaedackers and others have pioneered: giving an account of the natural and social history of something that seems relatively small and mundane, like a light bulb or a stick of butter or a blade of grass, and considering how that thing came to be what it is, approaching from multiple narratives and multiple scales.

This can be an especially powerful benefit of a universal-historical approach: incorporating very large scales in time and space into our histories, *not* to overwhelm or ignore the individual person or the small-scale event but to provide maximal contextualization for what happens at smaller scales, and to offer a broader set of perspectives on change and continuity over time.

Side Note: Social Constructs

Historians often refer to various aspects of a person's or a group's understanding of the world as "social constructs." To critics, this sometimes comes across as an empty relativism, as if there is no objective truth or reality. And certainly, both the term and the concept of social constructs can be overemphasized, and in some circles often are. But "constructivism," understood in a more nuanced way, can also be a powerful theoretical framework for historians trying to understand other cultures and cultural contexts, whether past or present.

What does it mean to say that, for example, the nation-state, or health and disease, or maps, or ideas about gender or race are socially constructed? It means that people use language, categories, and concepts to develop a shared understanding of the world. These understandings vary from group to group, but this does not mean that there is no reality behind them. Historians who take a constructivist approach (usually) agree that there *is* a real world, one that is "out there" and knowable. But they argue that people actively construct their knowledge and understanding of that world, sometimes in very different ways; that they

---

106. Walter Alvarez, *A Most Improbable Journey: A Big History of Our Planet and Ourselves*, p. 1.

do so in groups, socially; and that they use language and culture to do so. In the case of disease, for instance, a historian is unlikely to claim there is no such thing as biological pathogens that produce certain painful and even deadly effects in a human body. But how disease is understood, what defines a particular category of illness, and how people respond to it as a society—which in turn shape the experience of "having" the disease—all these are not given by nature. They are constructed culturally and socially. To take another example, the assertion that race is socially constructed is not to deny that there are phenotypic variations between people, such as differences of skin color; however, the association of these variations with ideas about other overarching distinctions—and, in particular, the lumping together of many different skin shades and ethnic backgrounds and labeling some "White" and others "Black" (to name just two)—is a social construct. Historical analysis demonstrates how such constructions came into being and changed over time, taking categories that seem "natural" and fixed and showing instead that they frequently are neither. This is another way of saying that historians *historicize* the categories.

Constructivism can also help historians think through the categories and labels they use in writing history. Historians' categories and models of reality (compare chapter 4, "Science") are not absolutes, and they may be subject to refinement or even wholesale change. For example, the French Revolution was an "overwhelming and bewildering concatenation of events"[107] for those who experienced it; it receives the simple label of "French Revolution" only in retrospect. This does not mean that historical categories and labels are mere fictions. To say that something like the idea of a nation-state or the French Revolution is "invented" does not mean that they are unreal, merely that they are ways of using the powers of human imagination to illuminate or interact with our world.[108]

Population

We have discussed a division of history into three major historical contexts for understanding the global human past: the era of foragers from 200,000 or 300,000 to 10,000 years ago, the agrarian era from 10,000 to 250 years ago, and the industrial era from 250 years ago to the present. One of the most basic changes over the course of these 300,000 years of human history is the number of people on the planet: a world of foraging societies could incorporate, at most, a few million people; the agrarian era saw the world population increase to several hundred million; and world population now stands at well over 7 billion. Precise numbers are not available until the very recent past, but the general trend of world population increase is clear enough. (See Figure 6.2.)

---

107. Benedict Anderson, *Imagined Communities*, p. 80.

108. Cf. Ibid., p. 6.

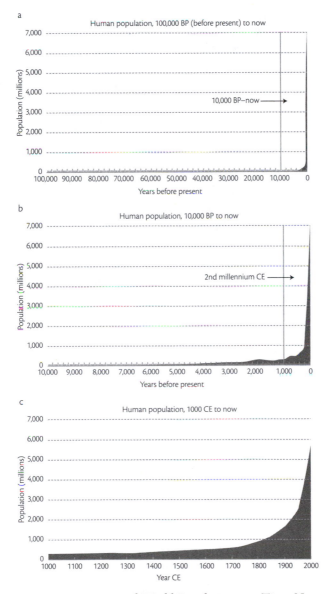

FIGURE 6.2 Estimated World Population over Time Note the different time scales in these three graphs, which portray world population over the past 1,000 years, 10,000 years, and 100,000 years of human history. Especially against the backdrop of the longer time scales, the present expansion of human population numbers is striking.

Source: Based on Figs. 6.1, Fig. 8.2, Fig. 11.1 in David Christian, *Maps of Time* (p. 142, p. 209, p. 343), in turn based on J.R. Biraben, "Essai sur l'evolution du nombre des homes," *Population* 34 (1979):13-25; Massimo Livi-Bacci, *A Concise History of World Population* (Oxford: Blackwell, 1992); and Chris Stringer and Robin McKie, *African Exodus* (London: Cape, 1996).

Our goal in engaging with world history is not just *describing* what happened, however, but *interpreting* and analyzing the dynamics of why changes happened the way they did. Hence, we need to understand something about population dynamics: *Why* did populations increase or decrease over time, globally and locally, and what consequences did population growth or decline have?

Population Dynamics in the Era of Foragers, the Agrarian Era, and the Modern Era

While DNA evidence can give some indication of genetic relationships between groups of people going back well into the era of foragers, a general understanding of how population dynamics worked in that period is mostly a product of reasoning and observation of modern foraging-society analogues.

As Marshall Sahlins and other anthropologists point out, hunter-gatherer populations do not typically spend all day looking for food, and most people in most foraging societies may average less time working to acquire food than do most people in most agricultural societies.[109] Also, with only a few known exceptions historically, foragers do not settle in one place, but rather move from place to place— sometimes seasonally, sometimes more often—in order to track the movements of preferred animals, to acquire preferred plants while they are in season, or to find more abundant locations. In some areas, foraging groups may endure a "hunger season," as when food sources become scarce in winter.

These constraints inform societal structures and practices around raising children. In particular, mothers in foraging societies today commonly breastfeed infants for two to five years, and they also nurse far more frequently (e.g., four times per hour during the day) than mothers in industrialized societies usually do.[110] Extended, high-frequency breastfeeding can delay the return of ovulation after giving birth, which produces considerably larger spacing between births, an important factor for a group of people that moves camp from place to place and must carry everything, including young children, with them whenever they move. While there is only a small amount of direct evidence,[111] it seems reasonable to assume that similar child-rearing and birth-spacing practices likely prevailed among the foragers of the deep past, at least in many instances, given similar biological and

---

109. See Marshall Sahlins, "Notes on the Original Affluent Society," pp. 85–89 in *Man the Hunter*, eds. Richard B. Lee and Irven DeVore with the assistance of Jill Nash-Mitchell.

110. Diamond, *The World Until Yesterday*, p. 182.

111. For an example of something closer to direct evidence, see, e.g., F. Clayton, J. Sealy, and S. Pfeiffer, "Weaning Age Among Foragers at Matjes River Rock Shelter, South Africa, from Stable Nitrogen and Carbon Isotope Analyses," *American Journal of Physical Anthropology* 129, no. 2 (2006):311–317.

physiological constraints—especially the lack of cow's milk (and baby formula) and soft cereal gruels to replace breast milk as a source of nourishment early in life. In short, practices around food acquisition, interactions between groups, and child-rearing meant that the era of foragers was likely a time of slow population growth: not because limitations on total resource constraints led to starvation, but because of social practices linked with modes of food acquisition.

What population growth did occur was probably supported by "extensification" more than by "intensification." If a local population grew too large to support itself fully on the land it usually occupied, people could potentially move to new, unoccupied areas, perhaps adapting technologically and behaviorally to new climates or ecosystems in the process (extensification). Once human groups already occupied the entire globe, however, further population growth would have required more efficient extraction of food from the local environment (intensification). This would also have been true on smaller scales long before the entire globe was populated: any group that could not simply move to a new territory (e.g. because all nearby territories were occupied) could potentially face resource limitations dictating how many people the local ecosystem could support.

Agriculture began appearing a few thousand years after all continents except Antarctica had been occupied. Archaeological evidence points to the transition from foraging to agriculture being a slow process, carried out over hundreds of years and many generations and not always irreversible: changing conditions might warrant a mix of foraging and agriculture, or a return to foraging after the adoption of agriculture. But the path from foraging to agriculture, albeit slow, became common in different parts of the world.

Social practices in agrarian societies display a different pattern than in foraging societies. In agrarian societies, groups of people are tied to a specific area of land and so do not have the same need for mobility, and they often have more ready access to alternative sources of nourishment for their young. Also, even young children can contribute to the work of a farm and a household—tending chickens or helping to care for younger siblings, for instance. Therefore, children are typically weaned from breastfeeding more quickly in agrarian societies, perhaps around two years earlier on average. This means that births can be spaced much closer together in an agricultural household, and since agriculture allows more intense exploitation of smaller pieces of land, larger populations usually inhabit a given area than in foraging societies.[112]

As discussed under "Technology" in chapter 5, agriculture was a mixed blessing. In many places, its introduction may have reduced average life span and, at least initially, made populations more vulnerable to disease (due to closer contact with disease-carrying animals and higher population densities). It also made people in

---

112. Agriculture may have even begun (at least in some places) as a response to growing populations and the need to feed more mouths with the same amount of land.

agricultural societies reliant on a much smaller range of plants and animals, so that even something as fickle as the weather could produce a bad harvest and lead to famine. (Foragers typically have a broader array of types of food to draw from, so that a failure of one type is not as likely to be catastrophic.)

Why, then, did agriculture tend, more often than not, to stick and then to grow? It may have been that turning to agriculture was exactly the kind of intensification that growing hunter-gatherer populations needed to feed all mouths; in other words, they developed a new technology as a response. And the new cultural practices that came along with the technological change allowed more rapid population growth, meaning that populations grew even larger, requiring the continued use of agriculture as long as environmental conditions in the area supported good crop growth.

A steadily increasing fraction of the world relied on agriculture over the last 11,000 years, and this produced global populations of a few hundred million around 1,000 to 3,000 years ago. These numbers increased even more swiftly over the past 500 years. After the initial ravages of disease that followed the joining of Old and New Worlds, leading to mass death among the peoples of the New World, disease resistance became more widespread, with fewer deaths resulting. And new crops from the Columbian Exchange led to increased food production in many parts of the world. In the 19th and early 20th centuries, innovations in both science and industry generated chemicals to promote crop growth and new fertilizers, greatly expanding food production to more than keep pace with population growth. And in the mid-20th century, scientific and technological innovation in crop breeding further increased crop yields in what has come to be known as the "Green Revolution."[113] While hundreds of millions of people are still undernourished and large famines are a terrible reality, they now result in almost every case from uneven distribution of food, not from total production of food, which if evenly distributed would be more than adequate for the world's needs. In fact, as world population has grown, the total amount of food worldwide *per capita* has also increased, even while the percentage of the world's population that works as farmers has declined. Between 1900 and 2000, for example, global population grew by a factor of approximately four, while grain production grew by a factor of approximately five.[114]

At the same time, the average human life span grew much longer across the globe in the modern era, especially in wealthier parts of the world, as evident from the plot shown in Figure 6.3. The agrarian era had seen very high infant mortality.

---

113. See, e.g., Antony Trewavas, "Malthus Foiled Again and Again," http://www.nature.com/nature/journal/v418/n6898/full/nature01013.html .

114. Adam Kucharski, "Will the Earth Ever Fill Up?," http://nautil.us/issue/29/scaling/will-the-earth-ever-fill-up . Note that in addition to new agricultural practices, there are also new technologies of storage and distribution (like refrigeration and long-haul trucking) that allow patterns of food distribution and consumption to change and more people to be supported by a smaller proportion of farmers.

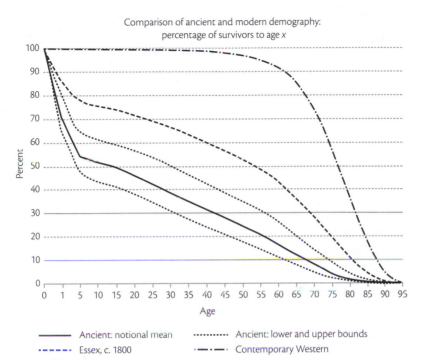

Comparison of ancient and modern demography:
percentage of survivors to age *x*

Ancient: notional mean .... Ancient: lower and upper bounds
----- Essex, c. 1800 ·—·—· Contemporary Western

FIGURE 6.3 Ancient and Modern Life Spans This graph shows estimates of the likelihood that a given person would live to be a certain age in the ancient world, in Essex c. 1800, and in the present-day West. The numbers can only serve as rough estimates, but they still give a sense of the difference in demographic regimes: in the ancient world, a given person had perhaps a 50-50 chance of living past age 5.[1] While it has always been the case that at least some people live to be quite old (70, 80, or even 90 years), death at a young age, especially before age 5, was far more common in every other time than our own. (Note that data on the ancient world comes from scattered sources, including census data in Roman Egypt, cemetery remains in various places, and more recent preindustrial age distributions.)

Source: Walter Scheidel, "Demography," Chapter 3 in Walter Scheidel, Ian Morris, and Richard P. Saller, eds., *The Cambridge Economic History of the Greco-Roman World* (Cambridge: Cambridge Univ. Press, 2007), p. 40.[2]

[1] Among other things, this likely means population estimates for the ancient world significantly undercount the total number of people because of all the unborn babies and infants who ended up dying within a short time and did not survive long enough to be counted.

[2] Thanks to Ian Moyer for pointing out this source.

But someone who lived through those first few years of childhood had a reasonably good chance of continuing to live, and it was not unheard of for a few individuals to live to very old age, 70 or even 80 years or beyond. The industrial era has seen tremendous declines in infant mortality, however, and higher probabilities of survival through young and middle adulthood as well. This resulted from a combination of innovations in food production, public health,[115] and disease control. Populations have grown so much that perhaps 8 to 10 percent of all the human beings who have ever lived are alive today, possibly almost as many as the total number of people who ever lived in the entire 200,000 or 300,000 years of the era of foragers.[116]

Malthusian Thinking About Population Dynamics

David Christian and many other authors have sought to make broader generalizations about the role that population numbers played in world history. For example, of the relationship between population growth and innovations in food acquisition, Christian writes:

> In the natural world, available resources are determined by the niches available to a particular species. But humans are different because they keep innovating: they explore, modify, improve, and even create new niches. Thus limits to human population growth are set only by the number and productivity of the niches that innovation has made available in any particular epoch. Every time there are significant innovations, the ceiling to population growth is lifted. When significant innovations occur, populations can climb until they overshoot the new ceiling. Then there will be a crash.[117]

Christian continues by arguing that during such a crash, famine, disease, and war will take many lives.

In writing this description, Christian draws on a particular explanatory framework, associated with Thomas Malthus. Writing around the year 1800, Malthus held that the resources of any given area of land can support a certain number of people and no more, and that because populations can grow exponentially in the absence of such constraints, there will constantly be "population pressure" bumping into that limit. Scarcity of food, the availability of which can grow at most linearly, keeps populations in check. (See Figure 6.4.) Malthus wrote of both "preventive" and "positive" checks on population size: preventive checks are reductions in the birth rate driven by the presence of too many people, while positive checks increase the death rate through war, disease, and famine. (Positive checks

---

115. Including the invention of modern urban sanitation, with (among other innovations) government boards of health, housing codes, indoor plumbing, sewer systems, and garbage pickup. These stopped cholera, for instance, well before there was a solid microbiological understanding of disease. See Martin S. Pernick, "Diseases in Motion," pp. 365–374 in *A Companion to World History*, ed. Douglas Northrop.

116. Extrapolated from Christian, *Maps of Time*, p. 208, drawing on Livi-Bacci, *A Concise History of World Population*.

117. Christian, *Maps of Time*, p. 311.

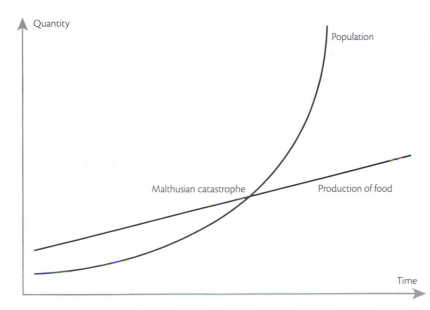

FIGURE 6.4 Malthus Illustrated This graph shows a simple illustration of the basic Malthusian premise: population grows exponentially, but food production (or "resource base") grows at best linearly, so population is bound to outstrip food: eventually, there will be too many mouths to feed. This model has been highly influential, but as discussed in the text, both its premises and its predictions have historically proven either incomplete or false.
Source: https://en.wikipedia.org/wiki/Malthusian_catastrophe#/media/File:Malthus_PL_en.svg
Image from Wikimedia user Kravietz, "Malthus PL en.svg"

are "positive" not in the sense of being good, but in the sense of "adding" a check to population growth.)[118]

Malthusian thinking tends to be seductive, especially in the context of large-scale, sweeping histories. The idea is intuitive—many mouths to feed, limited food with which to do it—and it provides a clear, unifying framework for population dynamics throughout history. Moreover, Darwin drew on Malthus in *The Origin of Species* and applied this way of thinking about resource scarcity and population dynamics to the animal kingdom, making it feel more natural for later thinkers to re-apply this sort of thinking to humans; in a science-based universal history, there is a certain appeal to emphasizing aspects of humanity that connect with the broader history of life.[119]

---

118. See Thomas Malthus, "An Essay on the Principle of Population": http://www.gutenberg.org/ebooks/4239 . Note that Malthus wrote several editions of this essay .

119. Darwin emphasized the Malthusian idea in an effort to convince people at the time that there truly is a "struggle for existence" throughout the living world. See *On the Origin of Species*, chapter 3. Also note that "invasive species" are an example of unchecked exponential population growth. When introduced into an environment in which nothing "checks" the growth of their population, they expand rapidly, often causing havoc within their new ecosystem.

But while Malthus's model of population dynamics is sometimes appropriate to apply locally to specific circumstances involving serious resource constraints, experience and evidence suggest that the model is not at all universally applicable among human beings. It argues that human population grows exponentially while food and other resources grow at most linearly, but neither premise is guaranteed—or even necessarily likely—to be true in a given case. Resources can, at least in some circumstances, grow much faster than linearly, since in many cases, people *produce* resources. For example, plants and animals we use for food constitute populations just as human beings do, and can grow rapidly under the right conditions.[120] Indeed, world food supplies during the industrial era have grown faster than population. (For the most recent decades, see Figure 6.5.) Meanwhile, population only grows exponentially if birth rates consistently exceed death rates,

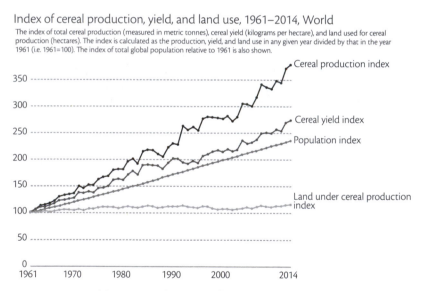

Index of cereal production, yield, and land use, 1961–2014, World

The index of total cereal production (measured in metric tonnes), cereal yield (kilograms per hectare), and land used for cereal production (hectares). The index is calculated as the production, yield, and land use in any given year divided by that in the year 1961 (i.e. 1961=100). The index of total global population relative to 1961 is also shown.

FIGURE 6.5 Malthus Contradicted Far from the catastrophic situation predicted by Malthus, total world cereal yield has so far more than kept pace with world population increase—including during the recent half-century represented in this graph, a period that saw the most rapid population growth ever. (Compare Figure 6.2.)
Source: Our World in Data

---

120. As Julian Simon argued, countering Paul Ehrlich's neo-Malthusian arguments. He also pointed out that there are times when one resource can be swapped out for another, more abundant version of the same thing. As Henry George wrote, "Both the jayhawk and the man eat chickens; but the more jayhawks, the fewer chickens, while the more men, the more chickens." (Quoted in John Tierney, "Betting on the Planet," https://www.nytimes.com/1990/12/02/magazine/betting-on-the-planet.html .) For more on Simon and Ehrlich, see "Sustainability" in chapter 8.

which cannot happen if death rates are too high for birth rates to keep up (or if, as in a number of modern nation-states like Japan and Italy, birth rates are too low to replace numbers as older generations die).

It seems that the agrarian era, at least for the most part, is best understood as a time when population growth was limited by high death rates more than by Malthusian resource ceilings. Fertility rates have to be quite high in order to keep up with the high death rates profiled in Figure 6.3. And even if the resources offered by an area of land set a certain "carrying capacity," the death rate may be too high to allow a given society to approach that limit. Disease and warfare may limit the population at a level well below the resource ceiling, particularly in areas of abundant harvests or foraging societies with abundant natural resources.[121] Infant mortality was high for much of this period, and adult deaths were a function of mass poverty and vulnerability to disease and violence at least as much as a function of ecological constraints. If people do not consistently survive to reproduce, there is never enough traction for the numbers to grow. So while some societies may have been up against a local Malthusian limit,[122] the general reality of the agrarian era was a "death-rate-limited demographic regime."[123]

Just as a death-rate-limited regime characterized the population dynamics of the agrarian era, the industrial era is characterized by a "demographic transition" in which death rates decline and then, after a period of usually a few decades, birth rates also fall. In between, population grows rapidly, while death rates are lower but birth rates are still high. France's growth period was from 1785 to 1970, Germany's from 1876 to 1965, Taiwan's from 1920 to 1990, and Mexico's from 1920 to 2000.[124] The eventual fall of birth rates was never purely the result of modern contraceptives, which during earlier transitions did not yet exist, and would not necessarily be viewed as desirable in societies that strongly value large families. Instead, industrialization and urbanization led to lower fertility rates. Children can work on a farm but do not generally participate in the labor force in industrial-urban settings

---

121. Note that disease and wars are not necessarily the result of "overpopulation." Wars are not always over resources; they often result from rivalries between groups, from the aspirations of power-hungry rulers, and the like. And disease vulnerability is a function of many things other than the resource base. Even famine is not always the result of a society maxing out the productivity of land and overshooting a Malthusian ceiling: it can also be provoked by the unequal distribution of resources, a political issue more than an ecological one.

122. The Malthusian framework should only be applied when it is relatively clear that a society was up against genuine resource constraints, as with foragers in especially resource-poor areas.

123. Thanks to Ian Moyer for introducing this term to us.

124. For these and other figures, see Livi-Bacci, *A Concise History of World Population*, p. 123, who cites J.-C. Chesnais, *La transition démographique*, pp. 294, 301.

until later in life.[125] Thus the same forces of industrial capitalism that enable population growth also turn children from producers of resources into consumers of resources for the first 10 to 20 years of their lives. Fertility rates tend to fall swiftly as people move away from the land and into cities, via mechanisms such as higher average age of marriage.[126]

Rather than seeing all this through a Malthusian lens, a more nuanced view places population growth against a regional backdrop, integrating developments in population with political and economic developments. When population growth is combined with industrialization and urbanization, it can be a force for economic growth, but great population growth in a given location without changes in economic and political structures may impoverish people and make the maintenance of living standards difficult. Population rarely determines anything on its own; it works in conjunction with other variables.

Still, especially since the 1960s, there has been no shortage of concern and warnings about looming future resource shortages. Universal histories have sometimes presented Malthusian limits as a totalizing reality, and human history as driven largely by ecological constraints. But while ecological considerations certainly deserve an important place in world history, the evidence is weak that Malthusian limits per se play such a constant, central, and defining role. Economic, technological, and social considerations are mediating factors: "Population size equilibrates with resources at a level mediated by technology and conventional living standards."[127] Birth rates are sensitive to economic and environmental conditions, via social variables like "average age at first marriage, the proportion of people ever marrying, and rates of remarriage,"[128] and "comparative evidence from other pre-modern societies suggests that temporary output fluctuations are more likely to activate preventive checks . . . than to raise mortality."[129] Also, as in Ester Boserup's model of population dynamics, nearness to a resource ceiling can drive innovation rather than overshoot and collapse.

---

125. Especially with the restrictions on child labor in many parts of the world starting in the 19th century.

126. "No single pattern or sequence of factors seems to explain this transition in all areas where it has been recorded, but it was usually accompanied by industrial development, immigration from rural areas to cities, and widespread changes both in family organization and in attitudes toward marriage and sexuality." (Joshua Cole, *The Power of Large Numbers*, p. 2.)

127. Walter Scheidel, "Demography," p. 50 in *The Cambridge Economic History of the Greco-Roman World*, eds. Walter Scheidel, Ian Morris, and Richard P. Saller.

128. Ibid., p. 68.

129. Ibid., p. 56.

Side Note: State Formation in Sumer

Various writers have given ecological limits and resource constraints more explanatory power than they probably deserve. An example is the initial formation of states in Sumer (southern Mesopotamia) over 5,000 years ago,[130] which some thinkers[131] have chalked up to population pressure. They argue that population growth is a primary driver of state formation in general, and in particular that expanding and urbanizing populations in Sumer were running up against resource constraints and so began warring for control of more land. According to this view, the needs to organize warfare and to create centralized ways of administering home territories and conquered areas were what led to the formation of states.

More recent scholarship using models that incorporate more likely estimates of ancient Sumer's population densities, however, has suggested that the city-states had sufficient land to feed their populations and were not running up against resource constraints that took them into one another's territories. Instead, leaders of incipient states may have been trying to control more *people*, not more *land*. Records at this time in Sumer suggest that conflicts were usually not between major powers running up against one another but, rather, were fought by major city-states trying to control (often rebellious) hinterlands, suggesting the scarce resource that incipient states were trying to control was people.[132] Given that people often flee the state and all its coercive apparatuses,[133] it makes sense that there would need to be some effort to subjugate people; the problems that states were solving may have been social rather than ecological.[134]

Biological Reductionism in Universal Histories

A deeper philosophical issue with treating population as a primary driver of historical change, or as the most important framework for the human story, lies in the implications of how Malthusian modeling thinks about human beings. Speaking of "population" treats people as numbers and biological entities only, and therefore is

---

130. Ian Moyer inspired the basic idea for this Side Note, and some of the details.

131. See, e.g., R. L. Carneiro, "A Theory of the Origin of the State," http://science.sciencemag.org/content/169/3947/733 .

132. Seth Richardson, "Early Mesopotamia: The Presumptive State," https://academic.oup.com/past/article-abstract/215/1/3/1479729 ; see also the work of Carrie Hritz .

133. See James C. Scott, *The Art of Not Being Governed: An Anarchist History of Upland Southeast Asia*.

134. See James C. Scott's other work concerning the initial formation of states, particularly *Against the Grain: A Deep History of the Earliest States*.

Extended Side Note: Easter Island

In *A Green History of the World*, the historian Clive Ponting[135] began a long trend of mobilizing the story of Easter Island as a warning about the dangers of overpopulation and overexploitation of resources. Authors including Jared Diamond[136] and David Christian,[137] as well as a large number of popular articles, have picked up Easter Island as a story with a "grim warning to the world."[138]

According to Ponting's version of the story, Polynesian voyagers arrived on the (extremely remote and isolated) island in the 400s, lived in relative prosperity for hundreds of years, and erected the massive stone statues for which the island is best known today as a form of competitive monument-building between rival clans. However, growing populations (peaking at 7,000 people on the island in 1550, according to Ponting, while Diamond estimates significantly larger numbers) gradually deforested the island, with trees cut down to provide clearings for agriculture, lumber for building, fuel for heating and cooking, and (most demandingly) rollers to transport the several-dozen-ton statues from quarries to their final standing positions. The tree shortage meant an end to building houses and canoes, so people lived in caves or stone shelters in hillsides or "flimsy reed huts,"[139] unable to leave the remote island. Exposed soil led to erosion and declining crop yields. Chronic warfare for scarce remaining resources ensued, weapons and slavery proliferated, the statues of rival clans were attacked and pulled down, population numbers collapsed to a fraction of what they were at the island's height, and the islanders even resorted to cannibalism. As Ponting summarizes: "The increasing numbers and cultural ambitions of the islanders proved too great for the limited resources available to them. When the environment was ruined by the pressure, the society very quickly collapsed with it, leading to a state of near barbarism."[140]

Master narrators like Ponting, Diamond, and Christian can make this story quite scary indeed, a terrifying parable for the modern world. Just as Easter Island was a remote island with significant resource constraints that the islanders overshot—leading to brutal warfare, a desperate scramble for remaining scarce resources, cannibalism, and mass death—so too the Earth itself is a remote island of habitability in space, with significant resource constraints that

135. See Clive Ponting, *A New Green History of the World: The Environment and the Collapse of Great Civilizations*, pp. 1–7.

136. See Jared Diamond, *Collapse: How Societies Choose to Fail or Succeed*, pp. 79–119.

137. See Christian, *Maps of Time*, pp. 472–475.

138. Ponting, *A New Green History of the World*, p. 1.

139. Ibid., pp. 5–6.

140. Ibid., p. 7.

we are also in danger of overshooting, or perhaps have already overshot. We may face a similarly terrifying future.

The problem with the Easter Island narrative is that almost every element may be false. The anthropologists Terry Hunt and Carl Lipo,[141] two of the foremost authorities on the archaeology of Easter Island, have been particularly vocal critics of the "ecocide" / "collapse" narrative, pointing out—among other things—that the island was probably not settled until much later than Ponting thought, perhaps as late as 1200. They argue that deforestation was probably not due primarily to direct human activity but rather to an invasive species of rat brought with the settlers: remains of palm nuts show clear signs of rat gnawing. These rats did not destroy trees, however, but rendered them unable to reproduce by consuming seeds, as is well-documented in parallel cases like New Zealand, Hawaii, and other Pacific islands.[142] And based on studies of the island's soil and the islanders' agricultural practices, deforestation may have ultimately *increased* the opportunities for productive agriculture rather than decreasing them. Moreover, the statues were ingeniously constructed so as to be "walked" across the island and hence did not need log rollers. (Hunt and Lipo demonstrated the walking mechanism by actually *doing* it with a model statue,[143] while also demonstrating the consistency of this mode of statue transport with the archaeological evidence.) The "weapons" that seemed to have proliferated were ineffective as weapons and so were almost certainly a different kind of tool. The statues most likely fell due to inattention and lack of maintenance after European first contact rather than from being intentionally pulled down. And there simply is no clear evidence of widespread, violent deaths or of significant warfare at all, or that the population had ever grown much larger than the roughly 3,000 that Europeans found when they first came upon the island in 1722. Hence, Hunt and Lipo argue, there was probably no collapse of population numbers at any point in the island's history— at least before European contact, which eventually introduced smallpox, other deadly pathogens, and slave raids, leading to a near-complete collapse before the population of Easter Islanders rebounded to its present several thousand people.

Instead of a parable of ecological disaster, pre-European-contact Easter Island becomes an encouraging story of surviving and even thriving in an isolated and resource-poor environment, in spite of the harm done by an invasive species. Whether or not their version of the story turns out to be completely accurate, Hunt and Lipo seriously undermine the evidential basis of the "ecological collapse" narrative.

---

141. See Hunt and Lipo, *The Statues that Walked*, and Hunt and Lipo, "Ecological Catastrophe, Collapse, and the Myth of 'Ecocide' on Rapa Nui (Easter Island)," pp. 21–44 in *Questioning Collapse*, eds. Patricia A. McAnany and Norman Yoffee.

142. See Hunt and Lipo, "Ecological Catastrophe, Collapse, and the Myth of 'Ecocide' on Rapa Nui (Easter Island)," p. 36.

143. National Geographic, "Terry Hunt and Carl Lipo: The Statues that Walked | Nat Geo Live," https://www.youtube.com/watch?v=rut16-AfoyA ; see, especially, 18:00.

at best a partial lens on human history. Speaking of "population pressure" is reminiscent of the way physicists or chemists speak of gases, with more molecules in a chamber producing pressure against its sides. More reductive still are biological comparisons:

> Humans have become, as Lynn Margulis and Dorion Sagan put it, "a sort of mammalian weed." Carlo Cipolla comments: "A biologist, looking at the diagram showing the recent growth of world population in a long-range perspective, said that he had the impression of being in the presence of the growth curve of a microbe population in a body suddenly struck by some infectious disease. The 'bacillus' man is taking over the world."[144]

That the unfavorably intended analogies are biological is not a coincidence: Talking about human "populations" has deep roots in thinking about humans biologically. The modern field of population ecology considers the dynamics of populations of organisms, whether humans or other living creatures, and so thinking in terms of populations implies a basic similarity between human and animal populations. Paul Ehrlich, a great modern proponent of neo-Malthusian thinking, was (and is) a population biologist who studied butterflies, and he and some of his colleagues have made rather free comparisons between human and insect populations.[145]

While humans do share many characteristics with the animal world, meaning that population thinking can yield insights, human culture, politics, and social structures also matter and go hand-in-hand with population dynamics. Making the story of human history primarily one of population numbers and ecological constraints fails to take this into account. A world with 8 billion people is certainly different in myriad ways from a world with 2 million, but it is not simply a story of greater resource usage: it is also a story of different scales of interaction among social and cultural creatures, different ways of organizing—and providing for the needs of—human lives. As we saw in the first pages of this section, even trying to understand why the numbers changed in the way they did turns the story into one of what happens within human communities, of cultural responses to environmental realities. This is part of why disciplinary historians are not fond of biologically reductive explanations, and why many different disciplines, not just population ecology, must be given weight and balanced with one another if we are to reach a properly nuanced view of human history as a whole.

---

144. Christian, *Maps of Time*, p. 342.

145. See, e.g., Paul Sabin, *The Bet: Paul Ehrlich, Julian Simon, and Our Gamble over Earth's Future*, pp. 26-28.

> ## To Ponder: Population and Culture in Other Animals
>
> Butterflies, bacteria, and many other organisms tend to overshoot their resource base if introduced to an area of particularly abundant resources, followed by a population collapse. We have argued that human cultural elements render this same analysis incomplete and incorrect for humans. Do you think this might also be true for, say, dolphins, whales, or elephants, the kind of social and (perhaps) cultural creatures that seem more "like us" in these regards?

Moreover, Malthusian thinking can quickly turn into a form of misanthropy: dislike or hatred of humanity. In *A Christmas Carol*, Charles Dickens puts these words on the cold-hearted and miserly Ebenezer Scrooge's lips: "If they would rather die, they had better do it, and decrease the surplus population."[146] Scrooge is referring to people in poverty, "those who are badly off."[147] Dickens, always a champion of the poor, highlights a rather common theme: the "surplus population," the "overpopulation,"[148] is usually identified as those masses of unnamed people living in poverty, not the wealthier elites who voice concerns about overpopulation and resource scarcity in political and scholarly circles. Or to put it differently, Malthusian thinking frames humans only as consumers, not producers—nothing more than mouths to feed, not persons with the potential to create.[149] As the environmental-policy author Ted Nordhaus writes, "We are not fruit flies, programmed to reproduce until our population collapses. Nor are we cattle, whose numbers must be managed."[150]

---

146. Charles Dickens, *A Christmas Carol*, Stave I: Marley's Ghost, https://www.gutenberg.org/files/46/46-h/46-h.htm .

147. Ibid.

148. The concept of overpopulation has become so familiar that it does not strike many people as intrinsically strange. But why look at it as too many people, rather than as not enough resources?

149. The development economist Peter Bauer wrote: "The birth of a child immediately reduces income per head for the family and also for the country as a whole. The death of the same child has the opposite effect. Yet for most people, the first event is a blessing, and the second a tragedy. Ironically, the birth of a child is registered as a reduction in national income per head, while the birth of a farm animal shows up as an improvement." (Bauer, *The Development Frontier: Essays in Applied Economics*, p. 22.) Similarly, Simon Kuznets argues, "More population means more creators and producers, both of goods along established production patterns and of new knowledge and inventions." (Quoted in Livi-Bacci, *A Concise History of World Population*, p. 112.)

150. Ted Nordhaus, "The Earth's Carrying Capacity for Human Life Is Not Fixed," https://aeon.co/ideas/the-earths-carrying-capacity-for-human-life-is-not-fixed .

Speaking of the global population of human beings adds a certain unity to a narrative of human history. The number of people is a basic statistic, and as such, it seems a reasonable candidate as a fundamental driver of local and global change. Numbers do make a difference, and ecological constraints in an agrarian / "organic" economy put hard limits on average standards of living and wealth. But drawing the inference that this means there were somehow "too many" people, either globally or locally, runs a serious risk of cheapening and even dismissing those lives. Framing world history in bio-ecological terms can be reductive and misleading.

Causation

Imagine a man slips and, tragically, falls off a cliff to his death while walking along a mountain path. We might ask, what was the *cause* of this fall?

A basic answer, of course, would be that the man slipped. As Marc Bloch, the source of this example, points out, that is the most direct influence on the fall, the most specific cause.[151] But a number of other factors play some role in the fall: the force of gravity, the geological forces that shaped the mountain, the economic incentives that helped to lead people in the past to create a path through the mountains.[152] These might not seem like causes of the fall in the same sense as the slip, but they each played a role. And the history of the universe, Earth, and life all become part of the story as well: the early universe produced a gravitational force of a certain strength; plate-tectonic processes produced the mountains; our evolutionary history gave human beings, unlike birds, no means to fly. Ordinarily, these would appear as "background conditions" taken for granted in an analysis of what "really" caused the fall, but even background conditions begin to look like causes if we make the time frame of our analysis long enough. How might we organize the different kinds of causes, without multiplying them to the point of senselessness?

The common idea of a "chain of causation," where one thing leads to another leads to another, will not work particularly well. Good historical explanations are virtually always *multicausal*. They recognize the influence of multiple causes, of multiple types, on multiple scales, playing different roles, with different significances—all the more so in universal histories, where deep time and cosmic context come into play. Linking events together in a single chain, a simple linear narrative of cause and effect, generally does not do justice to the messiness of the real world and the many causes that are simultaneously at play in any given event.

---

151. Bloch, *The Historian's Craft*, pp. 190–191.

152. Ibid., p. 191.

A given cause may be shorter-term or longer-term:[153] it may be the direct cause of an event (the slip, an "immediate" cause), a more distant but still influential cause (perhaps some loose gravel was on the path, a "proximate" cause), or a deeper underlying reason (perhaps the man was always careless when walking in the mountains, an "ultimate" cause). A cause may be of different types: personal, political, social, cultural, economic, ecological, or geological. It may be the result of individual choice, of collective human patterns like political structures or markets, or of an impersonal force, as in geology. It may be a *necessary condition* without being a *sufficient condition*. And a cause may function in different ways, such as to produce a change, to maintain conditions as they are in a steady state, or to reverse or undermine the effects of another cause.[154]

In any case, there is always a whole constellation of causes at work in any event. To make sense of this, one must assign relative weight to different causes. Carr writes, "Every historical argument revolves around the question of the priority of causes,"[155] and the "hierarchy of causes, the relative significance of one cause or set of causes or of another, is the essence of [the historian's] interpretation."[156] One cannot fixate on a single short-term cause to the exclusion of all others, but one also must not simply list all the causes and preconditions of an event. Instead, the art of historical interpretation lies in paying attention to which causes are most important, to which have maximal explanatory power for why things turned out the way they did.

Multicausal History

Some specific examples will help to illustrate the interplay of long-term and short-term causation, and different types of causes, in history.

1. Why was Rome sacked repeatedly by invading "barbarian" tribes? Factors internal to Rome made it more vulnerable, but there were external factors at work too. The newcomer "barbarian" tribes to Eastern Europe between 200 and 1000 were refugees; upheavals in steppe politics and wars between groups created the need for defeated groups to migrate.[157] To focus only on causes internal to Rome misses a major, world-historical cause of the "decline and fall" of Rome. Isolating a single society and attending only to the causes at work within that "box" does not work; one must pay

---

153. Using language adapted from Jared Diamond in *Guns, Germs, and Steel: The Fates of Human Societies*; see especially pp. 22–25.

154. Thanks to Bob Bain for inspiring this typology for talking about causation.

155. Carr, *What Is History?*, p. 117.

156. Ibid., p. 135.

157. McNeill and McNeill, *The Human Web*, pp. 100–101.

attention to long-range and geographically distant causes as well—a good argument in favor of keeping a world-historical perspective even while delving into details of a particular time and place.

2. Why were many societies indigenous to the Americas devastated by disease in the 1500s?[158] The introduction of European diseases and relative lack of immunity of the various Native American societies provides an immediate cause, but longer-term causes are at play too. After all, where did these sharp differences in immunity come from? Long-term causes may include extinction of the Pleistocene megafauna, which produced fewer potential domesticates that could make diseases endemic to American populations. Also, plate tectonics yielded a certain layout of the continents that would isolate American populations from the diseases of Afro-Eurasia.[159] These factors help to explain the relative immunity of Old World peoples and the relative vulnerability of New World peoples. Meanwhile, short-term causes influencing which American societies were most at risk had to do with how close people lived to one another in a given place (the great cities of the Inca and Aztecs were especially vulnerable), whether they were already malnourished, whether they suffered direct attacks by Europeans, and the character of their physical environments. As the historian Martin Pernick writes:

> Lack of immunity meant that Native Americans were likely to get sick when new germs were introduced, but it did not determine why some died while others recovered, nor did it determine whether or not the survivors rebuilt their population levels or preserved their cultures. Despite the fact that all Native Americans in 1492 lacked immunity, there were enormous differences in the severity and duration of the effects once new germs were introduced. Such differences in outcomes cannot be explained by immunity; they resulted from the interaction of biology, environment, and culture.[160]

---

158. Eric Wolf points out that there was not just one big disease epidemic but many distinct ones, including as many as 14 major smallpox and measles epidemics in Mesoamerica and as many as 17 smallpox and measles epidemics in the Andean region between 1520 and 1600. (Wolf, *Europe and the People Without History*, p. 133.)

159. The Atlantic and Pacific Oceans clearly produced much of this isolation, but as the historian Kären Wigen and the geographer Martin Lewis have argued, other demarcations between "continents" are more often matters of heuristic convenience than clear distinctions in space. In particular, there was much less to hinder human or animal movement between and across "Afro-Eurasia." Human societies did vary in crucial ways across this enormous landmass, but did so for other social and cultural reasons, not because of environmental or spatial separation. (Martin W. Lewis and Kären Wigen, *The Myth of Continents: A Critique of Metageography*.)

160. Martin S. Pernick, "Diseases in Motion," p. 367 in *A Companion to World History*, ed. Douglas Northrop.

PLATE 33 Two "Megacities" of the Modern World: Lagos, Nigeria, and Taipei, Taiwan Cities like (**a**) Lagos, Nigeria, and (**b**) Taipei, Taiwan, are unimaginably large by pre-modern standards, and they provide a strikingly different context for human life than even the biggest cities of the world before 1800. See the discussion under "Context" in chapter 6 and "Modernity" in chapter 7.

Source: (a) Michael Kraus / EyeEm/Getty Images (b) Photo by CEphoto, Uwe Aranas

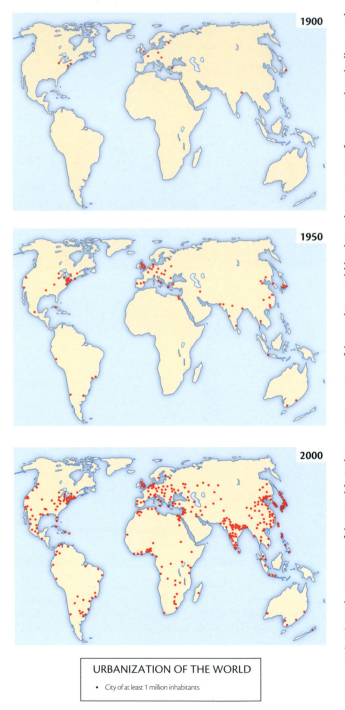

1900

1950

2000

URBANIZATION OF THE WORLD

• City of at least 1 million inhabitants

PLATE 34 **The Urbanization of the World** A characteristic pattern of the modern world has been the move away from agricultural villages and toward cities. Just 200 years ago, the world (population approximately 1 billion; see Figure 6.2) was overwhelmingly rural, but now more than half of the human population (which totals well over 7 billion) lives in urban settings, with several hundred cities holding populations of more than a million people each. See the discussion under "Context" in chapter 6.
Source: Sp 129 Map 2 2010 (file from OUP)

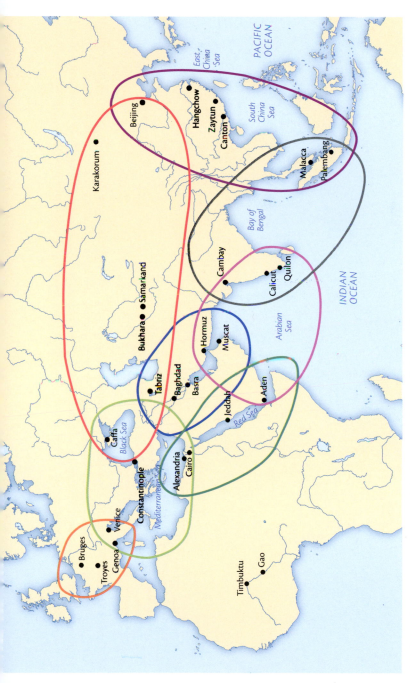

PLATE 35 Large-Scale Connections in 13th-Century Africa and Eurasia The historical sociologist Janet Abu-Lughod's map of this early "world system" shows the "circuits" that strongly connected groups of societies in 13th-century Afro-Eurasia. These circuits involved the large-scale circulation of goods, ideas, people, institutions, and diseases. The fate of any given society within this system was linked in crucial ways to the fates of all the rest. This system was devastated in the 1300s by pandemic disease and growing political conflict, but even this large-scale collapse indicated, and was enabled by, its level of connection. See chapter 7 (under "Connection") for a discussion of this and other examples of large-scale connections through world history.

Source: David Christian, Cynthia Stokes Brown, and Craig Benjamin, Big History: Between Nothing and Everything, p. 228, Map 10.4

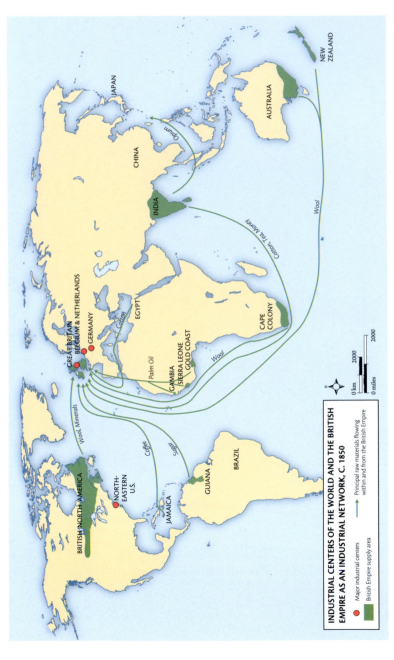

INDUSTRIAL CENTERS OF THE WORLD AND THE BRITISH EMPIRE AS AN INDUSTRIAL NETWORK, C. 1850

● Major industrial centers

■ British Empire supply area

→ Principal raw materials flowing within and from the British Empire

PLATE 36 Flow of Materials Within and From the British Empire The Industrial Revolution is often told as a story of Britain innovating and others following suit, but in fact, it was a globally dispersed story from the beginning. Britain's inventions at home would have meant little if not for shifting economic and political relationships abroad, including the heavy use of slavery and coerced labor, the colonial exploitation of raw materials from Egypt and India (sources of cotton), and the creation of new markets abroad, especially in Latin America, for industrially produced goods. See the discussion under "Modernity" in chapter 7.

Source: Based on map from OUP database

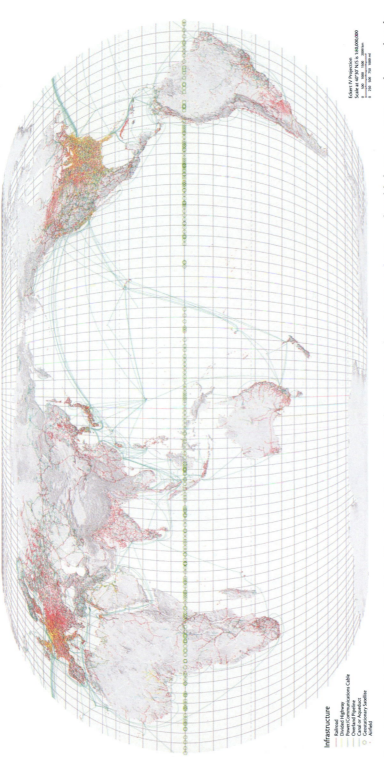

Infrastructure
Railroad
Divided Highway
Power/Communications Cable
Overland Pipeline
Canal or Aqueduct
Geostationary Satellite
Airfield

Eckert IV Projection
Scale at 40°30′ N/S is 1:160,000,000
0 500 1000 1500 2000 km
0 250 500 750 1000 mi

PLATE 37 Global Infrastructure Map The word "infrastructure" refers to systems that support, underpin, and enable human societies, such as railroads, highways, and the electrical grid. The modern era has seen a tremendous expansion of many kinds of infrastructure; individual lives and entire societies depend on infrastructural systems now more than ever before. To a large extent, questions about the sustainability and adaptability of human societies are questions of maintaining and adjusting infrastructure, including the social organization and institutions that support, maintain, and expand infrastructures. See the discussions under "Systems" in chapter 7 and "Sustainability" in chapter 8.

Source: Bill Rankin/Radical Cartography

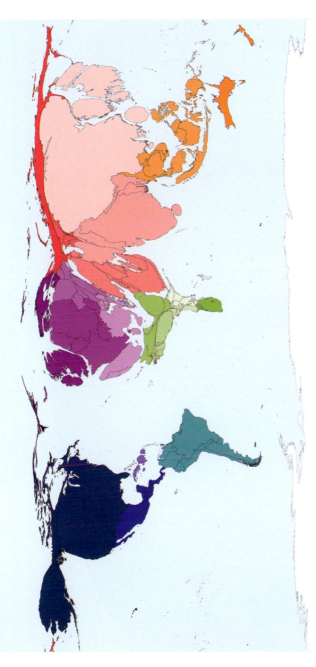

PLATE 38 Global GDP 500 Years Ago and Today (2018, Estimated) A comparison of global economic activity (**a**) in the year 1500 and (**b**) today can make useful points. For example, note the dominance of China and India 500 years ago, and their resurgence today, alongside the changes that can be seen in the Americas and Africa relative to the rest of the world. To some extent, however, this is an "apples and oranges" comparison: modern nation-states did not exist 500 years ago, and economic indicators like gross domestic product (GDP) also did not exist, at least not in their modern form. The use of statistics to characterize long-term historical change must be handled with care, since statistics themselves are a distinctively modern phenomenon and a distinctively modern way of knowing the world—as discussed under "Statistics" in chapter 7.

Source: World Mapper

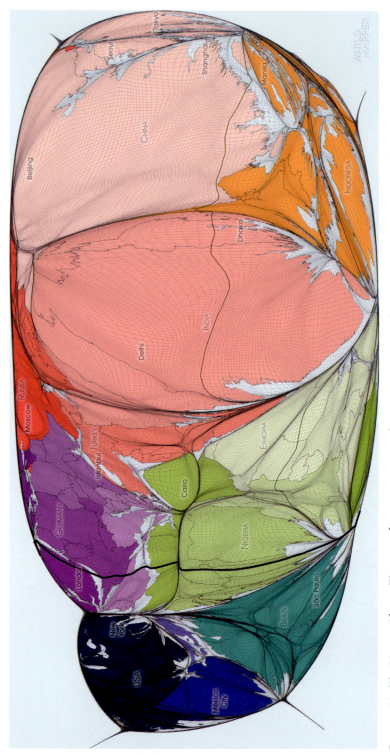

PLATE 39 The Human Planet The sizes of cities, countries, and regions are represented in proportion to the number of people who live there, giving a finer-grained sense than ordinary maps do of where population "centers of gravity" really are in today's world. See the discussion under "Statistics" in chapter 7.

Source: World Mapper

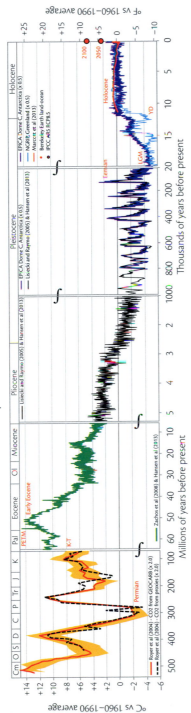

PLATE 40 History of Earth's Temperature The Earth has been hotter in the past than it will be this century, even if anthropogenic (human-induced) climate change results in the extreme warming predicted for 2050 and 2100 on the far right of this particular graph (which is a compilation of the results of ongoing research). But higher global temperatures in the past generally occurred before human beings existed, and certainly before they existed in settled societies, so the unprecedented aspects of predicted near-future climate change include the swiftness with which largely sedentary human societies will have to adapt. The fact that human-induced climate change also may produce effects that are visible on time scales of thousands to millions of years (note the shifts in time scales within the image) adds viability to the idea of naming a new geological epoch after human beings, the "Anthropocene." See the discussions under "Future" and "Sustainability" in chapter 8.

Source: Wikipedia

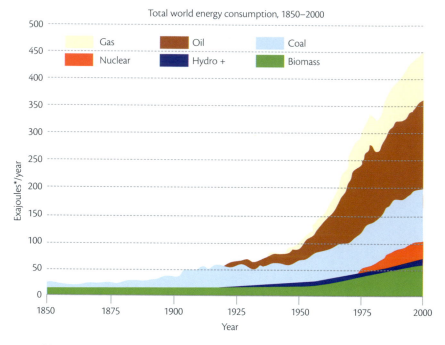

Total world energy consumption, 1850–2000

*Human energy consumption is measured in exajoules. A joule is the energy required to produce one watt for one second; an exajoule is a million million million joules.

PLATE 41 World Energy Consumption, 1850–2000 Modern industrial-capitalist societies have tremendously increased the scale of energy harnessing and resource extraction by human beings. The total human energy consumption multiplied many times in the 19th and 20th centuries. While Plate 42 shows *relative* contributions of different energy sources in the United States, this graphic shows the *absolute* growth in energy consumption in the world. Harnessing ever-greater quantities of energy increases the power of human beings and human institutions, with both constructive and destructive consequences. See the discussion under "Sustainability" in chapter 8.

Source: Based on David Christian, Cynthia Stokes Brown, and Craig Benjamin, *Big History: Between Nothing and Everything,* p. 216.

PLATE 42 Energy Transitions This ExxonMobil infographic presents the history of transitions in energy production in the United States. Represented is the relative fraction of U.S. energy demand satisfied by wood, coal, oil, gas, hydropower, nuclear energy, and modern renewables (wind and solar) from 1850 to 2030. This infographic was created in 2009, so the final two-plus decades are based on projections rather than actual data. Tremendous shifts in energy infrastructure will be required for any serious effort to sharply reduce carbon-dioxide emissions, and the relevant systems have a lot of inertia associated with them, but energy transitions do happen—on scales of decades, as shown here. See the discussion under "Sustainability" in chapter 8.

Source: Based on ExxonMobil, "Outlook for Energy: A View to 2030," pp. 2–4: http://81.47.175.201/flagship/attachments/exxon_mobil.pdf.

PLATE 43 Decline of the Aral Sea The modern history of Central Asia's Aral Sea shows that natural resources, vast as they may seem to people at the time, are finite. Soviet irrigation projects—aimed at growing crops, especially cotton, in the surrounding desert areas—redirected a huge volume of water from the two main rivers that fed the Aral. The effect, in just a few decades, was to reduce the Aral to only 10 percent of its original volume (it has since slightly recovered). At the same time, redirection of the rivers also led to the creation of new human communities that still exist, and today, it would be an existential threat to those communities to simply "turn the clock back" and fully direct the rivers back into the sea basin. The Aral Sea disaster is a reminder that environmental issues are about not only the natural world, but also human social organization, institutions, and infrastructure. See the discussion under "Sustainability" in chapter 8.

Source: NASA. Collage by Producercunningham/Wikipedia

Future World +50 Million Years

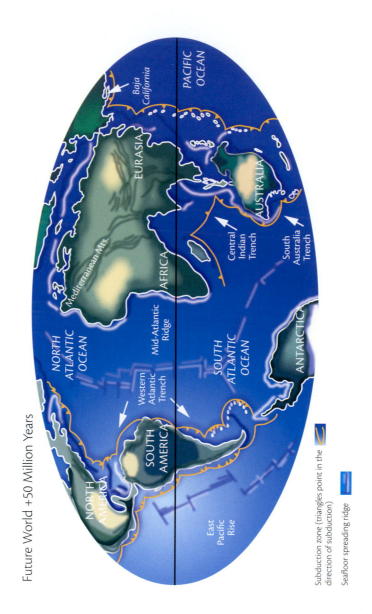

Baja California

PACIFIC OCEAN

EURASIA

AUSTRALIA

Mediterranean Mts.

AFRICA

Central Indian Trench

South Australia Trench

NORTH ATLANTIC OCEAN

Mid-Atlantic Ridge

Western Atlantic Trench

SOUTH ATLANTIC OCEAN

ANTARCTICA

NORTH AMERICA

SOUTH AMERICA

East Pacific Rise

Subduction zone (triangles point in the direction of subduction)

Seafloor spreading ridge

Future World +250 Million Years

PLATE 44 Future Continental Drift The future is partially and conditionally predictable, with certain aspects being easier to model and extrapolate than others. Some trends are so stable over time that they can be extrapolated millions of years into the future. Continental drift, for example, is a stable trend that appears to have been proceeding at about the same rate for hundreds of millions of years. If nothing interrupts or complicates this process, the Earth's surface will be noticeably reconfigured 50 million years from now, and a new "supercontinent" may emerge around a quarter-billion years from now. See the discussion under "Future" in chapter 8.

Source: Based on C. R. Scotese

PLATE 45 **The Sun as a White Dwarf** Astronomers expect that the Sun will continue fusing hydrogen into helium in its core for another 5 billion years or so, then will take about a billion years to slowly turn into a red giant after the hydrogen "fuel" in its core is finally depleted, and then will spend another billion years as a red giant before becoming increasingly unstable and ultimately "dying" by taking the form of a white dwarf. When this last "stage" comes about, the Solar System may look something like the Helix Nebula in this image: the nebula is another stellar system similar to our own, but at a later stage of its life cycle. See the discussion under "Future" in chapter 8.
Source: NASA

3. What caused the abolition of the Atlantic slave trade? Plausible answers include changing global economic conditions that made cheap wage labor more attractive than slave labor, fossil fuels making energy available without the need for slaveholding, the social-moral movement to abolish slavery, and the increasing costs of maintaining the system in the face of violent resistance and rebellion by enslaved people. The first two causes emphasize global environmental and economic developments, while the latter two emphasize the intentional action of specific individuals. The temptation for many works of history is to focus on the latter two at the expense of the former two, while the temptation for works of universal history is to focus on the former two at the expense of the latter two. But as usual, recognizing feedback and interaction between scales is key to producing the most powerful and complete explanations possible.

4. Why did a highly accurate scientific understanding of planetary motions emerge in the 1600s and 1700s? Popular accounts of the history of science often emphasize the contributions of "great men" like Kepler and Newton, with the implication that scientific understandings advance because of the contributions of a few geniuses. Historians of science, meanwhile, emphasize that social and cultural contexts matter a great deal. Kepler and Newton, however talented they may have been, found themselves in contexts with institutional or individual patronage for scientific work, a scholarly community in which to work, and access to observations and theoretical insights of past generations, which shaped their thinking.[161] And the natural world itself came into play: planetary motions as perceived from Earth are complex enough to have required many generations of effort to understand, yet simple enough that a neat theoretical framework of the Newtonian sort could make sufficiently good predictions to prove useful.

In all of these examples, the different types of causes, and the different scales at which the different causes operate, work together to produce an outcome; it is reductive to assign exclusive importance to one or the other. Just as it makes no sense to say that a long, skinny rectangle has a large area only because of its length—when its width, although small, is precisely the factor that multiples the length to produce the area—so too causes do not operate independently of one other.[162] It is

---

161. "Transformations in concepts and in styles of reasoning are the product of countless trickles rather than the intervention of single individuals. Marx, Darwin and Maxwell worked in a space in which there was something to find out. That means: in which various possibilities for truth-or-falsehood could already be formulated." (Ian Hacking, *The Taming of Chance*, p. 8.)

162. The rectangle example is inspired by the neuropsychologist Donald Hebb's similar comment about whether nature (genes) or nurture (environment) contributes more to the development of a human being's personality.

important to balance the individual and the collective, the short-term and the long-term, the personal and the impersonal. As much as one might be tempted to attribute immense causal powers to individuals like Lenin or Hitler, or to Newton or Einstein, these individuals did not exist apart from certain contexts that rewarded certain kinds of actions, gave them traction, and shaped their behavior. And neither did these contexts exist apart from the actions and decisions of those individuals. Looking only at small scales in space and time removes important context for understanding causes, while looking only at large scales removes concreteness and particularity.

Still, some causes must be emphasized more than others, or one will be left with nothing but a long list of causes having indeterminate importance. Here, the specific question one is asking really matters, and helps to narrow down what causes are important and most worth looking at.

Determinisms, Free Will, and the Writing of History

A related philosophical question involves the nature of a particular kind of cause—namely, individual choices. To examine the question, you can perform an experiment: Stand up. Now sit down.

What just happened? Did you move because you prompted the action by willing it, exerting causal influence over what happened to the matter that composes your body? Or was your sense of free choice in this matter an illusion, so that your action was predetermined—by your psychological makeup, by the way neurons in your brain were firing, or even by the laws of physics?

Determinism is the idea that our actions are predetermined; it is the rejection of free will. Determinists hold that each apparent choice a person makes is the inevitable result of prior conditions outside that person's control. There are many "flavors" of determinism, depending on what factor is identified as the determining cause. Physics-based determinism would claim that you stood up and sat down because the particles of which your brain and body are composed were following the laws of physics: you might have had the sense that you chose to do so, but it was actually just particles in deterministic motion.[163] Neuroscience-based determinism might make a similar claim about the neural firing in your brain, saying that electrical impulses and chemical reactions in your brain control your inner life, leaving no room for a conscious will to have any influence. These "hard determinist" positions claim that the building blocks—of matter, or of the brain—are the only entities with the ability to cause anything, and that deterministic building blocks

---

163. Physicists inherit the legacy of thinkers like Pierre-Simon Laplace, who articulated an early form of such determinism, arguing that an intelligence that knew the positions of every thing in the universe and all the forces acting at a given moment would, in principle, be able to predict the complete unfolding of the universe's future.

cannot be built into non-deterministic macroscopic objects, an idea that is related to the strong-reductionist position outlined in chapter 3 (see the discussion under "Reductionism").

Philosophers offer several alternatives to hard determinism, many of which can be referred to as forms of "libertarian free will." This is what most non-philosophers mean when they say simply "free will": the idea that people make choices and put them into action, that humans are *not* falling prey to an illusion in thinking that they have a will and can, at least some of the time, choose between genuinely possible alternatives. Philosophers who argue in favor of libertarian free will recognize that there may be significant constraints on human agency in any given situation. A person may be coerced to act in a certain way. Hormones and neurotransmitter levels may influence behavior and mood. And the laws of physics make a whole range of behaviors impossible (e.g., you cannot choose to fly by flapping your arms). But such philosophers argue that there is still such a thing as free choice, and that human wills can be regarded as causing human actions: An individual's behavior may be (sometimes profoundly) *influenced* by factors outside of that person's control, but it is not (in the usual course of events) *determined*.[164]

Determinism often has a strong appeal in the sciences. Disciplines like physics, chemistry, biology, and neuroscience seem to offer a universal deterministic framework of cause and effect at the level of elementary particles, or atoms, or chemicals, or neurons, and many scientists have a difficult time perceiving where there is "room" for free will to operate within such a framework.[165] And yet it is difficult to dispute that human life and human history are simply *not* deterministic, and that choices matter—sometimes a great deal. The rabbi and philosopher Jonathan Sacks writes, "We are free. We know that as surely as we know anything. We know what

---

164. A third alternative to hard determinism and libertarian free will is offered by "compatibilism," the philosophical position that free will and determinism are compatible with one another. Compatibilists may agree with hard determinists in thinking that all actions are determined by previous causes, and that any given action is predetermined and could not genuinely be otherwise. But they argue that it is still meaningful to speak of some actions as being "free," such as in the sense of not being coerced or too strongly influenced by factors outside a person's apparent control. E. H. Carr appears to take something of a compatibilist stance in writing that "all human actions are both free and determined" (Carr, *What Is History?*, p. 124). This is a popular position among philosophers, but most forms of it arguably change the meaning of human free will fairly radically.

165. Benjamin Libet's research provides experimental evidence that is widely cited as strong evidence against free will, but the experimental methodology, which involves people choosing when to perform a simple motion like pressing a button, does not really justify these conclusions. Intention may not be the beginning of the decision-making process, but that is not necessarily surprising, especially in a case so simple as pressing a button. Also, Libet's experiments arguably help very little in understanding anything like long-term decision-making. See, e.g., Ari N. Schulman, "Can Neuroscientists Measure Free Will?," https://web .archive.org/web/20181226032124/ https://www.bigquestionsonline.com/2017/09/21/ can-neuroscientists-measure-free-will/ .

it is to choose between alternatives, weigh the options, calculate the consequences, consult our conscience, ask the advice of others and so on."[166]

To doubt free will on the basis of science is, arguably, problematic. As Aristotle wrote in another context, "To rely on the non-obvious to establish the obvious is a sign of being incapable of distinguishing between what is and what is not intelligible in itself."[167] While some things are obvious and false (e.g., the Earth is motionless at the center of the universe) and other things are non-obvious and true (e.g., the Earth is in swift motion around the Sun and through the Milky Way Galaxy), radical skepticism about the foundations of human experience—including free will—comes close to undermining itself. Why be so confident of one or another scientific determinism if our most basic perceptions of human reality, which form a basis for science itself, are radically untrustworthy?

A hard-determinist stance also fails to make sense of why things at higher levels of organization, like blueprints or organisms or ideas, should have causal efficacy. If you stood up and sat down in response to reading the first paragraph of this section, it seems rather more reasonable to say that you understood and chose to follow our "command" than that the particles in your body were "mindlessly" following the laws of physics.[168] After all, the idea that a person can act as a cause is not really so strange; the idea that should perhaps seem stranger is that an atom or a neuron can act as a cause.

Moreover, a hard-determinist stance undermines the value of every discipline other than the one that studies the determining factor. Accordingly, most historians not only resist all these forms of determinism, but sometimes go so far as to reject a claim precisely *because* it seems deterministic—which stands in contrast to the usual pattern in the sciences. In the interests of recognizing multiple causation, they also reject "softer" forms of determinism like cultural determinism, or geographical determinism, or economic determinism, in which a single factor like culture, or geography, or economics has so much influence that one can safely ignore the influence of all other causes.[169]

At the same time, a professional allergy toward determinism can go too far if it leads to denying the possibility of large-scale patterns or the value of large-scale

166. Jonathan Sacks, *The Great Partnership: Science, Religion, and the Search for Meaning*, p. 124. Sacks continues: "Yet throughout history human beings have found almost endless ways of denying choice. . . . Our excuses become more sophisticated over time, but they remain just that, excuses" (pp. 124–125).

167. Aristotle, *Physics*, 193aI paragraph, p. 34.

168. Cf. our argument under "Reductionism" in chapter 3. While some thinkers have looked to quantum mechanics as a basis for free will, the problem with this is that it is still causal and *probabilities* are typically set in stone.

169. Another "softer" form of determinism—technological determinism—is one we saw under "Technology" in chapter 5 and will see again under "Transhumanism" in chapter 8.

narratives. And it is worth pointing out that individual or collective choices often exert much less direct influence over the direction of history than we sometimes like to think. Smail writes, "Yet, as with cases like the Internet, the intentions of the original designer, to whatever degree they are achieved, can be utterly dwarfed by the unintended things that happen as we adapt to the ecology that has emerged from someone's tinkering."[170] Likewise, Carr states, "the actions of individual human beings often have results which were not intended or desired by the actors or indeed by any other individual."[171] For example, the depression of the 1930s could not have been intended by practically anyone, yet it was "brought about by the actions of individuals, each consciously pursuing some totally different aim."[172]

Relationships Between Causation, Context, and Contingency

Universal histories show a great deal about how our lives today are conditioned by an immense array of things that happened in the past, including choices that people make. For instance, you would not be reading this book right now without millions of years of the Earth being shaped cosmically and geologically, and you would also not be reading it if the publisher had chosen not to accept the manuscript.

As we have seen, even very individual- and family-level actions like having and raising children can have consequences thousands of years down the road—not only if you lead a nation, or make a great discovery, or create an innovative technology, but even if you are someone whose name and work are "lost to history." In addition to individual actions, larger-scale trends are important too; impersonal phenomena like stellar nucleosynthesis and plate tectonics help to provide context for the present, the settings in which individual decisions are made and individual actions carried out. Context, in turn, shapes the possibilities for individual human actors making volitional choices, which are themselves contingent: human agency, within a particular context, produces contingent outcomes, which in turn produce new contexts for future actions. The ideas of contingency, context, and agency work together to show why history does not proceed according to abstract laws but, rather, according to particular sequences of choices and events, and why each individual story can still be located in, and illuminated by, many interlocking larger contexts.

---

170. Smail, *On Deep History and the Brain*, p. 110.

171. Carr, *What Is History?*, p. 62.

172. Ibid., p. 64.

7 MODERNITY

O ur purpose in this chapter is to identify some of the key aspects that make the modern world *different* than other past moments in the human story—a strikingly different social context for human dramas to play out—and to explore how this recent period fits into, extends, and also departs from the broader universal-historical picture we have been sketching. In "Modernity," we consider how this set of changes happened, and how the very idea of modernity structures the way that people today think about and relate to the past. In "Connection," we look at large-scale linkages between modern human groups and consider how historians can, and do, narrate the story of their emergence. In "Systems" and "Statistics," we examine two big, distinctly modern ideas that powerfully structure many people's view today of how our world works. And in "Purpose," we close the chapter by pondering how modern philosophies, histories, and worldviews have largely resisted certain questions of meaning and purpose, and ask what might be gained by reconsidering such questions.

Modernity

The world is not as it used to be.

While one might think that this statement would be true at any time in history, and thus not especially meaningful, in point of fact the past 250-plus years have been distinctive in both the speed and the magnitude of change—demographically, politically, economically, and culturally. The sweeping global changes of this recent period have affected the vast majority of people on Earth. So there is good reason to single out this period, even against the backdrop of a "history of everything" that reaches into a far deeper past.

Still, referring to the most recent period of world history as "modernity," or "the modern era," or "the modern world" is not a simple, straightforward description of what changed, but rather a storytelling device and a way of framing the present. It carries connotations and implications. It is, itself, an interpretation, and in some ways, crafting a rigorous, fair, and meaningful interpretation of the present social world, and of modernity's suite of global changes, may be the most difficult interpretive question in all of universal history. Writing about the recent past is always difficult for historians, because it is rarely straightforward to assess the significance of events and people until many years, or decades, or even centuries have passed. But even more than this, the political, economic, cultural, and philosophical circumstances of modernity are deeply embedded in how we all think the world works; it is exceptionally difficult to step far enough "outside" a modern mindset to interpret our own circumstances. We are like fish trying to interpret the water in which we swim.

Interpretations of modernity can focus on aspects that most people perceive as being largely positive: relatively better health, more wealth, and increased leisure for large numbers of people; longer life spans; elimination of mass poverty in large regions of the world; emergence of democracies and assorted political freedoms; new forms of political or social equality between persons; technologies that dramatically increase convenience and material comfort, and that enable connection at a distance; or the expansion of scientific knowledge. These developments go a long way toward explaining why the word "modern" so often has positive connotations in common usages like "modern science," or "modern medicine," or "modern democracy," or "modern technology."

On the other hand, different interpretations of modernity focus on aspects that most people perceive negatively: widespread environmental damage and climate change; hundreds of millions of people oppressed by totalitarian governments; perceived decline in standards of beauty in art and literature and music; unprecedented forms of surveillance and social control; colonial exploitation and economic inequality; the industrialized warfare of World War I, and the mushroom clouds and gas chambers of World War II; genocides and ethnic cleansings;[1] or the impersonal and alienating tendencies many people experience within modern societies.

Whether modernity is fundamentally a "good thing" or a "bad thing" is, perhaps, not an especially productive debate, given the danger of generalized and simplistic judgments of complex realities. The good and the bad are intertwined.

---

1. As in Zygmunt Bauman's contention that the Holocaust is a quintessentially modern phenomenon deeply rooted not only in modern forms of industrial production (gas chambers that apply modern chemistry to efficiently kill people en masse in a horrifying "economy of scale"), but also in modern political structures (strong states) and modern categories of social and philosophical thought, including a "rational" ordering of society. (See Bauman, *Modernity and the Holocaust*.)

Modern Changes: As Seen from the Informational Level

In its political and economic institutions, its cultural norms and philosophical at-titudes, its sense of the past and expectations for the future, almost every part of the world is substantially different today than it was during the agrarian era. For most people today, it is not easy to imagine a world in which only a small fraction of the Earth's surface is claimed politically by anything resembling a nation-state. It is not easy to imagine a world in which democracy would be primarily a part of *history* (e.g., Greek city-states) rather than a common feature of the present political world. It is not easy to imagine a world without industrial production and a worldwide market economy, or in which no one had ever traveled faster than a horse could carry them and no amount of wealth or power could protect you against many dis-eases that are easily cured or even prevented today. Nor is it easy to imagine a world where institutions, technologies, occupations, values, and cultures typically remain fairly stable not only from year to year, but from generation to generation. Yet such was the world of the year 1500, and in many ways the years 1600 and 1700 as well.

The agrarian era was not static; it was not a period in which nothing funda-mentally changed for human groups and individuals. As we have already seen, even the Paleolithic was not static. Human historical change has occurred for as long as there have been humans. But time scales for major societal and institutional change were longer then—often much longer than a human lifetime. Modernity, by con-trast, has brought with it far more rapid political, economic, and social change than any other era in history,[2] leading to a widespread sense of social dislocation and the eroding of traditional ways of life.

What are some of those changes? The historian Tamara Loos writes:

> Economically, modernity refers to the global expansion of trade, capital-ist development, and the institutionalization of market-driven economies, products, material wealth, and consumption. Politically, modernity's trans-formations include the shifts from absolutism, religious rule, and feudalism to secularity, bureaucratically administered states, popular forms of govern-ment, rule of law, and territorial sovereignty that are characteristic of the nation-state.[3]

Economically, "capitalism" is a system based on private ownership of the means of production in the pursuit of profit. ("Means of production" is a phrase that refers to facilities and implements useful for producing goods and services of economic

---

2. Anthony Giddens and Christopher Pierson, *Conversations with Anthony Giddens: Making Sense of Modernity*, p. 94. Note, however, that "modernity" is not universally accepted as a help-ful category by historians, as some argue that it is too vague and broad to be useful.

3. Tamara Loos, *Subject Siam: Family, Law, and Colonial Modernity in Thailand*, p. 19.

value, including machinery, tools, and raw materials, in addition to human labor.) The "capitalists" who own these means of production decide how to distribute or retain any resulting profits. Meanwhile, the majority of people, who are non-owners, live by selling the only "commodity" that they possess—namely, their ability to work, as "wage labor," thereby gaining money to pay for their needs and wants. Markets and wage labor existed, in some form, in various times and places before the modern period, alongside many other economic systems. But only in the modern era has capitalism emerged as a fully global, and globally integrated, system.

Combined with this shift to a capitalist economic system in most parts of the world, the Industrial Revolution enabled the transition to an "industrial capitalist" era, with sweeping consequences. Industrialization did not just mean the creation of new gadgets that increased the efficiency of agricultural production and manufacturing, but also led—in a reorganization of globally dispersed economic practices and relationships—to a "machine-based civilization"[4] of "endless invention, endless experiment,"[5] producing, among other things, an expectation of constant change and innovation in societies that had previously emphasized stability and tradition.[6] In general, industrial production led to greater surpluses than had techniques of manufacturing "by hand." These new methods of production, along with the use of fossil fuels to transition to a "high-energy society,"[7] enabled sustained population growth and sustained per-capita economic growth (in various places) that had been virtually unknown in the ancient world, while also producing unprecedented environmental consequences.[8]

Partly thanks to these developments, modernity has been characterized by increasing life spans and by luxury goods (beyond basic needs) becoming available to more than just a few people—in a word, by widespread affluence. At the same time, though, this affluence has its limits, because global industrial capitalism has also created tremendous inequalities, with a few dozen individuals controlling roughly the same amount of total wealth as the poorest 4 billion[9] and large gaps also opening up between rich and poor *countries*. Societies had displayed relative

---

4. Giddens and Pierson, *Conversations with Anthony Giddens*, p. 97.

5. T. S. Eliot, "The Rock," quoted in *The Complete Poems & Plays T.S. Eliot*, p. 147.

6. See Marshall Hodgson, *The Venture of Islam: Conscience and History in a World Civilization, Volume Three: The Gunpowder Empires and Modern Times*, pp. 176–205.

7. As discussed under "Context" in chapter 6.

8. Walter Scheidel in *The Cambridge Economic History of the Greco-Roman World*, eds. Walter Scheidel, Ian Morris, and Richard P. Saller, p. 66.

9. See, e.g., Peter Whiteford, "Do Eight Men Really Control the Same Wealth as the Poorest Half of the Global Population?," http://theconversation.com/do-eight-men-really-control-the-same-wealth-as-the-poorest-half-of-the-global-population-71406 .

parity before the modern age, but this has changed in the modern era, for reasons both political and economic.[10]

At around the same time these economic changes were taking shape, a set of political revolutions also transformed the ways people organized themselves and their interactions with each other. The French Revolution (1789–1799), for instance, has often been singled out, along with its antecedent American Revolution (1765–1783), as a focal point and exemplar for the spread of republics and democracies around the world.[11] (These political forms had existed in other places and times too—for example, centuries before in a variety of Greek city-states, or in less well-known places such as the Russian city of Novgorod—but what happened more globally after the late 18th century was distinctive.) This story, however, was not merely "French," but like industrial change, emerged only out of the interactions between many parts of the globe. The story of political change in France depended crucially on developments in its colonial empire, especially Haiti, and also on interactions with rebels in other places, such as the newly formed United States.

Industrialization, political upheaval, and the rise of powerful modern global empires all helped to usher in (often, in colonies, through forcible coercion) a whole set of new systems and institutions in economics, politics, and social organization. These included modern courts and legislatures with expanded power to create new laws or interpret old ones;[12] government-provisioned schools that made at least some education and literacy available (even obligatory) for the masses rather than exclusive to a small group of people; more expansive, elaborate, and powerful state bureaucracies; and joint-stock companies, modern corporations, and expanded insurance and finance arrangements that pooled resources for collective endeavors and deflected financial and legal risk from individuals to groups.[13] This meant a near-total shift of

---

10. Hodgson, *The Venture of Islam*, p. 200.

11. The French case in particular is also remembered for other, bleaker reasons—given the development of harshly coercive and violent practices in the Reign of Terror and subsequent Napoleonic dictatorship—but nevertheless included an expanded category of citizenship that over time encompassed most free French men, and created ways for them to participate more fully. This included voting in elections to a representative parliament and also in popular referendums, which were first used in 1793 and continued even under Napoleon. This democracy, however, was far from perfect. French women were long excluded from many of its benefits, not obtaining the right to vote until 1944–1945. And infamous new state practices of violence—such as the invention of the guillotine, ostensibly to allow more efficient executions—also shaped the Revolution and its legacies.

12. Marshall Hodgson points out that the idea of a body responsible for *regularly changing laws*, which seems completely natural to modern people, would have been alien to the premodern world (Hodgson, *The Venture of Islam*, p. 193)—even if laws and customs did nevertheless change with changing circumstances.

13. Some of these innovations, such as insurance, long predated the modern period and could be found in many earlier societies, but their extent, depth, and sophistication dramatically expanded.

the institutional landscape that oversaw human social interactions. The economist Clark Kerr has estimated that only "about 85 institutions in the Western World established by 1520 still exist in recognizable forms, with similar functions, and with unbroken histories," and 70 of these 85 are universities.[14] All others are new.

Military capacity and efficiency became a Darwinian imperative in the modern world, as the power of destructive technologies increased by leaps and bounds, and those who possessed such technologies enjoyed a huge advantage. Nationalist ideologies further supported the creation of mass armies drawn from the population at large rather than smaller forces of mercenaries, thereby dramatically expanding the size of armies, even as communication and manufacturing technologies transformed the character of warfare. The French Revolution had seen the formation of the first true mass army, a "nation in arms"; its sheer size allowed Napoleon to run roughshod over much of Europe and provided a powerful impetus for other European states to develop similar mechanisms of mass conscription. Warfare was reconceived as an affair of the entire nation rather than a contest between rulers or governments. Combined with mass armies, applying the techniques of industrial production to the problems of designing, creating, and then mass-producing technologies of killing made modern military forces tremendously formidable.

In many other ways as well, states tended to become much stronger than they had been before the modern era. As David Christian writes,

> France pioneered what has become the typical modern state: a huge bureaucratic organization with a scale, a power, a wealth, and a reach that would have been inconceivable in the premodern world. . . . On the one hand, the modern state regulates the lives of its citizens in ways that would have been inconceivable, and might often have seemed inappropriate, in the era of tributary states. It requires that children be taken from parents for compulsory education;[15] it demands detailed information on the lives of individuals, in areas ranging from their incomes to their religious beliefs; it regulates in detail how we may and may not behave. Moreover, these requirements are backed up by formidable police powers. The modern state has taken over many of the educational, economic, and policing functions once handled by households and local communities. In these ways, our lives are more regulated by the state than ever before.[16]

---

14. Quoted in Anne and James Duderstadt, "Universities of the World," p. 1, https://deepblue. lib.umich.edu/handle/2027.42/145450 .

15. Although, according to the framework set out by the Universal Declaration of Human Rights, governments are obligated to preserve the right of parents to "choose the kind of education that shall be given to their children" (Article 26.3; see http://www.un.org/en/universal-declaration-human-rights/).

16. David Christian, *Maps of Time*, pp. 428–430.

Similarly, the historian Marshall Hodgson writes of "the enormously extended role of the state, which entered every home in unprecedented detail and with inescapable efficiency."[17]

At the same time, Christian also points out that democratic states (at least ideally) include and even nurture their citizens, even to the point of making it a priority to defend many basic liberties. Many modern states also take an interest in public health and (at least in theory) encourage public debate, allow most ordinary citizens the opportunity to be elected to public office, and show restraint when constraints on economic activity might be counterproductive.[18] A paradox thus emerges in which some see the modern state, in its industrial-capitalist-democratic form, "as an ally and a defender of liberty and freedom,"[19] while others see an excessive buildup of power even in non-authoritarian regimes and worry about government overreach. This produces a "constant re-negotiation of this balance between regulation and support in the activities of the modern state."[20]

These economic and political changes have been accompanied by many new philosophical, cultural, and social trends. Writing decades ago, Hodgson noted that occupations became more and more technically specialized as industrialization took hold, creating a new set of attitudes toward work and cultural expectations in support of specialization and innovation.[21] (This also produced a much wider array of possible occupations, as well as growth in the number of occupations that were considered "professions" and thus accorded an elite status.[22]) Hence, many individuals do not know all the details even of the economic production process in which they are a part. Workers, for instance, who are involved in the manufacture of automobiles may understand their own part of the production line, but not necessarily all of the other systems that need to come together for a car to work.[23] This happens because each role tends toward specialization. Hodgson also identified a pattern of "gentling of manners" in modern societies, such as doing away with torture (at least officially),[24] along with a tendency to emphasize efficiency at the expense of all else,

---

17. Hodgson, *The Venture of Islam*, p. 194.

18. Christian, *Maps of Time*, p. 429.

19. Ibid., p. 430.

20. Ibid.

21. Hodgson, *The Venture of Islam*, pp. 186, 190.

22. Expanding from divinity, medicine, and law in the Middle Ages to include a wide variety of occupations by 1900.

23. Another memorable example: "No single person knows how to make a computer mouse" (Matt Ridley, *The Rational Optimist*, p. 5).

24. As in the United States' official prohibition of "cruel and unusual punishment."

"to subordinate all considerations of ethics or beauty or human commitments to maximizing technical efficiency"[25]—and in some cases, power or profit.

The Enlightenment, an 18th-century philosophical movement with consequences far beyond intellectual circles, sought to replace traditional sources of religious and political authority. Much of modern political philosophy and understanding of government derives from the Enlightenment-era (or slightly earlier) "social-contract theorists" like John Locke (1632–1704), Jean-Jacques Rousseau (1712–1778), and Thomas Hobbes (1588–1679), who held that governmental authority lies in the consent of the governed rather than in any inherent right of monarchs to rule,[26] and exists to protect the "natural rights"[27] of people under that authority.[28] Ideas associated with the Enlightenment became translated into political realities both through the actions of "enlightened despots"—monarchs who adopted various Enlightenment ideals but did not change the structures of political authority—and through revolutions, particularly the American, French, and Haitian revolutions, which explicitly drew on Enlightenment political philosophy to justify revolt against established forms of monarchical government. These ideas also gained traction elsewhere, and soon spread through many parts of the world.

The culture of modern science, and the construction of modern knowledge more generally, has also taken shape against the backdrop of Enlightenment philosophy. Those who today think of science as the only valid path to true knowledge (what we referred to as "scientistic" thinking in chapter 4) are in many ways the heirs of a certain strand of Enlightenment and post-Enlightenment rationality, which sought to use secular reasoning to ground everything from social order, to political authority, to morality—even as Enlightenment philosophers did not agree among themselves precisely how to go about this.[29] Postmodern critics who reject any objective

---

25. Hodgson, *The Venture of Islam*, p. 188.

26. Note that pre-Enlightenment approaches were *not* carte blanche for untrammeled authority. In many different societies, there were obligations that inhered to the position of king / sultan / chief, and rulers who fell short could be removed.

27. Like those to life, liberty, and property, in Locke's thinking.

28. Full equality of rights did not extend to all people for most Enlightenment-era thinkers, either in theory or in practice. For instance, women were excluded from the electoral franchise (in most places for centuries). Locke "invested heavily in the English Trans-Atlantic slave trade through the Royal African Company," and Voltaire also invested his money in the slave trade. (Dag Herbjørnsrud, "The African Enlightenment," https://aeon.co/essays/yacob-and-amo-africas-precursors-to-locke-hume-and-kant .)

29. See, e.g., Brad Gregory, *Rebel in the Ranks*, p. 219 ff., and Henry Martyn Lloyd, "Why the Enlightenment Was Not the Age of Reason," https://aeon.co/ideas/why-the-enlightenment-was-not-the-age-of-reason .

truth in scientific findings are responding, in part, to the proliferation of discordant philosophical systems all purportedly based in reason, which is a fair concern even if discarding the very idea of scientific truth is a rather extreme response to it.

Side Note: Sociology

Enlightenment thinkers' attempts to understand human nature and human societies provided impetus for the discipline of sociology, an approach to knowledge invented to analyze and better understand the workings of modern societies.[30] Specifically, sociology is the study of modern industrialized societies: their institutions and how they connect with each other, the functions they play, and how they change over time. And yet sociology is itself also an aspect of modernity. As the sociologist Anthony Giddens has pointed out, a unique feature of modernity is the extent to which its institutions are "reflexive," in the sense that knowledge about institutions—in everything from education to government to business—helps to change them.[31]

Karl Marx, Émile Durkheim, and Max Weber are regarded as founding figures in the discipline.[32] Marx emphasized economic factors as fundamental, while Weber emphasized questions of culture, religion, and politics. Durkheim thought that there existed a true, "inherent" nature of society with laws ("social facts") analogous to the laws of nature that scientists of his time believed could characterize all natural phenomena. Sociologists today are especially attuned to structures of power, and to analyzing where the power to change social systems may be located, within a society.

In this book, chapters 5 to 7 all draw on anthropology, history, and sociology, but chapter 5 draws especially on anthropology, chapter 6 on history, and chapter 7 on sociology (and history). These shifts in disciplinary focus parallel shifts in the type of evidence available in the different time frames that these chapters examine: in particular, historians and sociologists who deal with the modern world face the opportunity, and the many challenges, that come from having far larger quantities of data available for study, from a wider variety of sources.

30. "Sociology is concerned with the comparative study of social institutions, giving particular emphasis to those forms of society brought into being by the advent of modern industrialism" (Anthony Giddens, *Social Theory and Modern Sociology*, p. 1).

31. See, especially, Ibid., pp. 19–21. Giddens' theory is discussed by Martin O'Brien, Sue Penna, and Colin Hay (eds.) and other authors in *Theorising Modernity: Reflexivity, Environment and Identity in Giddens' Social Theory*.

32. Along with especially Auguste Comte.

Another broad cultural and political trend during the modern period has been the one toward secularization. It is important to note, however, that secularization does not mean, and has not meant, the disappearance of religion. Far from it: more than half of the world's population today self-identifies as either Christian or Muslim, and most of the rest assert some other religious affiliation. Only some 15 to 20 percent, by most measures, claim no religious adherence at all, and demographers do not expect this number to grow in the future.[33] Secularization in the sense we mean it here entails a dramatic set of institutional changes, with social and intellectual repercussions, as particular religions lose the claim, in many parts of the world, to any "official" status with state recognition: "the declining influence of religion in public life . . . politics, law, economics, education, social relationships, family life, morality, and the culture at large."[34] This shift brought important changes in how people thought about themselves, both individually and as members of groups.

Modernity is not just about vast scales and large trends, but also about the shaping of individual lives and minds in a distinctive way. The French social theorist Michel Foucault crafted a body of work, largely in the 1960s and 1970s, that illuminated how modern institutions like medical clinics, hospitals, psychiatric facilities, and prisons serve as instruments of social control, exercising their power not just over a person but *within* a person, subtly and even invisibly shaping the way people discipline their own bodies and minds.[35] Foucault argued that in many cases, modern institutions appear to be instruments of "progress," offering liberation from suffering and toil, but in practice, they can actually be *more* powerful instruments of social control than their predecessors. A certain presentiment of this vision can be found in Aldous Huxley's *Brave New World*, in which the rulers of the year 2540 have brought the entire population of the world under complete control, not by means of pain but by pleasurable distraction: their subjects accept and internalize this control willingly and gladly. Zygmunt Bauman has likewise argued that modernity, despite its assertions and claims to freedom, progress, and liberation, has been characterized by the sacrificing of freedom for security and apparent control over chaotic elements of human experience.[36]

---

33. See Pew Research Center, "The Changing Global Religious Landscape," http://assets .pewresearch.org/wp-content/uploads/sites/11/2017/04/07092755/FULL-REPORT-WITH-APPENDIXES-A-AND-B-APRIL-3.pdf, p. 5.

34. Brad Gregory, *Rebel in the Ranks*, p. 217. Gregory has argued that the declining influence of religion in public life is itself a long-term outcome of the Reformation era—a time when political authorities across Europe crafted and enforced distinctively religious laws, producing intractable political-religious conflicts, the "wars of more-than-religion."

35. The selves that work in the external world and manipulate it are themselves changed by it—and so, as in so many other things, there is a feedback loop.

36. See his *Modernity and the Holocaust*.

Similarly, the sociologist Peter Berger writes of how changes in the external world produce internal changes within people, forming a certain "modern consciousness."[37] Using a telephone, for instance, made available new possibilities of communication, required new skills, and in turn, impelled one to learn certain ways of thinking:

> It means to think in numbers, to absorb a considerably complex framework of cognitive abstractions (such as the network of area codes covering North America), to have some notion of what could go wrong with the machinery (even if one must call on an expert for repairs). . . . To use the telephone habitually also means to learn a specific style of dealing with others—a style marked by impersonality, precision, and (at least in this country [the United States]) a certain superficial civility.[38]

Or to give a different example, employers in the world today can now ask for workers' hours rather than just their product,[39] and time is measured mechanically and can therefore be separated, to some extent, from daily rhythms of the natural world, thus affecting fundamental aspects of human experience. As Berger concludes, "anyone today is not only situated in the modern world but is also situated within the structures of modern consciousness."[40]

Berger also writes of modernity "as a near-inconceivable expansion of the area of human life open to choices,"[41] standing in contrast to "traditional societies" in which one's identity and way of life were strongly dictated by the prevailing social order.[42] Berger argues that those who experience this transition to a more modern society often find it a double-edged sword: it can mean liberation "from the narrow confines of tradition, of poverty, of the bonds of clan and tribe," yet it also leaves a person profoundly alone, "uncertain of the norms by which his life is to be governed, [and] finally uncertain of who or what he is."[43] With the multiplication of plausible worldviews and ways of life that modernity makes possible, certainty about self and world can be "hard to come by."[44]

---

37. See, e.g., Peter Berger, *The Heretical Imperative*, p. 5.

38. Ibid., p. 6.

39. James Hannam, *The Genesis of Science*, p. 160.

40. Peter Berger, *The Heretical Imperative*, p. 7. This might not be literally true—there are still groups and individuals "outside." But they are usually treated by "modern" observers as curiosities, quaint "relics" of bygone eras.

41. Ibid., p. 3.

42. As immortalized in *Fiddler on the Roof*, in the song "Tradition."

43. Peter Berger, *The Heretical Imperative*, p. 23.

44. Ibid., p. 19.

All that said, many other structures of modern power have been neither hidden nor apologetic. That includes the realm of globally dispersed empires, which by the early 20th century controlled most of the Earth's surface, and also a variety of authoritarian governments—the most infamous cases being Nazi Germany, the Stalinist Soviet Union, and Maoist China, along with others such as Hoxha's Albania and the Kim family's rule of North Korea. State power is still very much on view today, partly through military campaigns around the world but also in internal practices of increasing surveillance, censorship, electronic control, and incarceration, in countries from China to much of the Middle East and parts of the former Soviet Union, among many other places.

In summary, there is no shortage of ideas with which to describe the changes associated with the modern world: industrialism, capitalism, secularism, imperialism, technical specialization, choice, innovation, gentling of manners, rapid social and technological change, global dissemination of political and economic forms combined with fragmentation of cultures and worldviews. And to these we could add urbanism, nationalism, and mobility, already explored under "Context" in chapter 6.

It is almost certainly reductive to think that any one change was ultimately fundamental and drove all others. Human societies are complex and interactive. Taking a single factor like capitalism or nationalism (or even the growing use of fossil fuels) as fundamental, to the exclusion of the other factors, will cause one to miss out on the feedback loops and interrelationships between changes. As discussed in chapter 6, a more nuanced, situationally informed analysis of historical change will yield different insights in different situations.[45]

It would also be inaccurate to think that all this happened in an instant: modernity was not built in a day. No single individual, or group, or event, or place "gave birth" to it. But from the perspective of universal history, the scope, scale, and speed of change in modernity is genuinely remarkable. The thin sliver of time represented by modernity plays an outsized role in evaluating the present moment in cosmic and human-historical context.[46]

Modernity as Interpretation and Storytelling

Nobody doubts that the world has changed dramatically in the past two or three centuries. But using the idea of "modernity" as a way to encompass these changes

---

45. As Christian points out, many theories attempt to understand the rise of modernity: demographic theories, geographical theories, idealist theories, commercial theories (explaining modernity using the expansion of trade networks, increased specialization, and corresponding increased rates of innovation), as well as theories that explain modernity in terms of the evolution of social structures.

46. At the same time, the things that have changed rapidly are the things that we are attuned to, and we are attuned to them because they have changed rapidly. The perceived speed of historical change really does depend on one's focus.

is not necessarily a value-neutral approach. Rather, the word itself is often charged with connotations, and it may imply several complicated, and sometimes mutually contradictory, value judgments.

Almost by definition, the idea of modernity drives a wedge between present and past. For if there is a modern, there is also a premodern, and the "pre-" subtly implies a dichotomy between the "us" of today and the "them" of the past. A further common, often unconscious implication is that *we* are fundamentally better now than *they* were then. Many scholars push back against the perceived superiority of the present, but the idea does not go away easily: it is typical of modern culture to value the "innovative" and the new as marking progress and improvement over what came before, which is labeled as "traditional" and/or old. And even in cases where premodern times are idealized as being the better side of the coin, there still remains a coin: history and society are split in two along an implied fault line in time.[47]

The conceptualization of time implied by splitting history into "modern" and "premodern" has at least two problems, however. The first is that no such neat dichotomy exists. Yes, there are real changes in today's world, and yet people today are not so completely cut off from the past. One need look no further than religion and literature. The religious traditions claiming the devotion, in one way or another, of four out of every five people in today's world took their fundamental shape well over a thousand years ago. The bestselling book in the world by far is still the Bible. Ancient works of literature like India's *Mahabharata* and *Ramayana*, or Greece's *Iliad* and *Odyssey*, remain deeply influential. Even some of the most influential and bestselling novels of all time (e.g., *Don Quixote*, *Dream of the Red Chamber*) were written hundreds of years ago, as were the plays and sonnets of Shakespeare. If the modern world had as little in common with the premodern world as we are sometimes tempted to imagine, then like the "civilized" people of Huxley's *Brave New World*, we might not even comprehend ancient religion or literature, because we would have no easy way of relating to it. Yet people continue to appreciate and engage with ancient texts, ideas, and people. Technological and cultural settings may change immensely, but many personal and social realities still bear strong resemblance to older patterns.

The second issue with a sharp division between the modern present and the premodern past is that it may produce a triumphalist sense that the world "we" live in today is the goal, and even the endpoint, of history, when in reality modernity itself is also always shifting, a *transitory phase*, just as much as any other condition of the human world in the past. Such triumphalist tendencies are connected with modern ideals of progress, the idea that societies have changed for the better with time. As the historian Herbert Butterfield noted in 1931, progress narratives tend

---

47. Daniel Lord Smail and Andrew Shryock, "History and the Pre," *American Historical Review* 118, no.3 (2013):709–737.

to lead to the writing of histories that are "the ratification if not the glorification of the present."[48] But making the present into the touchstone, the benchmark, or the goal of all history is methodologically suspect, to say the least. And at least some premodern people would presumably judge the modern world as negatively, or even more negatively, than modern people often judge the premodern world. This fact might at the very least give us pause, and make us more conscious of the ambiguous or negative connotations of the word "modernity." Moreover, that modernity is an interpretive device with the potential to make present societies an "in-group" and past societies an "out-group" may help to explain why modern people are sometimes quite defensive about the economic, political, philosophical, and ideological ideals and realities of modernity, asserting them to be superior to social arrangements of the past and "on the right side of history" even while recognizing that their effects have not been universally positive, and in many cases have been destructive.[49]

Modernity is also a much less universal idea than it may at first appear. By framing "the modern era" as associated with industrial capitalism, on the one hand, and with the political and cultural changes that are often traced to the Enlightenment project, on the other, this way of categorizing time may intentionally or unintentionally place European, or Euro-American, institutions and ideas at the center. There are historical reasons for this: as Loos writes, "Modernity refers to inseparable political, economic, social, and cultural processes—all of which evolved in relation to colonial conquest—that developed in eighteenth-century Western Europe,"[50] at a time when Europe had "reached a decisively higher level of *social power* than was to be found elsewhere."[51]

It is not accurate to say that modernity developed in Europe and was then exported, since it arose from global contexts and thus societies around the world had an active role in adopting and assimilating it.[52] But Europe's way of articulating the ideals, forms, and practices of modernity still "exerted power as a yardstick against which nonmodern societies and individuals were judged."[53] Ideas and theories about what modernity means were developed with the express purpose of bringing modern technology and ideologies to the world through colonialism

---

48. Herbert Butterfield, *The Whig Interpretation of History*, p. v.

49. Cf. Hodgson, *The Venture of Islam*, p. 200.

50. Loos, *Subject Siam*, p. 19.

51. Hodgson, *The Venture of Islam*, pp. 177–178.

52. In what are often called "alternative modernities." The idea that colonized peoples were trying to "catch up" implies that everybody was going to the same destination. But people innovated and became modern in their own way.

53. Loos, *Subject Siam*, p. 19; see also Marshall Hodgson, "The Interrelations of Societies in History," *Comparative Studies in Society and History* 5, no. 2 (963): 250.

and imperialism. And even today, when scholars across many disciplines explicitly reject this kind of Eurocentric perspective, part of modernity's "sense of self" is the idea that virtually everybody *must* want to move toward more "modern" political, economic, and social arrangements. Yet in fact, many people's relationships with modernity and modern institutions are fraught, especially considering the legacies of colonial and neocolonial power. Modernity was not often seen as a good thing by those who experienced its new institutions and ideologies as a cultural imposition by imperial powers that engaged in sometimes brutal resource extraction and human exploitation, mapped onto political, military, and economic structures that exerted dominance over people living in faraway places. This situation complicated any claims by modern states to be bringing freedom, autonomy, or prosperity to most regular people. By the early 1920s, in fact, countries that were either colonies or former colonies accounted for fully 84 percent of the planet's non-ice-covered land area.[54]

The presumed European roots of modernity and the tendency of modernity to distance the present from the past can come together in an insidious way: "Modernity imagines not only the present as superior to the past but also sees colonial peoples as historically locatable at an earlier stage of modern development that Europe had previously experienced."[55] In other words, certain groups of present-day people, such as Native Americans or Australian Aborigines, may be implicitly or explicitly treated as "premodern" and, therefore, of less value or relevance to the modern world. And yet when viewed holistically and globally, every present-day group is equally modern; after all, they live during the modern period. The idea that some people are culturally "backward" is itself a product of modernity.

Modernity, in short, is an ambivalent, complex, and sometimes fraught phenomenon. Today's world has amazing conveniences, opportunities, and scientific knowledge, and the Earth now supports well over 7 billion people, all of which can be considered a tremendous achievement insofar as it enables the lives of so many humans, and far more affluent ones on average than in the past. The modern world even allows many of these people to enjoy intercommunication with those on the other side of the globe in an instant. But modernity also carries new means of exploiting both other people and the planet. Meanwhile, the very *idea* of modernity is a human construction and a category we use to structure our thinking about history and the present. "Modernity" is a word worth using with care and awareness of its range of connotations. It is a word with real strengths (in expressing a whole range of global changes through a single, rich term) but also serious limitations (in separating us from, and potentially even making us arrogant toward, people

---

54. Julian Go and Anne L. Foster, eds., *The American Colonial State in the Philippines: Global Perspectives*, p. 17.

55. Loos, *Subject Siam*, p. 20.

of the past; in making certain contingent social trends seem inevitable because they appear to represent "progress"; and in its Eurocentric tendencies and implications).[56] As Peter Berger writes, "Modernity is a historical phenomenon like any other. As such, it is inevitably a mixture of admirable and deplorable features. And very likely it is also a mixture of truths and errors."[57]

Both sides of this observation shape the way people think about the world today, often at an unconscious level. The particular moment in the history of human thought at which this book is being written exerts tremendous influence on how all of us think about past and present, about society and the individual, about religion and philosophy. Much of what we take for granted about how the world works, whether in economics, politics, philosophy, or culture, is not automatic, essential, transparent, or basic to the human condition. Rather, it emerges as something contingent, unique to our own narrow sliver of time in history. And the perspectives associated with universal histories, including any reactions you may have to them as a reader, are shaped—for better or for worse, and often without conscious notice—by these same currents of modern thought.

Connection

Telling the story of modernity is, in part, telling the story of the origins of our *connected* world. While even relatively far-flung geographical areas had some limited contact with one another before modern times, and only rarely did any group of people remain totally isolated from surrounding areas, the modern world has developed ongoing political, economic, social, and cultural connections of a character and scope never before seen. The basic facts of interconnection, in other words, existed long ago; the striking part is how they developed—in both depth and extent—in the modern period.

By way of comparison, consider a well-known historical example. In the late 1200s and early 1300s, a man named Marco Polo became widely famous for traveling from Venice to China[58] and writing about what he encountered in his travels. Marco Polo was not the first inhabitant of Christendom to have contact with the "Far East"; he was the one whose memoirs were recorded.[59] But he inhabited a vastly different world than ours today, in which thousands of people travel between Europe and Asia every day via widely accessible commercial air travel, and countless more are in contact through nearly instantaneous electronic means of communication.

---

56. This discussion benefitted from input from Philip Deloria.

57. Peter Berger, *The Heretical Imperative*, p. 11.

58. It is debated whether he actually made it to China or whether these stories are fabrications.

59. Janet Abu-Lughod, *Before European Hegemony: The World System A.D. 1250–1350*, p. 29.

Connection Goes Far Back

Viewed from one perspective, connections between people, both as individuals and as groups, are at the core of the entire story of humanity's history. At the most basic level, it seems to be in our nature as "social animals" to connect with one another. Conception of a new human life results from an intimate connection between two people, and everyone spends the first nine months of their existence inside another human being. Connections with older caretakers enable young people to survive and even thrive during infancy and childhood. No art or technology was ever constructed, no way of life established, and no food collected or produced without some kind of cultural transmission and social learning. On the scale of individuals and families, connection is fundamental to being human.

Broader and larger-scale connections likewise run throughout humanity's long-term past. Though many fewer individuals traveled so far in their lifetime as compared with today, there was sufficient gene flow across the whole of Africa and Eurasia (and, later, the Americas and elsewhere) to keep *Homo sapiens* identifiable as a single species, albeit one dispersed widely over the Earth's surface, for tens of thousands of years. As an example of early forms of connection, the paleoanthropologist Genevieve von Petzinger has pointed out that cave paintings are often accompanied by abstract shapes or geometric signs that, at many sites, far outnumber the (better known) animal and human images, and that some of the *same* signs reappear over a long period of time and across a large geographical area. For example, roughly two dozen signs appear again and again over a 30,000-year time span within present-day Europe, some of them spanning thousands of kilometers, and some of these same signs even exist in Indonesia and Australia—suggesting a possible ultimate origin in Africa.[60]

As far as we can tell, early foragers moved and interacted (in an everyday sense) in comparatively small groups, likely framed by kinship connections. During the agrarian era of the past several thousand years, agricultural villages and cities emerged as a new form and, in some cases, larger scale of social organization and connection. Historians, archaeologists, and linguists have evidence of indirect links throughout Eurasia by about 5,000 years ago: languages, technologies, lifeways,

---

60. There are not nearly enough distinct signs to represent all the words in a language, and these signs do not repeat regularly enough to suggest that they are an alphabet-style writing system representing a language. But they are very likely a form of graphic communication—visual symbols or markings that communicated "specific, culturally recognized, agreed-upon meanings," allowing messages to be transmitted and preserved beyond a single moment in time. People at the time almost certainly knew what these signs meant, even if we do not today. (Genevieve von Petzinger, "Why Are These 32 Symbols Found in Ancient Caves All over Europe?," https://www.ted.com/talks/genevieve_von_petzinger_why_are_these_32_symbols_found_in_ancient_caves_all_over_europe?language=en ; see also Genevieve von Petzinger, *The First Signs*.)

goods, and crops all spread; no region was totally isolated.[61] Hodgson notes that during this time, speaking broadly, there were widely shared elements of culture, including literary and religious traditions, that cut across many geographical and political lines, even while political associations were more transient. Still, political associations also provided a means of connection: the largest empires of the past 4,000-plus years, in both Old World and New World, spanned larger and larger territories, even though premodern state systems remained smaller than those of the last 300 years.[62] Other mechanisms of connection between geographically disparate areas included trade, voluntary movement, "forced migrations as a result of war, skilled workers or intellectuals seeking opportunity, mercantile activity, and direct diplomatic contact."[63]

Many other forms of connection also reach far back into the past, including those enabled by particular technologies. One for which the evidence still survives is coins: the adoption of metal tokens as coinage allowed common standards of value and exchange across large areas, starting from their first known use in Lydia over 2,500 years ago, and coinage provided a notable form of connection across the Hellenistic world in particular.[64] The camel saddle was another important early technology, starting over 3,000 years ago, for connecting people across difficult landscapes, like the steppes and deserts of Central Asia and the Sahara in Africa.[65] Even earlier than this, the domestication of the horse and the invention of the wheel allowed nomadic peoples in Central Asia to use wagons to carry tents and supplies, helping transform the giant steppe grasslands of Eurasia "from a hostile ecological barrier to a corridor of transcontinental communication"[66] and, in turn, allowing the spread of Indo-European languages to encompass a huge swath of land from the western end of Eurasia to the Indian subcontinent and "forever chang[ing] the dynamics of Eurasian historical development."[67]

---

61. See, e.g., Barry Gills and Andre Gunder Frank, eds., *The World System: Five Hundred Years or Five Thousand?*

62. As mentioned under "Context" in chapter 6, state systems before the modern era never controlled more than one-third of the land area controlled by states today (Christian, *Maps of Time*, p. 305), but the "universal" rulers of empires like Rome or Sasanian Iran had parallel, mutually intelligible, and sometimes even similar rituals and understandings surrounding kingship. See Matthew P. Canepa, *The Two Eyes of the Earth: Art and Ritual of Kingship Between Rome and Sasanian Iran*.

63. Canepa, *The Two Eyes of the Earth*, pp. 24–31; quote from pp. 22–24.

64. J. R. McNeill and William McNeill, *The Human Web: A Bird's-Eye View of World History*, p. 70.

65. Ibid., p. 95.

66. David W. Anthony, *The Horse, the Wheel, and Language: How Bronze-Age Riders from the Eurasian Steppes Shaped the Modern World*, p. 6.

67. Ibid.

These mobile pastoralists of the Central Asian steppes played other important roles in long-distance connection for several thousand years, including connecting the "civilized" areas of Eurasia by prompting a common arms race. Violent conflict between steppe pastoralists and settled agrarian peoples helped to produce conditions in which Eurasian military technology became the most formidable in the world.[68] The Mongol conquests of the 1200s then produced the largest unified land-based empire in history and, with it, an impressively greater ease of connection and communication.[69]

World religions have, for at least the last few thousand years, also been a powerful integrating force over very large land areas. Long-range missionary efforts by universal religions, especially Buddhism, Christianity, and Islam, permeated the Afro-Eurasian zone and increased the level of interregional and intercultural contact.[70] Pilgrimage routes—such as those to Mecca, Jerusalem, or the Ganges River, and a whole host of others—established enduring personal and interregional connections. Ibn Battuta, another figure remembered today as having written in the 1300s about travels across wide geographical swaths, could move without much difficulty across the Islamic world given the "unusually strong social solidarity" among Muslims.[71] The Korean monk Hyecho, a pilgrim to Buddhist holy sites in India during the 700s, stands as a parallel figure within the Buddhist world.[72] And much of European Christendom, even while politically fragmented (and long before the label "European" came into existence as an identity), had a cultural and religious unity thanks to common ideological commitments to Christianity; pilgrims, scholars, and others traveled widely within Christendom, especially during the High Middle Ages.

By the 13th century, all of these forms of large-scale connection were sufficiently well-established that the historical sociologist Janet Abu-Lughod has argued that the globe then possessed a "world system" of interactivity across swaths of Africa,

---

68. McNeill and McNeill, *The Human Web*, p. 59.

69. The Americas saw the development of several large-scale communities, including grand empires like the Aztec and Inca, but the Americas did not have interactions between communities comparable to those between steppe nomadic pastoralists and the landed agricultural areas in Eurasia. Perhaps as a consequence, the Americas had less cause for an arms race of the sort that occurred in Afro-Eurasia. Cf. pages cited above from McNeill and McNeill, *The Human Web*. Cf. also the book *Culture and Conquest in Mongol Eurasia* by Thomas Allsen, who has shown the depth of connections across Eurasia by tracing the impact of a single individual who conveyed ideas between Persian and Mongol areas in the 13th century.

70. Hodgson, "The Interrelations of Societies in History," p. 241. See also Jerry H. Bentley, *Old World Encounters: Cross-Cultural Contacts and Exchanges in Pre-Modern Times*.

71. Hodgson, "The Interrelations of Societies in History," p. 237.

72. See Donald S. Lopez, Jr., *Hyecho's Journey: The World of Buddhism*. The Chinese Buddhist monk Faxian (c. 337–422) is a still earlier example of an important traveler-writer within the ancient Buddhist world.

Europe, and Asia, even if it lacked a hegemonic power like the imperial powers of later centuries. This, admittedly, was not a global or a worldwide system; in particular, it lacked the entire New World, and also Australia and the Pacific. But this 13th-century world had not just a "circulation system" for the transfer of goods, ideas, people, institutions, and diseases across large parts of Afro-Eurasia, but one "with many alternate routes"[73] and no significant internal gaps. By the mid-14th century, all the societies within this web "had become inextricably linked to the fates of the rest."[74] This world system did not survive: it was devastated in the 1300s by pandemic disease and growing political conflict, especially in the Mongol domains, but even this large-scale collapse indicated, and was enabled by, its level of connection.[75] (See Plate 35.)

Connections, whether interpersonal, linguistic, ecological, political, economic, technological, cultural, or religious, have decisively influenced the historical trajectory of every society for as long as we have records from human societies. And the sharing (or stealing) of people, technologies, ideas, and political and cultural forms have led to a kind of "cumulative growth" that "meant that possibilities open to later generations were markedly different from those open to earlier ones. . . . In every field the constant piling up of changes petty in themselves broadened the range of cultural activity, and so the number of points at which various cultures could be important to each other."[76] As David Christian and others have noted, such connection enabled collective learning.

Global Connections

And yet, even if the deeper story of humanity is rife with interconnections and exchange, the last 500 years have nevertheless seen these established at a new depth and scale, marking the modern period as one of fully global connection. Although both Pacific islanders and northern Europeans had long before reached the New World, the years following 1492 saw a starkly different kind of economic, political, and ecological connection: a giant reshuffling of crops, resources, and people on an immense scale, and the emergence of a fully global economy. During the 1500s and 1600s, the Atlantic Europeans became "the Mongols of the sea,"[77] integrating spaces across the oceans in ways that Pacific islanders had long done, but these new

---

73. Janet Abu-Lughod, *Before European Hegemony: The World System A.D. 1250–1350*, p. 37.

74. Ibid., p. 137.

75. Ibid. These connections, for instance, created sophisticated urban centers that facilitated trade exchange, but these were, in turn, particularly subject to diseases like the Black Death.

76. Hodgson, "The Interrelations of Societies in History," p. 240.

77. Phrase from Arnold Pacey, *Technology in World Civilization*, quoted in McNeill and McNeill, *The Human Web*, p. 178.

trans-Atlantic connections involved millions of people rather than thousands.[78] Even as new connections emerged, though, many of the old ones also held and remained influential. For example, religion stayed, and in some ways grew, as a connecting force; various religions, particularly Christianity, spread around the entire planet in the 1500s and beyond. Currency also grew in importance as New World silver (especially from the Potosí mine in South America) spread throughout the world. An immense influx of silver into the world economy enabled cultural and economic transactions by providing a greater supply of precious metals that served as a common term of exchange, in turn enabling a more ready flow of goods around the world. (See Figure 7.1.)

The interactions of the 16th and 17th centuries set the stage for, and enabled, the even deeper economic, political, and technological connections that then developed. The Industrial Revolution in the 18th century drew on, deepened, and

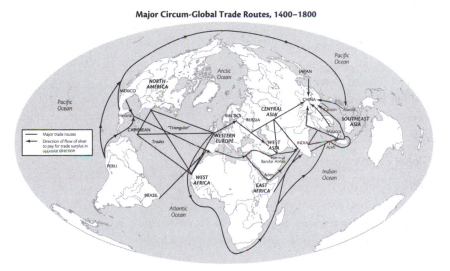

Major Circum-Global Trade Routes, 1400–1800

FIGURE 7.1 **Silver Transfers to Asia** Precious metals, especially gold and silver, had long served as common means of monetary exchange in much of the "Old World" (i.e., Afro-Eurasia). The incorporation of New World mines in the 16th century added new sources of these metals, in particular large amounts of silver from South America, further facilitating the flow of goods around the world. Until about 1800, the resulting global silver flows largely ended up in India and, especially, China, which was the wealthiest society in the world and a major exporter of a variety of luxury goods. This situation changed dramatically in the 19th century, following the expansion of European empires around the globe.

Source: Based on Andre Gunder Frank, *ReORIENT: Global Economy in the Asian Age* (Berkeley: University of California Press, 1998), p. 65.

---

78. "And like the Mongols, their conquests, slaughters, takeovers, co-optations, and absorptions of other peoples laid the groundwork for unprecedented consolidation of the webs of social and ecological interaction" (McNeill and McNeill, *The Human Web*, p. 178).

even transformed these connections into a new kind of global society. Though pop-ularly told as a story of Britain innovating and others following suit, the globally dispersed character of the Industrial Revolution was present from the beginning. Britain's inventions at home would have meant little if not for shifting economic and political relationships abroad, including the heavy use of slavery and coerced labor, the colonial exploitation of raw materials from Egypt and India (sources of cotton), and the creation of new markets abroad, especially in Latin America. Technologies preceding and underpinning the Industrial Revolution were drawn from throughout the world, including many parts of Afro-Eurasia. (See Plate 36.)

Before the 19th century, large-scale connection between world areas was lim-ited by practical considerations of distance, technological limits on speed and capacity, and constraints of a preindustrial economy that lacked the tremendous supply of energy opened up by fossil fuels and mechanization. The 1800s saw these constraints fall away.[79] Communication technologies like telegraphy and trans-portation technologies like the railroad and the steamship allowed far more rapid movement of ideas and goods, creating denser networks of communication and transportation around the world.[80] Such technologies facilitated worldwide con-vergence of social, economic, and political forms, including worldwide business cycles, economic depressions, and price convergence. (Price convergence means that the prices of a given good in different geographical regions converged with one another.[81]) Mass migrations of the 19th century also dwarfed previous popula-tion movements: between 1830 and 1914, over 100 million people migrated from India, China, and Europe across the Atlantic or to other parts of Eurasia.[82] The spread of the nation-state as a political form during this period may appear to have divided up the world among competing governments and peoples, but it also repre-sents a new, shared form of social organization and framework for self-identity and affiliation: at least in theory, all (or nearly all) people within a territory could regard themselves as "citizens" of a nation-state, in contrast to more exclusive notions of

---

79. "Between 12,000 and 5,000 years ago, at least seven societies around the world invented agriculture, in most cases quite independently: parallel pressures led to parallel solutions. But the steam engine did not have to be invented seven times to spread around the world: by the eighteenth century, once was enough." (Ibid., p. 7.)

80. Another technology of connection, like the camel saddle earlier, was silver. The Potosí mine (that produced three-fifths of the world's silver at its peak) and others, plus new technologies of extraction, lifted the constraints on long-distance trade by putting enough silver into circula-tion to "lubricate" the world economy. (Ibid., p. 202.)

81. Before the 1800s, goods could be valued radically differently in different parts of the world; one example is the cowrie, a type of mollusk whose shell in the 1300s carried a price 350 times greater in West Africa than in the Maldives. (Ibid., p. 204.)

82. Ibid., p. 261.

political-social identity in previous political forms.[83] The spread of nation-states also *enabled* connections and the flow of goods and people by creating "institutions that enforced customs laws in predictable ways, adhered to standardized means of diplomatic and commercial interaction, implemented international agreements, and provided predictable legal and commercial protections."[84]

The 1900s saw the rise of various attempts to unite the globe and connect people in new ways, including the emergence of international and transnational organizations like the United Nations, multinational corporations, and non-governmental organizations. Scientists crafted their own global community and, in many cases, actively worked to forge new ways of seeing the world as a whole, constructing categories like "global population," "global climate," and "global economy."[85] And even after former colonies gained political independence from European imperial powers, the connections between newly independent nation-states and the colonial powers remained in new forms: "Although many former colonies formed their national identities in the crucible of their fierce anticolonial struggles, once free, many of these former colonies found themselves still tied by history, blood, culture, and language to their former colonizers."[86] (See Figure 7.2.) Religion, for instance, ties many former colonies and colonizers together; in fact, it is not uncommon for people living in areas that were formerly colonies to be more devoted to the religion brought to them by colonial powers, such as Christianity, than are the former colonizers themselves.

These various forms of new global connection, especially in the 19th and 20th centuries, are often captured under the term "globalization," with an apparently straightforward definition: the modern world has become more integrated; diverse parts of the world have been drawn together across boundaries; participants in growing networks share economic life, culture, political standards, and forms

---

83. E.g., in the Roman Empire, where citizenship had been a specific category, with very limited membership. Even in the modern period discussed here, there were crucial exceptions, most obviously slaves (who were not legal citizens); and some people were categorized as less-than-full citizens, as in the French Revolutionary distinction between "active" and "passive" citizens—the details of which shifted over time, but which relied on inclusions and exclusions of people especially according to their wealth, race, and gender. See Immanuel Wallerstein, "Citizens All? Citizens Some! The Making of the Citizen," *Comparative Studies in Society and History* 45:4 (Oct. 2003).

84. Adam McKeown, "Periodizing Globalization," *History Workshop Journal* 63 (Spring 2007):223. James C. Scott writes, "The hegemony, in this past century, of the nation-state as the standard and nearly exclusive unit of sovereignty has proven profoundly inimical to non-state peoples. . . . Gone, in principle, are the large areas of no sovereignty or mutually canceling weak sovereignties." (Scott, *The Art of Not Being Governed*, p. 11.)

85. See Perrin Selcer, *The Postwar Origins of the Global Environment: How the United Nations Built Spaceship Earth*.

86. Alfred J. Andrea, "Series Editor's Preface," in Douglas Northrop, *An Imperial World: Empires and Colonies Since 1750*, p. vii.

Commonwealth of Nations (formerly British Commonwealth)

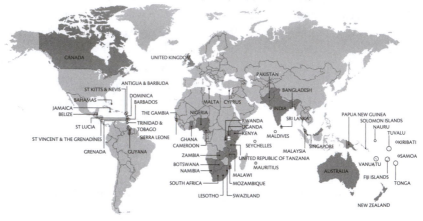

Organisation Internationale de la Francophonie

FIGURE 7.2 Former British and French Colonies Although the 20th century saw the political dissolution of European colonial powers' global empires, strong ties of language, religion, and culture often still connect former colonies to their former colonizers.
Source: Douglas Northrop, *An Imperial World: Empires and Colonies Since 1750* (Boston: Pearson, 2013), p. 201

of communication. Instead of having immediate experience only of local conditions and only vague or fanciful ideas about people in distant lands, it has become increasingly possible, even easy, to be aware of and knowledgeable about those on the other side of the world. This has led to a "real time, simultaneously-experienced global civilization";[87] "new intimacies and new forms of competition, rivalry, and

---

87. Howard Perlmutter, quoted in McKeown, "Periodizing Globalization," p. 218.

conflict";[88] "a sense of living in the midst of unprecedented change";[89] and a sense of the world as a "global village" (to use Marshall McLuhan's famous phrase) in which the peoples of the world have an opportunity to understand one another.

Commentators like McLuhan see great hope and great opportunity in the global connections of the 19th, 20th, and 21st centuries. But the consequences have been destructive as well as constructive. The Great Depression of the 1930s swept the world economy, not just local or regional economies. Global cholera and plague pandemics of the 19th century were enabled by the increased mobility afforded by transportation technologies that moved people—and their pathogens—much faster than before.[90] Languages now die out at a rate of one per week, continuing a striking trend of language consolidation and loss in the modern era. Wars in the modern world are fought with far more formidable weapons and techniques, and with far greater destructive capacity, than before. Negative environmental impacts affecting the entire planet have become possible. Although connection between people and between societies can multiply the possibilities of peace and security, so too they can open up new and bigger sources of vulnerability: to pandemics, to unimaginably destructive war, and to the dangerous consequences of changes to the entire Earth's climate. The words "connection" and "entanglement" may have different connotations, but they are two sides of the same coin.

The Limitations of Connection

Whether one looks at large-scale human interpersonal, economic, and political connection as, on balance, positive or negative, it is a defining phenomenon in history. Each society and culture in today's world has emerged from a process of interactions in which ideas and people and trade flow around, and they all have made each other what they are—for better and for worse. David Christian, for example, frames the history of the last few thousand years in terms of exchange networks, identifying "centers of gravity" where people, information, and goods collect as well as "hub regions" through which information and goods routinely flow.[91] From this perspective, the story of human history becomes fundamentally one of connection, in which the basic story is one of broadening networks and intersocietal ties, and where nothing emerges on its own.

This is a powerful idea, one formulated and best expressed by world historians and also by the writers of Big History, but even so, it has its limitations. When

---

88. Robert Park, quoted in McKeown, "Periodizing Globalization," p. 219.

89. McKeown, "Periodizing Globalization," p. 219.

90. See Martin S. Pernick, "Diseases in Motion," pp. 365–374 in *A Companion to World History*, ed. Douglas Northrop.

91. Christian, *Maps of Time*, pp. 291–293.

historians make *connections* the overriding story of world history, certain things may fall out of view, most notably the peoples who are not visibly connected to the largest networks. By focusing on connections around the world as a—or even the—central thrust to the story of human history, one gives center stage to some people (those in the most densely connected areas of the world) and marginalizes others (in less connected areas).

Another limitation of narratives focusing on connection is that such narratives can obscure the role of contingency in history, lending a sense of inexorability to the growth of connections over time and making modern global society, complete with electrical grid and internet, seem *inevitable*—always a perilous word to historians when narrating the past. While increased connectivity of societies results naturally enough from growing population densities and the spreading out of human communities, the precise forms and consequences of those connections are contingent, and the details arguably matter a great deal in what *kinds* of larger-scale connections endure over time.

Finally, a focus on broad-scale connections at the expense of smaller-scale connections runs the risk of obscuring the experience of individual lives, or small-scale events, that have always been colored heavily by the irreducibly local. The small-scale connections of family and local community remain crucial in every human life, even in today's global society, and have always been so, at every point in the past. Any newer and larger-scale connections have in no way replaced these older and smaller-scale ones, but they have added a certain complexity and additional levels of influence and framing to them. Keeping large-scale trends in view thus provides powerful context to individual lives, while keeping smaller scales in focus aligns historical writing more closely with people's lives as actually experienced.

The impulse to see human history in a world history or Big History "connective" framework brings many advantages. It allows one to keep a big picture in view, and it avoids fragmentation into an excessive range of small-scale or national stories. It has the potential to bring out just how fundamental connections on many scales are to human existence. But it is important to remember the limitations of this perspective too. The ideal is to make good use of the advantages of a wide point of view, while not forgetting to ask what even a panoramic[92] view of regional and global connections may leave out.

Systems

The rest of this chapter could go in any number of directions. Historians and sociologists who try to understand the development of modern societies have a much greater diversity of sources to work with than any anthropologist or historian who

---

92. Use of the word in this context inspired by Ross E. Dunn and Laura J. Mitchell's book *Panorama: A World History.*

studies the ancient world. Written sources in particular increase tremendously in the modern period, with state bureaucracies alone producing many millions, even billions, of pages of writing over the past 200 years, and even vaster quantities of electronic data over the past quarter-century. The sheer volume of available evidence opens up new opportunities for historians, but sometimes overwhelms their ability to analyze evidence comprehensively. Given this vast base of available evidence, any brief account of modernity will feel even more scattershot and incomplete than concise accounts of other time periods—despite the tiny amount of time occupied by the modern period.

We cannot map out a complete portrait of modernity, but instead only explore a few big ideas associated with the modern world that are of particular relevance in the context of universal histories. With this in mind, the chapter's remaining sections focus on *systems, statistics,* and *purpose.* These categories of thought are often overlooked, but they have strongly colored modern thinking about science, history, and society. Exploring them together presents an opportunity to consider ways in which modern universal histories, although they may seem all-embracing, are situated in a particular time period—the time we call the modern—and are products of a modern mindset.

The Idea of a System, and How It Structures Universal Histories

A "system" is a collection of parts that interact with one another in a stable way and that function together as a unit, a collective whole. Across many domains of modern scholarly thought, structures or arrangements that can be modeled and understood as systems have certain elements in common: "systems involve relationship, cycles, feedbacks, and movement,"[93] interdependent parts that work together and function as a whole. Stated so broadly, it comes as no surprise that just about anything can be characterized as a system: geological systems, living systems, social systems, economic systems, computer systems. The list could go on indefinitely.

The idea of a system in the abstract, as a way of thinking about a wide range of natural and social phenomena, is itself a concept tied especially to modern times, with the processes of industrialization and mechanization promoting "systemization" and the standardization of everything, from the manufacture of textiles to the assembly of automobiles. The concept of a system was in turn applied to everything from how a nation is governed ("political systems") to how knowledge is organized (e.g., the Dewey Decimal System). Emerging in English in the early 1600s, the word "system" was first applied to the living world in the late 1600s, to

---

93. Charles H. Langmuir and Wally Broecker, *How to Build a Habitable Planet: The Story of Earth from the Big Bang to Humankind,* p. 15.

thermodynamics[94] and the social world in the early 1800s, and to computers in the mid-1900s.[95]

Because of its wide applicability, the concept of a system offers a convenient framing device for many aspects of universal histories, both in the natural world and in the human social world. Cosmologists, for instance, develop ideas about the early universe by modeling it as a thermodynamic system. Astrophysicists study the Solar System and other planetary systems, and sometimes treat stars themselves as systems. Earth scientists study our planet's climate system and the various other systems profiled in chapter 3. Ecologists and evolutionary biologists speak of ecosystems. Biologists treat life at every scale as a set of interconnected systems, from the biosphere to a living cell or an organism, as we saw in chapter 4.[96] Anthropologists, historians, and social scientists speak of economic systems, political systems, social systems, and even "systems of thought."

Scholars in the humanities and social sciences sometimes speak of blended systems that are part human and part inanimate. An example is what some refer to as sociotechnical (or technopolitical,[97] or envirotechnical[98]) systems, which are characterized by interactions between individual people, social and political structures, and technological systems. The word "infrastructure" is often used to refer to sociotechnical systems that support, underpin, and enable human societies in ways that individuals are usually not aware of unless, and until, they malfunction: systems such as the electrical grid, water supplies, sewer systems, highway systems, and so forth.[99] (See Plate 37.) The concept of a system, in all of these ways, is always present in the background of everyday modern life, even if not often noticed as such, thanks sometimes to the intentional design that keeps them hidden from view. When pencils fit sharpeners, when screwdrivers fit screws, when tires fit cars, the underlying standardization is always the result of the individual artifacts being pre-defined as part of a much larger system.[100]

---

94. Originally in the work of Nicolas Léonard Sadi Carnot.

95. See Online Etymology Dictionary, "System," https://www.etymonline.com/word/system .

96. The field of "systems biology" at the cellular and molecular level attempts to investigate how each part of a system behaves in relation to the others as the system functions.

97. See, e.g., Gabrielle Hecht, *The Radiance of France: Nuclear Power and National Identity After World War II*, p. 15.

98. See, e.g., Sara B. Pritchard, "An Envirotechnical Disaster: Nature, Technology, and Politics at Fukushima," https://academic.oup.com/envhis/article-abstract/17/2/219/381273 .

99. Key aspects of many social systems may be computationally modeled as complex adaptive systems. See, e.g., John H. Miller and Scott E. Page, *Complex Adaptive Systems: An Introduction to Computational Models of Social Life*.

100. Note that some such infrastructural systems long predate the modern period—ancient irrigation networks in China or the Middle East, for instance. Modern sociotechnical systems influence how *knowledge* is generated and shared too. Data science and analytics are only a particularly prominent manifestation of the knowledge systems and knowledge infrastructure that are always around us but often invisible.

In addition to drawing implicitly on these various forms of "systems thinking," universal histories have sometimes gone further, making use of the concept as an explicit framing for understanding the past, present, and future. Perhaps the most explicit was that of Erich Jantsch, who wrote a book, published in 1980, called *The Self-Organizing Universe: Scientific and Human Implications of the Emerging Paradigm of Evolution*, which applied the emerging science of systems from the 1950s and 1960s.[101] He described a system as "a set of coherent, evolving, interactive processes which temporarily manifest in globally stable structures," and he spoke of universal history in terms of such systems.[102] One Big History pioneer, Fred Spier, has likewise given complex systems a prominent role in framing his universal history. He points to the concept of systems as a way of analyzing how wholes are greater than the sum of their parts,[103] and of "regimes" as a sort of generalized system and way of framing universal history.[104]

Advantages and Limitations of "Systems Thinking"

Like any conceptual lens, the idea of a system has its advantages and its disadvantages. Advantages include the ways in which it unifies disparate knowledge and helps to highlight real patterns that cross many scales. Disadvantages include the ways in which it tends to "systematically" overlook other patterns and scales.

It is reasonable to ask whether using the word "system" to characterize everything, from a set of planets around a star to an economy, is just a trick of language, an empty generalization without any specific meaning. But all these arrangements really *do* share certain properties, or common patterns in their inner workings. In at least this sense, the concept of systems can provide a unifying framework or common language for identifying principles that cross many scales and disciplines of study.

For example, the concept of feedback provides a common way of understanding what happens in a cell, an ecosystem, the Earth's climate, and the Sun. By "feedback," we mean that a process's output influences the process itself, either amplifying or diminishing it. In "positive" feedback, the original effect reinforces itself, so that the process is ramped up, as when a microphone picks up sound emitted by its own speaker and amplifies it in a runaway cycle. In "negative" feedback, the original effect tends to cancel itself, restoring the system to its earlier condition

---

101. Especially the idea of self-organizing systems, the stability of structures, and feedback.

102. Erich Jantsch, *The Self-Organizing Universe: Scientific and Human Implications of the Emerging Paradigm of Evolution*, p. 6.

103. Fred Spier, *Big History and the Future of Humanity*, p. 24.

104. See, e.g., Ibid., p. 21, and also Fred Spier, *The Structure of Big History: From the Big Bang Until Today*, p. 2 ff.

and maintaining a stable "equilibrium."[105] The Sun stays at a stable temperature, for example, because of negative-feedback effects in its core,[106] and the Earth's climate system is a balance between a large number of positive feedback loops and countervailing negative feedback loops that keep the climate relatively stable over time. Living systems from cells to organisms to ecosystems include many different feedback loops, including negative feedback loops that help maintain stable internal temperatures and solution concentrations. Any of these equilibrium conditions may look static and unchanging, but they often require active maintenance, as a systems-based analysis can help to reveal.

Feedback can likewise apply to social systems. Rapid social change, from the French Revolution to the fall of the Soviet Union to the Arab Spring, can sometimes be analyzed as a small change being amplified through positive feedback. Social stability, on the other hand, can, in some cases, be analyzed through the lens of negative feedback.

Thinking about a wide range of phenomena in terms of systems has other advantages as well. For example, some scientists have argued that "systems thinking" provides an alternative to reductionism. For example, Charles Langmuir and Wally Broecker speak of "systems thinking" as "including *relationship* in the understanding of phenomena,"[107] countering a common trend in 20th-century science of trying to understand things in isolation and analyzing parts at the expense of the whole.

A related example of the value of "systems thinking" in the social sphere comes from the field of "world-systems analysis," pioneered by the sociologist Immanuel Wallerstein. This field attempts to provide a holistic, historically informed understanding of how the modern social world has evolved over time—and thus to do better than any of the social sciences (including economics, psychology, political science, and especially sociology) can do individually. Wallerstein and other world-systems theorists treat today's capitalist "world-economy"—with its "vast international division of labor"[108] that integrates nearly all parts of the world in a single network of economic exchange cutting across otherwise well-defined political and cultural lines—as a single system.[109] Identifying this economic and

---

105. Note that the words "positive" and "negative" are not value judgments: positive feedback loops entail rapid change, and negative feedback loops entail stability. Either kind of feedback loop may be "good" or "bad" (or both!), depending on the situation.

106. Basically, if the Sun's core temperature fluctuated upward slightly, the resulting increase in the rate of nuclear fusion would lead to greater pressure and therefore expansion of the core; such expansion would lead to cooling, restoring the original temperature.

107. Langmuir and Broecker, *How to Build a Habitable Planet*, p. 13; italics added.

108. Janet Abu-Lughod, *Before European Hegemony*, p. 33.

109. Immanuel Wallerstein, "The Rise and Future Demise of the World Capitalist System: Concepts for Comparative Analysis," in *The Essential Wallerstein*, pp. 74–75.

social system as a single "unit of analysis"[110] makes it easier to recognize certain patterns that would not be as visible if this huge system were to be analyzed in terms of its smaller component parts, like countries or regions. For instance, a world-systems analysis makes clear that nation-states are not closed economic systems, but instead play particular roles as parts within the whole of the world-economy, such as when certain kinds of occupations, like industrial wage-work, are preferentially found in certain countries or geographic regions.[111]

Likewise, Wallerstein and colleagues use a world-systems approach to argue that "underdeveloped economies" are not simply primitive versions of developed economies that will eventually "catch up"[112] on their own. Rather, they argue that developed and underdeveloped economies are part of the same system, and the condition of developed economies rests in part on the exploitation of people and resources in other parts of the world. The legacies of colonialism and newer forms of economic exploitation appear more clearly with the recognition of national and regional economies all being part of a single, larger system.[113]

Systems are a powerful conceptual framework and bring certain patterns into better focus, but there are significant pitfalls in analyzing everything—both in the natural world and the social world—in terms of systems. For one, putting this concept at the center runs the risk of oversimplification: "systems thinking" attempts to model tremendously complicated natural, social, and technical realities like the Earth's climate, the world economy, or the electrical grid, and even a largely successful model of such complex realities will be bound to fail, some of the time, to capture important nuances of how something works. In addition, defining which components "count" as the parts of a given system by definition excludes others. But given the interlocking character of different scales and phenomena in the actual world (something that universal histories, at their core, set out to show), the act of highlighting some aspects at the expense of others limits one's ability to analyze other contributions to the system's inner workings. The political scientist and anthropologist James C. Scott writes that there are "limits, in principle, of what we are likely to know about complex, functioning order,"[114] in both human social organization and in the natural world.[115] Thinking in terms of systems, in other words,

---

110. See, e.g., Ibid., p. 71 ff.

111. Ibid., p. 92.

112. A phrasing that is itself associated with the "modernization theory" of sociologists like Max Weber, Talcott Parsons, et al.

113. The economic historian Andre Gunder Frank calls this the "development of underdevelopment."

114. James C. Scott, *Seeing Like a State*, p. 7.

115. See also Samuel Arbesman, "It's Complicated," https://aeon.co/essays/is-technology-making-the-world-indecipherable .

is no more than an attempt to model reality, and any such modeling may lead to an overconfidence that one understands the reality better than one actually does.

An example that straddles the human world and the natural world is the human body. The uncontroversial technique, used by doctors, biologists, and others, of dividing the body into multiple systems, like the circulatory system, the respiratory system, and the nervous system, certainly makes the body's functioning easier to understand and allows the establishment of medical specialties that greatly improve human health. In the real human body, however, each of the parts that medical professionals group into "systems" may well interact with one another, as parts of the same organism—including those located, ostensibly, in different subsystems. This happens in a complex way that the medical sciences only partially understand. The idealized conceptual definitions of distinct—that is, separate—systems can only capture so much of the functioning reality, and these definitions set up patterns of thinking that result in areas of specialty that sometimes fail to interact enough with each other to offer holistic medical care for the whole person.

Thinking of human history in terms of systems and social structures can likewise lead to an overemphasis on big, impersonal forces and large, long-scale trends at the expense of human agency, the individual, and small scales. To be sure, cultural, economic, and political systems that operate on large scales do strongly influence the behavior and mindsets of individuals. But social systems are, at the same time, composed of individuals. And as we have seen, there will always be feedback between levels. To give priority in historical analysis to the system over the individual and smaller-scale communities risks making individual people appear only as cogs in an ever-more-efficient machine.[116] (In turn, prioritizing small scales at the expense of large scales risks losing a wider perspective and appreciation of context, as explored especially under "Context" in chapter 6.)

Systems, in short, are a modern construct: a way of understanding, describing, and labeling aspects of the natural and social world that has emerged gradually during the modern period. For better and for worse, the idea of a system structures much of the thinking that underpins universal histories. It is important to keep in mind that this conceptual lens brings both strengths and limitations to the table.

---

116. Compare the dictum of Frederick Winslow Taylor: "In the past the man was first, in the future the system must be first" (quoted in Todd Rose, *The End of Average*, p. 42). Some poetic references to systems include Alfred, Lord Tennyson's "In Memoriam A. H. H.": "Our little systems have their day" (see http://www.online-literature.com/tennyson/718/), and what T. S. Eliot wrote of the people of the modern world in a poetic pageant-play called "The Rock": "They constantly try to escape / From the darkness outside and within / By dreaming of systems so perfect that no one will need to be good" (quoted in *The Complete Poems & Plays T. S. Eliot*, p. 159).

Statistics

Next, we turn to statistics.[117] How does your height compare with the average? How about your intelligence, perhaps as measured by IQ? What about the amount of sleep you get each night? How does your school, or workplace, or hometown "measure up" in comparison with national rankings or averages? How does your nation's GDP compare with other nations globally?

Statistics such as these have a powerful way of shaping how we think today. Perhaps surprisingly, however, most of these questions would not even have been formulated, let alone answered, by people living before the 1800s. While people surely always noticed differences in height, intelligence, economic prosperity, and the like, virtually no one before the 19th century would have phrased their observations about these variations in terms of numbers and statistics, and they would not have framed them as comparisons with an average. Although some premodern societies, like the Roman Empire or Imperial China, compiled numerical information about populations through (by present-day standards, very basic) censuses, such information was typically available and useful only to a select few, and was not a part of everyday life and ways of thinking about the world.

It may not be easy to fully grasp or appreciate how our very conceptualization of statistics and numerical information is a modern construct, rather than an inherent part of human nature. But the fact that our world is suffused with numbers, and that these numbers seem uniquely trustworthy and the most straightforward kind of "real" information, is the result of a particular set of cultural sensibilities and a feature of our particular historical context—a context where statistics are widely collected, published, and used. The widespread use of statistics may seem an expression of a perennial human desire both to categorize and know our world and to organize knowledge, but quantitative and statistical information is far from the only kind, or the only valuable kind, of knowledge. Examining the origins of the modern emphasis on numbers and statistics shows the emergence of some key features of modern thinking.

Statistics, the Social Sciences, and Modern Concepts

Statistics and modernity go together. In fact, the very existence of what we call "statistics" is tied to modern nation-states' interest in knowing as much as possible about their citizens, and in creating knowledge of broad patterns that simplify the complex social, economic, and political realities of millions of individuals. The word itself reflects this origin: it is not a coincidence that "statistics" very nearly contains the word "state." The word came into English from the German *Statistik*,

117. We are greatly indebted to Daniel Hirschman for both our general approach in this section and many specific points within it.

which was in turn coined in the mid-1700s to indicate the analysis of data about the state.[118]

To understand the connection between nation-states and statistics, it is important to recall that nation-states are specifically modern political forms that create, and sometimes impose, unity on culturally and linguistically diverse geographical regions. Consider the well-known European cases of France, Germany, and Italy. The territories of these modern nation-states initially included a wide range of languages and ethnicities, and neighbors on opposite sides of the French-Italian border, for example, were much closer linguistically and ethnically to one another than either was to Paris or to Rome. The creation of coherent identities within new nation-states' borders, distinct from other identities outside those borders, was the result of nationalistic cultural movements and generations of effort at the state and institutional levels. The language now known as Italian, say, was chosen from among dozens of (sometimes mutually unintelligible) local languages within Italian territory; in this case, it was the language of Florence that was chosen, because Petrarch, Dante, and Boccaccio had written in it centuries before. Similarly, the language now known as German was elevated to the status of a national language partly because Martin Luther had translated the Bible into it. Likewise, Parisian French was adopted as the national language of France in part because of Paris's status as the established institutional center. And while these three cases are European, the basic contours are not unique to Europe. The political scientist and historian Benedict Anderson, a specialist on Southeast Asia, has pointed out that the Indonesian language changed from a "strange language-of-state [based on] an ancient inter-insular lingua franca"[119] to a "national(-ist) language"[120] when newspapers and print moved it "out into the marketplace and the media."[121] Japan, too, likewise had tremendous internal diversity along linguistic, cultural, and social lines across its five major islands before it was unified into a single nation, with a single codified national language, in the modern period. And the same story could be told in many other locations around the world.

Numbers provided a key part of the nationalist program to craft communities. The philosopher of science Ian Hacking writes that "nation-states classified, counted and tabulated their subjects anew,"[122] helping to reinforce modern ideas of sovereignty and coherent national identities and grouping co-nationals as people who should be considered together. The world's first official bureau of statistics opened

118. See Online Etymology Dictionary, "Statistics," https://www.etymonline.com/word/statistics.

119. Benedict Anderson, *Imagined Communities*, p. 132.

120. Ibid., p. 133.

121. Ibid.

122. Ian Hacking, *The Taming of Chance*, p. 2.

in Paris in 1800, in the immediate wake of the French Revolution: "Uniformity of data collection, overseen by a centralised cadre of highly educated experts, was an integral part of the ideal of a centrally governed republic, which sought to establish a unified, egalitarian society."[123] But according to Hacking, "it was German thinkers and statesmen who brought to full consciousness the idea that the nation-state is essentially characterized by its statistics, and therefore demands a statistical office in order to define itself and its power."[124] Numbers regarding manufacturing, agriculture, birth and death rates, crime rates, and a host of other quantities began to be tracked—sometimes for the first time, sometimes in much greater detail than ever before[125]—and became widely available over the next half-century.

Statistics thus started out as a tool through which modern states could view, and thereby change, society, "but gradually developed into something that academics, civic reformers and businesses had a stake in"[126] as well. Statistics also sometimes served as a tool for conquest, as the collection of statistical information aided the standardization of military practices in modern nation-states, including conscription and provisioning of troops, helping states to assess and advance their prospects for imperial expansion.

No matter whose hands the numbers are in, though, numbers always represent the world in a selective way. To turn a social-cultural-political reality into a number, or a group of numbers—that is, to count something, or even to decide what to count—requires clear rules for inclusion and exclusion, lumping a "messy" and variegated world into discrete categories. And the social context of this information-gathering inspires particular ways of categorizing the world, at the expense of other ways. In the case of the initial number-gathering of numerically minded state bureaucracies, Hacking writes:

> There is a sense in which many of the facts presented by the bureaucracies did not even exist ahead of time. Categories had to be invented into which people could conveniently fall in order to be counted. The systematic collection of data about people has affected not only the ways in which we conceive of a society, but also the ways in which we describe our neighbor. It has profoundly transformed what we choose to do, who we try to be, and what we think of ourselves. Marx read the minutiae of official statistics, the reports from the factory inspectorate and the like. One can ask: who had

---

123. William Davies, "How Statistics Lost Their Power—And Why We Should Fear What Comes Next," https://www.theguardian.com/politics/2017/jan/19/crisis-of-statistics-big-data-democracy .

124. Hacking, *The Taming of Chance*, p. 18.

125. See, e.g., Joshua Cole, *The Power of Large Numbers*, pp. 25–26.

126. Davies, "How Statistics Lost Their Power."

more effect on class consciousness, Marx or the authors of the official reports which created the classifications into which people came to recognize
themselves?[127]

Many consequences for modern culture have followed from the counting and
categorization associated with statistics-gathering. One late-19th-century consequence was to introduce a style of reasoning that is common today: to examine
a quantity or a rate in one social group and compare it to that of another social
group, then drawing conclusions about both. For example, the sociologist Émile
Durkheim's foundational work *Suicide: A Study in Sociology* noted that suicide
rates are quite stable from year to year within a given country or region, varying
in some cases by as little as 1 or 2 percent.[128] In today's world, we are used to such
statistics being widely published and available, so this kind of stability may not be
surprising; but in the 19th century, it was a shocking discovery that suicide rates
(not to mention "figures for phenomena as diverse as births, deaths, marriages,
murders, and undeliverable letters at the post office"[129]) not only failed to exhibit
great and unpredictable year-to-year variation, but that those rates could be markedly *distinct* from one social setting to another. After all, suicide seems like a radically individual choice. But Durkheim argued that it is properly seen not only as an
individual matter, but as a social phenomenon. He argued that social factors, like
religious worldview or whether one's country was at war, therefore ought to be the
kind of factors invoked in trying to explain suicide and its statistical variations by
country. As he put it:

> If, instead of seeing in [suicides] only separate occurrences, unrelated and
> to be separately studied, the suicides committed in a given society during
> a given period of time are taken as a whole, it appears that this total is
> not simply a sum of independent units, a collective total, but is itself a
> new fact *sui generis*, with its own unity, individuality and consequently
> its own nature—a nature, furthermore, dominantly social. Indeed, pro-
> vided too long a period is not considered, the statistics for one and the
> same society are almost invariable. . . . This is because the environmental
> circumstances attending the life of peoples remain relatively unchanged
> from year to year.[130]

---

127. Hacking, *The Taming of Chance*, p. 3.

128. See, e.g., Émile Durkheim, *Suicide: A Study in Sociology*, ed. George Simpson and trans.
John A. Spaulding and George Simpson, p. 47 (Table 1).

129. Joshua Cole, *The Power of Large Numbers*, p. 16.

130. Durkheim, *Suicide*, p. 46.

In the 19th-century context where they were first noted, such observations inspired a certain "statistical fatalism"[131] and social determinism. The Belgian astronomer and sociologist Adolphe Quetelet famously wrote, "It is society that prepares the crime; the guilty person is only the instrument who executes it."[132] (On a related note, it is probably no coincidence that the system of philosophical ethics called utilitarianism emerged and became popular at this time, in the late 1700s through the mid-1800s, framed as it was around numbers: "the greatest good for the greatest number," in Jeremy Bentham's potent early formulation.) Even our present-day notion that reforms in public policy can decrease crime rates derives largely from this time, invoking chains of cause and effect that are entirely at the level of collections of people and that do not directly invoke individual choice (and, in fact, are sometimes criticized for minimizing, explaining, or even excusing individual choices).[133] All these developments were ultimately made possible by the "avalanche of numbers in 1820–[18]40, and the accompanying conception of statistical law."[134]

The effects of widely available statistics do not end there. As the education researcher and developmental psychologist Todd Rose points out in *The End of Average*, the mid-1800s is also the time when people first started thinking about features of the "average" person. Speaking of the average person with respect to a given trait is so common today that it is difficult to imagine what a change this represented, but the entire concept was invented and developed only in the past 200 years. The idea of measuring a human trait—like height, or weight, or intelligence—and then finding the *average* of that trait across a population was essentially never done before the 19th century.[135] Quetelet saw the average as a sort of normative ideal,[136] a notion that is still with us today when we grow concerned about a child who begins talking or walking "too late" relative to the average, or about an adult or child who deviates too far from the average in bodily dimensions, or personality, or quantifiable habits like time spent sleeping.[137] (Such things were

---

131. See Hacking, *The Taming of Chance*, p. 114 ff.

132. Quoted in Ibid., p. 114.

133. Some of the consequences of this way of thinking were, on balance, quite positive. For example, sanitation and other public-health measures increased life expectancies in many places.

134. Hacking, *The Taming of Chance*, p. 118. More common now than statistical fatalism is the idea that there are penchants or propensities for certain behaviors that are present at different rates in different populations, leading to different (but collectively relatively stable) statistics.

135. Rose, *The End of Average*, p. 27.

136. Ibid., p. 28.

137. Even the idea of a "social norm" is an extension of the idea of a "norm" in the industrial world: "The acquisition of numbers by the populace, and the professional lust for precision in measurement, were driven by familiar themes of manufacture, mining, trade, health, railways, war, empire. Similarly the idea of a norm became codified in these domains." (Hacking, *The Taming of Chance*, p. 5.)

surely capable of causing concern or consternation before 1800—but the framing in terms of deviation from the *average* is new.) Francis Galton contributed the idea that the average is not so much normative as a mediocre standard to be overcome or improved upon,[138] another concept that endures today, especially with regard to topics like intelligence and scholastic achievement or driving ability, where much more than half of the population wants to be "above average."

The 20th century saw the development of tools to assess "public opinion" through the introduction of yet more numbers, this time acquired through social surveys and public-opinion polls that asked people about their attitudes, behaviors, and opinions. More broadly, new statistical categories and the gathering of new kinds of numbers enabled the entire edifice of modern "social sciences" to take shape. For example, the very idea of "the economy" was created through the invention of economic measures like gross domestic product (GDP) and unemployment rate in the mid-20th century. Before that, "people wouldn't have thought of their nation or their society or their own lives in terms of the collective material production of their country. And they would not have marked success or failure by a series of indicators."[139] While *economic activity* certainly occurred before "the invention of the economy,"[140] and while people of the 1800s and before routinely spoke of trade, markets, industry, exchange, and so forth,[141] the invention of broad-scale economic indicators allowed the conception of a single unified entity called "the economy," which created its own patterns, judgments, and motivations:

> Before there were metrics and indicators, "the economy" didn't exist. . . . Until the 1940s, there was no "the economy." People did not use the term and they had only just begun to think of the material affairs of a nation as a coherent and cohesive subject that could be defined, measured, and tracked over time.[142]

Economic measures were carefully *constructed* by an international group of statisticians and economists to be comparable everywhere, so that, for instance, now every country calculates GDP in basically the same way and comparisons between countries are therefore possible. At the same time, the economic measures to which

---

138. Rose, *The End of Average*, p. 32 ff.

139. Zachary Karabell, *The Leading Indicators: A Short History of the Numbers That Rule Our World*, p. 77.

140. Ibid., p. 73 (chapter title).

141. And mercantilists, among others, took action based on their sense of collective economic power, often defined by the boundaries of the nation-state.

142. Ibid., p. 78.

we pay attention value some things more than others, and simply do not "see" crucial kinds of human activity, such as unpaid housework and child care. That in turn makes such activities seem less valuable—even though they are foundational to individual lives and critical to a functioning society. Economic indicators also tend to miss the environmental consequences of economic activity.[143]

Side Note: Eugenics and Theoretical Statistics

It is not just the most basic forms of counting things that have made statistics deeply intertwined with the social world, but also the development of more elaborate forms of theoretical statistics, in particular the work surrounding three major figures in the field's early development: Francis Galton, Karl Pearson, and R. A. Fisher. All three statistical theorists were also committed eugenicists, and the sociologist Donald MacKenzie has written that especially in the cases of Galton and Pearson, there is good reason to believe this interest in eugenics, and the broader social concerns of an emerging professional class in Britain, exerted heavy influence on the kinds of statistics they developed.

Galton's seminal contributions, for instance, often focused on developing statistics to assess the heritability of various characteristics that could be selected for or against through eugenics: "Regression was originally a means of summing up how the expected characteristics of an offspring depended on those of its parents; the bivariate normal distribution [another well-known statistical tool today] was first constructed by Galton in an investigation of the joint distribution of parental and offspring characteristics."[144] Pearson's research group pursued "an integrated research programme in which the demands of eugenic research generated, and conditioned the solution of, particular technical problems."[145] Eugenics was thus interwoven with the creation of some of the statistics that are most familiar to social scientists and statisticians today.

The problems that motivate the development of new mathematical techniques affect the direction in which those techniques develop, and personal and social interests may play a significant role in influencing why one would choose a particular motivating problem. It is worth pausing to ask what kinds of knowledge are produced by these specific statistical tools—and what kinds of knowing might be enabled if we asked for different numbers.[146]

---

143. See, e.g., Al Gore, *The Future: Six Drivers of Global Change*, p. xiv.

144. Donald MacKenzie, "Statistical Theory and Social Interests: A Case-Study," *Social Studies of Science* 8, no. 1 (1978):53.

145. Ibid., p. 62; see also p. 66.

146. Consider what one sees by looking at the mean, the median, and the mode. Which one you choose, and what you choose to take data on in the first place, will depend on what question you want to ask—not unlike Bayesians versus frequentists as profiled under "Science" in chapter 4.

Projecting Numerical Information Wherever We Look

The cultural context of how statistics became ubiquitous is important for understanding universal histories in at least two ways. First, this context helps to characterize what is unique about the modern world. Statistics and the social sciences are not only useful for describing the modern world, but have themselves been important distinguishing features of what makes modernity different from other cultural systems, for better and for worse. As Anthony Giddens writes:

> The gathering of social statistics also enters in a fundamental way into the constitution of modern societies. Modern societies could not exist were their demographic characteristics not regularly charted and analysed. In the study of class divisions, bureaucracy, urbanism, religion, and many other areas, sociological concepts regularly enter our lives and help redefine them.[147]

Statistics themselves are, as we have shown, a distinctively modern phenomenon and a distinctively modern way of knowing the world. Likewise, the categories of thought created by a societal emphasis on statistics affect how we think about an immense range of topics. We create categories like "the economy" and "the average person" through the use of numbers. This is not to say that such categories are invalid, merely that they are historically situated and particular to our time. They are not self-evident or fixed categories, and presumably, people will not think in these terms forever, without further change. Talk of such ideas, in other words, may be the kind of disposition or tendency that "dates" a piece of writing in the way that historically particular terms, such as "outdated" idioms, often do.

Second, universal histories, with their emphasis on broad-based, large-scale patterns in human history, often work at the level of generalization afforded by statistics and the modern conceptual categories they enable. The modern world is a thoroughly quantified world, and universal histories often draw heavily on highly quantified disciplines in the natural and social sciences. But again, what we choose to quantify in the first place relates to what stories we want to tell, and whose stories. One measures what one is interested in knowing; one counts what one most cares about. And that can become a framing for the rest of reality. (To see two examples of graphical displays of statistics relevant to universal histories, see Plates 38 and 39.)

In our times, this means that what counts as information—as "reality"— is largely what can be counted. But while there are (countless?) advantages to having statistical information widely available, and to being able to think in statistical categories, it is important to realize that taken on their own, numbers and

---

147. Giddens, *Social Theory and Modern Sociology*, p. 21.

averages provide a very particular, and sometimes narrow, way of thinking about the world. Information of any sort is never devoid of interpretive framing. Just as the Information Age could equally well be called the Misinformation Age, statistics give powerful tools for both understanding and misunderstanding the world.

Purpose

Does life have a purpose? Does the universe?

Such questions may strike you as out of place, or at least unusual, in a scholarly and scientific work. Scientific writing more often features comments like this one, already quoted in chapter 2, from the physicist Steven Weinberg: "The more the universe seems comprehensible, the more it also seems pointless."[148] And if scientists and other scholars speak about purpose in the context of human life, they tend to view purpose in a way that is highly focused on the individual: any purpose a human life may have revolves around what is meaningful and fulfilling to the individual, perhaps according to that person's particular values and priorities, but there is no *overall* purpose of human life, no general "end" or purpose that human beings pursue or exist for the sake of. The physicist Sean Carroll writes that meaning and purpose "aren't built into the architecture of the universe; they emerge as ways of talking about our human-scale environment."[149]

When asked to explain why a natural phenomenon happened, modern scientists usually speak about mechanisms rather than purposes—about *how* the phenomenon happened, not what outcome was being pursued or why. Instead of saying that a ball falls to the ground because it is seeking its natural resting place, modern physicists talk about the mechanism of gravity, and how the gravitational attraction between the ball and the Earth makes the ball fall. Strictly speaking, it may still be the case that the ball "naturally" seeks a resting place and "uses" gravity to get there: physics does not address the question of what purpose or purposes gravitational attraction may ultimately serve. The physical sciences describe the regular patterns associated with how physical objects move and change; they do not concern themselves with any purposes that may be served by those motions and changes. In other words, a scientific analysis is typically an analysis of *means*, not *ends*.

It was not always so. For the ancient Greek philosopher Aristotle, and for the medieval philosophers inspired by his thinking, knowing the end or purpose to which something was directed was the centerpiece of a full understanding of any phenomenon. But the Western philosophical and scientific intellectual tradition has seen a marked diminishment, even intentional avoidance, of purpose-based

---

148. Steven Weinberg, *The First Three Minutes*, p. 154.

149. Sean Carroll, *The Big Picture: On the Origins of Life, Meaning, and the Universe Itself*, p. 389.

Side Note: Philosophy in Modernity

The exclusion of purpose-based explanations in modern thought can be seen as part of the larger story of philosophy losing its central place in the modern intellectual world. In the premodern world, intellectuals interested in big universal questions were almost all well-versed in philosophy. And the classical philosophical traditions of the world—Western, Chinese, Indian, Islamic, and many others—present a rich terrain of people who have debated how the universe works in ways that are widely ignored today, by scientists as well as by most other people, even though their perspectives are often still relevant, valuable, and capable of seriously challenging modern ways of thinking about the world. This is why we bring some of their perspectives and ideas to bear in the "philosophical sections" that sit at the end of each chapter in this book.

---

explanations in the modern period. So while the range of meanings associated with the words "system" and "statistics" have steadily expanded in recent centuries, the concept of "purpose" now structures the thinking of scientists and philosophers far *less* than it typically did before, making the *rejection* of purpose-based explanations a characteristic of much modern thought.

In this section, we consider why purpose-based explanations have fallen out of favor in the modern period, why ideas about purpose are actually still more widely present in science and history than one might think (even though they are usually hidden), and what the idea of purpose—if called explicitly back into view—might contribute to modern universal histories.

A Brief History of Purpose in (Western) Philosophy

Aristotle laid many of the foundations for the "philosophy of nature" or "natural philosophy," the area of philosophical study in the ancient and medieval Western tradition that considered how the natural world works and what properties the entities present in nature have. Scientific inquiry in the modern world grew out of medieval Christian and Islamic natural philosophy, while strongly altering Aristotle's understanding of the proper way to go about explaining natural phenomena. Perhaps the major area of difference between the Aristotelian approach and the modern scientific one is in how to understand the *cause* of such phenomena, including change over time in animate beings and inanimate objects.

---

150. David C. Lindberg, *The Beginnings of Western Science*, p. 51.

Aristotle's approach to understanding the nature of change over time recognized four kinds of causes for any change. Here, the word "cause" has a broader meaning than it usually does today, and it includes all the "explanatory conditions and factors"[150] collectively responsible for a change. The classic example given by Aristotle is the making of a statue: One can ask, what caused the statue to come into being the way it did? The *material cause* is the material out of which the statue was formed, perhaps marble or bronze. The *formal cause* is the shape or pattern into which the matter was formed. The *efficient cause* is the agent that produced the change: in this case, the sculptor. The *final cause* is the purpose or end for which it was made, perhaps the beautification of a temple. Without all of these "causes," the statue would not have turned out the way it did.

Aristotle and his successors applied this framework beyond the human world to animals, plants, and inanimate objects. A comprehensive understanding of any event or pattern—like the ripening of a tomato,[151] or the development of an oak tree from an acorn—needs to consider *out of what, into what, by what,* and *for the sake of what* something was made: material, formal, efficient, and final causes, respectively.[152] Final cause is the end, purpose, aim, or goal of a phenomenon;[153] it is the "end result"[154] that a change is driving toward or is "ordered to." How things take shape over time is thus driven by the purpose of the change, as when an acorn undergoes an immense array of developmental changes at the molecular, cellular, and organismal levels *in order to* become an oak tree, or when heavy objects fall *in order to* move toward their natural place. As commentators on Aristotle have often put it, "nature acts for an end."[155] The end is realized through efficient causes, but final cause is what drives the efficient causes to act in the way that they do.

A general sense of purpose in accounting for the order of the natural world is present across many philosophical traditions in the world. But Aristotle's system has, arguably, the most fully articulated sense of purposes or ends present throughout the natural world: "Aristotle went so far as to give final cause priority over material cause, noting that the purpose of the saw determines the material (iron) of which it must be made, whereas the fact that we possess a piece of iron does nothing to determine that we will make it into a saw."[156]

---

151. Example from Mortimer J. Adler, *Aristotle for Everybody: Difficult Thought Made Easy*, pp. 44–45.

152. Adler, *Aristotle for Everybody*, p. 42.

153. The term "final" cause is derived from Latin word *finis*, meaning "goal," "purpose," or "end." (Lindberg, *The Beginnings of Western Science*, p. 52.)

154. Adler, *Aristotle for Everybody*, p. 45.

155. Thomas Aquinas, *Commentary on Aristotle's* Physics, Lecture 12 [198b10-33], #250, https://isidore.co/aquinas/english/Physics2.htm .

156. Lindberg, *The Beginnings of Western Science*, p. 52.

Modern thinkers usually speak of purpose as something that must be *intended* by an *agent*, but Aristotle's "teleology" (meaning purpose-laden philosophy; from the Greek word *telos*, which means "end" in the sense of "aim," "objective," or "goal") was not so much "external" as "internal," a distinction articulated by the philosopher Michael Ruse.[157] External teleology involves a mind that intends something to come about in the future, as when a human decides to boil water for the sake of making tea. Internal teleology like Aristotle's, however, involves intrinsic ends that are built into how the world works. The acorn could be said to pursue the goal of becoming an oak, but it is not doing so consciously, or because this "project" was necessarily imposed upon it from outside, but because it is *within its nature* to grow and develop into an oak. The future outcome of becoming an oak may not be *consciously intended*, but it could be said to drive all the changes that an acorn undergoes, which are intrinsic to its nature. As the historian of science David Lindberg has written:

> The world of Aristotle is not the inert, mechanistic world of the atomists, in which the individual atom pursues its own course mindless of all others. Aristotle's world is not a world of chance and coincidence, but an orderly, organized world, a world of purpose, in which things develop toward ends determined by their natures.[158]

Modern scientific thought does not proceed in this way. Instead, it tends to recognize efficient causes (like gravity, in the case of a falling ball, or reproductive and cellular processes, in the case of the acorn developing into an oak) and material causes (the matter of which the ball or acorn is made). But the language of forms (meaning a thing's essence or essential nature[159]) and formal causes has largely been replaced by a reductive approach that investigates the particles of which a thing is made, focusing on parts rather than wholes.[160] And final causes are usually not part of modern scientific analysis at all, at least not explicitly. Instead, scientific explanations of anything today, from stars to organisms, usually focus on the matter of which the thing is made and on the laws to which that matter is subject: "matter and motion" have taken the place of forms and ends.

---

157. Michael Ruse, *On Purpose*, pp. 1–2.

158. Lindberg, *The Beginnings of Western Science*, p. 52.

159. A "form" is a thing's essence or essential nature, "properties that make the thing what it is" (Lindberg, *The Beginnings of Western Science*, p. 47), disposing it to behave in a certain way, as "star-ness" makes a star behave like a star, or "oak-ness" makes an oak tree behave like an oak. The word "form" is somewhat abstract and technical, but it appears in some very familiar words, like "inform" and "transform": to trans-"form" is to give materials a new form that they did not previously have. (Adler, *Aristotle for Everybody*, p. 43.)

160. See "Reductionism" in chapter 3.

Why did this change occur? When and where did it happen, and who originated it? Early modern European thinkers between the 1500s and 1700s ceased to regard entities in the natural world as having intrinsic natures connected with purposes they strive toward. Part of the reason is that, as the English philosopher Francis Bacon argued in the 1500s and 1600s, the idea of (especially) final cause did not seem *useful* for understanding how to manipulate and control natural processes, which he and others regarded as the primary goal of science. Understanding how nature operates in its normal course is one thing, and Bacon never fully denied the existence of final causality in nature.[161] But Bacon, as a new kind of philosopher, was interested in the control and manipulation of nature,[162] and experiments isolating specific chains of (efficient) cause and effect were much more useful for that purpose, even if such experiments took phenomena out of their natural contexts and put them into a laboratory setting. Final causes as they operated in their natural contexts could not be manipulated in this way, only understood on their own terms.[163] Many early modern Western thinkers, including Bacon as well as Descartes, Boyle, Hobbes, Locke, and Hume, agreed that if knowledge is to be useful, one can generally ignore final cause. As Ruse explains, "A planet goes round and round the Sun; you want to know the mechanism by which it happens, not to imagine some higher purpose for it. In the same way, when you look at a clock you want to know what makes the hands go round the dial—you want the proximate causes."[164]

The principle of inertia in Newtonian mechanics also played a role in the overthrow of Aristotle's teleological explanations of motion. While Aristotle explained movement in terms of substances trying to reach their natural places (like earth / dirt moving downward to its natural place, which he regarded as the center of the Earth), Newton recognized that matter in motion tends to stay in motion, and he explained apparent "falling" motions in terms of gravitational attraction between bodies. There seemed to be no further need to invoke purposes or ends.

---

161. See, e.g., Étienne Gilson, *From Aristotle to Darwin and Back Again: A Journey in Final Causality, Species, and Evolution*, p. 23; see also David Bentley Hart, *The Experience of God: Being, Consciousness, Bliss*, p. 56.

162. "The knowledge of Causes, and secret motions of things; and the enlarging of the bounds of Human Empire, to the effecting of all things possible." (Francis Bacon, *New Atlantis*, in *Francis Bacon: The Major Works*, ed. Brian Vickers, p. 480.)

163. Cf. Gilson, *From Aristotle to Darwin and Back Again*, p. 23. Note that purpose is not a "testable" concept in the usual modern-scientific sense, but then again, neither is causation itself. The early-modern philosopher David Hume even went so far as to deny that belief in causation can be rationally justified. Specifically, he argued that effects do not follow causes by any kind of metaphysical necessity but only appear to do so, because some things are correlated and happen together. Most scientists and philosophers today are not deeply convinced by this argument, and concepts like causation are routinely used by modern science—and are arguably necessary. But not all of the concepts by which we make sense of the world are testable.

164. Michael Ruse, "Does Life Have a Purpose?," https://aeon.co/essays/what-s-a-stegosaur-for-why-life-is-design-like .

That said, the philosopher and historian of philosophy Lynn Joy argues that "the decline of explanations in terms of the four causes" did not occur "because the new conception of scientific explanation was shown to be rationally superior to Aristotle's conception."[165] Rather, the detailed debates of early modern natural philosophy made these concepts difficult to work with from a practical standpoint. As Lindberg writes, "It would be unfair and pointless to judge Aristotle's success by the degree to which he anticipated modern science (as though his goal was to answer our questions, rather than his own); it is nonetheless worth noting that the emphasis on functional explanation to which Aristotle's teleology leads would prove to be of profound significance for all of the sciences and remains to this day a dominant mode of explanation within the biological sciences."[166] Aristotle's questions were not our questions: he wanted to know how things worked *in their natural context*. Experimental science that seeks to understand mechanistic causation through laboratory manipulation outside of natural contexts would tend to miss the presence of teleology in nature even if it is there, focusing instead on how the "clock" keeps ticking (material and efficient causes) rather than on what the purpose (final cause) of the ticking is—although understanding the clock's purpose, to keep track of time, would be crucial if one wanted a full understanding of *why* the clock was ticking in the first place.

Purpose in Biology

Modern science and technology are the product of the kind of highly interconnected globe we traced earlier in this chapter (in the section on "Connection"), with roots and influences coming from many different regions. China, in particular, long ago produced a myriad of technological innovations that dazzled visitors and that have been chronicled at length by historians.[167] Many of the mathematical, scientific, and technical achievements of the ancient world were preserved and extended by Islamic scholars, only later slowly percolating to Europe and other areas. Once these connections helped such work to expand in the lands of Christendom, though, many of the approaches and philosophical underpinnings of what we today define as "science" took shape in early modern Europe. In short, the influence of Bacon and company was a contingent development. The philosophical foundations of modern science did not "have" to unfold the way they did—and present-day critics as diverse as Seyyed Hossein Nasr, Leon Kass, and Étienne Gilson (coming from Islamic, Jewish / humanistic, and

---

165. Lynn S. Joy, "Scientific Explanation from Formal Causes to Laws of Nature," in *The Cambridge History of Science*, eds. Katharine Park and Lorraine Daston, p. 73; original text is in italics.

166. Lindberg, *The Beginnings of Western Science*, p. 52.

167. See, e.g., Joseph Needham, *Science and Civilization in China*, many volumes, starting in the 1950s.

Christian intellectual traditions, respectively) have heavily criticized the effects of building science around the pursuit of control over nature and ignoring final cause.

Be that as it may, the actual dominant philosophical assumptions of modern science tend to default to a vision of the world as consisting of purposeless particles in purposeless (but "law-governed") motion, and physicists like Weinberg and Carroll draw on that vision when making declarations about the purposelessness of the universe. Yet despite such pronouncements, scientists and historians today still make implicit references to purpose and teleology in many fields that contribute to universal history. Probably the most prominent example of this, and the easiest place to see it, is in biology.

Biologists still routinely speak of purpose (and "function") as having a prominent place in the living world. The Nobel laureate Jacques Monod writes (in a book that otherwise speaks strongly against emphasizing purpose and final cause in the living world) that "the natural organ, the eye, represents the materialization of a 'purpose'—that of picking up images"[168] and that "one of the fundamental characteristics common to all living beings without exception [is] that of being *objects endowed with a purpose or project*."[169] He sees this kind of purpose as "essential to the very definition of living beings" and calls it "teleonomy."[170] He writes, "Objectivity . . . obliges us to recognize the teleonomic character of living organisms, to admit that in their structure and performance they decide on and pursue a purpose."[171] The physicist Vlatko Vedral writes, "Living things . . . appear to have a will of their own. They are best understood—perhaps even best defined—by what might be called purposiveness. They try to do things, and while they cannot violate the laws of nature, they certainly can exploit them in order to realise their goals."[172]

We could go further. Living things seem to have a *unity* of being beyond their parts, and they act toward ends. As Michael Ruse writes, "The parts of organisms serve the ends of the whole organism."[173] This is perhaps most evident in the development of seeds and embryos into mature plants and animals, and in the ongoing development and maintenance of the whole organism that continues throughout life:

It's a worthwhile exercise to keep this in mind while imagining whether a single, fertilized egg cell could, in any machine-like manner, determine

---

168. Jacques Monod, *Chance and Necessity*, p. 20.

169. Ibid., italics in original.

170. Ibid., p. 20.

171. Ibid., p. 31.

172. Vlatko Vedral, "What Life Wants," https://aeon.co/essays/across-the-wide-gulf-how-to-get-life-out-of-quantum-physics .

173. Ruse, *On Purpose*, p. 83.

or compute its own elaboration into the tissues, organs, and overall form of a developing, trillion-celled human being—and continue that precise, bottom-up, machine-like determination over several decades while repairing wounds, healing injuries, and adjusting to every new circumstance from minute to minute and year to year. And, of course, the machine design of that single, original cell would also have to provide for the actual performance of heart, liver, brain, and other organs, with their infinitely complex, moment-by-moment, mutual adjustment.[174]

The author of these words, Stephen Talbott, likewise points out, "All biological activity, even at the molecular level, can be characterized as purposive and goal-directed."[175] For example, speaking of "defects" in DNA replication and "errors" in gene expression is implicitly teleological: for something to be a *mistake*, there has to be a goal, since "physical interactions as such never *err*."[176] Talbott concludes that "purposiveness . . . is inseparable from life as such—you could almost say it defines those self-organizing, self-maintaining, and self-expressive activities we call 'living.'"[177]

The Advantages and Disadvantages of Including Purpose

Across the natural sciences and history, there are advantages and disadvantages of thinking with a purpose-based mindset.

The biggest shortfall of thinking in this way is that if you believe you know how the story ends, you may tell it in a way that ignores everything that does not lead to that ending. And that will leave out many other things, including actors or stories that might turn out to be essential. In other words, even if there really is an ultimate purpose to something, you may misidentify that purpose and miss important aspects of the story. Partly for this reason, historians are wary of teleological histories written as though the purpose of the past was to get to "us"—whether "us" means modern global society with capitalism and democracy[178] and computer

---

174. Stephen L. Talbott, "Evolution and the Purposes of Life," https://www.thenewatlantis. com/publications/evolution-and-the-purposes-of-life . Such behavior shows us, as Talbott puts it (drawing on E.S. Russell), that "*the purposive end is more constant than the physical means.*"

175. Ibid.

176. Ibid., italics added.

177. Ibid. Aristotle spent many years in intense study of living organisms, and may have been inspired to apply final cause widely through this set of experiences.

178. As in some of Francis Fukuyama's work, which identifies a condition of widespread liberal democracy as the "end of history," by which he did not mean that nothing more would happen, but that there would be no further "stage shifts" of human society. This suggestion, even with its caveats and qualifications, has been much criticized.

technology, or whatever one's favorite aspect of the present is. This is problematic insofar as it makes the present-day world seem inevitable, funneling everything into a single narrative and failing to properly account for contingency. As mentioned earlier in this chapter, the historian Herbert Butterfield famously pointed out that this combination of progress, purpose, and presentism makes for sloppy thinking about the past.

An analogous example from the realm of natural science, rather than human history, comes from the study of the nucleic acid RNA (see "Life" in chapter 4) and the roles it plays in the cell. For many years after its discovery, RNA was thought to serve as an intermediary in "translating" DNA blueprints into protein molecules. This is certainly a major role that RNA plays, but a considerable amount of RNA in cells does *not* participate in translation. In part because they thought of RNA as having just one particular purpose, biologists considered that this other RNA had no function in the cell—and even labeled it "junk RNA." But it turns out that this supposed "junk" actually performs a variety of functions that at the time were unknown.[179] Arguably, identifying the purpose of RNA too narrowly led cell biologists to miss significant parts of the overall picture of RNA's importance to the cell.

Similarly, in the evolutionary history of life, simple teleological progress narratives are problematic: "Extracting a single evolutionary progression from the fossil record can be misleading . . . it is like describing a bush as growing toward a single point by tracing only the branches that lead to that twig."[180] (See Figure 4.2.) The mechanism of natural selection provides explanations not in terms of future goals, but in terms of present environmental constraints. Accordingly, the evolutionary biologist Ernst Mayr stated that "adaptedness . . . is an a posteriori [after-the-fact] result rather than an a priori [preordained] goal-seeking."[181] Questions like "Why did humans become bipedal?" or "Why did brains develop?" are usually answered with proximate explanations, not with grand, overriding purposes.[182] Populations of organisms adapt to their surroundings, but they do not evolve toward some overall common goal identifiable to biology.

On the other hand, there are also many good reasons why teleological language and reasoning about purpose persist in both the sciences and history. In human history, after all, humans certainly *think* they pursue purposes—intentionally!—both

---

179. For details, see "Biochemistry" in chapter 4.

180. Neil A. Campbell et al., *Biology* (8th Edition), p. 531.

181. Ernst Mayr, "The Idea of Teleology," *Journal of the History of Ideas* 53, no. 1 (992):131.

182. Part of the reason is that grand, overriding purposes tend to deny the reality that things usually exist for more than one purpose. That is true even of obviously purposive artifacts of human making, and it is certainly true in an ecosystem.

individually and collectively.[183] And the biological world also presents many situations where thinking in terms of purpose is so helpful for understanding organisms that it is difficult to make sense of life, at any scale, entirely without it. Using ideas of purpose to understand life can lead scientists to discover things they might not have identified otherwise. The RNA example, for instance, shows that assuming the absence of purpose just because science has not yet identified something as being purposeful does not mean that it really is purposeless.

In evolutionary biology, where ideas about purpose may be most fraught, there are still good reasons to explicitly consider purpose. One reason is that the overarching Darwinian framework of natural selection leaves the ultimate origin of any teleological character of organisms largely unexplained. Most notably, it invokes survival and reproduction as given realities of life, but survival (self-maintenance) and reproduction are themselves *purposes* that organisms—all organisms—pursue. This is foundational, definitional, in the very category of "life." It is not that individual organisms "want" to evolve. But consciously or unconsciously, individual organisms do pursue purposes in surviving and reproducing, purposes that are basic to life at every level: cellular, organismal, species, and ecosystem. According to a founding figure in evolutionary biology, Theodosius Dobzhansky, "Living beings have an *internal*, or natural, teleology."[184] There is therefore a key sort of intrinsic goal-directedness. Or as J. B. S. Haldane, another founder of the modern evolutionary synthesis, quipped, "Teleology is like a mistress to a biologist: he cannot live without her but he's unwilling to be seen with her in public."[185]

The value of purpose-based thinking may extend to the physical sciences as well, although it can be harder to see. Ruse comments, "Nobody expects atoms and molecules to have purposes,"[186] and yet one could argue that atoms, the building blocks of matter, are perfectly ordered to be precisely that: the building blocks of matter. They are stable because the charge on the electron matches the charge on the proton, among many other properties; this basic fact is not something that any current fundamental theory of physics explains, but rather takes as a given. The structure of an atomic nucleus, including both protons and neutrons, allows the formation of different elements. The ability of a nucleus to undergo fission and fusion has allowed the creation of all manner of new elements in stars. It is completely consistent with

---

183. These purposes are multiple, and they often conflict with one another. There also are often unintended consequences of a given person or group's purposes. The possibility of unintended consequences is part of what makes it sensible to consider whether other purposes are being worked out—from Marxist structures to divine providence.

184. Quoted in Talbott, "Evolution and the Purposes of Life"; italics in source.

185. Quoted in Ernst Mayr, *Toward a New Philosophy of Biology: Observations of an Evolutionist*, p. 63, citing personal correspondence with Colin Pittendrigh.

186. Ruse, "Does Life Have a Purpose?"

everything we know about atoms to say that their *purpose* is to be the stable, fundamental building block of ordinary matter. Final cause can, in this way, throw light on why the atom is the way it is.[187]

Purpose, the Universe, and Emergence

On the largest scales, what does the idea of purpose mean for the universe? Are there grand purposes built into the cosmos itself? To begin investigating this question, imagine the early universe, a sea of particles almost identical in all directions. It is a striking fact, more than a little startling when one stops to think about it deeply, that this soup of particles had the *ability*, or the *potential*, to turn into the universe as we know it today, the home of all manner of entities, including animate and intelligent living things. The particles in the early universe *could* be shaped into stars, or rocks, or oceans, or flowers; we know this because that is what happened. And the fact that they were—and are—the sorts of things that could do that is not trivial: their particular physical properties made this the case, and almost every other conceivable arrangement of the early universe would have lacked this potentiality. Pause and consider that for a moment. Neutrons alone, for example, could never have become even a single planet, anywhere in the universe, without the existence of protons and electrons. Changes in the laws of physics could have resulted in the impossibility of all structure in the universe.

As we saw in chapter 3, universal-historical frameworks like David Christian's in *Maps of Time* often explain how entities in the universe came to be using the paradigm of "emergence," in which stars, planets, and life are built up over time from smaller building blocks. This pattern of "creative evolution," which continues to build on whatever things are already present in the universe at a given time, makes no explicit reference to purposes or teleology, relying only on mechanistic causation and the fact that some arrangements of particles (like stars or brown bears) turn out to be stable over some identifiable period of time. In this picture, there is no real point in asking the purpose-laden question "What is it all *for*"?

It is clear from the physical evidence that the universe really has taken its current shape in a gradual way, with smaller particles combining into larger wholes. That much, science makes clear. But as we have seen so many times in this book, the same set of facts can look very different if placed into different interpretive framings. How do the facts in this case look different if we consider the possibility that emergence has happened not because of pure mechanistic causation, but because purpose is "built in" to how the universe works just as much as the laws of physics are?

We might start to consider this question by remembering a property of the universe that we have seen throughout this book: its order and intelligibility. At every

---

187. Thanks to Lakhi Goenka for many observations and insights about atoms.

scale in space and time, the universe is not mere chaos, but rather an ordered whole—a *cosmos* (from the Greek root *kosmos*, which means "order").[188] While the details are sometimes formidably complicated, there is order and intelligibility all the way down, and also all the way up; the universe at both small and large scales "is more like a book than like an explosion in a print factory."[189] Without the basic intelligibility of things, universal history and the fields that comprise it would be impossible.

As the portrait of the early universe sketched here suggests, complexity and differentiation were not always the rule in the universe, but even the universe's infancy had a great deal of *order* to it—including the ordering principles we call "laws of physics"—and the *potential* for new forms of order to emerge over time. In other words, there was never a state of the universe in which mere chaos reigned; there was just an early time when much of the order was hidden, incipient, and potential rather than apparent and actual. (Framing the evolution of the universe in this way is consistent with the original meaning of the word "evolution," which comes from the Latin *evolvere*, meaning "to roll out" or "to unroll."[190] The original sense of "evolution" was one of "unrolling what already existed or maturing what was already preformed,"[191] not the emergence of something radically different and new. Looking at its roots, the phrase "cosmic evolution" could be taken to mean the *maturing of incipient order*.)

In short, the universe's order was there, in some sense, from the beginning. But arguably, this kind of always-already-there order sits uncomfortably within a purely mechanistic, "matter and motion" picture of reality, for order and ends usually go together. In the experience of human beings and other living things, purpose results in order. For example, a strong mission statement is intended to serve as the organizing principle of why a corporation is ordered the way it is; likewise, the purpose of eating eucalyptus leaves orders a koala's actions. And conversely, order is an indication of purpose: when we observe the order of a business, or an army, or a musical composition, or a plant's motion toward sunlight, we readily conclude that purposes are being pursued, consciously or unconsciously. Stable order often seems to be present for the sake of something; there is only a small step from "order" to "in order to."

---

188. Incidentally, this is why "cosmos" sounds like "cosmetic," and why cosmologists occasionally get confused with cosmetologists; *kosmos* also meant "ornamentation," hence the English word "cosmetic" has the same Greek root as "cosmos."

189. Peter Kreeft, "The Modern Scholar: The Philosophy of Thomas Aquinas," Recorded Books: 2009, Lecture 3, p. 20, in the reference guide available for download at https://www.audible.com/pd/The-Modern-Scholar-The-Philosophy-of-Thomas-Aquinas-Audiobook/B002UZHPWY .

190. The vehicle manufacturer Volvo takes its name from the Latin word meaning "I roll," a conjugation of *volvere*, "to roll."

191. Raymond Williams, *Keywords: A Vocabulary of Culture and Society* (New Edition), pp. 79–80.

Is it anthropomorphic or anthropocentric to draw this connection between order and purpose not only for the human and living worlds, but for the universe as well? Perhaps. But in some ways, the universe is more like us, and we are more like the universe, than people realized before modern science. The same laws of physics hold for the heavens and the Earth, and human bodies are made of the same atoms as comets and interstellar dust. In a way, bringing back the principle that "nature acts for an end" is a continuation, not an interruption, of this process of bringing together the character of life on Earth and the character of the universe within which that life exists.

A teleological framing for universal history would represent a serious philosophical paradigm shift. But positing inherent purpose in the universe, in the Aristotelian sense, arguably makes better sense of the inherent order in the universe—at all scales—than does positing only mechanistic causation. Perhaps at least one purpose of the universe is to bring forth life, on at least one planet and maybe elsewhere. As mentioned in chapter 2, the physicist Freeman Dyson has been quoted as saying: "As we look out into the Universe and identify the many accidents of physics and astronomy that have worked together to our benefit, it almost seems as if the Universe must in some sense have known that we were coming."[192] (Or making a similar point, the cosmologist Edward Robert Harrison once quipped, "Hydrogen is a light, odorless gas, which, given enough time, turns into people."[193]) If complex and living things emerge, perhaps it is because the universe was ordered toward complexity and life from the beginning.

This kind of explanation has the seemingly unusual feature of (apparently) reverse causation: the end dictates the means. The kind of "forward-looking"[194] causation implied by such a proposition, in which events happen the way they do because they are driving toward a certain kind of outcome, is exactly what the Aristotelian notion of final cause implies but is usually considered anathema to modern science. On the other hand, if we acknowledge that human purposes result in some events driving toward a certain outcome, and if we find reason to characterize other living things as teleological in many regards, it seems reasonable enough

---

192. Different versions of this quote appear in different places. This one is the version in John D. Barrow and Frank J. Tipler, *The Anthropic Cosmological Principle*, p. 318. A somewhat different version is quoted in Bill Bryson, *A Short History of Nearly Everything*, p. 237.

193. This is not a denial of contingency. There is a kind of openness in the way the universe develops, and perhaps many potentialities, but the range of possibilities is not unlimited. This is true as well in the development of oak from acorn. Development in the biological world is open to many influences and contingencies. An organism's DNA provides a certain level of preprogramming, but an acorn in fertile soil with consistent rainfall will develop very differently than one in a dry and arid land. It is not that one, and only one, end is contained in the beginning, but that a range of available possibilities, activated by historically contingent processes, is present from the start.

194. Ruse, *On Purpose*, p. 1.

to suspect that purpose could be embedded in how things work at an even more fundamental level.

There would be no threat to the scientific enterprise in admitting the possibility of teleological explanation in this sense, or of invoking final cause as an interpretive framework. The physical sciences still have their domain, not at all in danger, of identifying and explaining material and efficient causes. As Aristotle recognized long ago, final causes call forth efficient causes, as when the purpose of developing into an oak tree calls forth scientifically comprehensible mechanisms of cellular development in an acorn. Final causes also call forth material causes, as when the purpose of a saw dictates the matter of which it will be made. So too, perhaps the purpose of the universe dictates what matter it "needs" to include. Science takes the chunk of this particular pie that can be explained mechanistically. But there could be a different, and arguably bigger, picture that is not purely or solely mechanistic.

The mathematician and philosopher Alfred North Whitehead once commented, "Scientists animated by the purpose of proving that they are purposeless constitute an interesting subject for study."[195] Science can help us analyze how the cellular processes in an acorn proceed in order to develop into an oak, and it can go into great detail regarding how gravity operates. Yet there are other, larger questions, such as the purpose of life and the universe, that science does not touch. This does not mean science fails, but neither does it mean that those questions do not matter. Modern thinkers understand many aspects of the universe's workings through science, in great and continually expanding detail, yet they may miss major parts of the larger picture if they never consider purpose. At the very least, considering the possibility will cast a new, enriching, complementary light on the universe, and perhaps on our place within it.

---

195. Alfred North Whitehead, *The Function of Reason*, p. 16 (Beacon Press 1958 edition, book originally published in 1929). This often-quoted line comes in the context of Whitehead's critique of the "anti-empirical dogmatism" (p. 15) that leads scientists to dismiss purpose and final causation.

8 FUTURE

This chapter takes the framework developed in the rest of this book and applies it to the future—to the parts of universal history that have not yet happened. In "Future," we consider how experts go about making predictions of the short-term, medium-term, and long-term future, and to what extent these predictions should be seen as valid anticipations of the shape of things to come. In "Progress," we look at narratives of progress and decline, and ask whether directional narratives of this sort are helpful as a framework for thinking about what the future may hold. In "Sustainability" and "Transhumanism," we analyze two important themes that often appear in big-picture analyses of the future: environmental trends and technologies of human modification. We conclude with a multidisciplinary philosophical contemplation of the character of "Time" itself.

Future

Universal histories are primarily concerned with the broad sweep of the past and how that connects to the present: how the universe, Earth, life, and humanity came to be the way they are today. But history does not stop at the present moment, and universal histories also act as a springboard for contemplating the future. Some authors go so far as to imply that gaining insight about the future is the primary reason why people should care about history in general, or universal histories in particular.

An understanding of the past may certainly enable more insightful thinking about the future. But it is not just a matter of establishing which processes and trends have dominated the past and then extrapolating those into the future, or of learning from past mistakes so as not to repeat them. Instead, to think clearly about the future, its parameters, and its possibilities, apply the same approach that you would to think clearly about the past: develop a rigorous and reliable approach to thinking about causes and consequences, about constraints and contingencies, and about change over time.

Developing such an approach has been the major objective of this book. That is why we keep coming back to themes like causality, scale, discipline, and the relationship between "information" and "interpretation." We have argued that understanding the "how" and "why" of change over time—whether at the level of the universe, Earth, life, or humanity—requires an appreciation of how multiple causes, operating simultaneously at different scales, contribute to shaping virtually every historical event or process. We have focused on how the "lenses" of disciplines from cosmology to anthropology to history to sociology inform, shape, and also limit how experts construct explanations of historical change. We have provided many examples of how the same raw evidence can be interpreted in multiple ways, and put to the service of very different grand stories about how today's world has come to be. These same themes apply to the future just as much as they do to the past.

What Makes Something Predictable?

To what extent can evidence-based scholarship speak about the future? Is the future meaningfully predictable? One might argue, as many historians do, that the future is too unpredictable to justify contemplating it in any detail. This is surely true for many aspects of the future: If human agency matters, as we have argued it does, then there is an irreducible element of uncertainty in the prediction of any future that involves human choices and human action.[1] And if we remember that removing a single person from the world several thousand years ago could result in an entirely different set of people being alive today—as explored at the beginning of chapter 6—the prospects of being able to accurately envision any specifics of the long-term human future seem very dim indeed. Even in contemplating the relatively near-term future, many past predictions have been wildly off the mark, as in the case of early-20th-century predictions of soon-to-come socialist utopias or the end of war, or mid-20th-century predictions about soon-to-exist flying cars and two-day workweeks. And the "butterfly effect" (the principle, mentioned in chapter 3, that systems often display "chaotic" behavior where tiny differences in initial conditions lead to vastly different outcomes) seems to drive a nail into the coffin of predictability even in the non-human, natural world.

But while due caution and humility are always appropriate when thinking about the future, unpredictability does not always have the final word. First, some systems are *simple* enough, and have been confirmed as such to a sufficiently high

---

1. "Either something or nothing must depend on individual choices. And if something, who could set bounds to it?" (C. S. Lewis, *Perelandra*, p. 121.)

degree of confidence, that a good degree of predictability is possible even over very long time scales. The planets of the Solar System have stayed in stable orbits for billions of years, for instance, and we can reasonably expect them to remain in place for another billion or more. (From our perspective on Earth, we could say that it is reasonably safe to predict that the Sun will keep rising every morning for a good long time.) This is possible in part because very little about planetary orbits is actually complicated, and very little (as far as we know) could conceivably interfere with these orbits for a long time to come. The *regularity* or *periodicity* of the system, confirmed many times, adds to our confidence in its predictability.

Second, some past and present trends—again, especially those on large spatial and temporal scales—are also stable enough that they can be extrapolated into the future, with a level of confidence that may be less than perfect but that is still much greater than pure guesswork. Population and demography provide a good example: Based on current population trends (birth rates, death rates, etc.) in different parts of the world, experts can forecast how many people will be alive in, say, the year 2060. While any such forecast has a wide margin of error, and a global catastrophe like a nuclear war or meteorite impact could render these forecasts completely wrong, an informed estimate of the world population in 2060 could well turn out to be more

---

Side Note: Futurologists

Perhaps surprisingly, there is an academic field devoted to the study of the future, which is called "futurology" or "futures studies." The word "futures" here is plural because one cannot study "the future," given that it does not yet exist; one can only study potential futures. In fact, futurologists often refer to their field as being concerned with "3 p's and a w": possible futures, probable futures, preferable futures, and wildcards. We can simplify this scheme to "trends" and wildcards. Trends are historical patterns one can identify from observing the past and the present and trying to understand how they could extend into the future. Wildcards are departures, or twists in the story: the events or patterns that are difficult or impossible to anticipate based on the past and present, but that could derail the trends, for better or worse, and affect many aspects of the future.

Futurology, as a field, has a mixed reputation. Although its practitioners attempt to parallel the discipline of history in offering rigorous, evidence-based interpretations and predictions of the future, experts in disciplines like history or physics often view the methodologies and claims of futurologists as much less robust than those of their own discipline. This chapter engages with ideas about the future primarily through the established scientific and historical disciplines we have been engaging with throughout this book, making it a multidisciplinary exploration of ideas about the future rather than an exploration of futurology in its disciplinary particulars.

accurate than your personal estimate of how many children you will eventually have (at least for readers who are not yet past their reproductive life spans). Depending on how old you are now, the latter estimate could relatively easily be off by a factor of three or more, dependent as it is on a host of human choices and unforeseeable circumstances, while the worldwide estimate is arguably less likely to be off by so much, dependent as it is on aggregated human trends and patterns that are less likely to change as radically as the course of individual human lives.

Causality and Scale

How do such oases of relative or partial predictability fit into the larger landscape of the future? David Christian has argued that distinct levels of predictability are associated with short-term, medium-term, and long-term futures. By his definition, short-term futures look out to the next hundred years or so, medium-term futures look out to the next several thousand years, and long-term futures project millions or billions of years or more. Put differently, short-term futures concern time scales of 1 or 2 human life spans from the present, medium-term futures perhaps 10 to 1,000 human life spans, and long-term futures far more than 1,000 human life spans. (See Table 8.1.) Christian argues that the short term is difficult to predict, although certain trends will likely continue; that the medium term is almost purely speculative, because it will likely be dominated by unpredictable "wildcards"; and perhaps counterintuitively, that the long-term is actually easiest to predict in certain key regards, because the very long-term future relies on processes that are stable over millions to billions of years. For example, continental drift has been proceeding at roughly the same rate for millions of years and can be expected to continue, the life cycles of stars are regular and predictable, and the fate of the future expansion of the universe ultimately seems to rest on only a small number of variables.[2]

Christian has an insightful point here, but it should not be misunderstood as indicating that the long term is inherently more predictable than the short term. Quite the opposite, in fact: anything that is predictable in the long term is even *more*

Table 8.1 Short-Term, Medium-Term, and Long-Term Trends

Term	Length	Examples in This Section
Short	1–2 human life spans	Climate change
Medium	10–1,000 human life spans	Technology, biodiversity
Long	>1,000 human life spans	Plate tectonics, future of the Sun, future of the expanding universe

2. See David Christian, *Maps of Time*, pp. 467–491.

predictable in the short term and the medium term. For example, if we want to know the position of the continents, or where the planets will be in their orbits, or what state the Sun or the universe will be in, we can be more confident of the answer if we are predicting 10 years into the future than if we are predicting 10 million years into the future. While trends that have been going on for millions of years are often, almost by definition, exceptionally stable, and therefore predictable to some extent, patterns extrapolated into such a distant future may also be more vulnerable to disruption, due to the sheer amount of time in which disruption could occur and the difficulty of knowing with great confidence that no other factors are at play that could derail even exceptionally stable trends. Correspondingly, anything that is only somewhat predictable in the short term, like political structures or economic outcomes, becomes even less predictable in the medium term and the long term. Predictability and unpredictability depend much more on what question you are asking, on what kind of phenomenon you are considering, than on time scale, so whether we find predictability or unpredictability at a given scale depends on what we choose to look for.

It also helps to recall the central lessons of chapter 6 about context, contingency, and causality. In the history of humanity as well as of life and Earth, more than one cause is always at work: no single thing, no matter how important or powerful, drives all of history; the range of possibilities in any moment is always contingent upon what came before. And with the exception of an event that literally ends the world, no one cause will drive everything that happens afterward. Contingency and multicausality will continue to operate as they always have. As a result, we might say that at *all* scales, the future is *partially* and *conditionally*[3] predictable, with certain aspects of the future being easier to model and extrapolate than others.

An Example of Short-Term Prediction: Climate Change

To analyze an extended example, consider the issue of climate change. Earth's climate is one of the most comprehensively predicted aspects of the short-term (in David Christian's definition) future. This analysis relies on models of how the Earth's climate and weather patterns have responded and will respond to the changing composition of the atmosphere that results from emissions of greenhouse gases, which include carbon dioxide and methane.

The basic science underpinning climate change was identified well over 100 years ago. Predicted climate-change scenarios that have developed since then rest on the basic idea of the "greenhouse effect": the Sun produces light that streams in all directions, including the direction of the Earth; the Earth absorbs some of that radiation and re-radiates it in all directions as infrared radiation; and some of that infrared radiation, coming from the Earth's surface, is absorbed by certain

---

3. The word "conditionally" means, essentially, that if certain things happen, other things will follow.

components of the atmosphere: the greenhouse gases. This absorption of outgoing radiation has the result of keeping the surface of the Earth warmer than it would be without greenhouse gases, producing an effect much like that of a quilt, which traps heat radiated by a body underneath it.

To a great extent, the greenhouse effect is *good*; indeed, it is essential for life. If heat trapped through the greenhouse effect simply escaped, the Earth would be over 30 degrees Celsius colder than it is on average.[4] Water on Earth would exist almost entirely in the form of ice, and conditions on Earth's surface likely never would have allowed life as we know it today to thrive. But the present-day concern is about pumping more carbon dioxide (and methane) into the atmosphere, something that industrial societies have been doing at a very high rate for the last two or three centuries as they burn fossil fuels (coal, oil, and natural gas). The measured increase in atmospheric carbon dioxide—from a preindustrial 280 parts per million (ppm) to over 400 ppm now—corresponds to an increase in the strength of the greenhouse effect, leading to an increase in global temperatures. (See Figure 8.1.) Put succinctly, "Earth transforms sunlight's visible light energy into infrared light energy, which leaves Earth slowly because it is absorbed by greenhouse gases. When people produce greenhouse gases, energy leaves Earth even more slowly, raising Earth's temperature."[5]

Worldwide temperature data over the past several decades provide ample evidence that some warming has already happened. The fact that models of the Earth's climate system fit past temperature data much better when greenhouse-gas emissions are included presents a strong argument that these emissions are responsible for the warming trend, just as the basic physical science would lead one to expect.[6]

A warming atmosphere in and of itself may not seem especially perilous for most human communities, with certain key exceptions for people who already live in dangerously hot conditions or are especially vulnerable to heat. Likewise, the melting of polar ice and corresponding rise of sea levels in a warmer world would directly affect a select (albeit large) group of people—those who live in small island nations and coastal settlements, where sea-level rises represent an existential threat. Increased strength of storms, such as Atlantic hurricanes, could also produce potentially devastating effects for specific communities. But for the global human

---

4. See, e.g., NASA Earth Observatory, "Global Warming," https://earthobservatory.nasa.gov/Features/GlobalWarming/page2.php , or H. R. Treut et al., "Historical Overview of Climate Change," in *Climate Change 2007: The Physical Science Basis. Contribution of Working Group I to the Fourth Assessment Report of the Intergovernmental Panel on Climate Change*, eds. S. D. Solomon et al., p. 115, https://www.ipcc.ch/report/ar4/wg1/ .

5. Andrew Shtulman, *Scienceblind*, p. 123, quoting Michael Ranney, howglobalwarmingworks.org (old version of the website).

6. See, e.g., Markus Huber and Reto Knutti, "Anthropogenic and Natural Warming Inferred from Changes in Earth's Energy Balance," https://www.nature.com/articles/ngeo1327 .

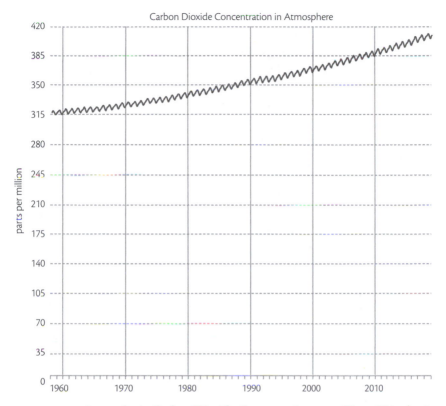

FIGURE 8.1 Atmospheric Carbon Dioxide Concentrations over Time This plot is called the "Keeling curve" after Charles David Keeling, the scientist who initiated the direct, continuous measurement and recording of atmospheric carbon dioxide levels in the late 1950s. The graph reflects how the ongoing burning of fossil fuels, which releases large amounts of carbon dioxide into the atmosphere, results in appreciable buildup of atmospheric carbon dioxide over time, strengthening the greenhouse effect.

Source: Based on raw data at https://scrippsco2.ucsd.edu/data/atmospheric_co2/primary_mlo_co2_record. html, and C. D. Keeling, S. C. Piper, R. B. Bacastow, M. Wahlen, T. P. Whorf, M. Heimann, and H. A. Meijer, "Exchanges of atmospheric CO_2 and $^{13}CO_2$ with the terrestrial biosphere and oceans from 1978 to 2000," SIO Reference Series, No. 01-06 (Global aspects), Scripps Institution of Oceanography (San Diego, 2001).

community as a whole, the greatest dangers may lie in the possibility of activating strong positive feedback loops in the climate system that could lead to very rapid climate change, globally and regionally, in a short period of time, to which all modern human societies would have great difficulty adapting. "Global warming" and "climate change" might better be termed "climate instability": destabilization of the climate is a primary danger, and a possible survival risk, for human societies.

Why? Because the climate system is not *linear*: increasing the amount of carbon dioxide in the atmosphere by a given amount does not lead to a predictable, steady amount of warming. Instead, the climate system is non-linear and metastable, meaning that it may stay in a relatively stable pattern for a long time until disturbed significantly, but once "tipped" out of this condition of stability, it may undergo rapid shifts to a new, possibly very different, stable state. This new state might be warmer or colder in any given location, with different seasonal weather patterns, regional precipitation, ocean-circulation patterns, and so forth. For instance, increasing greenhouse-gas concentrations in the atmosphere could melt permafrost at high northern latitudes, leading to the release of methane from the permafrost and, therefore, to a stronger greenhouse effect and more warming. That in turn could lead to still more methane release, producing a great deal of additional warming in a short time. Similarly, melting polar ice turns a shiny white reflective substance (ice) into a darker, less reflective substance (liquid water), which means that the more ice melts, the less sunlight will be reflected away from the Earth's surface. This tends to increase overall temperatures still further, leading to yet more melting, which leads to greater temperature increases, and so on in a continuing cycle. A final example of positive feedback (see "Systems" in chapter 7) is that warming leads to more water vapor in the atmosphere (higher specific humidity), and since water vapor is itself a greenhouse gas, this too creates conditions for further warming. (See Figure 8.2.)

The climate system also has negative feedback loops, in the sense that a temperature increase may activate other mechanisms that tend to *decrease* the temperature, restoring the original state.[7] An example of this is the radiative cooling of the Earth itself: as the Earth's temperature increases, its ability to radiate heat away from itself increases even faster,[8] which works to restore the original temperature. Clouds can also act as a source of negative feedback: as temperatures increase, more water vapor is released into the atmosphere, leading to more clouds, which reflect a certain amount of sunlight away from Earth's surface. These negative-feedback mechanisms are why the climate has substantial stability and a resistance to change—one that is very helpful to human societies as well as other forms of life, which depend on a certain level of stability and predictability in climate and weather.

Predictions of how Earth's climate patterns will change in response to changes in the composition of the atmosphere largely rely on modeling how these positive and negative feedback loops interact with one another, how much stability negative-feedback mechanisms lend to the climate system, and where positive feedback loops may be activated in ways that could produce large changes in a short time by crossing a *threshold* or *tipping point*, "overpowering" the negative feedback loops and changing the state of the climate system drastically. There is uncertainty in the details, making very complex simulations necessary, and even more detail is necessary

---

7. As in chapter 7 (see the discussion under "Systems"), note that the words "positive" and "negative" are not value judgments: positive feedback loops entail rapid change, and negative feedback loops entail stability. But either kind of feedback loop may be "good" or "bad" (or both, to some degree), depending on the situation.

8. In accord with a physical law called the Stefan-Boltzmann law.

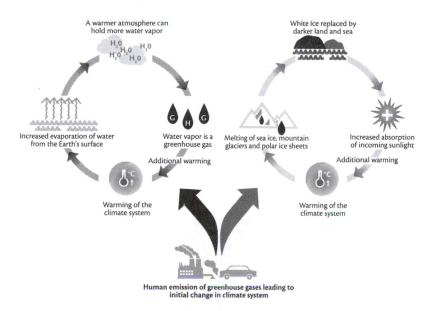

FIGURE 8.2 **Reinforcing the Warming** When atmospheric carbon dioxide concentrations increase, the greenhouse effect is strengthened, meaning that the atmosphere's ability to trap heat is strengthened. The warming that results from this in turn activates various feedback loops: positive feedback loops (pictured) amplify the warming, while negative feedback loops (not pictured) counteract the warming. The bottom line is clear: increasing carbon dioxide levels will ultimately lead to global warming, but how much warming occurs, and how fast it happens, depend to a great extent on the complicated details of how these feedback loops reinforce or counterbalance one another. (Note that positive feedback loops are not necessarily good. And negative feedback loops are not necessarily bad – in fact, they are crucial to Earth's ability to maintain stable climate conditions.)
Source: www.climatecommission.gov.au

to get a handle on how regional weather patterns might change, which is important for local responses and adaptations to climate change. While a true runaway greenhouse effect without eventual stabilization has never happened on Earth in the way that it seems to have on Venus (where average surface temperatures exceed 860 degrees Fahrenheit, or 460 degrees Celsius), and is still unlikely to happen here given the various mechanisms of negative feedback, rapid short-term warming could plausibly disturb many human systems that depend on stable regional weather patterns—like the South Asian monsoon rains, which enable food supply to hundreds of millions of people—and could be tremendously difficult to adapt to.[9]

---

9. Climate change, even on this scale, is not unprecedented in the planet's history. The deep history of the Earth's climate, studied by paleoclimatologists, shows that our planet has gone through many cycles where it was much warmer on average (or much colder) than it is today. But there has never been significant destabilization of climate with so many human beings on the planet, living in such difficult-to-move communities. (See Plate 40.)

Note why it is fair to say that the Earth's climate exhibits partial and conditional predictability. The basic science of the greenhouse effect, and the knowledge that burning fossil fuels adds carbon dioxide to the atmosphere, combine to produce the basic prediction that burning fossil fuels should lead to some amount of warming. Detailed climate models then allow more specific and quantitative predictions, and their reliability can be assessed, to some extent, by how well these models, when applied retroactively, match actual measurements of temperatures around the world in the past several decades. Predictions are in a range rather than absolutes (e.g., a 1.5- to 4.5-degree-Celsius increase in average global temperatures—which may not sound like a wide range, but when talking about average temperatures over the entire planet, it is), and the range of possible outcomes is contingent upon many details. Hence, there is predictability, but it is only partial, which makes sense given the complex modeling of a complex phenomenon. Predictions are also conditional: the behavior of the climate system depends, among many other things, on how much additional carbon dioxide is input into the atmosphere—and how much is able to be drawn out through technologies of carbon dioxide removal. This is just one example of how geological and socioeconomic variables can change how much warming would be predicted. The *impacts* of climate change on human societies have a similarly partial and conditional predictability. For example, *if* there is widespread melting of permafrost, *then* adaptation to climate change could become far more difficult.[10]

In imagining the future, it is tempting to think that climate change and its consequences will be the only major cause at play, that it will "take over" as the driver of historical change. But again, history is not monocausal or deterministic. Climate change may well drive a great deal of change in coming decades, and for some communities, it poses an existential threat. But the realities of climate, whatever precisely they end up being, will also continue to interact with social and biological systems, and humanity and other species will react and change in various ways. Some communities (cities? nations? regions?) will be affected more strongly than others, and some will adapt better than others. This will have political and economic consequences, which may in turn feed back into what happens with the future of the climate: societal responses to climate change could themselves affect the future climate. The overall pattern of a generally warming globe is simple to state as a prediction, but what it really means for how future events will play out is much more complicated, involving interactions and feedbacks at every level.

---

10. Climate change thus has at least a qualified predictability, even if its less predictable aspects—tipping points and feedback mechanisms—spark the greatest concern for the human-scale, short- and medium-term future. The combination of predictability and uncertainty in the climate system leads some authors to suggest that human adaptation to climate change should be thought of in terms of risk and its reduction rather than apocalyptic scenarios and their complete avoidance.

Medium-Term Futures

Medium-term futures are those that occupy the upcoming hundreds to thousands of years. Christian argues that medium-term futures are the least predictable of all, since many current human and planetary-level trends become harder to extrapolate this far into the future, while the very biggest and longest-term developments, at the level of stars, galaxies, and beyond, have been mapped by astrophysicists and cosmologists to a higher degree of confidence. At the medium term, however, Christian suggests that uncertainty is greatest, and proposes that science fiction may provide the best source of ideas and speculation about what the future might hold. As before, though, this conclusion hinges on presupposing certain kinds of predictability as the ones that matter. Looked at from another perspective, this medium scale of futures presents a continuum of relative predictability and uncertainty, just as shorter and longer scales do.

The suggestion of science fiction as a place to turn for medium-term visions reflects a larger contemporary cultural sense that technology is one of the key "forces" that will dominate what happens centuries to millennia from now. There is some reason for this expectation, thanks to the character of exponential growth—that is, the rapid growth that occurs when gains are proportional to what is already present. To take a monetary example, if we gave you a penny on the first day of May, and two on the second day, and four on the third, and eight on the fourth, so that we doubled the amount we were giving you each day, how much money would you have at the end of the month? The answer is over \$20 million. When a quantity increases in proportion to what is already there, this leads to exponential growth, which is counterintuitively rapid.[11]

How does this apply to technology and the future? "Moore's Law," formulated in the 1960s, states that various measures of computing power double roughly every 18 months. The exact time increment needed for each doubling has been debated and occasionally revised, but if, as in this case, the basic pattern is sustained over a sufficiently long period, the result will be a great deal of growth very quickly, leading to results that can be hard to anticipate. Arguably, this is why *Star Trek*, which debuted in 1966, included characters who could travel through space with ease but used communication devices that are in some ways less sophisticated than our existing smartphones today. *Star Trek*'s communications technology now looks like stuff from the past, even as other forms of technology, like space travel, have not grown as quickly as many science-fiction authors in the 20th century anticipated.[12] That is because communications technology has grown exponentially with a short doubling time, whereas spacefaring technology has developed more slowly.

---

11. Technically, this is not exponential growth. It is close enough, though, and it parallels Moore's Law.

12. We are grateful to John Laird for inspiring this point.

In other words, technological power may grow very, very rapidly, but not inevitably across the board. What it is that grows rapidly depends on many factors, including what people in the present (especially at the level of corporations and governments) prioritize in researching and developing. Moore's Law is a case in point: computing technology has been the subject of intensive research over the past half-century, and the physical world has "cooperated" in allowing Moore's Law to continue over this period of time. However, it is not a "law" in the sense of an immutable characteristic of the universe, and how long Moore's Law may continue to hold is unclear—and the subject of considerable ongoing debate.

The imaginations of science-fiction writers, technological innovators, world leaders, and big thinkers offer no shortage of suggestions for what the consequences of the growth of various technologies might be. Techno-utopians propose that the growth of technology will bring an end to

> every major social evil . . . that it will eliminate scarcity and disease, that it will significantly improve communications and education, and that it will undermine the environmental conditions which reinforce aggression, prejudice, sectarianism, nationalism, oppression, and exploitation.[13]

Alternatively, many books and movies have envisioned robots and artificial intelligences so powerful that they threaten to take over the world in a nightmarish, dystopian scenario.[14] Others imagine a world in which artificial and human intelligence merge in some way.[15] Space exploration looms large in some proposals, such as Carl Sagan's; time scales of centuries and millennia may be the most appropriate for envisioning human expansion to nearby stars within the Milky Way Galaxy, given the immense distances involved, the finite speed of light,[16] and the difficulty of setting up human-livable environments outside Earth's biosphere.[17] Meanwhile, transhumanists envision technologies that enable radical changes in human nature, possibly as early as the mid-21st century. In any case, the power of certain technologies may be reasonably judged as being likely to increase, but *which* technologies, and *what* they are used for, and *how* this in turn leads to further change, all depend on societal factors and on the choices people make, as well as on what turns out to be physically possible.

---

13. Bernard Gendron, *Technology and the Human Condition*, p. 3.

14. Like *The Terminator* or *The Matrix*.

15. As Ray Kurzweil does, e.g., in *The Age of Spiritual Machines*.

16. See chapter 2.

17. See, e.g., Carl Sagan's *Cosmos* or *Pale Blue Dot*. The Biosphere 2 project provides some vivid illustrations of the difficulties of sustaining human life outside Earth's biosphere (https://biosphere2.org/). See chapter 4 for more details on Earth's biosphere.

Some consequences of technology are, within the range of partial predictabilities, more likely to be destructive in the medium-term future. The cost to biodiversity is a case in point. Extinction is a natural phenomenon, and we know that more than 99.9 percent of all species that have ever existed have gone extinct.[18] Ecologists and conservation biologists, however, estimate that extinction rates are now somewhere between 100 and 1,000 times higher than they have typically been in Earth's history, leading to views of our present day as part of a "Sixth Mass Extinction," when extinction rates, if sustained over the next several human lifetimes, could result in the collapse of wider ecosystems and a fall in levels of biodiversity that parallels the five previous mass extinctions of the Phanerozoic.

While there have been hundreds of documented recent species extinctions, and much talk of certain prominent endangered species, the biggest concern about present extinction rates stems from *un*documented extinctions, including of species not among the approximately one and a half million that have been identified. Ecological models of habitat degradation and changes to ecosystems, largely based on human impacts (especially modern agricultural techniques and technologies that alter or destroy natural habitats), suggest that extinction rates are, in fact, much higher than we can directly observe. Once again, as with climate change, such conclusions depend on the application of modeling techniques to the observable aspects of a system, and these trends and their consequences exhibit partial and conditional predictability.

Long-Term Futures

Examined in isolation, long-term trends, which are seen on scales of millions to billions of years, seem fairly straightforward to predict. Continental drift, for example, is a stable trend that appears to have been proceeding at about the same rate for hundreds of millions of years. If no wildcards interrupt or complicate this process, extrapolating current observable drift directions and speeds shows that the Earth's surface will be reconfigured considerably 50 million years from now. (See Plate 44.) The Mediterranean Sea will have been replaced by the Mediterranean Mountains as plates collide. Many peaks in the Himalayas will be thousands of feet higher as the Indian subcontinent continues pushing farther into Asia, and many mountain ranges that are not at an active plate margin will have eroded and be thousands of feet shorter than they are now. The continents will, on average, be closer together than at present, having moved hundreds of miles, and Antarctica will no longer be nearly centered on the South Pole. In addition to changing the appearance of the Earth's surface, other global patterns will change in response to continental drift, such as how much water is locked up as ice at high altitudes (typically, the more

---

18. "To a first approximation, all species are extinct"—a saying often attributed to the paleontologist David Raup.

mountains there are over the Earth's surface, the more water takes this form), how much land is located near the equator versus near the poles, and how much near-coastline shallow water (habitats that tend to be rich in biodiversity) there will be. Just as these aspects of Earth's continental configuration have affected patterns of climate and biodiversity in the past, they will continue to affect such patterns in the future, assuming, again, that continental drift continues to operate in the way that it has (and geologists see no reason to believe that it will not).

Cosmic trends also exhibit this kind of partial and conditional, yet substantial, predictability. We know that the life span of a star is almost entirely dependent upon its mass; astronomers have calculated that a star with the mass of our Sun has a life span of about 10 billion years. We can therefore expect, in the absence of wild-cards, that the Sun will continue fusing hydrogen into helium in its core for another 5 billion years or so, that it will take about a billion years to slowly turn into a red giant after the hydrogen "fuel" in its core is finally depleted, and that it will then spend another billion years as a red giant before becoming increasingly unstable and ultimately "dying" by taking the form of a white dwarf. (See Plate 45.) The Earth may well be engulfed during the red-giant phase, and it will certainly be unin-habitable even if not engulfed—although the steadily increasing energy output of the Sun over time may make the Earth uninhabitable to most or even all life much more quickly than that, perhaps as "soon" as 1 billion years from now.

The fate of the universe as a whole likewise seems to depend upon a small number of variables. At some level, though, this biggest of all future questions is also less certain. Until about a quarter-century ago, the debate was over whether the uni-verse's expansion would continue forever, or whether there was a sufficient amount of matter in the universe, and thus sufficient gravitational pull of all matter on all other matter, to halt the expansion and produce a re-collapse—a "Big Crunch." However, since the discovery in the 1990s that the universe's expansion is accelerat-ing, discussions of the universe's future have turned to questions about how and why this could be occurring and have focused on the nature of dark energy, the putative energy that produces this acceleration. Depending on how powerful dark energy is, what it is, how it works, and how it can be expected to behave in the future—ques-tions to which the answers are unknown—the universe's expansion may continue to accelerate steadily, or it may accelerate so fast that at some point, billions of years from now, everything in the universe may be torn apart from everything else in a "Big Rip." On top of the predictive uncertainties introduced by dark energy, there may be other effects currently unforeseen by physicists that are at play. (Dark energy itself was not anticipated before it was inferred from observations.)

At this largest of views, therefore, some of the most basic questions about the future have not yet been answered. And even if compelling answers to this set of questions emerge, they will surely generate new questions and new mysteries for future scientists to consider. We are far from reaching the endpoint of our questions about possible cosmological futures.

Wildcards and Interactions Between Trends

No matter how carefully one analyzes current trends and tries to predict the future by extrapolating them, even stable trends can be disrupted: predictions are never certain. In many cases, this is a good thing. A classic—although possibly apocryphal—example is the increasing problem of horse manure (and urine, and carcasses) on the streets of large cities like London and New York in the 1890s, which led to a famous (but again, possibly apocryphal) prediction that London streets would be buried under nine feet of horse manure within 50 years.[19] Whether or not this prediction was actually made in the 1890s, mass-produced automobiles averted this outcome. Likewise, it is conceivable, even if perhaps unlikely, that new energy sources in our own near future might provide a viable solution to at least some problems of sustainability in a straightforward, scalable way. For example, energy generated by nuclear fusion may ultimately provide a part of the world's energy "portfolio," and even low-energy nuclear reactions (a term that is more scientifically acceptable and less misleading than "cold fusion") may yet hold promise for supplying the modern demand for energy—although the latter is a field of research that has been seen by many as a fantasy, and that has stayed far outside the mainstream of scientific work for decades.

Trends can also be derailed for the worse, however, including by apocalyptic scenarios that are all too familiar to anyone who tracks today's common predictions. The impact of a large meteorite, for example, would bring an abrupt end to most of the short-term and medium-term trends discussed in this chapter. So too would a nuclear war, perhaps even if "only" regional rather than worldwide—because agriculture and many other human activities throughout the world might become much more difficult due to "nuclear winter,"[20] and many people would die, possibly making the operation of technological society based on technical infrastructure far more difficult or even impossible. Given that large amounts of energy are required to operate this sort of technical infrastructure, and that most easily acquired energy sources have already been depleted and high-tech infrastructure is itself now required to obtain new energy sources, it is questionable whether another "Industrial Revolution" could occur in the aftermath of a massive population decline.[21]

---

19. For an interesting discussion, see Rose Wild, "We Were Buried in Fake News as Long Ago as 1894," https://www.thetimes.co.uk/article/we-were-buried-in-fake-news-as-long-ago-as-1894-ntr23ljd5 .

20. A prolonged period of global cooling predicted (somewhat controversially) for the aftermath of a nuclear war due to firestorms putting large quantities of sunlight-blocking soot into the upper atmosphere, which could produce widespread crop failure and, therefore, famine. The projected outcomes of a nuclear war depend crucially on the assumptions one makes—about size, location, duration of time that soot would stay in the atmosphere, weather patterns, and so forth.

21. See Lewis Dartnell, "Out of the Ashes," https://aeon.co/essays/could-we-reboot-a-modern-civilisation-without-fossil-fuels ; and Kevin Kelly, "Bootstrapping the Industrial Age," https://medium.com/@kevin2kelly/bootstrapping-the-industrial-age-dc8a100b351d .

Even in the long-term future, wildcards could derail even the most apparently stable trends—for better or for worse. The universe itself provides a good example: unanticipated physical effects could change all our predictions about what the future of the universe might hold. Dark energy itself was such an effect when it was first inferred, and this kind of discovery could happen again.

In addition to the possibility of wildcards, trends in different domains interact with one another, adding to the partialness and conditionality of any predictability. Climate trends, for example, may take a different course depending on the paths charted by human societies. And no matter what the climate system does in the future, it will set a context for politics and economics, as weather and climate always have—possibly a much more difficult context to adapt to, if weather patterns change greatly, storms increase, and sea levels rise enough to flood coastal cities. A similar observation could be made about interactions between other trends. The future of technology, for instance, interacts with politics and economics—the priorities people set in politics and business, what they invest in with their money and their energy and their time, will affect where and how technologies change. Human technological change could even, eventually, affect the long-term future of the Earth, Sun, and other stars in the Milky Way Galaxy. Scientists and science-fiction writers are fond of suggestions like the "Dyson sphere," in which a spacefaring civilization could theoretically set up a shell of material to completely enclose a star and capture a large fraction of the total energy it emits. Such scenarios seem far-fetched, at least for the present, but it is worth remembering that humans are already engaged in a planet-scale geoengineering experiment—namely, pumping greenhouse gases into the atmosphere to such an extent that the global climate could be affected for thousands of years to come.

None of this is exactly *knowledge* about what will happen in the future. An analysis of the sort that a universal history can provide deals only with what *may* happen, how *likely* given events or trends are, and how *desirable* they might be—whether they are possible, probable, and/or preferable futures. Even an analysis that takes into account the grand sweep of the past on multiple scales still must admit a great deal of unpredictability, and recognize the presence of multiple causes operating at multiple scales and interacting with one another in complex and at least partly unpredictable ways.

Interpreting the Future

And yet despite so many sources of unpredictability, if you ask yourself right now what you think the future is going to be like, you can probably conjure up at least a few ideas fairly quickly. Recent popular books and films offer no shortage of possibilities from which to select. The 2008 Disney/Pixar movie *Wall-E* offers a vision of soft and lazy humans in space who have no sense of ambition or self-sacrifice, cute robots who are more human than the humans, and planet Earth a desolate and decaying wasteland. Many works of young-adult fiction, such as Lois Lowry's *The Giver* and Suzanne Collins's *The Hunger Games*, offer futuristic visions of social control and oppressive or totalitarian government, with advanced technology put to inhumane or cruel uses. Cormac McCarthy's *The Road* envisions the near-complete destruction of life on Earth and a widespread descent into cannibalism among the few remaining humans. There are many dystopias premised upon ecological collapse, totalitarian society, a new rise of eugenics, robots taking over the world, nanotechnology used as a weapon of mass destruction, or biotechnology that dehumanizes and creates radical inequalities of a kind never seen before. Brighter and more utopian visions of the future, by contrast, seem to be on the wane in the 21st century, although not absent: scientific and science-fiction visions of physical immortality just around the corner, proposals for super-advanced transportation systems on Earth, or quick colonization of Mars and perhaps beyond. Visions of a future in which the advancement of technology and human goodwill combine to end many evils are not limited to 20th century science fiction, but continue to contribute to the array of envisioned futures available to the imagination today.

Few of these dystopian and utopian visions of the future, particularly those articulated through fiction, are intended as actual predictions about what will unfold. On the informational level, they usually aim for basic plausibility, but beyond that, in many cases they are highly imaginative stories of individual adventures set in wider worlds that are intended to provide commentary on present trends more than to prognosticate the future. For example, Suzanne Collins has said that she got the idea for *The Hunger Games*, in which an oppressive government annually selects 24 children to engage in televised combat to the death until only one is left alive, while channel-surfing between reality-TV shows and war coverage on the news.[22]

Still, what one imagines when thinking about the future, overall, is influenced both by these imaginative visions and by informational-level predictions. Like the interpretive level of analyzing the past, the interpretive level of predicting the future pulls together many pieces of information to create an overall vision of where we are headed and what it all means. And these overall visions may, in some ways, also shape the possibilities for what the actual future might hold.

Another way of saying this is that as with the past, what we think about the future often reflects present concerns. Imaginative visions tend to reflect the great preoccupations of the time in which they are written. Reading a broad-scale vision of the future may or may not tell you about the future in terms of what will "come true," but it will tell you much about the person who wrote it,

22. Suzanne Collins, *The Hunger Games*, p. 457; and The Telegraph, "The Hunger Games: Who Is Author Suzanne Collins?," https://www.telegraph.co.uk/culture/film/film-news/9161107/The-Hunger-Games-Who-is-author-Suzanne-Collins.html .

and probably the society it came out of—what its members thought about, were obsessed by, desired, or feared. Ideas about the future, in short, keep changing in ways that respond to current conditions, trends, hopes, and worries. It is notable, for instance, how extreme many visions of the future have been in literature and film over the past several decades: tending toward a vision of utopia or dystopia as an endpoint, whereas in reality one might say that many different trends are in play, that they usually tend to moderate each other, and that we might instead reasonably anticipate outcomes that are neither outright utopian nor dystopian.

None of this is to say that one overall vision of the future cannot hope to be better—more accurate, more insightful, more detailed—than another. Through the kind of careful and rigorous multicausal analysis we have discussed, it is surely possible to do better, and to watch for places where we are projecting our current narratives into the future without much evidence or legitimate confidence. At the same time, however, a story based on scientific and historical evidence is still, by its nature, a story: the framing of the story, the worldview behind it, and the context in which it is told will all influence which pieces of evidence feature most prominently, which elements are even included, how they form the basis for a central lesson or "moral," and what emotional registers are deployed to tell it. This is no less true when the story is about the future. If anything, the emotional power and resonance are then greater, because the stakes seem higher when framing interpretations, and making meaning out of raw evidence, to see a largely unknown future.

Progress

In the decades before World War I, European intellectual culture was dominated by the idea of "Progress." Inspired by the wonders of industry and machinery, the wealth and power they generated and underpinned, the advances of science and medicine, and the perceived superiority of Enlightenment philosophy over the philosophies that came before it, many European intellectuals assumed not only that certain aspects of life were getting better for certain people, but that humanity itself was advancing as a whole and, therefore, that the present generation was morally and intellectually superior to past generations. Many even saw European colonial conquests as progressive in the sense of helping to reform the "backward" ways of non-European cultures according to the new and "advanced" ways of Europe—hence, the now-infamous rhetoric of the "white man's burden" and "civilizing mission." To some, the dawn of a utopian world society seemed imminent. A few authors began to place utopian societies in the *future*, as in Edward Bellamy's 1888 novel *Looking Backward*, rather than on an island (as in Francis Bacon's *New Atlantis*, written in the early 1600s) or otherwise in the realm of the hypothetical (as in Plato's *Republic*, written well over 2,000 years ago).

Although it was published a bit later, after the end of World War I, one hears echoes of this optimism in the closing paragraph of H. G. Wells's concise universal history, *A Short History of the World*, expressed in some of the language then customary:

> Man is still only adolescent. His troubles are not the troubles of senility and exhaustion but of increasing and still undisciplined strength. . . . As yet we are hardly in the earliest dawn of human greatness. . . . Can we doubt that presently our race will more than realize our boldest imaginations, that it will achieve unity and peace, that it will live, the children of our blood and lives will live, in a world made more splendid and lovely than any palace or garden that we know, going on from strength to strength in an ever widening circle of adventure and achievement? What man has done, the little triumphs of his present state, and all this history we have told, form but the prelude to the things that man has yet to do.[23]

World War I dealt a hard blow to such cultural optimism, even if the effects of the blow did not settle in all at once.[24] The brutality of a conflict that claimed the lives of a generation of young men, fighting for reasons few really understood, using tools whose technological progress meant that mass killing was easier than ever, and embroiling the world in a horrifying but mostly futile war of attrition in the trenches—especially on the almost-static Western Front—left its mark on the notion that Progress was inevitable (or even underway), or that utopia was soon to be achieved. The postwar years saw a shift among European intellectuals from foreseeing an abrupt and drastic shift for the better in the near future to disillusionment. Then the years of global economic depression, followed by World War II and, especially, the Holocaust (which took place at the hands of Germany, ostensibly a leading country in education, statesmanship, high culture, and technical sophistication), dealt a further devastating blow. The Polish poet Wisława Szymborska wrote of the terrible disappointment felt by all those who had hoped that "Our twentieth century was going to improve on the others" in her 1993 poem "The Century's Decline":

> A couple of problems weren't going
> to come up anymore:
> hunger, for example,
> and war, and so forth.
>
> There was going to be respect
> for helpless people's helplessness,
> trust, that kind of stuff.[25]

---

23. H.G. Wells, *A Short History of the World*, p. 178.

24. For example, the first volume of Oswald Spengler's *The Decline of the West* was published in 1918, months before the end of World War I.

25. Wisława Szymborska, "The Century's Decline," https://reflections.yale.edu/article/faith-and-citizenship-turbulent-times/centurys-decline .

Yet in spite of the blows it has sustained, in spite of wars and rumors of wars, of environmental concerns and dystopian societies both real and imagined, the idea of Progress remains with us. The statement that the human condition always generally improves is perhaps no longer so convincing, but the general sense of our moral superiority today over people of the past, and (by implication) of future people's moral superiority over us, resurfaces and remains powerful in many contexts. It is embedded in subtle phrases within everyday language, at least in English: it is not a compliment to say that objects, ideas, or people are "archaic," or "mired in the past," or "behind the times." Conversely, if someone or something is "modern," or "ahead of the times," the implication is that these are good things. You might hear about a viewpoint being "on the wrong side of history" and be told that "people in the future will judge" those who continue to hold that view. Anything labeled "21st century" tends to be perceived as positive, while being seen as "medieval" or (worse) "Stone Age" tends to be negative. At least implicitly, there is still plenty of "chronological snobbery" (C. S. Lewis's phrase[26]) or "condescension of posterity" (E. P. Thompson's wording[27]) to go around.

And just as Wells's universal history participated in the Progress-minded mood of his time, so too do more recent universal histories. We have seen in chapters 4, 5, and 7 (under "Evolution," "Technology," and "Modernity," respectively) how progress narratives often implicitly structure one's understanding of the evolutionary history of life, of the history of human technologies, and of the modern period itself—even though a desire for greater nuance in thinking about the present and future should lead us to qualify precisely to what extent and in what senses life, or technology, or society can be said to progress.

Even beyond these specific instances, progress often serves as an unspoken structuring element to how all of universal history is told. For example, David Christian, in *Maps of Time* and *Origin Story*, speaks of "thresholds of increasing complexity," in which stars, elements, planets, life, human beings, agricultural human societies, and modern human societies succeed one another as the most complex entities in the universe. Readers may make a subconscious leap from "more complex" to "more advanced"—even if more complex entities are also understood, in Christian's work, to be inherently fragile. Christian explicitly says that complexity is not necessarily a good thing, and that increasing complexity does not necessarily make things better, but readers shaped by a modern mindset may well equate the two: the entire history of the universe can turn into a sort of progress narrative.

---

26. C. S. Lewis, *Surprised by Joy*, p. 252.

27. E. P. Thompson, *The Making of the English Working Class*, p. 12.

Problems with Progress

Historians have a difficult relationship with the idea of Progress, which could be defined as the notion that humanity, or the human condition, or human moral sensibilities naturally (or even inevitably) become better over time. A more limited sense of the word progress (which we will spell with a lowercase "p" when used in this latter sense) is, by contrast, not so much of a problem: if by "progress" we simply mean movement in the direction of a desired goal, most historians will certainly agree that there has been progress in many areas of human life, especially what we might call "material progress." In the modern period, the elimination of mass poverty, the harnessing of tremendous amounts of energy, the longer lives and greater health of many people and communities around the world compared to 100 or 1,000 years ago, the collective learning in science and technology that has made life much more healthy, convenient, and predictable for many—all these are forms of progress with respect to particular, widely desired, objectives.

Attaching value to the mere passage of time, however, or assuming a sort of general superiority of the present over the past, or of life now over life "back then," is a move that many historians have been unwilling to make. Writing in 1929, the historian Christopher Dawson questioned whether people were "happier or wiser or better" because of the "modern advance of material civilization."[28] Likewise, E. H. Carr wrote in 1961:

> At the present time, few people would, I think, question the fact of progress in the accumulation both of material resources and of scientific knowledge, of mastery over the environment in the technological sense. What is questioned is whether there has been in the twentieth century any progress in our ordering of society, in our mastery of the social environment, national or international, whether indeed there has not been a marked regression. Has not the evolution of man as a social being lagged fatally behind the progress of technology?[29]

The progress narratives that historians particularly question are the ones that imply that people today are smarter or morally superior compared with those in the past: the sense that things get better over time, not just in sophistication of technology but in overall human intelligence or moral sense as well. Herbert Butterfield, a 20th-century British historian, famously criticized the "tendency in many historians to . . . praise revolutions provided they have been successful, to emphasise certain principles of progress in the past and to produce a story which is

---

28. Christopher Dawson, *Progress and Religion*, p. 18.

29. E. H. Carr, *What Is History?*, p. 156.

the ratification if not the glorification of the present."[30] As noted in chapter 7, this "whig interpretation of history" (as Butterfield called it) warps the past by seeing it in terms of present issues and implying that everything led up to "us." But historians would contend that to take the lives of people in the past seriously, and to make sense of past lived experience, the past should be met on its own terms as much as possible. In writing about the past, we have to be careful not to write off the past.

To further complicate simplistic ideas about Progress, scientific and technological progress, when examined more closely, almost always benefits some at the expense of others: there are winners and losers. Colonialism, imperialism, slavery, and other mass cruelties are real parts of the story too, and they cannot be ignored. In today's world, the people who produce goods and services are often poor and exploited in comparison to those who purchase or receive them. And even for the beneficiaries, progress in the sophistication of technologies or the availability of goods and services—a kind of material progress—does not necessarily equate to "happier or wiser or better" lives. For example, modern medicine, which has certainly brought tremendous advantages, can also backfire, as when large numbers of people suffer and sometimes die from infections that they acquired in a (modern, technologized) hospital. This is just one example of a larger pattern: even widely beneficial historical changes have both pros and cons and, for some groups of people, may well have more disadvantages than advantages.

With all that in mind, some writers turn Progress on its head and claim that things have been getting *worse*. This inversion-of-progress narrative emphasizes the other side of the coin, stressing the science-enabled deadliness of modern weapons of war, the perils of climate change, or the existential threats to humanity now possible that 300 years ago were not. This is certainly one way to read the evidence, although it too leaves out many other possible threads. Perhaps, in contrast to both progress and decline narratives, there is no single overall direction to history. From this third point of view, people are people, they do things, and these things have consequences, many of which are unintended; it is often profoundly unclear what the net effect is. Countervailing trends may tend to moderate each other, so that utopias and dystopias alike are both easy to imagine but difficult to realize.

The Future as a Site for Discussing Present Moral Standards

Almost by definition, progress (or decline) must be measured with respect to some goal or standard.[31] This helps to explain why visions of future progress are so value-laden: practically everyone hopes for a better world, for their communities and world to move in a good direction. But different people often have seriously

---

30. Herbert Butterfield, *The Whig Interpretation of History*, p. v.

31. Compare our discussion of purpose in chapter 7.

differing visions of what would constitute a better world and a good direction. Does a better future have more or fewer people? More or fewer material goods? More privacy and less security or more security and less privacy? (Is it possible to have more of both?) More or less technology? More or less government? More or less taxation? More or less globalization? These are only a few examples of how discussions about the future, and about what constitutes progress, become proxies for discussions of *present* ethical and political controversies.

There is certainly nothing problematic about envisioning a better world, or arguing for a morally informed vision of the direction in which our world should move—activists, revolutionaries, and religious figures have done so for millennia. But it helps to be explicit about what we are doing. Different visions of progress may each be laudable in some regards, but their core virtues and values may conflict with one another: progress with respect to economic efficiency or standards of living, for instance, may clash with efforts to reduce economic inequality, or with the pursuit of leisure. And progress on the availability of convenient technology may create a tension with progress on environmental goals like curbing climate change and protecting biodiversity.

It is thus important to clarify what the costs, limits, and losses of a particular brand of progress might be. A "progressive" vision must clarify what kind of progress is being sought, and why it really represents change for the good, in order to avoid taking one's own cultural values for granted and elevating them to the apex of history without articulating explicitly why they belong there. Our next two sections consider these questions closely as we discuss framings of universal futures around issues of sustainability and human nature itself.

Sustainability

When universal histories consider the short-term to medium-term future, they often center their discussion on matters of environmental sustainability. "Sustainability" in this context has been defined in many ways, mostly related to preserving and restoring the natural world in such a way that humans and other forms of life can "flourish together"[32] in the timeframes of a planetary future. The fundamental reason why sustainability has become such an important concern in universal histories, and in public discourse generally, is that scholarly and scientific consensus maintains that many current environmental trends simply cannot be sustained indefinitely. For example, present-day emissions of greenhouse gases are unsustainable, because if continued indefinitely, they will lead to climate change that

---

32. "I define sustainability as the possibility that human and other life will flourish on the planet forever." (Quote from John R. Ehrenfeld, "Flourishing Forever: An interview with John R. Ehrenfeld," https://sloanreview.mit.edu/article/flourishing-forever/ .)

would be devastating to human societies.[33] As another example, certain agricultural practices—like the cutting down of rainforest to make room for "monocultures," in which huge swaths of land are devoted to planting a single crop—are considered unsustainable in part because they contribute to the loss of biodiversity, which has negative long-term impacts on ecosystems and on human societies.

Universal histories offer a particularly powerful way to approach questions of sustainability. They put the present moment into context, drawing on thousands of years of human history and hundreds of millions of years of Earth history. They encourage thinking about the future on scales of decades, centuries, millennia, and beyond, not just the next few months or years, offering a helpful antidote to an exclusive focus on short-term issues.[34] They highlight both the achievements and the vulnerabilities of modern global society, and chart a range of possible courses for the future, informed by the best evidence and interpretation available. At the same time, however, they run the risk of oversimplification of complex realities, in this as in any other area.

Universal History as Context for the Anthropocene

A key part of what makes universal histories a compelling tool for understanding environmental futures is their ability to put human activity into the context of the entire history of the biosphere. All species have some impact on their environment. To "environ" means to "surround," so "environment" in general simply means "surroundings." And it is almost essential to the definition of life that beings interact with their surroundings, both living and non-living. But the scales of present-day human interactions with our surroundings are, by many measures, unprecedented in Earth's history. Earth scientists therefore take seriously the idea of naming a new geological epoch after human beings: the Anthropocene, an idea we first met in chapter 3 (see the discussion under "Deep Time").

Throughout our history as a species, humans have interacted with their surroundings while trying to survive and thrive, but modern industrial-capitalist societies have tremendously increased the scale of humanity's energy harnessing and resource extraction. This is why most Earth scientists would date the origin of this proposed Anthropocene epoch to the 20th century, or to a few hundred years ago

---

33. Some climate change has already happened, and more is already "locked in" by the amount of greenhouse-gas emissions that have already occurred. But this amount is unlikely to be globally devastating, hence the concern to limit additional emissions in an effort to curb future climate change as much as possible. Also note that the burning of fossil fuels to produce energy is unsustainable both because of its contributions to climate change and because fossil fuels exist in limited supply. There has been extended debate over exactly how limited the supply is, but it seems certain that the supply is finite (given that the geological production of new supplies of fossil fuels, by any of the processes geologists are aware of, will take millions of years).

34. Cf. Jo Guldi and David Armitage, *The History Manifesto*.

at most. Along with changes in human institutions and social organization,[35] the increasing capacity to use fossil fuels for energy production has created the conditions for far more people to survive infancy and live longer, healthier lives; expanded the opportunities for global communication; and enabled human beings to monitor Earth systems in a way that would have been inconceivable centuries ago, such as tracking the average temperature of the entire planet.[36] Fossil fuels underpin most of the practices of modern industrial agriculture, allowing billions of people to eat,[37] and they power modern technology and science. In fact, as of 2018, these extremely concentrated sources of energy represented well over 80 percent of all energy use worldwide.[38] In short, fossil fuels have been essential to the creation of modern global society.

But with material progress, advanced technology, and increasing prosperity have come costs as well, as vast unforeseen changes. The total human energy consumption multiplied many times in the 19th and 20th centuries.[39] (See Plate 41.) Human activities, especially in industrial-capitalist societies, have radically altered ecosystems around the world. They have changed the composition of the atmosphere and the Earth's climate. They have drastically increased the numbers of some preferred species, like cows and chickens, while decreasing or rendering many others extinct, with parallel increases in the amounts of preferred crops like corn and wheat. They have produced artifacts—from plastic water bottles to cars—that, depending on the circumstances of disposal, can endure for very long time spans, even geological time spans, such that one might call them "technofossils."[40] They have produced trace elements that also will be detectable over geological time, such as those from the explosions of nuclear weapons.[41] The burning of fossil fuels consumes staggering reserves of ancient plant matter: according to calculations by Jeffrey Dukes, one gallon of gasoline requires "approximately 90

---

35. Like the creation of modern hospitals, municipal governments conscious of public health, huge multinational corporations that extract raw materials from the ground, and the expansion of the scientific community.

36. Modern science and technology enable both global warming and the monitoring of how much warming is happening.

37. J. R. McNeill, "Sustainable Survival," pp. 364–365 in *Questioning Collapse*, eds. Patricia A. McAnany and Norman Yoffee.

38. See, e.g., "BP Statistical Review of World Energy 2019," p. 11, https://www.bp.com/content/dam/bp/business-sites/en/global/corporate/pdfs/energy-economics/statistical-review/bp-stats-review-2019-full-report.pdf .

39. See, e.g., Christian, *Maps of Time*, pp. 140–141.

40. See, e.g., Starre Vartan, "Humans Produce So Much Junk, We Are Creating a New Geological Layer," http://www.slate.com/articles/technology/future_tense/2017/03/humans_are_creating_a_new_geological_layer_of_technofossils.html

41. Including plutonium-239, with a half-life of 24,100 years.

metric tons of ancient plant matter as precursor material."[42] Human agriculture, including croplands and pastures, currently occupies more than a third of Earth's ice-free land area.[43] Humans have co-opted as much as 25 to 40 percent of the net primary production of terrestrial (meaning "on land," as opposed to aquatic) organisms each year.[44] And fossil fuels presently burned in a single year derive from organic matter containing over 400 times the amount of carbon fixed by all the photosynthesis in the biosphere in a given year.[45] As Charles Langmuir and Wally Broecker argue, human beings have fundamentally changed the character of Earth as a planet:

> For the first time a single species dominates the entire surface, sits at the top of all terrestrial and oceanic food chains, and has taken over much of the biosphere for its own purposes. We are also influencing the physical environment by changing the composition of the atmosphere and ocean, modifying the water cycle, eliminating soils, and constructing huge communities on a scale never before seen. To an external observer there is also a change in the capabilities of the planet as a whole. Human beings permit access to planet scale sensing from space, land, and sea; we are capable of conscious direction of the planetary systems; and we could communicate with other planetary civilizations, should they exist. We have also vastly increased the rate of and capacity for planetary change through our access to energy, global communication, technology, and our developing ability to direct evolution through modification of DNA.[46]

---

42. Jeffrey S. Dukes, "Burning Buried Sunshine: Human Consumption of Ancient Solar Energy," *Climatic Change* 61, no. 1–2 (2003):31.

43. Jonathan A. Foley, Chad Monfreda, Navin Ramankutty, and David Zaks, "Our Share of the Planetary Pie," pp. 12,585–12,586 in *Proceedings of the National Academy of Sciences of the United States of America*, 104(31) (July 31, 2007), https://www.ncbi.nlm.nih.gov/pmc/articles/PMC1937509/ .

44. Christian, *Maps of Time*, p. 140, p. 459. See also Jonathan A. Foley, Chad Monfreda, Navin Ramankutty, and David Zaks, "Our Share of the Planetary Pie," and Peter M. Vitousek, Paul R. Ehrlich, Anne H. Ehrlich, and Pamela A. Matson, "Human Appropriation of the Products of Photosynthesis," pp. 368–373 in *BioScience*, Vol. 36, No. 6 (June 1986), https://www.jstor.org/stable/1310258 . Net primary production (NPP) is a measure of how much chemical energy in the form of biomass is produced by living things. The vast majority of this energy ultimately derives from sunlight, through photosynthesis. The exact percentage of terrestrial NPP co-opted for human use depends considerably on what exactly qualifies as "co-opting," since NPP directly used by humans and livestock "as food, fuel, fiber, or timber" (Vitousek et al., p. 368) represents a far smaller fraction; Vitousek et al. estimate this number at 3.2% (p. 369). The fraction of aquatic NPP co-opted by humans is considerably lower than the fraction of terrestrial NPP co-opted by humans.

45. Dukes, "Burning Buried Sunshine," p. 31.

46. Charles Langmuir and Wally Broecker, *How to Build a Habitable Planet*, p. 597.

The proposal to name the present moment in Earth's history after human beings ("Anthropocene" comes from *anthropos*, which means "human" in Greek) is an attempt to encapsulate, in a single word, this collection of planetary changes, some of which could be apparent to a hypothetical future visitor digging through Earth's strata thousands to millions of years from now.[47]

While there is a tendency to speak of human environmental impact as inherently or even exclusively destructive, few of the aspects that people value most about modernity could have been achieved without the use of fossil fuels and their corresponding effects. The idea of the Anthropocene thus should be seen as reflecting human *power* more than human *destructiveness*. That power is not inherently destructive; it is both constructive and destructive. The scale of human environmental impact also reflects the power not so much of humans per se but of humans organized into industrial-capitalist societies, with their accompanying technologies—despite what the *anthropos* in "Anthropocene" may imply. Should it instead be called the "Industrocene"? It is not the mere presence of humans that matters, after all, but specific human activities.[48] Still, these activities have an array of consequences, and present as well as future societies will live in a context that requires adapting to the many complex natural and social realities that are encapsulated by the word "Anthropocene."

Sustainability in the Anthropocene

Many aspects of the Anthropocene appear to be fundamentally unsustainable. Rises in sea levels and changing weather patterns represent existential threats to human communities living on islands[49] or coastal areas at current sea level.[50] Loss of biodiversity bodes ill for the biosphere in general and for humans in particular, relying as we do on biodiversity for "ecosystem services" like purification of water,

---

47. Langmuir and Broecker argue that even the term "Anthropocene" is not ambitious enough: "The vastness of planetary change and capability, however, is more equivalent to the great events of the past that mark boundaries between geological eras or even eons, such as the origin of life, the rise of oxygen, the origin of multicellular life, or the Permo-Triassic extinction" (*How to Build a Habitable Planet*, p. 597). "It appears, therefore, that we have not simply changed epochs from Holocene to Anthropocene; one could argue that we have changed eras and eons, from Cenozoic and Phanerozoic to Anthropozoic" (*How to Build a Habitable Planet*, p. 645). Their term "Anthropozoic era" echoes the Italian priest-geologist Antonio Stoppani, who used the term in the 1870s. See Paul J. Crutzen, "Geology of Mankind," http://www.geo.utexas.edu/courses/387H/PAPERS/Crutzen2002.pdf.

48. Another option would be "Capitalocene," which has been suggested before (see, e.g., Naomi Klein, "Capitalism Killed Our Climate Momentum, Not 'Human Nature,'" https://theintercept .com/2018/08/03/climate-change-new-york-times-magazine/). Other activities of industrial societies, such as the extraction of mineral resources from the Earth's crust, raise similar questions of sustainability. See, e.g., Stephen E. Kesler and Adam C. Simon, *Mineral Resources, Economics and the Environment*.

49. Such as the Maldives, nearly all of which may disappear or permanently flood.

50. Such as many areas in the lowlands of southern Florida.

decomposition of wastes, nutrient cycles, and soil formation. And fossil fuels are fundamentally *non-renewable*: once they are consumed, coal, oil, and natural gas are essentially not replenished, at least not on human time scales.

How should human societies respond to these sustainability challenges? Answering this question is much easier said than done, but directly addressing these issues would mean reducing greenhouse-gas emissions while adapting to the climate change that does occur,[51] conserving biodiversity, and transitioning to renewable energy sources—such as solar energy, wind energy, and hydropower—that provide a constantly replenished "stream" of energy.[52]

Universal histories have often tried to reduce the environmental issues of the Anthropocene to just two underlying problems: the growth in human population ("overpopulation") and economic growth ("overconsumption"). The Earth scientist Preston Cloud provides an early example in his 1978 book *Cosmos, Earth, and Man*, writing of "the excess of people and their ever-growing demands on the rest of nature"[53] and referring to the human "popollution"[54] of the planet and the need for "fewer descendants."[55] More recently, big historians like Cynthia Brown and David Christian have raised concerns about future population increase, especially in the context of a global economy predicated on growth. The twin ideas of overpopulation and overconsumption not only drive many discussions about the present and future, but color how authors tell a variety of stories about the past, as in Clive Ponting's *A New Green History of the World* or Jared Diamond's *Collapse*, books that profile and attempt to explain the decline or collapse of various societies in history.

This population-versus-resources narrative relies, in part, on Malthusian thinking of the sort we discussed under "Population" in chapter 6. In the 1960s and 1970s, Paul Ehrlich's *The Population Bomb* and the Club of Rome's *Limits to Growth* popularized "neo-Malthusian" thinking and promoted a strong agenda of population control. Ehrlich helped to develop the pithy acronym IPAT: Impact = Population × Affluence × Technology. This equation suggests that human impacts on the environment (especially based on practices in agriculture, mining, and other forms of resource production or extraction) are multiplied by any increase in population, by the affluence (ability to consume) of a group, and by how advanced their technology is.[56] In this framing, environmental impact is generally regarded

---

51. And ideally, drawing carbon dioxide out of the air through carbon-dioxide removal technologies and related means.

52. Nuclear power occupies a middle ground in that it is not technically based on a renewable source but has other advantages over fossil fuels (and distinctive disadvantages as well).

53. Preston Cloud, *Cosmos, Earth, and Man*, p. 349.

54. Ibid., p. 352.

55. Ibid., pp. xiv–xv.

56. More advanced technology in production and transportation of goods may encourage efficiency, but it also widens the availability and market of goods and, therefore, may increase environmental impact. Think of cell phones, for example.

as intrinsically negative, and the "solutions" to sustainability "problems" are thus seen as lying in decreasing human populations, affluence, and technology—in short, reducing our impact by "scaling down." This view sees the "carrying capacity" of the Earth as a hard upper limit on the degree to which humans can impact their environment without precipitating a catastrophic population collapse.

At first glance, this seems like a convincing picture: more mouths to feed would seem to imply less food and resources to go around, which would seem to indicate that the best response would be to curb human population and per-capita consumption of resources. It is true that there are always constraints on how many people an ecosystem (or the entire Earth) can support, given a particular arrangement of people and relationship with their environment: if all human societies had remained foragers, the Earth could probably never have supported more than a few million people total.

But IPAT simply does not work in practice. As we argued in chapter 6, the assumption that populations are subject to firm and unalterable resource constraints generally has not proven true in the past when applied to human societies. Growing population sizes have not always led to more consumption of the same resources, but instead have often fundamentally changed the patterns of resource use as new forms of social organization and new technologies come into play. This happened, for instance, when foraging societies developed agriculture and began drawing on a significantly different set of food resources than before.[57] People produce as well as consume, and they conserve and restore natural resources as well as destroy them. So larger populations create both new stresses *and* new opportunities—a pattern that has held for centuries and, presumably, will continue. Reducing the Anthropocene to a problem of too many people is not merely an oversimplification, but a fundamental misdiagnosis. (Not to mention that it creates other problems with sharp political and cultural implications, such as *who* is the "over" of "overpopulation."[58])

---

57. One might imagine environmental forecasters of the Pleistocene calling to curb population growth on the basis of then-prevailing patterns of resource consumption.

58. As Ted Nordhaus writes:

> The concept [of carrying capacity], tellingly, owes its origin to 19th-century shipping, referring to the payload capacities of steam ships. It jumped from the inanimate to the terrestrial at the end of the 19th century, describing the maximum number of livestock or wild game that grassland and rangeland ecosystems could sustain.
> Applied to ecology, the concept is problematic. Cargo doesn't multiply of its own volition. Nor can the capacity of an ecosystem be determined from an engineer's drawings. Nonetheless, environmental scientists have, for decades, applied the concept to human societies with a claimed precision that belies its nebulous nature. . . .
> To understand the human experience on the planet is to understand that we have remade the planet again and again to serve our needs and our dreams. Today, the aspirations of billions depend upon continuing to do just that." ("The Earth's Carrying Capacity for Human Life Is Not Fixed," https://aeon.co/ideas/the-earths-carrying-capacity-for-human-life-is-not-fixed .)

IPAT also fails empirically as a prediction of the future. Ehrlich used his reasoning about population growth to predict that the 1970s and 1980s would bring catastrophic global famines, disease, and consequent warfare, and he argued (in 1968) that it may already have been too late to avert the imminent death of hundreds of millions or even billions of people. Given that such outcomes did not occur on the predicted time scales, Ehrlich has since acknowledged that his timing was off, but maintains that his reasoning was fundamentally sound: overpopulation-induced global collapse is, he says, still on its way. Stewart Brand, formerly Ehrlich's disciple but now an opponent of his reasoning, counters: "How many years do you have to not have the world end to decide it didn't end because that reason was wrong?"[59]

Even in Ehrlich's heyday, the business economist Julian Simon opposed the view that humans are fundamentally resource drains, calling human beings "the ultimate resource,"[60] pointing out the many positive 20th-century trends in cleaning up pollution of air and water, and establishing a very different interpretive framework for thinking about environmental futures—one that instead emphasized the need for political and economic freedom. Simon, like Ehrlich, was prone to making extreme claims. But he, and those inspired by him, also correctly highlighted some real problems with Ehrlich's core narratives of overconsumption and, especially, overpopulation.

Environmental Sustainability as a Matter of Social Organization and Infrastructure

One way to understand the appeal of overpopulation narratives, despite their serious flaws, is to recognize their elegance and simplicity. Rooted in scientific observations and models of animal populations, they assume that a single variable (population size) has great explanatory power, and they posit that responses to environmental problems should be formulated while focusing on that variable. Thus, they utilize the reductive style of explanation common in the natural sciences, but do so in a situation where the insights of the social sciences and humanities are at least as necessary for full understanding. Universal histories are well-positioned to join the humanities and the natural sciences on equal footing, and to contemplate environmental futures not only as scientific issues but also as questions of *social organization* and *infrastructure*—namely, how future societies could organize themselves to change patterns of resource consumption, especially in the production of energy. There are several ways in which emphasizing the social dimensions

59. See New York Times Retro Report, "The Unrealized Horrors of Population Explosion," https://www.nytimes.com/2015/06/01/us/the-unrealized-horrors-of-population-explosion.html (quotation from video).

60. See Julian Simon, *The Ultimate Resource* and *The Ultimate Resource 2*.

of sustainability is more helpful than a population-focused approach for gaining a nuanced understanding of possible and probable (and preferable) futures.

First, analyzing the past and future as an issue of total population versus total resources makes it appear that responsibility for environmental impact is evenly distributed among individuals, and that individual consumption habits are the only thing that distinguishes one person from another as far as environmental impact is concerned. This leads to what the environmental scholar Michael Maniates has called the "individualization of responsibility": an emphasis on individual action, especially "green consumption," for the good of the environment.[61] But the problem is that social power is not evenly distributed.[62] People are embedded in larger social, political, and economic systems over which they have, for the most part, relatively little control. The primary sources of power over the environment lie with powerful *institutions*, especially governments and multinational corporations, and the sociotechnical systems (see "Systems" in chapter 7) they enable.

Rather than associating humanity itself, and by implication each human being individually, with environmental degradation, a more socially and institutionally focused lens considers where our choices are largely made for us, through social structures and practices. An example is recycling, which is often put forward as an environmentally virtuous practice. But its real impact on the planet is almost completely out of your hands as an individual, because local governments and waste-management corporations decide everything that happens to your waste after it leaves your possession. Another example is food production: the "ecological footprint" of the same diet may differ widely depending on *where* that particular diet is being consumed, because of differences in infrastructure used for the production and distribution of food, as well as differences in agricultural practices.

Adopting a more social and institutional lens is not fatalistic; in fact, it may be much less fatalistic than a point of view in which any hope for positive environmental change requires a huge number of people, one by one, to engage in highly effortful changes to their habits of consumption. An institutional lens focuses attention not on these individual consumption habits but on larger-scale and systemic change. From this perspective, individual people—including relatively less powerful ones—are able to influence the future by finding ways to influence systems, not just by persuading other individuals to adopt different consumption habits.

A second reason to prefer socially nuanced analysis rather than overpopulation narratives is that the latter set up unrealistic expectations. A population lens tends to rely on the idea of "overshoot," a concept drawn from population biology suggesting that sudden population collapse results when populations grow too much and exceed the

61. Michael F. Maniates, "Individualization: Plant a Tree, Buy a Bike, Save the World?," *Global Environmental Politics* 1, no. 3 (2001): 33.

62. Ibid., p. 33 ff.

carrying capacity of their environments. (This is the pattern that stories of a population collapse on Easter Island are intended to illustrate; see the Extended Side Note "Easter Island" in chapter 6.) The idea of an overpopulation-induced collapse leads to vivid illustrations of possible apocalyptic scenarios in the future, and also to a rather common hope that a serious global resource crisis like worldwide famine or a series of natural disasters might wake people up and drive them to work for a more sustainable world.[63]

Drawing on political science and sociology, however, Maniates points out that crises do not automatically make people band together and solve problems cooperatively; crises more often bring about favorable conditions for authoritarian governments, which are not typically more friendly to the environment (or anything else) than democratic governments. Also, there may well not be any single apocalyptic global crisis due to climate change, biodiversity loss, or resource scarcity. Instead, a changing climate may lead to a series of regional crises, creating more difficult contexts for future politics and economics, making political stability harder both nationally and internationally, and hitting the poor of the world hardest. This does not seem like the kind of scenario that would provide improved conditions for building more sustainable political, economic, and social structures—although it is hard to know for sure.[64]

More fundamentally, though, a focus on sociotechnical systems (rather than on individual efforts) shows that any environmentally conscious changes, particularly with respect to energy and climate, will necessarily be relatively slow and take place over an extended period of time, decades rather than just a few years. It is not merely a matter of mustering the collective willpower to transition rapidly. Energy infrastructure—the physical and social structures that produce, distribute, and enable consumption of energy drawn from coal, oil, natural gas, nuclear energy, solar energy, wind, water (hydropower), and the Earth (geothermal energy)— exists at a scale that is difficult to fully comprehend. Filling a car with gasoline, for instance, is a simple act, but the very availability of that gasoline relies on a huge and mostly hidden infrastructure: on an extraordinary array of technology from heavy machinery to pull petroleum out of the ground, to oil tankers to transport it, to the industrial behemoths called oil refineries.[65] It also relies, explicitly or implicitly, on the large-scale coordination of the several million people who work in the oil industry globally.[66] Shifting to electric cars, or hydrogen-powered cars for that matter, would require a massive shift in all of these areas. (And that is just for

---

63. Michael Maniates, "Teaching for Turbulence," in Worldwatch Institute, *State of the World 2013: Is Sustainability Still Possible?*, p. 260.

64. Ibid., pp. 260–264.

65. Thanks to John DeCicco for inspiring this example.

66. For more information, see, e.g., Statista, "Total Oil, Gas, and Petrochemical Employment in the United States in 2015, by Occupation," https://www.statista.com/statistics/539142/united-states-oil-gas-and-petrochemical-employment-by-occupation/ .

the gasoline. Equivalent infrastructural changes would be needed for the car itself.) The historian and information scientist Paul Edwards writes:

> Decarbonization is an infrastructure problem, the largest one humanity has ever faced. It involves not only energy production, but also transportation, lighting, heating, cooling, cooking and other basic systems and services. The global fossil fuel infrastructure includes not only oil and gas wells, coal mines, giant oil tankers, pipelines and refineries, but also millions of automobiles, gas stations, tank trucks, storage depots, electric power plants, coal trains, heating systems, stoves and ovens.[67]

None of this is a reason to abandon the pursuit of changes in our energy infrastructure to mitigate climate change and transition to more renewable energy sources. Energy transitions happen slowly and gradually, but they do happen: over the past 150 years, transitions—from wood to coal, or from coal to a mixture of coal, oil, natural gas, and nuclear—have occurred, but on scales of decades, not months or years. (See Plate 42.)

Edwards has suggested that one relatively plausible way to accomplish a transition from fossil fuels to renewable energy, and to do so on a reasonable time scale, would be to consistently replace fossil-fuel infrastructure with renewable-energy infrastructure whenever the former wears out. Energy infrastructure typically lasts decades; for example, coal-fired power plants have a typical lifetime of about 40 years.[68] And infrastructure is not only physical, it is also human: there are jobs on the line, and people whose training and livelihood rest with the fossil-fuel infrastructure, over similar time scales. Overly abrupt changes, or the wrong kind of changes, or changes made at the wrong time without mindfulness of how they will impact existing jobs and livelihoods will cause hardship and injustice, especially for those at the bottom who are "just getting by" as it is. The sociotechnical systems in play are complicated, with many stakeholders who have (often) legitimate but diverse and sometimes conflicting interests, and the lights need to stay on in the meantime for societies to keep functioning.[69]

But change of some sort will happen, even in the developed world, where reliance on fossil-fuel infrastructure is already deeply entrenched, and also in parts of the developing world, where some fossil-fuel infrastructure may never need to be built in the first place because renewable alternatives are already available. The

---

67. Paul Edwards, "How Fast Can We Transition to a Low-Carbon Energy System?," https://theconversation.com/how-fast-can-we-transition-to-a-low-carbon-energy-system-51018 .

68. Todd Woody, "Most Coal-Fired Power Plants in the US Are Nearing Retirement Age," https://qz.com/61423/coal-fired-power-plants-near-retirement/ .

69. The lights need to stay on, the agriculture and transportation sectors need to keep going, and so forth—energy is necessary for producing goods and maintaining society.

Side Note: The Aral Sea

The story of Central Asia's Aral Sea provides a demonstration of the principle that natural resources, vast as they may seem, are finite. In 1960, the Aral Sea still ranked as the fourth-largest lake in the world, but over several decades, Soviet irrigation projects—aimed at growing crops, especially cotton, in the surrounding desert areas—redirected a huge volume of water from the two main rivers that fed the Aral. The flow of water diminished steadily until it ultimately stopped, and the sea dramatically shrank. By the late 1990s, the Aral stood at only about 10 percent of its original volume. (See Plate 43.)

In the last few years, the remaining part of the sea that lies in Kazakhstan, called the North Aral Sea, has recovered a bit, after the Kazakhstani government began long-term efforts to replenish water levels and even to reintroduce fish. However, only so much can be done to restore the full Aral, the original basin of which is shared between the independent post-Soviet republics of Kazakhstan and Uzbekistan. Redirection of the rivers, which started long ago with the first canals (dating back hundreds of years) but expanded dramatically in scale when industrialized practices of agriculture rapidly grew during the Soviet period, created new human communities that still exist. Hundreds of villages appeared where rivers were diverted to make new cotton fields, and each of those villages held its own social world, with lives dependent on its survival. These midcentury irrigation decisions thus had long-term political, social, economic, and demographic consequences, and today, simply turning back the clock and directing the rivers into the sea basin once more would be an existential threat to those communities.

Taken as a whole, it adds up to a regional crisis that hits some individuals and communities much harder than others, with those living in the vicinity of what used to be the Aral Sea rendered especially destitute. These groups, such as the Karakalpaks of western Uzbekistan and Kazakhstan, are socially marginal and politically disempowered, as the centers of power and wealth are hundreds of miles away. This too makes it less likely that attempts to restore the Aral Sea (however quickly or slowly they might unfold) will become a top priority of those who are most able to do something about it. The Aral Sea disaster is a reminder that although resources like fresh water may be called "natural" resources, their distribution at local, regional, and global levels are profoundly *social* issues, and that choices surrounding resource distribution have ongoing, long-term consequences for the communities they affect.

slowness of transitions is, if anything, all the more reason to begin now, and conscientiously. Universal histories will not drive the process, but they can help by pointing out that technological change has always been a gradual process rather than a matter of instantaneous replacement. This was true in the deeper human past—farming was not immediately adopted, but took hundreds of years to catch on in many places, and several thousand years to grow around the world—and it is true now. Planning for the future has to reflect this nuanced understanding of the character of historical change. As much as possible, it needs to match the pace of change in physical infrastructure with the pace of change on the human side. And it must negotiate questions of who is responsible for initiating and implementing changes in social organization, resource use, and technology. What role do governments play? What role do corporations play? What role do extraordinarily wealthy investors play? What about ordinary individuals? These are all issues that need to be negotiated, and re-negotiated, in locations around the world.

Environmental Trade-Offs and the Future

The idea of "sustainability" was originally set up, at the level of the United Nations, as a core concept that could incorporate many interests, one that different people and nations could read different things into, but bringing everyone to the same table around a central environmental and economic goal. By design, it was a highly integrative term. Likewise, the word "environment" powerfully captures and unifies a whole range of concerns and realities of the natural and social worlds, triggering many associations: from the availability of clean water to the concentration of carbon dioxide in the atmosphere, from the extinction of species to the distribution of oil in the world, from toxic runoff to climate change. And while it may seem "natural" or even inevitable now that all these issues fit together into a single big picture, the ideas of sustainability and of the global environment were both carefully constructed by scientific experts and political elites in the 20th century.[70]

There is good reason for this. Many environmental / sustainability concerns are genuinely connected with one another, and one can readily perceive, for example, the connections between species diversity and climate: climate change can lead to the flourishing of some species and the extinction of others. Summing up those connections in two highly evocative words is a reasonable, effective, and perhaps even brilliant thing to do.

At the same time, however, the words can simplify extremely complex situations and mask the reality that some environmental goals may conflict with others—just as "progress" in one area can come into conflict with "progress" in another. Disposable diapers add to landfills, for example, but cloth diapers require constant cleaning, using energy and water. Which to use, when the worthy goal of cutting down material waste comes into conflict with the worthy goal of reducing energy and water usage?[71]

---

70. See Perrin Selcer, *The Postwar Origins of the Global Environment: How the United Nations Built Spaceship Earth*.

71. Plastic versus paper bags is another classic conundrum, though not a strict dichotomy given that there are cloth bags as well (which have their own advantages and disadvantages).

Messages like Preston Cloud's, earlier in this section, tend to suggest that the world's people have everything to gain and nothing to lose by controlling their population numbers and diminishing consumption. Jared Diamond implies something similar in his book *Collapse*, which features the subtitle *How Societies Choose to Fail or Succeed*. While Diamond does provide a degree of nuance to this point within the book, the subtitle and overall framing suggest that societies "choose to fail" when they fail to prioritize what matters—their resource base and relationship with the physical environment.

Yet here too, there are pros and cons to everything. Patricia McAnany and Norman Yoffee have written that they do not "suspect that rulers of the past— alleged to have been shortsighted—ruined their environments and failed. Rather . . . past societies (and their leaders as well as the opponents of leaders) experienced a variety of crises and responded to circumstances as best they could."[72] While one could certainly dispute the implication that leaders and societies consistently respond wisely to crisis situations, there is an important point here. As in the past, so too today: modern global society faces a series of complex, collective decisions in which sustainability considerations weigh strongly, but only rarely (if ever) is one option the clear-cut best one for everybody involved, even in the long term. Despite what the ostensibly universal framing of the words "sustainability" and "environment" might suggest, there are always trade-offs.

For example, we have already argued that environmental issues should not be reduced simply to concerns about the sheer size of a population. A growing population may face the need for changes in social organization and sociotechnical systems to improve patterns of resource use, especially the use of renewable sources of energy, preservation or provision of clean air and water, preservation of fertile soil and sources of food, mining of minerals, and mitigation and adaptation to climate change and ocean acidification. But so could a constant population, or even a population that declines in absolute numbers. And "depopulation" would present its own set of problems: if fewer people are born in the next generation, the size of the workforce of a society dwindles relative to the total number of people, especially relative to the number of elderly people who have aged out of the workforce— leaving more and more people who are out of work dependent on fewer and fewer people who do work.[73] There will always be challenges and problems, regardless of population size. But the changes necessary for an environmentally sustainable world may actually be more readily accomplished if that world has more people, if they are appropriately empowered and equipped.

---

72. Patricia A. McAnany and Norman Yoffee, "Why We Question Collapse," in *Questioning Collapse*, eds. Patricia A. McAnany and Norman Yoffee, p. 12.

73. Compare, e.g., the population structure in China after the government's long-time "one-child policy."

Solar energy and nuclear energy provide other examples of the trade-offs inherent in environmental choices. While solar energy is renewable, plentiful (more energy from the Sun strikes the Earth's surface in two hours than world energy consumption in 2015 from all sources combined[74]), and leaves behind far less pollution than fossil fuels, the acquisition of raw materials and manufacturing processes for solar panels still leave behind some (although comparatively small amounts of) pollution and carbon-dioxide emissions, and the intermittent nature of sunlight requires the storage of generated energy to be practical. Solar panels also have a limited life span, eventually wearing out and producing additional waste streams. Nuclear power, meanwhile, is a commercially viable way of generating large amounts of energy, and as proponents point out, it results in very low carbon-dioxide emissions. But the popularity of nuclear power is complicated by a history of accidents, ranging from the small-scale to the catastrophic (e.g., Chernobyl), and by the need for long-lasting storage of nuclear waste. Solar and nuclear are both better options than fossil fuels as far as climate change is concerned—that is, when measured by the standard of greenhouse-gas emissions—yet they are both complicated by other serious concerns. It is not necessarily indifferent to the environment or to future inhabitants of the Earth to suggest that we weigh the various considerations and attempt to balance multiple priorities.

And yet climate change, ocean acidification, soil erosion, and other environmental challenges present genuine threats that will bring about serious changes in human lifestyles around the globe, whether as proactive measures to head off these threats or as reactive measures to respond to their consequences—or both. At some point, there will surely be a transition to a world that looks much different than ours. What kind of changes that will mean, and how painful the transition will be, are serious questions. How much control any given individual, or even human beings collectively, will have over it is another. But the modern era of human history is not an endpoint, after which change ceases. Modern global society is developing and transitory, just like every other society in history. Things will change, although it is not easy to predict exactly how.

Envisioning the "progress" of modernity as ending in a "plateau" of stability is actually a relatively common pattern in modern utopian and dystopian thinking. The novels *Brave New World, Nineteen Eighty-Four*, and *We* (a Russian-language predecessor of the former two, written by Yevgeny Zamyatin in the early 1920s) all envisioned an "end of history," where social change effectively comes to a standstill

---

74. For the calculation and phrasing this example was based on, see Jeff Tsao, Nate Lewis, and George Crabtree, "Solar FAQs," https://www.sandia.gov/~jytsao/Solar%20FAQs.pdf . The numbers in this case are 643 exajoules for two hours of sunlight and 572 EJ for 2015 world energy consumption. The latter number was drawn from the International Energy Agency's "Total Primary Energy Supply (TPES) by Source" chart data for 2015; see https://www.iea.org/statistics/ . Note that conversion from ktoe to joules is necessary.

and millennial stability is achieved. So did Francis Fukuyama, who famously (or infamously) applied the phrase "end of history" (with some qualifications that are usually overlooked) to liberal democracy. But as Zamyatin also pointed out in *We*, the reality is that "there is no final revolution." Instability, change, and transition will continue as long as there are people. Or life. Or the Earth. Or the universe in anything like the form we know it. These are all dynamic, not static. Equilibria are not permanent—not as long as different scales interact, and not until (perhaps) the far, far distant cosmic future.

What modern global society actually craves is not so much sustainability as adaptability. Even over the very long term, as the astrophysicist Adam Frank points out, the habitability of Earth itself, or of any planet, is something that evolves and changes over time, reflecting constant adaptation more than a steady state:

> Astrobiology is fundamentally a study of planets and their "habitability" for life. But sustainability is really just a concern over the habitability of one planet (Earth) for a certain kind of species (*[H]omo sapiens*) with a certain kind of organization (modern civilization). That means our urgent questions about *sustainability* are a subset of questions about *habitability*. The key point, here, is the planets in our own solar system, like Mars, show us that habitability is not forever. It will likely be a moving target over time.[75]

So rather than trying to bequeath to future generations a world that looks like the current one, better to present one that is easier to adapt to, such as by working to mitigate climate change through the reduction of greenhouse-gas emissions, and set an example of adaptation ourselves. Instead of continuing to maintain the same systems but backing off the throttle by cutting population or individual consumption, perhaps system-level changes to the overall patterns of resource use are necessary, directly addressing the issues at hand and setting up templates for continued institutional, infrastructural, and social-systemic adaptation.

Transhumanism

Perhaps the most radical possibilities of technology are those proposed to fundamentally change human beings themselves. Such technologies are the focus of "transhumanism," a movement that advocates the fundamental transformation and "enhancement" of the human condition, especially through technological intervention. Areas of potential enhancement include radical extension of human life spans;

---

75. Adam Frank, "Climate Change and the Astrobiology of the Anthropocene," https://www.npr.org/sections/13.7/2016/10/01/495437158/climate-change-and-the-astrobiology-of-the-anthropocene .

physical modifications that confer "superhuman" strength, speed, or endurance; intellectual modifications that increase intelligence, concentration, or memory; and psychological modifications that confer desired changes to personality or mood. These could come through genetic modification, brain modification or implants, use of drugs, technologically mediated modification of human physiology and biochemistry, or a combination of these. Al Gore—who among his other activities wrote a book extrapolating present "megatrends" into the future—writes of

> the emergence of a revolutionary new set of powerful biological, biochemical, genetic, and materials science technologies that are enabling us to reconstitute the molecular design of all solid matter, reweave the fabric of life itself, alter the physical form, traits, characteristics, and properties of plants, animals, and people, seize active control over evolution, cross the ancient lines dividing species, and invent entirely new ones never imagined in nature.[76]

While such lists may seem like fantasy, or the stuff of science fiction, some preliminary aspects of a "transhuman" future are already present and widely accepted even today. To proponents of transhumanism, the possible improvement of human nature itself seems like a crowning achievement of progress, and perhaps even a natural culmination of universal history, while to critics, transhumanism seems dystopian and dangerously willing to discard some of the best aspects of humanity in service of a misguided technological ideal. Universal histories are well-situated to engage not only the scientific and technical dimensions of transhumanism, but also the serious cultural and ethical questions that it raises.

Technology and the Future of Human Evolution

Technologies of human modification and enhancement are sometimes framed as the "next stage" of human evolution. In a way, this is misleading. It is questionable whether there are distinct "stages" of human evolution at all, and implying this lends credence to misplaced progress narratives of the sort discussed under "Evolution" in chapter 4. On the other hand, it does make sense to think of technology as affecting the course of evolution: Juan Enriquez and Steve Gullans, for instance, have pointed out that we have many present-day and foreseeable-future

---

76. Al Gore, *The Future: Six Drivers of Global Change*, p. xiv. Gore advances this as one of six "megatrends" that will powerfully shape the future, alongside the deeply "interconnected global economy"; the "planet-wide electronic communications grid"; "a completely new balance of political, economic, and military power in the world"; "rapid unsustainable growth"; and a "new relationship between the aggregate power of human civilization and the Earth's ecological systems" (pp. xiv–xv).

technologies that induce "unnatural selection" and "nonrandom mutation"[77] to complement the usual mechanisms of evolution by "natural selection" and "random mutation." Julian Huxley—the brother of author Aldous Huxley and, in his own right, a prominent evolutionary biologist, eugenicist, and the first director of UNESCO—popularized the term "transhumanism" in a 1957 essay, framing transhumanism explicitly as an extension of human evolution: "the human species will be on the threshold of a new kind of existence, as different from ours as ours is from that of Pekin[g] man."[78]

To some extent, technology has played a role in evolution for a very long time, having consistently affected "natural" selection where human beings are concerned. In fact, biological evolution has, if anything, sped up in recent centuries: one study by Henry Harpending and John Hawks suggested "that over the past five thousand years alone, humans have evolved as much as a hundred times more quickly than at any time since the split of the earliest hominid from the ancestors of modern chimpanzees some 6 million years ago."[79]

Why is this? Because culture, technology, and biology have always intertwined in influencing the course of evolutionary change (as we explored in chapter 5 when discussing "co-evolutionary" frameworks). With rapid, human-driven, technology-enabled change to the physical and biological surroundings in which human beings live, natural selection responds with equally rapid change. As Enriquez and Gullans point out:

> Almost every aspect of human life has changed—moving from rural to urban; living in an antiseptic environment; eating very different sugars, fats, and preservatives; experiencing novel man-made stimuli; ingesting large quantities of medicines and chemicals; being sedentary; having children later; and living indoors. Given so many transformations, it would be surprising if our bodies and brains did not change as a result.[80]

It is also a basic evolutionary fact that larger populations tend to evolve faster, so the roughly sevenfold increase in the world's human population over the past 200 years—along with new foods, diseases, and medicines, as well as the increased opportunity for people with various disabilities and other serious medical conditions to survive and thrive (and to pass along their genetic heritage to future

77. Juan Enriquez and Steve Gullans, *Evolving Ourselves: Redesigning the Future of Humanity— One Gene at a Time*, p. 3.

78. See, e.g., https://web.archive.org/web/20160625132722/http://www.transhumanism .org/index.php/WTA/more/huxley . Huxley emphasized social and spiritual changes in human existence, not the technological shifts that became prominent for later writers.

79. As summarized by Peter Ward and Joe Kirschvink, *A New History of Life*, p. 352.

80. Enriquez and Gullans, *Evolving Ourselves*, p. 11.

generations)—makes the modern period especially likely to see to rapid evolution-ary change. As discussed in chapter 4, the key part of the phrase "survive and repro-duce" is "reproduce": rapid cultural changes that shift patterns of who reproduces, to what extent they reproduce, and with whom they reproduce, matter as much for human biological evolution as the factors that affect who lives and who dies. Among such cultural changes are the ease of international travel and marriage be-tween people who come from vastly different places and backgrounds.

In short, human evolution has responded to technological change for a very long time, as well as to the social change that both spurs and follows technological change. Still, the most radical possibilities for how human beings might change in the relatively near future seem to be based not on technologies that modify the environment in some of these existing ways, but on technologies that directly inter-vene in human bodies, human genetics, and human brains.

Technologies and Technical Limits of Human Modification

One sphere of transhumanist aspiration is extension of the human life span to pre-viously unheard-of lengths. During the modern period, public-health measures and the treatment and curing of diseases have dramatically increased the *average* human life span, especially in the developed world, principally by preventing large num-bers of deaths among children, young adults, and middle-aged adults. But aging still takes its toll on every human body, and even curing all forms of cancer would, by some calculations, further increase the overall average life span only by about 3 years.[81] What transhumanists promote instead is research into the underlying mechanisms of aging, with the hope that future medical interventions might slow or even stop the aging process itself, rendering typical life spans much longer than they are now.

Human genetic modification is another widely discussed area. The tools for modifying a person's genetic material have been available for decades. The first suc-cessful transfer of DNA into a person's cells for medical reasons ("gene therapy") happened in 1990, for example. A generation later, in the 2010s, a gene-editing tool called CRISPR made the direct modification of DNA sequences in living cells vastly more efficient and inexpensive. Before 2018, modification to the genetic

---

81. "Preventing and curing specific diseases can only have a limited impact on life expectancy in a population that already lives as long as people do in the industrialized world. If we cured *all* heart disease, life expectancy in the US would increase by only about 7 years. Curing *all* cancer would result in a gain of some 3 years." (Nick Bostrom and Rebecca Roache, "Ethical Issues in Human Enhancement," https://nickbostrom.com/ethics/human-enhancement.pdf , p. 4. They cite T. Thom et al., "Heart Disease and Stroke Statistics—2006 Update: A Report from the American Heart Association Statistics Committee and Stroke Statistics Subcommittee," *Circulation* [February 14, 2006], p. 4.) See also Peter Hoffman, "Physics Makes Aging Inevitable, Not Biology," http://nautil.us//issue/36/aging/physics-makes-aging-inevitable-not-biology .

material of human beings had treated only somatic (non-reproductive) cells and human embryos that went on to be destroyed; no child had yet been born who was directly experimented upon as an embryo, or whose parents' sperm or egg cells were genetically modified. In more technical terms, there had been no known modifications as yet to the "germline" in humans that reached birth—which means the cells that are capable of passing on genetic material to the next generation, such as sperm or egg cells within a given man or woman, the cells that divided to produce the sperm or egg cells, the cells that divided to produce those, and so on, all the way back to the single-celled zygote at the moment of that person's conception. The technical ability to modify a person's germline exists now, however, and was claimed to have been used by a researcher in China in 2018.[82] Any changes to the germline would be able to be inherited by all future descendants of the person whose germline had been modified. The effects of genetic modification of somatic cells are limited to that one person; the effects of modifying the germline, by contrast, extend to future generations.[83]

Perhaps the most radical visions of future human evolution are those having to do with intelligent machines and how humans might interact and merge with them. At the moment, artificial intelligence (AI) is not artificial *general* intelligence; even the most advanced current AI systems, as impressive as they are, are dedicated to fairly specific tasks. There are no "machines matching humans in general intelligence—that is, possessing common sense and an effective ability to learn, reason, and plan to meet complex information-processing challenges across a wide range of natural and abstract domains."[84] Human perceptual abilities, such as "analyzing visual scenes, recognizing objects, or [interacting] with a natural environment,"[85] have proven especially difficult for machines to achieve.

Machines of the future may or may not match human-level general intelligence, but even if machines themselves never reach this point, the philosopher Nick Bostrom points out that one "path to greater-than-current-human intelligence is to enhance the functioning of biological brains,"[86] especially through the "direct control of human genetics and neurobiology."[87] This parallels the thinking of the most

---

82. For some of the original reporting on this topic, see, e.g., Alexandra Harney and Kate Kelland, "China Orders Investigation After Scientist Claims First Gene-Edited Babies," https://www.reuters.com/article/us-health-china-babies-genes/china-orders-investigation-after-scientist-claims-first-gene-edited-babies-idUSKCN1NV19T .

83. CRISPR can also modify essentially any other organism, such as crops, which could take genetically modified organisms (GMOs) to a new level. Even ecosystems can be altered using a technique called "gene drives."

84. Nick Bostrom, *Superintelligence: Paths, Dangers, Strategies*, p. 4.

85. Ibid., p. 17.

86. Ibid., p. 43.

87. Ibid., p. 44.

widely known prognosticator of an "age of spiritual machines,"[88] the inventor and technologist Ray Kurzweil, who has argued that we are only decades, not centuries, away from an "intelligence explosion" (what he calls the "singularity"), which we should expect to arrive as early as the mid-21st century.

Rather than a scenario in which artificial intelligence displaces human intelligence, Kurzweil expects that the two will merge, as human beings first wear and then progressively internalize devices that grant them new and previously unimaginable physical as well as cognitive capabilities. Kurzweil extends the prospects of physical augmentation of the human body using robotic prosthetics and implants, seeking to "integrate human brains and nervous systems with various mechanical enhancements."[89] Currently, such technologies are typically used to repair what is broken, as when people with amputated limbs are given prosthetics they can control directly with their thoughts. But as Kurzweil and others have written, the future may hold opportunities not only to repair what is broken, but also to enhance what is not broken. For instance, he has suggested that nanoscale robots may be introduced into humans to feed the body from within, rendering ordinary consumption of food unnecessary.[90] He has also advanced the idea that microscopic devices like artificial red blood cells could change the physiology and biochemistry of the body so as to remove such fundamental limitations as the need to breathe more than once every few hours.[91] Kurzweil believes that too-small-to-see computers will be embedded throughout our environments, and "images will be written directly to our retina, providing full-immersion virtual reality."[92] He has even predicted the direct downloading of information into intelligent consciousness, access to other people's conscious experiences,[93] and the merging of (formerly distinct) people's consciousness.[94]

---

88. This is a Ray Kurzweil book title.

89. Enriquez and Gullans, *Evolving Ourselves*, p. 195.

90. Ray Kurzweil, *The Singularity Is Near: When Humans Transcend Biology*, pp. 303–305.

91. Ray Kurzweil, "The Accelerating Power of Technology," https://www.ted.com/talks/ray_kurzweil_on_how_technology_will_transform_us/transcript#t-893,772 . See also Kurzweil, *The Singularity Is Near*, pp. 305–306.

92. Kurzweil, "The Accelerating Power of Technology"; note that he actually predicted this outcome for the year 2010. See also Kurzweil, *The Singularity Is Near*, p. 312.

93. Through shared virtual environments that incorporate all the senses as well as the neural correlates of someone's conscious experience; see Kurzweil, *The Singularity Is Near*, pp. 314–317. Kurzweil also predicts that by the mid-2040s, "We will have version 3.0 human bodies, which we will be able to modify and reinstantiate into new forms at will. We will be able to quickly change our bodies in full-immersion visual-auditory virtual environments in the second decade of this century; in full-immersion virtual-reality environments incorporating all of the senses during the 2020s; and in real reality in the 2040s." (Kurzweil, *The Singularity Is Near*, p. 316.)

94. Kurzweil, *The Age of Spiritual Machines*, pp. 236–237.

Ultimately, Kurzweil predicts that the future of the Earth and universe will change radically as (merged human-artificial) intelligence that originated on Earth constantly finds new ways to manipulate energy and matter throughout the universe, spreading to other planets, stars, and galaxies and "waking up" the universe, turning it to its own ends. The future of the universe, Earth, life, and humanity would all be driven by Earth-originated intelligence.[95]

There are good reasons to be skeptical of Kurzweil, whose work may make for excellent science-fiction scenarios but may not be quite so good a description of the real world's future. Not only does he tend to predict that technology will move faster than it actually does, some or even all of the grandiose developments he predicts may turn out to be physically impossible. Kurzweil's basic argument, for instance, is based on the potential for technology to grow exponentially, as discussed earlier in this chapter.[96] But critics have been quick to point out that technology, particularly at the nanoscale, may run into fundamental physical limits that cannot be overcome.[97] Likewise, radical life extension may be impossible if aging is fundamentally an outcome of physics (because random thermal motion of molecules eventually leads to the irreversible accumulation of damage to living cells over time) rather than a reversible outcome of biology.[98] And many of the possibilities for merging people's conscious experiences and identities may turn out to be impossible, because the relationship between mind / consciousness and brain is not as straightforward as technological enthusiasts, many of whom are physicalists (see the discussion under "Mind" in chapter 5), assume that it is. On a less metaphysical note, Bostrom points out that "the rate-limiting step in human intelligence is not how fast raw data can be fed into the brain but rather how quickly the brain can extract meaning and make sense of the data."[99] In other words, downloading information directly into someone's brain may not much improve their knowledge and understanding.

Although new technologies do offer the humans who use them new capabilities, they always come with limitations too, and these limitations are often harder

---

95. Kurzweil, *The Singularity Is Near*, p. 349 ff.

96. Already, the scales of technological change are often shorter than the average human life span: the swiftness of social, technological, and economic change is why the 20th century saw so many parts of the world lose traditional means of livelihood as new technologies made old occupations obsolete. But how much shorter these scales can or will become is an open question.

97. And that Kurzweil's arguments that technology has grown exponentially throughout human history are seriously flawed.

98. "The scientific literature is full of explanations for aging: Protein aggregation, DNA damage, inflammation, telomeres. But these are the biological responses to an underlying cause, which is accumulating damage through thermal and chemical degradation." (Hoffman, "Physics Makes Aging Inevitable, Not Biology.")

99. Bostrom, *Superintelligence*, p. 56.

to foresee. As the AI expert Rodney Brooks points out, Isaac Newton could have foreseen neither the vast capabilities of smartphones nor the fact that they completely cease all function after a few days of routine use if they are not plugged into something called an electrical outlet.[100]

Universal Histories and Transhumanism

There are also social and human reasons why the course of technological change may not match Kurzweil's (and other transhumanists') most radical predictions. This human dimension is an especially productive one for universal histories to explore. Rather than providing a forum for undisciplined speculation about what the future of human evolution and technological development may hold, universal histories can use their integrative approach to bring together insights regarding the technical, ethical, and social dimensions of technologies of human modification, providing a more robust approach to thinking about which technological futures are possible, and also which are desirable.

First, considering the social context of new technologies, using approaches drawn from disciplinary history and the humanities, can help one to think with greater nuance about which technologies are likely to be pursued in the first place, and then to catch on and become widely accepted. Proponents of transhumanist philosophies and technologies, especially Kurzweil, often argue that the emergence of radical technologies is inevitable. This "technological determinist" view is based on the idea that technology "marches forward," growing exponentially, largely independent of social, cultural, political, and economic circumstances. Techno-determinists tend to see technology as something like an impersonal force that drives social structures and cultural values.

Historians, on the other hand, who are rarely techno-determinists, tend to see many factors at work, and the outcome (and direction) of technological change as being far from inevitable. People have to work on technology in order for it to develop or change in a given direction, after all, and they usually have to work in at least a somewhat coordinated fashion, have access to a range of sophisticated tools, and be materially supported for doing the work. All of those variables are tied up with economic, social, and political realities. And significant numbers of people have to be willing to adopt new technologies for their development to be profitable, which matters too, at least in the contemporary context of widespread industrial-capitalist economies. Power to influence the course of technological change therefore lies both with public acceptance of new technologies (the existence of a market for the technologies) and with the developers and others who stand to

---

100. Rodney Brooks, "The Seven Deadly Sins of AI Predictions," https://www.technologyreview.com/s/609048/the-seven-deadly-sins-of-ai-predictions/ .

benefit within the current economic-political system, not to mention any subsequent constraints, encouragements, or other nudges brought to bear by regulatory, administrative, or environmental contexts. Laws and regulations, culture and consumer demand, the ability of human institutions to adapt to changes—all these factors affect the pace and direction of technological change. What is physically possible is a constraint on, but not the only or even the primary determinant of, how the future of technology will unfold.

It is not always obvious that people have the power to affect the direction of technological change, in part because widespread cultural acceptance of a technology tends to obscure the fact that there was ever a choice. For example, dependence on caffeine (a "technology" that modifies human physiology) is today widely socially acceptable, and even encouraged by powerful commercial interests. But it did not have to turn out this way. The use of caffeine is not universal: it is forbidden or restricted in some religious communities, some people's bodies react quite negatively to it, and one can at least imagine a world in which caffeine had been widely banned alongside stronger, more dangerous stimulants like cocaine and methamphetamine. Schools and educational systems are currently working through similar questions concerning "smart drugs" or "study drugs." Specifically, many students around the world are willing to (modestly) improve their memory and concentration, even if these areas of cognitive function are in no way "impaired" to begin with, through the use of stimulants, which in turn increases the demand for such drugs from other students wishing to "keep up." In many educational contexts, a relatively small minority of students use such stimulants, and the drugs are acquired and used illegally. So it is clear to most that this "technology of human enhancement" can be resisted and need not be widely adopted. However, one can imagine a future world in which such drugs are so widely used and accepted that their popularity would seem to be *inevitable*, much like caffeine today. In other words, people in the present usually recognize (correctly) that we have a choice whether to accept or resist study drugs, or performance-enhancing drugs in sports, or any number of other "enhancement" technologies, but changing *cultural* contexts may obscure this reality.

As the caffeine example suggests, this pattern has held for a long time. The roots of human enhancement technologies go back more than just the last few decades, as does the tendency to retrospectively perceive the inevitability of their acceptance. J. B. S. Haldane (1892–1964, a founding figure in evolutionary biology whom we have met both in chapter 4 and in chapter 7) foresaw in 1923 that radical applications of biology would soon be possible, especially in "reproduction and heredity."[101] This expectation has been fulfilled in abundance, although reproductive

---

101. J. B. S. Haldane, "DAEDALUS or Science and the Future: A Paper Read to the Heretics, Cambridge, on February 4th, 1923," http://bactra.org/Daedalus.html .

technologies of human modification have become so widespread that it is no longer apparent to most people just how radical they are. For example, hormonal contraception systematically alters a woman's biochemistry to interrupt the body's normal operation and cause (usually temporary and reversible) sterility. The Pill, introduced in the late 1950s, was "based on chemical feedstock from a Mexican yam formerly used as fish poison."[102] Artificial insemination, on the other hand, in which a man's sperm is directly implanted into a woman's uterus or cervix, allows reproduction mediated by laboratory techniques rather than by sexual intercourse, and the emergence of "sperm banks" where donated sperm is preserved indefinitely. In vitro fertilization (IVF) is the creation of a new, genetically complete human being in a Petri dish (or "test tube"), with subsequent implantation into a woman's body for gestation. Among other things, it enables the possibility of producing children from the cells of two people who were not necessarily ever in the same place at the same time, or children for whom both biological parents are already dead. Whether attempting to prevent or enable pregnancy, these are all technological means of trying to bring human reproductive physiology under new and different forms of individual and social control.

IVF also enables further forms of human modification, as the procedure typically results in the production of several human embryos, only one or two of which are usually implanted in a woman's uterus and reach the point of being born. The rest may be discarded, or "saved" for implantation in another woman or for later experimentation (as in embryonic stem cell research). The criteria for selecting which embryo or embryos are implanted sometimes include preimplantation genetic diagnosis, in which embryos are genetically tested for various traits. Current restrictions on the use of this technology vary widely by country, but legal systems around the world favor its use for "screening out" embryos with life-threatening, disabling, or disadvantaging genetic conditions, while disfavoring its use for selecting other traits, such as sex, height, skin color, eye color, or intelligence. The use of preimplantation genetic diagnosis, however, gives rise to concerns about the possibility of "designer babies" in the future, selected from among a number of IVF-produced embryos for traits that the parents wish to prioritize. And current uses of the technology lead to concern about "ableism"—discrimination or prejudice against those perceived as being disabled in some way—given the potential for systematic elimination of those with "preventable" genetic conditions in the next generation and the systematic neglect of those already born with such conditions. (The same concern stems from the use of prenatal screening in general, since parents sometimes choose to abort babies who are found to have conditions like cystic fibrosis or Down syndrome.)

---

102. J. R. McNeill and William McNeill, *The Human Web: A Bird's-Eye View of World History*, p. 280. The yams are "barbasco yams" of the *Dioscorea* genus, which are a source of a chemical (diosgenin) used to produce synthetic hormones.

In all these matters, an awareness of the historical record reinforces why there are serious ethical concerns about reproductive technologies. Control over the genetic composition of future generations is exactly what advocates of 20th-century eugenics sought. Efforts to encourage those who were considered genetically "superior" to reproduce, and to prevent the reproduction of those who were considered genetically "inferior," led to eugenic policies including the state-sponsored sterilization of several hundred thousand people in Nazi Germany—and tens of thousands of people in the United States, whose eugenics laws were an inspiration to Nazi policy. Todd Rose has written that eugenics "has deservedly had a bad press; yet it is too often forgotten that it was motivated by very much the same philanthropic utilitarian considerations that underlie all 'liberal' attempts to modify a population."[103] Eugenics, birth control, and population control are all manifestations of the impulse to control and "improve" human reproduction, even if they are today usually, in most of the world, in the hands of couples and medical institutions rather than expressions of coercive state power.[104]

Such considerations seem to suggest that the future course of research and development of technologies for human modification will respond to social, cultural, moral, and ethical influences. If people refuse to accept certain modifications, the technology is much less likely to go in that direction. This is what eventually happened to early eugenicists' efforts to "enhance" the human population by sterilizing or otherwise preventing the reproduction of those considered less "fit": the broader culture turned against eugenics after seeing the horrors of Nazi applications—even in the United States, where much of the political and scientific development of eugenics occurred.

Criticisms of Transhumanism

Human modification has a strong appeal in some circles, in part because it brings the path of human evolution under direct human control. Nick Bostrom and Rebecca Roache argue, for instance, that "being able to think better would equip us to solve important political and social problems, make scientific breakthroughs, and so on"[105]—and that we should therefore seek and encourage it. Using technology to transcend normal human physical and cognitive limitations seems, at first glance, like it could be helpful. But as the comparison with eugenics suggests, "enhancement" technologies have a much darker side.

---

103. Todd Rose, *The End of Average*, p. 121.

104. There have been many cases of other state-level interventions in reproductive practices that do not lodge authority in individual hands, such as coercive population-control measures like China's "one-child policy," mentioned earlier.

105. Bostrom and Roache, "Ethical Issues in Human Enhancement," p. 15.

First, there have routinely been unforeseen consequences of major, large-scale experiments in the fundamental nature of human beings and the world we inhabit. Consider one large-scale experiment that has already been carried out, the global spread of industrial capitalism. As we have discussed in chapter 7 and this chapter, a great many consequences have flowed from this experiment, both positive and negative. One such consequence has been the emission of greenhouse gases into the atmosphere at a scale that may affect the Earth's climate for thousands of years. Greenhouse-gas emissions were not the primary objective of the industrial "experiment"; they were rather an unforeseen consequence, and one that human societies may have a very difficult time adapting to. Similarly, human lives and human societies may not be any more prepared for the consequences of widespread genetic or cognitive modification of human beings than they were, or are, for climate change. In fact, they may be far less prepared—perhaps especially in the case of germline modifications, which change parts of the huge and enormously complex human genome and could have both foreseen and unforeseen consequences for all descendants, in all future generations, of genetically modified persons.

Enhancement efforts are also culturally specific, not self-evidently applicable to all people and contexts. They enable much more powerful enforcement of prevailing social norms—as when children are given drugs to "treat" conditions that are deemed problematic but that arise primarily because of their social context, such as in schools. And there is the possibility of inscribing in human genetics whatever makes one valuable to *today's* society, in conformity with present norms of beauty, health, and productivity. As Aldous Huxley implied in *Brave New World*, technologies of human enhancement may empower the dominant social order and those who control it, while making the larger public shallow and quiescent. Bostrom even suggests that some countries might encourage reproduction through IVF with embryos selected from a huge number generated in order "to increase long-term social stability by selecting for traits like docility, obedience, submissiveness, conformity, risk-aversion, or cowardice, outside of the ruling clan."[106]

The desire to eliminate human limitations ignores the fact that those limitations are not just obstacles that impede human flourishing, but in some ways help to promote that flourishing. For example, limits on life spans and on physical and cognitive capacities are also limits on the destructive impact that a given person can have on others. In *That Hideous Strength*, C. S. Lewis pointed out the chilling prospect of "enhanced" and extended lives offering newly intense tortures that could last indefinitely, so long as a cruel person or group keeps an enemy alive for continuous torture.[107] This is an exaggerated threat, perhaps, but it is also a reminder that technology can be used for evil as well as for good, and that human modification

---

106. Bostrom, *Superintelligence*, p. 48.

107. C. S. Lewis, *That Hideous Strength*, pp. 175–176.

could make it easier, not harder, for the strong to dominate the weak. Indeed, if technological and physiological advantages of the "guns, germs, and steel" variety could enable the abuses of power and accelerate the loss of life that resulted from the collision of Old World and New World, imagine the possible abuses of enhancement technologies that grant "superhuman" physical or cognitive capacities to some while leaving behind those who cannot afford, or who do not wish to accept, such technologies.

Finally, genetic modification comes at the cost of manipulating and experimenting on human life in its earliest and most vulnerable stage.[108] Already, IVF does this routinely. Questioning the ethics of such manipulation is interlocked with deeply contested and fraught matters of culture, law, and policy, such as issues related to privacy, bodily integrity, and personal autonomy. But among other things, it is worth asking what consequences the manipulation of embryonic human life may have for the relationship between the present generation and the next generation(s). In the words of Leon Kass:

> Fewer people yet worried about the effects . . . on our embryo-using society of coming to look upon nascent human life as a natural resource to be mined, exploited, commodified. The little embryos are merely destroyed, but we—their users—are at risk of corruption. We are desensitized and denatured by a coarsening of sensibility that comes to regard these practices as natural, ordinary and fully unproblematic. People who can hold nascent human life in their hands coolly and without awe have deadened something in their souls.[109]

"Bioconservatives" like Kass, who broadly oppose human modification for purposes of "enhancement" (rather than therapy), give warnings to identify and preserve what is best in humanity, and they call for us to recognize that what a given culture sees as enhancement may well not turn out to be that at all. They emphasize that even well-meaning and apparently advantageous technologies may create new problems, even as they solve or mitigate others. They encourage us to see what is good in human life as it is now, even with its limitations, and to recognize the potential for serious abuse of enhancement technologies—and to pull back from the brink.

Enthusiasts for transhumanism may see great promise in present and near-future technologies for human modification, but certain forms of technological

---

108. Note that this is not true of gene *therapy* in adults.

109. Leon R. Kass, *Life, Liberty and the Defense of Dignity: The Challenge for Bioethics*, p. 10. His comments were directed at the debates about embryonic stem cell research in the United States but could reasonably apply to any process that exploits human embryos.

progress come at a steep cost. A careful, considered weighing of a given technology's potential future benefits against the warnings of critics, and against the lessons of a complicated and sometimes disastrous litany of past experience, can help us to make sound decisions in the present about what pathway would be best to pursue in the future.

Time

There is a certain set of time scales familiar to every human being who can read this book. We understand seconds, and we understand decades, and everything in between. Except perhaps for the very young, people usually have a sense of what those time scales "feel" like. We do not, however, have a sense of what a million years feels like, and we likewise have little sense of what a billionth of a second feels like. Or to put it a little differently, try imagining a million years. Now try imagining a trillion years. In your imagination, they may not feel very different. But they differ by the same factor as an hour differs from 114 years, and *those* are two time spans that, no doubt, feel quite different to a human reader. This is the difficulty of narrating history on large time scales, and part of why a universal history may feel "impersonal" at times: many relevant time scales in the universe are either too long or too short to be grasped intuitively by a human mind.

Your conception of time influences everything else. Your ideas about the "shape" or "direction" of history, your ideas about the universe and humanity's place in it— all these are bound up with conceptions of time. Time structures our lives and how we make sense of the world. It is at once physical, psychological, and social. It is connected with meaning, memory, and anticipation. And it is remarkable in its apparent familiarity: "time" is the most commonly used noun in English.[110] Yet thinking about and constructing a philosophy of time is extremely difficult. More than 1,600 years ago, Saint Augustine of Hippo wrote in his *Confessions*: "What

---

To Ponder: To Experience a Radically Extended Life Span

How might you narrate the history of the universe, Earth, life, and humanity if you actually experienced the whole thing through the eyes of a human being, "in real time," during a radically extended life span? If you lived billions of years, how would you divide your life into chapters, periods, stories?

---

110. Dean Buonomano, *Your Brain Is a Time Machine*, p. 3. "Year" and "day" are the third- and fifth-most common nouns, respectively.

then is time? I know what it is if no one asks me what it is; but if I want to explain it to someone who has asked me, I find that I do not know."[111]

One may tell a story linking past, present, and future without ever analyzing the ancient philosophical question of what time *is*. But one's vision, representation, and *feel* for the nature of time inform how one writes history at every level. As the historian of science Jimena Canales writes, "All historical accounts—explicitly or implicitly—make assumptions about what time is and how it progresses."[112] Differing visions of time also prevail within different disciplines, so it is fitting that this final end-of-chapter philosophical reflection should concern itself with the nature and meaning of time itself: time as a physical parameter, time as a social construct, time as a lived experience, and time as an underlying reality.

Philosophy, Physics, and Time

For many centuries, one of the biggest questions in philosophy has been the question of what time *is*. Specific questions about time discussed in philosophy—sometimes with considerable insight, but rarely with final resolution—include: What is the relationship between *being* and *becoming*? Is becoming, the "flow" or "advance" of time, an illusion? Is change an illusion, is permanence an illusion, or is the common-sense intuition that change and permanence are both real an accurate perception of reality? Does time exist apart from change, or is time simply a measure of change and not a separate thing? (If the latter, then "time" is really just "change.")

In this limited space, we cannot explore these questions comprehensively, but two figures in the history of Western philosophy who stand out for their views related to change and permanence are the ancient (pre-Socratic) Greek philosophers Heraclitus and Parmenides, both of whom were active around the early 5th century BCE. Heraclitus, famous for the saying "No man steps in the same river twice" (because both the man and the river have changed), thought that change and becoming was the only reality, and that permanence was an illusion. Parmenides occupied the opposite pole, arguing that change is an illusion and permanence the only reality. (Zeno's paradox, that a man walking to his destination should never arrive because he has to cross half the distance to his destination, then half again, then half again, was originally designed to show that motion is an illusion: Zeno was a disciple of Parmenides.) These two poles have continued to attract various thinkers over the centuries—Einstein, for instance, was squarely with Parmenides, as we will discuss shortly—but most have taken some middle ground, as Aristotle did, arguing (essentially) that a thing can change while remaining identifiably the same thing, that change and stability over time are both realities.

---

111. Augustine, *The Confessions of Saint Augustine*, trans. Rex Warner, p. 262.

112. Jimena Canales, *The Physicist and the Philosopher*, p. 359.

Centuries later, Augustine (354–430) wrote the long prayer known as his *Confessions*, which is half autobiography and half a seminal work of philosophy. One chapter of the *Confessions* is an extended meditation on what time is, and on the relationship between time and eternity. Augustine argued that God, the Creator of time, must exist outside of time, "in" timeless eternity. He considered only the present to be fully real, while the past and future exist only in memory and anticipation, but all moments of time are equally present "at once" to God. Augustine also carefully distinguished *time* from *intervals of time* and investigated the meaning of "duration": only intervals, but not time itself, can be "long" or "short." He concluded that we do not perceive the flow of time directly, but only have traces of the past in *memory* and of the future in *anticipation*.[113]

In the 1700s, the German philosopher Immanuel Kant (1724–1804) argued that space and time are not properties of "external" reality; instead, they are best understood as categories structuring human thought and experience. In this view, time is not a separate entity in the "outside world," and speaking of time does not necessarily reflect things as they are in themselves, but rather reflects how the human mind is structured.

The Greeks, Augustine, and Kant present but a few moments (so to speak) in the history of philosophy, at least Western philosophy, although they are well-remembered by the discipline today. They give a flavor for the kinds of philosophical investigations of time that have been going on for centuries, even millennia. Modern philosophy, however, has seen an important change. It addresses many of these same questions, but usually also with explicit input from, or engagement with, *physics*. The Stanford Encyclopedia of Philosophy explains:

> What is time, and is it real? If it is, does time flow or lapse or pass? Are the future or the past as real as the present? These metaphysical questions have been debated for more than two millennia, with no resolution in sight. Modern physics provides us, however, with tools that enable us to sharpen these old questions and generate new arguments.[114]

Why physics? What does modern physics have to say about time? There is no shortage of ideas. For example, Einstein's theory of relativity offers a view of time as a fourth "dimension" on the same footing as the three dimensions of space. But what, exactly, does it mean to put space and time together into a single four-dimensional framework? Physicists differ in their interpretations, though Einstein himself was unflinching in arguing that all of time exists "at once," just like the

---

113. See Augustine, *The Confessions of Saint Augustine*, pp. 251–280.

114. Stanford Encyclopedia of Philosophy, "Being and Becoming in Modern Physics," https://plato.stanford.edu/entries/spacetime-bebecome/ .

dimensions of space exist "at once." As he put it, "For us believing physicists, the distinction between past, present and future is only a stubbornly persistent illusion."[115] This view, denying the reality of time's "flowing" or "progressing," is commonly called the "block universe," since the picture of the universe it suggests is that of an unchanging, static, four-dimensional "block." This interpretation dovetails with the observation that nearly all fundamental laws of physics (in relativity and in quantum mechanics) are "time-symmetric"—meaning that the equations look identical whether time is seen as running forward or backward. Very rarely does anything in modern physics single out or require a direction for time.

The block universe is not universally accepted among physicists and philosophers, and it has some serious detractors. The philosopher John Randolph Lucas has objected as follows: "The block universe gives a deeply inadequate view of time. It fails to account for the passage of time, the pre-eminence of the present, the directedness of time and the difference between the future and the past."[116] Or as the physicist Richard Muller puts it, the error of elevating general relativity's representations of spacetime to the level of reality "is in interpreting a computational tool as a deep truth. It is fundamentally the error of physicalism: *if it isn't quantifiable, it isn't real*. In fact, it is based on an extreme fundamentalist version of physicalism: *if it isn't in our current theories, it isn't real*."[117] The theoretical cosmologist George Ellis has argued that the block-universe view does not "take complex physics or biology seriously"[118] or adequately address the reality of emergent complex systems in the real universe. He has argued instead that spacetime "grows" as time passes: the part of spacetime we call the "past" is fixed and unchangeable, while the "future" is open—a view known as "possibilism" or the "growing-universe theory," in contrast both with the "eternalism" of the block universe that assumes past, present, and future are equally real and on fully equal footing, and with "presentism," which assumes that only the present, not the past and future, is real.[119]

Another counterintuitive insight to come out of relativity is called the "relativity of simultaneity," which is the idea that two events that are simultaneous for one observer are not necessarily simultaneous for another observer who is in motion

---

115. Quoted in Dan Falk, "A Debate Over the Physics of Time," https://www.quantamagazine.org/a-debate-over-the-physics-of-time-20,160,719/ .

116. John Randolph Lucas, quoted in Lee Smolin, *Time Reborn: From the Crisis in Physics to the Future of the Universe*, p. 64.

117. Richard Muller, *Now: The Physics of Time*, pp. 303–304.

118. George F. R. Ellis, "Physics in the Real Universe: Time and Spacetime," *General Relativity and Gravitation* 38 (2006):1798.

119. One final philosophical objection to the block universe could be raised: Can time really be on exactly the same footing as space? An object is "extended" in space; it has different parts at different points in space. But it seems that it is fully present, not partly present, at each point in *time*.

with respect to the first observer. For example, if an observer on a train perceives two flashes of light—one at the back of the train and one at the front—to occur simultaneously, another observer who is standing still on the ground as the train passes will not perceive those flashes to be simultaneous.[120] Realistically, in order for the difference to be perceptible to a human visual system, as opposed to a much more precise set of scientific instruments, the train would have to be going at an appreciable fraction of the speed of light, a practical impossibility but a valid proof of principle. The key point is that the simultaneity of two events depends on the relative motion of observers. One consequence of the relativity of simultaneity is that two synchronized clocks that are moving with respect to one another do not stay synchronized: this has been experimentally verified, as when two originally synchronized clocks, one set onboard a commercial airliner flying west and the other set onboard a commercial airliner flying east, lost their synchronization (by a few hundred nanoseconds after flying around the world twice—not a huge difference by most measures, but precisely in accord with Einstein's predictions).[121]

The rate of time's passage is connected not only with motion but also with gravitational fields, since in general relativity, the curvature of spacetime is what generates gravity. As the physicist Carlo Rovelli puts it, "time passes faster in the mountains than it does at sea level."[122] Spacetime itself is dynamic and changing, so time itself can get stretched. Like the relativity of simultaneity, this is no purely theoretical result. It has been verified experimentally hundreds of times, and Global Positioning System (GPS) satellites have to correct for this "gravitational redshifting" effect constantly.[123]

Such results suggest that there is no truly "universal time"—that is, valid throughout the universe. Past, present, and future may be well-defined at a given event, from a particular observer's point of view, but there is no "single, universal distinction between past, present, and future."[124] The speculative edge of physics yields even more bizarre-sounding ideas, such as time travel through wormholes, or four-dimensional spacetime embedded in five-dimensional space (Randall-Sundrum brane theory). But even the most well-established ideas of relativity suggest a model of time that is intimately bound up with gravity and motion, and that

---

120. Fundamentally, this is due to the fact that light moves at a finite speed rather than moving instantaneously from one place to another.

121. The original version of this experiment is known as the Hafele-Keating experiment. The predicted results for such an experiment have to take into account both special and general relativity, since gravitational redshifting (the phenomenon described in the next paragraph of the main text) means that altitude matters for the passage of time as well.

122. Carlo Rovelli, *The Order of Time*, p. 9.

123. See, e.g., Muller, *Now*, p. 64.

124. Rovelli, *The Order of Time*, p. 48.

is well-defined only locally.[125] This means that instead of a Newtonian vision of absolute time that flows of its own accord, impervious to all possible influences, relativity shows us that time is not independent of everything else in the universe.

Finally, much has been written about the most important law of physics that *does* single out a direction for time, and one with strong implications for universal histories: the second law of thermodynamics. Physicists often invoke the increase of entropy, which is correlated with the forward "progress" of time, to *explain* the "arrow of time"—that is, why time only seems to flow in one "direction." But the proposal that entropy drives time in this way has several problems. First, there is no clear reason *why* entropy would be able to drive time's arrow, no physical mechanism identifying why entropy would have such "power." Rather, it makes much more sense to posit that time has directionality, with past and future being fundamentally distinct from one another, and then to explain entropy in terms of time rather than to explain time in terms of entropy. Additionally, how could time depend on entropy if the rate of time flow does not depend in any recognizable way on the precise rate of entropy increase in a given location?[126] And why should time flow not reverse locally when there are local decreases of entropy in a specific place at a particular scale, as there has often been in the formation of structure on Earth?[127] It is not clear that it really makes sense to explain the arrow of time using entropy.[128]

Physics gives us a view of time that is quite counterintuitive in extreme situations, but that reduces down to the uniform Newtonian-style "absolute time" in ordinary circumstances and, ultimately, may or may not explain fundamental aspects of time. Physicists often assume that since general relativity's model of space and time is wildly successful in describing the effects of gravity on everything smaller than galaxy-sized scales, and is at least partially successful in describing larger scales (though some argue that "detections" of dark matter and/or dark energy are actually exposing shortcomings of general relativity on the largest scales), time must "really" be like how it is represented in general relativity. But models only represent reality rather than being reality itself. And every physical model has flaws or limitations; powerful as it is, general relativity is no exception. Ellis writes that it is not clear whether

125. As the physicist Carlo Rovelli points out, it treats spacetime as a physical *field*—identical, in fact, to the gravitational field—meaning that time itself is a field interacting with other fields, like electromagnetic fields.

126. Muller, *Now*, p. 292.

127. Ibid., pp. 172, 292.

128. Ibid., p. 166. Muller points out another shortcoming of the entropy explanation: "Today, compelling evidence suggests that an arrow of time is built into the fundamental behavior of at least one additional realm of physics. It is in the physics of radioactive decay, historically referred to as the 'weak interaction,' and there is now evidence that 'time reversal symmetry' is violated in some such decays." (Ibid., p. 121.)

spacetime does *"indeed exist as a real physical entity."*[129] And general relativity and quantum theory are not fully compatible with one another, so relativity must break down in certain cases: relativity is not an absolute. As suggested in chapter 2, perhaps the laws of physics in general are simply not as all-encompassing as physicists think they are. And as Muller points out, physics is not generally good at handling the concept of "now," but this should be thought of as a shortcoming of *physics*, not of a commonsense or philosophical understanding of time. Physicists (or anyone else) who assume that all reality is within the domain of physics do not fully appreciate this.[130]

It is therefore unclear how much modern physics actually adds to ancient philosophical thought about time, although the two can work together to frame the questions differently and in a way that brings physics and philosophy together. Philosophy can help physics recognize fundamental issues about to what extent physical models and observations of time illuminate *reality*.

Time in Other Disciplines

A fairly standard view of time in modern science is that time is, *in reality*, "clock time." In other words, time is nothing more, and nothing less, than that which a clock measures, something that flows steadily onward, infinitely dividable into equal increments like minutes or seconds or milliseconds. On this view, human perceptions of time are, at best, experiential counterparts to the reality of measurable, physically real time—or, at worst, an illusion. But what if there is more to time than what a clock is ever, even in principle, capable of measuring? The political scientist and anthropologist James C. Scott points out (albeit in a very different context):

> Certain forms of knowledge and control require a narrowing of vision. The great advantage of such tunnel vision is that it brings into sharp focus certain limited aspects of an otherwise far more complex and unwieldy reality. This very simplification, in turn, makes the phenomenon at the center of the field of vision more legible and hence more susceptible to careful measurement and calculation. Combined with similar observations, an overall, aggregate, synoptic view of a selective reality is achieved, making possible a high degree of schematic knowledge, control, and manipulation.[131]

What if this is exactly what physics, and science more generally, has done with time? As Carlo Rovelli points out, physics shows that even clock time (physical

129. Ellis, "Physics in the Real Universe," p. 1822; italics in original.

130. See Muller, *Now*, pp. 255–265, 287, and 305–306.

131. James C. Scott, *Seeing Like a State: How Certain Schemes to Improve the Human Condition Have Failed*, p. 11.

time, or measurable time) is not a single thing: it is not an absolute, monolithic thing that exists independent of everything else, as Newton conceived. Observers in motion with respect to one another measure different rates of time—though in everyday life, these differences are completely unnoticeable—and gravity affects the rate at which time passes.[132] And what if there is more to time than what physics can identify in principle?

Historians, who might seem to be particularly interested in time, and perhaps to have a professional sophistication about it, are often not so much interested in clock time as they are in the socially constructed sense of time that different cultures have, how people experience and conceptualize time in different cultures past and present, and how they live within time given their understanding. The ancient Chinese dynastic cycle provides one example of a way to conceptualize time that is embedded within records of the past accessible to us today. Historical records left by early Chinese dynasties lack a "year zero" or "year one," for instance, a singular point in time of the sort found in the calendars of Christian, Islamic, and Jewish civilizations. Instead, they organize time according to cycles: the standard dynastic narrative is one of rise, decline, revival, decline, and fall; another dynasty follows. This way of organizing a historical narrative creates its own distinctive sense of time that connects the rhythm of years with people and politics in a way that emphasizes stability and repeating pattern more than progress, overall directionality, or one-time events like the birth of Jesus or Muhammad's establishment of the first Muslim community in Medina.[133]

Other ancient civilizations described their own versions of a cycle of time. Ancient Egypt, dependent on the reliable yearly flooding of the Nile for all subsistence, had two words to describe time: *neheh* and *djet*. The former described the cyclical, never-ending recurrence of the same patterns, "generated by the movement of the heavenly bodies and hence determined by the sun."[134] The latter described "a sacred dimension of everness,"[135] where time is suspended and things have attained immutability—that is, "time at a standstill."[136] Where modern industrialized societies tend to see linear time*line*s and a progression of past to present to future, the ancient Egyptian language and culture seem to have heavily emphasized cycles, stability, and permanence. Ancient Indian cultures likewise developed conceptions of time that included cycles, some covering truly huge time scales: the scriptures of Buddhism and Hinduism, for example, describe great cycles of billions of years or more.

---

132. See Rovelli, *The Order of Time*, p. 91.

133. Thanks to Christian de Pee for this point. Also see Shu-hsien Liu, "Time and Temporality: The Chinese Perspective," *Philosophy East and West* 24, no. 2 (1974):145–153.

134. Jan Assmann, *The Mind of Egypt: History and Meaning in the Time of the Pharaohs*, trans. Andrew Jenkins, p. 18.

135. Ibid., p. 18.

136. Ibid., p. 19.

Scientifically informed modern cultures, by contrast, provide another way of conceptualizing time, typically as a line rather than a cycle. As the historians Daniel Rosenberg and Anthony Grafton write in their book *Cartographies of Time: A History of the Timeline*, the timeline is so familiar to us that it seems practically inconceivable to think of time in any other way. Yet the timeline itself has a history, and it is put in service of particular kinds of historical narratives. The timeline "in its modern form, with a single axis and a regular, measured distribution of dates . . . is a relatively recent invention. Understood in this strict sense, the timeline is not even 250 years old."[137]

The timeline is a graphical representation tied to a way of conceptualizing time. Many modern cultures, underpinned both by the Abrahamic religions' proclamation of a beginning and end of time and by secular narratives of progress of the sort discussed in this chapter, tend to think of time as a line, and of "points in time" that can be tracked through the use of precise mechanical clocks. The political scientist and historian Benedict Anderson writes that "the date at the top of the newspaper, the single most important emblem on it," tracks "the steady onward clocking of homogeneous, empty time."[138] Still, as much as modern industrialized cultures around the world run on clock time and structure daily life around it, the historian Marc Bloch wrote that "human time will never conform to the implacable uniformity or fixed divisions of clock time. Reality demands that its measurements be suited to the variability of its rhythm, and that its boundaries have wide marginal zones."[139]

At the intersection of cross-cultural psychology and linguistics is the consideration of how language about time shapes thinking about time. An engineer by training and a serious student of linguistics, Benjamin Lee Whorf, of Sapir-Whorf fame (see "Language" in chapter 5), argued that a given speaker of the Hopi language

has no general notion or intuition of TIME as a smooth flowing continuum in which everything in the universe proceeds at an equal rate, out of a future, through a present, into a past . . . the Hopi language is seen to contain no words, grammatical forms, constructions or expressions that refer directly to what we call "time," or to past, present, or future.[140]

Whorf offered the "linguistic relativity" hypothesis discussed in chapter 5 as an argument that one's perceptions of time (and other realities) differ according to

137. Daniel Rosenberg and Anthony Grafton, *Cartographies of Time: A History of the Timeline*, p. 14.

138. Benedict Anderson, *Imagined Communities*, p. 33.

139. Marc Bloch, *The Historian's Craft*, p. 189. The great French historian was captured, tortured, and shot by the Nazis very shortly after penning those words.

140. See Benjamin Lee Whorf, "An American Indian Model of the Universe," in *Language, Thought, and Reality: Selected Writings of Benjamin Lee Whorf*, ed. John B. Carroll, p. 57.

linguistic circumstances, just as Einstein's "physical relativity" suggests that perceptions of time differ according to motion and gravity.[141] Other scholars have debated the accuracy of Whorf's assessment of the Hopi language, and how much the
Hopi way of conceiving temporal relations differs from those of speakers of modern
Indo-European languages. Later linguists showed conclusively that the Hopi *do*
mark both the passage of time and the feeling of time passing,[142] but at least part of
Whorf's underlying point may still stand, insofar as nuances of language may still
affect one's conception and experience of time in subtle ways.

Some languages have multiple words used to refer to time. The ancient
Egyptian language is one example, as is ancient Greek, which had the words *kairos*
and *chronos*.[143] *Chronos* is similar to modern ideas of clock time: quantitative, measurable, and regular. It is, appropriately, the root of English words like "chronol-
ogy." *Kairos*, meanwhile, expresses "the right time," as when (to use a classic example
from ancient Greece) a master of rhetoric recognizes precisely the right time to
raise an argument to which his listeners are now receptive. The word *kairos* refers to
an aspect of time that is qualitative, unquantifiable, and experiential: Hippocrates
wrote that every *kairos* is a *chronos*, but that not every *chronos* is a *kairos*. English
comes closest to making a similar distinction with the word "moment,"[144] which is
hard to reduce to something definable in terms of minutes and seconds. Other ways
of making similar distinctions between quantitative and qualitative time include
distinguishing, as Canales does, "the time of the universe" from "the time of our
lives,"[145] "clock time" from "time-in-general,"[146] "measured clock time" from "lived
time,"[147] "physical time" from "psychological time,"[148] "outer clock" from "inner
clock,"[149] or "mathematical time" from "real time."[150]

Specialists in psychology and neuroscience have sought to understand the
relationship between physical time and lived experiential time by considering

---

141. For a detailed discussion of to what extent Whorf intended an explicit parallel between physical and linguistic relativity, see Frank Heynick, "From Einstein to Whorf: Space, Time, Matter,
and Reference Frames in Physical and Linguistic Relativity," *Semiotica* 45, no. 1–2 (1983):35–64.

142. Especially Ekkehart Malotki; see his extensively documented critique in *Hopi Time: A
Linguistic Analysis of the Temporal Concepts in the Hopi Language*.

143. See, e.g., the discussion in James L. Kinneavy and Catherine R. Eskin, "Kairos in Aristotle's
Rhetoric," *Written Communication* 17, no. 3 (2000):433–434.

144. Compare also the words "timely" and "timing."

145. Canales, *The Physicist and the Philosopher*, p. vii.

146. Ibid., p. 24.

147. Ibid., p. 29.

148. Ibid., p. 46; drawing on Albert Einstein.

149. Ibid., p. 47; quoting Franz Kafka.

150. Ibid., p. 206; drawing on Jacques Maritain.

timekeeping mechanisms in the brain. The human brain, it seems, does not have a single "big" timekeeping mechanism, but rather many small ones. The 24-hour circadian rhythms of the human body, for example, are "managed" by a small cluster of neurons in the hypothalamus, called the suprachiasmatic nucleus.[151] Other "clocks" in the brain track time and regulate processes on other time scales, from fractions of a second on up. Damage to one timekeeping mechanism in the brain does not necessarily impair the brain's ability to keep track of time on other scales; the systems are largely independent.[152]

There are limits to the shortest time that human beings can be conscious of, the resolution with which we can distinguish temporal differences. A basic limit is set by the time it takes a neuron to fire, roughly one millisecond (one one-thousandth of a second). Two visual stimuli shown five milliseconds apart can be successfully distinguished as non-simultaneous.[153] Other sensory systems have slightly different resolutions, all measured in milliseconds. The neural and biochemical present is thus not instantaneous, but instead puts duration into our experience of the world. An impressive aspect of how the brain processes time is that although different systems in the brain operate at different speeds, we have a largely unified perception of what is happening when. The brain integrates stimuli that are received over a certain window of time, roughly 100 milliseconds or less. Movies and animation take advantage of the fact that a series of static images, played in sufficiently rapid succession, appears continuous. Likewise, the neuroscientist David Eagleman writes:

> In the early days of television broadcasting, engineers worried about the problem of keeping audio and video signals synchronized. Then they accidentally discovered that they had around a hundred milliseconds of slop: As long as the signals arrived within this window, viewers' brains would automatically resynchronize the signals; outside that tenth-of-a-second window, it suddenly looked like a badly dubbed movie.[154]

The standard "frame rate" in the film industry has long been 24 frames per second, meaning that one still image is displayed approximately every 42 milliseconds, which viewers' brains translate as continuous motion. (And even more so with modern computer games and films, which sometimes use 48 or 60 frames per second, meaning a new image appears approximately every 21 or 17 milliseconds, respectively.)

---

151. Really mashing together the Greek and Latin in "suprachiasmatic."

152. See Anil Ananthaswamy, "Your Brain Is a Time Machine: Why We Need to Talk About Time," https://www.newscientist.com/article/2132847-your-brain-is-a-time-machine-why-we-need-to-talk-about-time/ .

153. David M. Eagleman, "Brain Time," https://www.edge.org/conversation/brain-time .

154. Ibid.

How does the neuroscience of time intersect with a broader view of what time *is*? Whatever one's philosophical understanding of time, it seems important to be able to "derive" ordinary experience of the world from it. One intriguing possibility is that in the linguistic connections between time and space, as when we speak of "short" or "long" times, or of looking "forward" or "backward" in time—all of these are spatial metaphors—the brain is actually employing "the neural circuits that are used to represent space"[155] in an effort to represent time. This suggests the possibility of a deep connection between the architecture of the brain and ideas about physics, both of which draw analogies between time and space.[156] That said, it still seems that just as physics leaves room for multiple interpretations of what time is, so too do psychology and neuroscience, which do not touch questions of whether what is physically measurable and empirically observable is all that is real, such as whether the human existential experience of time is a mere byproduct of fundamental physics, or whether there is much more to time than what is accessible to physics, instruments, and empirical measurements. Neuroscience also does not fully settle the question of the relationship between brain activity and the reality of what the brain is perceiving. One might say that discussions of time perception usually touch the intersection of *chronos* and the brain, rather than deeply investigating broader or more qualitative understandings of time.

A final approach to pondering the character of time can be found in the study of religion, which contemplates the ways in which religious expressions and understandings of the world address human life in time. The time-bound character of human nature is intimately linked with the realities of birth and death. Our temporality is an expression of our finitude: we exist bit-by-bit rather than all at once. Religious ideas from the Australian Aboriginal Dreamtime, to the Abrahamic philosophical understanding of the transcendent and eternal God unlimited by time, to the unchanging unity of Brahman in classical Hindu philosophies all suggest that the contingent, time-bound reality of the ordinary world is open to, and perhaps enabled or permeated by, a more fundamental and timeless reality. Religious rituals not infrequently make "profane time" sacred by bringing time into contact with timeless eternity. Mircea Eliade, a prominent 20th-century scholar of comparative religion, put it this way: "All time of whatever kind 'opens' on to sacred time—in other words, is capable of revealing what we may for convenience call the *absolute*, the supernatural, the superhuman, the superhistoric."[157] Or to state a similar point from a different

---

155. Ananthaswamy, "Your Brain Is a Time Machine."

156. Ibid.

157. Mircea Eliade, *Patterns in Comparative Religion*, p. 389.

angle: "It would be impossible to overstress the tendency—observable in every society, however highly developed—to bring back that time, mythical time, the Great Time. For this bringing-back is effected without exception by every rite and every significant act."[158]

Time is not just one thing, and as we have seen, it raises many sets of questions. If time "belongs" to any one discipline, it is probably philosophy, as philosophy occupies a central position that draws on all of these other approaches. But time should not be regarded as belonging to any one discipline to the exclusion of others; disciplines rather stand alongside one another in expanding the thoughts we are able to think. After all, even philosophers think in categories associated with the culture and language of their "times."

With a myriad of ways to approach an *apprehension*, although perhaps not a *comprehension*, of time, neither physics nor philosophy, nor history, nor any other field stands over and above all other disciplines. All are speaking about time in ways that may or may not exhaust what one could say about a tremendously multi-faceted reality. As the neuroscientist Dean Buonomano writes, "our subjective sense of time sits at the center of a perfect storm of unsolved scientific mysteries: consciousness, free will, relativity, quantum mechanics, and the nature of time."[159] The writer and science journalist Anil Ananthaswamy goes even further: "all the profound scientific discoveries of the past century or so are struggling with a common enemy: time."[160]

---

158. Ibid., p. 395.

159. Buonomano, *Your Brain is a Time Machine*, p. 216.

160. Ananthaswamy, "Your Brain is a Time Machine."

9 INTERPRETATION

The final chapter of this book returns the focus to the bigger picture of grand stories and their interpretation. Having contemplated big questions about "the meaning of it all" throughout the book—from the size of the universe to the non-centrality of the Earth, from the "nature" of the living world to what it means to be human, from the large-scale course of human history to modernity and the future—we now consider again the interpretation and framing of universal history as a whole. In "Interpretation," we reconsider the general question of how to distinguish which approaches to universal history are most reasonable, insightful, and compelling. In "Complexity," we consider how viable complexity is as a framing device for the history of the universe, Earth, life, and humanity. In "Religion," we draw together critiques of naturalistic assumptions and consider the place of religious worldviews as framings for universal history. We then bring the book to a close in "Narrative," with a final look at the meanings attached to grand stories about the past.

Interpretation

We live in an ancient cosmos with a trillion galaxies or more, and on average, a hundred billion stars light each of those galaxies. Most of the elements in your body were manufactured in stars. The Earth under your feet was once molten, after having coalesced from a spinning disk of specks of matter around a newborn star. The continents, gigantic masses of rock that literally support our lives, move around, very slowly but steadily, and have taken a huge variety of configurations over geological time. Living creatures, some almost unimaginably different from those that now walk the land and swim the sea, have lived and died for many hundreds of millions of years—all from humble beginnings in the mists of time over 3 billion years ago. Your own body's origins, the literal "stuff" of which it is made, go back in an unbroken line to the origins of life and, in some ways, long before that. Much as the Book of Genesis says, you were formed from the dust of the ground, from the same stuff as the Earth. And the technology, the knowledge, the organization you see around you in the world today all rest on the contributions of millions, if not billions, of people who lived long before you were born.[1]

Such, in a single paragraph, is the story we hear in modern universal histories based in scientific and historical scholarship. It is, in many ways, a stunning and awe-inspiring story. Everything, even those bits of our world that seem most non-descript, has a history, a long story of how it came to be what it is, and can be placed in historical context—the terrain under your feet, the grass in a field, the Sun, the atoms in your body. When examined as a whole, new connections and new histories emerge.

And yet there is a rhythm to how these stories are usually constructed and told, a way in which these universal histories are customarily packaged. They are not mere collections of facts discovered by scientists and scholars, but are strongly *interpreted* in how these facts are selected, framed, and presented and in what lessons they are designed to communicate. At the core of our book is the idea that any such framing of a story is never simple, or straightforward, or automatic, or obvious. Despite declarations of loyalty only to the best, most current, most objective scholarship on how the universe came to be the way it is today, universal histories are not determined solely by the informational content of scientific and historical disciplines. Instead, they draw on the complete worldview of the authors who compose these stories. They are, after all, still *stories*.

What Is Interpretation?

Imagine that you have the ability to travel through space, anywhere you want, and also through time—to watch any and all events you choose in the history of the universe, Earth, life, and humanity. Such an ability would certainly increase your knowledge at the informational level. It would satisfy curiosity (to an immense degree!), give you the opportunity to fill the holes in your existing knowledge of "what happened" that brought humanity to where we are today, and most likely would also give you increased predictive powers for how the future will unfold.

It might not, however, give you a better understanding of *what it all means*. The additional knowledge could potentially even confuse or distract you from what is really *important* and *meaningful*. As the religious scholar Huston Smith once put

---

1. "That things are not so ill with you and me as they might have been, is half owing to the number who lived faithfully a hidden life, and rest in unvisited tombs." (The closing words of George Eliot's, *Middlemarch*.)

it, knowing the number and position of all the atoms in a great painting may not tell you anything about the point of the painting.[2] Or as the philosopher Bernard Lonergan writes:

> In the ideal detective story the reader is given all the clues yet fails to spot the criminal. . . . [The reader] can remain in the dark for the simple reason that reaching the solution is not the mere apprehension of any clue, not the mere memory of all, but a quite distinct activity of organizing intelligence that places the full set of clues in a unique explanatory perspective.[3]

In the real world, no one has access to "all the clues" that are important to understanding the history of everything. Perfect, complete, and total knowledge is impossible for finite beings like us. But this only increases the importance of the interpretive level in appreciating what lessons and implications we draw from a universal history. If we accept the basic content and evidence that scientific and historical disciplines have presented regarding the Big Bang, plate tectonics, evolution, humanity, history, and modernity—that is, if we accept, at least provisionally, their conclusions on the informational level as presented in this book—we can still narrate very different stories based on them, and we can answer many or all of the interpretive questions listed earlier quite differently. As stated in chapter 1, the *story* of the history of everything can be framed or interpreted in many different ways, and can be invested with distinct kinds of meaning and very different "takeaways." Anyone who has had trouble making sense of a stream of data or information can relate: the purpose of the story, what information is available, and one's broader views about how the world works all go into forming one's interpretive dispositions. As Stephen Jay Gould has written:

> All grand theories are expansive, and all notions so rich in scope and implication are underpinned by visions about the nature of things. You may call these visions "philosophy," or "metaphor," or "organizing principle," but one thing they are surely not—they are not simple inductions from observed facts of the natural world.[4]

This is not to say that any interpretation of the history of everything will do just as well as any other interpretation. All are not created equal. An interpretation can be *in*valid or *un*compelling, maybe because it is based on faulty assumptions,

---

2. Huston Smith, *The World's Religions*, p. 24.

3. Bernard Lonergan, *Insight: A Study of Human Understanding*, in *Collected Works of Bernard Lonergan, Vol. 3*, eds. Frederick E. Crowe and Robert M. Doran, p. 3.

4. Stephen Jay Gould, *Time's Arrow, Time's Cycle*, p. 9.

incorrect or incomplete information, or a lack of insight. And there are limits to how fully the story of the history of everything can be told, given the information available. Rigor is necessary. But many crucial interpretive questions are also more open to alternative interpretations than most existing universal histories admit. We contend that the best answers to the big interpretive questions are rarely, if ever, self-evident.

The question of what the scale of the universe tells us about the place of humans in the cosmos is an excellent example. The intellectual vantage point of modern universal histories usually assumes a certain kind of answer, put aptly by the cosmologist Sean Carroll:

> We human beings, by contrast, are quite tiny—a recent arrival on an insignificant planet orbiting a non-descript star. . . . A person is a diminutive, ephemeral thing, standing smaller in comparison with the universe than a single atom stands in comparison with the Earth. Can any one individual existence really *matter*?[5]

Carroll thinks that the answer is ultimately yes, but even so, this quotation shows one aspect of why framing the question of human significance around scale is misguided: our physical size stands in a similar relationship with the universe as an atom stands in relationship with the Earth. In other words, we as humans sit in the middle of the universe's scales. The reality is that the argument really does run both ways: we are big by many standards, we are small by other standards, and we would not be here today if not for *both* the big scales (stars creating elements and the Sun heating the planet) *and* the small scales (atoms, molecules, and the cells making up our bodies). Even if this were not the case, does size really imply anything about importance? As Jonathan Sacks writes:

> The fact that we occupy a small space in the universe and a small stretch of the totality of time says nothing about our significance or lack of it. . . . In plain language, [inferring human insignificance from our relative size] is mere cynicism and its effect is to undermine the trust on which human relationships and institutions depend.[6]

This example shows how one might *reason* through interpretive questions, as we have attempted to do at many points throughout this book. Suppose, for the sake of argument, that someone reading the previous paragraph had started out convinced of humanity's cosmic insignificance. After reading the paragraph, that

---

5. Sean Carroll, *The Big Picture: On the Origins of Life, Meaning, and the Universe Itself*, p. 2.

6. Jonathan Sacks, *The Great Partnership: Science, Religion, and the Search for Meaning*, p. 118.

person may, or may not, have had their convictions shaken, but if they now accept that humanity's size and physical position in the universe do not automatically imply cosmic insignificance, they can enter into a conversation about *why* they think what they do. Meanwhile, someone who is—or becomes—convinced of humanity's significance could likewise enter the conversation. Explicitly opening this up as a topic of conversation is a way to make progress on the range of interpretive and synthetic questions subject to reasoned discussion and analysis.

With all this in mind, go back to the beginning of this chapter and re-read the second paragraph (the first that appears under the section heading of "Interpretation"). What strikes you? Words in that paragraph strike a certain tone: "huge," "unimaginably," "humble beginnings." Implicit in this framing is a set of pointers to make you feel small in the vastness of space and time. But imagine that our purpose had been the opposite—namely, to highlight the cosmic significance of human beings. In that case, we could well have written, with equal accuracy, of the unbelievably intricate microscopic and submicroscopic world that enables our existence, of the long and laborious development of the Earth into a place fit for human habitation, of the grandeur of the universe that is our home, of the way that scales larger than us and scales smaller than us contribute to making our existence possible, and of the profound marvel that is human consciousness, language, reasoning, and the capacity to know the true, to admire the beautiful, and to love the good. Putting different perspectives in conversation with one another, challenging currently dominant interpretive views, has been a major point of this book.

Interpretation and the Integration of Disciplines, Worldviews, and People

We have argued that interpretation, while perhaps harder to pin down as fully as the "facts" at the informational level, is still a productive arena for rigorous discussion. Historians already know this very well, because contesting alternative interpretations of the same basic information is where historical research almost always happens. This is one fundamental reason why historians have something to contribute even to the most science-based portions of a universal history, and why collaborations between historians and scientists open up new possibilities for how research in Big History (and its various related or ancillary fields, like environmental history) can be conducted: historians' disciplinary training is designed to give them insight regarding how to construct multiple stories from a collection of raw evidence, and how to sift through those stories to evaluate which are the most insightful, the most accurate, and the most fair, while rarely staking any final or absolute claim to total truth or completeness.[7]

---

7. "A study is an advance if it is more incisive—whatever that may mean—than those that preceded it; but it less stands on their shoulders than, challenged and challenging, runs by their side" (Clifford Geertz, *The Interpretation of Cultures*, p. 25).

Universal histories deal with a large number of big, synthetic, holistic ideas at the level of worldview. Such "big ideas" are usually "born from insight, not from reasoning."[8] Assessing claims at the interpretive level requires both careful reasoning and *insight*: the same kind of insight that allows new ideas, or new formulations of old ideas, to come into being in science and history and every field of inquiry. Insight can be generated and recognized, but not deduced. It can be augmented by reasoning and evidence, but not reduced to them. It is the foundation for ways of knowing in literary, philosophical, and humanistic domains, and it provides the material for new theories (like Darwin's insights about living things, or Newton's insights about gravity) in the sciences.

As mentioned in the Preface, many of the insights necessary for an all-encompassing work of history are those that experts working in disciplines isolated from one another cannot necessarily "get to," precisely because they are isolated from one another. Moreover, experts in different disciplines construct explanations of historical change in ways that are not always consistent, as when historians emphasize contingency while natural scientists emphasize seemingly deterministic "laws," or when historians seek multicausal complexity while scientists more often prize elegant simplicity, explaining phenomena using as few variables as possible. How to integrate such different approaches? We think that our approach to fully collaborative, cross-disciplinary writing, as outlined in the Preface, and our ideal of "deep multidisciplinarity"—the full integration of thinking across fields, also described in the Preface—go a long way toward answering this question. The integration of disciplines requires the integration of people, and the depth of the former is often proportional to the depth of the latter.

Interpretation and Universal Histories

Grounded throughout in evidence-based scholarship, universal histories seek, and often seem, to give an "unbiased" and "objective" view of the past; as the 19th-century Swiss-American naturalist Louis Agassiz said, "Go to Nature; take the facts into your own hands; look, and see for yourself!"[9] But to some extent, the grander in scope a history is, the more heavily interpreted it is. After all, how do you decide what to include in your universal history in the first place?

A universal history can never be truly universal, never truly a history of *everything*. Reading past universal histories helps to make this clear, because they often express and reflect the spirit of their times—as when world

---

8. James Lovelock wrote these words about the origins of the Gaia hypothesis; see James Lovelock, *Gaia*, p. x. See also our chapter 3.

9. See, e.g., William James, *Memories and Studies*, p. 7.

population looms particularly large in Preston Cloud's universal history, written in the strongly overpopulation-minded 1970s,[10] or as when Erich Jantsch frames his universal history (published in 1980) by talking about the counterculture of the 1960s and 1970s,[11] or as when Robert Chambers discusses issues of Victorian-era natural theology at some length in his *Vestiges of the Natural History of Creation* (1844).[12] This is also easier to see in those efforts that were made long ago, precisely because such local influences are unlike our own today. It is much harder to perceive how similar influences work on us, in the here and now: how they shape our own thoughts, our own way of conceiving the universe. Without critical attention to how the story is packaged, though, universal histories risk reflecting the metaphysical and political moods of their times more than they mean to, perhaps more than they ought to, and in extreme cases turning into a "dated" expression of the latest intellectual fads. As William Ralph Inge wrote, "Whoever marries the spirit of this age will find himself a widower in the next."[13]

Yet this is not a reason to abandon the project. Even if there are limits to how free from contemporary interpretive tendencies a history of everything can be, and even if future scientific or historical discoveries require many details to be rewritten, this big picture still matters. Partnerships of people who can integrate disciplines while carefully attending to issues of worldview and interpretation offer the promise of a more powerful understanding of how to interpret our world. Everything influences everything else; there are many interlocking stories. And yet history is not utter chaos. There is always continuity, change, and connection, and the vast range of scales in time and space all shape and interact with one another. Narratives and histories about these connections, these changes, and these continuities will keep emerging; we can only hope (and work) to make them sharper, and grow in accuracy and in insight.

Complexity

Narrating history often drives authors to speak in terms of periods, stages, and thresholds. Such markers of where one *is* in history—from the "age of foragers" to the "modern period," from the "Phanerozoic" eon of the Earth's history to the "main-sequence stage" of the Sun's life cycle—are themselves interpretive

---

10. See Preston Cloud, *Cosmos, Earth, and Man*, and our chapter 8.

11. See Erich Jantsch, *The Self-Organizing Universe*.

12. See Robert Chambers, *Vestiges of the Natural History of Creation*.

13. Quoted by Peter Hitchens, "In Defense of George Bell," *First Things: A Monthly Journal of Religion and Public Life*, no. 267 (2016):60.

devices, ways of organizing and selecting what is most important. For many works of universal history, particularly those within the field of Big History, *complexity* and *thresholds of increasing complexity* serve as central framing devices that thread through the history of the universe, Earth, life, and humanity. David Christian's sequence of thresholds has become a standard approach for periodizing Big History: first the Big Bang, then the emergence of stars and the production of elements in stars, followed by the emergence of planets, life, human beings capable of collective learning, agriculture, and the "modern revolution." The emergence of each form depends on the emergence of all the forms before it:

> The fundamental rule seems to be that complexity normally emerges step by step, linking already existing patterns into larger and more complex patterns at different scales. Once achieved, some patterns seem to lock their constituents into new arrangements that are more stable and more durable than the simpler arrangements from which they are created.[14]

Complexity, a quality of systems that have interdependent parts and where the whole might be said to be greater than the sum of its parts,[15] is a useful structuring device. It allows one to keep track of "where one is" in a grand narrative of the history of everything. It allows one to trace how composite entities like planets and people came into being, starting from component parts. It also guides the choice of which among the infinite possible threads in a universal history are to be followed. Thinking about complexity in these ways illuminates important aspects of the universe's history, and it may be an antidote to reductionism, highlighting the reality of complex systems and the problems with thinking that smaller, component entities are all that matter.[16]

At the same time, the idea of complexity runs the risk of obscuring more than it reveals. In particular, it seems to offer an objective justification for dwelling on modern global society as a sort of scientifically affirmed, teleological pinnacle of all history, when in reality, the definition of what counts as "complexity" is at least somewhat arbitrary (see Figure 9.1). And it takes the focus off everything that happened in the history of everything that does *not* neatly fit into a narrow view of the buildup of increasing complexity. This also risks promoting a kind of

---

14. David Christian, *Maps of Time*, pp. 510–511.

15. See, e.g., Fred Spier, *Big History and the Future of Humanity*, p. 24.

16. As explored under "Reductionism" in chapter 3, though we also explored in chapter 7 (see the discussion under "Purpose") how a paradigm of complexity and emergence can encourage a form of reductionism as well.

FIGURE 9.1 Earth at Night Putting modern global society into context is a major goal of many universal histories, and the idea of complexity often frames the story of how Earth's surface came to look like this at night, with the spread of electric lighting, especially in urban areas. Useful as it is, this approach is not without its problems and drawbacks, however.
Source: NASA

tunnel vision. The challenge is to consider how a universal history might trace the history of *both* the apparently complex and the apparently simple, and gauge the importance of both.

Measuring Complexity

Any narrative of increasing complexity raises a natural question: How can one define what complexity *is*, and then measure it, in such a way that it becomes possible to, for example, meaningfully compare the complexity of a star with that of an agrarian civilization? To justify any such cross-domain comparison, one needs a metric—a way of assessing, and of quantitatively measuring, complexity.

The astrophysicist Eric Chaisson has proposed one such metric, widely used in Big History circles, that quantifies the *rate of energy flow* through an object. Called the "free energy rate density" or "power density," it is defined as the energy passing through a given system per second per gram of material in the system (or equivalently, power per gram). When applied to systems such as galaxies, stars, planets, plants, animals, human brains, and human societies, this metric is, indeed, quantitatively larger for those systems in which we perceive greater complexity: more energy passes through a plant per gram of plant matter than passes through a star per gram of star matter. (Stars are huge and have large amounts of energy passing through them, but they are also diffuse.) Likewise, forms of human social organization from villages to towns, cities, states and empires, and modern global society form a progression of increasing power density: there is more power per gram flowing through the "later" forms of social organization than through the "earlier" ones.[17]

But does this actually represent a progression of increasing complexity? Fred Spier points out that by this measure, birds, not humans, come out as the vertebrates that exhibit the largest power densities. Power densities in human societies that set large-scale fires (as for intentional management of vegetation, or for cooking food and safety from predators) rank higher than industrial societies.[18] Chaisson's metric, like any other, may lead to inappropriate conclusions if taken to have general validity. It is just one way to operationalize complexity, however, and it suffers from what one might call the "microchip bias": faster and smaller comes out looking better—and not for any particularly profound reasons, but because that is how the metric is designed.[19]

Mathematically sophisticated work characterizing complex systems does yield serious insights, especially through the recognition of "scaling laws": patterns in "how a system responds when its size changes."[20] Insights into everything from the metabolism of mammals to the nature of cities become visible when applying the approaches of the academic field known as "complexity science." But while the study of complex systems does provide rigorous approaches to analyzing complex systems from a "hard-sciences" point of view, even a quantitative metric can be a storytelling device and a way of selecting what a given thinker believes to be important. As we explored under "Statistics" in chapter 7, and in many other places within this book, the question of what you care about, what you value, comes before quantification: you count what you value. This means that the many other things not being counted are judged, implicitly or explicitly, not to matter. The same pattern holds here: complexity and power density may give the appearance of an objective criterion that justifies placing modern human societies at the pinnacle of history, but complexity is too loose and ill-defined a concept, and power density too arbitrary a metric, to do such heavy lifting on its own. Putting modern societies front and

---

17. Chaisson prefers the notion of energy flow, because it is more basic and meaningful than the notion of "information," which he regards as a looser concept without the same potential for a common understanding from one field to another. See Eric J. Chaisson, "The Natural Science Underlying Big History," pp. 3–4 in *The Scientific World Journal*, Volume 2014, Article ID 384912, http://dx.doi.org/10.1155/2014/384912 , pp. 3–4. The details of how to apply this power-per-gram metric to social entities like an empire are complex, and Chaisson has tried to develop a protocol for applying his concept in disparate places (see pp. 26–30 of the same article).

18. Spier, *Big History*, p. 33–34.

19. Marvin Croy, personal conversation.

20. Geoffrey West, *Scale: The Universal Laws of Life, Growth, and Death in Organisms, Cities, and Companies*, p. 15.

center and trying to trace how human structures took shape over time may well be worth doing, because it leads to fascinating stories and solid integrative thinking, but not necessarily because it illuminates anything in particular about complexity.

Complexity in the Physical, Biological, and Social Worlds

Even if we could find a metric that gave more consistently valid results, any narrative structure that assumes a progressive increase in complexity tends to systematically bias the narrative, obscuring aspects of the physical, biological, and social worlds that seem to run contrary to—or have little to do with—this story of increasing complexity.

In the physical and biological worlds, there is tremendous hidden complexity at small scales, from subatomic particles and atoms to living cells. Small scales, it turns out, can be incredibly intricate and display deep forms of order. For example, an atom is not indivisible. It is a very complicated set of parts in complex relationships with one another, with electrons orbiting a nucleus composed of protons and neutrons, which are themselves composed of quarks. Electrons are capable of taking on a wide variety of configurations, which enable bonding and chemistry. Electrons and protons are bound together by the electromagnetic force, while protons and neutrons in the nucleus are bound together by the strong nuclear force. Physicists look at each of these entities and forces and see a rich world of complexity and deep inner structure that works according to physical laws impressive in both their mathematical elegance and their potential to give rise to an enormously complicated variety of interactions at the subatomic level.

A similar pattern holds true in the biological world. Judged by the sheer number of "moving parts" working in concert, cells have a level of complexity and internal organization that defies easy comprehension. They are assembled from billions of molecules constantly buffeted by atomic-scale thermal motion that still somehow combine into coherent structures like ribosomes, cell membranes, or mitochondria.

A narrative of increasing complexity can certainly accommodate building blocks that are themselves also complex—no one thinks human beings are less complex as individuals merely because they also collect themselves into societies—but atoms and cells are rarely singled out in Big History circles as principal elements of a sequence of increasing complexity. And their forms of deep internal structure and intricacy are not usually seen as a potential challenge to the overall narrative of increasing complexity in the universe. They are more often regarded as only the building blocks of more complex, larger structures.

Meanwhile, the idea of complexity runs into a different set of issues within the macroscopic living world. Complexity is not particularly well-defined for organisms, and any progression of increasing complexity is bound to be misleading in certain regards. For instance, one way we might try to "objectively" define complexity in the living world would be according to something like "genetic complexity," as measured by, say, the size of an organism's genome (the total number of DNA base pairs, or the number of genes). But it turns out that defining complexity genetically fails to track macroscopic complexity of structure and function, or the range of capacities that an organism displays. The marbled lungfish, as an example, does not seem exceptionally complex as organisms go, but it has a huge genome, with around 40 times more DNA base pairs than the human genome. The genome size in some salamander species is over 20 times greater than in humans.[21] On the whole, there is no clear relationship of any sort between the apparent complexity of an organism and the amount of DNA in its genome.[22]

Even purely at a macroscopic level, an emphasis on complexity tends to train our vision to perceive only one relatively small strand within the history of life. It is an important strand and a fascinating story, one that leads to human beings and the animal and plant life that we interact with regularly. But as Robert Bellah has argued (taking his words from arguments articulated by Stephen Jay Gould), "the primary trend of biological evolution is toward diversity, variety, rather than toward greater complexity, which is only a marginal and minor development taking life as a whole."[23] Note that populations of organisms often *lose* complex body parts over time, because that can be advantageous within a given environment: winged stick insects seem to have evolved from wingless stick insects, which in turn evolved from winged ancestors,[24] and blind mole rats had sighted ancestors.[25] These are only a few examples out of many. Taken as a whole, organisms appear to "stand an equal chance of becoming simpler or more complex over millions of years."[26] The evolutionary path to any given species is almost always a back-and-forth across matters of complexity, rather than a steady, let alone triumphal, march in one direction.

---

21. T. R. Gregory, Animal Genome Size Database, http://www.genomesize.com . There are approximately 3 billion DNA base pairs in the human genome (haploid), or about 3 picograms of DNA. Since there is non-coding DNA, the total number of DNA base pairs is not strictly correlated with the total number of genes in a given organism, but the perceived complexity of an organism is not tied directly to the number of genes either.

22. Some species of amoebas have been assessed as having hundreds of times as many DNA base pairs than humans, although there is debate about this conclusion. See http://www. genomesize.com/statistics.php .

23. Robert Bellah, *Religion in Human Evolution: From the Paleolithic to the Axial Age*, p. 59.

24. Amy Maxmen, "Evolution, You're Drunk," http://nautil.us/issue/9/time/evolution-youre-drunk , citing M. F. Whiting, S., Bradler, and T. Maxwell, "Loss and Recovery of Wings in Stick Insects," *Nature* 421 (2003):264–267.

25. See, e.g., S. Sanyal et al., "The Eye of the Blind Mole Rat, *Spalax ehrenbergi*. Rudiment with Hidden Function?," *Investigative Ophthalmology and Visual Science* 31, no. 7 (1990):1398–1404. The species *Spalax ehrenbergi* appears to lack vision but to still be able to perceive (using the rudiments of an eye) the approximate time of day.

26. Maxmen, "Evolution, You're Drunk."

Another potential pitfall of increasing-complexity narratives is that it is easy to forget that the "earlier" forms of complexity typically are not superseded or replaced by new forms of complexity, but instead continue to exist in their own right, not only as building blocks but also alongside "newer" or "more complex" forms. Unicellular organisms, for instance, are not simply a stepping stone on the way to multicellular organisms; they are a crucial and ongoing part of a world inhabited by both unicellular and multicellular organisms alike, in complicated relationships with one another. A similar pattern shows up in the social world. As some practitioners of deep history (discussed in chapter 6) point out:

> Historians have long been fascinated by the idea that human history is the story of how small family groups turned into nations ... But we have never stopped living in groups reminiscent of the families, clans, and tribes described by political anthropologists. ... Historically, each new level of social integration is shaped by the dynamics of the social forms that predate it and may still, in diverse ways, be embedded within it.[27]

Foraging societies may have been largely replaced by states and agrarian societies, at least in most places, but family and kinship networks were not replaced when this happened. More broadly, the development of human political structures is not linear, not a simple matter of larger-scale forms of political organization replacing smaller-scale ones; instead, "there are movements between large and small, hierarchical and flat, organized and anarchic, imperial and national, etc., which are not linear at all but cyclical or amorphous."[28]

---

27. Mary C. Stiner, Timothy Earle, Daniel Lord Smail, and Andrew Shryock, "Scale," in *Deep History: The Architecture of Past and Present*, p. 247.

28. Timothy Burke, "Particularism as a Big Idea," https://blogs.swarthmore.edu/burke/blog/2013/02/20/particularism-as-a-big-idea/ . See also James C. Scott, *The Art of Not Being Governed*:

> The temporal, civilizational series—from foraging to swiddening (or to pastoralism), to sedentary grain cultivation, to irrigated wet-rice farming—and its near-twin, the series from roving forest bands to small clearings, to hamlets, to villages, to towns, to court centers: these are the underpinning of the valley state's sense of superiority. What if the presumptive "stages" of these series were, in fact, an array of social options, each of which represented a distinctive positioning vis-à-vis the state? And what if, over considerable periods of time, many groups have moved strategically among these options toward more presumptively "primitive" forms in order to keep the state at arm's length? On this view, the civilizational discourse of the valley states—and not a few earlier theorists of social evolution—is not much more than a self-inflating way of confounding the status of state-subject with civilization and that of self-governing peoples with primitivism. (pp. 8–9)

A final potential issue with emphasizing complexity is that it is easy, but misleading, to equate *more complex* with *more capable* or *better*. David Bentley Hart points out that

> one object may have a far greater range of powers than another precisely because it is simpler in structure; a broadax and a guillotine can both perform one very similar unpleasant task, but the former can do innumerable other things as well, not nearly as unpleasant, like cutting down a dead tree or hacking a guillotine to pieces.[29]

Like the broadax, bacteria can do a great many things that more "complex" multicellular eukaryotic organisms cannot. As Lynn Margulis and many others have emphasized, bacteria "run" all the biogeochemical cycles on Earth; they put oxygen into the atmosphere over 2 billion years ago; they probably outnumber human cells within the human body; almost nothing in the living world would function the way it does without them. We need them; yet they only sometimes need us, even if they have played, and continue to play, a huge role in making the Earth a habitable planet for us.

Evaluating Complexity

The idea of complexity seems to offer a single unifying frame for the physical and social worlds. But there are dangers associated with relying too heavily on any single big idea. Complexity is tricky to define in a coherent way, and emphasizing increases in complexity as the main track of historical development can create misleading impressions. When narratives of increasing complexity turn into progress narratives, it begins to seem as though human societies themselves are being said to increase in value because they increase in complexity. Relative simplicity and relative complexity, however, both have their roles and importance in any setting—physical, biological, or social.

An alternative to emphasizing complexity would be to explicitly trace the emergence of, and the relationship between, different forms of complexity and simplicity alongside one another, as in how bacteria help to produce an environment habitable for (complex) macroscopic life, and how macroscopic life provides new niches and new opportunities for (comparatively simple) bacteria. Both the more simple and the more complex, then, appear as expressions of underlying order in the universe, which changes form over time. This general approach is the one we have pursued throughout this book: examining feedback loops and interactions

---

29. David Bentley Hart, *The Experience of God: Being, Consciousness, Bliss*, p. 136.

between different scales in time and space, and between different levels of apparent complexity, rather than trying to fit everything into a single, all-encompassing framework. The loop, more than the line, becomes a fundamental metaphor.

Religion

Science-based universal histories typically draw on the culture of the modern Western secular intellectual world, which usually adopts naturalism as a default worldview and overall interpretive framing. "Naturalism" is the idea that the natural world is all there is, that there is nothing "supernatural" beyond nature, and that natural causes are the only kinds of causes that are real.[30] The word is closely related to the words "materialism" and "physicalism," which we have seen before in different contexts.[31]

While naturalistic views are not universal among researchers and scholars, many historians and scientists directly articulate and defend some form of naturalism as the only professionally appropriate fundamental view of the world. The historian E. H. Carr, for instance, writes that he finds it difficult "to reconcile the integrity of history with belief in some super-historical force on which its meaning and significance depend,"[32] and assertions of atheism are also common in popular-science writing. Naturalism shows up in more subtle ways too, many of which we have seen in this book. It appears in Carl Sagan's definition that "the Cosmos is all that is or ever was or ever will be,"[33] which would seem to exclude the reality of anything beyond the natural world, and in philosophies of mind that deny any realities that are not strictly physical. Less directly, naturalism informs discussions of humanity's place in the universe that argue for our complete insignificance, or the assumption that an explanation for the origin of life in terms of natural causes would imply that there is no Creator. And arguably, a naturalistic worldview lies at the root of the argument that Big History should have a unique place as *the* modern origin story— finding a place in the universe and a meaning of life for modern people who, since they are "modern," are assumed to "no longer" believe in religion.

Several sections of this book, however, have called into question an exclusively naturalistic framing for universal history, or at least have questioned some of the conclusions drawn in naturalistic accounts of universal history. Our general approach has been one of what might be called pluralism, rather than naturalism:

---

30. See, e.g., Carroll, *The Big Picture*, p. 11.

31. See explicit examples in chapter 2 (under "Universe"), chapter 5 (under "Mind"), and chapter 8 (under "Transhumanism" and "Time").

32. E. H. Carr, *What Is History?*, p. 96.

33. Carl Sagan, *Cosmos*, p. 1.

throughout this book, we have included reflections of various religious thinkers alongside and integrated with secular forms of scholarship. As part of this final chapter, which considers the overall interpretive framings of universal history, we suggest here that pluralism is a better framing for universal histories than naturalism alone. Pluralism allows one to see the possible defects in, or limits of, a solely naturalistic framework, and it also better encapsulates the history of human thought: religions are an integral part of the human dimensions of universal history; for that matter, naturalism has its own history of how it came to be a prominent worldview among many intellectual elites. Robustly including religion as part of this pluralist approach has the potential to make universal histories both more universal and more historical.

Naturalism as One Worldview Among Several

Counts vary, but out of 7.3 billion people alive in the year 2015, there were approximately 2.3 billion Christians, 1.8 billion Muslims, 1.2 billion who considered themselves without religion, 1.1 billion Hindus, 500 million Buddhists, and 400 million practitioners of a variety of Chinese, African, Native American, or Australian Aborigine traditional religions. Jews, another group that has exerted major influence in world history, numbered around 14 million.[34] (See Figure 9.2.) Several other religions also have millions or tens of millions of adherents. Each of these religious categories grows very complicated when examined closely, as a wide range of beliefs, practices, spiritualities, and communities co-exist under any of the overall headings. But the raw numbers alone tell a story: one of global religious pluralism, in which no one religion dominates the world or claims a majority of the world's people as adherents.

Religious demographers do not generally expect this basic situation to change in coming decades. Taking into account demographic trends like fertility rates within different religious communities and people switching between religious groups, the number of religiously unaffiliated people has been predicted to shrink as a percentage of the worldwide "pie," with Christianity growing slightly and Islam growing rapidly.[35] Within Western intellectual circles, secularism is more dominant than

---

34. Pew Research Center, "The Changing Global Religious Landscape," http://assets.pewresearch .org/wp-content/uploads/sites/11/2017/04/07092755/FULL-REPORT-WITH-APPENDIXES-A-AND-B-APRIL-3.pdf, p. 10. Note that many "secular Jews" do not consider themselves religious at all, even though they may be ethnically and/or culturally Jewish, and a small handful of people are not ethnically Jewish but observe Jewish religion. The numbers cited in the main text "are based on estimates of people who self-identify as Jewish when asked about their religion on national censuses and large-scale surveys. They do not include 'cultural' or 'ethnic' Jews … who describe themselves, religiously, as atheist, agnostic or nothing in particular." (Ibid., p. 9.)

35. Ibid., p. 8.

Global religious demographics in 2015

% of world population

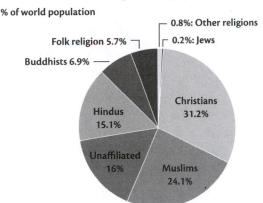

0.8%: Other religions
0.2%: Jews
Folk religion 5.7%
Buddhists 6.9%
Hindus 15.1%
Unaffiliated 16%
Christians 31.2%
Muslims 24.1%

Number of people in 2015, in billions

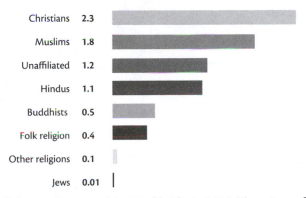

Christians	2.3
Muslims	1.8
Unaffiliated	1.2
Hindus	1.1
Buddhists	0.5
Folk religion	0.4
Other religions	0.1
Jews	0.01

FIGURE 9.2 Religious Demographics Worldwide, in 2015 The writers of universal histories usually hope to appeal to human beings across all political and social boundaries, but to do so, they must take into account a wide variety of audiences with a wide variety of worldviews.

Source: Pew Research Center

among the general public, but again, it is not universal. For example, scientists in the United States split about half-and-half between those who do not claim a religious affiliation and those who do; a nearly 50-50 split also holds for those who believe in God or a "higher power" and those who do not.[36] Based on these numbers, it may be fair to say that naturalism makes a strong showing among worldviews in

36. See, e.g., Pew Research Center, "Scientists and Belief," https://www.pewforum.org/2009/11/05/scientists-and-belief/ . The United States is admittedly a somewhat exceptional case among Western nations in its levels of religiosity, but in the context of the world as a whole, most Western nations are unusual for their lower levels of religiosity.

the modern world, but the numbers alone do not suggest that naturalism is auto-matically the right framing for a universal story—not if the goal is for that story to resonate with the entire "human family." Naturalism is one worldview among many others.

Naturalism has certainly been a worldview held by many scientists and schol-ars who founded major scientific ideas or developed universal-historical nar-ratives. However, many other key contributors have been deeply religious: the priest-astrophysicist Georges Lemaître, who first proposed the Big Bang; the monk-geneticist Gregor Mendel, who laid some of the foundations for modern genetics; the astronomer and mathematician Johannes Kepler, who formulated the laws of planetary motion; the polymath Isaac Newton, whose contributions to mathematics and physics were innumerable; and the visionary educator Maria Montessori, a pioneer of universal-historical narratives in educational contexts—to name just a few.

Treating naturalism as a default, or as the only legitimate way to frame a story about the universe, rather than as one worldview among many, makes it seem like these scholars mentioned here are aberrations, exceptions to the rule. But the real-ity of scientific and historical scholarship, past and present, is that while naturalism has been widespread as a *methodology* (e.g., scientists focus on characterizing and explaining natural phenomena, without invoking supernatural explanations), reli-gious and secularist *worldviews* have both been well-represented in these fields for a long time.[37]

Religious Worldviews and the Foundations of Universal History

Universal histories stand to gain from the philosophical categories and insights of multiple religious traditions, as we have attempted to show at various points throughout this book. But the incorporation of religious worldviews has its pit-falls and its potential abuses too. For example, in *The Demon-Haunted World*, Carl Sagan offered a rather common objection to invoking divinity or divine agency in thinking about the way the natural world works:

> But he [Hippocrates, famous physician in ancient Greece] is chiefly cele-brated because of his efforts to bring medicine out of the pall of superstition and into the light of science. In a typical passage Hippocrates wrote: "Men think epilepsy divine, merely because they do not understand it. But if they called everything divine which they do not understand, why, there would be

---

37. For relevant commentaries, see, e.g., Peter Harrison, "Why Religion Is Not Going Away and Science Will Not Destroy It," https://aeon.co/ideas/why-religion-is-not-going-away-and-science-will-not-destroy-it ; or Steven Shapin, *The Scientific Revolution* (1st Edition), p. 195. Shapin writes a parallel passage in the second edition of the same book, pp. 204–205.

no end of divine things." Instead of acknowledging that in many areas we are ignorant, we have tended to say things like the Universe is permeated with the ineffable. A God of the Gaps is assigned responsibility for what we do not yet understand.[38]

In a related and often-cited story, the 18th- and 19th-century French physicist and astronomer Pierre-Simon Laplace is said to have commented, when Napoleon inquired where God was in Laplace's model of the Solar System, "I had no need of that hypothesis."[39]

Sagan voices a common concern among scientists (and historians) about supernatural explanations. The worry is that invoking the supernatural is ad hoc and, at root, intellectually lazy, and that it takes the place of real explanation in terms of natural causes—a valid concern if supernatural explanations are deployed in an undisciplined way, as they sometimes have been in practice.

But a moment's reflection shows that the religious individuals who helped shape modern science and history could not, as a rule, have been operating according to a God of the Gaps framing—constantly using the divine to explain away that which they did not understand. If they had, they would not have contributed to a scientific or historical understanding of how the world works, at least not in terms that could form a foundation for modern secular scholarship. As noted under "Mathematics" in chapter 2, belief in a Creator who behaves consistently and not arbitrarily can help to justify and support a search for comprehensible natural mechanisms in science and history: the opposite effect of believing in a God of the Gaps. Even Lemaître, who when proposing the Big Bang model of the universe's beginning could rather understandably have spoken of God, was careful to speak of his then-speculative scientific theory in strictly natural terms; while as a priest he certainly did not doubt that God is the Creator of the universe, any number of natural mechanisms for how the universe has unfolded could be compatible with one and the same "supernatural" origin. The role of the natural sciences is to distinguish between those possible mechanisms, determining which ones the relevant evidence most strongly supports.

A key point is that religious intellectuals who helped form some of the foundations of universal history generally did so in the context of recognizing an intelligent Creator whose mind they desired to know more intimately by better knowing the Creation. Rather than supernatural explanations taking the place of natural explanations when the latter failed, devotion to God and to the search for natural explanations were often deeply intertwined. Kepler's notebooks feature calculations

---

38. Carl Sagan, *The Demon-Haunted World*, p. 8.

39. Probably an embellishment of a real conversation that took place.

that are "punctuated with mystical speculation and prayers."[40] When preaching, Mendel was able to draw imagery, seamlessly integrated, from both science and the Bible.[41] And Lemaître commented in an interview:

> I was interested in truth from the standpoint of salvation, you see, as well as in truth from the standpoint of scientific certainty. There were two ways of arriving at the truth. I decided to follow them both. . . . I have no conflict to reconcile. Science has not shaken my faith in religion, and religion has never caused me to question the conclusions I reached by strictly scientific methods.[42]

It is a misinterpretation to write off any type of religious argument as implying a God of the Gaps conceptualization, and to ignore the rich intellectual religious traditions from which foundational building blocks of universal history were, to some extent, derived. This is not to say that Big History or related fields should become explicitly religious disciplines, staying within the boundaries of any particular religion. On the contrary, incorporating more religious thought from religious intellectuals, alongside scientific, historical, and literary approaches to understanding the world, can help to prevent universal histories from becoming narrowly antireligious, leaving naturalism unchecked and universal histories appealing only to those who embrace naturalism.

The Reasonability of Religious Worldviews

All that said, truth is not settled by a majority vote, whether among scholars in the past, scholars in the present, or the general public. A pluralistic framing might be helpful in practice and fairer to the diversity of worldviews found within most scholarly communities past and present, but if naturalism really *is* the only correct worldview, then it should be the privileged interpretive framing for universal history. So what makes it reasonable to seriously consider worldviews that hold naturalism to be an incorrect or incomplete picture of reality?

One consideration, which we have explored in various parts of this book,[43] is that the existence, order, and intelligibility of the natural world do not seem

---

40. James Hannam, *The Genesis of Science*, p. 296.

41. See, e.g., "A Brief Portion of an Easter Sermon by Gregor Mendel," https://www.vofoundation.org/faith-and-science/brief-portion-easter-sermon-gregor-mendel/ .

42. Duncan Aikman, "Lemaître Follows Two Paths to Truth," https://www.nytimes.com/1933/02/19/archives/lemaitre-follows-two-paths-to-truth-the-famous-physicist-who-is.html .

43. See especially chapter 2 ("Mathematics"), as well as chapter 1 ("Creation") and chapter 4 ("Biochemistry").

to explain themselves. The supernatural—a reality "above nature," or "beyond nature"—need not come into conflict with or be set in opposition to the natural world, but instead can help to make sense of the natural world, underpinning and enabling it. The whole natural order might actually make *more* sense, and have *more* integrity, if we put it within a broader context rather than viewing it as internally self-sufficient. Supernatural explanations should not, in general, *conflict* with natural explanations. A God of the Gaps, who steps in as an explanation of things we do not (yet) know the natural causes of, is in a certain sense not supernatural *enough*— that is, too close to being part of the natural order, "just" an extremely powerful being, whose role is eclipsed by the natural causes that science discovers.

The potential for conflict between supernatural and natural causes is much reduced if we take the view of divine causality broadly present in classical monotheistic philosophy. According to this understanding, God is the uncaused condition for the existence and intelligibility of all things. As the Orthodox Christian writer David Bentley Hart writes, asking for evidence of God is rather like asking for evidence of Tolstoy in *Anna Karenina*. In a sense, *everything* is evidence: the characters and the story would have no existence, order, or intelligibility without the author. The author explains the existence of the entire universe in which the characters exist at a *primary* level, but if you ask why a character behaved in one way and not another, *secondary* causes (what happens in the plot) are generally the proper level to invoke.[44] These secondary causes can be studied in their own right, without explicit reference to the author, but without the author—who exists at a level completely beyond the characters' universe—there would be no secondary causes. So if universal history really is like the plot of a book in this way, and if natural causes really are secondary causes, then perhaps there is, indeed, "no end of divine things" in universal history, but in a different sense than Sagan meant it.

Even if one grants the reality of the supernatural in this sense, the claims of any given religion go beyond this level. Almost every religion in the world, from those with global spread to geographically localized ones with comparatively small numbers of practitioners, makes more specific claims about how "God, gods, spirits, supernatural beings, deceased ancestors, and the like"[45] *relate to* human beings and the natural world, and most include stories or reports of miracles, where highly unusual phenomena signal the presence or working of powers that go beyond the ordinary course of nature.[46] Claims of individual religions should be evaluated

---

44. Hart, *The Experience of God*, p. 303.

45. Matt Rossano, *Supernatural Selection: How Religion Evolved*, p. 19.

46. Note that the distinction between natural and supernatural does not always map neatly onto the categories people use to describe their own beliefs. Still, as Kenneth Woodward writes, "Miracles—and miracle workers—are found in all the major world religions. My contention is that without some knowledge of such stories and what they mean, no religion can be fully appreciated or understood." (Kenneth Woodward, *The Book of Miracles*, p. 18.)

individually: Did the Buddha really achieve, and show the path to, enlightenment? Did Jesus really rise from the dead? Did God's revelation to humanity really reach its pinnacle in Muhammad and the Qur'an? But the general idea of miracles, and of the direct impinging of the supernatural order on the natural world, can also be discussed at a general level.

On the one hand, if there is a supernatural order, it makes sense that natural causes may not always be sufficient to explain a powerful or extraordinary phenomenon. To posit that miracles are axiomatically impossible is essentially equivalent to positing naturalism, which denies the existence of causes not inherent in the natural world. But a thought experiment from the Jewish philosopher Emil Fackenheim casts light on why naturalistic worldviews and religious worldviews not based in naturalism often seem to "talk past each other." In the book *God's Presence in History*, Fackenheim imagines a modern naturalistic skeptic being sent back in time to observe the Exodus of the Israelites from Egypt and the parting of the Red Sea— which Fackenheim takes, for the purposes of this thought experiment, to have happened exactly as described in the Bible. The skeptic observes these great events with utter astonishment. However, after the event has passed, the skeptic dissects both the physical event (the parting of the sea) and the psychological response it produced in him (astonishment) and explains it all away. The skeptic leaves unconvinced that God exists, let alone was present in this ostensibly mighty work.

The naturalistic skeptic may think that a shallower-than-expected body of water and a good strong wind can go a long way toward explaining the parting of the Red Sea, and a little bit of mass credulity, and perhaps mass hallucination, can take care of whatever explanatory work is left. But Fackenheim perceives that the situation is different for the believer, who stands in wonder at what seems to be the most awe-inspiring of miracles. Fackenheim argues that for the believer, causal explanations of an awe-inspiring phenomenon like the parting of the Red Sea—that is, explanations of how, exactly, the phenomenon took place—could only deepen the sense of God's presence and wondrous working of a miracle, while for the non-believer, an explanation in terms of natural causes would invalidate the idea that God had anything to do with what happened.

The dynamic of skepticism and belief described by Fackenheim plays out in the work of Richard Dawkins, the famous British biologist and atheist, and Stanley Jaki, a Hungarian physicist and Catholic priest. Both have tried to explain the "Miracle of the Sun" in Fátima, Portugal, an October 1917 event in which many eyewitnesses among a crowd of tens of thousands described the Sun as having danced and zigzagged in the sky during an appearance of the Virgin Mary. The crowd had gathered because three shepherd children, who had previously claimed to have seen appearances of the Virgin Mary, said that she told them there would be another appearance, accompanied by a miraculous sign, that day. Dawkins devotes two paragraphs of *The God Delusion* to "debunking" the event by proposing that simultaneous delusion, collusion in a mass lie, mistakes in historical accounts of the event, or the simultaneous perception of a mirage could explain it all.[47] Jaki devotes an entire book (*God and the Sun at Fatima*) to considering Fátima and identifying possible atmospheric phenomena through which the Sun could have taken on the appearances described by eyewitnesses, without anyone outside Portugal perceiving anything unusual about the Sun that day. Despite the much greater attention to detail in Jaki's causal account, it is Jaki, not Dawkins, who maintains—based on the evidence of eyewitness accounts and the singular coming together of these natural phenomena at the time and place predicted—that this was ultimately a profound sign from God and not a meaningless coincidence of natural phenomena, or an example of people seeing something because they wanted to see something. Proposed causal explanations deepen Jaki's sense of the profundity and significance of the event, while Dawkins dismisses out of hand any proposed miraculous character of what happened.

Fackenheim's thought experiment goes a long way toward explaining why the evidence for a given religious worldview can look completely compelling to some and yet weak, or even ridiculous, to others who are their intellectual equals. And there is a lesson here for evaluating claims of miraculous events or profound individual or collective religious experience, including everything from inspirations in prayer to visions to states of mystical ecstasy. Fackenheim, for his part, thinks that the interpretive dispositions of the skeptic and the believer are not only mutually irreconcilable, but also mutually irrefutable: neither the skeptic nor the believer can convince the other, because they reason from such completely different premises and starting points. And yet Fackenheim does not think the story ends there:

> The secularist, therefore, cannot refute but only *convert* the religious believer. This possibility, too, is mutual. We have above projected the modern, scientifically inspired secularist among the maidservants at the Red Sea, and observed him persist in his secularism. One possibility, however, was then not considered. Conceivably the secularist might partake of an astonishment radical enough to sweep aside all mere curiosity, to overwhelm all destructive reflection, and to assume a permanent quality which could only be deepened by causal explanations. Were this to occur, the secularist would have turned away from his secularism: he would have turned to, and have been turned by, the presence of God.[48]

---

47. See Richard Dawkins, *The God Delusion*, pp. 91–92. The proposals of a mass lie or that the historical account is mistaken seem especially implausible; skeptical secular newspapers and at least one magazine reported the phenomenon almost immediately after it occurred. For one of the original accounts, see *Ilustraçao Portuguesa*, October 29, 1917, pp. 353–356, available online at http://hemerotecadigital.cm-lisboa.pt/OBRAS/IlustracaoPort/1917/N610/N610_master/N610.pdf. See also John Haffert, *Meet the Witnesses of the Miracle of the Sun*.

48. Emil L. Fackenheim, *God's Presence in History: Jewish Affirmations and Philosophical Reflections*, p. 45.

Incorporating Religion in Universal History

Each of the major worldwide religious traditions has its own historical context, and naturalism is no exception. The universal religions with sacred texts—such as Hinduism, Buddhism, Christianity, Judaism, Islam, Sikhism, Daoism, Confucianism, the Baháʾí Faith, Jainism, and Zoroastrianism—are extraordinarily long-lived social phenomena, ones that have provided communities of people with "ultimate concern"[49] and an overall orientation to the world and that have maintained continuity of beliefs, rituals, and texts for hundreds or thousands of years. (Portions of Hinduism's sacred texts, for example, go back well over 3,000 years.)

For most people today, many of these religions are so familiar, at least in name, that their impressive scale in space and time can be easy to forget. Yet almost no basic human pattern has been as long-lasting through time or as widespread today as religion. As Jacques-Bénigne Bossuet (1627–1704) wrote in his *Discourse on Universal History*, published in 1681, "Empires crumble: religion alone endures."[50] Jonathan Sacks writes of Christianity as "the largest movement of any kind in the history of the world";[51] Islam likely stands as a close second.

At the same time, seen from the perspective of the 300,000-year history of *Homo sapiens*, these "world religions" are all very recent phenomena: they each originated within only the past 5,000 years. Before the comparatively recent invention of writing, "scriptures" as such could not exist, and before the dense connectivity across the world in the past few thousand years, the widespread transmission of specific religious ideas and practices would have been far more difficult.[52]

Naturalism too is part of this story of "recent developments." Naturalism has its own premodern roots, including in ancient Greece,[53] and its presence as a widespread phenomenon is a feature of modernity. But it has few (if any) known, explicit precedents from more than a few thousand years ago. In important ways, it can be regarded as a kind of religious worldview—one that broadly denies ideas

---

49. The Lutheran theologian Paul Tillich's phrase.

50. Quoted in John McManners, "Introduction," in *The Oxford Illustrated History of Christianity*, ed. John McManners, p. 1.

51. Sacks, *The Great Partnership*, p. 8.

52. On the other hand, the archaeological site of Göbekli Tepe, a temple built before agriculture, provides intriguing hints that some orally transmitted religions might have been surprisingly widespread over comparatively large geographical areas. Building this site required the coordination of a large number of people over a large area. Combine this with Genevieve von Petzinger's insight that some graphic communication signs were shared over entire continents during a period of tens of thousands of years, and there are tantalizing hints that even the now-lost religions of the deep human past may not always have been purely local affairs. Unfortunately, most of the relevant evidence needed to evaluate this issue is gone.

53. See., e.g., Tim Whitmarsh, *Battling the Gods: Atheism in the Ancient World*.

held by the world's other major religious traditions, but that addresses many of the same questions. This does not mean that naturalism should not be taken seriously; rather, a wide variety of worldviews, religious and secular alike, deserve to be taken seriously.

Many scholars have attempted to explain religious impulses, from modern textual faiths to ancient Paleolithic practices, as outcomes of *other* factors that are viewed as more fundamental: the byproduct of the impulse to create highly cohesive social groups that function as a single unit in the "battle for survival," for example, or a source of control over disease, death, fickle weather, and the other fearfully unpredictable aspects of life.[54] And yet naturalism could, equally well, be "explained away" as an outcome of the desire not to be held ultimately accountable for one's actions, or as a result of the impulse to explain away any phenomenon that threatens the comfortable predictability and (partial) mastery of nature associated with modern science.[55] But putting dismissive explanations aside, at the end of the day you have to have a worldview. Everyone does. And religious worldviews with sophisticated philosophical traditions would not have persisted over time if they were not, at a fundamental level, *reasonable*—if they did not provide ways of making compelling and convincing sense of the world. If writers of universal history wish to be both universal and historical, to appeal to the entire "human family," they should be open to the possibility of incorporating a breadth of global religious and philosophical traditions as well as traditions across history.

Narrative

Carl Sagan once wrote: "In every culture we imagined something like our own political system running the Universe. Few found the similarity suspicious."[56] In its original context, this line was intended to challenge the "prescientific" views of cultures not based in modern science—cultures like ancient China or ancient Egypt, which depicted the cosmos as having a universal ruler or rulers similar to an emperor or pharaoh, or like ancient Greece, which envisioned a pantheon of gods with problems, challenges, and behaviors that strongly resembled those of the society they governed.[57] But what if we turned this maxim on its head and asked how it also now applies to modern, scientific universal histories and the cultures that produce them?

---

54. For a discussion, see Matt Rossano, *Supernatural Selection*, pp. 2–8.

55. See, e.g., Sacks, *The Great Partnership*, p. 27.

56. Carl Sagan, *Pale Blue Dot: A Vision of the Human Future in Space*, p. 43.

57. Extrapolating a little from the original context in Sagan's writing, which does not mention China, Egypt, or Greece in this context, but the point is similar.

Not only political systems, but ideas drawn from practically every area of thought, culture, and human activity have the potential to inform how one tells a story about the history of everything. Philosophy, economics, popular culture—all go into the mix. E. H. Carr writes that "the historian's work closely mirrors the society in which he works,"[58] or taking a different angle on the same phenomenon, that "there is no more significant pointer to the character of a society than the kind of history it writes or fails to write."[59] The same is true of the future: "Nothing dates an era more than its vision of the future."[60] These insights hold true whether the visions of history and the future are derived from conventional disciplinary history or from the natural sciences. The art of storytelling, the metaphors and lines of thought that are used, will always draw on far more than just a list of well-established facts.

The Atheist and the Orthodox Jew: Visions of Reality

A particularly poignant example of this pattern comes from two polymaths of different eras, philosophies, and religions: the atheist Bertrand Russell (1872–1970) and the Orthodox Jew Jonathan Sacks (b. 1948). Russell articulated his vision of reality, and of the human place in the cosmos, with particular eloquence in the essay "A Free Man's Worship." After narrating a kind of universal history in a single paragraph,[61] he writes:

> Such, in outline, but even more purposeless, more void of meaning, is the world which Science presents for our belief. Amid such a world, if anywhere, our ideals henceforward must find a home. That Man is the product of causes which had no prevision of the end they were achieving; that his origin, his growth, his hopes and fears, his loves and his beliefs, are but the outcome of accidental collocations of atoms; that no fire, no heroism, no intensity of thought and feeling, can preserve an individual life beyond the grave; that all the labors of the ages, all the devotion, all the inspiration, all the noonday brightness of human genius, are destined to extinction in the vast death of the solar system, and that the whole temple of Man's achievement must inevitably be buried beneath the debris of a universe in ruins—all these things, if not quite beyond dispute, are yet so nearly certain, that

---

58. Carr, *What Is History?*, p. 51.

59. Ibid., p. 53.

60. Paul Pottinger, "Sci-Fidelity," *Sydney Morning Herald*, March 6, 1992, Metro section, p. 1.

61. A universal history that he puts into the mouth of a demon (Mephistopheles).

no philosophy which rejects them can hope to stand. Only within the scaffolding of these truths, only on the firm foundation of unyielding despair, can the soul's habitation henceforth be safely built.[62]

Since Russell wrote these words in 1903, the basic scientific picture of the universe has changed immensely. No one had yet proposed the Big Bang; no one even knew for sure that there were galaxies beyond the Milky Way until some 20 years later. Chemistry textbooks still expressed uncertainty as to whether atoms were real.[63] General relativity, quantum mechanics, plate tectonics, and the modern evolutionary synthesis had not yet been conceived. In other words, the great unifying theories of today, whether in cosmology, physics, geoscience, chemistry, or biology, existed only in incipient form, if at all. And yet the philosophy that Russell stated, and for which he claimed near-certainty on the basis of empirical evidence, still informs a wide range of writing in popular science and universal history. One hears echoes in statements like Roy Scranton's: "For a growth of carbon scum on a spinning rock in the backwater of an unremarkable galaxy light years from anywhere to develop the technology to send radio telescopes into space to measure the age of the universe is a prodigious achievement."[64] From Robert Chambers to H. G. Wells to David Christian, the factual information in a universal history gets updated continuously, sometimes changing immensely, and yet the basic framing and the storytelling devices either remain similar or change in ways that reflect changes in culture rather than in science. At the very least, this seems "suspicious," to use Sagan's word. It turns out that not only can you tell a different story with the same set of facts, but you can tell the same story with a different set of facts.

Many assert that Russell's basic philosophy was something *discovered* by modern science: as the story goes, Copernicus started in motion the "demotion" of humanity by kicking people out of the center of the universe, while Darwin completed it by making us just another animal. The reality, however, is that this secular, naturalistic philosophy became associated with modern science through specific, contingent choices of scientists and other thinkers. That Russell's way of narrating the basic framework is a philosophy grafted onto science, not a necessary outcome of that science, is further supported by the fact that Russell was not the first to make statements like this—not by a wide margin. A compelling presentation of the same

---

62. Bertrand Russell, "A Free Man's Worship," in Louis P. Pojman, *Ethical Theory: Classic and Contemporary Readings*, p. 607.

63. See, e.g., Alexander Smith, *Introduction to Inorganic Chemistry* (revised edition), pp. 224–225. This popular textbook was published in 1910. Thanks to James Penner-Hahn for pointing this passage out.

64. Roy Scranton, *Learning to Die in the Anthropocene: Reflections on the End of a Civilization*, p. 116.

underlying set of ideas (even though the author disagrees with them) is found, for example, in the Hellenistic-era Jewish Book of Wisdom, referring to Greek philosophies like Epicureanism:

> Short and sorrowful is our life . . . we were born by mere chance, and hereafter we shall be as though we had never been; because the breath in our nostrils is smoke, and reason is a spark kindled by the beating of our hearts. . . . Our name will be forgotten in time, and no one will remember our works; our life will pass away like the traces of a cloud . . . For our allotted time is the passing of a shadow, and there is no return from our death.[65]

If the universe seems amoral, indifferent to our existence, or even hostile,[66] we might remember, as Robert Bellah puts it, that "only persons can be hostile or deaf and indifferent."[67] Personifying the universe is part of the storytelling. To see just how different a vision can be compatible with the same basic set of facts, Jonathan Sacks offers the following articulation, based on Russell's and phrased in much the same language:

> That man, despite being the product of seemingly blind causes, is not blind; that being in the image of God he is more than an accidental collocation of atoms; that being free, he can rise above his fears, and, with the help of God, create oases of justice and compassion in the wilderness of space and time; that though his life is short he can achieve immortality by his fire and heroism, his intensity of thought and feeling; that humanity too, though it may one day cease to be, can create before night falls a noonday brightness of the human spirit, trusting that, though none of our kind will be here to remember, yet in the mind of God, none of our achievements is forgotten—all these things, if not beyond dispute, have proven themselves time and again in history. We are made great by our faith, small by our lack of it. Only within the scaffolding of these truths, only on the firm foundation of unyielding hope, can the soul's salvation be safely built.[68]

Sacks writes of stories like Russell's vision and his: "The science is the same in both stories. The difference lies in how far we are willing to push the question,

---

65. Wisdom (of Solomon) 2:1b-5, trans. *Revised Standard Version, Second Catholic Edition.* The book is typically included in Catholic and Orthodox, but not Protestant, Old Testaments, and it is not part of the Jewish canon.

66. Cf. Steven Weinberg: "It is very hard to realize that this all is just a tiny part of an overwhelmingly hostile universe" (Weinberg, *The First Three Minutes*, p. 154).

67. Bellah, *Religion in Human Evolution*, pp. 104–105.

68. Sacks, *The Great Partnership*, p. 27.

'Why?' The first story says there is no why. The second says there is."[69] Constructing an interpretive narrative "is about the question that remains when all the science is done. When we know all that can be known about what happened and how, we may still disagree on the *meaning* of what happened."[70]

Metanarrative

History—as a form of writing and scholarship—is usually about charting a pathway, or pathways, through time rather than identifying general principles that play out in a predetermined way. It is convenient that the word "history" contains the word "story": histories lend themselves to stories, to narratives.[71] The purpose of this book has been to summarize the way scientists and historians of the recent past have told the story of the universe as a "history of everything," and to analyze that story *as a story*: understanding its cultural, philosophical, and interpretive context, as well as how a history of everything that wishes to remain true to modern scientific evidence and historical scholarship could look substantially different with a different set of interpretive choices. We have suggested many different directions that stories of the history of everything—or of any particular thing—could go, given altered philosophical foundations, cultural worldviews, or sets of disciplinary concerns.

Stories are also central to being human. A culture's stories are a huge part of cultural continuity: history helps to give a culture the sense of being the same culture over time, like memory helps to give a person the sense of being the same person over time. At a psychological level, stories are more easily memorized than unconnected facts, and they help us make sense of things.[72] Stories help us to draw connections and process the world. As a Buddhist saying states, "Objects of knowledge are limitless";[73] stories help us to identify and remember what matters. Narratives of any sort are used to create understandings that stretch beyond the bounds of individual facts and details. They turn unrelated, arbitrary events into something coherent, memorable, and recognizable.

---

69. Ibid., p. 24.

70. Ibid., p. 24.

71. Indeed, the word "story" derives from the same root as "history," derived from Latin, and in turn ancient Greek.

72. Cf., e.g., the classic psychological experiment by John Bransford and Marcia Johnson, "Contextual Prerequisites for Understanding: Some Investigations of Comprehension and Recall," *Journal of Verbal Learning and Verbal Behavior*, 11:6 (1972:Dec.):717-726. There is also research showing that reading or listening to a story has much the same impact in a human brain as if one is actually living the story.

73. See Donald Lopez, *Buddhism & Science: A Guide for the Perplexed*, p. 194.

The metanarratives of universal history are no different. A "metanarrative" is an ultimate story about how everything fits together: "a narrative that, in the eyes of its users, frames and explains all other narratives and can be framed and explained by none."[74] The point of bringing a critical eye to universal history is not to eliminate metanarratives but to refine them, to evaluate them, to make them explicit; to point out how crucial it is to return again and again to questions of framing; to bring multiple metanarratives into conversation with one another; and to see what each captures, and misses. While universal histories often claim to be shared among all people, a given metanarrative tends to resonate with only a limited group. Universal metanarratives, it turns out, are usually not so universal after all. Yet a metanarrative that is aware of its own limitations may actually become more powerful.

A Many-Branched Stream

How do you end a book that seeks to provide "A Guide to the History of Everything"? If, as we pointed out in the second sentence of chapter 1, books like this one tend to begin in a certain way, there are also patterns in how they end: with a grand message about humanity's place in the whole of space, time, and the universe;[75] with a call to collective human responsibility in building a better future or a wider perspective on the consequences of human actions;[76] or with an expression of admiration for the grandeur of science or a reflection on the prospects for future scientific discovery.[77]

But that is not how this book will end. It will end instead by returning to the question, raised in chapter 6, of what it means to write "a" history of everything rather than "the" history of everything.

The early-20th-century Jewish philosopher Franz Rosenzweig (1886–1929) once spoke of each individual person as a "many-branched stream."[78] Perhaps so too is history. Rather than seeing the essence of universal history as a single, unified,

---

74. Paul J. Griffiths, "Impossible Pluralism," https://www.firstthings.com/article/2013/06/impossible-pluralism .

75. Like Carl Sagan's *Cosmos*, Eric Chaisson's *Epic of Evolution*, Cynthia Stokes Brown's *Big History: From the Big Bang to the Present*, or David Christian's *Maps of Time*.

76. Like Walter Alvarez's *A Most Improbable Journey: A Big History of Our Planet and Ourselves*; Robert Hazen's *The Story of Earth: The First 4.5 Billion Years, From Stardust to Living Planet*; David Christian's *This Fleeting World: A Short History of Humanity*; or Fred Spier's *Big History and the Future of Humanity*.

77. Like Steven Weinberg's *The First Three Minutes* or Stephen Hawking's *A Brief History of Time*.

78. *Franz Rosenzweig: His Life and Thought*, ed. Nahum N. Glatzer, p. 161: "Which goes to show that man is not a channeled stream but a many-branched one."

grand, and sweeping metanarrative that catches everything up in its flow, one in which a single master story (about, say, complexity) applies to everything and plays out on all scales of space and time as *the* story of the universe, we might instead take a multifaceted approach to understanding and linking the past, present, and future: incorporating new forms of evidence, examining a broad array of scales in time and space, and seeing human history in its broader context on several different levels—astronomical, geological, biological, and social.

Such an approach can be more expansive, and less narrow, than attempting to write a singular through-line, a modern creation myth. Our hyperspecialized world needs general visions of reality and ways to see how things fit together, but this requires *multiple* stories: more narratives, interweaving and interlocking, and not a single, totalizing one. Narratives are helpful, and constructive, and "good to think with."[79] They clarify many aspects of our lives, identify or produce meaning, and organize many aspects of human thought. We need compelling and persuasive stories to understand our lives, what we are doing, and who we are, both in a wider, universal sense and in our own particular stories. And we need settings, like universal histories, to bring grand stories and worldviews and understandings of the world together, and to consider their dimensions. We need to provide a habitat where they can live and grow together, a place to discuss and integrate them with rigor, with fidelity to empirical evidence, with deep philosophical thought and a high regard for the whole breadth of the history and present of human thought—in all its dizzying variations—and with a genuine desire to better understand multiple perspectives on the cosmos, its history, and what it means to be human within it.

---

79. A phrase taken from the anthropologist Claude Lévi-Strauss.

How Old is the Earth? How Old is the Universe?

In the 1800s, physicists and geologists came up with a variety of ways of estimating Earth's age (see Plate 1). Estimates that were based on physics (especially the thermodynamics of how long it would take Earth to cool from a molten state) were generally in the tens of millions of years, while estimates based on uniformitarian geology (estimating how long it would take for geological processes, operating uniformly over long time scales, to produce the Earth we currently observe) were generally in the hundreds of millions of years. Following the discovery, around the turn of the 20th century, of radioactivity and radiometric dating of rocks, scientists realized that these 19th-century estimates had relied on problematic assumptions or problematic measurements. Radiometric dating led to higher estimates, in the range of billions of years, ultimately converging on 4.5 to 4.6 billion years by the 1950s.

Meanwhile, the discovery in the 1920s that the universe is expanding allowed cosmologists to "rewind" the universe's expansion history to estimate how long it had existed. This provided a way for scientists to estimate the universe's age where there had been no clear basis for making such estimates before. However, the expansion rate (Hubble constant) proved very difficult to measure, leading to much debate and sometimes mutually incompatible age estimates. Twentieth-century estimates of the universe's age ranged from less than 2 billion to more than 20 billion years, but by around the year 2010, estimates had converged between 13.6 and 13.9 billion years.

Although in the first two decades of the 21st century a relatively clear picture has emerged, in which the Earth is 4.5 billion years old and the universe is about three times older, Plate 1 shows that these age estimates varied a great deal in the 19th and 20th centuries, and that there was even a period of time—in the 1940s—when the best estimates of the Earth's age were greater than that of the universe.

Notes: (1) While estimates of Earth's age in the 1800s tended to cluster in the tens to hundreds of millions of years, as shown in Plate 1, a few estimates were higher. (2) Although it is not shown here, there was a period of time in the second half of the 20th century when the age of the oldest stars was estimated to be greater than that of the universe. This issue too has been largely resolved (as common sense would suggest it somehow would have to be!). (3) Note that the ranges shown in Plate 1 (blue and orange bars) do not generally reflect error bars or estimated uncertainty ranges, since these were often not rigorously and reliably estimated until the 1950s for Earth estimates, and 2000s for Universe estimates. The range bars instead reflect some of the most dominant views among experts about the likely ages of the Earth and the universe.

Sources: Information about the Earth's age drawn from Phillips 1860, Kelvin 1862, Darwin 1862, Geikie 1868, Geikie 1892, King 1893, Kelvin 1895, Kelvin 1897, Goodchild 1897, Joly 1899, Geikie 1899, Dubois 1901, Joly 1904, Boltwood 1907, Sollas 1909, Becker 1910–15, Holmes 1913, Russell 1921, Rutherford 1927, Holmes 1927, Holmes 1946, and Patterson 1956. See *Scientific American Classics: Geochronology*, "Determining the Age of the Earth," Number 17, 2013, and Paul S. Braterman, "How Science Figured Out the Age of Earth," *Scientific American*, October 20, 2013, https://www.scientificamerican.com/article/how-science-figured-out-the-age-of-the-earth/. Information about the Universe's age drawn from Lemaître 1927, Hubble 1929, Baade 1952, Humason, Mayall, & Sandage 1956, Sandage 1958, vandenBergh 1960, Sandage 1968, Sandage & Tammann 1975, deVaucouleurs & Bollinger 1979, deVaucouleurs & Peters 1984, Sandage & Tammann 1985, deVaucouleurs 1993, Sandage & Tammann 1995, Freedman et al. 2001, WMAP collaboration 2003, 2006, 2008, 2010, 2012, and Planck collaboration 2013, 2015, 2018. See John Huchra, "Estimates of the Hubble Constant," last updated October 7, 2010, https://www.cfa.harvard.edu/~dfabricant/huchra/hubble.plot.dat (this file copyright by John Huchra at the Harvard-Smithsonian Center for Astrophysics; it was assembled as part of the NASA/HST Key Project on the Extragalactic Distance Scale).

INDEX